ABORTION AND WOMAN'S CHOICE

The State, Sexuality, and Reproductive Freedom

Rosalind Pollack Petchesky

Longman Series in Feminist Theory

Longman
New York & London

Abortion and Woman's Choice
The State, Sexuality, and Reproductive Freedom

Longman Inc., 1560 Broadway, New York, N.Y. 10036
Associated companies, branches, and representatives
throughout the world.

The Introduction has been adapted from an article that originally appeared
in the Summer 1980 issue of *Signs.*

Chapter 7 has been adapted from an article that originally appeared
in the Summer 1981 issue of *Feminist Studies.*

Developmental Editor: Nicole Benevento
Editorial and Design Supervisor: Harriet Sigerman
Production Supervisor: Ferne Y. Kawahara
Manufacturing Supervisor: Marion Hess

Library of Congress Cataloging in Publication Data

Petchesky, Rosalind P.
    Abortion and woman's choice.

    (Longman series in feminist theory)
    Includes bibliographical references and index.
    1. Abortion.   2. Abortion—Political aspects.
3. Birth control.   I. Title.   II. Series.
HQ767.P49   1983   363.4'6   83-11342
ISBN 0-582-28215-2

Manufactured in the United States of America
Printing: 9 8 7 6 5 4 3 2 1   Year: 92 91 90 89 88 87 86 85 84

IN LOVING MEMORY OF

SARAH EISENSTEIN

AND

JOAN KELLY —

THEIR COURAGE, THEIR FRIENDSHIP, THEIR COMMITMENT

TO THE FIGHT FOR HUMAN LIBERATION

Contents

Preface

Reproductive politics prompted the writing of this book, and a feminist movement for women's reproductive rights made it a vital project. I began working on the book in the fall of 1978, a little more than a year after Congress passed the first Hyde Amendment restricting Medicaid funding for abortions. By then it was clear that abortion was only the most volatile among a range of issues—teenage sexuality, homosexuality, family relations (including domestic violence), birth control, childbearing—that had once been regarded as "personal" but, after a decade of feminist organizing, were capturing center stage in mainstream political controversy. This was the domain of reproductive politics—the public debate over power and control in family, sexual, and procreative relations. Feminists and gay rights advocates had politicized those issues by putting pressure on the state for legalization, services, funding, and legitimacy in regard to them; now the organized right wing was trying to reverse the immediate past in a campaign that focused on revoking legal abortion.

Why abortion? What made it a symbol—and more than a symbol—of all that the right found menacing in ideas about sexual freedom and women's liberation from the traditional strictures of male-dominated family life? Increasingly, abortion has become the cutting edge of reproductive and sex-gender politics for two reasons: Not only has a determined antiabortion movement and its New Right allies pushed the issue to the forefront but autonomy over the abortion decision epitomizes the capacity of individual women and women collectively to control fertility and to control the consequences of heterosexual sex—especially for young, unmarried women. In this book, therefore, I aim for a holistic understanding of abortion from a feminist perspective, including the history of its practice and state policies to contain it; the social, economic, and cultural conditions under which women utilize it; and the legal, moral, and political battles that surround it. In doing so I have two purposes: (1) to analyze and defend women's need for safe, legal abortion; and (2) to use this analysis to develop a theory of the social relations of reproduction and a feminist concept of reproductive freedom.

For readers who are interested, I offer a word about the theoretical premises of *Abortion and Woman's Choice*. They grow out of a dialogue that has ensued for the past decade among writers identifying themselves as Marxist-feminists, a dialogue that has revolved around the concept of "reproduction." Marxism, from which it was borrowed, understood "social reproduction" as simply a dimension of the system of economic production: the continual replacement of the system of production as a whole, its goods, capital, raw materials, as well as labor power.[1] In this meaning, there was nothing distinct or specific about the activities related to reproduction, and certainly nothing in Marx's thinking to identify it with the social conditions of women. Children, and decisions about whether or not to have them, became an epiphenomenon of the labor market. Recognizing that Marxist theoretical inquiry ignored or distorted whole realms of activity that define human life—such as the bearing and socialization of children, sexual desire and relations, family structure and power, and fertility and its control—feminists tried to reinvent the concept of reproduction in a Marxist-feminist framework. This effort generated two new meanings of "reproduction": (1) the processes of intergenerational reproduction and the "reproduction of daily life," which include many of the maintenance and socialization activities of the home and family and, increasingly, institutions—the work of women; and (2) the narrower but also socially mediated processes of human biological reproduction and sexuality.[2]

Both meanings contain serious problems. The first tends to make reproduction the mirror image of Marx's concept of production, calling it "women's domestic labor" or simply "housework." Although it recognizes that women's situation within the family is distinct, it constructs a false analogy that reduces the complexity of family relations and their class and cultural variations. In particular, it ignores their sexual and psychological dimensions and the specificity of child development.[3] The second meaning was taken up by radical and structuralist feminists as an affirmation of the idea that women *are* their bodies; that the body is the locus of women's oppression and therefore the genesis of a specifically "female" language and epistemology. The problem here is that women's association with reproduction in the narrower sense becomes indistinguishable from traditional biologically based theories of gender difference. When we start to locate women's specific experience and oppression in their bodies we edge dangerously close to asserting "a true and eternal nature" of Woman. This "denies the existence and the power of *social mediations*, which are precisely what oppress us in our bodies."[4] Moreover, analyses of pregnancy, childbearing, and fertility changes in naturalistic or biological terms either become vulnerable to conservative efforts to dislocate women from realms of power and public activity, or lend themselves to a Malthusian determinism in which human populations fluctuate like those of any animal species and women's bodies are merely the passive instruments.

The value of these feminist theories of reproduction is that they begin to see reproduction as a distinct realm of activity that not only structures the lives of women but is culturally, consciously shaped by them. A problem they leave—one that a number of feminist theorists are currently trying to solve[5]—is to demonstrate that the connection between women's reproductive activities and their social and political situation is historical, not "biological" (i.e., "natural" and unchanging). This book attempts to reconnect, in a way that is sensitive to historical and cultural variations, the body and its gender-specific processes; the "social mediations" of the body; the larger systems—the capitalist patriarchal state and political economy—from which those mediations arise; and women's consciousness. Because the analytical framework is mostly limited to the United States (with some reference in Chapter 1 to the history of fertility control in Western Europe), the cross-cultural dimension is regrettably weak. But the principle of historical, class, and cultural particularity figures prominently in the book. And so does the role of women as conscious agents of reproductive processes.

I start from the premise that reproduction generally, and fertility control in particular, must be understood as a historically determined, socially organized activity (separate from the activity of mothering), encompassing decisions about whether, when, under what conditions, and with whom to bear or avoid bearing children; the material/technological conditions of contraception, abortion, and childbirth; and the network of social and sexual relations in which those decisions and conditions exist. These relations include those between "providers" (doctors, family planners, population controllers) and "consumers" (women), between women and their male sexual and procreative partners, and between parents and children. It is out of these relations, which are dynamic and historically changing, that women's consciousness develops and acts upon reproductive life.

Feminist theory requires this social perspective in order to explain the great differences—of class, culture, occupation, locale, and history—in women's reproductive experience. We need it to free us and our theory from the oppressive persistence of the "body eternal." A theory and analysis of the social relations of reproduction is necessary to make concrete the idea of reproduction as a domain that constructs women as a gender and women's own consciousness. This is a difficult and complex task to achieve in theory. In practice, feminists of many varieties and in many countries, by fighting for abortion rights, birth control, maternity and child care, and free sexual expression, have implied their agreement that ". . . *the way in which the biology of human reproduction is integrated into social relations is not a biological question: it is a political issue.*"[6]

This book will not appeal to those who question women's right and need for abortion or the justice of the feminist struggle for equality. It is written for feminists, liberal-minded professionals and policy makers, students, educators, clergy, journalists, and others who already feel some conviction about these things but need a deeper kind of understanding. Why has the abortion issue become a seething political and social controversy? What historical developments and social and cultural conditions have led to both rising abortion practice and state policies and moral ideologies related to that practice? How do these conditions and policies affect the changing position and consciousness of women? What are the elements of a feminist vision of abortion and its relation to the total conditions of women's reproductive freedom? Beyond theory, these are the questions the book addresses—and they are political questions.

The collective knowledge and resources that contributed to my work on this book over the last five years are enormous. The initial research was done thanks to a year's fellowship at the Hastings Center, with valuable support from many on its staff, its fine library, and its director, Daniel Callahan. In subsequent years, time off for writing was made possible by an appointment as a Rockefeller Fellow at the Center for the Study of Human Rights, Columbia University; and most particularly by the office space, hospitality, and warm encouragement I received from Frank Grad and his staff at the Legislative Drafting Fund, Columbia University School of Law. I would also like to thank my colleagues and students at Ramapo College of New Jersey for allowing me leave time during those years and awarding me release time for research during my teaching years. These grants were precious gifts without which the book would have remained a slim hope.

Ideas do not emerge from a vacuum. They move along, carried by the work of many others. Mine have owed a tremendous debt to feminist activists, lawyers, and writers working on these issues. I could not have begun to write this book without the historical and theoretical groundwork laid by Linda Gordon in her book *Woman's Body, Woman's Right*. Nor would I have gotten very far without many hours of talk with Rhonda Copelon, in which she shared her legal knowledge and experience; or Ellen Willis' thoughtful writing on abortion, which seemed so often the spark of truth that got me going. In whatever I understand of the relations between liberalism and feminism, or between patriarchal power and the capitalist state, I have been influenced by the thinking of Zillah Eisenstein and her *Radical Future of Liberal Feminism*, the first book in this series. At every point in the writing process, in more ways than I could recount, I have relied on the analytical clarity, social scientific knowledge, and practical sense of Hal Benenson. Most important, my inspiration for writing the book and my commitment to completing it came from the women's reproductive rights movement, especially CARASA and its members. Knowing they were out there, fighting to make reproductive freedom a practical reality, was what gave the book its reason to be.

Many individual friends and loved ones helped me at various stages of research and in the preparation of the manuscript—reading and editing, brainstorming, and generously sharing their ideas, their sources, and their time. Among these, I owe the most special and loving thanks to Hal Benenson, Rhonda Copelon, Zillah Eisenstein, Marty Fleisher, Kris Glen, and Karen Judd. And to Joan Kelly, who listened to me describe parts of the manuscript from her hospital bed and, in the depths of illness, offered me her very special wisdom. You are not responsible, any of you, for what finally emerged, but are deeply appreciated for your guidance and support. Also very helpful in providing sources and reading and critiquing parts of the manuscript were Wendy Chavkin, Martha Francois, Nick Freudenberg, Janet Gallagher, Dick Glendon, Mary Katzenstein, Rayna Rapp, Ellen Ross, Meredith Tax, Ann Teicher, and Sharon Thompson. I am grateful, too, to my father, Simon Pollack, M.D., for sending me a continual stream of useful medical materials; and to my brother, Nathan Pollack, M.D., for trying to soften my biases about medical practice. Shirley Driks, who typed and retyped the manuscript drafts during more than three years, was cheering and supportive as well as amazingly skilled. Lynn Berkeley was a fine research assistant, helping me with many details at the end. Nicole Benevento, my editor, believed in the book enough to take it on when it was barely a conceptus; to wait for it patiently through an interminable gestation; and to push it to birth. Finally, and most of all, I thank Jonah, Hal, and my parents, Roberta and Simon Pollack, for being there for me and with me through these years.

Rosalind Petchesky

NOTES

1. Karl Marx, *Capital,* trans. Ben Fowkes (New York: Vintage, 1977), 1:711–24.

2. Veronica Beechey, "On Patriarchy," *Feminist Review* 3 (1979): 78–79; and F. Edholme, O. Harris, and K. Young, "Conceptualizing Women," *Critique of Anthropology* 3 (1977): 111.

3. See my critique of the "housework" debate in R. Petchesky, "Reproduction, Production, and Class Differences Among Women," in *Class, Race and Sex: Exploring Contradictions, Affirming Connections,* ed. Amy Swerdlow (New York: G. K.

Hall, 1983), and the references cited there; also see the references cited in Renate Bridenthal, "The Family: The View from a Room of Her Own," in *Rethinking the Family,* ed. Barrie Thorne (New York: Longman, 1982), p. 238n.

4. Editorial, "Variations on Some Common Themes," *Questions Féministes* 1 (Summer 1980): 10. See also Ann Rosalind Jones, "Writing the Body: Toward an Understanding of *L'Ecriture Féminine,"* *Feminist Studies* 7 (Summer 1981): 247–63. This contains a useful summary and critique of some of the new French structuralist-feminist writing.

5. For example, Michele Barrett, *Women's Oppression Today* (London: Verso, 1980); Mary O'Brien, *The Politics of Reproduction* (London: Routledge and Kegan Paul, 1981); Beechey; Janet Sayers, *Biological Politics: Feminist and Anti-Feminist Perspectives* (London: Tavistock, 1982); and Zillah Eisenstein, *Feminism and Sexual Equality: The Crisis of Liberal America* (New York: Monthly Review, forthcoming).

6. Barrett, p. 76; emphasis added.

Introduction:
Beyond "A Woman's Right
to Choose"—
Feminist Ideas about
Reproductive Rights

. . . that all the while the *Foetus* is forming . . . even to the Moment
that the Soul is infused, so long it is absolutely not in her Power
only, but in her right, to kill or keep alive, save or destroy, the Thing
she goes with, she won't call it Child; and that therefore till then
she resolves to use all manner of Art, to the help of Drugs and
Physicians, whether Astringents, Diuretics, Emeticks, or of whatever
kind, nay even to Purgations, Potions, Poisons, or any thing that
Apothecaries or Druggists can supply. . . .

DANIEL DEFOE

Behind Defoe's scathing condemnation of female malice in the act of
abortion lies the presence of not only "right-to-life" antecedents in seventeenth-century England but the idea among women that abortion is a
"woman's right." Linda Gordon lays the groundwork for a feminist theory
of reproductive freedom, observing that, throughout history, women have
practiced forms of birth control and abortion; recurrent moral or legal
prohibitions against such practices merely "forced women underground
in their search for reproductive control."[1] Similarly, George Devereux,
surveying 350 primitive, ancient, and preindustrial societies, asserts "that
there is every indication that abortion is an absolutely universal phenomenon, and that it is impossible even to construct an imaginary social sys-

1

tem in which no woman would ever feel at least impelled to abort."[2]

The universality in birth control practices helps us to understand that reproductive freedom for women is not simply a matter of developing more sophisticated techniques. While the ascent from "purgations, potions, and poisons" to vacuum aspiration doubtless represents a gain for women, abortion and reproductive freedom remain political, not technological, agendas—which feminists find necessary to mobilize over and over again. Because we are in the thick of that mobilization at present, it is important to examine the political ideas that have informed movements for reproductive freedom historically and today.

Two essential ideas underlie a feminist view of reproductive freedom. The first is derived from the biological connection between women's bodies, sexuality, and reproduction. It is an extension of the general principle of "bodily integrity," or "bodily self-determination," to the notion that women must be able to control their bodies and procreative capacities. The second is a "historical and moral argument" based on the social position of women and the needs that such a position generates. It states that, insofar as women, under the existing division of labor between the sexes, are the ones most affected by pregnancy, since they are the ones responsible for the care and rearing of children, it is women who must decide about contraception, abortion, and childbearing.

These two ideas grow out of different philosophical traditions and have different, sometimes contradictory, reference points and political priorities. The first emphasizes the *individual* dimensions of reproduction, the second the *social* dimensions. The first appeals to a "fixed" level of the biological person, while the other implies a set of social arrangements, a sexual division of labor, developed historically, that may be changed under new conditions. Finally, one is rooted in the conceptual framework of "natural rights," while the other invokes the legitimating principle of "socially determined needs."

In what follows I analyze the origins and theoretical implications of these two ideas; I take account of the radical and conservative elements in each and highlight tensions between them that may never be totally resolved. My argument is that reproductive freedom—indeed, the very nature of reproduction—is social and individual at the same time; it operates "at the core of social life" as well as within and upon women's individual bodies.

Thus, a coherent analysis of reproductive freedom requires a perspective that is both Marxist and feminist.[3] This dual perspective is also necessary on the level of political practice. For even if it were true, as some "right-to-lifers" have charged, that the women's movement is self-contradictory in demanding both control by women over reproductive matters and greater sharing of responsibility for such matters between women and men, both these goals are indispensable to a feminist program for reproductive freedom. We have to struggle for a society in which responsibility for contraception, procreation, and childrearing is no longer relegated to women primarily; and, at the same time, we have to defend the principle of control over our bodies and our reproductive capacities. In the long run, we have to ask whether women's control over reproduction is what we want, whether it is consistent with equality; in the short run, we have never experienced the concrete historical conditions under which we could afford to give it up.

Controlling Our Bodies

The principle that grounds women's reproductive freedom in a "right to bodily self-determination," or "control over one's body," has three distinct but related bases: liberalism, neo-Marxism, and biological contingency. Its liberal roots may be traced to the Puritan revolution in seventeenth-century England. In that period, the Leveller idea of a "property in one's own person" was linked explicitly to nature and paralleled the idea of a "natural right" to property in goods: "To every individual in nature is given an individual property by nature, not to be invaded or usurped by any: for every one as he is himselfe, so he hath a selfe propriety, else could he not be himselfe, and on this no second may presume to deprive any of without manifest violation and affront to the very principles of nature, and of the Rules of equity and justice between man and man. . . ."[4] A person, to be a person, must have control over himself or herself, in body as well as in mind. This Leveller notion of individual selfhood, although phrased in masculine terms, had specific applications to the conditions of women in the seventeenth century: the enactment of the Puritan idea of marriage as a contract, restrictions against wife beating, and the liberalization of divorce.[5] It had other applications that affected men and women: the introduction of habeas corpus in 1628 (bodies cannot be detained without cause); and, above all, a resistance to the idea of selling, or alienating, one's body to another through wage labor. Thus, the original notion of "property in one's person" was not only an assertion of individualism in an abstract sense but had a particular radical edge that rejected the commoditization of bodies through an emergent labor market. The Levellers were saying: My body is not property; it is not transferable; it belongs only to me.

While the liberal origins of the "bodily integrity" principle are clear, its radical implications should not be forgotten. In its more recent juridical expressions, for example the so-called right to privacy, the principle has been applied to defend prisoners from physical abuse, undocumented aliens from bodily searches, and patients from involuntary treatment or medical experimentation, as well as in the well-known "reproductive rights" cases.[6] While privacy, like property, has a distinctly negative connotation that is exclusionary and asocial, when applied to persons as persons—in their concrete, physical being—it also has a positive sense that roughly coincides with the notion of "individual self-determination." Control over one's body is an essential part of being an individual with needs and rights, a concept that is the most powerful legacy of the liberal political tradition.

This principle clearly applies to persons as persons and not only to women. Nevertheless, it was the soil that nourished the growth of feminism in the eighteenth and nineteenth centuries, and many of the gains sought by women under the rubrics of "liberty" and "equality" still have not been won.[7] A certain idea of individuality is also not antithetical to a Marxist tradition, which distinguishes between the idea of individual human beings as historically determined, concrete, and particular in their needs and the ideology of "individualism" (i.e., "the individual" conceived as isolated, atomized, exclusive in *his* possessions, disconnected from larger social fabrics). As Agnes Heller puts it, the former idea recognizes that the end of socialist transformation is ultimately the satisfaction of individual needs, which are always concrete and specific (unlike rights, which belong to "citizens" or "persons" in the abstract). Thus, "Marx recognizes no needs other than those of individual people"; while understanding needs as generally social or "socially produced," such needs "are the needs of individual human beings." "When the domination of things over human beings ceases, when relations between human beings no longer appear as relations between things, then *every* need governs 'the need for the development of the individual,' the need for the self-realization of the human personality."[8]

Similarly, Marcuse argues in favor of restoring a sense of individual "happiness" to a revolutionary ethic ("general happiness apart from the happiness of individuals is a meaningless phrase"). Through his analysis of contemporary forms of domination and repression that alienate individuals from a sense of connectedness with their own bodies and thus with the physical and social world, Marcuse arrives at a hedonism containing a liberatory element. That element is a sense of "complete immediacy," of "sensuality," which is a necessary precondition for the "development of personality" and the participation of individuals in social life. The link between eroticism and politics is a "receptivity that is open and that opens itself [to experience]."[9] Control over one's body is a fundamental aspect of this immediacy, this "receptivity," a requirement of being a person and engaging in conscious activity. Understood thus, it is a principle of radical ethics that should never be abandoned.

The direct connection between "control over one's body" and feminist claims regarding women's control over reproduction seemed obvious to early birth control advocates. Ezra Heywood, an anarchist birth controller in the 1870s, asserted "Woman's Natural Right to ownership of and control over her own body-self—a right inseparable from Women's intelligent existence."[10] This connection is as real today. Because pregnancies occur in women's bodies, the continued possibility of an "unwanted" pregnancy affects women in a very specific sense, not only as potential bearers of fetuses, but also in their capacity to enjoy sexuality and maintain their health. A woman's right to decide on abortion when her health and her sexual self-determination are at stake is "nearly allied to her right to be."[11]

Reproduction affects women as women; it transcends class divisions and penetrates everything—work, political and community involvements, sexuality, creativity, dreams. Gordon illustrates this point with reference to the conditions that generated the nineteenth-century birth control movement:

> The desire for and the problems in securing abortion and contraception made up a *shared female experience*. Abortion technique was apparently not much safer among upper-class doctors than among working-class midwives. The most commonly used contraceptives—douches, withdrawal—were accessible to women of every class. And what evidence there is of the subjective experience of women in their birth-control attempts also suggests that the desire for spaced motherhood and smaller families existed in every class, and that the desire was so passionate that women would take severe risks to win a little space and control in their lives. *The individual theory and practice of birth control stems from a biological female condition that is more basic even than class.*[12]

It is surprising to find Gordon reverting to a "biological female condition" in the midst of an analysis of the social construction of women's reproductive experience. Yet it reminds us that the "bodily integrity" principle has an undeniable biological component. As long as women's bodies remain the medium for pregnancies, the connection between women's reproductive freedom and control over their bodies represents not only a moral and political claim but also, on some level, a material necessity. This acknowledgment of biological reality should not be mistaken for biological determinist thinking about women; my point is simply that biology is a *capacity* as well as a limit.[13] That it is women who get pregnant has been the source of our confinement (in all senses) and our (limited) power. An abundance of feminist anthropological literature reminds us that pollution rituals, fertility cults, prohibitions against abortion, and chastity rules imposed on wives and daughters are signs of men's envy and fear of women's reproductive capacity. Indeed, the current attack on abortion in the United States and elsewhere in the West has been interpreted by some feminists as a massive recurrence of male "womb envy."

I would be the last to romanticize the control that comes from our biological connection to childbearing, or to underestimate its repressive social aspects. On the other hand, women's control over their bodies is not like preindustrial workers' control over their tools; it cannot be wrested away through changes in technology or legal prohibitions and repression— which is why no modern society has succeeded for long in outlawing abortion or birth control, only in driving it "underground."

It is important, however, to keep in mind that woman's reproductive situation is never the result of biology alone, but of biology mediated by social and cultural organization. That is, it is not inevitable that women, and not men, should bear the main consequences of unintended pregnancy and thus that their sexual expression be inhibited by it. Rather, it is the result of the socially ascribed primacy of motherhood in women's lives. Yet biology as it is socially mediated by male-dominant institutions affects all women. Today there is prolific evidence of this "shared female experience." The cutbacks in abortion funding, whose hardest impact has been on low-income women, have spearheaded a right-wing movement to curtail abortion services and reimbursements for working-class and middle-class women dependent on health insurance plans as well. While sterilization abuse has mainly been directed at poor, Third World, and mentally disabled women, the ultimatum to well-paid women chemical workers that they get sterilized or lose their jobs has widened our perspective on this issue.[14] Indeed, the fact that female sterilization, an irreversible procedure, has become the most widely used, medically encouraged, and economically reimbursable method of contraception among all but the very young in the United States,[15] as evidence grows of the pill's dangers to health and abortions are restricted, raises questions about reproductive "choices" for *most* women. That the two major birth control methods in current use are, on the one hand, irreversible, and, on the other hand, dangerous to health, affects women of all classes. It is a condition set, not by reproductive technology, but by a reproductive politics that seeks to curtail the efforts of women "to win a little space and control in their lives" and freely to express their sexuality.

The principle of "control over our bodies," then, has a material as well as a moral and a political basis. The "liberal," the "radical" or "neo-Marxist," and the "biological" elements of this principle should not be seen as alternatives to one another but as different levels of meaning that give the principle its force and complexity. Sorting out these levels should make it easier for us to distinguish between situations when we are describing "control over our bodies" as a *material fact*, when we are asserting it as a *right*, and when we are defining it as part of a larger set of socially determined *human needs*.

Yet the idea of "a woman's right to choose" as the main principle of reproductive freedom is insufficient and problematic at the same time as it is politically compelling. For one thing, this principle evades moral questions about when, under what conditions, and for what purposes reproductive decisions should be made. Feminists writing on abortion usually have not claimed that a pregnant woman "owns" the fetus or that it is part of her body. On the contrary, feminists have generally characterized an unwanted pregnancy as a kind of bodily "invasion."[16] Recognizing a real conflict between the survival of the fetus and the needs of the woman and those dependent on her, the feminist position says merely that women must decide because it is their bodies that are involved, and because they have primary responsibility for the care and development of any children born.

But determining who should decide—the political question—does not tell us anything about the moral and social values women ought to bring to this decision.[17] Should women get an abortion on the grounds that they prefer a different gender, which amniocentesis can now determine? Such a decision would be blatantly sexist, and nobody's claim to "control over her body" could make it right or compatible with feminist principles. That is, "a woman's right to control her body" is not absolute, but we have not developed a socialist-feminist morality that would tell us what the exceptions should be.

Admitting that we have not fully articulated a feminist morality of abortion does not imply that all or most women who get abortions do so thoughtlessly or irresponsibly. On the contrary, women who seek abortions know and experience better than anyone else the difficulty of that decision. Much more serious is the potential danger in the assertion of women's right to control over reproduction as absolute or exclusive, for it can be turned back on us to reinforce the view of all reproductive activity as the special, biologically destined province of women. This danger grows out of the concept of "rights" in general, a concept that is inherently static and abstracted from social conditions. Rights are by definition claims staked within a given order of things. They are demands for access for oneself, or for "no admittance" to others; but they do not challenge the social structure, the social relations of production and reproduction.[18] The claim for "abortion rights" seeks access to a necessary service, but by itself it fails to address the social relations and sexual divisions around which responsibility for pregnancy and children is assigned. In real-life struggles, this limitation exacts a price, for it lets men and society neatly off the hook.

The notion of rights has tremendous polemical power, but rights tend to be seen as isolated, rather than as part of a total revolutionary program. This is different from Marx and Engels's view of "bourgeois rights" as necessary preconditions and as means to building a class-conscious movement but not as ends in themselves (as feminists often think of them). It is also different from the more radical concept of control

over one's body as a social and individual need, implicit in the requirements of personality and sensual "receptivity." Needs, unlike rights, exist
only in connection with individuals and within concrete historical circumstances. For a Native American woman on welfare, who every time she
appears in the clinic for prenatal care is asked whether she would like
an abortion, "the right to choose an abortion" may appear dubious if
not offensive.[19]

Finally, the idea of a "woman's right to choose" is vulnerable to
political manipulation, as demonstrated in recent legislative and judicial
debates. Thus "right-to-lifers" exploit the liberal concept of "informed
consent" by promoting legislation that would require abortion patients
to be "informed" in graphic detail of a fetus' physiological characteristics
at each stage of development. Physicians opposing the federal, California,
and New York City regulations to curb involuntary sterilization, particularly the requirement of a thirty-day waiting period, have claimed that
such regulation is "paternalistic" and inhibits women's "right to choose"
sterilization.[20] During hearings before the House Select Committee on
Population in 1978, a spokesman for the Upjohn Company, manufacturer
of Depo-Provera (an injectible contraceptive drug currently banned from
U.S. distribution because of evidence it is carcinogenic), opposed FDA
regulation of contraceptives on the ground that it "deprives the public
of free choice": ". . . safety cannot be absolute—it can be defined *only
in relative and personal terms.* The individual with advice from his or her
physician—not a governmental regulatory agency—should decide which
risks are 'reasonable' under these circumstances."[21]

That judgments about contraceptive safety can be made only "in
relative and personal terms" assails the commitment to establishing and
enforcing generalizable standards of health and safety that transcend individual judgments. Moreover, when the risks include thromboembolisms,
myocardial infarction, breast cancer, and cervical cancer, the need for
social standards and their vigorous enforcement is a matter of life and
death. Recent applications of laissez-faire ideology to reproductive policy
are clearly part of a larger right-wing push that seeks "deregulation" in
many spheres; seen within this general political context, they are to be
expected. But the ease with which the principle of individuality and control over one's own body may be perverted into bourgeois individualism—
and capitalist greed—should make us pause, clear our heads, and think
through more rigorously the social conditions of individual control.

The Social Relations of Reproduction

The idea that biological reproduction is a social activity, distinct from
the activity of childrearing and determined by changing material conditions and social relations, is essentially Marxist. In *The German Ideology,*

Marx defines "three aspects of social activity": along with "the production of material life" and "the production of new needs," human procreation—reproduction within the family—is also a "social relationship." That is, it involves not only "natural," or biological, relations but social, cooperative relations among men and women through sexual and procreative practices. That activity is social insofar as it is cooperative, purposive, and above all conscious.[22] We can extend this view to human sexuality in general, which, whether heterosexual, homosexual, or bisexual, is fundamentally social, involving reciprocity, the conscious articulation and re-creation of desire; not merely satisfying a need but doing so in an interactive context that people create together. Moreover, sexual meanings and practices, like the meanings and practices of motherhood, vary enormously through history, across cultures, and within the same culture—indicating that these "natural" realms of human experience are incessantly mediated by social praxis and design.[23]

If this variability characterizes sexual and maternal experience, how much more is it true of contraception, abortion, and childrearing practices—all domains that, throughout civilization, have been transformed by conscious human interventions.[24] A woman does not simply "get pregnant" and "give birth" like the flowing of tides and seasons. She does so under the constraint of *material conditions* that set limits on "natural" reproductive processes—for example, existing birth control methods and technology and access to them; class divisions and the distribution/financing of health care; nutrition; employment, particularly of women; and the state of the economy generally. And she does so within a specific network of *social relations* and social arrangements involving herself, her sexual partner(s), her children and kin, neighbors, doctors, family planners, birth control providers and manufacturers, employers, the church, and the state.

Georg Lukács takes up the idea of a "metabolism," or necessary interaction, between the natural and social aspects of human life. He suggests that the progressive socialization of "natural being" through "social practice" is the essence of history.[25] To dichotomize "nature" and "society" is false; and, by inference, it is also false to assume a split between women's "biological" functions and her "social" ones. Hilda Scott similarly reflects this view in paraphrasing the Czech demographer Helena Svarcova: "Marx's observation . . . suggests looking for the dialectical relationship between the natural and social sides of reproduction, instead of regarding them as two parallel but independent processes. In this view, human population is seen as the unity of biological and social aspects which condition each other, the social aspects being the chief but not the only factor."[26]

The attempt to develop a social conception of reproduction is, of course, not limited to Marxists. Demographers, for example, conventionally acknowledge the importance of social conditions in determining population, but within a set of completely mechanistic assumptions. A social phenomenon such as changing birthrates is thus viewed solely in terms of statistically measurable demographic events (numbers of women in a given childbearing cohort, numbers entering the labor force, availability and use of contraceptives, and so on) as though it were a natural, unintended occurrence.[27] Population-oriented anthropologists emphasize not only the tremendous variability but the rational, deliberate character of methods for controlling population and fertility among all societies, including the most primitive.[28] However, they view such activity from a functionalist perspective, as "adaptive mechanisms" adopted by the culture as a whole, undifferentiated by sexual divisions or divisions of power. Utterly lacking is any sense that the methods and goals of reproduction, and control over them, may themselves be a contested area within the culture—particularly between women and men.

In contrast, an analysis of reproductive activity in terms of the "social relations of reproduction" would emphasize the historical dynamism of consciousness and social conflict and the historical agency of social groups. Social divisions, based on differing relationships to power and resources, mediate the institutional and cultural arrangements through which biology, sexuality, and reproduction among human beings are expressed, and such relations are essentially antagonistic and complex. At the most basic level they involve gender divisions, or the sexual division of labor (itself a predominantly cultural product); but in class-divided societies, they are also entangled with divisions based on class. Gordon's book is laced with examples of the ways in which, in nineteenth- and twentieth-century America, women's birth control possibilities were directly affected by their class position, which determined their relationship to medical and family planning distribution systems. Thus the diaphragm—"the most effective available contraceptive in the 1930s"—was virtually inaccessible to working-class and poor women, due to material conditions such as the lack of privacy, running water, and access to private clinics and medical instruction through which diaphragms were dispensed.[29] Today, class and race divisions in reproductive health care determine not only women's access to decent gynecological services, counseling, and the like, but their risk of exposure to involuntary sterilization, dangerous contraceptive drugs, or unnecessary hysterectomy.

The social relations of reproduction are also complicated by the forms of consciousness and struggle through which they are expressed in different historical periods. Sometimes antagonisms remain implicit or repressed; sometimes, under conditions that need to be understood more precisely, birth control and abortion become areas of open sexual and class conflict. Anthropological and historical studies, while scant, record the particularity of reproductive relations to class and culture and the ways those relations are recurrently ones of social division. Devereux, for example, describes societies in which abortion, or retaliation against involuntarily-induced abortion, represented a clear act of female defiance.[30] Flandrin, in his analysis of late medieval church views toward contraception and sexual relations, points out that the evidence of widespread contraceptive practice indicates that conscious, even unrepentant resistance to the dominant ecclesiastical morality must have been common in Europe from the fifteenth to the eighteenth centuries.[31]

These examples suggest that the critical issue for feminists is not so much the content of women's choices, or even the "right to choose," as it is the social and material conditions under which choices are made. The "right to choose" means little when women are powerless. In cultures where "illegitimacy" is stigmatized or where female infants are devalued, women may resort to abortion or infanticide with impunity; but that option clearly grows out of female subordination. Similarly, women may have autonomy over reproduction and childbirth, as in New Guinea, while being totally excluded from everything else.[32] Or, like the women employees at the American Cyanamid plant in West Virginia, they may "choose" sterilization as the alternative to losing their jobs. To paraphrase Marx, women make their own reproductive choices, but they do not make them just as they please; they do not make them under conditions they create but under conditions and constraints they, as mere individuals, are powerless to change.[33] That individuals do not determine the social framework in which they act does not nullify their choices nor their moral capacity to make them. It only suggests that we have to focus less on "choice" and more on how to transform the social conditions of choosing, working, and reproducing.

At present, the organized forces that shape the class-specific socially constructed character of women's reproductive experience in the United States are powerful and diverse. The intervention of doctors, particularly obstetrician-gynecologists, in women's control over their reproductive lives has been pervasive; yet medical control over reproduction is far from monolithic. Private and public population control agencies have cooperated with the medical profession, as "medical indications" and "medical effectiveness" became euphemisms for technical efficiency in population control. But these agencies maintain a financial and institutional power base independent of doctors. Further, the large-scale commercialization of birth control products and services has meant that other interests, such as pharmaceutical and insurance companies, have become important influences on the methods available to women, their safety or risk, and whether they will be reimbursed.

This conjuncture of medical, corporate, and state interests in the "management" of reproduction has defined the choices of all women, but in a way that is crucially different depending on one's class and race. Still the major providers of birth control and abortion information and services to women, physicians are widely known to vary the information and the quality of services they provide based on the class and race of their patients. For example, private doctors in Maryland were found to provide abortions with much greater regularity to their middle-class than to their lower-class patients.[34] Similarly, cases of sterilization abuse by physicians in the public health services have occurred almost entirely among black, Native American, and Mexican-American welfare recipients, as well as women who are prisoners or mentally retarded.[35] Low-income and non-English-speaking women are regularly denied information about safer, "nonmedical" methods of birth control because of racist and class-biased assumptions that they are not "competent" to "manage" such methods. Moreover, it is poor and Third World women who are likely to be used as experimental subjects in international population control programs for testing or "dumping" contraceptive chemicals or implants whose safety has been questioned by the FDA.[36] Finally, in a capitalist society, class is the mightiest determinant of the material resources that help make having and raising children joyful rather than burdensome.

It would be wrong, however, to picture women of any class as the passive victims of medical, commercial, and state policies of reproductive control. In hearings before the House Select Committee on Population and in lawsuits, women of all classes have successfully challenged drug companies and doctors regarding the severe health hazards of the pill, Depo-Provera, and other synthetic hormones.[37] Groups of Mexican American, Native American, black, and other women have joined with women's health and reproductive rights groups to fight against involuntary sterilization in the courts and through extensive federal and state regulations. An active, vocal movement to defend women's reproductive freedom and "abortion rights" is growing in the United States and Western Europe and is currently a major force in the feminist movement.

What is "reproductive freedom" from the standpoint of historical materialism? On what principle is women's struggle to secure control over the terms and conditions of reproduction based? A materialist view of reproductive freedom would justify this struggle in terms of the principle of socially determined need. The moral imperative grows out of the historically and culturally defined position that women find themselves in through motherhood. Because it is primarily women who bear the consequences of pregnancy and the responsibility for children, the conditions of reproduction and contraception affect them directly and in every aspect of their lives. Therefore, it is women primarily who should have control over whether, when, and under what conditions to have children. Moreover, an emphasis on the social rather than biological basis of reproductive activity implies that such activity is once and for all removed from any "privatized" or "personal sphere" and may legitimately be claimed for political and social intervention. That intervention may take the form of measures to protect or regulate reproductive health—for example, to assure the safety and voluntariness of contraceptive methods— or to transform the material conditions that currently divide women's reproductive options according to class and race.

On the other hand, a materialist view of reproductive freedom recognizes the historical contingency of the conditions in which women seek reproductive control. For most of history, women's "choices" over reproduction have been exercised in a framework in which reproduction and motherhood have determined their relationship to society. A materialist (and feminist) view looks forward to an eventual transcendence of the existing social relations of reproduction so that gender is not ultimately the determinant of responsibility. This implies that society be transformed so that men, or society itself, bear an equal responsibility for nurturance and child care. Then the basis of the need would have changed and control over reproduction might not belong primarily to women.[38]

It is here, however, that a contrary feminist sensibility begins to rankle and the limitations of a historical materialist, or traditional Marxist, framework for defining reproductive freedom become apparent. These limitations are disturbingly suggested in Alison Jaggar's "Marxist feminist" defense of abortion, which argues that the "right" of women to an abortion is "contingent" upon "women's situation in our society": ". . . if the whole community assumes the responsibility for the welfare of mothers and children, [then] the community as a whole should now have a share in judging whether or not a particular abortion should be performed. . . ."[39]

Can we really imagine the social conditions in which we would be ready to renounce control over our bodies and reproductive lives—to give over the decision as to whether, when, and with whom we will bear children to the "community as a whole"? The reality behind this nagging question is that control over reproductive decisions, particularly abortion, has to do not only with "the welfare of mothers and children" but very fundamentally with sexuality and with women's bodies as such. The analysis emphasizing the social relations of reproduction tends to ignore, or deny, the level of reality most immediate for individual women: that it is their bodies in which pregnancies occur. Indeed, that analysis becomes false insofar as it disregards the immediate, sensual reality of individuals altogether. In order to make this connection, a theory of reproductive freedom has to have recourse to other conceptual frameworks, particularly one that is more commonly associated with a feminist tradition and asserts women's right to and need for bodily self-determination.

Reproductive Politics, Past and Future

"Even if contraception were perfected to infallibility, so that no woman need ever again bear an unwanted child; even if laws and customs change—as long as women and women only are the nurturers of children, our sons will grow up looking only to women for compassion, resenting strength in women as 'control,' clinging to women when we try to move into a a new mode of relationship."[40]

How do we break out of the apparent contradiction between "women's right to control" over reproduction and their need not to be defined by reproduction? How do we transform the social relations of reproduction to bring men, as potential fathers, into those relations on an equal basis? How would such a transformation affect the principle of "control over our bodies"? The two ideas of reproductive freedom discussed here must be incorporated into a revolutionary feminist and socialist politics. Despite the real tensions between these ideas—stressing changes in the social relations of reproduction and stressing women's control over their bodies—neither is dispensable for feminists. Yet no political movement for "reproductive rights" or women's emancipation, including our own, has yet sustained this double agenda in a systematic and consistent way.

The failure to integrate these two ideas in practice in a political movement is illustrated dramatically by Attina Grossman's account of the abortion struggle that united feminists, socialists, and communists in Weimar Germany.[41] "The Communist left and its women's movement" saw abortion as primarily "a class issue": the proposed law making abortion a criminal act would affect working-class women most severely, since middle-class women could both afford and get access to illegal abortion and contraception. Feminists emphasized "women's right to sexual pleasure and control of their bodies," suggesting that maternity is a special female realm of experience that cuts across class divisions.

Grossman correctly stresses the positive aspects of this political campaign: It brought together in a single coalition the women's movement and the working-class movement; it appealed to women of all classes on the basis of their oppression as women in reproduction; it moved even the German Communist party (KPD), for mainly tactical reasons, to put forward a feminist slogan: "Your body belongs to you." Yet the different ideological bases on which groups supported the abortion struggle implied differing senses of why that campaign was important and must have had an impact on the cohesiveness of the movement and its ability to make its ideas felt, for "the politics of reproduction were never . . . adequately integrated into Communist ideology."[42] Thus a theory that related the need of individual women for control over their bodies to the needs of the working class as a whole was not—nor has it yet been—articulated.

Reproductive politics in the context of socialist revolutions have been still less cohesive or consciously feminist. In general, where liberalized abortion and divorce reforms have been introduced as a fundamental aspect of socialist revolutions—for example, in the Soviet Union and Eastern Europe—the purpose has been mainly to facilitate women's participation in industry and the breakup of feudal and patriarchal forms. Such measures have not been inspired by either of the ideas I have been examining, nor by a feminist movement self-consciously struggling to put those ideas into practice. Accounts of the Soviet Union in the 1920s and 1930s[43] and of Czechoslovakia in the 1950s and 1960s[44] richly and poignantly illustrate the limits of "reproductive reforms" when they are neither accompanied by material changes that would augment women's real power in society nor brought into effect through a mass independent women's movement. Foreshadowing experience in the United States since *Roe* v. *Wade,* such reforms were used in a later, reactionary period as a pretext for sexual and reproductive repression. The tendency these cases point to is a reactive chain of developments in which measures such as liberalized abortion and abolishing illegitimacy unleash a rise in sexual activity, abortions, and divorce followed by a period of backlash in which there is an outcry against the "breakup of the family," women are blamed and accused of "selfishness," and the society is chided by population experts about its declining birthrate. In the absence of either adequate material support (incomes, child care, health care, housing) or shared male responsibility for contraception and childrearing, women are left, after these reforms, in some ways more vulnerable than before.[45]

Scott's assessment of the situation in Czechoslovakia, while critical of the repressiveness for women of the later, backward shifts in abortion policy, tends nevertheless to focus the blame on abortion. She intimates that abortion is intrinsically a method of birth control that puts women at a disadvantage and "encourages irresponsibility on the part of men." "Abortion as a birth control method puts all the responsibility for the future of the unborn child [*sic*] on the woman. She makes the application, she agrees to the operation, she pays the fee. If, as in Czechoslovakia, she must go before an interruption commission, she is the one who receives the lecture, is subjected to pressure to have the child, is reproached for getting herself 'into trouble.' " [46] What is most striking in this account is the absence (as in Russia) of any women's organization, movement, or tradition that made reproductive freedom a value in its own right. Clearly, there is nothing inevitable, nothing written into "nature," about the presumed relationship between abortion and male "irresponsibility." One could perfectly well imagine a system of abortion decision making that involved potential fathers to the same degree as potential mothers, although whether women would or should give up their control over this decision is another question. What reinforces male irresponsibility is the reliance on abortion *in a social context in which the sex-gender division remains unchanged and in a political context in which that division remains unchallenged.*

That a socialist revolution is a necessary but far from sufficient basis for reproductive freedom is illustrated in a different way by the current antinatalist drive in China. The effort of the Chinese government to limit births to two per couple, through a massive campaign of propaganda and education as well as economic incentives,[47] raises numerous questions. While the political decision that the Chinese economy and educational system cannot support an increasingly young population may be rational on some level, one wonders, first, whether the economic sanctions on households are accompanied by as vigorous efforts to equalize the position of women in work, economic, and political life; or to develop birth control education and methods for men. Moreover, do the measures fall more heavily on some groups so that poorer families feel a greater pressure to comply? Finally, how and by whom were the decisions made? Were those most affected by them (parents) involved in the process? One disturbing aspect of the Chinese policy is its emphasis on chemical contraceptives and IUDs, with all the known risks and side effects.[48] Once again it is women whose bodies are subjected to reproductive and contraceptive risk.

Strategies for establishing reproductive freedom must distinguish between different historical and political contexts. Under the conditions of advanced capitalism existing in the United States today—particularly as the right wing seeks to restore patriarchal control over whether, how, and with whom women have children—reproductive politics necessarily become a struggle for control. Moreover, that struggle is greatly complicated by persistent class and race divisions. For most women in capitalist society, the idea of reproductive control (or "choice") is unthinkable short of a vast array of social changes that are themselves predicated upon a socialist revolution. In the meantime, "control" in a more limited sense may mean different things to different women (birth control information is one thing, possession of your reproductive organs and custody of your children is another). In a class- and race-divided society, "pronatalist" and "antinatalist" policies coincide (e.g., restrictions on abortion *and* involuntary sterilization), making it necessary for "reproductive rights" proponents to articulate continually that "reproductive freedom means the freedom to have as well as not to have children."[49] Because women are subordinate economically, politically, and legally, a policy emphasizing male sharing of childrearing responsibility could well operate to divest women of control over their children in a situation where they have little else. (We are currently getting a foretaste of this danger, with increasing losses of custody fights by women, particularly lesbian mothers.) The "collective" principle could play into the suggestions of "right-to-lifers" that the responsibility for childbearing is too important to be left to women.

On the other hand, because the sexual division of labor around childrearing prevails and defines women's position, a policy emphasizing improved benefits and services to encourage childbearing may ease the material burdens of motherhood; but it may also operate to perpetuate the existing sexual division of labor and women's social subordination. This has certainly been the case in Eastern Europe. And in the United States it is easy to imagine an accretion of reforms such as pregnancy disability benefits, child-care centers, and maternity leave provisions, which, if unaccompanied by demands for transforming the total position of women, can be used to rationalize that position.[50] The point is not that present attempts to secure funded abortion, pregnancy and maternity benefits, child-care services, and other reforms should be abandoned but that those attempts must be moved beyond the framework of "a woman's right to choose" and connected to a broader revolutionary movement that addresses all the conditions for women's liberation.

A feminist and socialist transformation of the existing conditions of reproduction would seek to unleash the possibilities for material (economic and technological) improvements in reproduction from traditional family and sexual forms, to place those positive changes in a new set of social relations. Foremost among these new relations is that concerned with the care of children. Men must be "ready to share the responsibilities of full-time, universal child care as a social priority"—that is, the responsibility for children must be dissociated from gender, which necessarily means that it becomes dissociated from heterosexuality. The writings of feminist theorists[51] reveal deeply rooted cultural and psychic bases of traditional childrearing arrangements; they help explain why it is this aspect of presocialist patriarchy that seems most intractable in postrevolutionary societies. The changes we require are total; ". . . no decisive changes can be brought about by measures aimed at women alone, but, rather, the division of functions between the sexes must be changed in such a way that men and women have the same opportunities to be active parents and to be gainfully employed. This makes of women's emancipation not a 'woman question' but a function of the general drive for greater equality which affects everyone. . . . The care of children becomes a fact which society has to take into consideration."[52]

Under different conditions from any that now exist, it may become possible to transcend some of the individualist elements of feminist thinking about reproductive freedom and move toward a concept of reproduction as an activity that concerns all of society. At the same time, a basis could be created for the genuine reproductive freedom of individuals, ending systems of domination that inhibit their control over their bodies. We need to envision what those conditions would be, even though they seem far from present reality. Charting the development of reproductive politics in the past, especially abortion, and rigorously analyzing their conditions in the present, ought to help us transform those politics in the future.

NOTES

1. Linda Gordon, *Woman's Body, Woman's Right: A Social History of Birth Control in America* (Harmondsworth, England, and Baltimore: Penguin, 1977), p. 47.

2. George Devereux, "A Typological Study of Abortion in 350 Primitive, Ancient, and Pre-Industrial Societies," in *Abortion in America,* ed. Harold Rosen (Boston: Beacon, 1967), p. 98.

3. I am indebted to Zillah Eisenstein for this important clarification.

4. Quoted in C. B. MacPherson, *The Political Theory of Possessive Individualism* (London: Oxford University Press, 1962), p. 140.

5. See Keith Thomas, "Women and the Civil War Sects," *Past and Present* 13 (1958): 332–52. For accounts of Leveller doctrine as well as the ideas of more radical sects about women and individualism in this period, see Christopher Hill, *The World Turned Upside Down* (New York: Viking, 1972); idem, *The Century of Revolution, 1603–1714* (New York: Norton, 1961), Chaps. 4, 7, and 8; and MacPherson, Chap. 3.

6. *Griswold* v. *Connecticut,* 381 U.S. 479 (1965); *Eisenstadt* v. *Baird,* 405 U.S. 438 (1972); *Roe* v. *Wade,* 410 U.S. 113 (1973); and *Doe* v. *Bolton,* 410 U.S. 179 (1973). See also the fine summary and analysis of these cases as well as the June 1977 Supreme Court decisions on abortion in Kristin Booth Glen, "Abortion in the Courts: A Laywoman's Historical Guide to the New Disaster Area," *Feminist Studies* 4 (February 1978): 1–26.

7. Juliet Mitchell, "Women and Equality," in *The Rights and Wrongs of Women,* ed. Juliet Mitchell and Ann Oakley (Harmondsworth, England: Penguin, 1976).

8. Agnes Heller, *The Theory of Need in Marx* (New York: St. Martin's, 1976), pp. 67, 73.

9. Herbert Marcuse, *Negations: Essays in Critical Theory* (Boston: Beacon, 1968), pp. 166–71.

10. Gordon, p. 66.

11. Judge Dooling in *McRae* v. *Califano,* 491 F. Supp. 630 (1980), p. 742.

12. Gordon, p. 70; emphasis added.

13. Cf. Sara Ruddick: "Neither our own ambivalence toward our women's bodies nor the bigoted, repressive uses men, colonizers and racists have made of biology, should blind us to biology's possibilities. On the other hand, our belief in the biological body's psychosocial efficacy may be an illusion created by the fact that the people who engage in maternal practices almost always have female bodies." "Maternal Thinking," *Feminist Studies* (Summer 1980), p. 346.

14. "Four Women Assert Jobs Were Linked to Sterilization," *New York Times,* 5 January 1979; Rosalind Petchesky, "Workers, Reproductive Hazards and the Politics of Protection: An Introduction," *Feminist Studies* 5 (Summer 1979): 233–45; Michael J. Wright, "Reproductive Hazards and 'Protective' Discrimination," ibid., pp. 302–9; Wendy Chavkin, "Occupational Hazards to Reproduction—a Review of the Literature," ibid., pp. 310–25.

15. Committee for Abortion Rights and against Sterilization Abuse [CARASA], *Women Under Attack: Abortion, Sterilization Abuse, and Reproductive Freedom* (New York: CARASA, 1979); Rosalind Petchesky, "Reproduction, Ethics and Public Policy: The Federal Sterilization Regulations," *Hastings Center Report* 9 (October 1979): 29–42; Charles F. Westoff and James McCarthy, "Sterilization in the United States," *Family Planning Perspectives* 11 (May/June 1979): 147–52; and Charlotte F. Muller, "Insurance Coverage of Abortion, Contraception and Sterilization," *Family Planning Perspectives* 10 (March–April 1978): 71–77.

16. "There is no way a pregnant woman can passively let the fetus live; she must create and nurture it with her own body, a symbiosis that is often difficult, sometimes dangerous, uniquely intimate. However gratifying pregnancy may be to a woman who desires it, for the unwilling it is literally an invasion— the closest analogy is to the difference between lovemaking and rape. . . . Clearly, abortion is by normal standards an act of self-defense." Ellen Willis, *Beginning to See the Light* (New York: Alfred A. Knopf, 1981), p. 208. Cf. Judith Jarvis Thomson's classic essay, "A Defense of Abortion," in *The Rights and Wrongs of Abortion*, ed. John Finnis et al. (Princeton: Princeton University Press, 1974), pp. 10, 12. Thomson uses philosophical sleight of hand to arrive at the same conclusion.

17. This point is made persuasively by Daniel Callahan, *Abortion: Law, Choice and Morality* (New York: Macmillan, 1970), p. 494; cf. Alison Jaggar, "Abortion and a Woman's Right to Decide," in *Women and Philosophy*, ed. Carol C. Gould and Marx W. Wartofsky (New York: Capricorn, 1976), p. 347.

18. Cf. Mitchell, pp. 384–85.

19. Meredith Tax, citing a remark by Pat Bellanger, representative of WARN (Women of All Red Nations), St. Paul, Minnesota.

20. Patricia Donovan, "Sterilizing the Poor and Incompetent," *Hastings Center Report* 6 (October 1976): 5; and Petchesky, "Reproduction, Ethics and Public Policy," p. 35.

21. U.S. Congress, House, Select Committee on Population, *Fertility and Contraception in the United States*, 95th Cong., 2d sess., December 1978, p. 110.

22. Karl Marx, *The German Ideology*, in *Writings of the Young Marx on Philosophy and Society*, ed. Lloyd D. Easton and Kurt H. Guddat (Garden City, N.Y.: Anchor, 1967), pp. 419–22.

23. Rayna Rapp and Ellen Ross, "Sex and Society: A Research Note from Social History and Anthropology," *Comparative Studies in Society and History* 23 (January 1981): 51–72; Jeffrey Weeks, *Sex, Politics and Society: The Regulation of Sexuality since 1800* (London: Longman, 1981); *Radical History Review* 20 (Spring/Summer 1979): special issue on "Sexuality in History," esp. articles by Robert A. Padgug ("Sexual Matters: On Conceptualizing Sexuality in History," pp. 3–23) and Jeffrey Weeks ("Movements of Affirmation: Sexual Meanings and Homosexual Identities," pp. 164–79); Jean-Louis Flandrin, "Contraception, Marriage, and Sexual Relations in the Christian West," in *Biology of Man in History*, ed. Robert Forster and Orest Ranum (Baltimore: Johns Hopkins University Press, 1975); Michel Foucault, *The History of Sexuality*, vol. 1, *An Introduction* (New York: Pantheon, 1978); Gayle Rubin, "The Traffic in Women," in *Toward an Anthropology of Women*, ed. Rayna (Rapp) Reiter (New York: Monthly Review, 1975), pp. 157–210.

24. See, e.g., Gordon, Chaps. 1 and 2; Norman E. Himes, *Medical History of Contraception* (New York: Gamut, 1963); John T. Noonan, Jr., *Contraception* (Cambridge, Mass.: Harvard University Press, 1966); Devereux; Steven Polgar, "Popula-

tion History and Population Policies from an Anthropological Perspective," *Current Anthropology* 13 (April 1972): 203–11.

25. Georg Lukács, *The Ontology of Social Being—2. Marx* (London: Merlin, 1978), pp. 5–7, 38–39.

26. Hilda Scott, *Does Socialism Liberate Women?* (Boston: Beacon, 1974), p. 159.

27. Thanks to Ellen Ross and Hal Benenson for reminding me of this point.

28. See Polgar; and Alexander Alland, *Adaptation in Human Evolution: An Approach to Medical Anthropology* (New York: Columbia University Press, 1970).

29. Gordon, pp. 309–12.

30. Devereux, pp. 113, 117.

31. Flandrin, pp. 25–28.

32. Sherry B. Ortner, "The Virgin and the State," *Feminist Studies* 4 (October 1978): 25; and Gordon, who cites similar examples from anthropological evidence and concludes: "These are women's choices, but hardly choices coming from positions of power" (p. 34).

33. Karl Marx, *The Eighteenth Brumaire of Louis Bonaparte* (New York: International Publishers, 1963), p. 15.

34. Constance A. Nathanson and Marshall H. Becker, "The Influence of Physicians' Attitudes on Abortion Performance, Patient Management and Professional Fees," *Family Planning Perspectives* 9 (July/August 1977): 158–63.

35. Ad Hoc Women's Studies Committee against Sterilization Abuse, *Workbook on Sterilization and Sterilization Abuse* (Bronxville, N.Y.: Women's Studies, Sarah Lawrence College, 1978); and CARASA, pp. 49–53.

36. See Barbara Ehrenreich, Mark Dowie, and Stephen Minkin, "The Charge, Gynocide; the Accused, the U.S. Government," reprinted in *CARASA News* 4 (January 1980): 13; Deborah Maine, "Depo: The Debate Continues," *Family Planning Perspectives* 10 (November/December 1978): 392.

37. U.S. Congress, House, Select Committee on Population, pp. 109–10.

38. The position presented here is obviously different from the technological determinism of Shulamith Firestone in *The Dialectic of Sex* (New York: Bantam, 1970). Firestone's simplistic view that women's position could be "revolutionized" by the introduction of *in vitro* fertilization, artificial uteruses, and other "advanced" features of reproductive technology ignores the social aspects of reproduction and the political question of who controls that technology, how control is organized socially and institutionally, and for what ends.

39. Jaggar, pp. 351, 356, 358.

40. Adrienne Rich, *Of Woman Born* (New York: Norton, 1976), p. 211.

41. Attina Grossman, "Abortion and the Economic Crisis: The 1931 Campaign against §218 in Germany," *New German Critique* 14 (Spring 1978): 119–37.

42. Ibid., p. 134.

43. Richard Stites shows how the revolutionary Russian Family Code, which abolished illegitimacy, eased divorce, and recognized de facto marriages, worked to women's disadvantage in the absence of either adequate means of material support for women and children or a feminist politics emphasizing men's role in reproduction. Similarly, the liberalized abortion law of 1920 became a pretext not only for abandonment and nonrecognition of paternity but for the lax and exploitative sexual relations that characterized this period. In these conditions of insecurity, the return to a traditional sanctification of marriage and motherhood

in the 1930s, with heavy restrictions on abortion and divorce, was actually welcomed by many women, insofar as the new (1936) provisions reinforced men's responsibility for providing protection to wife and children. Richard Stites, *The Women's Liberation Movement in Russia* (Princeton: Princeton University Press, 1978), pp. 367–69, 374, 386–87.

44. Scott documents the introduction of liberal abortion laws during the 1950s in Czechoslovakia, Hungary, and Rumania and its repressive aftermath. Following a major birthrate decline, as well as an apparently significant increase in the abortion rate, in the 1960s policy makers and population "experts" in these countries not only blamed abortion for social and demographic problems but accused women of "selfishness" and irresponsibility for seeking abortion and getting pregnant in the first place. A series of "maternal incentive" policies was introduced, including extended paid maternity leave, housewives' allowances, bonuses for additional children, etc., and "abortions for other than medical reasons in the case of childless married women and those with one child" were restricted. Scott, pp. 141, 132–33, 153.

45. A very moving and amusing expression of this pattern, and of people's confusion and personal conflict over heterosexual relations, marriage, and abortion in the 1920s in Russia, is the fine Soviet film *Bed and Sofa* (*Tretya Meshchanskaya*), produced by V. Shklovsky and A. Room (1927).

46. Scott, p. 144. Cf. Kristin Luker's similar argument that abortion reform in the United States in the early 1970s encouraged "male disengagement from responsibility," in *Taking Chances: Abortion and the Decision Not to Contracept* (Berkeley: University of California Press, 1975), pp. 134–35.

47. James P. Sterba, "Chinese Will Try to Halt Growth of Population by End of Century," *New York Times*, 13 August 1979, p. A4; Walter Sullivan, "A Tough New Drive on Births in China," *New York Times*, 10 October 1979, pp. C1, C11.

48. Sullivan reports that "while various contraceptive preparations are taken by millions of Chinese women, only 10,000 men are taking the birth control substance gossypol experimentally." On the commune he visited, 95 percent of the sterilizations performed had been done on women. Sullivan, pp. C1, C11.

49. CARASA, p. 9.

50. To offset the birthrate decline in the United States, Princeton demographer Charles Westoff suggests a variation on a pronatalist incentives policy that would divide all American women into one-third who would "never have any children" and another two-thirds who "would have to reproduce at an average rate of three births per woman to maintain a replacement." While the former group would presumably be channeled into full-time employment, the latter would be drawn into their role of "breeders" through "a serious investment in child-care institutions" and other government-sponsored reproductive subsidies. "Some Speculations on the Future of Marriage and Fertility," *Family Planning Perspectives* 10 (March/April 1978): 79–82.

51. Nancy Chodorow, *The Reproduction of Mothering* (Berkeley: University of California Press, 1975); Dorothy Dinnerstein, *The Mermaid and the Minotaur* (New York: Harper & Row, 1976); Rich, *Of Woman Born*.

52. Scott, p. 190.

PART

I FERTILITY CONTROL IN THEORY AND HISTORY

1

Fertility, Gender, and Class

Conscious activity to control human fertility is as intrinsic to the social being of human groups as the activity to control and organize the production of food. What changes over time and from one social context to another is who controls fertility, under what conditions, through what means, and for what purposes. The techniques of fertility control change less than the value bestowed on children and the social conditions and consciousness of the women who bear them. These changes concern the cultural symbolism and social relations of fertility control, suggesting that, as with the economic distribution of goods, control over fertility is a matter not only of technology but of the total arrangement of power in society.

A basic proposition of this book is that gender divisions and the position of women in society have a direct and specific influence on fertility control practices and therefore on birthrates. How, when, and whether to have a child involve different issues for women than for men; yet they do so in ways that vary depending on a woman's class, age, and occupation, as well as the time and culture in which she lives. Because gender and class relations are negotiated through political struggles (struggles for power and control), fertility becomes an area of conflict and negotiation, between women and men and between different social classes. Fertility control is not, then, simply a private strategy of individuals or families to help them cope with economic or other pressures. It occurs within definite social contexts and sexual power relations that women individually and collectively try to accommodate and sometimes resist.

We need to distinguish between fertility control as it has been practiced in all cultures by individuals, particularly women, and as it has been practiced recurrently by male-dominated ruling elites. This distinction is often expressed as the difference between "birth control," or control by individuals over their own childbearing, and "population control," or control by authorities or elites over population size and composition.[1]

But the concept of population control is too simplified and too "gender neutral" to encompass the multiple and crisscrossing grounds through which public authorities or "centers of power" historically have sought to channel biological reproduction. At the least, these include not only population control but control over the sexuality and physical health of women, the terms and conditions of motherhood, and the structure of the family.

Public, organized strategies of fertility control—the subject of Chapter 2—do not emerge in a vacuum; they are responses to popular practices and changing ideologies about fertility, which are the subject of this chapter. Whatever the dominant norms, women persist in trying to calibrate fertility to their own life rhythms and needs. A classic historical survey of contraception concluded that "the human race has in all ages and in all geographical locations desired to control its own fertility; that while women have always wanted babies, they have wanted them when they wanted them. And they have wanted neither too few nor too many."[2] But women's changing wants in regard to fertility, and the demands of "the race," as represented by male rulers, churchmen and moralists, chiefs of clans or households, and medical and population authorities, have often diverged. Fertility rates are the negotiated outcomes of struggles, whether overtly political or waged surreptitiously and "underground," between these sometimes overlapping, sometimes conflicting sets of interests.

The remarkable thing is not that those in power have attempted to control population by controlling the fertility of women but that they have been so unsuccessful. They continually run up against the everyday practices of ordinary women, in having or not having children according to their own sense of their needs.[3] Toward this end, abortion has been the means to which women have resorted with greatest persistence over time.

State, church, and medical strategies to regulate fertility in industrial societies, including those that would restrict or suppress abortion, have an impact on women's ability to control their fertility, but it is partial and reactive rather than absolute. Such strategies are part of a range of limiting conditions that include social and economic forces that those in power do not always direct or plan. More than anything else, changes in fertility and abortion rates represent women's own responses to conditions they as individuals did not create but against which their collective practices, such as illegal or clandestine abortion and birth control, become strategies of survival and resistance. Indeed, more than the suppression of abortion, its endurance on a large scale, through diverse historical contexts, tells us something important about women's specific relation to fertility and the terms and conditions of fertility control and reproductive freedom for them.

The point here is not to romanticize women's fertility behavior as "liberating" or morally defensible in itself, or to collapse all cultural and historical situations into modern concepts of birth control. The late feminist anthropologist Michele Rosaldo warned against the tendency in feminist theory to mystify premodern women "as the bearer of primordial human need," "the image of ourselves undressed," thus erasing "the historical specificity of their lives and of our own." "There is something wrong—indeed, morally disturbing—in an argument which claims that the practitioners of infanticide in the past are ultimately our predecessors in an endless and essentially unchanging fight to keep men from making claims to female bodies."[4] A precise social analysis requires that we pay attention to the specific conditions of history, culture, and locale that give any act of fertility control its meaning. Women make the "choice" to get or induce an abortion under an enormous range of conditions, some of which are oppressive, desperate, or even dehumanized. But in most cases they do so consciously, as active agents of their fertility and not merely victims of their biology or pawns of "natural" forces like population movements. If we are going to understand changes in fertility, we have to look at women, the conditions in which they live, and their own consciousness.

The Role of Technology

Many people think that birth control is the "modern" invention of industrial societies, associated with techniques or methods that preindustrial peoples could not have known. This belief echoes in everyday usage, which links birth control to methods (e.g., the pill) that require medical intervention and commercial distribution. But such belief stems from the intellectual error of technological determinism, since it confuses the *activity* of birth control (including abortion) with the techniques through which it is achieved. It is like thinking that steam-driven engines or computers inaugurated the industrial or "information" revolution, rather than the social relations that produced the machines. In this view, birthrates decline mainly because of "the diffusion of new contraceptive aspirations, techniques and information," an event associated conventionally with industrialization.[5]

In fact, historical and anthropological evidence weighs heavily against technological determinism in the analysis of fertility changes. Most human societies have attempted to control their fertility, whether this was a systematic aim or not. Not only through rules governing marriage patterns and taboos on sexual intercourse at certain times, but through the deliberate use of contraceptives, abortion, and infanticide, fertility control has been a constant of human life.[6] From the Hutterites to the Kung San, the fertility of women fluctuates over a wide spectrum in which a woman's "biological capacity" is defined in relation to a specific social and ecological context and intent. This intent has everything to do not only with scarce resources or the division of property but with the specific problems of women in their nearly universal assignment to the bearing and care of children.

Evidence concerning preindustrial hunting and gathering and pastoral societies calls into question the assumption that they normally suffered from population scarcity as a result of high mortality rates. Rather, high reproduction rates and limited resources often meant that such societies risked a population surplus, resulting in deliberate efforts to curb population growth.[7] The "mode of life" among nomadic hunters and gatherers necessitated the reliance on deliberate means (e.g., postpartum abstinence or twin infanticide) of controlling and spacing births "because of the difficulty of transporting more than one baby at a time."[8] But these concerns particularly affected women. For example, postpartum abstinence in precolonial East and West African societies was a fertility control method instigated and sustained by women. Not only was it based on a belief that pregnancy or sexual intercourse during lactation might be harmful to a nursing child; it also reflected the practical problems of transporting too many children under nomadic or tribal conditions.

The criteria of "too many" in this case grew, not out of the high economic "costs" of children, but out of the needs and perceptions of women as childtenders. Indeed, "too many" children is not an absolute but a historically specific desideratum. Himes describes in detail the numerous methods of contraception used among East and Central European peasant women in the fifteenth and sixteenth centuries, leaving no doubt that these methods were the product of a folklore and situation specific to women. Alongside the numerous herbal and magical remedies, methods such as a molded disk of melted beeswax inserted into the vagina to cover the cervix or a sponge soaked in lemon juice as a spermicide attest to the tenacity and ingenuity of women in their desire—often successful— to control pregnancies.[9]

Also, throughout history and to the present day, even when effective methods of contraception are known, women have continued to rely on abortion. Among all fertility control methods, abortion has been the most persistent and prevalent. Formulas for abortion in ancient Chinese medical texts date from nearly three thousand years before Christ; there are references to abortion throughout ancient Greek and Roman literature (e.g., in the writings of the physician Soranos of Ephesus) and among Islamic medical writers of the Middle Ages. Methods included not only herbal remedies but also abdominal massage, hot baths, and jumping or other "violent movements."[10] George Devereux, who surveyed 350 primitive, ancient, and preindustrial societies in the Yale Human Relations Area Files, found a range of abortion methods including herbs, chemicals, mechanical means, violence, and magic. Customs and values related to abortion practices also vary enormously. Nevertheless, within this diversity, "there is every indication that abortion is an absolutely universal phenomenon, and that it is impossible even to construct an imaginary social system in which no woman would ever feel at least impelled to abort."[11] The historical demographer E. A. Wrigley echoes this conviction: "It is clear that abortions were attempted at times in all populations."[12]

It is important to ask why, even when effective methods of contraception are available, the practice of abortion persists. The answer has to do with the specific nature of abortion. An abortion intervenes after the fact, to end a particular pregnancy; its focus is the pregnancy itself, not sexuality, not a woman's reproductive cycle or capacity. But more than anything else, abortion, however sordid and dangerous, has in most times and places been accessible to women. Abortion is a "uniquely female practice, which men could neither control nor prevent."[13] While methods of contraception are known and practiced in "primitive peasant cultures," they tend to be used in a hit-or-miss fashion. More important, methods like coitus interruptus, which rely on the man's cooperation, may be incompatible with the reality that "the physical burden and danger of childbearing, and the responsibility for nourishing and rearing the child, fall mainly on the mother" and that "a wish to avoid childbirth . . . is apt to be hers rather than her husband's."[14] Abortion does not require male cooperation, is technically simple and completely effective, and responds to the problem at hand. In fact, it is incorrect to refer to abortion as a "technique" of fertility control. Abortion is the prevention of a pregnancy that has already begun from going to term, from eventuating in childbirth; and abortion may be accomplished through a variety of methods—chemical, herbal, mechanical, surgical. It is a *timing* of birth control, rather than a specific technique, and its usefulness derives from the many reasons—historical, economic, psychological—why "planning ahead" might be neither effective nor appropriate to the situation.

When does a pregnancy begin? That question has confused the meaning of abortion through many historical periods, revealing once again that human biological experiences are always mediated by social life. The very concept of an abortion is a particular way of constructing an event whose boundaries and content have differed in different situations. Can we always identify the markers on the continuum between a "spontaneous" abortion and one that is "helped along," or between the latter and a whole series of possible interventions through different means and at different points during a pregnancy? Women in preindustrial Europe do not seem to have drawn any sharp distinction between "potions" that intervened before or after conception, since conception (as opposed to "animation") had no special meaning. In England and America prior to the mid-nineteenth century, pregnancy as a biological event was not thought to begin until "quickening," at which time there was a "child." Before that, a woman was "irregular"; herbal potions and purgatives, hot baths, or vigorous jumping were natural, not medical, strategies to make her "regular" again.[15] Moreover, since most abortions until the present century either were self-induced or were administered by midwives or through the remedies of local lay healers, herbalists, or female kin or neighbors, they have no recorded history; they are not "cases" in a medical sense. Only in France in the late eighteenth and nineteenth centuries and in America and England in the nineteenth century, when a rising male-dominated medical profession exposed the practice of abortion and its lay practitioners to scrutiny and attack, did abortion acquire a history, both demographic and medical. Under the "surveillance" of physicians and populationists, it acquired an incidence (social measurement) and a politic (state regulation). In this regard, abortion is similar to mental illness and homosexuality; it is historically constructed and takes a particular ideological form through the scrutiny and "recordings" of positivist medicine.[16] Its very meaning—as act of "deviance" (defiance?) or act of "nature"—reflects cultural inscription and social change.

Contrary to the thesis that fertility control is a product of modernization, some historical demographers have established that major declines in fertility occurred in rural areas of England, France, and America long before "mature" industrialization. These declines were due mainly to the deliberate use of birth control and abortion within marriage, rather than the postponement of marriage. A classic study of the village of Colyton, England, for example, demonstrated that as early as the mid-seventeenth century, villagers were using systematic methods of "family limitation"— probably abortion and coitus interruptus, and possibly infanticide. Family reconstitution methods show changes in the age-specific fertility rate and the age at which wives had their last birth. One can quite reasonably infer the use of fertility control methods from the fact that married women were restricting childbearing to the early years of their fertile period and reducing their total number of children.[17]

Although they document these facts, historical demographers are reluctant to acknowledge their social implications. E. A. Wrigley remains fixed in the cultural biases of modernization theory when he argues that people in preindustrial societies adopt methods to limit births or population as an adaptive behavior geared toward group survival, not unlike that exhibited by "robins and rooks." Fertility control in premodern contexts is thus a form of "unconscious rationality," which contrasts sharply with the "conscious rationality" of modern couples when they exercise "private choice" to use birth control.[18] This notion of unconscious rationality is based on ignorance of the specific activities and knowledge of women in preindustrial societies as well as the presence in those societies of conscious, materially based motives for limiting births. Demographers cannot explain birth control in preindustrial, particularly preagricultural, societies—before there was a systematic ideology of "birth planning"—because of their inattention to the sexual division of labor in those societies and women's work as childbearers and rearers.

By contrast, Linda Gordon notes the "different interests of men and women in the practice of birth control" and emphasizes the existence of birth control and abortion methods in traditional societies as "part of the folklore and folk culture . . . developed by women and handed down from generation to generation."[19] The methods used most frequently in preindustrial societies—magic, potions, or other means to induce abortion, as well as abstinence and infanticide—were "more amenable" to secret use by women. Such methods did not depend on male compliance or cooperation. (Gordon argues persuasively that even magical or obviously ineffective methods may be *rational* insofar as they are *believed* to have a causal effect on fertility and, at the least, indicate a conscious acceptance of birth control as a legitimate aim.)

Nevertheless, recognizing that women's use of birth control crosses many cultures and predates modern times should not suggest a false universality. The degree to which women use or even have any notion of fertility control methods, effective or ineffective, may vary tremendously within the same country or time period, even from one town or village to the next. How do we explain the absence of "techniques" when techniques have already been invented? How do we understand the *social* transmission of knowledge or lore, except in terms of social life?

The argument I am making here assumes that abortion and contraceptive practices, like changing rates of fertility, have to do with changes in the social relations of reproduction, which are inherently gender relations, and not in the first instance with technology. What a feminist perspective on historical demography would lead us to expect is that where conditions exist that enhance women's power—strong female networks of kin or neighbors, matrilocal or matrilineal patterns of kinship, or direct female access to the material resources of survival (employment or land)—methods of contraception and abortion will be systematic and effective. Conversely, where childbearing is the only source of prestige for women and relationship to men the only means of survival, fertility control methods may be less accessible to women. But these conditions vary perhaps even more among tribal, horticultural, peasant, and preindustrial societies than they do among industrial ones.

An example of this variation and its impact on fertility in one preindustrial context is offered by David Levine, who compares fertility patterns in four rural villages in "protoindustrial" (seventeenth- to eighteenth-century) England. Levine adopts the concept of "family strategy" to show the deliberate use of fertility control among working-class families even before industrialization and urbanization. That strategy differed depending on economic conditions, especially shifts in the demand for labor, in different locales.[20] This analysis reveals that while economic shifts affect fertility patterns, they do so in ways that are not mechanical or readily predictable but that depend on particular circumstances of class, occupation, and locality.

Some historians recognize that land enclosures and the rapid proletarianization of the rural population in England created a different relationship to an economic future and to children than did traditions of peasant proprietorship. For cottagers and laborers, in the late seventeenth through the mid-nineteenth centuries, a "marginal and precarious" existence and the development within capitalist "protoindustry" of a demand for child labor and occasional labor created disincentives to delay marriage and pregnancy and a generally rising rate of fertility.[21] But while these conditions pertained to the large majority of rural proletarians (thereby keeping English fertility high well into the nineteenth century), skill and occupational divisions and local labor markets created significant variations in working-class fertility patterns. In seventeenth-century Terling, for example, the complete and early pauperization of the rural proletariat removed all hope of improved circumstances or acquiring land; thus "a calculating approach to reproductive behavior . . . was undermined," and earlier marriages and more childbearing were the result.[22] In contrast, skilled framework knitters in Shepshed accommodated their fertility to the need for domestic labor (wife and children) in a family mode of production, resulting in early marriage and childbearing combined with *low* overall fertility.[23]

But the care with which Levine considers class and occupational influences on fertility contrasts with his carelessness concerning how fertility was controlled and by whom. In the village of Colyton, deteriorating conditions in the woolen industry and a high level of unemployment among men were accompanied, not by higher fertility, but by lowered fertility within marriage.[24] Apparently, then, "a calculating approach" to fertility was not "undermined" in this case, but Levine's explanation of this discrepancy is confusing because he defines the proletarian family's "fertility strategy" and its economic situation solely from the viewpoint of the male wage earner. Thus, Levine focuses on age at first marriage rather than fertility control within marriage as the predominant "strategy" of fertility control, even though Wrigley's earlier study had demonstrated that it was *marital* birth control and abortion that mainly accounted for reduced fertility in Colyton. Specifically, Levine argues that men, in response to rising unemployment, "chose older brides."[25] This is a striking example of male bias, since it assumes that decisions about marriage and fertility are invariably made by men. Nor does it explain why the loss of male economic opportunities in Colyton should lead to the opposite strategy from that which prevailed in Terling. Given that Colyton women, unlike men, were regularly and continually employed outside the home, why should we not assume that it was women who chose to delay marriage? Indeed, the major difference between Colyton and Terling is that the former maintained a high rate of female employment in a thriving lacemaking industry. "Sixty percent of all women over 15 . . . were engaged in lacemaking" in 1695, so that *"throughout the whole period . . .* women in Colyton would find employment in activities which tied them to a larger, extralocal economy. . . ."[26]

> . . . these phenomena must be seen in the context of an increase in independent *women's work.* The spread of lacemaking in Colyton was probably crucially important in freeing women from the strict confines of family economies.[27]

While Levine recognizes this "independence" in relation to illegitimacy and early marriage in the eighteenth century, he does not ask whether delayed marriage and low marital fertility in seventeenth-century Colyton may not have had the same roots, that is, may not have been a *female* strategy based on the economic and social conditions of women. Proletarianized women of Colyton were less dependent than women of other locales on marriage for their economic survival, while their work outside the home no doubt exerted pressures on their time and capacity as childbearers and brought them into contact with other women. But this interpretation does not fit easily within Levine's overall framework, which fails to consider how women's work may have different implications for marital (and premarital) fertility than men's, given the sexual division of labor around child care.[28] A crucial result of this shortsightedness is that Levine ignores Wrigley's evidence that seventeenth-century Colyton women not only delayed marriage but controlled their fertility within marriage and that this was the main factor in their reduced childbearing. The likelihood is that decreased fertility among Colyton residents was achieved mainly through abortion and contraception and that these were strategies initiated by, learned through, and shared collectively among a community of working women.

Birth control practices do not fall from the sky. Their development and use follow from specific social conditions that have to do with economic shifts or gender relations or some interaction of the two. These constants do not mean that there are no fundamental changes or cleavages in the practice of fertility control but that such changes generally occur in the realm of ideas, social organization, and politics, rather than technology, and that they have social and economic roots. Thus, with the development of a capitalist market and long before industrialization, a new consciousness about fertility control began to arise (its predecessor, presumably, was not "unconsciousness" but *different,* preindustrial forms of consciousness). This new fertility ethic focused on children as a "value" and, in the true spirit of capitalist accounting, on the calculation and "rational planning" of family size in accordance with family resources.[29] But for children to be perceived as an "investment" to the husband, rather than security against old age, extra hands, or extra kin, presupposed definite conditions that transform the meaning of having and raising children. Central among these conditions in Western Europe were (1) a system of production in which land and its products become commodities of exchange (so that the economics of consolidating and appropriating supersede the custom of parceling out); (2) a wage-labor economy that is sufficiently pervasive that families are dependent on it to survive and sufficiently expansive that they have some hope of a future to plan for; (3) a sociomedical context in which infant and child mortality is low enough to make "frugality" in childbearing worth the risk; and (4) a family structure whose core is the married couple and whose central purpose is the production and maintenance of *children as values.*

In other words, what was necessary was an idealized version of the nuclear family, which eventually would be inherited, in a bourgeois society, by most of the working class.[30] These conditions historically have arisen according to different timetables for different classes; moreover, their implications at a given moment may differ for women and men within those classes. But whatever the class and gender specifics, the conditions give rise to the techniques, not the other way around; the need and desire for fertility control necessarily precede the practice of it and the forms that practice takes.

Malthusian Ideology and Bourgeois Culture

If not new techniques, what is specifically modern about a "contraceptive society"? Until the twentieth century, statistical data regarding contraception and abortion did not exist. Historical demographers inferred patterns and practices indirectly, either from data on age-specific fertility or from literary evidence. But since we know that contraceptives and abortion have nearly always been used, "modernity" here cannot be simply the use of fertility control or even its enlarged scale, but must lie in the attitudes, reasons, or circumstances surrounding that use.[31] Moreover, since no essentially new methods of fertility control were developed from ancient times until the twentieth century (unless we count the introduction of antiseptics in the mid-nineteenth century, which made abortions a good deal safer), "technology" obviously is not an explanation. In order to explain a rising incidence of deliberate fertility control, demography must go outside its usual circular reasoning (new methods are adopted because they exist, fertility declines because it is "adaptive" that fertility should decline) and begin to look at the social, economic, and ideological changes that may affect fertility practices in a particular historical context.

Not surprisingly, Thomas Malthus was merely the codifier of a mode of thought about fertility that predated his work and the industrializing context surrounding it by two hundred years. Both Noonan and Ariès trace the roots of the "economic ethic," or the idea that one should limit one's children to only so many as one could support, to the rise of a market in land, labor, and goods—to early capitalism. At least since the sixteenth century, French landowners practiced inheritance customs and marriage patterns designed to restrict numbers of heirs and thus preserve the patrimony. These included packing off surplus daughters to convents and sons to monasteries or military service, as well as delaying their own marriages. They were the traditional fertility control methods of preindustrial patriarchs, who controlled not only land but households, wives, servants, and children.[32] Women too, especially those of the artisan and laboring classes, had economic motives for postponing marriage and thereby limiting fertility. Many such women in Western Europe, from the sixteenth to the eighteenth centuries—during the rise of capitalism— were obliged to work to save money for a dowry or acquire a craft or skills before marriage.[33]

Moreover, the bourgeois ethic was rapidly imposed on the poor in preindustrial programs of population control. The enforcement of the Act of Settlement by English Poor Law overseers throughout the late seventeenth and the eighteenth centuries was infused with the notion that young couples should be prevented from marrying "before they have provided themselves with a settling," lest they become a burden on the parish.[34] The application of a "moral economy" of fertility control to the poor probably has much older roots. Noonan finds its traces among the medieval church fathers as early as the eleventh century; Bede justified an exception to the church's prohibition on contraception and abortion for *paupercula* (poor women), whom he distinguished from "fornicators" (women who don't have poverty as an excuse).[35] While one case has to do with coercion and the other with permissiveness, the point is that, where the poor are concerned, the relation between fertility control and economic necessity was taken for granted. In the early modern period landowners throughout much of continental Europe began to impose this idea on their daughters and younger sons, who were pressured to delay or forsake marriage in order to avoid "diluting the inheritance."[36] Having too many children was a definite economic liability; family limitation was a way of thinking that arose in a particular economic and social setting.

Yet the practice of birth control (contraception and abortion), as distinct from delayed marriage, acquired its own ideology in a bourgeois patriarchal culture. Ariès describes this new ideology in Weberian terms, as a "spirit" of family planning, an ethic that dictates that births should be "calculated" in accordance with one's "means" (*"la notion de 'calcul,' de 'politique' et de niveau de vie"*), that families should plan ahead for children and not have more children than they can "afford."[37] While this ethic may have its prototype in the behavior of the preindustrial noble or peasant landholder—absolute in his patriarchal authority over household and kin, calculating the value of his property for purposes of succession—it is different in one fundamental respect. Here, the value being cultivated is not land but children; the purpose of controlling fertility is to make children into assets, not merely to prevent them from becoming liabilities. This objective coincides with a mode of fertility control that is different from the earlier forms of delayed marriage (also economically motivated), a mode that is particular in both the methods it entails and the values those methods reflect.

One element of the "demographic transition" that seems to be verified by family reconstitution studies is a dramatic shift, in various countries at different times, in the average married woman's age at last birth. What occurs is "a new and different type of fertility control" involving "stopping behavior" or the projection and achievement of a "target family size" and the deliberate cessation of childbearing once that size is reached.[38] This behavior is not a function of industrialization, as evidenced by the fact that France experienced a major fertility decline in most regions during the eighteenth century, when it was mainly a country of peasants.[39] But the ideology that elevates the behavior to a "moral economy" is particular to the rising bourgeoisie.

It is not easy to disentangle "moral" from "economic" elements in this ideology. For one thing, economic interests and strategies are invariably legitimated by moral dicta, with which they easily become confused; the classic example in capitalist culture is the work ethic and high productivity. Ultimately, as Marxist theory shows, economic conditions determine moral values, but the relation between them is complicated and enmeshed. Second, the social consequences of moral values may be different depending on the people to whom they are applied; the idea that one *ought* not have more children than one can support has a different content when applied to/by the upper class than when applied to/by the poor.

Nowhere are the moralistic implications of Malthusian ideology clearer than in the writings of Malthus himself (whose first *Essay on the Principle of Population* appeared in 1798), particularly in his application of his ideas to the working class. Malthusianism, it must be understood, is not a scientific analysis but a moral ideology and prescription for action that would gradually become part of bourgeois consciousness. The core of Malthus' doctrine was "a new moral economy," rationalized as science, whose central thrust was to exhort the poor to restrain from sexual "excess" and early marriage.[40] In his first essay Malthus evoked a tone of dire fatalism, suggesting that "misery and vice," "vices . . . continually involving both sexes," were the inevitable price of checking exorbitant population growth.[41] The "vices" Malthus had in mind were presumably various forms of nonprocreative sex, including the use of abortion and birth control. In later versions of the essay, however, "moral restraint" is added as a major form of "preventive check," especially in regard to the English poor. Yet Malthus continues to condemn birth control (still a "vice") while admonishing the laboring *man* to delay marriage and *"not to bring beings into the world for whom he cannot find the means of support."*[42] Hence is the working class blamed for its misery and the "solution" to poverty and hunger seen to lie in abstinence from childbearing and sex.[43] With time, this moralistic core would be leavened with the assumptions of bourgeois economics concerning the "rationality" of market behavior and the appropriateness of economic planning and calculation in the production of children as of everything else. But, from its origins, bourgeois population theory, like bourgeois economics, is primarily a moral code: Too many children, like too little money (or too much sex), are an evil.

Turned inward, on the upper and middle classes, Malthusian moral precepts become a prescription for action, a strategy to secure personal wealth and class cohesion. Ariès argues that in seventeenth- and eighteenth-century texts, especially those critical of the new "family planning" ethos, economic motives were "much more powerful" than ideas about sexual freedom. In the second half of the eighteenth century in France, contraception was so common among respectable married couples, convinced of its propriety in achieving respectable worldly ends, that it was no longer confessed.[44] A study by André Burgière correlates the areas of greatest fertility decline and contraceptive practice in France in the late seventeenth and early eighteenth centuries with the influence of Jansenism and religious asceticism. "Family limitation," in this view, emerges as the operating principle of a new family type for which children are no longer the instruments to forge alliances or perpetuate the lineage but become both the content and the emblems whereby the household establishes its independence and "[improves] its social status. . . . Sexual asceticism [delayed marriage as well as abstinence and withdrawal] plays the same role in this spirit of matrimonial enterprise that the sense of thrift played in the spirit of capitalist enterprise."[45]

While "fewer and better" would become a practical strategy for bourgeois self-improvement, it was also perceived by the eighteenth century in France as a "badge of identity" certifying upper-class moral superiority. One of the authors in the *Encyclopédie* cites "luxury, the love of pleasure, the idea of conserving one's beauty, the embarrassment of pregnancy, the even greater embarrassment of a numerous family" as common reasons why upper-class women were thought to use contraception.[46] What this quote reveals is not only an upper bourgeoisie attempting to demarcate its identity through smaller families but also the link, for bourgeois male republicans, between "luxury," rebellious women, and birth control and between patriotism, domestic order, and procreation. By the nineteenth century, the "embarrassment of a numerous family" had become firmly entrenched in the bourgeoisie's sense of its status and respectability— including that of the bourgeois woman. A character in an 1858 novel, queried about whether he might have twelve children, replies: "Never in the wise and enlightened bourgeoisie. Twelve children, maître Pierre! This unrestrained multiplication of the human species occurs only in the lower classes. . . ."[47]

As a bourgeois ideology, Malthusian thought is thus multidimensional. It is a *moral prescription* that is at once about capitalist values and about sexual values; the means toward family limitation are forms of sexual restraint (in themselves a "thrift" or "economy"), whereas its rewards are material prosperity and well-educated (male) children. It is also a *signifier* through which the bourgeois class identifies itself as against an expanding proletariat and, especially in the towns, *les classes dangereuses*. Finally, it is a set of *practices* that reflects capitalist values (saving, investment, individual achievement) and the objective material conditions of a rising bourgeoisie.[48]

To describe an ideology is not to explain its social origins, however. The new definition of the value of children contained in early "family planning" doctrine arises out of a market society in which command of both commerce and the state required increasing literacy and scientific knowledge. These requirements entailed a new emphasis on educating children (mainly sons), which in turn resulted in a new relationship between parents and children. With the development of schools and "childhood" in its modern meaning, upper- and middle-class parents in Western Europe became responsible for their children in new ways and for a longer period of time: for their food and clothing, for the costs of their education, and most of all for their "future."[49] Hence, the bourgeois model of "the family"—the nuclear family "concentrated on the child," individual achievement, and well-being—is inseparable from the bourgeois model of fertility—the admonition to have a *certain number* of children of a *certain quality,* who, like "fruit trees," are articles of investment, cultivation, and long-term growth. The rise of a "Malthusian mentality" is connected to the historical development of this family form.

But there is a fourth dimension of Malthusianism. Although it often remains implicit rather than explicit, it is the foundation of the whole edifice: the precept that "quality children" are produced by "good mothers." On one level, this precept is an ideological construct that gets advanced most strenuously as a pronatalist dogma. In eighteenth-century France, political writers articulated it in the most virulent terms, binding women to home and motherhood and excoriating those who ventured out of this sphere. Rousseau and Moheau (one a Calvinist, the other a Catholic) railed against such "unnatural" and "perverse" practices as abortion, contraception, and wet nursing, accusing women who indulged in them of betraying their duty (procreation) to their husbands and the state for hedonistic ends.[50] Now, these writers are well-known anti-Malthusians, the Cassandras of "depopulation" in France. But what is important is that the same basic ideological premise they invoked underlay both pronatalist and antinatalist strategies: the necessity of woman's domestication, her confinement to nurturance and maternal duty. The new dogma of maternal duty and the abominable "selfishness" of women who abandon that duty was addressed to all women but particularly those of the upper and middle classes. For the new bourgeois ethic of family planning, "quality" must supersede "quantity"; but it is through the ministrations of Mother that "quality children" are planned and produced. Thus the interconnected strands of the bourgeois family form include not only the legal and moral power of the father and "fewer and better" children but also the subordination of women's sexuality to maternity.

Given the changing situation of bourgeois women as mothers, it is not difficult to understand why these women became principal supporters of the new Malthusian ideology, as well as its practitioners. The increasing dependency of children requires the increasing responsibility of mothers, now not only as breeders but also as caretakers. Ironically, the emphasis on limiting the family's number of children entails an expansion and intensification of maternal "duties," as the idea of "quality"—education, manners, a "better standard of living," good character, piety, and so forth—attains finer and finer ramifications. In fact, the two notions, fewer children and better mothering, reinforce one another; expanded childrearing responsibilities stimulate women's interest in limiting births. The motor force driving the (bourgeois) "family economy" is *'les soucis du calcul de l'avenir des enfants'*; the family member most caught up in these concerns is Mother. She is "more confined to the domestic economy, closer to children," and thus more attuned to the values of birth control and school, as vehicles toward economic security and social betterment.[51] The economic security and social betterment of her children are in fact *her job*. The rise of schooling and the decline in fertility are interconnected developments in capitalist society not only because schooling costs money but because it leaves mothers isolated in child care, without the aid of older children to mind younger ones. For Ariès, the function of bourgeois housewives within the "family economy," though it is outside the market, clearly has economic as well as cultural and sexual dimensions; the two are different aspects of the same social relationship. Thus his analysis points to the interconnections between a bourgeois culture of fertility (including a particular family form, which is the locus of the family planning ethos) and bourgeois economic interests.

Grasping the breadth and complexity of Malthusian and neo-Malthusian ideology makes it easier to come to terms with its powerful hold, even among its critics. Marxists, trade unionists, radical birth controllers, and feminists in the nineteenth century were opposed to various aspects of Malthusian doctrine; yet their thinking became trapped in some of its basic assumptions. Marx's critique of Malthus (whom he accused of gross plagiarism) struck directly at the naturalistic, mechanistic bias of a theory of population that claimed abstract, universal validity ("an abstract law of population exists only for plants and animals, and even then only in the absence of any historical intervention by man"). The critical point about Marx's anti-Malthusian concept of a "relative surplus population" was not only that "overpopulation" is a product of the cyclical processes of capital accumulation (which create unemployment and deteriorated housing), but, more generally, that shifts in human population, presumably including fertility, are always the result of particular historical circumstances and social purposes.[52] But since Marx did not see women as an integral part of the proletariat, as both reproducers and producers, he had no basis for theorizing a "law of population" whose dynamics included women's need for fertility control, apart from the shifts in the capitalist demand for labor; he did not see fertility control as part of the class struggle, much less the gender struggle. Thus the Marxist critique of Malthus was partial rather than total. It recognized the social basis of population, but it ignored the progressive and potentially liberating dimension of human efforts to control reproduction as well as production.

Engels, writing in the 1840s and 1880s, expressed sympathy with the anti-birth-control sentiments that characterized many of the British male trade unionists throughout the nineteenth century. In 1844, for example, referring to Malthus' doctrine as a "repulsive blasphemy against man and nature," he asserted that *"children are like trees,* returning abundantly the expenditure laid out on them, . . . that a *large family* would be a most desirable *gift to the community.*"[53] The idea that controlling fertility is a "blasphemy against nature" and that large families, not small, are morally desirable clearly reflects a reversion to an ahistorical, naturalistic concept of fertility, not a transcendence of it. Though less explicitly, Engels here evokes the same Jacobin conception of a male-dominated patriarchal family expressed in William Godwin's *On Population* (1820):

> . . . it is one of the clearest duties of a citizen to give birth to
> his like, and bring offspring to the state. *Without this he is hardly*
> *a citizen: his children and his wife are pledges he gives to the public for*
> *good behavior;* they are his securities, that he will truly enter into

the feeling of a common interest, and be desirous of
perpetuating and increasing the immunities of his country
from generation to generation.[54]

Reproduction through the male-dominated nuclear family is the tie that
binds the proletarian male to the state; *more* children, not fewer, signal
woman's domestication *within* the working class. Thus, the radical attack
on Malthus rests on the same bourgeois model of family relations and
woman's confinement to reproduction as does Malthusianism.

Historians of nineteenth-century feminism and birth control correctly
distinguish both the radical birth control movement and the feminist
movement (which were themselves distinct) from the neo-Malthusian
movement, whose main practical goal was to curb the fertility of the
working class.[55] But they underestimate the extent to which both groups
managed to incorporate or accommodate certain basic elements of neo-
Malthusian ideology into their thinking. In particular, the emphasis on
(1) economic, moral, or eugenic justifications for "fewer and better" children (as contrasted with justifications concerning women's health and
self-determination) and (2) motherhood as woman's highest duty were
embedded in feminist ideas about voluntary control over childbearing.
Feminists who opposed mechanical means of birth control in favor of
the practice of "voluntary motherhood" were committed to a policy of
sexual restraint or abstinence that fitted well with Malthusian notions
of sexual or "moral" economy. Let us recall that, at least from the seventeenth century, the bourgeois ethic of family limitation had been directed
as much at the bourgeois class, its self-regulation and self-definition, as
at the proliferating working class. The twin precepts of sexual prudence
and smaller families were embraced by feminists, not only as a means
toward women's protection within marriage (although that was an important part of it), but also as an expression of female virtue—maternal
duty to children, to class, to "the race."

In short, feminist thinking (in the nineteenth and early twentieth
centuries) about fertility and its control embodied a basic contradiction,
which reflects the influence of Malthusian and neo-Malthusian ideology.
Along with the idea of the wife's "right to be her own person, and her
sacred right to deny her husband if need be and to decide how often
and when she should become a mother,"[56] was a firm belief in motherhood
as "an exalted, sacred profession" that was woman's main responsibility
as well as her virtue. Later feminists, who believed fervently in birth
control, alloyed their feminism with a neo-Malthusian commitment to
"quality over quantity," and even eugenic arguments about "racial betterment." The South African feminist Olive Schreiner wrote in 1911 that
the commitment of "modern" woman was not simply " 'Thou shalt bear,'
but rather, 'Thou shalt not bear in excess of thy power to rear and train

satisfactorily.'" She argued that "to the family as well as to the state unlimited fecundity on the part of the female has already . . . become an irremediable evil. . . ."[57] American feminists like Charlotte Perkins Gilman and Frances Willard aimed at the "professionalization" of mother-hood, making childrearing rational and scientific—in the name of "race progress" and eugenics as well as emancipated womanhood.[58] Even Emma Goldman, writing in 1914, opposed the "race suicide" propaganda of Roo-sevelt with an amalgam of feminist-libertarian and eugenic ideas:

> Woman no longer wants to be a party to the production of a race of sickly, feeble, decrepit, wretched human beings, who would have neither the strength nor moral courage to throw off the yoke of poverty and slavery. Instead she desires fewer and better children, begotten and reared in love and through free choice; not by compulsion, as marriage imposes.[59]

Birth Control in the Bourgeois Family

I have been suggesting that Malthusian (and neo-Malthusian) doc-trine developed historically within an ideological framework that assumed patriarchal control over women and women's confinement to motherhood. It was this framework, as well as its repressive application to the poor, that gave the doctrine its conservative thrust, even though it contained an unmistakably progressive element as well. One group of historians interprets the cultural origins and implications of the new family/fertility ideology very differently, however, associating both with the rise of sexual "egalitarianism" and female "power" within the "modern family." Jean-Louis Flandrin argues that contraception (by which he means primarily coitus interruptus) arose in eighteenth-century France on a large scale because of the "construction of a new family morality." This morality involves an increase of sentiment and reciprocity in the relations between parents and children as well as husbands and wives, but its center is the introduction of a "courtly" tradition into conjugal relations beginning in the late seventeenth century, which effectively enhanced women's power within marriage. As a result, women's physical and health needs became a matter of greater common concern; the assumption of painful labor and death in childbirth as woman's fate gave way to a desire to avert the risks of constant childbearing. Moreover, it became increasingly possible for women to avoid the iron dictum of the "conjugal due" (wom-an's duty, according to church doctrine, not to deny her husband his sexual "rights"), either through feigned headaches or simply through the growing assumption that *mutual consent* ought to be the basis of sexuality between married couples as it was between lovers.[60] The Enlightenment idea that sexual pleasure and procreation could be separated, that this was a specifically *human* capacity, became the basis for both women's sexual autonomy and contraception in marriage. Hence the increase in abstinence and coitus interruptus as methods for controlling fertility. According to Flandrin's reasoning, these methods involve a reduction of male sexual pleasure and therefore can only be "practiced when women were in a position to persuade men to practice [them]"; they necessarily involve an element of reciprocity and even female power in heterosexual relations.[61]

There is an important strength in Flandrin's argument in that, unlike many of the more economically oriented theories of fertility change, it understands the situation and needs of women as central in constructing patterns of fertility behavior. It assumes that major declines in fertility based on conscious planning, while involving the cooperation of men, are probably initiated by women. Even coitus interruptus, which has conventionally been considered a "male method," can in this view be due as much to female "quick-mindedness" or self-assertion as to male courtesy.[62] In an argument similar to Flandrin's, Daniel Scott-Smith explains the declining birthrate throughout the nineteenth century in the United States in terms of what he calls "domestic feminism," a historical change whereby "the average woman experienced a great increase in power and autonomy within the family." This "new autonomy of women within the family" made possible "the power of the wife to persuade or coerce her husband into practicing birth control," mainly abstinence and withdrawal, and even gave her "sexual control" over her husband.[63]

Apart from their failure to cite any evidence of what women thought about birth control and sexuality (rather than the fragmentary literary voices of male authors of advice manuals and moral tracts), these arguments suffer from two major problems. First, to the extent that they describe a partial reality in women's family and marital conditions, it is a reality that pertains almost exclusively to bourgeois or upper-class families, although they claim to be accounting for declines in fertility that were general rather than class specific. Second, even with regard to women of the bourgeoisie, the argument that their status and power increased *within* the family ignores their restriction *to* the family within bourgeois culture and the emergent capitalist economy, and the moral imperatives with which that status was hedged. Thus maternal duty becomes "power," sexual abstinence becomes "sexual control," and domestic confinement becomes "domestic feminism." Indeed, these authors ignore that a feminist ideology and movement arose in the first place because upper- and middle-class women had so *little* power, within the state and the economy *and* within the domestic sphere, and that their subordination in one was directly related to their subordination in the other. The glorification of maternity and domesticity that would become part of the culture and of the new republic had to do not so much with women's empowerment as with their social control by church, state, and husbands. To understand that "feminism itself grew from the upward mobility that made small families more economical"[64] is to say that feminism had a particular class base in the rising bourgeoisie. It is not to argue that the women of that class were "rising" in the same way as the men. The imperative toward smaller families was not only a sign of "upward mobility" of the class as a whole but a necessity dictated by the specific conditions of women.

Feminist scholarship shows that women's position within the family, for women of all classes in early industrial France, England, and America, became increasingly defined by the primary and exclusive responsibilities of motherhood—not only the bearing but also the care and rearing of children.[65] This fact more than any other would shape women's needs and desires regarding fertility and the "demographic transition" that resulted—but differently for middle-class and for poor women. For neither group, however, does it make sense to draw a sharp distinction between "economic" and "cultural," or "moral," motives for limiting children. Rather, motherhood and domestic management *were* the economic functions of bourgeois wives, as industrialization increasingly removed productive tasks from the home and segregated housewives. For poor women, especially those without dependable men to support them, children were first and foremost an economic problem and motherhood an economic task. But for women of all classes, historically as today, their objective relationship to pregnancy and children has necessarily made their motives for limiting fertility different from and more immediate than men's.

Feminist thinking in the late nineteenth and early twentieth centuries continued to rest in an uneasy tension between the notion of fertility control as woman's moral duty (to "enlightened motherhood" or to "the race"), rooted in eugenics, and the notion of fertility control as woman's fundamental right to control over her body. But even the idea of woman's right to control fertility, or "voluntary motherhood," had complicated layers of meaning. On the broadest level, that principle involved a " 'right of self-defense' . . . against venereal disease, male sexual demands or pregnancy"; it represented a resistance of Victorian bourgeois women to sexuality as such, which they perceived to be riddled with danger, contamination (through prostitution), and the perpetual double standard.[66] While "voluntary motherhood" rested on a "false consciousness" that subscribed to the "cult of motherhood,"[67] even this dimension contained a radical edge. For its proponents were not only proclaiming motherhood as woman's highest function but also demanding complete control and autonomy for women over motherhood—over when, whether, and how it would be undertaken.

The opposition of nineteenth-century feminists to abortion must be seen in this light. Apparently many feminists, including Elizabeth Cady

Stanton, saw abortion as a necessary evil prompted by men's sexual oppression of women and their refusal to accord their wives proper respect, "to check their sensualism, and leave their wives free to choose their periods of maternity."[68] Because of this association of abortion with the degradation and exploitation of women, many feminists responded positively to the physician-led political campaign in the post–Civil War period to outlaw abortion (see pp. 78–84). But, read carefully, these feminist protests were aimed, not at abortion per se, but at the one-sided and exploitative sexual relations that often made abortion necessary; they were aimed at the causes, not the consequences, of abortion. Mohr quotes the wife of a Christian physician, writing to a leader of the physicians' antiabortion campaign in 1866: "[T]he *greatest* cause of abortion is one hidden from the world, *viz.:* unhappiness and want of consideration towards wives in the marriage relation, the more refined education of girls, and their subsequent revolting from the degradation of being a mere thing—an appendage."[69]

Yet there is also an element of class and race division and class and race identity in the idea of "voluntary motherhood" that cuts through its resistant feminist aspects and separates middle-class feminists from working-class, immigrant, and black women. The vision of a "womanhood" that transcends domesticity and a privileged maternity is unavailable to these nineteenth-century women, not because of an absence of feminist consciousness, but because of the hegemony of class consciousness. The new ideology of family limitation and responsible motherhood defined the superiority of bourgeois mothers; within the context of bourgeois material conditions and class privilege, it created a cultural armature through which the bourgeois lady could recognize and display the class content of her gender identity. "Fewer and better" children and sexual "purity" became dual badges of class and racial identity for white bourgeois women at the same time as they were being asserted as pledges of resistance to men's domestic and sexual power. For women whose material conditions differed, the dominant ideology would be difficult if not impossible to realize.

Class Divisions, Motherhood, and Fertility Control among the Poor

In the course of the eighteenth century in France, the tendency to send infants off to wet nurses, the high incidence of child neglect and abandonment, and the declining fertility rate and increasing use of contraception were trends that cut across classes, occupational groups, and rural-urban distinctions.[70] But they clearly had different meanings and motivations depending on who the women were. For women of the salons, a smaller family and fewer maternal duties meant a way of being "free" and *at the same time* of distinguishing their status from that of middle-class and poor women. For the silk weaver in Lyons or the wife of a craftsman, the wet-nurse system and fertility control (including abortion) were necessities dictated by the conditions of her work and economic constraints.

Most European historians agree that the infant mortality rate in late-eighteenth-century France was exceedingly high; in some regions, about one in four infants sent out to the country to wet nurses died before the age of one year. This was a serious problem.[71] But the causes of high mortality had to do with the entire social organization of child care, in particular, long-distance travel under arduous conditions; the poverty and malnourishment of many wet nurses, even if infants managed to arrive safely; and the absence of alternative child-care arrangements other than foundling homes for working women, who made up a large part of the clientele of rural wet nurses. These conditions obviously affected some classes more harshly than others; they were class specific. In fact, mortality rates were much lower for infants who were not sent long distances, and "most of the infants placed in the country did not die there, but returned to their natural mothers in the city after the period of their nursing."[72] It is thus remarkable that demographic historians today echo the eighteenth-century writers in blaming infant deaths on the presumed callousness, indifference, and "selfishness" of mothers, rather than on a range of conditions that clearly structured child-care practices, especially for poor and working-class women.

Legal sanctions, as well as moral and economic ones, in France in the late eighteenth and early nineteenth centuries also affected social classes differently. These sanctions reinforced women's exclusive respon-sibility for children and therefore their special concern to limit their num-ber of children. Unlike English law, French law gave fathers few absolute rights over children, but it also gave them few responsibilities.[73] Both legal and economic burdens of fertility tended to fall most heavily on poor women. Poor and laboring women were not likely to read moral tracts on maternal nursing or literature on domestic manners and morals; nor, we might suppose, were they the objects of sexual chivalry. Especially if they were single and working in towns, away from kin and native village, they were vulnerable to seduction and abandonment and confined to a pool of working-class men, as potential lovers and husbands, that was occupationally itinerant, unstable, and small. (In Lyons, for example, women silk workers outnumbered men in the town, and 40 percent of the women remained unmarried at age fifty.[74]) These conditions resulted in high rates of illegitimacy, often the result of expectations thwarted by circumstance, which were reinforced by the tendency of French law to put all the burden of responsibility and proof for illegitimate children on the woman. Whereas a sixteenth-century law providing for *déclarations de grossesse* had required that a father's identity be revealed in court and that he be obliged to make payment to the girl,

> . . . in the course of the 18th century, bourgeois opinion would no longer tolerate that procedure, and the girl had to prove the culpability of the man she claimed to be the father of her child. It became very difficult and time-consuming to get indemnification. After the French Revolution, the Civil Code forbade even searching for the father of an illegitimate child [*recherche de paternité*]. *Henceforth an unmarried mother would be considered solely responsible for the conception of her child, and she alone would pay.*[75]

Married women among the working class and poor were also compelled by material conditions and the prevailing marriage laws to assume most of the burden of maintaining children. The "family economy" among the poor in prerevolutionary France relied greatly on "the earning capacity, the labor and the sheer ingenuity of women"; they, not their husbands, were generally regarded as responsible for providing the children with food. Not only was it "easier for a father to opt out than for a mother to do so," but *bureaux de charité* assumed that the mother was the one responsible, "dealt directly" with her, and made eligibility for relief contingent upon *her* "piety, thrift and readiness to work."[76] Moreover, many women with children were neither single nor married; rather, they were partners in a "free union" in which both the male and the state had little legal obligation to provide them with financial support in the care of their children. Such women did not regard themselves as "debauched" or "matriarchal" but as victims of economic and social injustice. Working-class women active in the revolutionary movements of 1789, 1848, and 1871 continually put forward demands for family allowances, state pensions, and the status of "legitimacy" for children born in such unions.[77] This suggests that they would have preferred to keep their children and raise them if they had had the necessary social supports.

The major consequence of the lack of such supports was an extraordinarily high rate of infant abandonment among both single and married poor women. "In the second half of the eighteenth century, there were 20 to 40 foundlings for every 100 births in Paris"—some 40,000 abandoned infants every year in the decade before the revolution.[78] While there is certainly evidence that many abandonments arose out of conditions of misery and destitution, it is also true that the class composition and situation of the parents varied, as did their motives in abandoning their infants. A carefully detailed study shows a definite correlation between "'the curve of abandoned children" in Paris between the 1720s and the 1780s and "the curve of the price of wheat."[79] Yet abandonment did not occur only among the poorest or as a temporary remedy, but almost as frequently among a cross section of Parisian "bourgeois," including artisans, shopkeepers, domestic servants, and even the well-to-do, who were themselves experiencing hard times. Among both the very poor and the quasi-middle-class (artisans and shopkeepers) from the center of Paris, who "appear most frequently in the admission records," there were many who had no intention of reclaiming their children, increasingly so in the immediate prerevolutionary years. This is evident from the fact that they left no identification and that increasingly the hospital became filled with new-borns rather than older children. Abandonment was "a step frequently decided upon before the infant's birth," a deliberately chosen method of "family limitation."[80] This decision nearly always stemmed from "the material difficulties of life" rather than "immorality," callousness, or "con-cealed infanticide"; most such parents were honestly ignorant of the high risk of mortality to which they exposed their children and thought they were providing them with food and shelter. It should be noted that, despite the high number of "illegitimate" children among the abandoned, the majority were probably either the legitimate offspring of married couples or the offspring of the "free unions" so common among the work-ing class. Out of their own needs, these couples (especially the women among them) put into practice the view that deliberate abandonment of infants one "could not support" was an acceptable "family limitation" practice.

In sum, the following facts seem clear. First, abandonment was a popularly accepted method of "fertility control," though one practiced mainly by the working class and the poor. Thus, the adoption of "Malthu-sian" thinking and behavior is surely not limited in this period to the upper classes, although both the conditions prompting it and the methods used differ among the poor and artisan classes. Fertility control practices do not "trickle down" from the upper to the lower classes, but are accom-modated by different social groups to their particular circumstances.[81] To limit the analysis of changing fertility control practices during the French "transition" to coitus interruptus, abstinence, and bourgeois family relations is to exclude from that analysis the particular forms of control upon which the masses actively relied.

Second, incentives for abandonment, as for abortion and infanticide—which were also practiced widely among the lower classes throughout the eighteenth century[82]—included not only economic constraints but also a cultural and legal context that placed disproportionate burdens for children's care on mothers. The failure or inability of fathers to support infants, the difficulties in securing declarations of paternity or indemnifi-cations for illegitimate children or children of "free unions," no doubt contributed significantly in this period to the rise in abandonments, infan-ticide, and abortion. But to understand this is greatly to expand our analy-sis of the French fertility decline—to see that it had different implications and contours for different groups of women. Understanding changes in fertility is clearly impossible without considering the situation of women, the class and occupational differences among them, and the place of abortion in their consciousness and their daily life.

The Place of Abortion

The concept of "cultural diffusion" begs all the important questions of *how* ideas and practices get transmitted from one class or group to another and how those ideas get accommodated and transformed under different circumstances. "Cultural" theorists of fertility trends assume that techniques get introduced among elite groups and then, by means never quite specified, make their way down the social hierarchy.[83] We have seen, however, that effective methods of "family limitation"—including abandonment and abortion—were widely practiced among the poor and working class in preindustrial France, for reasons growing out of their economic and social conditions. Family limitation, both as an ideology and as a set of practices, was never exclusive to the dominant classes nor imposed by them unilaterally and coercively on the poor. Some demographers argue that the high incidence of abandonments in the late eighteenth century is itself evidence that birth control methods were not available to these parents. Yet this assumption is puzzling, given other evidence that various "potions of sterility" and abortifacients were available in towns and villages, purveyed through the local midwives and crones.[84] Indeed, a central part of Moheau's complaint is that the law making abortion and infanticide punishable by death (which dated from 1556) could not be enforced and that the lives of fetuses, in the countryside as well as the cities, were jeopardized because "their mothers form homicidal motives against them."[85] A survey of French physicians from all over the country found the commonly held view that "charlatans and empirics contribute to the country's depopulation . . ." and that "the matrons and 'so-called wise women' " were particularly responsible.[86] The occasion for the distribution of "drugs and . . . balms, . . . purgative pills, poultices, herbs" was often the small-town fair or market—in other words, meeting places frequented by ordinary folk. Even allowing for the biases of physicians, who campaigned against "charlatans" and midwives throughout the late eighteenth and nineteenth centuries, there is no reason to believe these reports are false.

Aside from anecdotal evidence, there is another, more inductive way to think about the importance of abortion to declining preindustrial fertility rates. For we cannot account for a decline that is national in scope by referring to cultural *mentalités* and habits that affected only a small segment of the population or to a method as notoriously ineffective as coitus interruptus. McLaren makes the compelling argument that even in the absence of direct evidence, we must assume the importance of abortion in preindustrial contexts where marital fertility is known to have been low. For the premodern contraceptive methods most likely to have been used, especially coitus interruptus, have very high failure rates. A "rise in contraceptive practices" and a decline in fertility in such situations must have been "accompanied by an increase in abortion" used as a "back-up method."[87] The evidence is that abortion was traditionally, and remains today, a more "female" method of fertility control and a more popular method than many forms of contraception. The relative importance of abandonment among the poor in late-eighteenth-century France may be exaggerated because foundling homes collected the evidence, whereas abortions were lost to history. At the same time, abortion use appears to have been specific to particular conditions; it was not uniformly available in all regions or among all occupational groups. It is the nature of this specificity we must try to understand.

By the late nineteenth century, a now vigilant and powerful medical profession provides us with more systematic reports about contraceptive and abortion use. A number of reasonably effective mechanical methods of contraception—sponges, pessaries, rubber condoms, sheaths—were used among middle-class couples. Most sources, however, tell us that these methods, and the private physicians who distributed them, were too expensive for poor and working-class women; besides, they often had husbands who were hostile to contraception.[88] French working-class women, whose birthrate continued to decline in this period, had little choice but to rely on abortion:

> If there was no education to provide or fortune to pass on, family size restriction would be primarily the woman's concern, especially if she controlled the family budget. And to control fertility, she did not wait passively for new information, but took advantage of whatever means were already at her disposal including inducement of miscarriage.[89]

The question of the health dangers posed by various abortifacients common among poor and working-class women is ambiguous. On the one hand, it seems clear that such women were forced to rely on "home remedies" and "quack cures"—drugs that sometimes contained poisons (such as the lead-based Diachylon), knitting needles and quills, or injections of harsh substances such as Lysol into the womb—because they had no access to physicians and antiseptics (even after antiseptics were in common use for other purposes).[90] Nevertheless, it is not certain that such home remedies are always dangerous; drugs in small doses or even a sharp implement—if sterile, used carefully, and in an early stage of pregnancy—were apparently effective without serious injury to the pregnant woman.[91] A survey of one hundred patients by a Berlin doctor in 1919 regarding their birth control and abortion methods contains references to many "folk" methods reported to have been effective abortifa-cients, apparently without dire consequences: hot baths, jumping off chairs and stools, douching with soapy water or Lysol, using a commercial "pe-riod remedy," drinking various drugs and teas, and "[poking] around with a quill a little bit until blood came and then a doctor scraped me out."[92]

Because of insufficient evidence, it is probably impossible to make a definitive judgment about risks and mortality in the days of illegal abortions. But the extent of risk is not my point. Rather, two things seem clear about abortion in the nineteenth century. First, the cause of fatalities had less to do with medical technology than with medical politics and economics—the distribution of knowledgable and decent care. Second, whatever the risks, women wanted and sought abortions. Far from being pushed on women by quacks and hucksters (although some ineffective or useless methods undoubtedly were), abortifacients were "diffused" among women because women demanded them, often knowing there was danger. It is simply incorrect to assume that, prior to the availability of safe (i.e., antiseptic) methods, abortion was an infrequent mode of fertility control.[93]

This is dramatically illustrated in accounts about working-class women in the 1890s and during World War I in England who took pills containing lead or deliberately exposed themselves to lead in factories in order to induce miscarriage or sterility. Such examples call for detailed examination because they reveal something important about "cultural diffusion" among working-class women. An outbreak of lead poisoning in Sheffield, owing to contamination of the local water supply, gave women the information that small amounts of lead acted as an abortifa-cient. The knowledge spread rapidly from one town to another—"a home remedy passed on by word of mouth"—and was easily put to use, since the lead compound Diachylon was already "at hand in every working-class home" for various healing purposes.[94] This suggests two important theoretical possibilities about how birth control and abortion information gets transmitted on a mass scale: (1) The process occurs effectively because the idea and the practice of fertility control are already embedded in popular ways of life; and (2) it occurs, not vertically (from the elites to the masses), but horizontally, from one working-class woman to another (her neighbor, coworker, or kin) or from one factory or shop to another or from one working-class town to another. This is of course a hypothesis, and needs to be tested through precise data comparing patterns of abortion use among different women's communities and different occupational groups, towns, and regions. Yet it seems borne out by the fragments of information we have regarding abortion practices in nineteenth-century England, France, and the United States. These suggest that where there are strong and cohesive women's communities, either through shared neighborhood cultures or shared work, and where women have access to local "wise women" or midwives or active communication networks, abortion practices flourish.[95]

Studies showing that declines in working-class fertility in late-nineteenth-century England were greatest among particular occupational sectors, especially among families where wives worked and most especially in the textile industry, confirm this view of the "cultural diffusion" process. For women socialized into networks of coworkers or workers' wives (e.g., among better-paid skilled workers), not only were fertility rates consistently lower than for other working-class groups but abortion was apparently well known and widely practiced.[96] The explanation for this lies in their obvious need for effective fertility control and in the socialized nature of their conditions, which made it possible to meet that need. In other words, I am assuming that women who work in factories have a particularly viable social basis for information sharing and self-help. A look at the communities in northern England where lead-based abortifacients were widely used in the 1890s confirms this line of argument. Nottingham, Leicester, Burnley, and Sheffield were precisely the towns where married women's employment was high and thus where women were brought into regular contact with one another in factories and workshops.[97] That regular birth control and abortion practice was a long-standing part of working-class life in such towns seems evident. A variety of herbal and other folk remedies had been rooted in popular health culture since preindustrial times.[98] Moreover, as early as the 1830s the radical birth control pamphlets and handbills of Francis Place, Richard Carlile, and Charles Knowlton enjoyed "a quite large circulation," aimed "specifically towards the working classes" in the northern industrial districts.[99]

McLaren's study of abortion in France in the late nineteenth and early twentieth centuries similarly emphasizes the importance among the working classes of women's "self-help," community, and cross-generational networks in the diffusion of abortion methods. Medical and government sources report casual and unashamed conversations among female neighbors about where to find the local midwife or purveyor, what to take that will be safe, or how to elude abusive husbands.[100] Similarly, in the German survey from 1913, mentioned earlier, where women noted an "accomplice" or helper in their abortions, it was either a midwife, a coworker, or in one case "the wife of a coworker of my husband's [who] has helped the whole block."[101] While these accounts involve urban women, the phenomenon of women's communities and networks that act as conduits of abortion lore is not limited to towns. Mohr suggests that such sharing of abortion information among female kin and neighbors characterized the rise of abortion rates in the nineteenth-century United States not only in the towns but also on the frontier.[102]

That abortion flourished where women's ties to one another were strongest does not mean that husbands were uninvolved in or always hostile to their wives having abortions. Sometimes husbands assisted or procured the drugs, although very often, as among the Berlin women, there was a strong desire to keep the abortion secret from husbands, a sense that he "must know nothing." But in most cases, regardless of husbands' attitudes or role, the source of the woman's knowledge about methods and her sense of abortion as a legitimate, accepted practice was other women.[103]

As a popular method of conscious fertility control, abortion among poor and working-class women never abates but increases with time. In addition to cost, accessibility, and the desire to avoid methods requiring the husband's cooperation, there is a very practical reason why abortion, even when risky, may be the most useful method of fertility control for working-class women: "In allowing the working class couple to postpone the decision of controlling pregnancy to a later date in the reproductive cycle, abortion gave the family living at subsistence level time to assess whether they could support an additional child."[104] "Planning" clearly involves different constraints and timetables for different social groups. It is thus not surprising that abortion was by all estimates extremely widespread among working-class and poor women in England and America in the late nineteenth and early twentieth centuries, when it was everywhere illegal. "In the 1890s, doctors were estimating two million abortions a year" in America, probably an underestimate.[105] Caroline Hadley Robinson, who surveyed U.S. birth control clinics in the 1920s, found that 47 percent of the clientele of one clinic in Chicago, who were all poor Jews on welfare, were "already practicing abortion" before they came to the clinic and estimated that "one half to nine tenths of all interruptions of pregnancy in the general population are voluntary, illegal acts."[106]

Conscious ideologies legitimating abortion do not always accompany or fit neatly with its widespread practice. What of the consciousness of working-class women in the nineteenth century? Did they articulate an idea of abortion as "a woman's right"? Here again, there seems to be agreement among historians writing about France, Britain, and the United States. Perhaps differently from middle-class feminists, working-class women in all three countries commonly believed that, regardless of the law, there was no baby, hence nothing "wrong" in ending a pregnancy, prior to "quickening."[107] Numerous medical and state observers, in England and France, were dismayed at working-class women's casual attitude about abortion and their widespread assumption that it was only "a perfectly legitimate measure" and not a question of "killing" anything. Rather, for many, who openly came to doctors for help, abortion was a question of making *themselves*, their own bodies, "regular": "Until animation they perceived themselves, not as pregnant, but as 'irregular'; they took drugs, not to abort, but to restore the menses."[108] Thus, between the collectively shared norms of these women and the medical scrutinizers who recorded those norms, the very meaning of "abortion" was contested.

Working-class women in the nineteenth and early twentieth centuries defended their right to abortion on at least two grounds, reflecting two different ideologies of fertility control. On the one hand, there is the strong and impassioned plea for women's own lives and humanity, an end to constant childbearing and physical exhaustion. "It is not right," says one Englishwoman in 1915, "it is wicked that a woman should be killed by having children at this rate."[109] Indeed, the idea "that the woman must have the freedom of her body" was apparently not unknown to European working-class women at that time. But, like the feminist proponents of "voluntary motherhood," the freedom these women were seeking was a (negative) freedom *from* unwanted sex and unwanted childbearing, from what they saw as sexual and biological abuse of their bodies; it was not a (positive) freedom to seek sexual fulfillment.

On the other hand, by the late nineteenth century there is ample evidence, at least among the wives of skilled workers in England and possibly among the poor as well, that the Malthusian ethic of "fewer and better" and having no more children than one could afford had taken hold. In fact, the "economic" morality seems to have gotten entangled and hung in an uneasy suspension with the "feminist" morality defending women's bodily integrity. A poignant, though rather late, example of this confusion is a letter sent to Dr. Marie Stopes, the English sex counselor and birth control reformer, in 1922:

> Could you be kind enough to tell me the safest Means for Prevention of Children as my age is 37 I have had 14 children nine living . . . we are very poor People I have my last at the Maternity home the Matron and Dr. told me I have a very Weak Heart if i have any more it might prove fatal *my inside is quite exhausted* I have Prolapsed Womb, *its wicked to bring children into the world to Practicly starve and be a burden to the ratepayers* as that is what it Means in my case as my Husband is only a jobing Gardener his work is most uncertain I cannot feed baby myself I realy must try something as my Husband is not a careful man in that respect *I dont want any more* if I should sink with having another what would become of all the other little ones my nerves are getting quite bad worrying from one month to another. . . .[110]

In fact, by the 1870s in England, especially with the enactment of compulsory elementary schooling, conditions were created that would transform working-class culture and working-class family life and would make them more amenable to neo-Malthusian ideas. As a result of compulsory education, which abolished the value of children as potential wage earners, higher wages, and a consumption-oriented living standard among the more privileged sectors, and because of the influence of social reformers, charity workers, public investigators, and public health agents, "the [working class] home was to become increasingly central to the life of the worker and the question of restricting the number of children it housed ever more important."[111] This process was not one of bourgeois values merely "trickling down," but of those values being externally imposed and internally transformed.

The role of social workers and public health clinicians in communicating the dominant bourgeois values of "rational," child-focused mothering and restricted childbearing for the sake of higher consumption seems particularly important. It raises major questions about the cultural diffusion theory, suggesting that, at least in part, such "diffusion" occurs through the deliberate imposition of values rather than by osmosis. The idea that "maternal duty" involved rational planning and budgeting, of children as well as household economies, was clearly geared to the economics of the capitalist market in labor and goods; it was also transmitted by agents of the bourgeois state. From whom but social workers and preachers does a poor woman learn that "its wicked to bring children into the world to Practicly starve and be a burden to the ratepayers"? Yet the "modern" ideology of fertility control is not simply transposed mechanically or wholesale from one class to another, like a lesson taught in Sunday school. The conditions of working-class life, which are not the same as those of the middle class, result in an accommodation of that ideology to a new situation. The language of neo-Malthusian thinking takes on a different sense within a working-class context. For example, letters from working-class women in England written in 1913–14, and published by the Women's Cooperative Guild, to the extent that they explicitly approve of birth control and abortion, do so in terms resonant with the middle-class idea that fewer children mean giving "more advantages," that children deserve certain "advantages" as a precondition to being born:

> . . . that we would only have what little lives we could make happy, and give a chance in life.

> I have not had children as fast as some . . . not because I do not love them, but because if I had more I do not think I could have done *my duty to them* under the circumstances.

> . . . as to mechanical prevention of family, I know it is a delicate subject, but it is an urgent one, as it is due to low-paid wages and the unearthly struggle to live *respectably.* All the beautiful in motherhood is very nice if one has plenty to bring up a family

on, but what *real mother* is going to bring life into the world
to be pushed into the drudgery of the world at the earliest
possible moment because of the strain on the family
exchequer. . . .[112]

The emphasis on "maternal duty" here, on the value of fewer children
who must be provided with a certain "standard of living," reflects both
sides of the double bourgeois ideology of fertility control: the definition
of children as "consumption goods" rather than "production goods"[113]
and the definition of motherhood as intensive and exclusive. Moreover,
the letters written to the Guild were mostly not from the poorest women
but from the (unemployed) wives of skilled workers, who were literate
and saw their children as having some possibility of "moving up." Yet
even here, and certainly among women less privileged, there is a class-
specific meaning to the idea of limiting births to give children "a chance
in life." Margaret Llewelyn Davies interprets the birthrate decline in the
late nineteenth and early twentieth centuries among better-paid workers
in England in terms that imply resistance more than accommodation: a
"refusal to have children," "a kind of strike against large families," which
grew out of the transcendence of fatalism and the growing consciousness
"that there are other things in life besides poverty and work," "something
better than bare existence."[114]

We have to distinguish between the origins of an idea and the social
context in which it is applied. Words like "respectability," "drudgery,"
and even "maternal duty" have concrete meanings depending on the circumstances of those espousing them, the "life chances" specific to them.
It is one thing to hope children will acquire professions (or professional
husbands); it is another to hope they will grow up—and maybe go to
school. At the same time, a distinctly patriarchal standard of "woman's
place" in domesticity and childrearing permeates the working-class variant
of Malthusianism, just as it does the working-class ideology of the "family
wage," to which it is closely related. When a working-class wife argues
that birth control will give her "better health to serve my husband and
children, and more advantages to give them,"[115] she is utilizing the bourgeois ideology of upward mobility and "true motherhood" to justify her
decision to use birth control. Yet, while accommodating bourgeois patriarchal assumptions, her statement also embodies a determination, for herself
and her children, to push beyond the limits of their lives.

We have journeyed far into the complexities of history and theory
to reach some fairly simple conclusions: Abortion has nearly always been
a crucial form of fertility control for women; its availability and practice
are in some ways a measure of the position of different groups of women
in society; and a scientific understanding of fertility trends has to encom-

pass these facts. We have also found that the extent to which abortion and other forms of birth control are available to women is specific to certain social conditions. Where women are connected by strong ties of work and community, where they have access to nondomestic sources of support and livelihood, where mothering is not the only work culturally valued for them or their sense of their autonomy over "domesticity" is bolstered by feminist bonds, and where alternative systems of reproductive health care thrive because they are supported by vital women's communities—there, and mainly there, does a *culture* of fertility control, including abortion, develop. If these have been the historical conditions in which abortion as a popular practice exists, then it becomes clear that political efforts to suppress abortion are aimed not only at women's control over their fertility and their sexuality but at the social and economic roots of their collective power.

NOTES

1. Linda Gordon, *Woman's Body, Woman's Right* (New York: Grossman, 1976). This book laid the groundwork for much recent feminist thinking about such issues. See esp. Chaps. 13 and 14.

2. Norman E. Himes, *Medical History of Contraception* (New York: Schocken, 1970), p. 185.

3. "Clearly, the history of fertility sustains those who argue that public policy by itself cannot influence fertility behavior. Ordinary people will not be persuaded by a massive educational campaign . . . or by elite spokesmen for what has been termed the Population Coalition. Rather, people will determine for themselves the family size that seems most appropriate to their lives." Michael B. Katz and Mark J. Stern, "History and the Limits of Population Policy," *Politics and Society* 10, no. 2 (1980): 242. This is an exaggerated version of my point. Events in Eastern Europe, China, and perhaps to some extent the United States belie such a "spontanist" view and show how difficult population policies are to enforce.

4. M. Z. Rosaldo, "The Use and Abuse of Anthropology: Reflections on Feminism and Cross-Cultural Understanding," *Signs* 5 (Spring 1980): 392.

5. Charles Tilly, "Historical Study of Vital Processes," in *Historical Studies of Changing Fertility,* ed. Charles Tilly (Princeton: Princeton University Press, 1978), pp. 18–20, 42–43. The theory of the "demographic transition" posits a two-stage process in which, first, early industrialization results in diminished mortality (due to improved nutrition, sanitary conditions, etc.) and thus in population growth; and, second, later industrialization brings the "diffusion" of both "new aspirations" and "contraceptive knowledge," thus producing lower fertility. The theory cannot explain some major anomalies, such as the widespread fertility decline in preindustrial France.

6. See, among others, Tilly; Ronald Lee, "Models of Preindustrial Population Dynamics with Application to England," in Tilly, p. 155; Himes, pp. xii–

xiii and throughout; Gordon, Chap. 2; Steven Polgar, "Population History and Population Policies from an Anthropological Perspective," *Current Anthropology* 13 (April 1972): 205–6; and George Devereux, *A Study of Abortion in Primitive Societies,* rev. ed. (New York: International Universities Press, 1976).

7. Polgar, pp. 205–6; and E. A. Wrigley, "Fertility Strategy for the Individual and the Group," in Tilly, p. 136. Richard Easterlin, for example, seems curiously unaware of this fact when he argues that only in modern societies, with a decline in mortality, do people experience the "potential problem of unwanted children." "The Economics and Sociology of Fertility: A Synthesis," in Tilly, pp. 132–33.

8. Moni Nag, "How Modernization Can Also Increase Fertility," *Current Anthropology* 21 (October 1980): 576; and Polgar, pp. 205–6. Nag quotes one anthropological source reporting on the Tonga tribe of Northern Rhodesia that the older women "said that they did not dare to have another child before the existing one could run, because of the possibility of raids by neighboring tribes."

9. Himes, pp. 182–84. This source is outdated but still the best we have on birth control lore in early societies.

10. Ibid., pp. 111–12, 89, 138; see also D. V. Glass, *Population Policies and Movements in Europe* (London: Frank Cass, 1967), pp. 28–29, 422. Soranos, going beyond Hippocrates' prohibition of abortion, made a clear distinction between abortions necessary for preserving the woman's life or health and those "desired as a consequence of adultery or as the consequence of the desire to maintain beauty." With a science of medicine, we seem to have the distinction between therapeutic abortions and those in which women are seen as selfish, or acting out of their own "convenience."

11. Devereux, p. 98.

12. E. A. Wrigley, *Population and History* (New York: McGraw-Hill, 1969), p. 125.

13. James C. Mohr, *Abortion in America* (New York: Oxford University Press, 1978), p. 103; and Kingsley Davis and Judith Blake, "Social Structure and Fertility: An Analytical Framework," *Economic Development and Cultural Change* 4 (April 1956): 230: "It is a woman's method and can be practiced without the man's knowledge." The "female" character of abortion is true in the sense that women are able to practice it without male consent, but it is inaccurate to say that abortion is a "woman only" method. Devereux cites numerous examples of forced abortion committed on pregnant women by angry, violent husbands.

14. Davis and Blake, pp. 224–25.

15. Angus McLaren, *Birth Control in Nineteenth Century England* (London: Croom Helm, 1978), p. 35. See also Keith Hopkins, "Contraception in the Roman Empire," *Comparative Studies in Society and History* 8 (1965–66): 124, 136–38. Hopkins emphasizes that Romans of the upper class typically "confused" contraception and abortion, "both in method and conceptualization," since their understanding of the timing of conception and the length of gestation was in error.

16. Cf. Michel Foucault, *Madness and Civilization: A History of Insanity in the Age of Reason,* trans. Richard Howard (New York: Vintage, 1974); and Jeffrey Weeks, *Sex, Politics and Society* (London and New York: Longman, 1981).

17. E. A. Wrigley, "Family Limitation in Pre-Industrial England," *Economic History Review* 19 (1966): 82–109. See also Etienne Van de Walle, "Alone in Europe: The French Fertility Decline until 1850," in Tilly, pp. 257–88; Lee, in Tilly, pp.

191–94; Tilly, p. 54; and E. Shorter, "Female Emancipation, Birth Control and Fertility in European History," *American Historical Review* 78 (1973): 611.

18. "All the foregoing [concerning birth control in preindustrial society] does not imply that the individual man or woman was conscious of this range of issues in the least, any more than the individual robin or rook is conscious of the problems of avoiding too large a population, but like robins and rooks people respond sensitively to social pressures." Wrigley, 1966, p. 104; and Tilly, pp. 148, 152. Tilly uncritically accepts this distinction between conscious and unconscious rationality, characterizing fertility control in preindustrial societies as a "self-regulating system" (p. 54).

19. Gordon, pp. 28–30. For a general look at feminist revisions of male-biased anthropology and the importance of gender divisions in preclass, prestate societies, see Rayna (Rapp) Reiter, ed., *Toward an Anthropology of Women* (New York: Monthly Review, 1975).

20. David Levine, *Family Formation in an Age of Nascent Capitalism* (New York: Academic Press, 1977). Cf. Katz and Stern, pp. 225–45, who also attempt a Marxist analysis of fertility changes, here focused on Erie County, N.Y., in the late nineteenth and early twentieth centuries. Their study relies mainly on a neoclassical emphasis on social status, "rising levels of consumption" and educational costs, rather than a Marxist emphasis on labor conditions. Like Levine, they understand the family as a decision-making unity, ignoring gender divisions even more than he does.

21. See, for example, Lawrence Stone, *The Family, Sex and Marriage in England, 1500–1800* (New York: Harper & Row, 1977), pp. 421, 637–39; and Tilly, p. 40.

22. Levine, pp. 120–21.

23. Ibid., pp. 80–84. Cf. Katz and Stern, p. 239; they find a similar pattern among skilled workers in early-twentieth-century America.

24. Levine, p. 112. Levine's "revisit" to Colyton is a critique and expansion of Wrigley's (1966) study.

25. Ibid., p. 108.

26. Ibid., pp. 111*n*, 144.

27. Levine, pp. 144, 137. The argument relating rising illegitimacy to women's increased "expectation of marriage" was originally made with regard to France by Louise A. Tilly, Joan W. Scott, and Miriam Cohen, "Women's Work and European Fertility Patterns," *Journal of Interdisciplinary History* 6 (1976): 447–76. See also Cissie Fairchilds, "Female Sexual Attitudes and the Rise of Illegitimacy: A Case Study," *Journal of Interdisciplinary History* 8 (1978): 627–77.

28. Compare Dov Friedlander, "Demographic Patterns and Socionomic Characteristics of the Coal-Mining Population in England and Wales in the 19th Century," *Economic Development and Cultural Change* 22 (October 1973): 39–51. He shows that, for coal-mining populations in England, the absence of available employment for women was an important social condition leading to higher levels of fertility.

29. Philippe Ariès, "Interprétation pour une Histoire des Mentalités," in *La Prévention des Naissances dans la Famille,* ed. Hélène Bergues (Paris: Institut National d'Etudes Démographiques, 1960), pp. 314–18.

30. See Andras Hegedus, Agnes Heller, Maria Markus, and Mihaly Vajda, *The Humanisation of Socialism: Writings of the Budapest School* (London: Allison & Busby,

1976), pp. 15–16; Michael Drake, *Historical Demography: Problems and Projects* (Milton Keynes, England: Open University Press, 1974), p. 20; and André Berguière, "From Malthus to Max Weber: Belated Marriage and the Spirit of Enterprise," in *Family and Society*, ed. Robert Forster and Orest Ranum (Baltimore: Johns Hopkins University Press, 1976), pp. 239, 245.

31. The debate over whether motivations or techniques are more important in determining changes in fertility continues to divide U.S. demographers. On the motivations side, see Judith Blake and Prithwis Das Gupta, "Reproductive Motivation Versus Contraceptive Technology: Is Recent American Experience an Exception?" *Population and Development Review* 1 (December 1975): 229–49; and Richard Easterlin, *Birth and Fortune* (New York: Basic Books, 1980), pp. 55–57. Unfortunately, the analysis by Blake and Das Gupta tends to ignore social and economic conditions responsible for changing motivations. Those who espouse a technological theory include Norman Ryder, Larry Bumpass, and Charles Westoff (see notes 2, 7, and 8); and, more recently, Henri Leridon, "Fertility and Contraception in 12 Developed Countries," *Family Planning Perspectives* 13 (March/April 1981): 93–102. Etienne Van de Walle summarizes this debate and attempts to take a position that acknowledges *both* motivations and technology as important determinants of fertility, in "Motivations and Technology in the Decline of French Fertility," in *Family and Sexuality in French History*, ed. Robert Wheaton and Tamara K. Hareven (Philadelphia: University of Pennsylvania Press, 1980), pp. 135–38. But most of the evidence he cites regarding eighteenth-century France involves coitus interruptus, abstinence, and abortion—"techniques" that did not have to be "invented."

32. Van de Walle, in Wheaton and Hareven, pp. 158–61; and Jean-Louis Flandrin, *Families in Former Times: Kinship, Household and Sexuality*, trans. Richard Southern (Cambridge: Cambridge University Press, 1976), pp. 185–86. See also Joan Kelly, "The Preindustrial Household," in *Household and Kin*, ed. Amy Swerdlow, Renate Bridenthal, Joan Kelly, and Phyllis Vine (Old Westbury, N.Y.: Feminist Press, 1981), pp. 9–13.

33. See Louise A. Tilly and Joan W. Scott, *Women, Work, and Family* (New York: Holt, Rinehart and Winston, 1978), pp. 24–26, 94–95.

34. Alice Clark, *Working Life of Women in the Seventeenth Century* (New York: Augustus M. Kelley, 1968), p. 83. The Act of Settlement was passed in 1662 to keep the poor from migrating to parishes other than those of their birth. See Karl Polanyi, *The Great Transformation* (Boston: Beacon, 1957), p. 88; and Christopher Hill, *The World Turned Upside Down* (New York: Viking, 1972), p. 282. See also Ariès, in Bergues, pp. 314–16.

35. John T. Noonan, Jr., *Contraception: A History of Its Treatment by the Catholic Theologians and Canonists* (Cambridge, Mass.: Harvard University Press, 1966), p. 160.

36. Van de Walle, in Wheaton and Hareven, pp. 158–60.

37. Ariès, in Bergues, pp. 314–18.

38. John Knodel and Etienne Van de Walle, "Lessons from the Past: Policy Implications of Historical Fertility Studies," *Population and Development Review* 5 (June 1979): 217–45, 233.

39. See Van de Walle, in Tilly.

40. McLaren, pp. 43–46; see also Drake, pp. 12–13.

41. *An Essay on the Principle of Population*, ed. Anthony Flew (Harmondsworth, England: Penguin, 1976), pp. 92, 103.

42. T. R. Malthus, *An Essay on Population*, based on the 7th ed. of the Second Essay (London: J. M. Dent, 1958), 2: 151, 169.

43. It should be noted that this moralism was present from the beginning in Malthus' thought. In the First Essay, he writes: "Dependent poverty ought to be held disgraceful. . . . A laborer who marries without being able to support a family may in some respects be considered as an enemy to all his fellow-laborers." Flew ed., p. 98.

44. Ariès, pp. 318–19.

45. Berguière, pp. 242–43, 250.

46. In Wheaton and Hareven, p. 156. This association of "family limitation" and the use of wet nurses with luxury and a corrupt aristocracy reaches its apogee in Rousseau's *Emile*.

47. Quoted from Edmond About's *Maître Pierre*, in Angus McLaren, "Abortion in France: Women and the Regulation of Family Size 1800–1914," *French Historical Studies* 10 (Spring 1978): 461–85.

48. Cf. Weeks, p. 10: "[citing Foucault] that the sexual apparatus and the nuclear family were produced by the bourgeoisie as an aspect of its own self-affirmation, not as a means of controlling the working class; that there are class sexualities (and different gender sexualities); that indeed there are sexualities, not a single uniform sexuality."

49. See P. Ariès, *Centuries of Childhood: A Social History of Family Life*, trans. Robert Baldick (New York: Vintage, 1962), pp. 333–36; and Ivy Pinchbeck and Margaret Hewitt, *Children in English Society* (London: Routledge & Kegan Paul, 1969), 1: 36, 41–42.

50. Flandrin, pp. 212–13.

51. Ariès, in Bergues, p. 323.

52. Karl Marx, *Capital*, trans. Ben Fowkes (New York: Vintage, 1977), 1: 783–84, 849n.

53. In Ronald L. Meek, ed., *Marx and Engels on Malthus* (London: Lawrence and Wishart, 1955), p. 61. Only under communism, wrote Engels to Kautsky in 1881, could it be decided "whether, when, and how" population, or fertility, might be limited (p. 109).

54. Quoted in McLaren, p. 71; emphasis added.

55. See ibid., pp. 94–95; Gordon, Chap. 4; and Daniel Scott Smith, "Family Limitation, Sexual Control, and Domestic Feminism in Victorian America," in *A Heritage of Her Own*, ed. Nancy F. Cott and Elizabeth H. Pleck (New York: Simon and Schuster, 1979), p. 236. I am using the term "neo-Malthusian" here to refer to those late nineteenth- and early twentieth-century successors of Malthus who, unlike him, approved of the use of artificial means of fertility control.

56. Quoted from Dio Lewis, *Chastity, or Our Secret Sins* (1888), in Smith, p. 234.

57. Olive Schreiner, *Women and Labour* (London: Virago, 1978), p. 63.

58. Gordon, pp. 127–29, 144–45.

59. Emma Goldman, "Love and Marriage," in *Woman Rebel*, ed. Alex Baskin (New York: Archives of Social History, 1976), p. 3.

60. Flandrin, pp. 216–19, 224–25.

61. Ibid., pp. 221–23. Lawrence Stone has partially applied the cultural perspective, based on the ideas of Ariès and Flandrin, to explain the sharp decline in the fertility of the English nobility in the seventeenth and eighteenth centuries. Stone associates this decline with the increased use of contraception, which he too attributes to the growth of "companionate marriage," "more child-oriented family attitudes, and . . . a shift away from the patriarchal traditions of the 17th century . . . [toward] more egalitarian relations between husbands and wives. . ." (pp. 417, 432). But while Stone is more careful than Flandrin to distinguish between the demographic and social situation of the propertied classes and that of poor laborers and cottagers, he seems totally unaware that particular groups within the English working class in the seventeenth and eighteenth centuries evidently did have incentives—and knowledge—to use contraception (see discussion of Levine). Moreover, he emphasizes shifts in Protestant theology as the motor force behind the conceptual separation of "pleasure from procreation," ignoring evidence that that "mentality" first took hold in Catholic France.

62. Van de Walle, in Hareven, pp. 148–51, quotes from a letter attributed to Francis Place, the English birth control advocate, that holds the woman responsible for not producing "a spurious issue" and recounts a popular story in which a pregnant marquise rues her lack of "quick-mindedness" during the act of love. See also Davis and Blake (1956), who cite evidence that, among some African tribes, "sometimes the woman, by moving her hips so as to extrude the penis just before ejaculation, accomplishes coitus interruptus without the male's cooperation" (p. 224n).

63. Smith, pp. 223, 226–27. This argument comes close to that of Edward Shorter, "Female Emancipation, Birth Control, and Fertility in European History," *American Historical Review* 78 (1973): 605–40. Shorter's virtually undocumented claim that the rise in marital and nonmarital fertility in late-eighteenth-century Europe and its decline in the subsequent century were due to "female emancipation"—specifically, sexual emancipation—was firmly taken to task by Tilly, Scott, and Cohen and by Fairchilds.

64. Gordon, p. 151.

65. See, e.g., Kelly, pp. 18–33; Ann Oakley, *Woman's Work* (New York: Pantheon, 1974), Chap. 3; Mary Ryan, *Womanhood in America from Colonial Times to the Present* (New York: Franklin Watts, 1975); and Barbara Welter, "The Cult of True Womanhood," in *The American Family in Social-Historical Perspective*, 2nd ed., ed. Michael Gordon (New York: St. Martin's Press, 1978), pp. 313–33.

66. McLaren, pp. 197–98; and L. Gordon, pp. 103, 109–11.

67. Gordon points out (pp. 112–13) that many "voluntary motherhood advocates shared the general belief that mothers of young children ought not to work outside their homes but should make mothering their full-time occupation." Even those who thought motherhood could be combined with other functions, such as Victoria Woodhull and Tennessee Claflin, still regarded it as her "most holy" function. L. Gordon, p. 110 and Chap. 5, passim; and Scott-Smith, p. 236.

68. Mohr, p. 112.

69. Ibid., p. 114.

70. See Flandrin, pp. 226–30; Edward Shorter, *The Making of the Modern Family* (New York: Basic Books, 1975), Chap. 5; and Tilly and Scott, pp. 132–34. Some

historians suggest that neglect or poor treatment was a "conscious strategy" of premodern French women to limit the number of children in the family.
71. Flandrin, pp. 198–206, 236–37. Shorter, pp. 169–90, and Badinter, pp. 109–112, overstate the "maternal indifference and callousness" argument. Their account is glazed with a heavy dose of high-minded retrospective moralizing— reading backward from what is then constructed as "modern" maternal sensibility.
72. The best source on these conditions is George D. Sussman, "Parisian Infants and Norman Wet Nurses in the Early Nineteenth Century: A Statistical Study," in *Marriage and Fertility: Studies in Interdisciplinary History,* ed. Robert I. Rotberg and Theodore K. Rabb (Princeton: Princeton University Press, 1980), pp. 249–65.
73. Mauricette Craffe, *La Puissance Paternelle en Droit Anglais* (Paris: R. Pichon et R. Durand-Anzias, 1971), pp. 65–66.
74. Tilly, Scott, and Cohen, "Women's Work and European Fertility Patterns," in Rotberg and Rabb, pp. 236–41; and Scott and Tilly, pp. 26–27.
75. J.-L. Flandrin, "Repression and Change in the Sexual Life of Young People in Medieval and Early Modern Times," in Wheaton and Hareven, p. 38; emphasis added.
76. Olwen Hufton, "Women in Revolution," *Past and Present* 53 (November 1971): 91–94 and 15n.
77. See Sheila Rowbotham, *Women, Resistance and Revolution* (New York: Pantheon, 1972), pp. 104–6; Edith Thomas, *The Women Incendiaries* (New York: George Braziller, 1966), Chaps. 2, 7, and 12; and Elizabeth Racz, "The Women's Rights Movement in the French Revolution," *Science and Society* 16 (Spring 1952): 152–53. Racz mentions that one of the *cahiers* probably submitted by women to the Estates General during the French Revolution asked for " 'means of rendering celibacy less frequent, of granting civil and political status to illegitimate children, of extending relief to heads of large families and improving public education for both sexes.' Other *cahiers* recommended a more equitable arrangement of dowries and a double tax on bachelors." This suggests that the abandonment of children may frequently have been a byproduct of the abandonment of women.
78. Van de Walle, in Wheaton and Hareven, p. 147; Olwen H. Hufton, *The Poor of Eighteenth Century France* (Oxford: Clarendon Press, 1974), p. 318; and Claude Delasselle, "Abandoned Children in 18th Century Paris," in *Deviants and the Abandoned in French Society,* ed. Robert Forster and Orest Ranum, Selections from the *Annales,* Vol. 4 (Baltimore: Johns Hopkins University Press, 1978), pp. 47–82.
79. Delasselle, pp. 70–73; see also Hufton, 1974, p. 332. The social reality behind these curves included the "large, floating population of men, women, and children" who continually drifted to Paris from the countryside "during periods of high prices," who sought the foundling home as a temporary refuge for their children from starvation but often intended to take the children back. See also Elisabeth Badinter, *Mother Love: Myth and Reality* (New York: Macmillan, 1981), pp. 111–12, regarding the mixed social and occupational composition of parents who abandoned their children at La Couche in Paris. This pattern was probably truer in Paris than it was in the provincial foundling hospitals, where stark poverty was more often the rule. The classic example of the good *petit bourgeois* is Rousseau,

who, notwithstanding his views on motherhood and childrearing, unrepentantly deposited all five of his children at the foundling hospital.

80. Delasselle, pp. 74–76; and Hufton, 1974, p. 333.

81. Stone's observation regarding the fertility of poor cottagers and laborers in England during the same period is applicable to the French case. He distinguishes between incentives to get pregnant and marry and incentives to raise children, pointing out that while most of the English poor had high fertility until late in the nineteenth century, they also had "fewer surviving children," due to both high rates of (socially induced) mortality and practices of abandonment and neglect (p. 421). See also Clark, p. 86, who cites figures from Gregory King indicating a surprisingly small average family size, of two to four children per family, among laborers in late-seventeenth-century English towns. Clark attributes this to "starvation and misery," "underfeeding and bad housing," especially for poor mothers and their children, who, in addition, were chased from one parish to another when the local officials found their maintenance a burden.

82. That abortion methods were well known among the French working class and poor in most towns and villages, and were widely practiced, is affirmed by Van de Walle, in Wheaton and Hareven, pp. 144–46; and Hufton, 1974, p. 331.

83. Knodel and Van de Walle, pp. 235–38, are an example of this erroneous thinking; McLaren, *Birth Control in Nineteenth Century England*, pp. 219–20, gives an excellent critique of it.

84. Van de Walle, in Wheaton and Hareven, pp. 144–45; and Hufton, 1974, p. 331.

85. Moheau, p. 100.

86. Jean-Pierre Goubert, "The Art of Healing: Learned Medicine and Popular Medicine in the France of 1790," in *Medicine and Society in France*, ed. R. Forster and O. Ranum, Selections from the *Annales*, vol. 6 (Baltimore: Johns Hopkins University Press, 1980), pp. 8, 16.

87. McLaren, "Abortion in France . . . ," pp. 462, 468–69, 484.

88. Gordon, pp. 66–70, 310–12; and McLaren, "Abortion in France . . . ," p. 484. On the methods of birth control known and used in nineteenth-century Europe, especially the condom and its development and spread, see Himes, Chap. 8; and Eleanor S. Riemer and John C. Fout, eds., *European Women: A Documentary History, 1789–1945* (New York: Schocken, 1980), pp. 202–3.

89. McLaren, "Abortion in France . . . ," p. 484.

90. McLaren, *Birth Control in Nineteenth Century England*, pp. 240, 249. Mohr, pp. 239–40, points out that abortion was suppressed in the United States just at the time when antiseptics had been developed and safe procedures could have been made available.

91. Both Gordon and McLaren, writing about America and England respectively, suggest that "most abortions [in the nineteenth century] were safe and successful" (Gordon, p. 52). McLaren, *Birth Control in Nineteenth Century England*, argues that "the very fact that certain drugs were recommended as abortifacients by midwives and older women generation after generation [e.g., common herbs like "garden rue" and "black hellebore"] implies that some were found to be relatively effective, as well as relatively safe (pp. 34, 241).

92. Excerpts from this physician's report, translated from the German, are

included as Document 46 in Riemer and Fout, pp. 206–8. The tactic of using an implement to begin the abortion and then going to a doctor or hospital to have it completed is also mentioned by McLaren, "Abortion in France . . . ," p. 478. It is an indication of the degree to which male professionals had come to mediate the abortion process by the twentieth century.

93. Knodel and Van de Walle, pp. 217, 219, make this assumption.

94. McLaren, *Birth Control in Nineteenth Century England,* pp. 228, 242.

95. McLaren, who provides much of the historical material that informs the argument I am making, arrives at a similar conclusion (*Birth Control in Nineteenth Century England,* pp. 219–220), in his strong critique of the "cultural diffusion" thesis and its misunderstanding of class divisions. But he neglects to fully develop a counterthesis about how, precisely, fertility control information and methods were transmitted from one working-class woman or community to another.

96. Margaret Hewitt, *Wives and Mothers in Victorian Industry* (Westport, Conn.: Greenwood, 1975; reprinted from the 1958 ed.), Chap. 7; McLaren, *Birth Control in Nineteenth Century England,* p. 220; and Margaret Llewelyn Davies, ed., *Maternity: Letters from Working Women* (New York: Norton, 1978), p. 13. Hewitt, pp. 90–93, 95, argues that lower fertility was a characteristic of Victorian women's employment away from home and not of particular conditions in any one occupation; it cut across numerous occupational groups. The reason was clearly economic and social. With meager incomes and no options for child care that were not "expensive and dangerous," limiting fertility was the working woman's only solution.

97. Hewitt, pp. 96–97, 222.

98. McLaren, *Birth Control in Nineteenth Century England,* pp. 34, 241.

99. Hewitt, p. 94, points out that the circulation of birth control pamphlets in Manchester in the mid-1830s rivaled the works of Thomas Paine in the same period.

100. McLaren, "Abortion in France . . . ," pp. 475–76.

101. In Riemer and Fout, pp. 207–9.

102. Mohr, pp. 106–7.

103. Ibid. Mohr argues, mostly on the basis of court records, that "most abortion decisions" in nineteenth-century America were mutually undertaken by husbands and wives, or that husbands at least concurred and usually paid the costs: "There is no record of any man's ever having sued any woman for aborting his [sic] child" (p. 115). This proves nothing about the number of abortions that may have occurred without the husband's knowledge and without having been prosecuted; it also reflects the middle-class bias in Mohr's sources. For statements of working-class women's efforts to keep abortions secret from their husbands, see McLaren, *Birth Control in Nineteenth Century England,* pp. 226–28; and Riemer and Fout, pp. 207–9.

104. McLaren, *Birth Control in Nineteenth Century England,* pp. 244–45.

105. L. Gordon, p. 53.

106. *Seventy Birth Control Clinics* (New York: Arno, 1972; reprinted from the 1930 ed.), p. 66.

107. McLaren, *Birth Control in Nineteenth Century England,* pp. 243, 246; idem, "Abortion in France . . . ," p. 476; and Mohr, pp. 73–74.

108. McLaren, *Birth Control in Nineteenth Century England,* pp. 35, 246; idem,

"Abortion in France . . . ," p. 476. McLaren quotes a French physician writing in 1878: "One has to hear how freely they relate their adventure, without the shadow of shame or remorse, because they say, *'the woman must have the freedom of her body,'* and, after all *she 'hurts no one in freeing herself,'* since the child which was going to be born was not yet born.' "

109. McLaren, *Birth Control in Nineteenth Century England*, p. 248.

110. Ruth Hall, ed., *Dear Dr. Stopes: Sex in the 1920s* (Harmondsworth, England: Penguin, 1981), p. 16; emphasis added.

111. McLaren, *Birth Control in Nineteenth Century England*, pp. 207, 218. See also Katz and Stern, pp. 233, 239–40, regarding similar patterns among the skilled working class in the United States in the same period. On the rise of compulsory schooling, see J. S. Hurt, *Elementary Schooling and the Working Classes, 1860–1918* (London: Routledge & Kegan Paul, 1980), Chap. 8.

112. Davies, pp. 74, 81, 89–90.

113. Drake, p. 20.

114. Davies, p. 14.

115. Ibid., p. 94.

2

Abortion and the State: Nineteenth-Century Criminalization

Privacy, like individualism, is a historical product; it emerges only when there is a public domain, that is, in relation to the state. The concept of a private, personal realm encompassing family, sexuality, and childbearing did not exist among hunters and gatherers nor in the medieval world. In ancient and modern states in the West, the division between public and private, city and household, acquired salience in political theory and in the everyday structures that separate male from female, denoting, not woman's autonomy within the "private" sphere, but her confinement to it. Throughout history, states have recurrently invaded the private domain, attempting to organize, rechannel, restrict, or expand the fertility and sexual practices of ordinary people. Their reasons, in most historical periods, have to do with two essential purposes related to the nature of the state: the control of populations (their size and composition) and the control of sexuality, especially that of married women and young girls. In practice, however, these two aspects of state intervention in personal life result in complex and sometimes contradictory policies.

This chapter examines the role of the state in channeling fertility control practices, first in a general and speculative way and then in the context of a historical case study: the criminalization of abortion in nineteenth-century America. My argument is that state policies of fertility, population control, and sexual control are attempts to contain, not only women's spontaneous practices, but also the contradictions inherent in these different, but inevitably related, "public" purposes.

Population control, as an organized, centralized policy administered by a hierarchically concentrated power structure, is a feature of both the ancient and modern state. One can argue that the size, composition, and productivity of its population were important formative elements in determining the cohesiveness and power of early states. Historically, the state arose within or as a constellation of newly "public" functions, which Stanley Diamond calls the "census-tax-conscription system":

> The territorial thrust of the early state, along with its vertical social entrenchment, demanded conscription of labor, the mustering of an army, the levying of taxes and tribute, the maintenance of a bureaucracy, and the assessment of the extent, location, and numbers of the population being subjected. These were the major direct or indirect occasions for the development of civil law.[1]

These functions presuppose a certain stage of production, expansion, and exchange, in particular, (1) a mode of production (field agriculture, mining) that is labor intensive and produces a surplus sufficient to make available not only "extractible resources" but disposable wealth that can supply revenues; (2) an institutionalized system of militarism and military conquest, requiring a constant supply of "manpower" and revenues for its upkeep; and (3) a territorial base that supports a stable population whose primary affiliations and loyalties can be appropriated from (declining) kin groups in the service of the rising central power. Census taking (counting affiliation by residence or domicile rather than blood ties), taxation, and military and labor conscription are the principal methods whereby individual loyalties and tributes are tallied and extracted—a process that is invariably coercive and bloody.[2]

Within such a system, human beings—workers, slaves, taxpayers, citizens, soldiers, and *breeders* of all these—assume a value they did not have in a social organization based on kinship and horizontally shared resources. They become an object of *appropriation* for the state, its principal source of wealth; and *births,* along with conquests, migrations, and involuntary confinement or servitude, become a matter of state policy, perceived as a basis of political, military, and economic power. Thus the eighteenth-century French writer Moheau urged the mercantilist monarchy to value numbers of people more highly "than the gold and silver coins that enter the public treasury"; he castigated the practice of birth control among the French upper class and rural women as "a terrible and secret cause of depopulation that imperceptibly *drains the nation"* and is *"deadly to the state";* and he reviled women who put their children out to nurse as "betraying . . . their duties as a citizen."[3]

Because women are the reproducers of children, the formation of the state—whether in ancient society, the African kingdom of Dahomey, or early modern Western Europe—has invariably brought drastic changes in the position of women, usually in the direction of a decline in their power and status. A growing feminist literature documents various historical cases in which state formation has attempted to reduce women to their procreative capacity at the same time as it has involved the appropriation by male rulers and patriarchs of women's power and symbolic authority (in horticultural society) over fertility, children, and their own sexual being. This process has had multiple dimensions: the deposition of archaic fertility goddesses by male deities who took upon themselves the power to create life, the consequent demystification and "domestication" of women's social and biological role in childbearing, the establishment of patterns of patrilineal descent and male control over property inheritance within kin groups, the consolidation of those patterns through laws enforcing female chastity (of virgins and wives) and regulating population, and the confinement of women (especially of the upper classes) to domestic spaces and tasks.[4] In ancient Athens as in mercantilist France, woman's "duties as a citizen" were to remain chaste within marriage and to procreate—to provide heirs/citizens/soldiers/slaves/workers—but not to rule either in the city or the household. To secure the loyalty of men as taxpayers, property owners, and soldiers, the ancient and the early modern state in Europe promised them authority in their own house and the "legitimacy" of their children. Thus, far from being separate from the private sphere of family and childbearing, the public realm of the state depends on that sphere and tries to shape it. In feminist theory, the origins of the state are inseparable from the origins of patriarchy, a system of power in which men as fathers and husbands govern the labor, sexuality, and fertility of their daughters and wives. And the specific link between the two is the politicization and appropriation of fertility. Both public and private control over women as sexual and reproductive beings helps define the terms and boundaries of public power in the state.[5]

Sorting out the populationist (political-economic) and the sexist (patriarchal) dimensions of fertility control policies imposed by those in power in any period is a difficult task. Radical feminist theorists such as Adrienne Rich and Mary Daly cite the manifold ways in which, historically, institutions representing patriarchal authority in the state—the church, lay moralists, the husband-dominated nuclear family, and later the medical profession—attempted to define women's relationship to their fertility: when and whether they had sex and became pregnant, with whom, and how. Through moral injunctions, heterosexual and conjugal prescriptions, motherhood cults and fetishes, personal and sexual domination, and appropriation of the techniques of birth control and childbirth, these institutions sought to control women and their activities even more than the quantity or "quality" of their issue.[6] But while the politics of fertility can never be reduced to sheer numbers (birthrates), neither can the question of population control as an economic motive be divorced from those politics. The frequent practice of female infanticide in the ancient world, for example, represented a fusion of population control and misogynist strategies, an "efficient" method of controlling future births that both devalued women as reproducers and denigrated them as social beings. Likewise, cults of virginity not only restrained and appropriated the sexuality of young girls but also helped define the limits of marriage and childbearing in economic conditions where partible land was scarce.

The complex interrelation of class, sexual, and populationist elements in the state's reproductive policy can be illustrated by the Roman Empire, whose population measures were a precarious balancing act. As early as the first century, Roman law manifested concern with a falling birthrate—among married *upper-class* couples. For this class, procreation was viewed as a civic duty, and the law, under decrees of Augustus, constructed a number of rewards and penalties to promote at least three children per couple and to discourage childlessness. This pronatalist policy reflected the state's awareness that chemical, magical, surgical, and mechanical methods of abortion and contraception were known and practiced by Roman women and accounted for the birthrate decline.[7] Yet these methods were, as they have been through much of history, class specific; contraceptive potions and abortifacients were the "prerogative of those able to afford them," while the poor resorted to abandonment and infanticide. The Empire did not prohibit these latter methods, but it did impose the punishment of exile on wives who procured an abortion without the husband's consent and on women (probably midwives) who administered drugs or potions connected to children or conception (contraceptives and abortifacients).[8] Such wives and midwives were seen as setting "a bad example in the state," forsaking the duty of procreation among citizens and—worse still—taking reproduction into their own hands.

State-organized programs to reduce or increase fertility vary enormously according to historical and national circumstances, but certain commonalities stretch across time and place and link programs of pronatalist marriage and family laws, involuntary sterilization, infanticide, or prohibitions on contraception and abortion. Because state societies are hierarchically organized—divided into dominant and subordinate classes and races—these policies, whether pronatalist or antinatalist, have a distinct class and frequently ethnic dimension. Often they aim at reducing the underclasses—the surplus poor, the unemployed, racial and ethnic minorities, or the otherwise "unfit"—and increasing birthrates among the middle class, the "wellborn," and dominant racial and ethnic groups. In this way the state attempts to direct who will raise and socialize children and to shape the composition and size of the different classes. This was true in ancient Greece and the Roman Empire, as it was in the "race suicide" and eugenic campaigns in America in the late nineteenth and early twentieth centuries.

At other times, dominant groups consecrate to themselves the "rationality" and practical benefits of safe methods of fertility control, denying them to the lower classes. In late-eighteenth-century France or early-twentieth-century America, fears of the mushrooming *classes dangereuses* and white Anglo-Saxon "race suicide" contend with the bourgeoisie's or Yankees' pride in "fewer and better" children as signifying their moral purity and demarcating them from the lower classes. Ultimately, the recurrent policy of imposing patriarchal controls over women's fertility and sexuality is difficult to balance with a policy of population control aimed at the poor or racial minorities. The state's promotion of fertility control measures in the service of populationist ends may unwittingly facilitate their use by the "wrong" women (ruling-class wives and unmarried daughters), in the service of their sexual and reproductive freedom. Eugenicists in the early twentieth century in England and the United States, for example, found that tax incentives or subsidies to encourage "better breeding" among the upper classes actually encouraged the lower classes; whereas the dissemination of birth control information aimed at curbing the poor and the "unfit" had a greater, though unintended, impact on the middle class.[9] In other words, while population control and sexual control over women are coexistent strategies in state societies (which are also male-dominated societies), at various historical junctures they come into serious conflict.

The role of the state is to mediate this conflict by developing fertility policies that authorize population control measures and set limits on the legitimate boundaries of women's control over their fertility and sexuality, especially women who are the concern of patriarchal authority: wives and unmarried dependent daughters. In this mediating function, state powers recurrently seek to prohibit abortion, a means of fertility control that is particularly incompatible with orderly sex-gender relations. But even here, tensions between population control and sexual control infiltrate public policy. Moreover, the state must balance these two goals with a third, overriding purpose: to maintain internal order and its own legitimacy, which sometimes requires accommodating popular demands.

We have been talking about "the state" abstractly, as though it were a monolith. In fact, in the history of the Western capitalist state, policies affecting reproduction and sexuality have emerged out of a changing nexus of mediating forces, in which and through which women have negotiated their relationship to childbearing and sexuality. There has been no "center," no monolithic power structure, but a complex weave of multiple "centers of power" whose composition has shifted historically."[10] The pivotal, though far from decisive, role of the church in influencing popular thinking and practices about fertility was displaced to some extent by the medical profession in the nineteenth century, which in turn found its influence challenged in the mid-twentieth by population planners and governmental agencies. Throughout the eighteenth to twentieth centuries, all four power centers coexisted and exerted an influence on state policies. Yet the absence of any absolute center does not mean that "power is everywhere";[11] it remains possible to specify its locus in a given instance and to analyze the dynamics through which one group dominates and another resists within the total conjuncture. In the long run, women's fertility options in state societies are affected by a complex network of institutions and social forces including religion, medicine, law, the economy, and the family, which are all hierarchically organized by gender, class, and race. In the short run, we can still identify the disproportionate impact of, say, poor law officials, physicians, or family planners on the fertility practices of groups of women at particular moments.

In America in the late nineteenth and early twentieth centuries, the configuration of "powers" and "discourses" around fertility control began to shift markedly in a number of ways that still affect struggles for reproductive freedom. The official organizers of a fertility politics, one that represented the dominant groups in society, were increasingly secularized and professionalized— physicians, social welfare agents, academics, scientists—in short, the same middle-class configuration that designed policies of state intervention in many other arenas of "family life" from the Progressive era onward.[17] Ideologically, they combined a focus on eugenics, or a belief in "selective breeding" that would promote the propagation of "fitter" populations and discourage that of the "unfit"; an epidemiological, or public health, approach that provided a hygienic rationale for birth limitation and sexual restraint, especially among the lower classes; and an emphasis on "quality" mothering, guided by "experts" in childrearing. Sex, in this formulation, becomes a subtext of hygiene; yet it was also perceived as a "point of access" to population control and therefore a legitimate object of public scrutiny.[13] The "control" of sexuality is not an end in itself. It is a means toward the production of "good" children, "stable" families, "pure" races, higher (or lower) birthrates, and an orderly (class-based) society; rather than "repress" sexuality, it *defines* sexuality within history. A historical analysis that would reduce this complex nexus of political agencies and ideologies to "population" or "eugenics" alone would obscure the aspect of direct sexual regulation they involve, including the direction of women's sexuality into maternity. On the other hand, subsuming all "population" questions under the "history of sexuality" risks overlooking the intense ideological effort by twentieth-century agents of population control to sanitize the subject of fertility control, to desexualize it under a veil of medical and technocratic rationality.[14]

Increasing measures by the state and other powerful agencies to regulate fertility and women's control over it, beginning with the outlawing of abortion in the 1860s and 1870s, were part of a much larger tendency in late-nineteenth-century America that marked the early origins of the welfare state. It involved the centralization and rationalization of control over the movement, passions, reproduction, and secretions of bodies— what Foucault calls "bio-power." New state boards of charity, hygiene, child welfare, and the like aimed not only at the sexuality and reproductivity of women but the mobility of the poor and immigrants, the containment of deviants, and the activity and welfare of children—at all "surplus populations" in a period when industrial capitalism and immigration were spewing forth surplus people as quickly as surplus goods.[15] The forms in which these regulations appeared were positivistic science and medicine and the newly specialized and professionalized interests that practiced them: criminologists, psychiatrists, child welfare agents, obstetrician-gynecologists. The methods the social regulators used were those of measurement and surveillance: census taking, birth registries, population statistics, case histories, and "expert testimony."[16] Indeed, with the development of an organized medical profession, it became possible for agents of upper-class and patriarchal authority to scrutinize the fertility behavior of ordinary women at first hand. (Without the medical reports of physicians in late-eighteenth-century France and nineteenth-century America, we would probably know little or nothing about that behavior today.) Systematic measurement and scrutiny of women's fertility and sexual practices were part of a process of *politicization* that made visible an arena of social life that had previously been invisible, private. Laws criminalizing abortion in the latter half of the nineteenth century did not suppress abortion as much as they revealed it, regulated it, certified it as a legitimate domain of public intervention and control.

The question is, Why does the state begin to centralize and "technocracize" its control over bodies—their numbers, movement, passions, and so on? Why, in particular, does a traditional female practice, abortion, become subject to organized political control? Historically, state and church policies regulating fertility tend to be reactions to the perceived practices and values of women. The state attempts to accommodate, rechannel, or delegitimate women's everyday practices and values around fertility; rarely is it possible to wipe them out. Thus ordinary women play a dynamic part in determining the politics of reproduction and sexuality, through their practices and sometimes their consciously articulated ideas. Yet both state policies regarding fertility and the popular practices they aim to regulate must be seen in relation to historically varying social and economic conditions. These conditions proceed, as Marx says, independently of the "will" of either women or the state.

Falling Birthrates and Rising Abortions

The total white fertility rate in the United States decreased by half between 1800 and 1900, the number of children born per married woman falling from 7.04 to 3.56. Demographers have established that this decline began "at least as early as 1810" and that three-quarters of the pre-1940 decline (among whites) occurred before 1900 and much of it before the

Civil War.[17] Because this trend was well under way when much of the population was still living in rural areas, it cannot be attributed simply to urbanization and industrialization or declining mortality in the wake of improved living standards. Rather, the immediate cause of the decline was a drop in marital fertility (as measured by the changing ratio of young children to women of childrearing age) due to the widespread practice of abstinence, contraception, and abortion in the decades before the Civil War.[18] We thus have to look at the changing conditions of families and the position of women within families to explain the growing use of measures to limit births.

The conditions determining declining national fertility in mid-nineteenth-century America were material and ideological, but on both counts they had to do with changing definitions of motherhood. It is true that the decline was related in some general way to the growth of capitalist production and its separation from the home, changes in the standards of consumption, and a rise in urban employment along with a shrinkage in available land.[19] But these "background" conditions tell us only that changes in fertility had to do with broad changes in the society; they do not tell us about the processes and social relations through which smaller family size becomes a response to those conditions. There is the further problem that fertility declined not only among the urban bourgeoisie most affected by an industrial economy but among rural and frontier populations. In the previous chapter I suggested that smaller family size coincided with bourgeois class interests, thus enlisting the cooperation of husbands. In regard to rural fertility declines in the nineteenth century, some demographers point to an explanation that relates to property relations and patrilineal inheritance: the increasing scarcity of cultivable land in older, more settled areas.[20] Still, these class and sectoral conditions translated into conscious decisions about childbearing through processes that directly involved the perceptions of women, both urban and rural, about their identities and responsibilities as mothers. More than anything else, smaller family size accommodated the new definition of women as primarily mothers, under a cultural mandate that more and more defined motherhood in terms of the care and socialization of children, as opposed to the physical bearing of them.

Social historians have revealed the many levels on which the nineteenth century came to veil womanhood in the "cult of domesticity" and to crown her the "mother of civilization." It would charge her with forming "the moral and intellectual character of the young," and make "home" her "appropriate and appointed sphere of action."[21] "The 'empire of the mother,' as defined by nineteenth-century writers, was more than a feminine mystique. It conferred upon women the function of socialization. . . ."[22] As such, it organized a distinctly economic as well as a cultural, or "moral," reality. For poor women, especially those without dependable men to support them, children were always first and foremost an economic problem. In the nineteenth century, motherhood and domestic management became the central economic functions of bourgeois wives as well, circumscribing their work, as industrialization increasingly removed productive tasks from the home and segregated/differentiated its purposes. This fact more than any other—that motherhood was now their central social as well as moral end—shaped women's needs and desires regarding fertility.

What is important for a theoretical account of the decline in fertility and the rise in abortion during the nineteenth century is the means by which and the people to whom that ideology got transmitted. For I suggest that the ideology itself may have had a decisive impact on women's fertility control practices. We may assume that declining rates of national (white) fertility, both urban and rural, were related in a fundamental way to the changing consciousness of white women. That consciousness was shaped by changing conditions of motherhood and a dominant ideology of motherhood that had come to pervade the "national culture." The "cult of motherhood" in antebellum America was propagated and transmitted through a newly created "national cultural industry," burgeoning out of the invention of inexpensive printing machinery and based in the Northeast. The major products of this industry were sentimental novels and ladies' magazines, such as the famous *Godey's Lady's Book*, which represented the ideal woman as maternalism personified. Although addressed to and imaging the urban bourgeois "lady," these magazines and books were distributed all over the country, to women of different classes. Pioneer women took the new ideas about femininity and motherhood with them to the West, and a new "transportation network" of turnpikes, canals, and railroads carried them not only westward but to rural areas.[23]

Now, to argue that nineteenth-century motherhood ideology was a major influence on decisions to limit fertility is not to say that it was the most important influence for all women or that the conditions it addressed even pertained to the lives of some women. Particularly among blacks and immigrants, and among segments of the rural population, conditions of poverty and the continued reliance on child labor (and sometimes that of wives as well) made idealized maternal devotion and restricted childbearing beside the point. For these women, the dominant ideology may have seemed a standard beyond their reach, thus reinforcing a sense of their personal and moral failure. (Devotion to the home and to "fewer and better" children was now considered a divine as well as a natural prescription.)

On the other hand, while fewer than 5 percent of all white married women worked outside the home during most of the nineteenth century,[24] the women who did work—factory workers, domestic servants, farm laborers—undoubtedly restricted their fertility not in order to be "better mothers" but in order to function as providers. Moreover, labor force participation rates were substantially higher among young unmarried women, causing at least some of the fertility decline by leading young working women to delay marriage.[25] Also important, though we lack empirical data to verify it, may be the influence that having worked outside the home as single women had on the consciousness of married women. If the experience of wage earning gave young women "a greater sense of personal independence that they carried with them into their marriage," this may well have encouraged them to exercise independence in resorting to abstinence, contraception, and abortion to limit marital pregnancies.[26]

Women's consciousness regarding not only motherhood and work but also sexuality affected their behavior in reducing fertility. Historians agree that abstinence was probably a major form of fertility control, although abortion and contraception were widely in use. Abstinence reflected and supported the orthodoxy, proclaimed most effectively by physicians, that the maternal nature of woman precluded sexual instincts:

> The medical proponents of the sacred obligations of motherhood sought to free conception itself from unseemly passions, declaring that a child conceived in fits of lust was subject to all sorts of character disorders, especially the solitary vice of masturbation. In short, the suppression of the female sex drive and the use of abstinence as a mode of family limitation were additional byproducts of the cult of motherhood.[27]

But physicians were not simply arch-conspirators in a patriarchal plot to suppress women's sexuality. Nineteenth-century feminists were among the strongest advocates of sexual abstinence for women—as a measure of female self-defense against sexual exploitation and in support of "voluntary motherhood." For the same reasons, feminists and free lovers opposed abortion and contraception, seeing them as symptoms of women's sexual exploitation rather than means toward the "right to choose" motherhood, which they heartily endorsed.[28] Abstinence, however, was not only a birth control tactic but the expression of an ideology of moral virtue, one that manifested woman's nature as asexual and pure. In participating in and elaborating this ideology, Victorian feminists were at once asserting their procreative freedom and limiting their own sexuality, subscribing to the idea of sex as dangerous and taboo.[29] Their reasons for doing so—for participating in a kind of sexual false consciousness— were probably tied to issues of class and race, particularly in a period of rising immigration and class division and agitation against slavery. For the connotation of asexual purity contained in the ideology of the "lady" was a distinguishing feature by which white middle-class women were defined, and defined themselves, in relation to poor, black, and immigrant women. Fewer children were evidence of a chaste and spiritual, hence "ladylike," life.

These conditions underlay the decline in fertility in the nineteenth century; they involve economic, social, and cultural/ideological elements that are complexly interwoven and cannot be pried apart. Similarly, in the absence of survey data or any evidence other than physicians' observations, it is impossible to determine the weight of different methods— abstinence, contraception, or abortion—in determining the reduction in marital fertility. All we can know for sure is that all three approaches were used, and as is generally true in a period of fertility decline, they tend to coincide and reinforce one another (i.e., their use rises simultaneously). We might also apply McLaren's argument, inferring a probable rise in abortions from the combination of (1) falling birthrates and (2) our knowledge that the contraceptive methods used were highly ineffective. Vaginal injections of carbolic acid; douches made of cold- or warmwater solutions, bicarbonate of soda, Borax, vinegar, Lysol, or other agents to remove or sterilize sperm; cotton or sponge tampons; vigorous exercising after intercourse—all were of dubious reliability. Even periodic abstinence was unreliable, since it was combined with mistaken notions about the fertile time in a woman's reproductive cycle.[30] Increased recourse by nineteenth-century women to faulty birth control methods undoubtedly reinforced their need for abortions.

Based on different kinds of historical evidence, Mohr estimates a "great upsurge of abortion" during the middle of the century. First, during the 1840s abortifacient preparations emerged as a "booming business," which reflected an existing market of women who were seeking abortions and in turn gave abortion greater visibility and legitimacy, thereby undoubtedly increasing its incidence.[31] A proliferation of "female remedies" and emetics, advertised widely in newspapers and popular magazines, signaled the growth of a highly profitable drug industry that had, from its birth, targeted the "female market." In addition to drug companies, local apothecaries began an active over-the-counter trade in herbal and other substances thought to induce abortion, and various medical purveyors of the popular health movement—Thomsonians, botanics—became involved in prescribing home remedies, writing guidebooks, and setting up clinics to instruct women in the use of home techniques.[32]

We cannot know precisely what proportion of the advertised methods were effective and therefore their actual, or even approximate, impact on birthrates. What is important politically, however, is not the *actual* relation between abortion practices and fertility but the *apparent* relation; as in the present (when we do know something about this relation), it is the *visibility* of abortion rather than its incidence that arouses organized opposition. Thus it is for political even more than demographic reasons that we should find it significant to hear physicians in the late nineteenth century making estimates, based on clinical experience, about rising abortion rates. For example, Dr. Edwin M. Hale, a homeopathic leader writing in 1860, " 'safely asserted that there is *not one married female in ten who has not had an abortion, or at least attempted one!'* In the nation as a whole he believed that one in every five pregnancies ended in abortion. . . ."[33]

This may be evidence about upward trends, but if so, it reflects the reality of a specific class of women—those who sought the services of physicians and could pay for them. Mohr echoes the widely held view of nineteenth-century physicians when he claims that before 1840 abortion was a "recourse of the desperate"; after that time, it became the "systematic practice" of "respectable" women—those who were married, middle or upper-middle class, native-born Protestants.[34] Despite the opposition of some feminists to abortion and birth control, then, in practice Victorian middle-class women were apparently relying on abortion with growing frequency in order to assert control over the spacing and number of their children and thus over the situation within "their sphere."

The shifting *class base* of abortion, even more than its overall rise, undoubtedly accounts for the severity of the political attack against it. Abortion in the mid-nineteenth century became the object of organized opposition, not because of the numbers of women practicing it, but because of who those women were and the sex-race-class implications of their conduct. For abortion, unlike abstinence, directly communicates that women who utilize it are engaging in sex without the intention to procreate, are having sex for its "own sake" (to satisfy "male lust" if not their own). Abortion brings the *sexual* aspect of fertility and its control into the open; and for this to occur among married "respectable" women was to shatter delicately established boundaries of class, race, and gender.

The Medical Attack

If abortion "came out" in the 1860s and 1870s, it was the doing not of the women who practiced it so much as of the medical authorities who exposed and indicted it. Falling birthrates and rising abortion in the United States—and the greater sexual autonomy of middle-class women they seemed to denote—generated a two-sided political response: a propaganda campaign systematically attacking abortion and birth control use among middle-class "native" women; and a program of "negative eugenics" to limit the propagation of the poor, the foreign-born, and the "unfit." The first of these responses was led by the newly consolidated medical profession, whose ideological and lobbying efforts forged the national abortion policy that would prevail for the next century. The physicians' campaign was double-edged, representing both a gender and a class and ethnic conflict. It was aimed first at the redomestication of married WASP women, who made up the physicians' primary clientele. At the same time, it was aimed at the defense of the WASP establishment against rising immigration and proletarianization, a goal that would be taken on more directly by early-twentieth-century eugenicists.

Just as the Yankee woman was duty-bound to "propagate the race" and defend "the home," the immigrant, poor, or black woman, regarded as a carrier of disease and a breeder of "bad stock," was admonished to avoid reproducing.[35] Thus misogyny and sexual control clearly interact with population control; pronatalism geared toward the upper classes and antinatalism geared toward the lower classes presuppose that for women to control fertility is a dangerous and subversive thing. But there is also an underlying tension. It would take over forty years before upper-class fears of lower-class *sexuality* would be reconciled with their fears of lower-class *fertility,* to allow the provision of state-sponsored birth control services for the poor. In what follows we look at the role of the medical profession, the eugenics movement, and birth control radicals, including feminists, in forging a national fertility policy. The record shows that if the relationship between these groups has at times been one of ideological and political conflict, it has also been one of mutual influence and accommodation.

Prior to the mid-twentieth century, if there was a state policy on population and fertility, it was created not directly by the state apparatus but by emerging elites who sought control over the dispensing of private reproductive health care and the state's backing to legitimate that control. In its first stage it was a policy created through the pressure of the "regular" medical profession, particularly its ob-gyn specialists. The American Medical Association, more than any other group, led the campaign in the post–Civil War years to criminalize abortion, until then regarded by most Americans as "morally neutral" prior to "quickening" (the stage of pregnancy when fetal movements are noticed):

> From the Louisville convention of 1859 through the rest of the nineteenth century, the steadily growing AMA would remain steadfastly and officially committed to outlawing the practice of abortion in the United States, both inside and outside that organization, and the vigorous efforts of America's regular physicians would prove in the long run to be *the single most important factor in altering the legal policies toward abortion in this country.* [36]

The 1859 convention was the first of many occasions on which the AMA took a stand favoring the "general suppression" of abortion. Until that time abortion had in most states been legal, or at worst a misdemeanor, if performed before quickening. Not only did the AMA oppose the doctrine of quickening on biomedical grounds; it also called for the nonparticipation of physicians in abortion practices and asserted the "moral" view that the fetus was a "living being" at all stages of gestation, a being with civil rights.[37] For the next two decades, AMA leaders such as the singleminded Horatio Storer engaged in a concerted campaign of propagandizing and lobbying among state medical societies, state legislatures, professional journals, and the popular press, using their growing influence to secure the criminalization of abortion at any point in a pregnancy.[38] The criminal statutes that resulted and lasted in most states until 1973 prohibited abortion unless necessary to save a pregnant woman's life.

Before examining the reasons behind the medical profession's initiative, two points deserve emphasis. The first and most striking is that the doctors' crusade was overwhelmingly a *moral* crusade; health or health-related matters—for example, the high mortality and morbidity rates associated with abortion—were never the principal issue. The sharpest evidence that concern for women's health had little to do with the "regular" physicians' attack on abortion is the fact that the attack came "at the very time abortion might theoretically have become an obviously safer procedure than it had been earlier in the century. . . ."

> By 1890 the vast majority of American physicians had been taught the great advantage of antiseptic techniques, and antiseptic techniques might have rendered abortion—which had always been simple surgery in any event—safer, in all likelihood, than childbirth.[39]

Indeed, many physicians acknowledged that abortion was relatively safe and that only its illegality and practice under unhygienic conditions made it dangerous.

The second point is that the churches, even the Catholic church, remained lukewarm toward the issue. Unlike doctors, leaders of organized religion never played a central role in the late-nineteenth-century delegitimation of abortion in this country, despite medical leaders' efforts to recruit them. An 1871 AMA report on abortion shows the peculiar "moral leadership" exerted by the medical profession, appealing to "the clergy of all denominations" to heed "the perverted views of morality entertained by a large class of females—aye, and men also, on this important question."[40] Clearly, the AMA saw itself as shepherding the clergy on this issue, not the other way around.

Historically, the position of physicians with regard to abortion has been ridden with contradiction. On the one hand, the profession has never disguised its contempt for the practice; to this day, abortion is considered by many doctors as the boundary dividing professionals from charlatans and quacks.[41] On the other hand, for all its disdain, the profession has never been successful in wiping out abortion (as opposed to quashing its legality and respectability) and has been constantly preoccupied with how to bring the practice under medical control. In mid-nineteenth-century America, before the medical profession had secured a monopoly over health care, including fertility-related care, controlling abortion required enlisting the powers of the state. By the same token, the ideological and legal campaign against abortion helped the profession to establish its monopolistic control over health care. During this period, "regular" physicians (those who had received formal training and commanded capital-intensive techniques) sought the systematic regulation of lay competitors, using the instrumentalities of the state (e.g., legislation to impose stricter training, credentialing and licensing requirements, and penalties for their violation). "Doctors as a group" came to discredit the popular health movement and midwives by defining their activities as "unladylike" while defining their own as technically superior—the "best" care. "Doctors worried that, if midwives were allowed to deliver the upper classes, women would turn to them for treatment of other illnesses and male doctors would lose half their clientele. . . . Doctors had to eliminate midwives in order to protect the gateway to their whole practice."[42] Widespread abortion and family limitation clearly threatened the newfound status (to say nothing of potential profits) of male physicians as "attenders" of birth. The moral and legal attack on abortion therefore became an essential part of an exclusionary process that used discrediting tactics. Midwives were expelled from large-scale medical/obstetric practice through their delegitimation as incompetents ("quacks"), as "females," and as purveyors of wickedness.

On one level, then, the leadership of regular physicians in the antiabortion campaign clearly reflects the economic position of the medical profession in the mid-nineteenth century, its push to monopolize the market in health and childbirth, a particularly female market. It is more than an analogy to characterize this process as a stage in the capitalization and consolidation of medical practice in which regular physicians attempted to drive petty craftswomen and tradesmen from the market. In this pursuit the use of state laws to regulate, rationalize, and delegitimate traditional practices assisted in centralizing the autonomy of the professions and the bureaucratization of "social welfare" functions in the state.

But the growth of the medical profession was distinct from that of, say, the steel industry or textile manufacture in that its "product" was a certain kind of woman, a certain kind of female behavior and consciousness. In fact, social and ideological control over reproduction were inseparable. The economic interests of physicians cannot explain either the moralistic rhetoric or the misogyny of the antiabortion campaign. By 1860 the male "regulars" had more or less secured their dominance over American medical practice, at least to the extent that formal medical training was seen as a prerequisite to reliable care.[43] What remained was to establish an ideological hegemony that would give them an *exclusive* authority over their principal clientele—upper- and middle-class married women. Historians portray physicians more than any other group as the social agents who, through their popular writings as much as their medical treatises, propagated the Victorian ideology of "true womanhood."[44] Through its moralizing function as well as its claim to scientific knowledge, the profession attempted to establish its elite credentials.

Nowhere was the moralizing tendency of regular physicians more striking than in their relentless campaign against contraception and abortion. Medical school curricula and teachers were silent on these subjects; an address by the president of the American Gynecological Society in 1890 implied that "physicians should have nothing to do with the nasty business."[45] Both contraception and abortion were associated by a male, upper-middle-class, WASP medical profession with obscenity, lewdness, sex, and, worst of all, rebellious women. Physicians condemned the abortion practices of married women as "self-indulgence in the most disgusting forms," abandonment of maternal and child-care duties to "selfish and personal ends."[46] Their "medical" views of abortion and contraception cannot easily be separated from the conservative sexual values of their class, particularly the view that "female chastity is necessary to protect the family and its descent; that female chastity must be enforced with severe social and legal sanctions, among which fear of pregnancy functioned effectively and naturally."[47]

Physicians' active participation in shaping the ideology of female chastity and maternalism and giving it concrete political form (the anti-abortion campaign) was motivated, then, not only by economic interest but by class and culture. It was part of a conservative reaction, in the postbellum period, against women's rights activists—who were well organized and outspoken—and more generally against middle-class women's perceived rejection of their "traditional role." One side of this cultural reaction was sexual; the other side, inextricably tied to the first, had to do with class and race. Medical tracts opposing abortion stressed not only women's "self-indulgence" but abortion's prevalence among the "wrong" women (white middle-class Protestant married women), while immigrant and Catholic birthrates climbed. "Respectable" women—that is, the appointed clientele of the "regulars"—would find themselves out-bred by "the ignorant, the low lived and the alien."[48] Along with this pronatalist class message, the practice of physicians itself communicated, and embodied, a strong class and race division. Regular physicians scorned and dissociated themselves from anything connected to popular health, "female doctors," midwifery, and abortionists precisely because these practices administered to the reproductive needs of immigrants and the poor.

Thus, sexual conservatism, professional elitism and aggrandizement, and class and race bias entwined to determine the unique role of medical professionals in formulating a state policy criminalizing abortion in the nineteenth century. At the same time, the antiabortion campaign was a significant part of the historical process that produced a capitalist system of medical care in the United States, one that sharply divided along lines of class, race, and gender. Other non-Catholic countries developed policies that combined opposition to abortion with promotion of racist eugenics— for example, Germany and England. But the absence in the United States of either a strong centralized church or a national "public hygiene" implementation system meant that a policy to contain the fertility of the poor and foreign-born and to promote racial and sexual "purity" appeared as an emanation of "science." Privatism both legitimated and obscured the policy. Well into the mid-twentieth century, the medical profession, which both influenced and reflected the policy of the state, rejected any form of fertility control other than abstinence or "eugenic" sterilization.

Given this staunch and nearly universal opposition of the AMA and its adherents, how did a medical paradigm of abortion develop? A look at the reasoning of the handful of medical supporters of birth control in the late nineteenth century gives some clues as to how the medical arguments would evolve. A few argued that "preventive measures" should be supported by physicians as an antidote to abortion. Other medical practitioners, voicing a restrained support of birth control, revealed a concern that was primarily eugenic—the idea that "regulation of reproduction would be one effective remedy . . . [for] poverty, pauperism, prostitution, drunkenness, crime, imbecility, insanity, infanticide, etc."[49] Increasingly during the twentieth century, physicians would come to endorse eugenics and population control, and for some this might also sustain a conditional support of abortion, although they continued to prefer sterilization as a "solution."

The most telling sign that physicians might eventually alter their hostile position on birth control and abortion emanated less from moral or even eugenic concerns than from issues of professional control. Those few physicians, such as Robert Latou Dickinson, who became active campaigners among their colleagues for a more liberal view toward birth control were concerned that birth control practices, which were clearly not going to disappear, at least be brought under medical control and exercised according to medical standards.[50] Contributions to medical journals show that, as early as the 1880s, regular medical practitioners felt themselves under pressure from patients to supply birth control information. The inference that these doctors were beginning to draw was that if they were to avoid losing patients—to lay practitioners or abortionists or to fatal risks—it would be better to "keep the matter in our own hands":

The demand upon the practitioner to prevent conception is an unquestionable fact. Under these circumstances, *it is the duty of the profession to define more clearly what conditions justify and what do not justify interference,* and then to settle upon some safe, efficient measures to meet the demand.[51]

What is being articulated here is the impulse toward defining a medical paradigm of birth control, later to be extended to abortion. Another contributor to the same journal spells out the terms of this paradigm more precisely:

I would always advise [contraceptive measures] where puerperal or uraemic convulsions accompanied pregnancy; where vomiting was severe during pregnancy; where any pelvic deformity existed, or any uterine or ovarian growth was present; where excessive hemorrhage accompanied labor; where the perineum or other parts had been lacerated much during labor; where any hernia of the intestines was present; and where any heart, kidney or lung mischief was present—in fact, in all cases in which the medical attendant was of the opinion that evil results would follow conception; *but never merely for social or economic reasons.*[52]

Here, then, is the origin of (1) the distinction between "medical" and "socioeconomic" indications, or "therapeutic" versus "elective" procedures, and (2) the idea that the "medical attendant" alone (meaning a certified physician) is qualified to judge when "evil results [will] follow conception." This application of the "medical model" to birth control occurs within the context of a general shift among American medical practitioners from a moralistic to a positivistic mode of discourse. But the concept of "medical necessity" also reflects a conflict between medical professionals and their patients as well as midwives and lay practitioners. It represents a narrow accommodation by some medical practitioners to the popular demand for birth control, an accommodation that absorbed the feminist idea of women controlling their pregnancies into the framework of medical control over disease.

The Eugenics Movement and Sterilization

Immediately following the campaign against abortion in the 1860s and 1870s, a profusion of hereditarian and biological determinist theories emerged that would lay the groundwork for the eugenics movement. Rooted in social Darwinism, Italian criminal anthropology, phrenology, and genealogical studies of "degenerate" families, such theories were widely accepted by American penal and social reformers, as well as by physicians. The assumption that crime, insanity, poverty, and prostitution and other forms of illicit sex were the manifestations of inherited diseases that could "be shown to run in the blood," as Oliver Wendell Holmes put it, became a dominant ideology in a social context of accelerated immigration and labor unrest. That context gave the ideology its importance as a political tool to control class, racial, and ethnic conflicts.[53] Biological determinist ideology conjured up a peculiar confusion of genetic, behavioral, and moralistic ideas, particularly regarding lower-class sexuality. Typical is this passage by the social reformer Charles Loring Brace:

> It is well known to those familiar with the criminal classes that certain appetites or habits, if indulged abnormally or excessively through two or more generations come to have an almost irresistible force, and no doubt, modify the brain so as to constitute almost an insane condition. This is especially true of the appetite for liquor and of the sexual passion and sometimes of the peculiar weakness, dependence and laziness which make confirmed paupers. . . .
>
> [Describing a young girl of "licentious habits and desires"] the "gemmules," or latent tendencies, or forces, or cells of her immediate ancestors were in her blood, producing irresistible effects on her brain, nerves, and mental emotions, and finally, not being met early enough by other moral, mental and physical influences, they have modified her organization, until she is scarcely able to control them and she gives herself up to them.[54]

There is a neat fit between the revival in the early twentieth century of neo-Malthusian thinking about the dire consequences of "overbreeding" among poor and "unfit" populations and hereditarian explanations of the inevitable, incurable deficiencies of those populations. Both lay the moral blame for poverty and social distress on the poor themselves rather than the conditions they must contend with. In the 1920s the eugenics movement arose out of these two connected ideological strands, along with the timely rediscovery of Mendelian genetics, to present an allegedly scientific basis for controlling both the quantity and "quality" of births.

The racist, nativist, and class-biased thinking of eugenicists is familiar but cannot be overstressed. American intellectuals, scientists, and physicians were strongly influenced by the ideas of Francis Galton, a cousin of Darwin and founder and leader of the eugenics movement in England. They borrowed from Galtonian eugenics its belief in the innate superiority of famous and "successful men" and the innate inferiority of lower-class and delinquent members of the population, along with a belief in the existence of biologically superior and inferior races. It was common for eugenicists to equate biological "fitness" with social class and to conclude "that college-educated, native, white Protestants (like themselves) were the bearers of the valuable genes of society."[55]

Eugenicists rested their claims to scientific objectivity on a positivistic methodology that armed them with a number of newly developed quantitative tools: the census, intelligence testing, and the use of statistics to measure every sort of social problem; "populations" became subject to comparison and measurement.[56] Measuring devices lent the eugenics movement an aura of optimism and activism, an emphasis on "social engineering" to improve "the race" that went beyond the grim predictions of their Malthusian forerunners. Whether focused on "positive eugenics"—schemes of education, tax incentives, and the like to increase the propagation of the "superior"—or "negative eugenics"—schemes involving involuntary confinement, immigration restrictions, and surgical sterilization to diminish the numbers of the "inferior"—the assumption of eugenicists was that the manipulation of populations was a worthy object of social intervention. In the long run, the negative (antinatalist) strategies were the ones developed beyond rhetoric into government policy. These measures (e.g., a proliferation of institutions for the "feebleminded," a rash of compulsory sterilizations) were justified on explicitly social and racial (i.e., "eugenic") grounds: "to cut off defective germ plasm through the medium of segregation" and "to protect society from the menace [of the feebleminded]."[57]

The eugenics movement spread rapidly across the country during the 1920s. Eugenics became part of the curricula of many major universities and prompted the establishment of numerous publications, international congresses, and local and national organizations.[58] The general public was less influenced by the propaganda of the Eugenics Record Office and its organizational affiliates, however, than was the growing group of professionals who had become stalwarts of hereditarianism. The "new professions"—social workers, prison wardens, psychiatrists in prisons and mental asylums, and administrators of institutions for the alcoholic and the feebleminded—had arisen with custodial institutions, and their "direct responsibility was with persons who became wards of the state for care and cure." These new agents of "public welfare" found hereditary explanations most amenable to their professional outlook and thus became, along with academics and social scientists, the major promoters of eugenics as a "cause." The transformation of eugenics from a creed into public policy in the legislative campaigns of the 1920s was achieved, not through public demand, but primarily through "expert testimony before legislative committees" by specialists and practitioners of eugenics.[59] Like the medical profession earlier, these specialists derived their autonomy and centralized bureaucratic authority in part from an assertion of control over the fertility of women—in this case, women of the poor rather than the middle class.

It seems clear how an ideology linking deviant behavior to hereditarian and germ theories would lend itself to penal and social welfare policies that involved, in the late-nineteenth-century seaboard states such as Massachusetts and New York, increasing bureaucratization and centralized state control. Assumptions about "incurability" helped justify larger public appropriations for institutional "quarantine" and custodial incarceration. But while "the numbers cared for in institutions nearly tripled from 1904 to 1923,"[60] in the next decade the method that came to typify the eugenic approach to limiting "deviant" populations was surgical sterilization, mostly of women. Eugenicists, unlike their pessimistic Malthusian and social-Darwinist predecessors, established the premise that some deliberate technical intervention could be applied to deal with social deviance, differential population growth, and their sexual roots. This interventionist thrust of the eugenic period bridged the gap between the previous era and the later development of family planning and population control organizations. Compulsory sterilization epitomized the two-sided character of eugenics as a means of social-sexual control. It concentrated an attack on populations deemed expendable or socially threatening (poor, uneducated women, who were its usual victims), and a symbolic attack on sex and the sexual danger or contagion that *those* women were felt (by middle-class professionals and reformers) to represent.

Efforts at *"systematic asexualization* in the United States for eugenic purposes" had taken place in the 1890s, but a major turning point came somewhat later with the development of the relatively simple surgical procedures of vasectomy and salpingectomy, making it possible to sterilize people without destroying sexual feeling. Thereafter, there were many proposals in favor of legalizing sterilization, followed by the enactment of eugenic—and sometimes punitive—sterilization laws in thirty-two states. The first such law, that of Indiana in 1907, authorized the compulsory sterilization, upon recommendation of a "board of experts," of "confirmed criminals, idiots, imbeciles, and rapists in state institutions."[61] In 1914 a report of the Eugenics Section of the American Breeders' Association, under Harry Laughlin, advocated sterilization as a "means of reducing defective germ plasma," estimating that 10 percent of the total population was "socially inadequate." Laughlin proposed that such eugenic sterilization be directed at the insane, the "criminalistic," the feebleminded, orphans, vagrants, and paupers, among others.[62] All this activity resulted in the involuntary sterilization of over 45,000 persons in the United States in the years between 1907 and 1945, half of them mentally ill (as opposed to mentally defective) and the great majority of them poor women. The systematic character of sterilization procedures reached the point where "many mentally retarded or unstable persons were being admitted to the institutions merely to be sterilized and then released."[63]

Carrie Buck was one such person. In 1926 the U.S. Supreme Court finally gave its stamp of approval to the compulsory sterilization laws when Justice Holmes, in *Buck* v. *Bell,* delivered his famous defense of Carrie Buck's sterilization on the grounds of "a compelling state interest in preventing the procreation of children who will become a burden on the state":

> It is better for all the world, if instead of waiting to execute degenerate offspring for crime, or let them starve for their imbecility, society can prevent those who are manifestly unfit from continuing their kind. The principle that sustains compulsory vaccination is broad enough to cover cutting the Fallopian tubes. . . . Three generations of imbeciles are enough.[64]

Compulsory sterilization, more than any other eugenic "remedy," symbolizes the urge to exorcise danger, to "purify," to cut off social deviance and unrest at its (presumed) source. As a populationist strategy, it aims to eliminate the "unfit" or the expendable by simply preventing them from being born; the class and racial interests it perpetuates are transparent. A poor and unskilled mass of unemployed comprises not only a cheap labor reserve economically but also a potential source of social rebellion and hence a threat to the established order. Eugenic techniques of social control such as involuntary sterilization, insofar as they promised literally to extirpate this threat, must have furnished a comforting safety valve in the eyes of a predominantly white Anglo-Saxon bourgeoisie. But the focus of compulsory sterilization laws—most of which are still on the books—was population control *and* sexual control. Their aim was not only to reduce numbers or root out "defective genes" but also to attack and punish sexual "promiscuity" and the sexual danger thought to emanate from the lower classes, especially lower-class women. That surgical sterilization directly affects not sexuality but pregnancy is irrelevant to its implicit sexually punitive intent. In particular for women, in a patriarchal culture that defines women's sexuality in terms of their reproductive capacity, involuntary sterilization does indeed mean "systematic asexualization."

The message of Holmes' pronouncement on the violability of the Fallopian tubes is that the state may and will penetrate the body—its sexuality, its reproductivity—in its function as moral police. It will "vaccinate" society (or its elite classes) against "degenerates" and "pollutants," will regulate populations through the regulation of women's bodies and claim jurisdiction over women's bodies through the exigencies of population. *Buck* v. *Bell* is the first major policy statement by an arm of the U.S. government legitimating its direct role in fertility control politics. The sexual message of this decision speaks directly and menacingly to women. For there is little question that, to the institution where she was incarcerated as to the court, Carrie Buck's sterilization was the condition for her release. Its punitive meaning is absolutely clear. She would be not only "sanitized" and "neutralized" as a "carrier" of "bad genes" but also stigmatized and made an example for her promiscuity and her lust.

Abortion, Sterilization, and the Socialist-Feminist Birth Control Movement

The historical analysis of abortion prohibition and eugenic sterilization laws illustrates the argument that state policies to control fertility are policies directed at women's sexual autonomy and reproductive freedom as well as at control of population quantity and "quality." These policies take different forms for women of different classes, yet the denial that *any* women should be the final arbiters of their relation to motherhood and their sexuality clearly underlies all such policies, whatever their class and racial dimensions. This would seem a potential unifying basis around which feminists might have developed a program that could transcend the barriers of class and race to address the forms of oppression specific to women as a whole. But it was precisely the strength of class and race divisions and the translation of these divisions into the sex-race-class dichotomy of "pure women" and "lustful women" that prevented such unity, or even a perception of common interests. Instead of feminists of the "first wave" ardently supporting legal abortion and expressly opposing compulsory sterilization, the opposite was the case. And the stand they took—opposing abortion and supporting involuntary sterilization of the "unfit"—was a direct product of the classist and racist biases of feminists and their dissociation of sex from the birth control issue.

This was particularly true of the accommodationist leadership of the feminist birth control movement, especially Margaret Sanger. There is no need to retell Sanger's story. It is her ideas and her political influence, particularly in regard to the medical profession and abortion and to the eugenics movement, that I wish to highlight. Sanger's early sympathies unquestionably lay with socialism, feminism, and the sex radicalism she learned from Havelock Ellis. In *Woman and the New Race* (1920), she strongly identifies the "problem of birth control" with the struggle of women for their emancipation and woman's fundamental need to "own and control her body," sexually and productively. She insists "that no woman should be a mother against her will." "Woman must have her freedom— the fundamental freedom of choosing whether or not she shall be a mother and how many children she will have. Regardless of what man's attitude may be, that problem is hers—and before it can be his, it is hers alone."[65] She condemns "the church's code of sex morals," which violates women's "basic sex rights" and condones "lawful rape" in marriage, advocating instead the spread of birth control information as a means of "removing the fear of unwanted children" and helping woman to "know her own body, . . . her sexual nature."[66]

But Sanger's main focus throughout the 1920s and 1930s was to win acceptance for birth control and establish its legality, and this single-mindedness made for serious contradictions in her ideology and her politics. On the one hand, she consistently opposed the restriction of birth control to "medical indications," believing that social and economic problems were at least as valid, and far more frequent, justifications. On the other hand, her consuming desire to gain legitimacy and respectability for the movement led her, in the 1920s, to seek the endorsement of "influential doctors," courting their favor and in large measure deferring to a medical model of birth control dissemination. Strategically, this meant: (1) on the level of her own clinic, always referring patients to a doctor for prescribing and fitting birth control devices; (2) on the national level, making political compromises to win medical support for her organization, the American Birth Control League; and (3) on the level of confronting the state, pursuing legal loopholes that seemed to allow birth control if confined to the supervision of licensed doctors for purposes of preventing disease.[67]

Thus, Sanger's major legal strategy for years was to push for "doctors only" bills in state legislatures, which would allow birth control dissemination on the condition that licensed M.D.s would be in charge. While the bills failed in most cases, the politics they grew out of were successful in "drawing doctors into the birth control movement."[68] In turn, the support of the medical profession undoubtedly contributed to the *legitimation* of birth control, but on terms that doctors could live with. Paradoxically, the long-standing disdain of the medical profession for birth control led to the proliferation of private birth control clinics, operating outside hospitals and physicians' offices; yet these same clinics (constantly vulnerable to police harassment) ultimately achieved their legitimacy through deference to a "very strong medical bias," including "a highly conservative attitude toward abortion, sterilization, publicity, and non-medical personnel."[69]

Sanger's eagerness to win over the medical profession to birth control helps to explain her persistent opposition to abortion. Her grim experiences as a public health nurse and her rage over the death of Sadie Sachs notwithstanding, a look at what she writes about abortion reveals an uncritical acceptance of the current medical dogma. Like many feminists before her, she sympathized with poor women who were the victims of an experience that was "humiliating, repulsive, painful and too often gravely dangerous."[70] But rather than blame the illegal and unhygienic conditions under which poor women's abortions were performed, she blamed the procedure, characterizing it as intrinsically "horrible" and associating it with the "savage" methods of fertility control, infanticide and abandonment. Citing many medical sources, she claimed that the numerous risks to health and life, such as uterine perforation, sepsis, and subsequent sterility are "always" present in abortion, without specifying factors of age, timing, or the use of antiseptics and sterile facilities. These risks, as we now know, were mainly the result of inadequate conditions and care rather than inadequate technology; and if this "knowledge" was absent in 1920, it was the dominant political discourse, which cast abortion as evil and unsavory, and not the limits of medical science that made it so.

If abortion once again in the late nineteenth and early twentieth centuries became a "recourse of the desperate," this had not always been the case. If upper- and middle-class women's use of abortion declined in that period, and that of poor women became more dangerous, it was largely because of the harsh ideological campaign and the stigma of criminality perpetrated by the medical profession. Sanger's object in attacking abortion so intensively is forthrightly polemical: to persuade that same medical profession that contraception is the only possible antidote to abortion. The crux of her argument in *Woman and the New Race* is to portray abortion as the "cruel" and "repressive" *alternative* to legal contraception, an alternative that no woman would resort to if she were "not denied the knowledge of scientific, effective contraceptives":

> The question that society must answer is this: Shall family limitation be achieved through birth control or abortion? Shall normal, safe, effective contraceptives be employed, or shall we continue to force women to the abnormal, often dangerous surgical operation?
> "Contraceptives or Abortion—which shall it be?"[71]

Not all feminist birth control advocates accepted a medically oriented strategy or opposed abortion. Mary Ware Dennett of the Voluntary Parenthood League, for example, expressed a more feminist view than Sanger's when she argued that "doctors only" bills "removed the technique of birth control from a woman's own control" and left her susceptible to doctors' moral censure. Antoinette Konikow, the socialist doctor, argued that the effect was to suppress mass interest in birth control as a popular issue, a women's issue, and to transform it into a medical interest.[72] Indeed, this warning turned out to be prophetic. Constrained in a medical straitjacket to secure legitimacy, birth control and abortion would not again become the focus of a mass movement until the late 1960s. Even in the early twentieth century, however, strong-voiced feminists consistently supported the need for and potential safety of abortion for masses of women, against the feminist mainstream. Stella Browne, the English socialist-feminist and ardent birth control activist, took Sanger to task (without naming her) for her position on abortion. Writing in 1922, Browne unveiled the medical and misogynist politics behind the appeal to "safety" when it was society that denied antiseptics and hygienic facilities to poor women:

> . . . I am profoundly convinced that [abortion] is a woman's right, and have argued the case for that right in the Press, both in England and America. I am told, however, by one of the leaders of our movement, to whose penetrating judgment and wide nursing experience I give the highest honour, that abortion is *physiologically injurious* and to be deprecated. It is open, perhaps, to question whether the effects of abortion itself have been sufficiently separated from the appalling bad conditions of nervous terror, lack of rest and lack of surgical cleanliness in which it is generally performed. . . .
>
> It is up to science to meet the demands of humanity . . . that life shall be given . . . "frankly, gaily," or —not at all. Which shall it be?[73]

In its quest for legitimacy, the birth control movement, under Sanger's leadership, turned increasingly to the medical profession and the elite professionals who espoused eugenics. The story of the conservatizing influence of eugenics ideology on birth control activism has been told amply by historians. According to the pessimistic judgment of David Kennedy, Sanger's biographer, by the late 1920s "eugenics dominated birth control propaganda and underscored the conversion of the birth control movement from a radical program of social disruption to a conservative program of social control."[74] Linda Gordon recapitulates this theme in her notion that birth control from the 1920s through the following decades shifted "from women's rights to family planning." Sanger's strategy, which became that of Planned Parenthood, was to give birth control an aura of scientific and medical respectability by assimilating it within the framework of social engineering ("planning") and public policy. In practical terms, this meant forging alliances with professions closest to organized power in the domains of reproduction and population—physicians, eugenic-minded academics, and administrators of the incipient "social welfare" bureaucracies. Such alliances inevitably meant ideological and political compromises. The costs to a radical (i.e., socialist and feminist) birth control movement were (1) the continued suppression of abortion, (2) the indelible linking of birth control as public policy with racist and class-biased assumptions about who should reproduce and who should not, and (3) the relinquishing of control over the administration and conditions of fertility control to medical professionals and planners. Historically this meant a shift away from a focus on individual women's right to and need for sexual and reproductive autonomy (i.e., feminist criteria) and toward a focus on "medical necessity" in a narrow sense, populationism, and the fiscal problems of the state.

What is often unseen is that the "professionalization" of birth control, the perversion of its feminist aspects, also involved the *desexualization* of the birth control issue. Family planning, as propagated by the new coalition of professional birth controllers (in 1942 Sanger's Birth Control Federation of America became the Planned Parenthood Federation of America), eugenicists, and physicians, attempted to "decontaminate" as it medicalized and technocracized fertility control. This meant depoliticizing it, removing its sexual connotations by reinforcing a "hygienic" concept of sex as not only strictly marital, monogamous, and heterosexual but also an aspect of "good adjustment" to marriage.[75] If birth control were to appeal to the sexually conservative medical profession and their likeminded colleagues in eugenic circles, it could hardly feature woman's discovery of her "sexual nature," of which Sanger had been among the most passionate exponents.

Feminist activists did not create the essentially eugenic-minded nonfeminist alliance that dominated fertility control politics in the United States from the 1920s to the 1970s. Ironically, however, some feminists, through their ideas and their practical affiliations, served as "midwives" to a configuration of powers that legitimated birth control by (1) extracting from it any feminist or sexual content and (2) linking it to programs of coercive population control. Many prominent birth control advocates, from the 1910s to the 1930s, in England and America, "had strong eugenic backgrounds."[76] Like their nineteenth-century predecessors, they participated in the dominant ideology that surrounded them. Sanger's eagerness to court the middle-class professionals who promoted eugenics sometimes caused her to adopt their rhetoric. "More children from the fit, less from the unfit—that is the chief issue of birth control," she wrote in 1919. And while she "usually strove to avoid an ethnic definition of 'unfit,' " she occasionally cast aspersions on "foreigners" and allowed rank racists like Paul Popenoe to write in the *Birth Control Review*.[77] The "myth of the menace of feeblemindedness" and the notion of "unfitness" (based on physical rather than class, racial, or ethnic characteristics) had broad currency in the early twentieth century and were uncritically accepted by many socialists, feminists, and progressive reformers. Emma Goldmann certainly had a notion of the "sickly, feeble and decrepit" whose birth ought to be prevented. Caroline Hadley Robinson was not only blatantly hostile to abortion but just as blatantly supportive of eugenic sterilization of the "unfit" (by whom she meant the feebleminded, deaf-mutes, the blind or crippled, and other such "defectives").

While embracing elements of eugenic ideology, did white middleclass feminists in some ways transform that ideology? Like the proponents of "voluntary motherhood" in the late nineteenth century, feminists such as Sanger and Charlotte Perkins Gilman took strands of the dominant ideology—in this case, eugenics—and fashioned them into a peculiarly feminist variation that combined the notion of individual choice with the notion of moral duty. In her vision of a "new race" Sanger distinctly avoids racist or biological determinist arguments to explain the "social handicaps" of the poor, arguing instead that "the cell plasms of these peoples [immigrants] are freighted with the potentialities of the best in Old World civilization."[78] Yet, while Sanger seems to blame the conditions and not the poor for the horrors that oppress their lives, the antidote she envisages is the standard eugenic one: "The most immoral practice of the day" is not economic exploitation but "breeding too many children."[79] Thus, birth control and woman's "right to choose" become vehicles toward bettering "the race" and achieving the ideal of a "melting pot"; motherhood, freely chosen, is eugenic:

> We know that in each of these submerged and semi-submerged elements of the population there are rich factors of racial culture. Motherhood is the channel through which these cultures flow. Motherhood, when free to choose the father, free to choose the time and the number of children who shall result from the union, automatically works in wondrous ways. It refuses to bring forth weaklings; refuses to bring forth slaves; refuses to bear children who must live under the conditions described. It withholds the unfit, brings forth the fit; brings few children into homes where there is not sufficient to provide for them. Instinctively it avoids all those things which multiply racial handicaps. Under such circumstances, we can hope that the "melting pot" will refine. . . .[80]

The appeal to "maternal instinct" and "responsible" childbearing became a central element of eugenic ideology, just as it had been of Malthusian ideology in an earlier period. Feminists such as Sanger and Gilman may well have played a key role in fabricating this ideological synthesis and thereby in softening the eugenic creed and winning it broader legitimacy. In so doing, however, they were demanding that maternity become a realm of individual self-determination and full human dignity, and this was far from the aims of eugenicists like Davenport and Popenoe. Indeed, eugenicists became disenchanted with birth control when it seemed to be having a greater impact on middle-class women's fertility and sexual practices than on the poor.[81] Despite political and institutional alliances, the tension between sexual control and population control remains deep, and so does that between feminists and populationists.

In the final analysis, the deradicalization of the birth control movement in the interwar period did not result from the failures of feminism or individual feminists, but from a much broader set of conditions that contained the power of radical social movements as a whole and kept birth control radicalism, feminism, sexual liberation, and socialism from coming together in a single movement. Sanger's reliance on the medical profession and eugenicists was not the result of opportunism or ambition but of the absence of a mass feminist *and* working-class movement that wholeheartedly struggled for sexual liberation and reproductive freedom. Gordon attributes this absence in the pre–World War I period in part to the deliberate "silence" of the American left on the subject of birth control. Socialists such as Kate Richards O'Hare and the male-dominated organs of the Socialist Party accepted a traditional Victorian view of woman's place in the family and the primacy of her childbearing function. The major feminist organizations—the National American Woman Suffrage Association, the Woman's party, and the Women's Trade Union League—also shied away from an active commitment to birth control, to say nothing of abortion. This reticence grew out of feminists' acceptance of "race suicide" and "maternal instinct" dogma and still more, at least for the older generation of suffragists and feminists, out of their fears of the sex radicalism and "promiscuity" they associated with birth control politics.[82] These two tendencies—the sexual puritanism of first- and second-generation feminists and their sense of class and racial superiority—were deeply connected.

Thus, feminist sexual conservatism and socialist antifeminism combined to effectively cut off the birth control movement from links with broader socialist and feminist organizations. In the next two decades, what had been serious lapses in consciousness among feminists and socialists—a failure to transcend barriers of race and class and divisions of gender—were compounded by, first, political and ideological repression and then an economic depression that swept up all radical forces into the struggle for jobs, social welfare, and industrial unionism. The now professionalized birth control organizations existed completely separate from this struggle, and separate too from the lives and identities of poor and working-class women. Harboring a missionary, eugenic purpose vis-à-vis the poor—a purpose that would be assisted but never fully taken over by the state from private agencies—these organizations reflected the split in reproductive services and policies between the dispensing of population control to the poor and the private market in services for the middle class and the wealthy.

This capitalist dualism, which the state upholds through laws and institutions that codify the dichotomy between "private choice" and "public service," itself contradicts a feminist vision. It precludes a concept of control over reproduction that unites the needs and conditions of *all* women, as a common *social* question, and assumes that all women are fundamentally capable of exercising "choice."[83] The dominant population organizations in twentieth-century America have, to their credit, disseminated birth control among women throughout the world. But they have done so in a way that is consistent with the interests of the capitalist state by maintaining a class-divided system of distribution and a professional doctrine that divorces fertility control from women's need for sexual self-determination. This is the foundation of the fertility control policy adopted by the state in the mid-twentieth century.

NOTES

1. Stanley Diamond, "The Rule of Law Versus the Order of Custom," in *The Rule of Law,* ed. Robert Wolff (New York: Simon and Schuster, 1971), p. 126.

2. For historical analyses of this process in various periods in the West, see, along with Diamond, Charles Tilly, ed., *The Formation of National States in Western Europe* (Princeton: Princeton University Press, 1975); Frederick Engels, *The Origin of the Family, Private Property and the State,* ed. Eleanor Burke Leacock (New York: International Publishers, 1972); Gerhard Ritter, "Origins of the Modern State," in *The Development of the Modern State,* ed. Heinz Lubasz (New York: Macmillan, 1964); and Marc Bloch, *Feudal Society,* trans. L. A. Manyon (Chicago: University of Chicago Press, 1964), Vol. 1, pt. 3.

3. M. Moheau, *Recherches et Considérations sur la Population de la France* (Paris: Moutard, 1778), 1: 12, 2: 102–3.

4. See, e.g., Zillah Eisenstein, *The Radical Future of Liberal Feminism* (New York: Longman, 1981), Chaps. 2 and 3; Joan Kelly-Gadol, "Did Women Have a Renaissance?," in *Becoming Visible: Women in European History,* ed. Renate Bridenthal and Claudia Koonz (Boston: Houghton Mifflin, 1977), pp. 137–64; Sarah Pomeroy, *Goddesses, Whores, Wives and Slaves: Women in Classical Antiquity* (New York: Schocken, 1977), Chaps. 4 and 5; Sherry B. Ortner, "The Virgin and the State," *Feminist Studies* 4 (October 1978): 19–36; and Ruby Rohrlich, "State Formation in Sumer and the Subjugation of Women," *Feminist Studies* 6 (Spring 1980): 76–102.

5. See Eisenstein, Chap. 2, especially on this point.

6. Adrienne Rich, "Compulsory Heterosexuality and Lesbian Existence," *Signs* 5 (Summer 1980), pp. 69–71; and Mary Daly, *Gyn-Ecology: The Metaethics of Radical Feminism* (Boston: Beacon, 1978).

7. Noonan, *Contraception,* pp. 21–22.

8. Ibid., pp. 24–27. See also Pomeroy, pp. 166–68; and Keith Hopkins, "Contraception in the Roman Empire," *Comparative Studies in Society and History* 8 (1965–66): 124–51. Noonan quotes St. Ambrose in the fourth century: "The poor women abandon their children; rich women deny their own fetus in their uterus and by parricidal [*sic*] potions extinguish the pledges of their womb in their genital belly" (p. 19).

9. Weeks, *Sex, Politics and Society,* p. 135; and David M. Kennedy, *Birth Control in America: The Career of Margaret Sanger* (New Haven: Yale University Press, 1970), p. 120.

10. This term comes from Foucault, *The History of Sexuality,* Vol. 1.

11. Martha Vicinus, "Sexuality and Power: A Review of Current Work in the History of Sexuality," *Feminist Studies* 8 (Spring 1982): 139. A very thoughtful critique of Foucault.

12. See Eli Zaretsky, "The Place of the Family in the Origins of the Welfare State," in *Rethinking the Family: Some Feminist Questions,* ed. Barrie Thorne and Marilyn Yalom (New York: Longman, 1982), pp. 188–224; and generally, Barbara Ehrenreich and Deirdre English, *For Her Own Good: 150 Years of the Experts' Advice to Women* (Garden City, N.Y.: Anchor, 1979); and Jacques Donzelot, *The Policing of Families,* trans. Robert Hurley (New York: Pantheon, 1979).

13. Weeks, *Sex, Politics and Society,* p. 122 and Chap. 7.

14. An analogous intervention was the control of prostitution in the late nineteenth century, instigated by an alliance of religious and feminist moral reformers who saw contagious disease and sexual license as intertwined, indeed identical, targets. See, on England, Judith R. Walkowitz, *Prostitution and Victorian Society: Women, Class, and the State* (New York: Cambridge University Press, 1980); and on America, David J. Pivar, *Purity Crusade: Sexual Morality and Social Control, 1868–1900* (Westport, Conn.: Greenwood, 1973).

15. For interesting accounts of this process, see Zaretsky; Gerald Grob, *Mental Institutions in America* (New York: Free Press, 1973), pp. 262–65; and Barbara G. Rosenkrantz, *Public Health and the State: Changing Views in Massachusetts, 1842–1936* (Cambridge, Mass.: Harvard University Press, 1962).

16. Weeks, *Sex, Politics and Society,* p. 123; and R. Petchesky, "Treatment as a Model of Social Control: Ideology, Technique, and Political Organization" (Ph.D. dissertation, Columbia University, 1974), Chap. 1.

17. Smith, "Family Limitation . . . ," in *A Heritage of Her Own,* ed. N. Cott and E. Pleck, p. 226; and Wilson H. Grabill, Clyde V. Kiser, and Pascal K. Whelpton, "A Long View," in *The American Family in Social-Historical Perspective,* ed. Michael Gordon (New York: St. Martin's, 1973), pp. 383–84.

18. Grabill, Kiser and Whelpton, pp. 393–94.

19. William Leach, *True Love and Perfect Union* (New York: Basic Books, 1980), p. 83; Mary P. Ryan, *Womanhood in America, from Colonial Times to the Present* (New York: New Viewpoints, 1975), p. 162; and Richard A. Easterlin, "Factors in the Decline of Farm Family Fertility in the United States: Some Preliminary Research Results," in *The American Family in Socio-Historical Perspective,* 2d ed., ed. Michael Gordon (New York: St. Martin's, 1978), pp. 533–45.

20. See Easterlin, pp. 540–42.

21. Catherine Beecher, "The Peculiar Responsibilities of American Women," in *Root of Bitterness,* ed. Nancy F. Cott (New York: Dutton, 1972), pp. 173–74. See also Ryan, Chap. 4; Barbara Welter, "The Cult of True Womanhood: 1820–1860," in M. Gordon, pp. 313–33; and Nancy F. Cott, *The Bonds of Womanhood: "Woman's Sphere" in New England, 1780–1835* (New Haven: Yale University Press, 1977).

22. Ryan, p. 165.

23. Ibid., pp. 140–43.

24. Smith, p. 225, Table 2; and Stanley Lebergott, *Manpower in Economic Growth* (New York: McGraw-Hill, 1964), p. 519, Table A-10.

25. Smith makes a central point of this to support his theory that fertility decline was the result of "domestic feminism" (pp. 225–26). Cf. Tamara K. Hareven and Maris A. Vinovskis, "Patterns of Childbearing in Late 19th Century America: The Determinants of Marital Fertility in Five Massachusetts Towns in 1880," in *Family and Population in Nineteenth Century America,* ed. Hareven and Vinovskis

(Princeton: Princeton University Press, 1978). "The opportunity to work outside the home in textile and shoe communities such as Lawrence and Lynn was likely to influence the curtailment of fertility more through the postponement of marriage than through direct family limitation." Preliminary analysis of their small set of cases, however, indicated "that working, married women had lower fertility ratios than married women who were not gainfully employed outside the home" (p. 125).

26. Hareven and Vinovskis, note 47.

27. Ryan, p. 164.

28. L. Gordon, *Woman's Body, Woman's Right,* pp. 108–9.

29. Linda Gordon and Ellen DuBois, "Seeking Ecstasy on the Battlefield: Danger and Pleasure in Nineteenth-Century Feminist Sexual Thought," *Feminist Studies* 9 (Spring 1983): 7–25.

30. John S. Haller and Robin M. Haller, *The Physician and Sexuality in Victorian America* (New York: Norton, 1974), pp. 118–19.

31. Mohr, *Abortion in America,* pp. 53–55. His estimate that "abortion rates in the United States may have risen from an order of magnitude approximating one abortion for every 25 or 30 live births during the first three decades of the 19th century to an order of magnitude possibly as high as one abortion for every 5 or 6 live births by the 1850s and 1860s" is, he admits, "frankly speculative," based on "virtually no quantitative data" (pp. 50, 275*n*).

32. Ibid., pp. 59–61.

33. Ibid., p. 76.

34. Ibid., p. 86.

35. L. Gordon, *Woman's Body, Woman's Right,* pp. 140–42. She notes the ambiguity in Theodore Roosevelt's use of the term "race," as in that of many eugenic-minded contemporaries: "it could mean the human race, or the white race; the emotional significance of this usage lay in the fact that it connoted both meanings simultaneously, encouraging a tendency to identify the human race with the white race."

36. Mohr, p. 157; emphasis added.

37. *Roe* v. *Wade,* 410 U.S. 113 (1973), p. 141, contains an excellent historical review of changes in state and medical policy on abortion.

38. Mohr, p. 200.

39. Ibid., p. 240. In England, the "antiseptic principle" had first been applied and reported in the 1860s, through the work of Joseph Lister, and by the 1870s and 1880s, the knowledge that wound sepsis and puerperal fever were caused by bacteria spread through human contact was well established. A decade later, antiseptic techniques were surely known and practiced among American doctors for purposes other than abortion. See George Rosen, *A History of Public Health* (New York: MD Publications, 1958), pp. 315–19.

40. *Roe* v. *Wade,* p. 142.

41. Lawrence Lader, *Abortion II: Making the Revolution* (Boston: Beacon, 1973), p. 21.

42. Richard W. Wertz and Dorothy C. Wertz, *Lying-In: A History of Childbirth in America* (New York: Schocken, 1979), pp. 55, 58–59.

43. Joseph F. Kett, *The Formation of the American Medical Profession: The Role of Institutions, 1780–1860* (New Haven: Yale University Press, 1968), p. 164.

44. See Haller and Haller; Ryan; Wertz and Wertz; and Carroll Smith-Rosenberg, "Puberty to Menopause: The Cycle of Femininity in Nineteenth-Century America," in *Clio's Consciousness Raised,* ed. Mary Hartman and Lois W. Banner (New York: Harper & Row, 1974), pp. 23–37.

45. Himes, pp. 282–84.

46. Mohr, pp. 165–66, 174.

47. L. Gordon, *Woman's Body, Woman's Right,* p. 261.

48. Mohr, p. 167.

49. See Himes, pp. 281–82, quoting Dr. Edward Foote, a noted birth control advocate of the period.

50. L. Gordon, *Woman's Body, Woman's Right,* pp. 262–63.

51. Himes, pp. 292–93, quoting from the 1888 *Medical and Surgical Reporter,* published in Philadelphia.

52. Himes, p. 297; emphasis added.

53. See Petchesky, Chap. 2; Mark Haller, *Eugenics: Hereditarian Attitudes in American Thought* (New Brunswick, N.J.: Rutgers University Press, 1963); Allan Chase, *The Legacy of Malthus* (New York: Knopf, 1977); and L. Gordon, *Woman's Body, Woman's Right,* Chaps. 6 and 7. All offer historical accounts of the eugenics movement and its impact.

54. Charles L. Brace, *The Dangerous Classes of New York and Twenty Years' Work Among Them* (New York, 1872), p. 43.

55. Haller, pp. 160, 163. See also his account of the relationship between emerging racist ideology in the United States and criminal anthropology, social Darwinism and the eugenics movement, pp. 50–57.

56. Weeks, pp. 123–24.

57. Haller, pp. 95–97, 113.

58. Most important among the latter were the Committee on Eugenics of the American Breeders' Association, set up in 1906 "to investigate and report on heredity in the human race" and "to emphasize the value of superior blood and the menace to society of inferior blood." Its principal propaganda agency was the Eugenics Record Office, in Cold Spring Harbor, Long Island. See Haller, pp. 62, 72–73.

59. Ibid., pp. 24–25, 77, 124. Cf. Weeks' account of the similar professional and class base of the eugenics movement in England. Weeks, pp. 131–32.

60. Haller, p. 129.

61. Ibid., pp. 47–50; and Julius Paul, "The Psychiatrist as Public Administrator, Case in Point: State Sterilization Laws," *American Journal of Orthopsychiatry* 38 (January 1968): 77.

62. Haller, p. 133.

63. Ibid., p. 138; and Paul, p. 78.

64. *Buck* v. *Bell,* 274 U.S. 200 (1926), p. 207.

65. Margaret Sanger, *Woman and the New Race* (New York: Brentano's, 1920), pp. 93–94, 100, 230.

66. Ibid., pp. 168–69, 180–83.

67. Section 1145 of the New York State Penal Code was such a loophole, Sanger thought. See L. Gordon, *Woman's Body, Woman's Right,* pp. 258–59, 263, 271.

68. Ibid., p. 264.

69. Ibid., p. 271, quoting J. Mayone Stycos; see also Himes, pp. 326–30.

70. Sanger, pp. 119–21.

71. Ibid., pp. 121–22, 129.

72. L. Gordon, *Woman's Body, Woman's Right,* p. 265.

73. From "The Feminine Aspect of Birth Control," in *European Women: A Documentary History, 1789–1945,* ed. Eleanor S. Riemer and John C. Fout (New York: Schocken, 1980), pp. 213–14.

74. Kennedy, p. 121.

75. See L. Gordon, *Woman's Body, Woman's Right,* p. 341 and Chaps. 10 and 12, for an excellent history of the "professionalization of birth control" and the development of Planned Parenthood in the 1940s and 1950s.

76. Weeks, pp. 136, and 192–93. He compares the similar role that Dr. Marie Stopes played in England to that of Sanger in the United States and her similar deference to both the medical profession and the eugenicists.

77. Kennedy, pp. 115, 117–18.

78. Sanger, p. 37.

79. Ibid., p. 57.

80. Ibid., pp. 45–46.

81. Kennedy, p. 120.

82. L. Gordon, *Woman's Body, Woman's Right,* pp. 236–37, 243.

83. Ibid. She suggests that middle-class feminists of the 1920s themselves embodied this tension, becoming "estranged" from a "mass base" and losing the "vision of a common womanhood" (p. 300).

3

Abortion and the State: Twentieth-Century Legalization

Legal abortion in the 1970s was neither given nor imposed. Yet, if it was "won," it was won in a form that, like civil rights legislation, by itself could not and would not assure that abortion services were provided to any woman who needed them in a context where choice was meaningful. Abortion was and is a social necessity that grew out of pressing needs and popular practices and became legitimated through state law. Why a shift in abortion policy occurred is a story that reflects a familiar pattern of conflict and accommodation between corporate and popular agendas in the shaping of the liberal welfare state.

Most analyses of the welfare state in the United States and Britain work from an inadequate theoretical base, for they ignore the state's concern with maintaining gender hierarchy and regulating family life. In contrast, recent feminist analysis emphasizes that the welfare state "is not just a set of services, it is also a set of ideas about society, about the family, and—not least important—about women, who have a centrally important role within the family, as its linchpin"; its policies amount to *"the State organization of domestic life."*[1] Keeping this feminist perspective in mind, we can nevertheless adapt certain useful insights about the contradictory origins and purposes of the welfare state from neo-Marxist theories.

On the one hand, the centralized state instruments created to soften the impact of the capitalist market on families and the poor are invariably geared toward social control. Ensconced in a rhetoric emphasizing "human services" and "needs assessment," programs aimed at family and income maintenance are designed and administered to fit families and households to a particular structural and behavioral norm and to stigmatize those who deviate. The welfare state aims to reproduce the dominant class, race, and gender relations—including the "stable" male-headed nuclear family. On the other hand, the programs emerge historically out of pressures exerted from below—sometimes through organized popular movements pressing the state for protection from economic assaults (jobs, health and safety regulations, decent public schools) and sometimes through spontaneous popular practices or self-help that threaten established interests (popular health movements, illegal abortion). The fact that the programs originate as a response to these pressures, in the state's need to accommodate or conciliate popular resistance, has meant that the programs really achieve the satisfaction of certain minimal human needs, if partially and inadequately.[2]

Ian Gough points out that social programs frequently seem to be the product of simultaneous pressures from conflicting classes (capital and labor), which organize separately or in coalition, to achieve "reforms" (well-known examples are workmen's compensation and social security). This creates the illusion of a "harmony of interests" among classes; but in reality the reforms are usually "supported by different groups for quite distinct or opposed reasons" and the ruling class and the state are not moved to institute social welfare measures until popular pressure has reached the point of being virtually irresistible: ". . . it is the threat of a powerful working-class movement which galvanises the ruling class to think more cohesively and strategically, and to restructure the state apparatus to this end." Once programs are in effect, the illusion of harmony breaks down in "conflicts over the nature of the service or the way it is organized . . . or over the level of benefits and the conditions attached to their receipt" and finally over who controls.[3]

This analysis, though drawn too narrowly in terms of the conflict between the organized working class and capital, may be fittingly applied to political conflicts over reproductive health services and reproductive rights, including legal abortion. To know why abortion was nationally legalized in 1973, we have to look not only at the "actors" (feminists, liberals, population control advocates) who articulated the need for change but at the conditions that brought those actors to political consciousness.

This chapter puts *Roe* v. *Wade* in its larger social context to explain that the Supreme Court legitimated but did not initiate a rise in abortions. As with other dimensions of welfare state policy, shifts in state policies regarding abortion or fertility have usually been responses to, rather than determinants of, changes in the economic and social conditions that structure women's work and marital patterns and birth control practices. These conditions give rise to movements and organizations that put pressure on the state to change its policies, but out of "distinct or opposed reasons."

Falling Birthrates and Rising Abortion Rates in the 1960s and 1970s

In over a dozen states and the District of Columbia in the several years preceding the Supreme Court decision, there was a groundswell of judicial and legislative activity to liberalize or, in a few cases, repeal existing abortion statutes. The activity was so sudden, so sweeping, that it caught even proabortion organizers by surprise. In the words of one activist: "We rode the crest of something I still can't define—but that something was clearly changing attitudes on the part of the American public. . . ."[4] "That something" was a complex cluster of political and social forces that need to be sorted out in order to clarify—and strengthen—the misunderstood and obscure role that feminist ideas often play in reproductive rights struggles.

What were the contributions of population control politics, feminist politics, and social changes to the restoration of legal abortion in the United States? Both the women's liberation movement and the population control establishment played instrumental roles in speeding up the process of legitimation and giving voice to the ideas that made legitimation possible. Feminists and abortion repeal activists in liberal church, political, legal, and medical circles provided the critical material and human network through which old laws could be exposed, challenged, and, for the first time, openly and collectively defied. Without that energy and organizing, it might have been years more before a *Roe* v. *Wade* got decided. Yet we still have to explain why a mass feminist movement reawakened at that moment and, unlike its predecessors, included "abortion on demand" as one of its central goals; and why a population control establishment that had for years regarded abortion with disdain suddenly lobbied for its legalization.

Contrary to common belief, the Supreme Court decision in 1973 was not the "cause" of rising abortion rates but an accommodation to social changes that began long before *Roe* v. *Wade* was decided. These changes were rooted in the same cluster of interacting conditions that produced the overall fertility decline among U.S. women that began in the early 1960s, as can be seen in Figure 3.1. They included (1) later marriage and childbearing among young women, along with their increasing levels of college attendance; (2) the rising labor force participation of young women, married and unmarried, still in low-paid jobs and in a context of high inflation during the Vietnam war years; and (3) rising divorce rates and proportions of female-headed households. These changes combined with several enduring conditions: a sexual division of labor that makes women still the primary ones responsible for children; a lack of commitment to government-funded social services, especially

FIGURE 3-1. U.S. TOTAL FERTILITY RATE, 1917–1975

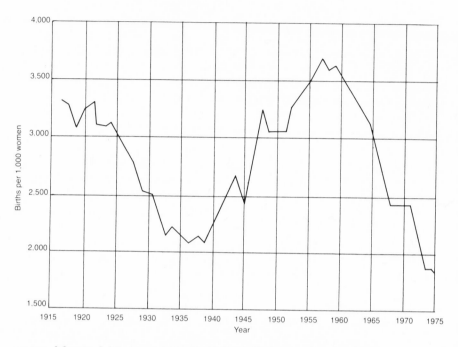

SOURCE: Maurice J. Moore and Martin O'Connell, *Perspectives on American Fertility,* U.S. Department of Commerce, Bureau of the Census, Current Population Reports, Series P-23, No. 70 (July 1978).

child care and health care; and the need of all women to avoid unwanted pregnancy for reasons of health, sexual self-determination, and social self-actualization.

These new and old circumstances cut across class and ethnic-racial divisions, resulting in lower fertility and a greater need for safe, reliable methods of fertility control among diverse groups of women. Certainly there are social differences in fertility rates. For example, more educated women, unmarried women, divorced/separated women, and most of all, women working outside the home or looking for work have significantly fewer children than do women who left school early or do not work outside the home.[5] Nevertheless, these differences merely underscore the importance of the changing conditions listed above. The conscious activity of most women in the pre-*Roe* period to limit their fertility, often through illegal abortion, must be understood in its social and economic setting.

While never reducible to an economic question, deciding whether to have a child has distinct economic implications. But today (as historically), the economic aspects of the question stem not from women's income levels but from women's work. The continued primary responsibility of mothers for children, along with the steadily increasing labor force participation of women, especially mothers, is the major contradiction for women under late capitalism and defines the outer limit of the social conditions determining decisions about having and not having children. As a consequence of the sexual division of labor around childbearing, the main responsibility for contraception and pregnancy lies not with "couples" but with women. This is true not only for the growing numbers of women who head families, which rose throughout the 1960s and 1970s in direct relation to rising divorce rates, but also for married working women, who make up the largest proportion of working women and the fastest-growing cohort in the labor force.[6] Most of these women retain the primary responsibility for household maintenance and child care, despite working hard and long hours outside the home—a situation commonly known as the "double day."

Meanwhile, the participation rate of women in full-time and part-time work continues to rise. The increased demand for women workers, especially in the low-paid clerical and service sectors, is experienced by individual women in the context of inflation and economic crisis and the inability of families to maintain a decent standard of living on a single wage. For most working-class and even middle-class people, the costs of having a baby—obstetrician's and insurance bills, hospitalization, clothing and diapers—are staggering. This situation inevitably affects decisions about childbearing and contraception, but women's reproductive choices are even more constrained by a series of related economic, political, and social realities. These include severe shortages in government-funded social services, especially child care and health care; the low pay of jobs generally available to women (women still earn one-half to two-thirds of what men earn in comparable jobs); and the rise of wife battering and child abuse within the male-dominated family, which raises serious questions about that institution's capacity to "protect" women and children. If a woman chooses to bear or raise a child outside heterosexual marriage, she encounters difficulties in securing custody or the right to participate in mothering at all. The legal and social attack on lesbian mothers suggests that although women remain primarily responsible for children, their responsibility is expected to be exercised within traditionally accepted frameworks of kinship and sexuality—that is, within heterosexual coupling and marriage.

These conditions affect women differently, depending on their class, race, age, sexual orientation, and occupation. Whether as black, Hispanic, and Asian women employed in hospitals, laundries, and sweatshops, where the worst kinds of reproductive hazards go unremedied, or as clerical workers, mostly unorganized and working without pregnancy or maternity benefits, or as welfare mothers confronted with the virtual abolition of Medicaid funds for abortion and cuts in child health and other benefits, or as lesbian mothers fighting for child custody and against patriarchal norms of childrearing, different groups of women experience different forms of reproductive oppression. But, for many women, economic crisis and the loss of the family as a safe refuge must be understood as an important structural determinant of decisions to avoid or terminate pregnancy. Yet, declining fertility among American women in the 1960s and 1970s was not simply due to economic distress, as in the 1930s; even more, it reflected limited but real economic *advances* for women.[7] These advances were related to the sharp rise in women's labor force participation. Even where—as in most cases—the gains made were in low-paying, sex-segregated service and clerical jobs, they meant more resources than women had had in the decades before. The consequences for their fertility of women's working outside the home, however, may be different for women of different classes and occupations. Let us look at these differences, keeping in mind the basic argument that the overall drop in fertility in this period is related to a general *improvement* in the conditions of women, of which greater economic independence is a critical aspect.

A woman's type and location of employment, her occupational status, and her educational level—in short, her class and racial-ethnic position— affect the work-fertility relationship. Where women's jobs are low paying, dead-end, menial, and seen as temporary or makeshift, employment outside the home may coincide with high rather than low fertility. Where they are employed in home-based industries or family-owned retailing or crafts, fertility may remain high because it is compatible with the need for more "hands" and for the mother's presence at home. Where women's jobs offer some "alternative gratifications," decent pay, and a modicum of security, on the other hand, low fertility is almost certain to result.[8] During the "baby boom" of the 1950s when fertility rates rose sharply among all socioeconomic groups, lifetime fertility varied greatly among employed married women by occupation. Women who reached their main childbearing years in the late 1940s and early 1950s and were employed in clerical, professional/technical, and managerial/ administrative fields had significantly lower fertility than women employed as operatives, nonfarm laborers, service workers, and agricultural workers (see Table 3-1). In most societies, the former are occupations for women that require more education and hence postponed marriage and childbearing and more efficient use of contraception, as well as provide a greater sense of permanent recruitment into the labor force and possibilities for advancement. In general, demographers have found an inverse correlation between women's level of education and their lifetime fertility.

While women's overall labor force participation rose steadily during the postwar years, this increase reflected different realities at different

TABLE 3-1. CUMULATIVE FERTILITY OF EMPLOYED MARRIED
WOMEN BORN 1925–29, BY OCCUPATION GROUP

Occupational Group	Cumulative Fertility (per 1,000 women)
Professional-technical	2,316
Managerial-administrative	2,277
Sales	2,718
Clerical	2,311
Crafts	2,591
Operatives	2,823
Laborers (nonfarm)	2,972
Service workers	3,205
Agriculture	3,607

SOURCE: U.S. Department of Commerce, Bureau of the Census, *Childspacing and Current Fertility*, 1970 Census of Population Subject Reports, PC(2)-3B (August 1975), Tables 9 and 12.

times. Starting in the early 1960s, it came to reflect not so much an increase in the absolute numbers of women working outside the home but changes in women's life cycle and the fact that more women were working through more of their lives—before, during, and after marriage.[9] Between 1950 and 1970, the labor force participation rate of white married women nearly doubled. Age also has been an important variable in structuring the pattern of women's rising labor force participation, and the tendency for women in their prime childbearing years to spend more of those years working outside the home emerged over a decade before *Roe*. As Figure 3-2 shows, the 1960s experienced a qualitative leap in the labor force participation of all women, but most strikingly of those aged twenty to thirty-five. This is in contrast to the earlier increase (indicated by the graph line for 1960), which was clustered among women in the post-childbearing years. By 1970, women in their early twenties, increasing numbers of them unmarried, had achieved the highest labor force participation rates of any age cohort. This trend would deepen in the 1970s and dramatically would come to include mothers in their late twenties and early thirties. But the trend was well under way in the 1960s (see Figure 3-2).

In addition, the occupational distribution of women in the labor force changed significantly during the 1960s and early 1970s. While the proportion of working women who were operatives, sales workers, and farm workers declined between 1959 and 1974, the proportion who were clerical workers increased from 30 to nearly 35 percent, or from 6.3 million to nearly 11.5 million, making clerical workers the largest and fastest-growing category of employed women. Professional and technical workers increased from 12 to 16 percent, and nonhousehold service workers from

FIGURE 3-2. LABOR FORCE PARTICIPATION RATES OF WOMEN BY AGE, 1940–1977

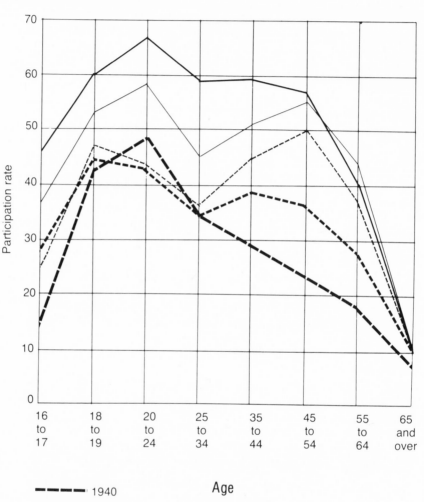

- - - - - 1940
- - - - - - 1950
-------- 1960
———— 1970
———— 1977

Age

SOURCE: Francine D. Blau, "Women in the Labor Force: An Overview," in *Women: A Feminist Perspective,* ed. by Jo Freeman, 2d ed. (Palo Alto, Calif.: Mayfield, 1979).

14 to 17 percent.[10] Except for service workers, these women represent a more educated as well as a less childbearing-oriented population, corresponding to the growing rates of women's college attendance during the 1960s and 1970s. The numbers and percentages of women who both attended and graduated from college began to rise around 1960 and continued rising sharply during the subsequent two decades, but most significantly during the 1960s.[11] Table 3-2 indicates that the trend toward equal proportions of women and men enrolled in colleges was established by the early 1970s.

Thus the conditions we would expect to result in lowered fertility were very much in evidence in the 1960s, long before abortion became legal. While we cannot establish a direct "causal" link with rising (illegal) abortions and pill use (the pill was introduced in 1960), it is safe to assume that the growing labor force participation and college attendance of women in their childbearing years motivated at least as much as they were "caused" by those trends. This is not because childbearing and work or school are intrinsically incompatible; countless women, particularly black women, have combined them for centuries. It is because the dominant institutions for childrearing in the United States are still organized around their separation.

Because of her continued association with domestic tasks, a woman's working conditions include the conditions of family and reproductive labor, and these in turn are shaped by class.[12] The concrete impact that childbearing has on women's lives, specifically their labor force participation, differs markedly depending on whether they are able to organize or afford substitutes for maternal child care—a question of class, culture, and public policy. With adequate income, upper-, middle-, and even working-class women may be able "to substitute purchased inputs [babysitters, housekeepers, nursery schools] for the wife's time in child rearing." Elsewhere, extended families, neighborhood or kin networks, older siblings, or other "surrogates" may reduce what sociologists call "role incompatibility" between mothers working and taking care of children.[13]

TABLE 3-2. PERCENT OF MEN AND WOMEN ENROLLED IN COLLEGE, 1960–1979

Year	Women	Men
1960	38	54
1965	45	57
1970	49	55
1975	49	53
1979	48	50

SOURCE: U.S. Department of Labor, Bureau of Labor Statistics, *Perspectives on Working Women: A Databook*, Bulletin 2080 (October 1980), Table 39.

But the dominant reality in the contemporary United States, more so than in any other advanced capitalist society, is that child-care alternatives for employed mothers are widely unavailable. Compelled economically and encouraged socially to work outside the home, people with children are told that infant and child care is not a public concern. This fact, which lies at the core of U.S. "family policy," has a direct bearing on fertility. A study of census data from 1977 found a relationship between fertility behavior, employment, and the availability of suitable child care. A substantial percentage (17.4 percent) of unemployed mothers with children under five years said that they would be working if they could find "satisfactory child care at reasonable cost"; nearly 25 percent of mothers of young children currently working part-time indicated their desire to work longer hours, if not constrained by the lack of child care.[14] Moreover, women "who feel prevented from working" or working full-time because of the absence of low-cost child care have fertility rates and fertility expectations that are closer to those of full-time employed mothers of young children. This suggests "that fertility differentials by labor-force status would be greater if we took into account the extent to which women with young children reduce their labor-force participation as a result of child care constraint."[15]

Probably the most important change in the 1960s and 1970s affecting women's position in the family, the work force, and childbearing was the phenomenon of postponed marriage, which generally results in lower fertility. During those decades, women's age at first marriage rose, and the rate of first marriages declined.[16] More telling is the growing percentage of single women under age thirty. Table 3-3 indicates that the increase in the proportion of single women under 25 had begun by 1960, although for women aged 25–29 that increase occurred in the 1970s. For younger women since 1960, this increase has been remarkable; over half of those aged 20–24 are unmarried today, compared with a little more than one-quarter in 1960. For them, as for women aged 18–19, much of the change came in the pre-*Roe* years.

TABLE 3-3. PERCENT SINGLE (NEVER MARRIED) WOMEN BY AGE: 1960, 1970, AND 1980

Age	1960	1970	1980
18–19 years	67.7	75.4	82.8
20–24 years	28.4	35.8	50.2
25–29 years	10.5	10.5	20.8

SOURCE: U.S. Department of Commerce, Bureau of the Census, *Marital Status and Living Arrangements: March 1978*, Current Population Reports, Series P-20, No. 338 (May 1979), Table B; and *Marital Status and Living Arrangements: March 1980*, Current Population Reports, Series P-20, No. 365 (October 1981), Table B.

O'Connell and Moore present another dimension of this picture by showing that the legitimation ratio (percentage of premaritally conceived first births legitimated by marriage) in the United States reached its peak in the "baby boom" years of 1955–58, after which it began to decline, particularly for women aged 15–17 and 20–24. The most significant decline in "legitimated" pregnancies for these women was during the late 1960s and early 1970s (to 1974).[17] Similarly, first-birth rates for women aged 15–24 began to decline in the 1960s, although the decline accelerated in the 1970s. Conversely, the proportion of white women who were "childless" at the ages of 25 and 30 began to climb (after having reaching an all-time low) in about 1964–65 and continued to climb dramatically through the 1970s.[18]

In other words, young women in the pre-*Roe* decade were well along in the trend of deferring marriage and motherhood to work and school that would characterize the years of legal abortion. O'Connell and Moore suggest that the availability of legal abortion was what made the decline in legitimation ratios possible. But it is more plausible, given the dates of the decline, to argue that changed social conditions for young women created a need and a demand for more readily available abortion and contraception. (Chapter 5 discusses why the two needs are inevitably bound together.)

If the age and rate of first marriage began to change by 1960, so too did the divorce rate. In fact, it starts its infamous climb at about the time the "baby boom" is ending and the contemporary rise in younger women's labor force participation begins.[19] This simply underlines the complex interrelationships of all these conditions—labor force participation, education, age at first marriage, fertility, and consequently patterns of abortion and birth control use. We cannot untangle whether women postpone marriage and childbearing because of the greater availability of jobs and educational possibilities or seek jobs and education because they are less encumbered with marriage and motherhood, for the simple reason that the two processes are mutually reinforcing. Yet the totality of these conditions adds up to a situation in which more women are spending more years of their lives outside marriage and without direct dependence on men, focused on activities other than domesticity and childrearing. To the extent (assumed rather than demonstrated) that the majority of these women remain heterosexual and sexually engaged outside marriage, the increase in their need for reliable contraception and safe abortion follows as night follows day. It particularly follows in a male-dominant culture in which women lack the resources to raise children easily on their own. And it was the case, in an increasingly pressing way, throughout the decade preceding the Court's decision in *Roe* v. *Wade*. To say this is to state the most obvious, simple fact. Yet polemicists of the twentieth-century crusade against abortion, like those of the nineteenth, disregard the basic elements of social reality in favor of misogynist moralism.

We look at the extension of these social and demographic patterns into the 1970s and their differential impact on different groups of women in the next chapter. Here, they merely lay the analytical groundwork for understanding why a rising need and demand for abortion were not the consequence of availability (legalization) so much as they were its stimulus. This analysis is reinforced when we consider the available information about birth control and abortion practices during the decades before the pill and legal abortion. It is well established that fertility declined to an unprecedented extent in the Great Depression, before the development of the pill; this was due to the deliberate use of contraception, sterilization, and abortion. An important study of white, ever-married women born between 1901 and 1910—the cohort of women who reached their prime childbearing years in the 1930s—found "a lower completed family size than any other cohort," in an era when the pill and the IUD were unavailable and abortion was everywhere a crime. By age fifty, around 42 percent of these women had had either one or no children, and many of the others had planned the spacing and termination of their childbearing. They did this through widespread use of the contraceptive methods that were then available—the condom, douche, withdrawal, rhythm, and diaphragm (in that order of importance). But evidence also suggests that they had high rates of surgical sterilization (often reported as "medical" in intent), and many also practiced abortion.[20]

If the decline in fertility during the 1930s was not caused by a "technological breakthrough," neither was the "baby boom" of the 1950s caused by a technological blackout. In both periods, effective *techniques* of contraception were available, including (illegal) abortion, but different social conditions determined differences in their use.[21] Survey data from the "baby boom" period indicate that some 70 percent of white married couples used contraception prior to 1955. In 1955–60, there was an increase in contraceptive use among white married couples of different socioeconomic backgrounds from 70 to 81 percent, with the majority using condoms, diaphragms, or rhythm. Surveyors report that "the use or prospective use of contraception [in 1955–60] is nearly universal among fecund couples, and there are strong attitudes to support this practice. Most wives, regardless of their religion, educational attainment, or position in society, feel that it is entirely proper for couples to try to control the number and spacing of their children."[22] Moreover, data on the mean age at which "baby boom mothers," who averaged 3.3 children, had their third or higher-order births suggest that even those women who had three or more children terminated their childbearing some ten to fifteen years before menopause.[23] Unless these women were abstaining from sex, birth control and abortion use must have become part of a new family structure and family ideology. Regarding abortion specifically, a committee headed by Dr. Mary Calderone concluded in the mid-1950s that "the frequency of induced abortions in the United States could be as low as 200,000 and as high as 1,200,000 per year. . . . There is no objective basis for the selection of a particular figure between these two estimates as an approximation of the actual frequency."[24]

It is impossible to know with much precision the incidence of abortion in the days of illegality. Demographers suggest that many women in the 1950s were either failing to report abortions or reporting them as miscarriages; thus abortion, despite its illegality and despite the ideological emphasis on motherhood, was an important means of fertility control. They estimate further "that about two-thirds of all legal abortions in the early years of legalization replaced formerly illegal procedures."[25] In other words, formal legalization was a *response* to a rising social need, expressed in women's persistent practice during the preceding (post–"baby boom") decade. These practices occurred through underground abortion services, church and other community-based referrals, and cooperative doctors' networks that emerged in populous cities and states in the 1960s, themselves a stark testament to growing popular demand as well as the political consciousness about abortion and women's rights generated by a growing women's liberation movement.

In conscious statements as well as behavior, "clearly changing attitudes on the part of the American public" prefigured and prompted *Roe v. Wade*. These new attitudes, like the revised state laws, undoubtedly grew out of social changes in women's conditions. According to one study of national survey data, "the largest part of the change in abortion attitudes [toward greater approval for *all* reasons, including economic, being unmarried, or simply not wanting any more children] occurred before 1970, simultaneously with campaigns to liberalize state abortion laws." While the Court's decision may have "boosted levels of approval further," it in fact reflected a dominant trend already established in popular practice and in the easing of restrictive laws in some seventeen states.[26] In 1969, a Louis Harris poll of a nationwide sample indicated that 64 percent "believed that the decision on abortion should be a private one." In the same year, two separate polls among physicians showed a majority favoring *repeal* of abortion laws.[27] This is significant because the AMA at the same time was officially taking a more conservative stand on abortion.

The conditions of declining fertility in the 1960s and 1970s are not historically unique but resemble those surrounding American women born in the late nineteenth and early twentieth centuries. Women born between 1870 and 1910 tended to postpone marriage into their mid-twenties as well as maintaining high rates of lifetime celibacy. Over 20 percent remained childless throughout their lives. This is a lower percentage of "childlessness" than demographers predict for white women at present in their childbearing years but twice as high as among the childbearing cohorts of the late 1940s through early 1960s.[28] And turn-of-the-century women who did bear children had lower fertility rates, higher rates of contraceptive use, and probably higher rates of abortion (even without legality) than their daughters and granddaughters. It is not the trends of today but the "baby boom" pattern of early and teenage marriage, legitimated pregnancies, and early and more frequent childbearing that constitutes the anomaly of the twentieth century. The cold-war decades were years of American economic expansion, political repression, and, above all, the absence of a visible feminist movement or a visible female presence in the labor market. "Family life" became the only acceptable channel through which women might enter adulthood. The "absence" of abortion (of course, women continued to get abortions clandestinely) was a political and ideological, not a technological, fact, and one to which women may have felt resigned out of a sense of hopelessness rather than conviction:

> "I still remember how much I didn't want to get married. I wanted to get a job and have some things. I was afraid if I got married it would be the end of my chance for a better life. I wasn't wrong about that either. . . ."
> "Did you ever consider abortion?"
> "Never! I could never do that. God, I remember even now how terrified I was. I kept thinking it couldn't be true. I remember even thinking that I would take my mom's car and drive it off a cliff. I knew he'd marry me; I never doubted that. *But I didn't want to get married.* I wanted to *do* things and *have* things."[29]

Although women who worked outside the home in professional and clerical occupations in the 1950s had fewer children than others, they were deviant—and made to feel so.

What is particular to the lives of earlier women (1900–1919) is that they arrived at young girlhood when the labor force participation rates of women, especially young unmarried women, were growing faster than they ever had, undoubtedly affecting not only childbearing and fertility control practices but women's consciousness. These were also years when vocal radical and feminist movements that believed in women's right to control their bodies and the terms of motherhood spread their ideas vigorously, influencing young working-class women as well as middle-class women.[30] The parallels with today should be obvious, although there are important differences as well. In both cases, fertility and abortion trends have to be understood in relation to the complex interworkings of changing social conditions and ideologically powerful political movements.

In the 1960s and 1970s, the conjunction of abortion and delayed marriage and childbearing—they are mutually reinforcing—became a pervasive social force in a context in which education, training, and jobs became viable long-term options for the majority of young women, displacing marriage and maternity, in time if not in value. In the 1970s, college enrollment among women aged 16–34 increased by 57 percent for white women and by 112 percent for black women; and the enrollment of women in undergraduate institutions for the first time exceeded that of men. By 1978, the labor force participation rate of women aged 16–19 was 54 percent, an increase of ten percentage points from 1970; for women aged 20–24 years, it was 69 percent, an increase of eleven percentage points from 1970.[31] These trends occurred within a changing capitalist economy that, from the standpoint of women's labor, was if anything complex. In the midst of a widening recession, a deteriorating industrial base, and declining productivity in heavy industry, the singular growth areas in the American economy were business services, health services, retail trade, eating and drinking places, and state and local governments— precisely the low-paying, dead-end, and largely unorganized job sectors that employ women.[32] In other words, the capitalist economy required reliable means of fertility control to support a growing demand for female labor power.

While these developments have not meant increased earnings or status or an exit from sex-segregated work ghettos, they have meant an expectation of more options and an expanded world that surely affects how young women think about marriage and childbearing. And that expectation has been powerfully enhanced for a wide range of women by the growth of feminism. Women who became activists in the women's liberation movement were the beneficiaries of the social changes described above. In the late 1960s and early 1970s they were primarily white, middle-class, college-educated women who had begun thinking about "women's issues" in relation to their situation as professionals or students or their involvement in other movements for radical social change, particularly the civil rights and antiwar movements.[32] An active and vocal feminist movement in this period was both effect and cause of a new sense of women's possibilities; it grew out of the social changes that were occurring for women and moved, in its vision, far beyond them. It also made "abortion on demand" a primary political goal. In so doing, the new feminists differed from previous feminist movements; their actions helped create a climate of visibility and legitimacy around abortion that did not exist for women early in the century. In turn, legal, accessible abortion, especially for young unmarried women, helped make it possible for women to postpone or reject marriage in favor of school and work, and for a feminist consciousness to grow and flourish.

The argument I am making does not locate the changes that occurred during the 1960s and 1970s within a framework of expanded "individual choices" or individual achievement, but within a new range of social conditions that redefined the terms of a "normal life" for women. We might say that the "standard of childbearing" is a "historical and moral" question, just as Marx noted regarding the standard of living. It is a product of social forces and not just of individual preferences. Thus, women's conformity to it may reflect not only a widening of their sphere of action but also a raising of the threshold of their basic needs. In this respect, it is significant that women's college enrollment has gone up at precisely the moment when a college degree has been devalued from a sign of prestige to an entrance-level requirement for skilled and even semiskilled jobs. It is not out of "privilege" that most people today go to college; it is part of their normal life course, if not economically necessary. Similarly, the outer limit of women's choice to get an abortion is that while their responsibilities (not just "opportunities") for study, training, and work have greatly enlarged, those of men, or of society as a whole, for the care and rearing of children have remained virtually unchanged. There has been no liberation of women in the past decade, but a furthering and deepening of the conditions making it necessary for them to maximize control over their lives. In that context legal abortion became, by the early 1970s, an acknowledged social imperative.

Population Control and the Legalization of Abortion

When President Dwight D. Eisenhower was asked in 1959 about the federal government's relation to birth control, he replied: "I cannot imagine anything more emphatically a subject that is not a proper political or governmental activity or function or responsibility. . . . That's not our business." Four years later, however, President John F. Kennedy hesitantly voiced his approval in principle of federal support for contraceptive research. By 1965, Eisenhower had reversed his position on public support for family planning, and had become, with former president Harry S. Truman, a co-chairman of Planned Parenthood–World Population. . . . By 1967, the Agency for International Development was spending almost nine million dollars annually on birth control abroad, and the Department of Health, Education and Welfare, with the Office of Economic Opportunity, spent over twenty million dollars for contraceptive programs in this country.[34]

State intervention in fertility control occurs for three different purposes, called forth by a combination of social conditions and conscious political activity. These purposes are population control, the regulation of sexual behavior and sexual norms, and the state's need to maintain social order and the legitimacy of its rules and rule-making system. When legitimacy breaks down and the state is no longer able to enforce its policies, as happened with the draft and U.S. military intervention in Vietnam, then "concessions" have to be made that will restore legitimacy without seeming to compromise the dominant ideology informing a given policy (and thus the authority of the state).[35]

In the early 1970s, abortion became legal in the United States, and the "right to abortion" was given constitutional protection because essentially it could not remain illegal, because the old laws could no longer be enforced, even symbolically. They had lost their credibility and their power when so many women (1) were clearly willing to defy the law in order to get abortions and were able to find cooperative providers, (2) were defining their lives increasingly in terms of work and education more than marriage and childbearing, and (3) were claiming these acts in the name of "women's liberation." And they contradicted the capitalist economy's tendency to draw on expanding pools of younger (married and unmarried) women workers. But in making concessions to the movement for legal abortion, the state—and the population policy establishment that had become the architect of state policy on fertility—carefully avoided concessions to feminist ideology about reproductive freedom. To accommodate popular pressures without legitimating feminism—or acknowledging the true causes of the need for abortion—state and population planners subsumed abortion politics under the rubric of population control.

The relegalization of abortion by the Supreme Court in 1973 (prior to that in some states) in part paralleled the gradual emergence of the state as the central coordinating agency and terrain of fertility control politics in the United States and internationally. But this process had little connection to women's right to legal abortion, either in theory or in practice. It was spearheaded by a coalition of private and family planning organizations, foundations, and corporate interests organized around the population issue. Groups like the International Planned Parenthood Foundation (IPPF) and the Population Council, formed in the late 1940s and early 1950s, together shaped what was to become population and fertility policy in this country and its dependents in the Third World for the next thirty years, persistently seeking government funding and support and with astonishing success achieving it. In this way, the federal government—in spite of politicians' traditional avoidance of confrontations with the church and their extreme discomfort with "sexual" issues—became recruited, rather late in the day, into the "population" field.

From the 1930s through the 1950s, the federal government had steered away from visible involvement in family planning. By 1965 it was clear that birth control had achieved a new public presence and legitimacy; as early as 1960 a government agency, the Food and Drug Administration, had approved oral contraceptives for commercial distribution. In 1965, following five years of pill use by American women, the Supreme Court denied the constitutionality of state laws prohibiting the sale of contraceptives to married couples; the OEO was given its "first sizable project grants" for family planning; Truman and Eisenhower, paternal symbols of state authority, joined the board of IPPF; and the Gruening Committee began its influential Population Crisis Hearings in the Senate, which mainly focused on the need for population control in the Third World.[36] All these developments, and the mushrooming of federal government activity and spending that succeeded them, were responses to two sets of pressures: (1) population control ideology, as put forward by the population policy establishment, and (2) the growth of birth control practice.

These two developments were and are relatively independent. In reality, state officials and the population control agencies that in effect shaped population policy from the 1950s to 1970s would have avoided legal abortion if they could have. Abortion has never been an efficient method of reducing fertility from the standpoint of population controllers. While relatively inexpensive, it is impermanent, works after the fact rather than preventively, and in that sense is a direct response to a woman's own decision about a pregnancy at hand rather than a technical answer to her "fertility status"—all in contrast to the preferred methods of population controllers: surgical sterilization and long-acting hormonal injections (see Chapter 5). Besides, abortion arouses a far more intense, organized political opposition, particularly from the Catholic church, than these other methods do. When it became clear that legal abortion could not be avoided, the population establishment rationalized the change in law by invoking the specter of the "population explosion."

Beginning in the mid-1950s, statistical demographers, geographers, family planners, and econometricians began to signal a "population explosion," particularly in the Third World (the image of a bomb exploding was meant to resonate with the atom bomb). "Excess population," they warned, would devour food supplies, accelerate poverty and unemployment, "destabilize" the political climate, and therefore endanger both foreign investments and world peace.[37] Thus, the idea of a population explosion seemed to give neo-Malthusian thinking and practices "a new scientific basis," a new source of legitimation, which it had lost after the Nazi horrors.[38] Despite voluminous statistics and numerical projections marshaled in support of this idea, the aura of "scientific" authority barely disguised old-fashioned racist and eugenic images. Brochures published by population groups like the Draper Fund and the Population Council showed hordes of black and brown faces spilling over a tiny earth, while ads in the *New York Times,* signed by prominent industrialists, appealed to middle-class urban dwellers' fears of slums, riots, violent crime, and the poor. Proposals were entertained to put sterilants in the water or food of Third World countries and to tie foreign aid to such countries to their participation in family planning programs. (The latter, of course, became U.S. policy, through the Agency for International Development.[39]) Now that the idea of "overpopulation" as a "crisis" may be waning, it is hard to recapture the intensity with which that idea seized the imagination of businessmen, academics, middle-class professionals, and policy makers in the pre–*Roe* v. *Wade* period.

The centers of power most responsible for promoting the ideology of overpopulation were private foundations and organizations whose founders and directors consisted mainly of top corporate and financial leaders and biomedical scientists representing elite population research centers. Central among them was the Population Council, founded by John D. Rockefeller III in 1952 to "rally scientific and political support" for population control; to finance "the scientific information, the technical plans, the training programs and the professional personnel" necessary for its execution; and, above all, to help formulate an overall public policy in the population field.[40] Also important was the Hugh Moore Fund, set up by the owner of the Dixie Cup Corporation in 1954 and instrumental in developing the propaganda campaigns that succeeded in winning over many businessmen to the population control bandwagon.[41] Both prior to and during the U.S. government's active involvement, such corporate groups functioned as central agencies of policy formation, organizational and professional coordination, and ideological dissemination of a dominant population strategy. The larger political and social context of all this activity was the development of the United States as a major imperialist power with enormous economic and military interests throughout the Third World; and the development in Third World countries of national liberation movements that threatened U.S. power and investments. The equation of "political instability" with population growth rates, while incorrect even from the imperialists' viewpoint, nevertheless provided a simple, technically manageable way to rationalize political conflict as well as lagging development in the Third World.

There was also a domestic side of this context in the migration of blacks to northern cities and the growing militance of the civil rights movement. Thomas Littlewood analyzes the extent to which shifting alignments around the increase in government-sponsored family planning programs in the 1960s reflected racial conflicts and a deeply embedded racism within the dominant power structures. He points out that racial and ethnic population patterns affect "voting blocs," especially in populous northern and midwestern cities and states, and can often tip the balance in elections. Thus the migration of many blacks into New York, New Jersey, Ohio, Detroit, and Chicago threatened political machines rooted in white "Catholic European ethnic groups," as well as the power of the Catholic church.[42] But the racism of population control politics runs deeper than calculations of voting blocs. When demographers publish "scientific" studies warning about the "racial aspects of zero population growth" and citing projections about what proportions of the population will be black or Hispanic by the year 2000 if differential birthrates continue,[43] the clear message to white elites is no different from that of the eugenicists earlier in the century.

A population politics embedded in racism and corporate capitalism's need for "stability" may, however, collide with a sexual politics that seeks to curtail the sexual options of young people outside of heterosexual marriage and defer to the moral codes of organized religion. That is why the United States has never developed a coherent population *or* sexual policy. Until the mid-1960s, "opposition from Catholic organizations . . . remained an obstacle to the adoption of government-financed population planning programs domestically, or as a component of foreign aid."[44] Even afterward—certainly with enormous vigor by the mid-1970s—the church was able to wield its political power to intimidate politicians from tampering with the "divisive" issue of birth control. Every president beginning with Eisenhower has at least publicly deferred to the views of the church on birth control and abortion. This influence, if not successful in stopping family planning programs, has had a decisive impact on their scope so that, for example, early family planning grants were restricted to married women living with their husbands.[45] No president has openly supported legal abortion. In a particularly revealing chronicle of a situation in the early 1960s in Illinois, where the church held formidable political power, Littlewood shows the tactics and equivocations of the church in its campaign to block the establishment of state-sponsored birth control services available to *all* women (i.e., in public hospitals without restrictions on age or marital status). Registering strong opposition to a legislative proposal to provide birth control services in Cook County Hospital, the vicar general of the Chicago diocese sent a telegram to the members of the County Board of Commissioners "to make the Catholic stand perfectly clear." The message not only voiced the "vehement" objections of the church to the proposal but did so in terms that strongly threatened retaliation at the polls[46]—foreshadowing the antiabortion tactics launched by the National Conference of Catholic Bishops in 1975.

The reasons for the church's militant position on government-sponsored family planning are not purely doctrinal; they are also political. On one level, there is a sense in which the government's involvement in family- and sex-related issues represents a jurisdictional challenge to the church, a threat to its institutional role as guardian of "morality." It is the public legitimation of fertility control practices and not the practices themselves that the church actively campaigns against. On another level, the church's numbers are surely a source of its power in terms of congregants, schoolchildren, and activists in church-related causes, as well as potential voting blocs. This reality helps explain the otherwise puzzling outcome of the Illinois family planning dispute. For finally, after months of adamant opposition from the church and Catholic politicians, legislation was passed in Cook County to provide birth control services to welfare mothers over the age of fifteen, regardless of their marital status—and the church quietly, in the end, complied! Littlewood suggests that the reason had to do with racial and ethnic divisions—specifically, the fear in Catholic ethnic parishes and neighborhoods of the growth of black populations in their districts. He implies that in some locales deals were made between Planned Parenthood affiliates and the church to concentrate family planning centers in black neighborhoods and keep them out of Hispanic and white ethnic neighborhoods where the church had its base.[47] Thus, while decrying the "evil" and "immorality" of government-sponsored family planning services, the church's position in practice may not have been so far from that of the (now closely allied) business leaders and government bureaucrats whose main concern was to lower welfare rolls and "dependency rates."

Under the Nixon administration, government population policy reached a new level of organization as well as manifesting all the contradictions that characterize it today. In 1970 Congress passed the Family Planning Services and Population Research Act, which set up an Office of Population Affairs and a National Center for Family Planning Services in the Department of Health, Education, and Welfare. In essence, it committed the government to "providing services on a voluntary basis to every wanting woman," and to allocating resources to make this possible. The Senate passed this legislation unanimously and with "little debate," in a moment when population control ideology was at its peak; yet, to "mollify the U.S. Catholic Conference," it included a provision "that none of the funds could be used for any program that included abortion as a method of family planning."[48] Similarly, the same Nixon who asked for an increase in federal spending for family planning remained publicly opposed to abortion. Having appointed a special Presidential Commission on Population Growth and the American Future—chaired by none other than John D. Rockefeller III and studded with population establishment and high corporate luminaries—he nevertheless rejected the portions of its final report that endorsed legal abortion and providing birth control services to minors:

> . . . I want to reaffirm and reemphasize that I do not support unrestricted abortion policies. . . . I consider abortion an *unacceptable form of population control.* In my judgment, unrestricted abortion policies would demean human life. I also want to make

it clear that I do not support the unrestricted distribution of family planning services and devices to minors. Such measures would do nothing to preserve and strengthen close family relationships.[49]

What Nixon was "reaffirming" here was not only a conservative sexual politics but an idea of government-supported family planning as legitimate *only* for population control. Yet, while Nixon took this position publicly and in relation to the church, he never did anything in practice to stop HEW's policy of supporting the delivery of birth control services to minors, and it was during his administration that *Roe* v. *Wade* was decided. It was also in this period that involuntary, or nonconsenting, sterilization of poor women through federally sponsored family planning clinics, particularly in the South, "took off"—apparently with executive knowledge, if not blessing.[50] Clearly, Nixon (and every other president) wished to appear to oppose abortion in order to preserve the political support of the church, but also to flow with the heavily corporate-backed population control movement, which by now favored not only govern-ment-sponsored family planning services but also legalized abortions. The Nixon administration's aim, though perhaps served by little more than rhetoric, was to mediate the conflict between population control (sup-ported by a powerful array of private corporate foundation and institu-tional interests as well as liberal politicians) and sexual control (supported by the Catholic church and many conservative and right-wing political groups whose allegiance Nixon still tried to gain). Foreshadowing the Carter and Reagan administrations, Nixon carefully targeted the issues of abortion and teenage access to birth control to define the cutting edge of the sexually illegitimate, although in a general context that approved of state-sponsored population control.

In fact, in the late 1960s and early 1970s—the period of the Vietnam war and the transition of the black civil rights movement from nonviolence to militance—the pendulum of the sexual control–population control di-chotomy swung far in the direction of the latter. That fact plus the persua-siveness of "overpopulation" ideology helped rationalize a growing lobby-ing campaign among population control groups to liberalize the abortion laws. The Commission on Population Growth's positive recommendation on abortion in 1972 followed years of active soliciting for "abortion law reform" in which John D. Rockefeller and other establishment leaders had played an important role. Some of the tenor of their thinking is conveyed in a talk that Rockefeller gave at an international conference on abortion in Virginia in 1968, where he carefully placed the justifications for "reform" within a "moral" framework.[51] Three major themes were sounded by Rockefeller, all of which he defined as "moral problems" and all of which became important bases of the *public* policy, including the Supreme Court's decision, that would congeal in 1973. These themes were the ideological core around which a proabortion consensus among population groups, family planners, medical organizations, and government officials was being worked out.

First, and most significantly, Rockefeller made the utilitarian argument that abortion is inevitable and unstoppable, that its prohibition leads to large-scale "disrespect for the law," which in turn creates a "gradual erosion of the moral fabric that holds society together." Thus abortion should be legalized for the sake of social order and stability. Second, he presented a public health rationale and a set of medical conditions for liberalizing abortion: that it should be performed in hospitals by "duly licensed physicians," with a broadening of the "mental health" criteria (as presumably determined by doctors). Finally came an argument on behalf of the "unwanted child," who should have the right to "a life of dignity and self-fulfillment" or, it is implied, no life at all ("children's rights"). Nowhere was there any mention of the needs of women, much less the right of women to control pregnancy.

We should not exaggerate the role of the population control establishment in achieving legal abortion but should recall that eugenic and Malthusian ideas had never been used to defend legal abortion. Quite the contrary. Fears of "tainting" the now sanitized family planning field kept abortion a taboo and isolated subject. Only in the late 1960s did population control advocates and family planners begin to draw these connections, and then with pronounced caution and reluctance. (Rockefeller in 1968 spoke of the need for abortion as "regrettable" and "always a tragedy.") In fact, the neo-Malthusian ideology of the population explosion and the medical ideology of "therapeutic" or "mental health" reasons for abortion combined to provide a "respectable" rationale for a legal reform that many liberal professionals, academics, clergy, businessmen, and policy makers had already come to see as inevitable.

The reasons for this sense of inevitability are revealing and take us back to the arguments of Rockefeller that the criminal statutes *could not be enforced* and that this situation threatened "respect for law." The laws that made abortion a felony, except in cases of life endangerment, could not be enforced because millions of women, and some doctors, were determined to defy them—out of a sense (for the women) of pressing personal need. Abortion had to be legalized because the pressure of popular practice on doctors, health facilities, and finally the state had become irresistible. Indeed, the frequent emphasis of abortion reformers in pre-*Roe* days on rising reported deaths and serious complications reflected a reality caused by the increase in illegal abortions. It was an increase rooted in conditions that were massively changing women's position, family life, and sexuality in American society: not only the rise in women's labor force participation and college attendance, their later age at marriage and increased divorce rates, but the increase in contraceptive use (see Chapter 5). The population controllers' and physicians' participation in the abortion repeal campaign was an accommodative response to a trend they could not stop; their commitment was one not of principle but of pragmatism.

Along with the population control organizations, both the medical and the family planning professions were moving toward a proreform position by the late 1960s. For both groups—strong working allies for decades—two planks of the incipient policy mapped out by Rockefeller were compelling: (1) the guarantee of medical means and medical control, which family planners had long welcomed; and (2) the association with eugenic ends, to which doctors have often been sympathetic. The AMA passed a cautious, medically oriented resolution in 1967 in favor of a somewhat liberalized abortion law. The American Public Health Association, always more socially conscious than the AMA, followed this pronouncement with a more far-reaching resolution in 1968, which called for the *repeal* of restrictive abortion laws. Finally, the family planning establishment, under the leadership of Dr. Alan Guttmacher (himself an ob-gyn), joined the movement for safe, legal abortions. Planned Parenthood members in 1969 approved the proposal that existing criminal statutes be abolished (this had already occurred, at least on a partial basis, in some ten states), and its affiliates began to work with the movement to establish referral services and freestanding clinics.[52] These policy changes reflected a broad and growing sentiment among middle-class professionals, particularly liberals in the public health, social work, and family planning fields, as well as civil liberties lawyers and socially oriented clergy, in favor of abortion reform. It was a sentiment stimulated in part by humane considerations, by direct contact with the horrendous social consequences of illegality; and it became organized into effective lobbies.

In 1970, acknowledging the growing trend in state legislatures and courts "to make abortion more freely available," the AMA's House of Delegates resolved that this liberalizing trend should be contained within a medically defined and medically controlled framework. "Sound clinical judgment" and "the best interests of the patient," rather than "mere acquiescence to the patient's demand," should govern the procedure, which "should be performed by a licensed physician in an accredited hospital only after consultation with two other physicians. . . ."[53] While the conservatism and professional self-protection inherent in this statement are clear, it also marks a distinct shift in AMA policy on abortion. After a century of strictly moral opposition to abortion on practically any grounds, the AMA was now conceding that abortion for "medically necessary" reasons was legitimate.

What accounted for this sudden shift? It is surely the case that growing numbers of physicians and public health nurses were witnessing a virtual epidemic of perforated uteruses, infections, and deaths caused by illegal abortions in the 1960s; their awareness grew that this was an unnecessary tragedy. But public health reasons cannot fully explain the shift. Sensitive clinicians had been aware of the health risks to women, especially poor women, from illegal abortions since the late nineteenth century. Rather, both the change in medical policy and the changes in the law—which were mutually reinforcing—reflected the larger social and political context in which they occurred. This context included the population control movement pushing on one side and the activists in the feminist health movement and liberal reform organizations pushing on the other. But more than anything else, it included masses of women who, regardless of legal constraints and personal risk, were determined to get abortions.

The Role of Popular Organizing: Feminists and Libertarians

Birth control politics throughout most of the twentieth century in America have been laced with a tension between the ideas and methods of popular organizers and mass movements on the one hand and those of liberal reformers and sympathetic medical and legal professionals on the other. "Abortion on demand" and "a woman's right to control over her body" were never ideas that carried much weight in family planning conferences and AMA committees, in the legislative hearings and courtrooms where abortion policy was made, even though those ideas created important pressures on clinicians and policy makers to find more "moderate" principles to accommodate women's demands. Among such accommodationist principles the most important was the legitimacy of "therapeutic" abortion. This is the concept that the conditions justifying abortion are those that involve a woman's health, though "health" may be broadly defined to include a woman's mental or emotional health as well as fetal health. Those exclusively qualified to determine when such conditions, or "medical indications," exist, and to administer the procedures, are certified physicians.

Feminists have strongly opposed the distinction between therapeutic ("necessary") and elective ("unnecessary"?) abortions. Ellen Willis recalls this debate during the campaign for legalization in the late 1960s:

> When the radical feminist campaign for repeal of the abortion laws began in 1969, our first target was the "reformers" who sat around splitting hairs over how sick or poor or multiparous a pregnant woman had to be to deserve exemption from reproductive duty. It was the feminist demand for the *unconditional right to abortion* that galvanized women *and created effective pressure*

> *for legalization.* Now the idea that abortions without some special
> justification are not necessary but merely "convenient"—as
> if unwanted pregnancy were an annoyance comparable to,
> say, standing in a long line at the supermarket—has been
> revived with a vengeance.[54]

Radical and socialist feminists, working through organizations such as
the Chicago Women's Liberation Union, NOW, Redstockings, and wom-
en's health activist groups, consciously rejected both the medical model
of reproductive health and (though not always) populationist goals as
the basis of birth control. In contrast to family planners and public health
practitioners, feminists put forward a libertarian view of "abortion on
demand" as a necessary condition of women's right to control their bodies
and pregnancy:

> All the excellent supporting reasons—improved health, lower
> birth and death rates, freer medical practice, the separation of
> church and state, happier families, sexual privacy, lower welfare
> expenditures—are only embroidery on the basic fabric: *woman's
> right to limit her own reproduction.* It is *this* rationale that the new
> woman's movement has done so much to bring to the fore. Those
> who caution us to play down the women's rights argument are
> only trying to put off the inevitable day when the society must
> face and eradicate the misogynistic roots of the present situation.
> And anyone who has spoken publicly about abortion from the
> feminist point of view knows all too well that it is *feminism*—
> not abortion—that is the really disturbing idea.[55]

Contrasting "reform" to the more radical demand for repeal, feminists
argued that the former was steeped in conditions that denied women's
capacity and right to make reproductive decisions. Medical and legalistic
models of abortion, they pointed out, focused on "hardship" situations—
rubella, rape, mental illness—and thus "always pictured women as victims, . . . never as possible shapers of their own destinies."[56] And these
models implicitly suggested that women were incompetent to act as moral
agents on their own behalf. Repeal, on the other hand, would simply
abolish any restrictive, discriminatory conditions impeding abortion so
that medical authorities could no longer be moral gatekeepers.

Legal abortions had always been possible in some states to save a
woman's life or spare her "serious" health problems, or for the other
classic "hard" reasons: the fetus was known to be defective or the pregnancy resulted from rape or incest. But to obtain an abortion even under
these conditions involved going through hospital committees and private
networks that were penetrable only to privileged women. When the laws
of some states underwent reform in the late 1960s, these restrictive condi-

tions continued and, if anything, became more apparent under the rubric of (now legal) "therapeutic" abortions. Punitive therapeutic abortion committees put women through intense and often moralizing inquiries to determine whether their abortion request was truly justified on "health" grounds. Physicians and hospital authorities in California and Colorado, for example, imposed enormous red tape, requiring written consent from at least two physicians as well as the hospital committee and insisting on inpatient (hence much costlier) procedures. Many hospitals, particularly smaller ones, feared the label "abortion mill" or had chiefs of service opposed to abortion; thus they refused to perform abortions or imposed strict residency requirements.[57] These restrictions effectively excluded poor women, who lacked the personal connections to private doctors and the funds necessary to obtain a safe hospital abortion.

In the radical political context that existed from 1968 through the early 1970s, however, feminists and other proabortion activists sometimes found it possible to use "health" and "mental health" provisions expansively, to push them to their limits. Abortion referral groups in California, for example, were able to use "psychiatric indications" to sidestep much of the red tape that encumbered hospital abortions—evidently finding cooperative physicians with less difficulty—and thus to process most abortion cases.[58] Along with abortion activists in progressive church groups and radical health groups, civil libertarians, and some sympathetic doctors, organized feminists functioned as shock troops in the struggle to break through legal barriers. By pushing at the soft spots in existing laws (utilizing "health" and "mental health" provisions, testing hospital rules), they were able to open a wedge through which the growing need of women for access to abortion services could make itself felt even among the most resistant physicians.[59]

These tactics affected only a small number of women and were really test cases. The most important action feminists took to expand women's access to abortion and change the medical profession's position was through providing information and a network of alternative—and in at least one case, underground—services. Popular feminist pamphlets published from 1969 to 1971, especially *The Birth Control Handbook* and the now classic *Our Bodies, Ourselves,* circulated in the many thousands of copies, giving practical information about abortion procedures, risks, and sources of information and service.[60] As in the early twentieth century, alternative clinics and a network of cooperating private doctors were set up in the vacuum created by the institutionalized medical profession's refusal to provide care even after liberal abortion laws were passed.

In New York, for example, after the state passed one of the most permissive laws in the country in 1970, state health officials immediately tried to implement "guidelines" that, contrary to the law's spirit, once again would restrict abortions to "accredited hospitals and their clinics."

Despite the new law, hospitals continued to refuse abortion services to women past the first trimester, or from out of the hospital catchment area, or without either ready cash or insurance coverage. In the face of such roadblocks, feminists and other abortion activists set up their own alternatives: an abortion "underground" that provided counseling and referrals to safe, reliable practitioners; and eventually, a national network of freestanding abortion clinics. Members of the medical hierarchy have consistently opposed such clinics, have refused to cooperate with them, and have ostracized gynecologists who did. The reality is that the clinics have provided more and better abortion services, with significantly lower complication rates, more attention to counseling and birth control, and at much lower cost, than have the nation's hospitals.[61]

Politically, the impact of confronting the medical profession and the state with a rival set of institutions that could clearly meet people's needs, and do so at a lower cost, was powerful. More than anything else, it illustrated that the criminal statutes could not be enforced. Feminists believed—and they were not altogether wrong—that new abortion techniques, when used early in a pregnancy and under safe conditions, were so simple they could be "seized" from medical control.[62] Indeed, it is ironic to speculate that the fact of abortion's technical simplicity and lack of "heroic" surgical challenge is one reason why many doctors disdain it. Acting on this belief, at least one group of feminists set up an underground abortion clinic in Chicago that operated over a four-year period (1969–73) practically under the eyes of the police, providing eleven thousand illegal abortions.

Known as Jane and originating out of the Chicago Women's Liberation Union, the clinic delivered services to women of all ages and stages of pregnancy. At first it contracted with illegal abortionists, trying to bargain down their fees, but then Jane volunteers learned to perform the operation themselves, using the aspiration technique, which made it possible to reduce fees to an average of $50, although "no one was turned away for lack of funds."[63] In this way, the theory and practice of self-help became an essential part of the struggle for legal abortion, proving "that abortions could be performed safely, humanely and very inexpensively by non-professional paramedics working in apartments." Jane maintained a safety record that compared "favorably with that of licensed medical facilities in New York and California" in the early years of legal abortion, and it was able to provide its services primarily to low-income women. It not only monitored clients' reproductive health (through Pap smears, taking blood pressure, referrals for complications) but focused on counseling as "the heart of the procedure"—a form of counseling that attempted to give the woman sisterly support and to demystify the abortion experience.[64]

In part, the threat posed by Jane and the freestanding (legal) clinics that succeeded it was economic. Low fees made "the bottom fall out of the abortion black market," hence undercutting what had long been a boondoggle for some doctors.[65] Even more important, the fact that these clinics provided (and continue to provide) a vital service that thousands of women desperately need, under safe conditions, has been the major determinant of their "unstoppability." It is interesting that in four years of illegal operation involving dozens of activists, only seven members of Jane were arrested; the charges were dropped in 1973. "The police were not interested in stopping them, . . . the police had known what they were doing and had not intervened . . . since they were providing a necessary service for policemen's wives, mistresses and daughters and for all policewomen," and did so in a manner that left women healthy and well rather than bloody or dying.[66]

From 1968 to 1973, the organized feminist movement used a variety of direct-action methods to put pressure on the medical profession, state legislatures, and popular consciousness to repeal abortion laws. The 1969 AMA Convention in New York was surrounded by picketers from the women's movement wielding signs and leaflets "demanding that doctors sign a petition for repeal."[67] Feminists from NOW and other women's liberation groups invaded the AMA meeting, as well as courtrooms, legislative hearing rooms, district attorneys' offices, and the streets—no bastion of patriarchy was sacrosanct—and provided the most visible external pressure for change in the abortion laws. Joined by radical health and welfare rights groups, they sat-in at public hospitals and health agencies to demand that abortion services be provided to poor women. Redstockings (a New York women's liberation group) sponsored a "speakout on abortion" at which dozens of women testified publicly about the horrors of their illegal abortions.[68]

The shift in medical and family planning policy from 1969 to 1971 was a response to this political pressure, as well as to the threatened growth of alternative abortion services outside the control of the medical hierarchy. These two factors—the militant organizing of feminists and the threat of "alternative services"—were crucial political influences toward loosening population establishment and medical abortion policy. The role of feminist activists as "shock troops"—doing underground abortion referrals and counseling, conducting speakouts, sit-ins, and demonstrations—was critical for the timing of the Supreme Court decision and earlier decriminalization statutes in several states.

Unfortunately, the impact of feminist *ideas* about abortion and birth control was less clear. Part of this confusion was the failure of women's liberationists of the pre-*Roe* period—unlike the present reproductive rights movement—to distinguish sharply between the demand for birth control and abortion services on behalf of women's choice and the aims of population control. As in the late nineteenth and early twentieth centuries, some feminists of the "second wave" conflated their values about abortion as a social need and right of all women with arguments about "overpopulation," echoing the dominant ideology and state policy.[69] The result was, in the late 1960s, a deepening of divisions between the mainly white women's liberation movement and the black liberation movement, whose predominantly male leadership, from its most militant to its most conservative wings, had long been suspicious of any government-sponsored family planning program as a weapon of racial "genocide." Given the racist policies of government-funded clinics and family planners—targeting minority neighborhoods for family planning services; providing birth control devices and "follow-up" in abundance, but not jobs, decent housing, basic health care, maternity care or child care; sterilizing poor black, Hispanic, and Native American women without their informed consent—these suspicions grew out of a stark reality.

But the polemic about genocide has usually overlooked the distinction between birth control and population control. It has ignored the question of *who* controls, and the very real need of black and other ethnic minority women to control their fertility, which necessarily requires government funding and services. Occasionally it has carried a populationist-misogynist message of its own, such as the statement of one Florida NAACP official that "our women need to produce more babies, not less . . . ; until we comprise 30 to 35 percent of the population we won't really be able to affect the power structure in this country."[70] Black women, speaking out of their identity within the black movement but with a feminist voice, responded forcefully to such statements and the male supremacy they implied. Acknowledging the racism of population control policies, Toni Cade Bambara, Shirley Chisholm, and others argued that the "male rhetoric" of genocide went against the needs and feelings of black and Puerto Rican women growing out of their own responsibilities for children and could not be heeded at the expense of those women's lives or the well-being of their children.[71] Opposition to population control and support for birth control and abortion *as paired feminist values* originated here, in the political thinking and experience of black women.

Another ambiguity in the white feminist movement's ideas about abortion arose from its emphasis on the practical rather than the theoretical or broadly social aspects of abortion. During the New York State campaign, radical feminists made clear the differences between their approach, which emphasized concrete access to abortion for all women, and that of more liberally oriented groups (e.g., the National Association for Repeal of Abortion Laws, which became the National Abortion Rights Action League, or NARAL), which emphasized the legal "right to choose." Feminists consistently opposed legislative proposals that restricted legal abortion to licensed physicians, therapeutic criteria, and so forth, insisting on the importance of paramedicals and nonhierarchical forms of reproductive health care if all women were to have access to services.[72] This was a practical way to critique the elitism of the medical care system and the abstract idea of abortion as a private matter between "a woman and her doctor." For the majority of women did not and do not have access to a cozy, confidential relationship with a private physician, traditionally the ticket to a safe abortion. Thus the feminist position implicitly called for substantive changes in the quality and conditions of reproductive health care. But this practical approach was not developed into an analysis and an ideology that could communicate to popular understanding the sexual and social as well as the health reasons why women of all classes and age groups, married and unmarried, ought to have access to abortion; why legal abortion is a positive benefit and not a "necessary evil."

The philosophy of removing the state from abortion decisions altogether, of repeal pure and simple (implied in the slogan "Get the State's laws off our bodies") is at bottom one of laissez-faire. It contains an implicit presumption that the "right to choose," or the relegation of abortion to the private sphere, will in itself guarantee that good, safe abortions will be provided. Many feminists have understood that this is not a reasonable presumption; the existing medical-care system, like other capitalist markets, does not adequately meet people's needs; how and by whom abortions (or other health services) are provided is a critical dimension of whether real needs will be met. This deeper understanding was often implicit in how radical feminists conducted the abortion struggle, but it failed to be translated either into a popular feminist discourse or into public policy. More seriously, the powerful idea that restricting abortion means compelling motherhood, that motherhood is a social relationship and not a punishment or a destiny, remained—remains still—far removed from the consciousness of most people. As a result, feminists in the campaign for legal abortion won the battle but not the war. On the level of public discourse—policy, law, media representation—the feminist voice on the abortion question was and remains barely audible. More disturbing, within popular consciousness, it would seem that medical and neo-Malthusian, not feminist, justifications for abortion prevail.

Yet, in a vague and diffuse way, on some deeper cultural level, articulated in a negative sense by the antifeminist right wing, the women's liberation movement of the 1960s and 1970s brought to light the taboo sexual meanings of fertility control politics that the family planning and population control establishment had tried so methodically to conceal. More than anything else, the fight for "abortion on demand," as a demand of and by women, asserted these meanings even when some feminists were not eager to, or when their ideas about abortion remained rhetorical and confused. When a large and clamoring body of women—single, lesbian, and divorced, as well as married with kids, or grandmothers—began marching by the thousands for legal abortion, it created a political context that by definition exposed the connections between fertility control and women's sexuality. As a reaction to this feminist movement, the conservative forces now in power and the sexual/family ideology they represent are a challenge not only to feminism but to the hegemony and contradictions in the previous thirty years of population control and family planning policy. For the former policy hoped to make birth control (and, later, abortion) available but without any radical sexual or gender-related consequences.

In the late 1970s, the pendulum began to swing back again, and the preoccupation of policy makers, public and private, with population control receded before their growing concern to refortify the boundaries of sexual control. This was apparent in the first Hyde Amendment, passed in 1977, to cut off most federal funds for abortion services. There the impulse of legislators to curb "promiscuous sex" among poor young women seemed to take priority over their more recent urge (since the 1940s) to reduce the fertility of the poor. The past two decades of liberalized policies around fertility control, including abortion, are perceived as having unleashed a wave of "illicit" sexual activity, especially among young unmarried middle-class women but also among welfare recipients. Thus the policies must be revised; the connection between fertility control and sexual freedom must be contained. But it should be clear that this readjustment of policy has little to do with political parties, nor is it the invention of the New Right. Antiabortion policies have been a constant under every president since Eisenhower, and the constitutionality of abortion was declared in spite of verbal presidential opposition. These shifts reflect, not partisan leanings, but the tensions embedded in the patriarchal state between population control and sexual control; and the persistent view of abortion as uniquely subversive.

There is a lesson to be learned from Roe v. Wade, a lesson that could have a bearing on its sequel in the 1980s. If, after a century of medical and eugenicist domination of reproductive politics, abortion became legal in the first place, it was because at a particular historical moment social need, feminist activism, and populationist ideology came together. This was sufficient to change state policy, but in order for that change to have been radical—a liberating force for masses of women, and lasting— social need and feminist activism would have had to merge with a popular feminist ideology, one that turned the accepted meanings of abortion upside down. And this did not happen.

NOTES

1. Elizabeth Wilson, *Women and the Welfare State* (London: Tavistock, 1977), p. 9. Although it deals primarily with Britain, Wilson's study is the major feminist work on this subject and is extremely comprehensive. See also Zillah Eisenstein, "The Sexual Politics of the New Right: Understanding the 'Crisis of Liberalism' for the 1980s," *Signs* 7 (Spring 1982): 567–88, which situates the feminist critique of the welfare state in the contemporary neoconservative politics in the United States.

2. See Ian Gough, *The Political Economy of the Welfare State* (London: Macmillan, 1979), pp. 11–14; Frances Fox Piven and Richard A. Cloward, *The New Class War* (New York: Pantheon, 1982), Chap. 1; and James O'Connor, *The Fiscal Crisis of the State* (New York: St. Martin's, 1973), pp. 162–68. These analyses of the welfare state relate to the United States and Britain. Social welfare policies, and the state apparatus that implements them, can develop differently in other national and historical contexts. See Carolyn Teich Adams and Kathryn Teich Winston, *Mothers At Work: Public Policies in the United States, Sweden, and China* (New York: Longman, 1980), pp. 156–57.

3. Gough, pp. 65–66.

4. Lawrence Lader, *Abortion II*, p. 117.

5. See U.S. Department of Commerce, Bureau of the Census, "Fertility of American Women: June 1980," *Current Population Reports*, Series P-20, No. 364 (1981).

6. U.S. Department of Labor, Bureau of Labor Statistics, *Perspectives on Working Women: A Databook*, Bulletin 2080 (October 1980), Tables 26–28.

7. Demographers have long pointed to the close relationship between lowered fertility among women and their higher labor force participation rates. Yet the enormous literature on this subject leads to the conclusion that it is a complex and variable relationship, not subject to generalization. In the postwar United States, where the relationship seems strongest, it may be true both that women have fewer babies in order to work or when work opportunities expand and that they more readily seek work when there are fewer children to care for. In fact, numerous studies of the relationship between women's work and fertility indicate the complexity of that relationship and its failure to conform to any uniform pattern from one country or occupation group to another. For a sampling of the literature, see James L. McCabe and Mark R. Rosenzweig, "Female Employment Creation and Family Size, in *Population and Development: The Search for Selective Interventions*, ed. Ronald G. Ridker (Baltimore: Johns Hopkins University Press, 1976); H. Theodore Groat, Randy L. Workman and Arthur G. Neal, "Labor Force Participation and Family Formation: A Study of Working Mothers," *Demography* 13 (February 1976); J. Mayone Stycos and Robert H. Weller, "Female Working Roles and Fertility," *Demography* 4 (1967): 210–219; and Elise F. Jones, "The Impact of Women's Employment on Marital Fertility in the U.S., 1970–75," *Population Studies* 35 (July 1981): 161–62, 172–73.

8. McCabe and Rosenzweig, pp. 323–24, 341–42; and Lourdes Benería and Gita Sen, "Accumulation Reproduction, and Women's Role in Economic Development," *Signs* 7 (Winter 1981): 295–97.

9. Juanita Kreps and Robert Clark, *Sex, Age, and Work: The Changing Composition of the Labor Force* (Baltimore: Johns Hopkins University Press, 1975), pp. 8–12.

10. U.S. Department of Labor, Women's Bureau, *1975 Handbook on Women Workers*, Bulletin 297 (1975), Table 36; and *Perspectives on Working Women: Databook*, Table 10.

11. *1975 Handbook on Women Workers*, Table 89; and U.S. Department of Commerce, Bureau of the Census, *A Statistical Portrait of Women in the United States: 1978*, Current Population Reports, Special Studies Series P-23, No. 100 (February 1980), Fig. 5–1.

12. For an earlier statement of this intersection, see R. Petchesky, "Dissolving the Hyphen: A Report on Marxist-Feminist Groups 1–5," in *Capitalist Patriarchy and the Case for Socialist Feminism*, ed. Zillah R. Eisenstein (New York: Monthly Review Press, 1979), pp. 378–81.

13. Lois Wladis Hoffman and Martin L. Hoffman, "The Value of Children to Parents," in *Psychological Perspectives on Population*, ed. James T. Fawcett (New York: Basic Books, 1973), p. 65; and McCabe and Rosenzweig, p. 324.

14. Harriet Presser and Wendy Baldwin, "Child Care as a Constraint on Employment: Prevalence, Correlates, and Bearing on the Work and Fertility Nexus," *American Journal of Sociology* 85 (March 1980): 1202–13, 1205, 1209.

15. Ibid., p. 1211.

16. U.S. Department of Health, Education, and Welfare, National Center for Health Statistics, *First Marriages: United States, 1968–1976, Vital and Health Statistics*, Series 21, No. 35 (September 1979), Table 8.

17. Martin O'Connell and Maurice J. Moore, "The Legitimacy Status of First Births to U.S. Women Aged 15–24, 1939–1978," *Family Planning Perspectives* 12 (January/February 1980), p. 22, Table 5.

18. Stephanie J. Ventura, "Trends in First Births to Older Mothers, 1970–79," National Center for Health Statistics, *Monthly Vital Statistics Report* 31 (27 May 1982): 2–3 and Fig. 3. The proportions of childless women at age thirty among black and Hispanic women are, and continue to be, substantially smaller than those of white Anglo women.

19. U.S. Department of Commerce, Bureau of the Census, *Divorce, Child Custody, and Child Support,* Current Population Reports, Series P-23, No. 84 (1979), p. 1; and U.S. Department of Commerce, Bureau of the Census, *Marital Status and Living Arrangements: March 1980,* Current Population Reports, Series P-20, No. 365, Table C.

20. Deborah Dawson, Denise Meny, and Jeanne Ridley, "Fertility Control in the United States Before the Contraceptive Revolution," *Family Planning Perspectives* 12 (March/April 1980): 76–86. Of the women in this survey, 28 percent had been surgically sterilized before age fifty, a figure close to that reported in the 1976 National Survey of Family Growth.

21. Richard A. Easterlin, *Birth and Fortune* (New York: Basic Books, 1980), pp. 55–57, makes this argument cogently.

22. Pascal K. Whelpton, Arthur A. Campbell and John E. Patterson, *Fertility and Family Planning in the United States* (Princeton: Princeton University Press, 1966), pp. 276–79, 221.

23. U.S. Department of Commerce, Bureau of the Census, *Child-Spacing and Current Fertility,* Subject Reports PC(2)-3B (1975), Tables 90 and 91.

24. Quoted in Christopher Tietze, *Induced Abortion: A World Review*, 4th ed. (New York: Population Council, 1981), p. 21.

25. Ronald Freedman, Pascal K. Whelpton, and Arthur A. Campbell, *Family Planning, Sterility and Population Growth* (New York: McGraw-Hill, 1959), p. 32; and Frederick S. Jaffe, Barbara L. Lindheim, and Philip R. Lee, *Abortion Politics: Private Morality and Public Policy* (New York: McGraw-Hill, 1981), p. 14.

26. Donald Granberg and Beth Wellman Granberg, "Abortion Attitudes, 1965–1980: Trends and Determinants," *Family Planning Perspectives* 12 (September/ October 1980): 250–61, 252, and Table 1. They note "the time lag between the adoption of a social practice and its acceptance as a social norm"; but this is to equate "social norms" with the positive pronouncements of the state, denying their connection with popular practice.

27. Lucinda Cisler, "Unfinished Business: Birth Control and Women's Liberation," in *Sisterhood Is Powerful*, ed. Robin Morgan (New York: Vintage, 1970), pp. 277–78.

28. See U.S. Department of Commerce, Bureau of the Census, *Fertility of American Women: June 1979*, Current Population Reports, Series P-20, No. 358 (December 1980): 2–4; Maurice J. Moore and Martin O'Connell, *Perspectives on American Fertility*, U.S. Department of Commerce, Bureau of the Census, Current Population Reports, Series P-23, No. 70 (July 1978): Tables 1–4, 1–6, 2–5; and Anne R. Pebley, "Changing Attitudes Toward the Timing of First Births," *Family Planning Perspectives* 13 (July/August 1981): 171–75.

29. Quoted in Lillian Breslow Rubin, *Worlds of Pain: Life in the Working-Class Family* (New York: Basic Books, 1976), p. 66.

30. See L. Gordon, *Woman's Body, Woman's Right*, Chap. 9, on the relationship between birth control agitation and working-class movements.

31. *Statistical Portrait of Women in the U.S.: 1978*, p. 35 and Tables 5–2, 6–2.

32. See Emma Rothschild, "Reagan and the Real America," *New York Review of Books* 8 (5 February 1981): 12–17.

33. See Jo Freeman, "The Women's Liberation Movement: Its Origins, Organizations, Activities, and Ideas," in *Women: A Feminist Perspective*, 2d ed. (Palo Alto, Calif.: Mayfield, 1979), pp. 557–74; and Sara Evans, *Personal Politics: The Roots of Women's Liberation in the Civil Rights Movement and the New Left* (New York: Knopf, 1979). Both are accounts of the origins and social composition of the recent women's liberation movement.

34. Kennedy, *Birth Control in America*, p. viii.

35. For Marxist theories of the "relative autonomy" of the state and of its "legitimization" functions, see O'Connor, pp. 6–7, 69–70; Gough, Introduction and Chaps. 3 and 4; Ralph Miliband, *Marxism and Politics* (New York: Oxford University Press, 1977), Chap. 4; Fred Block, "The Ruling Class Does Not Rule: Notes on the Marxist Theory of the State," *Socialist Revolution* 7 (May/June 1977): 6–28; and Nicos Poulantzas, "The Problem of the Capitalist State," *New Left Review* 58 (1969).

36. See Kennedy, pp. viii–ix; Mohr, *Abortion in America*, pp. 250–51; and Bonnie Mass, *Population Target: The Political Economy of Population Control in Latin America* (Toronto: Women's Educational Press, 1976), pp. 45–46.

37. Mass, pp. 36, 40, 43, 161–62.

38. Thomas M. Shapiro, "Capitalist Class Influence and Social Policy: The Population Council and Population Control" (unpublished ms., 1981), p. 19.

39. Mass, p. 161; and Thomas B. Littlewood, *The Politics of Population Control* (Notre Dame: University of Notre Dame Press, 1977), p. 61.

40. Shapiro, pp. 17, 20–22; and Mass, p. 40.

41. Steven Polgar, "Birth Planning: Between Neglect and Coercion," in *Population and Social Organization,* ed. Moni Nag (The Hague: Mouton, 1975), pp. 191–92; and Mass, p. 40.

42. Littlewood, pp. 10–11, 21–22.

43. A study done by the Center for Continuing Study of the California Economy and published in 1982 predicts, based on trends indicated in the 1980 census, that "the proportion of Americans who are white and of European ancestry, the nation's basic ethnic stock since Colonial days, will decline at an accelerating rate in the next two decades," and that "more than half of the U.S. population growth in the next two decades will come from minority groups," particularly Hispanics. "Study Sees Shift in U.S. Population," *New York Times,* 19 July 1982, p. A10. Once again, in ever more sober and refined technocratic language, the message is distinctly racist.

44. Mass, p. 42.

45. Littlewood, pp. 44–45.

46. Ibid., pp. 27–30.

47. Ibid., pp. 40–41, 146–47.

48. Ibid., p. 55.

49. Quoted ibid., pp. 61–62.

50. Littlewood describes the complicity of the Nixon administration in federal sterilization programs geared toward population control, under the direction of Dr. Louis Hellman in the new Office of Population Affairs and goaded on by warnings of social scientists like Daniel Patrick Moynihan about rising "illegitimacy rates" and "dependency ratios" (ibid., Chaps. 4 and 5).

51. John D. Rockefeller III, "Abortion Law Reform—The Moral Basis," in *Abortion in a Changing World,* ed. Robert E. Hall (New York: Columbia University Press, 1970), pp. xv–xx.

52. Lader, p. 84; and Alan F. Guttmacher, *The Case for Legalized Abortion Now* (Berkeley: Diablo Press, 1967). Guttmacher was the national head of Planned Parenthood and a leader among ob-gyn practitioners who fought against the mainstream of their profession in favor of legalized abortion.

53. The resolution is quoted in *Roe* v. *Wade,* 410 U.S. 142 (1973), p. 143. By 1970 at least thirteen states had liberalized their abortion statutes, allowing abortions in at least some circumstances.

54. Ellen Willis, *Village Voice,* 3 March 1980, p. 8.

55. Cisler, p. 276.

56. Ibid., p. 275.

57. Lader, pp. 22, 114; and Daniel Callahan, *Abortion: Law, Choice and Morality* (New York: Macmillan, 1970), pp. 137–42.

58. Lader, p. 111.

59. Failure to grant a hospital abortion in cases of rubella or severe emotional distress might be grounds for a malpractice suit.

60. The Boston Women's Health Book Collective, *Our Bodies, Ourselves* (New York: Simon and Schuster, 1971); there were two subsequent printings and two later editions. Donna Cherniak and Shirley Gardiner, *Birth Control Handbook* (Montreal: Montreal Health Press, 1973).

61. Barbara L. Lindheim, "Services, Policies and Costs in U.S. Abortion Facilities," *Family Planning Perspectives* 11 (September/October 1979): 283; and Pauline Bart, "Seizing the Means of Reproduction: An Illegal Feminist Abortion Collective, How and Why It Worked" (unpublished ms., n.d.). Bart cites the case of the Florida Medical Association, which accused the Feminist Women's Health Center in Tallahassee of failing to work with local doctors or provide adequate medical backup, yet "itself prevented local physicians from cooperating" (p. 4).

62. Cisler, p. 265; and Bart.

63. Bart, pp. 4, 10. This unpublished manuscript is the only written source available documenting the story of Jane.

64. Ibid., pp. 4, 7.

65. Ibid., p. 5.

66. Ibid., p. 6 and note 2.

67. Lader, p. 82.

68. Cisler, pp. 271, 278; and Florynce Kennedy and Diane Schulder, *Abortion Rap* (New York: McGraw-Hill, 1971).

69. See, for example, Cisler, p. 287.

70. Quoted in Littlewood, p. 75.

71. See Shirley Chisolm, "Facing the Abortion Question," in *Black Women in White America: A Documentary History*, ed. Gerda Lerner (New York: Vintage, 1973), pp. 602–607; and Toni Cade (Bambara), "The Pill: Genocide or Liberation," in *The Black Woman*, ed. Toni Cade Bambara (New York: New American Library, 1970). ". . . I've been made aware of the national call to the Sisters to abandon birth controls, to not cooperate with an enemy all too determined to solve his problem with the bomb, the gun, the pill; to instruct the welfare mammas to resist the sterilization plan that has become ruthless policy for a great many state agencies; to picket family-planning centers and abortion-referral groups, and to raise revolutionaries. And it seems to me that once again the woman has demonstrated the utmost in patience and reasonableness when she counters, "What plans do you have for the care of me and the child? Am I to persist in the role of Amazon workhorse and house slave? How do we break the cycle of child-abandonment–ADC-child?" (pp. 163–64).

72. Lader, pp. 126, 130.

PART

II

ABORTION PRACTICE IN THE 1970s

4

The Social and Economic Conditions of Women Who Get Abortions

Only a generation ago, social assumptions about the consequences that must follow from premarital sexual activity and premarital conception were radically different from what they are today. In the "baby boom" years of the 1950s, social norms prescribed that an out-of-wedlock conception lead inexorably to marriage and the bearing of a "legitimate" child. A group of working-class adults who had married in the 1950s and early 1960s, for example, reported during interviews that for them abortion was simply "not a choice" and that getting married was the only imaginable outcome to a premarital pregnancy. "Of course if you get pregnant, you get married; everybody does. Everybody just expected us to get married when I got pregnant—my parents, his parents, our friends."[1] Today, most young people, whatever their level of sexual activity, seem to have a different expectation. Access to birth control and legal abortion have contributed to a changing consciousness among women that they might legitimately defer marriage and childbearing to other goals and needs, without deferring sex. This consciousness, the growing demand for abortion services, and legalization itself were products of the changing social conditions discussed in the previous chapter.

Nevertheless, this fundamental alteration of consciousness has affected different women differently, particularly as collective experiences are shaped by class, race, age, or life cycle. Depending on her relatively higher or lower class position, a woman might have seen abortion in the 1970s as a condition of either her expanded possibilities or her ability to maintain some control over a highly constrained set of circumstances. In either case, it was a socially determined need. Examining the precise contours of that need in different circumstances can show us the given limits on "choice." This analysis can help clarify the demographic commonalities and social differences underlying abortion practices in the

141

1970s. It can show us that if access to abortion is a need of women collectively, that need presents itself with particular urgency at certain ages and in certain life conditions.

Recent Trends in Abortion Practice

Legalization, public funding, and public legitimacy have contributed to a significant rise in abortions in the United States since 1970 (see Figure 4-1). The proportion of pregnant women who legally terminate their pregnancy has risen steadily, from 19 percent in 1973 to 30 percent in 1979, an increase of 58 percent in six years.[2] As we saw in the previous chapter, this increase and its social determinants reflect patterns that emerged quite distinctly by the 1960s. Their impact has been concentrated on women in particular age groups and social situations.

To understand the specificity of abortion trends in the 1970s, it is important to look at the social characteristics of women who get abortions.

FIGURE 4-1.   U.S. ABORTION RATE PER 1,000 WOMEN AGED
15–44, 1973–1980

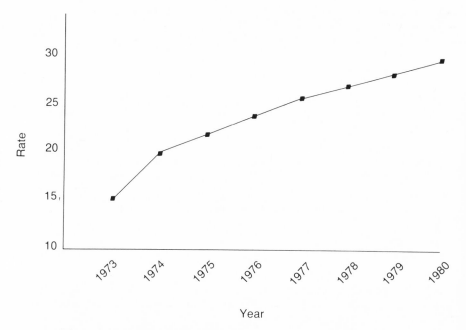

SOURCE: Adapted from Stanley K. Henshaw et al., "Abortion Services in the United States, 1979 and 1980," in *Family Planning Perspectives* 14 (January/February 1982), p. 7.

At the present time in the United States these women tend overwhelmingly to be *young and unmarried*. Two-thirds (65 percent) of all women getting abortions each year since 1975 have been between the ages of fifteen and twenty-four, and three-quarters (75 percent) have been unmarried.[3] This pattern contrasts with earlier periods when abortion was a practice mainly of older married women with children, who used it as a regular means of fertility control rather than a "backup method."[4] It is true that in the 1880s and 1890s most abortions also occurred among young unmarried women, but then it was a sign of the delegitimation that physicians had brought about; abortion became a phenomenon of "the poor, the socially desperate, and the unwed—usually seduced or misled."[5] Today the youth and single status of most abortion clients is a sign of the legitimacy of abortion, its association with normal reproductive conditions, and the increasing visibility of women's sexuality outside the patriarchal family.

Two groups of women in particular have contributed to the recent increase in abortion rates: teenage women, especially whites, and slightly older poor and minority women. They have been the primary beneficiaries of legalization and expanded services. The centrality of white middle-class teenagers in this development has had far-reaching political implications. It has become the basis of a distorted ideological construction of teenage sexuality and teenage abortion as a pathology requiring therapeutic intervention, or a sin requiring political and "moral" restrictions. But the trend itself—the fact that significantly more teenage girls today than twenty years ago get pregnant out of wedlock and have abortions—is undeniable. Its social roots have to be distinguished carefully from the ideological and political struggles that occur in its wake. Among those social roots are a set of factors that have reshaped the life situations of many teenage and young adult women. These include an overall shift toward later marriage, a resultant increase in premarital heterosexual activity and intimate relationships, and the increased primary involvement of young women of reproductive age in school or work rather than childbearing in marriage.

Young American women during the 1970s married later than their predecessors and tended with greater frequency to live as "single" women, either with male (or female) partners or alone. In 1980, 50 percent of all women aged 20–24 were unmarried, compared with 36 percent in 1970.[6] (See Table 3-3.) A similar trend away from marriage occurred for eighteen- and nineteen-year-olds. These developments were linked to important changes in the domestic living arrangements of young women. Between 1970 and 1980 the number of female "single-person households" involving women under twenty-five years of age more than doubled, while households consisting of an unmarried couple tripled.[7] And for women who entered marriage, the tendency toward greater regulation of childbearing could be seen in the increasing delay of childbearing after marriage and also the spacing of children closer together.[8]

The postponement of marriage and childbearing has lengthened the years of young women's premarital sexual life by advancing the endpoint of this stage in the life cycle. Its beginning point has stretched as well, since the average age at menarche, or onset of menstruation, has lowered in the course of the last few generations due to improvements in health and nutrition. Taken by itself, this extension in the potential time span of premarital sexual activity could be expected to generate a higher incidence of unwanted pregnancy and thus the need for, and recourse to, abortion.[9] This consequence, however, is not a "natural" or "biological" phenomenon, like the mating of birds. It occurs because of a changed consciousness among young women about the sequence of their life events; their capacity, as young women, to be self-sufficient; and the diminished social penalties of sexual activity.

A related development, which also reflects young women's changed attitudes and practice concerning premarital pregnancy, is the rise in out-of-wedlock births. Young American women, especially whites, in the 1970s were much less inclined than their mothers and grandmothers to "legitimate" the first pregnancy through marriage.[10] The percentage of premaritally pregnant white girls aged 15–19 who legitimated their pregnancies fell from 51 percent in 1971 to 31 percent in 1976, down to 20 percent in 1979. For blacks, the decline was from 8.5 percent in 1971 to 4 percent in 1979. In historical perspective, the recent decline in the proportion of legitimated pregnancies represents a return to the lower levels characteristic of the World War II period, which antedated the peak in legitimation of the late 1950s and early 1960s.[11]

Why has this change occurred? To what extent is it the result of legal abortion, relieving the pressure on young people to marry? That postponed marriages and legal abortion are independent developments is evident from the fact that the increase in the numbers of pregnant teenage women who chose to give birth without getting married began in the late 1960s, prior to the legalization of abortion. This suggests that changing consciousness concerning unlegitimated births is not merely an attitudinal by-product of a change in the law.[12] Rather, its social roots are deeper and more complex.

The rise in out-of-wedlock first births occurred at the same time that a growing percentage of young women were resolving their pregnancies through abortion. In this context "postponement of marriage" is not just an interesting but isolated demographic fact. It is part of a larger set of social and cultural changes that have resulted in *both* rising abortion rates *and* rising out-of-wedlock birthrates among young American women, especially if they are white and middle class. In Chapter 3 we found that these changes include (1) the expansion in higher education and technical training for women and (2) an expanding (if sex-segregated) capitalist market for women's labor. These conditions of the 1960s and 1970s, although far from uniform in their impact on women, created an expectation—reflected in and brought to consciousness by the feminist movement—that women's situation and possibilities were improving.

If aborting an out-of-wedlock pregnancy or giving birth to an unlegitimated baby seem to be opposite choices, they are linked by this common element of consciousness, which in turn arises out of the social changes I have described. Both involve the rejection of early marriage as the defining objective in women's lives, and at least an expectation of economic independence. Fewer young women "feel obligated to marry as soon as possible for lack of an alternative, socially acceptable role" or in order to legitimate their pregnancy.[13] Without minimizing the constraining conditions of class and race that affect contraceptive practice and unplanned pregnancies, or the hardships of single motherhood, it is possible to recognize the decline of compulsory marriage as a progressive development. To an increasing extent, young women sense that they can consider abortion or single motherhood from the standpoint of their own needs rather than from the dictates of family pressure or traditional social stigmatization. In so doing they are seeking to reconcile their reproductive decision with a self-determined life, even as their achievement of such a life is undermined by the social relations of male domination and class and racial inequality.

This interpretation of recent developments in young women's reproductive experience differs from two alternative perspectives: (1) the widely circulated image of an "epidemic" of adolescent pregnancy and childbearing, and (2) the explanation of changing behavior as a response to economic hardship. The first perspective, which describes pregnancy on the model of a communicable disease, is not supported by evidence concerning teenage patterns of sexuality, pregnancy, and childbirth. While teenagers as a group have experienced a rising pregnancy rate, their birthrate, like that of every other group of U.S. women, has declined since the 1960s. This is largely because of access to abortion. The rising number of out-of-wedlock births among whites (that of black women of all ages declined in the 1970s) was occurring by the late 1970s among all unmarried white women, not only teenagers; in fact, the rate of "illegitimacy" among teenagers still represents the *lowest* rate of any group of unmarried women under thirty. Moreover, this increase in "illegitimate" births among teenagers is partly a result of the fact that the teenage birthrate as a whole has declined, so out-of-wedlock births become a larger proportion of the total.[14]

It is spurious to call this an "epidemic," when in fact two-thirds of all "sexually active" teenagers manage not to get pregnant. Figure 4-2 reveals that pregnancy, particularly out-of-wedlock childbearing, is a

Figure 4-2. Pregnancies and Sexual Activity Among Teenage Women, 1978 and 1979

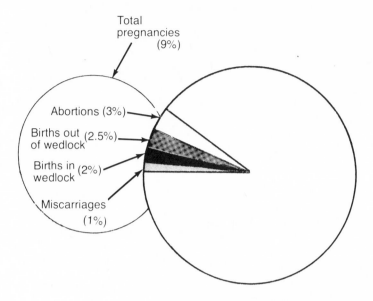

Total
pregnancies
(9%)

Abortions (3%)

Births out (2.5%)
of wedlock

Births in (2%)
wedlock

Miscarriages
(1%)

Teenage Women, 13–19 (1978)

SOURCE: Adapted from Alan Guttmacher Institute, *Teenage Pregnancy: The Problem That Hasn't Gone Away* (New York, 1981), Fig. 10.

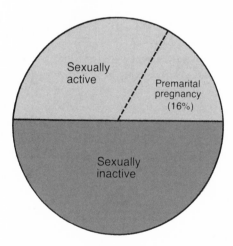

Sexually
active

Premarital
pregnancy
(16%)

Sexually
inactive

Metropolitan-Area Teenage Women, 15–19 (1979)

SOURCE: Adapted from Melvin Zelnik and John F. Kantner, "Sexual Activity, Contraceptive Use and Pregnancy Among Metropolitan-Area Teenagers: 1971–1979," in *Family Planning Perspectives* 12 (September/October 1980).

rather small slice of reality when seen from the perspective of teenage women taken as a whole. Only 8.5 percent had pregnancies that were resolved in 1978, and only 2.5 percent bore out-of-wedlock babies. Nearly two out of three unmarried teenage pregnancies (62 percent) in 1978 resulted in abortions or miscarriages, slightly more than one out of three (38 percent) in live births.[15] Among metropolitan-area women surveyed, aged 15–19, only 16 percent had ever had a premarital pregnancy, or slightly less than one-third of those who had ever had premarital intercourse. Not "illegitimacy," then, but the urge to be sexually active, to delay or avoid marriage and childbearing, to continue school, and to utilize abortion if necessary to make that possible became major patterns for teenage women in the 1970s.

The second perspective explains delayed marriage as a response to male unemployment (as opposed to female independence). This approach appears especially applicable to the late 1970s, when high inflation combined with a deepening recession. It suggests that young women were putting off marriage—even when they were pregnant and rejected abortion—because economic hardships made men unavailable to them.[16]

Without discounting the probable reality of aspects of this description for some women, especially the poorest and least educated, we can see certain problems with it as a general explanation. First, the postwar rise in illegitimacy rates occurred throughout the "baby boom" for all age groups and, except for a slight decline in the late 1960s among women in their twenties, characterized the years of economic expansion prior to the recent recession. Second, it is important to recall that the Great Depression in the 1930s was characterized not by a rise in illegitimacy but by a fall, corresponding to declining fertility rates generally.[17] The explanation in terms of economic hardship appears mistaken in asserting an invariant relation between economic stress and increased illegitimacy. Finally, that recent increases in out-of-wedlock childbearing, like those in abortion, exist among white middle-class women confirms the present interpretation that their source is not economic stress so much as "the changing relationships between sexual behavior and the social mechanisms controlling it," especially "the role of the family as the principal regulator of sexual expression."[18]

While the moralizing reactionaries of the New Right bemoan the decline of family "regulation" of sexuality, I am arguing, on the contrary, that important aspects of this change are the progressive, inevitable consequence of young women's gains, during the 1960s and 1970s, in access to economic and educational resources. I am not suggesting that frequent pregnancies and abortions among very young women are healthy or desirable[19] or that there are no serious problems among teenagers that impede a successful (and preferable) reliance on regular birth control use. These impediments, as we see in Chapter 6, have to do with both consciousness and sociopolitical structure—with the pervasive ideas about sexuality that teenage women themselves reflect, and the institutional and cultural forces that sometimes make recourse to contraception difficult or risky for them. Abortion has become a central part of the "facts of life" for teenage women because of a set of changing social conditions that, on the whole, have improved their prospects as women in a male-dominated society. In the long run, while unsettling to parents and threatening to sexual conservatives, these conditions enhance young women's sense of control over their futures and their sexuality. Moreover, available public health data suggest that when abortion is conducted early, under safe and sanitary conditions, the health risks of even repeated abortions among teenage women are much less serious than the health risks from childbirth.[20]

What is dangerous is the tendency of some girls to deny they are pregnant and thus delay seeking an abortion until late in the pregnancy—often so late that health risks increase greatly. This pattern of denial and delay results from teenagers' fears that their parents (especially fathers) will find out and be angry and punitive. Both late abortions and an untold number of births to teenage women are the product, not of liberalization, but of continued sexual conservatism in the midst of greater access to safe early abortion.

In the analysis presented to this point, I have placed women's increased reliance on abortion in the general framework of consciousness and expectation of improved economic and social conditions for women in the United States. This is a very different approach from one that sees abortion as a "desperate measure," a "last resort," or else an act of careless "hedonism," which distorts the actual situation of most women getting abortions. It is important, however, to examine how social conditions of class and racial inequality differentiate women's experience of abortion. These conditions may severely limit the fulfillment of the promise of a better, self-determined life for women, which society's provision of legalized abortion services appears to offer.

Class and Race Differences in Resolving Nonmarital Pregnancies

Out-of-wedlock childbearing—involving the decision neither to get an abortion nor to marry—remains more prevalent among working-class and poor than among middle-class teenagers. While the majority of middle- and upper-class pregnant teenagers, even in predominantly Catholic areas, terminate their pregnancies in abortion, the likelihood is much greater that working-class teenagers will carry their pregnancies to term.[21] Studies of young women who had unintended premarital pregnancies in the early 1970s (just after legalization) concluded that women's choice of outcome—whether to marry and have the child, to become a single parent, to get an abortion, or to deliver and put the baby up for adoption— was strongly influenced by class background. A survey of women in Hawaii found that "when women who chose abortion are compared with women with similar options who chose to have a child, the abortion patients are consistently more middle class in both objective social characteristics and basic value orientations." More of these women tended to be from professional or lower-middle-class families and had at least some college education. Women choosing childbirth, either within or outside marriage, tended to be from families whose adults were employed in "blue-collar or service occupations" and to have a high school education or less.[22]

A study of pregnant unmarried adolescents in California done in the same period found class, age, and ethnic differences between women who got abortions and those who brought the pregnancy to term. These differences characterized married and unmarried women. The women who took their pregnancies to term were more likely to be younger, Mexican-American, and from working-class families.[23] Their decision to have the baby rather than seek an abortion had to do with the actual conditions that gave different shape to their lives. The abortion groups made better grades in school, had higher school attendance, and were more likely to be earning money of their own; the "term" groups had significantly poorer school records and were more likely to have dropped out of school.[24] The extent to which teenage women experience their lives as purposeful, moving according to some plan, is centrally related to school experience; the quality of that experience in turn depends on their class and race. These circumstances have a critical bearing on the decision about abortion or childbirth.

Many working-class students find high school oppressive, crowded, and essentially custodial, a place that is sometimes alien to their culture and language if they are Latin or West Indian. They realistically see little connection between earning a diploma and going on to an adequate job or to college. In contrast, their cultures may regard having a baby as an achievement and a mark of adulthood and esteem. In this context abortion may not seem a desirable alternative. The well-publicized trend in the 1970s for teenage mothers, white as well as black, to keep their babies rather than give them up for adoption is associated with the narrow socioeconomic options of many of these women, as well as the growing tolerance for unwed motherhood.[25]

Lack of adequate educational and occupational opportunities helps explain the class and racial contexts of a significant proportion of teenage motherhood. On the other hand, the *effect* of early childbearing, for working-class and to some extent middle-class teenagers, is to foreclose present and future educational and occupational attainment. The possibility of accumulating work experience, training, and the necessary resources for a consistent relation to work may be drastically affected by early child-bearing. The earlier a woman has a baby, it seems, the more likely she is to drop out of school; the less education she gets, the more likely she is to remain poorly paid, peripheral to the labor market, or unemployed, and the more children she will have—between one and three more than her working childless counterpart. Conversely, a sample of young adult women who had reached age twenty-four by 1972 found that for each year the birth of the first child was postponed, a woman was able to attain an additional half year of schooling.[26]

In addition to having a strong influence on dropping out of school, the bearing of her first baby as a teenager is associated with a young woman's high subsequent fertility. Major responsibilities for child care at an early age, combined with limited education, may mean that she will "never catch up," never get out from under the weight of child-care responsibilities and lack of skills to improve her situation. Her relation to the job market is likely to be marginal, centered on unskilled, low-wage sectors, if it exists at all. As a result, teenage childbearing thrusts a young woman into economic dependency on welfare assistance, support from her parents, or support from her husband's earnings. For working-class women, dependency in these circumstances frequently amounts to a condition of persistent poverty or, when poverty is avoided, to an inability to develop labor market skills. The long-term effect of early childbearing is thus cumulative, resulting in the loss of employment and resources in later years.[27] Racism compounds this picture. All girls who drop out of high school to become mothers have a difficult time finding employment, but the unemployment rate of black high school girls with babies is nearly twice that of white girls in the same situation.[28]

Recently some small steps have been taken to alleviate the harsh consequences that social institutions impose on teenage women who become pregnant and bear a child. To a large extent these measures have come as a response to the changed consciousness of teenage women themselves. During the 1970s a significantly greater number of pregnant teenagers, especially black girls, was able to continue and complete high school even if they decided to carry through their pregnancy. This change was partly eased by a shift in school board policy allowing pregnant girls to stay in school.[29] But school boards were only responding to recent changes in young women's lives. As we have seen, the likelihood that teenage pregnant women will get married to legitimate a pregnancy declined drastically during the 1970s, for whites and blacks, while the proportion who remain unmarried increased. Later marriage, higher college attendance and labor force participation, and recognition by the courts of a girl's maturity outside marriage (the "mature minor" doctrine) have combined to make teenage out-of-wedlock childbearing not easy, but more compatible with self-development.

The positive change in school board policies regarding pregnant teen-agers reflects not only more generally supportive social attitudes but also a specific realization that early marriage, even more than early childbear-ing, is a disaster for students who become pregnant. If a pregnant teenager gets married, she is more likely to drop out of school permanently than if she remains single, living with her parents.[30] School boards have recog-nized that pregnant teenagers are not going to get married and be taken care of, or to disappear conveniently into "homes," and thus have granted their right to an education. These progressive developments—in the con-text of an active feminist movement—have in turn encouraged the found-ing and funding of self-help organizations, such as the Sisterhood of Black Single Mothers in New York, which have helped to meet the survival needs of some black teenage mothers.[31]

The tendency for teenage mothers to stay in school and not to marry (the two seem to go together), while increasing among all groups, is much more prevalent among black teenagers. In 1979 the likelihood of teenage mothers remaining unmarried was much greater among blacks than whites; 76 percent of white teenage mothers who were high school drop-outs had married, whereas only 19 percent of comparable black teenage mothers had. Black teenage mothers were much more likely to be living with parents or other relatives than with a spouse; in sharp contrast, three-quarters of the young white mothers were living with either a hus-band or (in a few cases) a "male partner."[32] For the black girl, the family network provides a base of support that cushions the experience of early childbearing; she is still a daughter and, above all, she has her mother at home to help her out. For the white girl, despite rising rates of "illegiti-macy," marriage is still the dominant recourse; she becomes a wife and relies on the support of a young man whose resources and experience are nearly as limited as her own.

If the black girl's situation reflects the traditional value placed by black families on childbearing, on providing extended family and commu-nity support to young single mothers, it is nonetheless a value born of harsh reality. If teenage black women avoid marriage after becoming preg-nant, it may be because racism and its impact on young black men (particu-larly on their prospects of adequate employment) make that a prudent choice. If these young women look to motherhood for a sense of esteem and self-worth, it may be because so few alternative sources of esteem are available to them. If black parents and other kin are supportive of their pregnant daughters, providing them with a home, child-care assis-tance, and a "positive attitude," it may reflect not only a set of traditional norms valuing children but a situation in which the parental family knows it can count on the contribution of the daughter's welfare benefits. Finally, poverty and institutional racism may increase the value placed on babies and childbearing, regardless of the mother's age or circumstances, because of the precariousness of life. Infant, neonatal, and perinatal mortality rates among blacks and other minorities remained nearly twice as high as those of the dominant white majority in 1979—a fact determined partly by poor nutrition and inadequate or unavailable maternity and child health services.[33]

Yet the fact of having coped with teenage motherhood for generations and having done so outside the framework of marriage may have made that experience a more viable one for black women than for white. Field studies of communities of urban and rural black women point out how the scarcity of black men able to get steady jobs and the frequently voiced conviction of black mothers that "you can't trust men" create in young black women a set of values about marriage rooted in caution. From mother to daughter, from daughter to sister, the idea is passed down that a woman cannot rely on having a man to take care of her; pregnancy alone is no reason to get married.[34]

These distinct features of the social and family context of childbearing for black teenagers help account for the pattern of timing of reproductive events in black women's lives and the difference between this pattern and that of white women. Black women tend to bear children earlier in life, with children spaced more closely together, and to have abortions at a somewhat later age than white women, after they have borne at least one child. The difference between racial groups in the timing of abortion is marked. Table 4-1 shows that nearly two-thirds of black women who had abortions in 1978 in eight reporting states were mothers; conversely, nearly two-thirds of white women had no previous children at the time of their abortion. Figure 4-3 reflects the fact that the peak age for abortions among black women is higher than it is among white women. While abortion ratios (per 1,000 live births) are higher among black women than white women at all ages over 20, those among white teenagers are consistently higher than they are among black teenagers.

Although the timing of abortions shows persistent differences between blacks and whites, certain recent improvements in educational and employment conditions for some black women have altered the context

TABLE 4-1. PERCENT DISTRIBUTION OF REPORTED ABORTIONS BY RACE AND PREVIOUS CHILDBEARING EXPERIENCE, 1978

	White	Black
No previous live birth	64	36
One or more previous live births	35	64

SOURCE: Drusilla Burnham, "Induced Termination of Pregnancy: Reporting States, 1977 and 1978." U.S. Department of Health and Human Services, *Monthly Vital Statistics Report* (Hyattsville, Md., 1981), Table 5.

FIGURE 4-3. WHITE AND BLACK WOMEN WHO HAD ABORTIONS IN 1978, PERCENT DISTRIBUTION BY AGE.

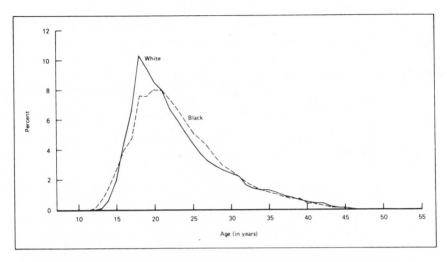

SOURCE: Drusilla Burnham, "Induced Terminations of Pregnancy: Reporting States, 1977 and 1978," U.S. Department of Health and Human Services, *Monthly Vital Statistics Report* 30 (Hyattsville, Md., 1981), Fig. 1.

in which they experienced the need for abortion. These improvements underlie an important part of the rise in the rate of abortions among black women in this decade and the decline in childbearing among black teenagers.[35]

Educational advances at the college level and access to better jobs and higher earnings within the female labor force represent gains that have enhanced the prospect of self-determined life choices for middle-class and many working-class black women. Enrollment of black women in U.S. colleges during the 1970s increased by nearly twice the margin of white female enrollment. By 1978 "the proportion of black women enrolled in college (11 percent of those between fourteen and thirty-four years of age) was not significantly different from the proportion of comparable white women."[36]

For broader groups of black women, there were important advances in occupational position as the proportion of employed black women holding traditional service and domestic worker jobs declined by over one-quarter and that in clerical positions increased by one-half between 1970 and 1979. During roughly the same period, the earnings of black women in employment as a whole came close to those of white women (although the earnings of all women remained at less than 60 percent of the earnings of white men). In 1970 black women's median earnings for year-round, full-time work were $6,940, or 82 percent of those of comparable white women. By 1978 black women's median earnings had increased to $9,020, or 93 percent of the median for white women.[37]

The prospect of more education, more rewarding employment, and higher earnings has been associated for many black women with an increasing tendency to postpone (or avoid) marriage. Between 1970 and 1978 the percentage of black women over age 14 who had never married increased from 28 to 35 percent (the corresponding figures for white women were 21 and 22 percent).[38] In the past, reasons for marriage or nonmarriage among black women have been related to the economic conditions confronting black men and the reality-based ethic of self-reliance of black women. In the light of recent educational and occupational gains, however, these patterns in marriage must be evaluated as well in terms of the new awareness of black women of an expanded range of options. One key decision is that regarding entry into, and maintenance of, employment. High labor force participation is not a new phenomenon for black women. It is nonetheless significant that the rate of participation for black women between twenty-five and thirty-four years old had risen to the very high level of 70 percent by 1979.[39]

These important advances have resulted not only from shifts in the needs of the capitalist economy but also from the impact of the civil rights and women's liberation movements. Although they are not the "cause" of rising abortion rates, they provide a context for understanding the decline in fertility, increased use of abortion, and the shifting role of maternity in the lives and cultural self-definition of black women. It is important to recognize that the linked trends of rising college attendance and employment, later marriage, and higher abortion rates are specific to middle-class and working-class women, both black and white, as distinct from the poor. Indeed, as members of a racial minority who are trying to attain or maintain a middle-class position in a capitalist patriarchal society, black women college and graduate students have been observed to exhibit sexual attitudes and behavior that involve "taking very few risks," being much more "careful" than white women, thus defying traditional racist-sexist stereotypes.[40] The availability of legal, funded abortion has diminished the magnitude of risk for these women and thus has helped them achieve important goals.

Here too, changes in social conditions reflect and reinforce changes in women's consciousness. Abortion is and always has been for black women an important "fact of life," a well-known option practiced by them despite its illegality, despite moral and religious opposition to it in the black community, and despite its association with genocide by black male political figures. Black women's relation to abortion reveals a strong basis of support for their right to choose, which underlies the relative absence of public agitation for, and generalized discussion of, abortion in the black community.[41] Writing in *Essence*, Bebe Moore Campbell decries the "shame" and "silence" that cloaked abortion practices of generations of black women and calls on black women to be strong and outspoken in their defense of abortion rights.[42] Moreover, a recent poll in *Life* magazine revealed that 80 percent of "all nonwhite women" in a national sample agreed that women should have the legal right to get an abortion if they want one, as compared to 67 percent of white women.[43] Their situation and needs, not ideology, underline the importance of this right for them in daily life.

Abortion Access for Poor Women

The legalization of abortion following *Roe* v. *Wade* had a crucial, positive impact on the life choices available to all women. However, its contribution to women's basic health and well-being was most dramatic for poor women, who disproportionately are women of color. For it occurred in a context involving major changes in the composition of the poor, specifically the growing number and economic burdens of poor women who support families. This development has been succinctly described as the "feminization of poverty" in the United States.[44] While it denotes a contrast with the situation discussed above, in that it describes a group of women whose economic and social conditions worsened rather than improved over the decade, the point is that access to safe, legal, funded abortion helped greatly to relieve those conditions.

By 1980, 15 percent of all white families, over 20 percent of all Hispanic families, and 42 percent of all black families were headed by women, and these families constituted over half of all families living in poverty. About one-third of all female-headed families are officially classified as poor (the percentages are much higher among black and Hispanic female-headed families). They depend on food stamps, Medicaid, welfare—the very social programs that the state in the late 1970s began systematically cutting back. If the women heading these families work outside the home, they undoubtedly find themselves in marginal, low-paying service and clerical jobs. Their median income is roughly one-half that of married-couple families.[45] Medicaid is virtually their only source of health care.

The importance of legal, funded abortion services in the lives of poor women dependent on Medicaid is a matter for them, as it is for all women, of gaining control over their sexual circumstances and the conditions of motherhood. But it is also a matter critically involving their physical health and their mortality. Legalization has radically changed the conditions under which poor women resolve the problem of an unwanted pregnancy. The illegal status of abortions prior to 1973 did not prevent poor women from having them, but they did so in circumstances that were frightening, unhygienic, and sometimes life threatening.

Before *Roe* v. *Wade,* the practical consequence of physicians' control over hospital abortions was the virtual exclusion of poor and minority women from "therapeutic" services.[46] The main feature of the days of illegality was not the absence of abortions but their invisibility. Abortions—hundreds of thousands of them a year—were performed in a class-divided system that relegated poor women to the sordid conditions of back-alley abortionists, while rich and middle-class women usually had access to safe, sanitary abortions in hospitals and physicians' offices. The medical profession enforced this division under the aegis of the "therapeutic" rationale and the incentive of the profit motive. Through rigid requirements and hierarchical committee procedures, physicians maintained a strict monitoring process over hospital abortions that limited the number and types of abortions performed, legally and illegally. Restrictive abortion laws were widely disregarded to accommodate middle-class private patients, who could more easily find a doctor to attest that they had "psychiatric problems" or rubella.[47] Moreover, there is evidence that state prosecutors were highly selective in their enforcement of abortion laws, seeking out clinics and back-alley abortionists as targets for prosecution but never prestigious hospitals where illegal abortions were performed routinely. Cost alone ($600 to $800) prohibited most women from securing hospital abortions, even if restrictive rules and the elitist structure of proprietary medicine did not. As a result, surveys done in the 1960s in New York City found that "four times" as many hospital abortions were done "on the private services as on the ward services" and that only a tiny number were done in the municipal hospitals that serviced primarily poor black and Puerto Rican women.[48] This is in sharp contrast to the much greater number of ward patients hospitalized during the 1960s for complications from illegal, out-of-hospital abortions.[51]

A major effect of legalization and Medicaid funding of abortion was to make abortion a "safe and legal" medical service that for the first time was available to poor women. And poor and minority women seem by their numbers to have been eager to take advantage of this fact. Black and Hispanic women typically are somewhat older than white women when they get their abortions, but they are reportedly three times more likely than white women to get abortions. Similarly, Medicaid-eligible women, a disproportionate number of whom are women of color, have an abortion rate that is three times higher than that of the white, unmarried, middle- or working-class majority.[49] The percentage of abortion recipients before the Medicaid cutbacks who were either "black and other" (33 percent) or Medicaid patients (22 percent nationally, 25 percent in New York State) substantially exceeded their proportion in the population at large.[50] Even if these differences are inflated (e.g., by the likelihood of underreported abortions among middle-class women in private, non-clinic settings), they still indicate an important shift from prelegal days.

Moreover, legalization and the increased availability of abortion services have meant definite public health benefits for poor and minority women. Maternal mortality in the United States has dropped sharply in the last two decades; specifically, since 1973, "abortion-related deaths have decreased by 73 percent." Similarly, hospital data from New York City show that morbidity such as infections and uterine perforations caused by illegal abortions dropped substantially after legalization in 1970.[52] Since poor and minority women are the main ones to suffer such deaths and morbidity, these declines are an important indication that legalized abortion has meant better reproductive health for them.

Neither the undeniable benefits to their health nor the high rate of use of abortion has guaranteed adequate access to abortion services for poor women. The reverse is true. Poor women are *both* three times more likely than other women to get abortions *and* much more likely to be denied access to abortion. The years following *Roe* v. *Wade* painfully brought home the lesson that abstract legal guarantees of "a woman's right to choose" are not equivalent to the actual delivery of adequate abortion services to all women who need and want them. Most poor and minority people in the United States rely for their routine health care on the outpatient services of government (federal, county, municipal) hospitals and clinics. But even after abortion became legal throughout the United States and supposedly a "woman's right," it did not become widely available. Surveys done by the Alan Guttmacher Institute and the Centers for Disease Control showed that "only a minority of all American doctors, about half of the ob-gyns who specialize in women's health care, and only a few non-Catholic hospitals provide abortion services."[53] Moreover, they indicated that "eight out of 10 public hospitals and six in 10 non-Catholic private hospitals," particularly in rural areas, provided *no* abortion services.[54] Even hospitals that provide abortion services tend not to provide them on an outpatient basis (although the vacuum aspiration technique is decidedly cheaper and safer in the early stages of pregnancy) nor to accompany them with counseling or birth control services. And their costs range from one and a half to two times as high as those charged by private clinics. In fact, the total participation of U.S. hospitals in providing abortion services has declined in relative terms from 1973 to 1977, and absolutely since 1977. All of the growth in abortion service providers must be attributed to freestanding abortion clinics, which provide three-fifths of all U.S. abortions.[55] Despite the clinics' excellent record of service,

the estrangement of mainstream health providers from the provision of abortion . . . hinders better integration of health

services and makes the development of adequate referral
and informational resources for abortion more difficult. . . .
By limiting the accessibility of abortion services in the many
less densely populated areas not feasibly served by clinics, it is
likely to affect adversely those least capable of easily obtaining
abortion services—rural women, the very young and the
poor.[56]

The major reason for this "estrangement" has been found by researchers to be physicians' negative attitudes about abortion and the decisive
influence of attending physicians on hospitals' abortion practices. Constance Nathanson and Marshall Becker have analyzed these attitudes and
their impact on abortion availability in an important survey of practicing
obstetrician-gynecologists in Maryland.[57] (Maryland was one of the first
states to legalize abortion in the late 1960s.) They point out that "since
no state has enacted legislation authorizing nonphysicians to perform
abortions, *medical practitioners effectively control access to legal abortion services.*"[58]
This is true regarding ob-gyn practice in both private offices and hospitals.
With respect to the latter, the personal values and attitudes of staff obstetricians in the private non-Catholic hospitals surveyed were the *main* factor
determining numbers of abortions performed in those hospitals; and where
attending physicians were opposed to abortion psychologically or philosophically, their affiliated hospitals "were much less likely to perform
abortions"—even when hospital policy favored providing abortion and
contraceptive services.[59]

Equally interesting are Nathanson and Becker's findings regarding
abortion performance, both in terms of scope and conditions, in physicians' private practice. As would be expected, the study found religion
to be "the most powerful predictor of abortion performance," with 85
percent of Catholic doctors performing no abortions, as opposed to 28
percent of Protestant and 9 percent of Jewish doctors. Moreover, doctors
refusing to perform abortions tended to have "conservative" views on
the ethics of bodily self-determination, on the expansion of reproductive
health and family planning services, and on the role of women in contemporary society.[60] The most interesting aspect of this study is what it
tells us about Maryland physicians who *do* perform abortions as part of
their ob-gyn practice. Among *providing* physicians (who are the majority),
"close to 40 percent . . . request women to obtain consent for the abortion
from their husbands or parents," and "over half . . . report that they
do not accept Medicaid as payment for the abortion." Fees average $250 for a
first-trimester abortion and $300 for a later abortion.[61] In other words,
the abortion practices of providing physicians reflect a pronounced class
bias. Physicians who have "liberal" values regarding the role of women
in society and who are less likely to request parental or spousal consent
are also those who refuse to treat Medicaid patients:

These are physicians with *largely middle-class and predominantly white practices.* Their comments in connection with fee policies reflect a generally suspicious and defensive attitude toward any patient who is personally unknown or is referred by an unknown physician. The patient management procedures of these physicians are the outcome of *an abortion practice limited to women of their own social status with whom a prior personal or professional relationship exists.* This relationship precludes the need for consent or for payment in advance; *the abortion is done mainly as an accommodation.* Medicaid patients are not accepted because they do not meet the physician's interpersonal criteria for abortion performance.[62]

Thus, an intimate, personal doctor-patient relationship around abortion decisions is alive and well—for white middle-class women! Conversely, private, proprietary medical care in this country continues to function as an exclusionary device to deny poor women access to abortion services.

There is a striking contrast between the failure of the U.S. hospital system (particularly public hospitals) to provide abortion services to poor women and its central role in their sterilization. Hospitals are the *major* providers of contraceptive sterilizations, which increased threefold in the United States during the 1970s. (It was in 1970 that the AMA loosened its traditional abortion policy and decided to lift all parity and age restrictions on sterilization procedures.) It has been well documented that low-income women are disproportionately represented among those who have been surgically sterilized, and this would seem to be particularly true for Puerto Rican and Native American women.[63] Beginning in 1973, court suits began to mount involving both private practicing and health-service physicians engaged in the involuntary sterilization of poor, minority, and retarded young women. At the same time, evidence accumulated concerning doctors' attitudes favoring sterilization of AFDC mothers with illegitimate children; the routine performance of "elective hysterectomies" on poor minority women patients in teaching hospitals; and the requirements in these hospitals that abortion services be made contingent on consent to sterilization (the famous "package deal").[64] Moreover, physicians, particularly the American College of Obstetricians and Gynecologists, have consistently opposed federal and local sterilization regulations that attempt to impose strict conditions assuring voluntary consent, claiming that such regulations are a violation of their First Amendment rights.

Apparently, physicians' attitudes and practices regarding sterilization are very different from their attitudes and practices regarding abortion, and these differences are directly related to class and race. It would appear that, for the ob-gyn profession as a whole, abortion is taboo on moral grounds or is treated as a *privilege* reserved for white middle-class women, a "private" matter between the physician and "his" patients. Sterilization, today as fifty years ago, is deemed more appropriate for poor and minority women.

Passage by Congress of the Hyde Amendment in the late 1970s, which cut off Medicaid funds for abortion, made de facto denial to poor women of access to abortions a national policy. The virtual curtailment of publicly financed abortions in most states following Hyde aroused the apprehension of many feminists that poor women would be forced to bear unwanted children, to get unwanted sterilizations, or to risk death or injury from illegal abortions. Although it is too soon to gauge the impact of the loss of federal funding, these effects have not occurred. Rather, the immediate result of the Hyde Amendment was that an estimated *94 percent of the Medicaid-dependent women needing abortions continued to get them.*[65]

That the Hyde Amendment "did not deter the majority of low-income women from obtaining legal abortions" should not be surprising, for it reflects two social realities that historically underlie abortion use and its restriction. First, the provision of legal abortion services to Medicaid recipients was always concentrated in a relative handful of states. These states have continued Medicaid funding for abortion on the state level. The high level of abortion use among Medicaid-dependent women since Hyde reflects the restricted geographic availability of abortion to poor women and the maintenance of funding in this limited group of states. More important, even in states where Medicaid funding was cut off, "between 65 percent and 80 percent of Medicaid-eligible women" wanting abortions managed to get them legally—and an undetermined number got them illegally. Legal abortions were at times available because local practitioners continued to provide them, despite loss of funding, under the pressure of popular demand. Elsewhere, however, poor women undoubtedly borrowed from friends or relatives, depleted clothing or food money, relied on charity or clinic goodwill, or traveled out of state and thus risked delay and medical complications. "Plenty of rent checks have gone unpaid, and plenty of food bills have been snipped in half, in order to pay for abortions—with disastrous results to poor women's health and that of their families."[66] These facts remind us of a lesson of history: Women will persist in getting abortions out of their own sense of need and right, even under substantial economic, legal, and medical obstacles.

Denying poor women access to abortion, thus forcing them to have children they do not want, and restricting their reproductive capacity through coercive measures such as sterilization abuse, would seem to be contradictory policies. Yet, as I suggested earlier, these ambiguities are inherent in a society geared historically to the need to control both its "relative surplus population" and the sexual and reproductive maneuverability of women. These goals hang in an uneasy tension and may be tentatively worked out differently at different times or in different regions.

At present, when neoconservatism and antifeminism are the ascendant political tendencies, the denial of access to abortion is a pressing threat to poor women (and others).[67] But this is only one dimension of the loss of reproductive control that poor women face. Especially in locales with large concentrations of poor blacks, Puerto Ricans, Haitians, Chicanos, and Native Americans, a more serious problem regarding abortion may stem, not from its denial, but from its forced imposition. The limited evidence regarding this practice comes from firsthand accounts of Third World women patients and women who have worked in proprietary abortion clinics.[68] They report that poor women of color may find that a positive pregnancy test automatically results in an aggressive attempt to persuade them to undergo abortion. Instead of being offered a choice, they are presumed to be too poor or too young or to have too many children already to bear a child. This is in part a function of the population control mentality, but it also reflects economic interests. In profit-making abortion establishments, Medicaid reimbursement and unregulated fee schedules operate as an incentive to some doctors to process as many abortion cases as possible.

All these situations make up a complicated reality. Poor women often cannot get abortions when they want them and are sometimes pressured to get abortions when they do not want them. But most frequently, they seek and get abortions because they need to—necessity, not freedom, dictates choice. All dimensions of this totality exist at present, and all are different in important ways from the reality of abortion for most middle-class women. It is not surprising that abortion has different meanings for different women, depending on their social conditions. But this does not contradict the fact that the rise in legal abortions coincides with major gains for women as a whole, gains that affect most women, but differentially, in a society structured on class and race divisions. While access to abortion services and contraception hardly guarantees "upward mobility" in such a context, those services provide one important material circumstance that can broaden a woman's range of possibilities and give her a little more control over her life, especially if she is poor.

NOTES

1. Quoted in Lillian Breslow Rubin, *Worlds of Pain: Life in the Working-Class Family* (New York: Basic Books, 1976), pp. 66–67.

2. Stanley Henshaw et al., "Abortion in the United States, 1978–1979," *Family Planning Perspectives* 13 (January/February 1981): 7, 10–11; and idem., "Abor-

tion Services in the United States, 1979 and 1980," *Family Planning Perspectives* 14 (January/February 1982), p. 7.

3. Henshaw et al. (1981), Table 10; and Jacqueline Darroch Forrest, Christopher Tietze, and Ellen Sullivan, "Abortion in the United States, 1977–1978," *Family Planning Perspectives* 11 (November/December 1979): 337, Table 4.

4. Carl Djerassi, *The Politics of Contraception* (New York: Norton, 1979), pp. 25–26, points out that this is the case in present-day China, Cuba, Eastern Europe, Japan, and North Africa, as contrasted with the United States, Sweden, and Canada, where abortion prevails among young, unmarried, low-parity women. See also International Fertility Research Program, *Traditional Abortion Practices* (Triangle Park, N.C., 1981).

5. James C. Mohr, *Abortion in America* (New York: Oxford University Press, 1978), pp. 46–49, 76–83, 88–91. Mohr's assumption that abortion rates in the nineteenth century increased absolutely and not only among the native middle-class married women who patronized physicians is based on inferences from physicians' reports, newspaper accounts, and advertisements for commercial abortion products and services. We cannot be sure about trends in abortion use among poor and working-class women based on these sources.

6. U.S. Department of Commerce, Bureau of the Census, "Marital Status and Living Arrangements: March 1980," *Current Population Reports*, Series P-20, No. 365 (October 1981), pp. 1–5 and Table B.

7. Ibid., p. 5, Table F, and p. 4, Table E. These changes may not be uniform for all social groups. For example, data correlating age at first marriage with education levels show that in 1970–75 there was no change in the first-marriage age of persons with a high school education or less, whereas there was a "distinct rise in the median age at first marriage among brides and grooms who had attended or completed college." See U.S. Department of Health, Education and Welfare, "First Marriages, United States, 1968–1976," *Vital and Health Statistics*, Series 21, No. 35 (Hyattsville, Md.: National Center for Health Statistics, September 1979), pp. 20–21.

8. U.S. Department of Commerce, Bureau of the Census, *Fertility of American Women: June 1979*, Current Population Reports, Series P-20, No. 358 (December 1980), pp. 2–4; and Maurice J. Moore and Martin O'Connell, *Perspectives on American Fertility*, U.S. Department of Commerce, Bureau of the Census, Current Population Reports, Series P-23, No. 70 (Washington, D.C.: Government Printing Office, July 1978), p. 20, Table 2-5.

The women with the highest age at first birth of this century were those born in 1910–19—the low-fertility mothers of the depression and war years. These were also the women who had the lowest fertility and highest rates of birth control use prior to the current period. Yet, as Moore and O'Connell and the Census Bureau study suggest, these rates really reflect the fact that lower fertility and rising ages at marriage and first birth are *trends characterizing most of the twentieth century*. It is the "baby boom" period that is, in every respect, anomalous. See also Anne R. Pebley, "Changing Attitudes Toward the Timing of First Births," *Family Planning Perspectives* 13 (July/August 1981): 171–75.

9. This argument is assuming the risks and inadequacies of contraceptive methods discussed in Chapter 5.

10. "Legitimated" pregnancies are those conceived premaritally and made "legitimate" by the couple marrying sometime before the birth. The concept obviously contains the same normative assumptions as does the concept of "illegitimacy"; the state only recognizes children who are the product of patriarchal marriage.

11. Martin O'Connell and Maurice J. Moore, "The Legitimacy Status of First Births to U.S. Women Aged 15–34, 1939–1978," *Family Planning Perspectives* 12 (January/February 1980): 16, 21–23; and Melvin Zelnik and John F. Kantner, "First Pregnancies to Women Aged 15–19: 1976 and 1971," in *Teenage Sexuality, Pregnancy, and Childbearing,* ed. Frank F. Furstenberg, Richard Lincoln, and Jane Menken (Philadelphia: University of Pennsylvania Press, 1981), pp. 97–101 and Tables 3, 7.

12. O'Connell and Moore, pp. 22–23, make this argument, attributing the decline of the "legitimation ratio," as well as the phenomenon of postponed marriage, to the availability of legal abortion.

13. Wendy Baldwin, *Adolescent Pregnancy and Childbearing—Growing Concerns for Americans* (Washington, D.C.: Population Reference Bureau, 1977), p. 10. This is a comprehensive and balanced analysis of many of the issues related to teenage pregnancy, sexuality, and childbearing. See also Furstenberg, Lincoln, and Menken, for a collection of many of the important articles written during the 1970s on these issues.

14. See Moore and O'Connell, pp. 40–41; and Frank F. Furstenberg, Jr., "Schweiker Is Wrong on Teen Pregnancy," *New York Times,* 15 February 1981, p. E19.

15. Zelnik and Kantner, in Furstenberg, p. 98; Melvin Zelnik and John F. Kantner, "Sexual Activity, Contraceptive Use and Pregnancy Among Metropolitan-Area Teenagers: 1971–1979," *Family Planning Perspectives* 12 (September/October 1980), Table 5 and p. 230; and Alan Guttmacher Institute, *Teenage Pregnancy: The Problem That Hasn't Gone Away* (New York, 1981), pp. 6–8, 17 and Figs. 1–2, 10.

16. This is, in essence, the argument of Easterlin in *Birth and Fortune.* He tends to apply a simplistic economism to the question of "illegitimacy" and, in the process, explains it entirely in terms of male motivations, male employment status, etc.: "[If times are bad] the young man, in particular, will question whether or not he can support a family." And, "some couples will break up because of the young man's inability or unwillingness to shoulder the burden of family responsibilities. The result will be illegitimate births that, had times been better, might have been legitimated" (pp. 90–91).

17. See Phillips Cutright, "Illegitimacy in the United States: 1920–1968," in *Demographic and Social Aspects of Population Growth,* ed. Charles F. Westoff and Robert Parke, Jr. (Washington, D.C.: Commission on Population Growth and the American Future, 1972), pp. 383–84.

18. Daniel Scott Smith and Michael S. Hindus, "Premarital Pregnancy in America, 1640–1971: An Overview and Interpretation," in *Marriage and Fertility,* ed. Robert I. Rotberg and Theodore K. Rabb (Princeton: Princeton, 1980), p. 343.

19. See Jane Menken, "The Health and Social Consequences of Teenage Childbearing," in Furstenberg, Lincoln, and Menken, pp. 167–83.

20. Willard Cates et al., "Mortality from Abortion and Childbirth: Are the Statistics Biased?" *Journal of the American Medical Association* 248 (9 July 1982): 192

96; Willard Cates, Jr., "Legal Abortion: The Public Health Record," *Science* 215 (26 March 1982): 1586–90; and Susan Harlap et al., "A Prospective Study of Spontaneous Fetal Losses after Induced Abortions," *New England Journal of Medicine* 301 (27 September 1979): 677–81. In 1978, 98 percent of all first-trimester abortions and 83 percent of all second-trimester abortions were performed using the suction method, which involves minimal risks of injury or subsequent infection.

21. A study of pregnant teenagers in Rhode Island in 1978 found that 56 percent of those "in the highest socioeconomic status areas" chose to get abortions, whereas 32 percent of these gave birth. In contrast, only 22 percent of "teenagers living in poverty areas" terminated their out-of-wedlock pregnancies in abortion, while 63 percent of these had live births. *Teenage Pregnancy: The Problem That Hasn't Gone Away* (New York: Alan Guttmacher Institute, 1981), p. 52 and Fig. 50.

This class difference remains. Nevertheless, what is politically significant is that it is among *white* teenagers, many of them middle class, that the *increase* in out-of-wedlock childbearing during the past decade has occurred.

22. Patricia Steinhoff, "Premarital Pregnancy and the First Birth," in *The First Child and Family Formation,* ed. Warren B. Miller and Lucille F. Newman (Chapel Hill, N.C.: Carolina Population Center, 1978), p. 199. Steinhoff hinges much of her analysis, however, on a rather stereotyped understanding of "working-class values" (e.g., "a passive orientation to life events") as opposed to "middle-class values" (e.g., "future-orientation" and an emphasis on "planning" one's life).

23. Jerome R. Evans, Georgiana Selstad, and Wayne H. Welcher, "Teenagers: Fertility Control Behavior and Attitudes Before and After Abortion, Childbearing, or Negative Pregnancy Test," in Furstenberg, Lincoln, and Menken, pp. 355–56 and Table 1.

24. Ibid., pp. 357–58 and Table 2.

25. See Baldwin, pp. 10–11. She cites a spokesperson from the Child Welfare League testifying before a congressional committee in 1975 that, prior to 1970, 80 percent of all illegitimate births among white young women had been placed for adoption; only five years later, 80 percent were being kept! See also Marie Hoeppner, "Where Have All the Children Gone? The Adoption Market Today," Rand Paper Series, No. P-5990 (Santa Monica, Calif.: Rand Corp., September 1977), pp. 6, 13; Kathleen Rudd Scharf, "Teenage Pregnancy: Why the Epidemic?" *Working Papers* 6 (March/April 1979): 64–70; and Helen L. Friedman, "Why Are They Keeping Their Babies?" *Social Work* 20 (July 1975): 322–23.

26. Calculated from Kristin A. Moore and Linda J. Waite, "Early Childbearing and Educational Attainment," *Family Planning Perspectives* 9 (September/October 1977): 220–25, Table 1.

27. Moore and Waite; Baldwin, pp. 26–27; and Harold Benenson, "The Theory of Class and Structural Developments in American Society: A Study of Occupational and Family Change, 1945–1970" (Ph.D. dissertation, New York University, 1980), pp. 166–69, 173–79.

28. Frank L. Mott and Nan L. Maxwell, "School-Age Mothers: 1968 and 1979," *Family Planning Perspectives* 13 (November/December 1981): 291.

29. Ibid., p. 289.

30. Wendy Baldwin cites a study indicating that the reasons unmarried first-time mothers gave for not wishing to marry the man who had fathered their child "reflected a thoughtful assessment of the roles of father and husband and

the conclusion that the man involved could not fulfill them. He may have been an alcoholic, a drug user, in jail, or irresponsible. Marrying him could have resulted in more problems than another solution to an untimely pregnancy" (p. 9).

31. Nadine Brozan, "Single Mothers Sharing a Difficult Time," *New York Times,* 14 May 1979, p. A16.

32. Mott and Maxwell, 1981, p. 289, Table 4. Cf. Moore and Waite, pp. 224–25, who found that "for black but not for white women, no educational advantage is derived from delaying the onset of motherhood beyond 18," mainly because extended family and community support systems and "accepting social attitudes" made possible the combination of early childbearing and continued schooling and work for black young women.

33. See U.S. Department of Health and Human Services, *Monthly Vital Statistics Report,* Annual Summary for the U.S., 1979, DHHS Publication No. (PHS) 81–1120 (Hyattsville, Md.: National Center for Health Statistics, 1980), Table 6.

34. See Joyce Ladner, *Tomorrow's Tomorrow: The Black Woman* (Garden City, N.Y.: Anchor, 1972), pp. 236–41.

35. The 7 percent decline in black adolescent childbearing out of wedlock between 1970 and 1978 had as a necessary condition the legalization and accessibility of abortion. See *Teenage Pregnancy: The Problem That Hasn't Gone Away,* p. 25 and Fig. 20.

36. U.S. Department of Commerce, Bureau of the Census, *A Statistical Portrait of Women in the United States: 1978,* Current Population Reports, Series P-23, No. 100 (Washington, D.C.: Government Printing Office, 1980), Tables 12-9, 12-10, 12-12. By 1978, virtually the same proportions of black women and white women 25–29 years of age had completed 4 years of high school and 1–3 years of college. Although a significant racial gap remained in this age cohort for college graduates, among those 20–24 years old in 1978 the difference between the percent of black women and the percent of white women who had graduated from college had shrunk from 9 percentage points to 5.

37. U.S. Department of Labor, Bureau of Labor Statistics, *Perspectives on Working Women: A Databook,* Bulletin 2080 (Washington, D.C.: Government Printing Office, 1980), Tables 74 and 76.

38. *A Statistical Portrait of Women in the United States: 1978,* Table 12-5.

39. *Perspectives on Working Women,* 1980, Table 67.

40. In her study of black women in a northeastern city who were first-generation college graduates, Elizabeth Higginbotham illustrates how class may structure the fertility experience of some black women differently from others. Higginbotham identifies her subjects as "part of an ever increasing population of younger, more highly educated black people" who have been completing high school and attending "traditionally predominantly white universities and colleges." Most of the women had completed advanced degrees or were pursuing graduate degrees in professional fields, or were working in highly skilled professional occupations. Their class backgrounds ranged from working class (6) to lower middle class (25) to middle class (25). While most were married or in "stable relationships" with a man, the married women nearly all continued to work after marriage and half of them remained childless. Higginbotham remarks the high rate of childlessness among the married women as well as the fact that only one woman among the 56 had had an out-of-wedlock child prior to coming to college. In

Higginbotham's judgment, most of them would have had an abortion rather than bear a child during the years of their education and establishing their careers. Elizabeth Higginbotham, "Educated Black Women: An Exploration into Life Chances and Choices" (Ph.D. dissertation, Brandeis University, 1980), and personal interview.

41. The absence of public discussion and organizing around abortion by black feminists has stemmed not only from certain black male leaders linking abortion to genocide and the feelings against abortion in the black community traditionally. It has also been the result of the inadequate and often racist relationship of the mainstream feminist movement to the needs of black women, as well as the focus of black women's organizations on other priorities.

42. Bebe Moore Campbell, "Abortion: The New Facts of Life," *Essence* 12 (September 1981): 129.

43. "Abortion: Women Speak Out," *Life* 4 (November 1981): 46–47. The poll was conducted by Yankelovich, Skelly, and White and based on a random national sample.

44. Barbara Ehrenreich and Karin Stallard, "The Nouveau Poor," *Ms.* 11 (August 1982): 217–24.

45. U.S. Department of Commerce, Bureau of the Census, *Household and Family Characteristics: March 1980,* Current Population Reports, Series P-20, No. 366 (September 1981), Table 5; and *Money Income and Poverty Status of Families and Persons in the United States: 1980,* Current Population Reports, Series P-60, No. 127 (August 1981), Table 21.

46. See the discussion in Chapter 3.

47. Daniel Callahan, *Abortion: Law, Choice and Morality* (New York: Macmillan, 1970), p. 137; and Lader, p. 22.

48. Callahan, p. 139.

49. Frederick Jaffe, Barbara L. Lindheim, and Philip R. Lee, *Abortion Politics: Private Morality and Public Policy* (New York: McGraw-Hill, 1981), p. 128; and *Safe and Legal: 10 Years' Experience with Legal Abortion in New York State* (New York: Alan Guttmacher Institute, 1980), p. 30.

50. Henshaw et al., Table 10; and Forrest, Tietze, and Sullivan, pp. 333, 340.

51. Cutright, pp. 400–493.

52. Cates, pp. 1586–87; and *Safe and Legal,* p. 23.

53. Jaffe, Lindheim, and Lee, p. 32.

54. Forrest, Tietze, and Sullivan, p. 279.

55. Ibid., pp. 276–79; and Barbara L. Lindheim, "Services, Policies and Costs in U.S. Abortion Facilities," *Family Planning Perspectives* 11 (September/October 1979): 283.

56. Lindheim, p. 289.

57. See Constance A. Nathanson and Marshall H. Becker, "The Influence of Physicians' Attitudes on Abortion Performance, Patient Management and Professional Fees," *Family Planning Perspectives* 9 (July/August, 1977): 158–63; and idem, "Obstetricians' Attitudes and Hospital Abortion Services," *Family Planning Perspectives* 12 (January/February 1980): 26–32.

58. Nathanson and Becker, 1977, p. 158.

59. Nathanson and Becker, 1980, pp. 26, 30–31.

60. Nathanson and Becker, 1977, pp. 161–62 and Tables 4-5. Jaffe, Lindheim, and Lee, p. 41n, estimate that "between 45 and 60 percent" of ob-gyns perform abortions.

61. Nathanson and Becker, 1977, p. 160.

62. Ibid., pp. 161–62.

63. See R. Petchesky, " 'Reproductive Choice' in the Contemporary United States: A Social Analysis of Female Sterilization," in *And the Poor Get Children: Radical Perspectives on Population Dynamics,* ed. Karen L. Michaelson (New York: Monthly Review Press, 1981), pp. 76–80; Helen Rodriguez-Trias, *Sterilization Abuse: The Women's Center Reid Lectureship* (New York: Barnard College, 1978); Ad Hoc Women's Studies Committee Against Sterilization Abuse, *Workbook on Sterilization and Sterilization Abuse* (Bronxville, N.Y.: Sarah Lawrence College, 1978); and pp. 178–182, below.

64. Richard C. Dicker et al., "Hysterectomy Among Women of Reproductive Age, Trends in the United States, 1970–1978," *Journal of the American Medical Association* 248 (16 July 1982): 323–27; and Ad Hoc Women's Studies Committee Against Sterilization Abuse, p. 17.

65. Willard Cates, "The Hyde Amendment in Action," *Journal of the American Medical Association* 10 (4 September 1981): 1109–12. Cates reports on a Center for Disease Control survey of the impact of the Hyde Amendment on low-income pregnant women between 1977 and 1980. The Hyde Amendment cut off federal Medicaid funding for nearly all abortions. In the first year of the amendment (1977), funding was allowed for abortions when pregnancy would result in severe danger to the woman's health or was the result of rape or incest. By 1980, however, federal Medicaid funds would pay for abortions only when the woman's life was in danger.

66. Campbell, p. 126.

67. ". . . the conservatives don't want women with insufficient funds—and that often means black women—to be in control of their bodies because that would put us in control of our lives. States will *still* pay for the births of unwanted children." Ibid., p. 87.

68. Evidence of coercive or overly zealous abortion practices in clinics servicing poor and Third World women comes from firsthand accounts by women who work in such clinics and have observed the "Medicaid mill," as well as from remarks by Pat Bellanger, representing Women of All Red Nations, as cited by Meredith Tax.

5

Considering the Alternatives: The Problems of Contraception

[Bertha] Barnes was on birth control pills, but gave them up because of high blood pressure. When she went to a Galveston clinic to be fitted for an intrauterine device, she was told that their schedule was full. When her contraceptive foam ran out, she did not have the $5 for a new supply. That is when she became pregnant.

STEVEN ROBERTS, *New York Times*

Abortion and contraception are not simply alternatives. They are, as family planning specialists tell us, complexly interrelated, even interdependent. After all, the main reason why women require abortions is because contraceptive methods fail—in many ways, not only the obvious ones. From the standpoint of a woman seeking to avoid pregnancy, a method "fails" when she errs in its use or the method is flawed or too expensive *and* when its risks or side effects, or its irreversibility, make its costs prohibitive to her. In the latter case the method fails because it does not meet her basic needs, which include the need to maintain her essential health and well-being and, perhaps, to keep her options about future childbearing open.

Physicians and family planners place priority on technical "efficacy" in evaluating contraceptive methods in a way that sometimes minimizes or denies women's concerns about their health and personal needs. At first glance, they would seem to have both the historical and public health records on their side. As we have seen, women have repeatedly chosen to risk their health, sometimes their lives, to achieve effective fertility control. Moreover, for women in certain age and socioeconomic groups or with specific health problems, carrying a pregnancy to term is no doubt more hazardous than taking the pill.[1] Nevertheless, the social context of the 1970s was one in which the idea of health as a basic right and the activism of feminist health advocates and Third World liberation groups transformed the discourse of reproductive rights politics. In part, this was possible because of the availability of abortion, which altered the basic terms of reproductive choice and risk. In the current framework, the "choice" between effectiveness and safety, or between effectiveness and future fertility, is no longer politically tolerable. At the same time, the tension in women's experience and in feminist thought between the desire for control and the desire to minimize, or socialize, risk remains. In the area of contraception, it is especially intense.

The Politics of Contraception

The questions, Why do there have to be so many abortions? Why don't more women use contraception? are wrongly put. Most women who seek abortion *are* contraceptive users; they have not "substituted" abortion for contraception. The increase in abortions and the increase in contraceptive use in the 1970s occurred simultaneously. Until a "perfect" method of contraception is developed, which will probably never happen, periods of heightened consciousness and extended practice of birth control will inevitably mean a rise in abortions. One jarring reminder of this interdependence is the fact that clinical studies of new contraceptive methods cannot proceed under conditions in which abortion is illegal (as in the 1950s and 1960s) or federal funding for abortion is curtailed (as now) because human subjects will not accept the risk of unwanted pregnancy without the availability of abortion as a backup.[2] Thus we have to expand our analysis of why abortion rates increased in the United States in the 1970s to include an important contributing factor: A uniquely effective, but not foolproof, method of contraception had been developed, distributed, and absorbed into popular practice on an unprecedented scale. What was the impact of the pill and the "pill culture" on rising abortion rates? To what extent did the reality and the "aura" of the pill—themselves the *product* at least as much as the cause of a growing demand—create changed expectations about reliable fertility control that helped also to legitimate abortion? On the other hand, to what extent did the pill's failure to meet these expectations directly increase the need for abortion?

Feminist demographer Susan Scrimshaw has argued that the pill, with all its flaws, acted as a kind of catalyst that helped change women's expectations to include the possibility and the right of reliable contraception: "It can be argued that even among women who discontinued or never initiated pill use, their heightened perception of the life alternatives open to them increased their motivation to use other contraceptive methods more effectively. This change in expectations has resulted in increased pressure from women for the development of a true contraceptive panacea."[3] Scrimshaw credits "the advent of the pill" with having produced a whole range of "new" social forces: women's greater sexual self-assertiveness, the increasing entrance of women into higher education and careers, the postponement and reduction of childbearing, an increased "honesty and joy in sex," and the development of aggressive feminist health networks. But the pill did not "cause" these changes, any more than the changes effected the "liberation" of most women. The case for the "contraceptive revolution" is reductionist; it ignores the fact that certain conditions and relationships created a pill "market" to begin with and that it was the *conjunction* of an effective new technology with other social conditions, such as an expanding job market for women, that led to changes in consciousness among women. As I suggested in Chapter 4, the evidence strongly supports the view that changing conditions of women (increased labor force participation, more schooling, delayed marriage) underlay their need for and consciousness about effective birth control. The successful marketing of the pill was a response to that need more than its "catalyst." (This interpretation is reinforced by the fact that the fertility decline started *before* the "pill era.")

But Scrimshaw reminds us that the pill, as a more effective method of reversible contraception than women had ever known, contributed to a climate of expectations that women need not and should not have to fear an unwanted pregnancy. Having a baby when you didn't want a baby became "unthinkable" for new generations of women, or for older generations at new stages in their lives. This changed consciousness undoubtedly contributed to the rise in abortions, for women who did not use the pill as well as those who did. It meant that if there were not more unwanted pregnancies, there were at any rate more women willing and prepared to do something about them. It meant that the shadow of fear and furtiveness, sometimes of danger and death, that had surrounded abortion for a hundred years would increasingly become an anachronism. The pill, as the apparent embodiment of "perfect" birth control, helped propagate that idea among women, to close up the margin of uncertainty and fatalism that had previously clouded fertility control.

That women wanted and expected unfailing fertility control as a normal part of life, however, does not mean that they wanted or expected serious health risks and side effects in return. In fact, the actual circumstances in which the pill was developed and commercially introduced reinforce the claims of feminist health activists that the needs of women, especially Third World women, were not foremost in the minds of oral contraceptive researchers. Gregory Pincus, the biochemist who along with John Rock developed the first commercially successfully oral contraceptive, tells us that in 1951 he was visited by Margaret Sanger, who impressed upon him the gravity of the "population explosion" and urged that he use his research knowledge to devise a "foolproof method" for use in "underdeveloped areas of the world." Thus, during the height of the U.S. "baby boom," the pill was conceived as an instrument of population control in the Third World. The sources of funding for research included major pharmaceutical companies as well as every major international population control institution (Planned Parenthood, Population Council, Pathfinder Fund, etc.).[4] And the populations among whom the initial clinical trials were conducted, using dosages and combinations now known to be extremely hazardous, were poor women in Haiti and Puerto Rico. The decision to manufacture a pill containing high dosages of estrogen was made in spite of the fact that clinical literature since the 1940s had linked estrogen to carcinogenesis. Moreover, case reports associating the pill with sometimes fatal thromboembolisms began to appear soon after the pill was marketed (1960); yet pharmaceutical companies, researchers, and physicians suppressed or downplayed this information until the press and the Congress made it public in the late 1960s.[5]

There is no denying that the health hazards of the pill are serious or that the history of the pill is sullied with racism, profiteering, and collusion among researchers and drug companies. But the tendency of some feminists to view the pill entirely as a male medical conspiracy seems unnecessarily crude. The self-interested motives of some physicians, the drug industry, or population controllers cannot explain the fact that by 1965 oral contraceptives had become the number-one method of fertility control in the United States any more than the existence of highly profitable, proprietary abortion clinics can explain women's growing demand for abortion. In a capitalist economy, it is hardly surprising that commercial interests attempt to exploit and expand any potential market. But the market is never conjured up out of the air; it exists in a social context of relationships and needs that are distinct from it even as they become shaped by it.[6] We have seen that, even when women have been aware of risks to their health and life, they have been willing to take those risks in order to assure their control over pregnancy; control, for most women, has historically taken priority over safety, and certainly over "sharing the responsibility." Where male partners are hostile to birth control or unwilling to take any responsibility, women may prefer the method (e.g., the pill or sterilization) that seems least conspicuous, surest, and least dependent on male cooperation. In middle- and working-class families where women are saddled with most of the responsibility for children as well as a job outside the home, this may be especially true. As a working-class wife put it in the 1950s:

He doesn't care how many times I get that way; he'd never do anything. The wife [should be responsible] because after the first pleasure the man has no more to do. It's the woman who carries the baby and goes through all the suffering at birth. He goes off to work or gets out of the house and that's all he cares about. He wouldn't use anything at all, he just lets fly.[7]

Similarly, in 1969, before knowledge of the pill's health hazards was widespread, black feminist Toni Cade (Bambara) challenged the view of the pill as genocidal, emphasizing its importance for black women as a means of self-control:

. . . I would never agree that the pill really liberates women. It only helps . . . the pill gives her choice, gives her control over at least some of the major events in her life. And it gives her time to fight for liberation in those other areas.

I find it criminal of people on the podium or in print or wherever to tell young girls not to go to clinics, or advise welfare ladies to go on producing, or to suggest to women with flabby skills and uncertain options but who are trying to get up off their knees that the pill is counterrevolutionary. It would be a greater service to us all to introduce them to the pill first, to focus on preparation of the self, rather than on abandonment of controls.[8]

An argument that emphasizes the burdensome and inequitable side of women's responsibility for contraception is made by Kristin Luker in her book *Taking Chances*. She asserts that the domination of the contraceptive field by the pill is the result of a "deliberate" clinical and research decision in the late 1950s to shift emphasis to "female-oriented methods" whose use would be removed from sexual intercourse. Before the pill, "virtually all contraceptives . . . were intercourse-related," meaning that they involved at least some degree of shared responsibility by men. The shift to "female methods" (the pill, IUD, and abortion) worked primarily to reinforce, through technology and clinical practice, the patriarchal ideology of women's exclusive responsibility for reproduction.[9] But Luker's liberal feminist ("egalitarian") analysis of the pill's advent and its impact suffers from technological determinism as well as romanticizing the past. It ignores the fact that some methods used "prior to the pill" were not "intercourse-related" (e.g., illegal abortion or sterilization) and that even those that were (e.g., the condom, abstinence, or withdrawal) may have been used *effectively* only when women asserted their own sense of need.[10]

In other words, the "male" or "female" responsibility involved in a fertility control method is not a question intrinsic to its technology or form but is determined by the social relations of its use. (The question of risks to health is another matter.) Above all, Luker's argument disregards women's desire and need for control, even if it means assuming *all* the risks. This no doubt includes even single young women who may also feel resentful that the pill signals their "availability" and seems to get men "off the hook."[11] That such women might prefer to hand over their responsibility—and risks—to men conveniently overlooks the fact that the women Luker inverviewed ended up, on their own steam, in an abortion clinic. It also glosses over the reality of "male responsibility" in the 1950s: women passively waiting for a man to "do something," to "pull out," or to wear a condom. Whatever the motives of the researchers, the pill met a ready and eager market. Finally, Luker's position ignores the feminist understanding that *pregnancy involves an irreducible biological dimension for which the experience, and therefore the responsibility, cannot totally be transferred.* "Control over our bodies" is more than a slogan.

Where reproductive risks are concerned, however, we are dealing with a contradictory reality. I have tried to underline the persistent desire of women in nearly all circumstances to maintain and maximize control over their reproductive lives. If the planning and application of fertility control methods are sometimes shared with male partners, the relentless fact that the *consequences* of an unwanted pregnancy fall more heavily on the woman has meant that she would often rather assume the risks herself than trust the man, whose stakes are different. Yet it is also true that institutional and clinical practices have intensified the exclusivity of women's burdens and reified the identification of reproduction as a female activity, for reasons that are historical rather than governed by biological necessity. With the exception of vasectomy, all the existing "medical" methods of contraception are geared toward females *because* females have been the traditional clientele of reproductive medicine since its inception in the nineteenth century. A "male pill," while technically possible, has never been developed for a number of telling reasons: (1) Much more is known about female reproductive biology than about male *because* women's bodies have historically been the objects of (male-dominated) clinical practice and research; (2) insufficient numbers of men volunteer for clinical trials in fertility control studies, for similar reasons of gender-defined tradition; (3) both researchers and male subjects are extremely concerned about the possibilities of "undesirable side effects" that chemical contraceptives could cause in men, especially the risk of impotence and a "loss of male libido."[12] Male researchers rarely express a similar concern for side effects and libidinal loss in women due to synthetic hormones, although they surely occur. One senses that where sex (as opposed to reproduction) is at issue, the male of the species is still regarded by a patriarchal culture and medicine as the delicate and vulnerable one.

If feminists remain distrustful of physicians' and family planners' assurances that lower-dosage pills are safe, except for women who are "predisposed" to risk (i.e., smokers, diabetics, or women with hypertension), it is because of a systematic history of careless experimentation with women's bodies and denial of our reality by medical professionals.[13] A striking example of the misogynistic values that shaped the original development of the pill can be found in Pincus' account of it. Contrary to everything that would be revealed four years later, Pincus in 1956 flatly dismissed the issue of mortality related to clotting disorders: ". . . there is no proof of any causal relation between thrombotic disease and the use of oral contraceptives . . . no evidence for a role of either estrogen or progestin in thromboembolism in women."[14] He glossed over the issue of carcinogenicity, saying the work had been too "exhaustive" even to summarize, and then attributed possible metabolic disorders, especially weight gain, to a "loss of anxiety about accidental pregnancy with consequent appetite improvement"![15] Noting women's frequent complaints of nausea, headache, and malaise related to pill use, he called them "reactions" (in quotes) and suggested a "suspected . . . *psychogenic basis,*" since the "reactions" are most severe in the earlier stages of pill use. To persuade us of the validity of this argument, he cited experiments done on Puerto Rican women *who were unknowingly given placebos instead of contraceptive pills!* He also mentioned, in passing, experiments done during the 1950s and 1960s in which synthetic hormones were administered to pregnant women with a history of miscarriage, resulting in "masculinizing effects on the female fetus"; to nursing mothers, who transmitted them through their milk; and even to "suppress menstruation in sexually precocious girls. . . ." At the same time, Pincus waxed ecstatic about the benefits of the pill in reducing menstrual flow and menstrual disorders, as well as causing "a definite improvement in sexual adjustment" in women.[16]

Misogynic and sexist attitudes among male clinicians and researchers, however, are less important in determining the oppressive features of contraceptive practice for women than are certain structural characteristics of today's contraceptive market. For if that market exists only because of women's socially determined need, if it is not the creature of a conspiracy, it is also true that a few powerful interests monopolize the fertility control "industry" and therefore subject it to distortions.

The consumer market in contraceptives is dominated by two methods: the pill, which involves serious health hazards; and sterilization, which, for women, involves major surgery and is irreversible. This extremely narrow range of choice reflects both the medicalization and the commercialization of birth control in the mid-twentieth century—two processes that are closely related. The proclivity of male-dominated U.S. medicine to "treat disease" rather than sustain health has had a particularly distorting impact on reproduction. Natural or daily maintenance processes such as childbirth, fertility control, and prenatal and infant care either are fitted into an inappropriate model of pathology—hence subjected to "heroic" interventions, surgery, or chemical regulation—or are disregarded altogether as "health needs" and as a result are denied reimbursement.[17] Procedures that most readily assume a commodity form in an advanced capitalist market (costly, rapidly consumed, or highly technologized) become "preferred" birth control methods. Indeed, untold millions of women throughout the world, who need an item for *daily* consumption over fifteen or twenty years of their lives, constitute an ideal consumer market, as the vast pharmaceutical industry is well aware.

It is the ordinary dynamics of the capitalist market that in some ways determine the narrowness of contraceptive choices. But it is also the nature of health-care institutions in our society as ones that are hierarchically organized and geared toward managerial models of control. The pill and the IUD in part function as means to connect women patients on a regular basis to the medical-care system, since they can be acquired only by prescription (this is true of the diaphragm as well) and must be periodically renewed or checked by a doctor. They require little time or instruction to be administered and thus may be rapidly processed, with little need for auxiliary services or counseling. Private doctors are notoriously unwilling (and also untrained) to take the time necessary to instruct teenagers or poor women in the use of a diaphragm or condom. Clinics, in addition to the predilections of their medical personnel, have other structural constraints that operate to reinforce "pill pushing." In particular, their dependence on federal reimbursements, which are tied to total numbers of cases processed, results in a relentless pressure on birth control counselors to process cases quickly and thus to recommend the method that is most time effective from a managerial point of view.[18] Thus, in both the private and the public sector, birth control patients become not simply users of a service but routinely integrated objects in a system of social intervention designed to control population.

The symbiosis between an increasingly hierarchical and elite medical profession and a multinational pharmaceutical industry is mirrored in the tendency of insurance companies to reimburse only those procedures that qualify as "medical" (i.e., that require a prescription, surgery, or hospitalization) and in the medical profession's increasing reliance for its profits on third-party payments. At the same time, as we saw earlier, birth control organizations in this country began in the 1920s and 1930s to look to the medical profession and to the imprimatur of medical procedures for their legitimation; they succeeded in forging this alliance by yielding both to medical control over procedures and to eugenicist ideas, convincing the (white upper-middle-class) clinicians that birth control was an expedient way to limit the numbers of the poor. Thus, the commoditization of birth control reflects the ideological perspectives and interests of a network of power centers that includes physicians, pharmaceutical companies, and family planning and population control agencies. Generally speaking, these groups share an acceptance of population control as a major political priority and family planning as a means to deal with poverty and social instability, a definition of "efficacy" in terms of control by physicians and technicians rather than the health and safety of users, and a preference for methods that are the most technologically sophisticated, the most cost effective, and therefore the most profitable and efficient. Hence the predominance of the so-called medically effective methods.

A vivid example of the alignment of interests around contraceptive politics is the recent struggle over the injectable synthetic hormone (progestin) known as Depo-Provera. Manufactured by the Upjohn Company and administered as a contraceptive to some 10 million women throughout the Third World and in Western Europe over the past decade,[19] Depo-Provera is a highly effective contraceptive that keeps women sterile for up to six months. It was banned by the FDA in 1978 for distribution as a contraceptive in the United States because of studies linking it to breast cancer in dogs and endometrial cancer in monkeys, and after evidence of congenital malformation of infants accidentally exposed to it *in utero.* Feminists in organizations like the National Women's Health Network and the feminist and socialist caucuses of the American Public Health Association (APHA) have fought strenuously against the unethical "dumping" of a product considered unsafe for North American women on millions of women in the Third World. (Manufacturers and suppliers get around the illegality of exporting a product banned for domestic sale by producing it through their foreign subsidiaries in Europe and Canada.) As with high-dosage oral contraceptives in the past, these women are essentially being used as guinea pigs, and the goals of population control, as usual, are being put before women's health.[19] Feminist opposition has confronted a solid wall of Depo-Provera supporters, who would like not only to expand its international sale but to lift the ban in the United States. The "pro-Depo" alliance consists of the Upjohn Company and its industrial allies; the International Planned Parenthood Federation (IPPF), which "is one of the largest international suppliers of Depo," and its research arm, the International Fertility Research Program (IFRP) in North Carolina; the U.S. Agency for International Development (AID), from whom IPPF gets most of its funds; and a substantial number of physicians and population researchers who have controlling voices in the APHA, the American College of Obstetricians and Gynecologists (ACOG), and the Population Association of America (PAA). These interests have parried criticisms of Depo-Provera by discrediting the animal studies as inconclusive, failing to conduct thorough clinical studies where evidence of the relation to cancer in women was available to them,[20] and arguing that the "benefits" of avoiding pregnancy in countries where fertility rates and maternal mortality are extremely high outweigh any long-range health risks the women may incur. The principle that a drug may be used indiscriminately on human beings until clinical trials prove it harmful is the opposite of that on which the FDA is supposedly founded: that no drug may be commercially sold until clinical trials have proven it safe. Applying the perverted principle to millions of nonwhite women sets up an imperialist double standard; it says, in effect, the risk of cancer matters less for these women than it does for North American women. Particular national and local conditions and levels of development do make a difference; in some countries, a poor woman's risk of dying in childbirth may be much higher than any risk of cancer she incurs from Depo-Provera, which may in fact diminish her maternal mortality risks. But the internationalization of reproductive rights struggles through the Depo-Provera issue can only strengthen women's position in the long run, since it applies to all women, whatever their economic or national identity, the standard that women's health cannot be traded off for "efficacy." To be saved from death in childbirth only to die from cervical or endometrial cancer is hardly an unmixed blessing of advanced technology; raising the issue forcefully puts manufacturers on notice that, as with oral contraceptive pills in the United States, they will be continually monitored by a politically conscious public concerned about health and safety standards.

Indeed, the seriousness with which the Depo-Provera alignment has had to meet its feminist critics, and its failure thus far to lift the ban in the United States, shows that the concentration of interests controlling the contraceptive market is not all-powerful. It has to accommodate the self-perceived needs and organized demands of women through a subtle process of negotiation and struggle. When we try to analyze why medical professionals and population experts favor one fertility control method over another at a given time, the reasons often have as much to do with strategies for securing control, political legitimacy, and the absence of vocal resistance to a method as with technological sophistication and profits. In this process, women have made real gains. The producers and purveyors of birth control commodities have had to contend with a new political consciousness, within this country and increasingly in the Third World as well, about not only the need for birth control but also its hazards. This consciousness has arisen since the late 1960s as the result of a growing consumer and feminist health movement on the one hand and the awareness in Third World communities of the threat of population control on the other.

Today women in all groups seek control over pregnancy, bolstered by a popular ethos that sees that control as a fundamental right. But they seek control that is compatible with their health and safety as well as their personal and ethnic autonomy. The "choice" between effectiveness and safety no longer seems reasonable or tolerable because that "choice," given the possibility of safe, early abortion, is *unnecessary*. What is clear is that it is not only the anticipated risks of mortality and morbidity associated with the pill that more and more women find unacceptable; it is also, and perhaps more often, the day-to-day experience of unpleasant side effects. At the same time, the health hazards of the pill may be viewed by a growing number of black, Native American, Puerto Rican, and Mexican-American women on a continuum with involuntary sterilization, toxic environments, and other conditions that diminish not only their reproductive capacity but also the length of their lives.

The Inadequacies of Contraception

Sterilization

By the late 1970s in the United States, surgical sterilization had become the most prevalent form of contraception among women over the age of twenty-five.[21] A good deal has been written about sterilization, and my purpose here is not to analyze it in depth but to understand the nature of its relationship to abortion. Common sense and a glance at the demography of sterilization suggest that that relationship should be remote. For surgical sterilization remains an irreversible method of fertility control that ends a woman's fertility permanently, whereas abortion is aimed at ending a given pregnancy. Procedures have been developed for reversing surgical sterilizations, but they are extremely expensive and difficult and have a very unreliable rate of success.[22] Its virtual irreversibility puts sterilization into a different category of fertility control from abortion or nonpermanent contraception. The great majority of women getting sterilized for contraceptive purposes are different from most women getting abortions. Women who seek sterilization are married at the time of being sterilized (87 percent), and their peak ages are around 30–34 (as opposed to 18–19 among women getting abortions).[23] They do not want or expect to have any more children (unless they have been sterilized involuntarily or have not been informed that the operation is irreversible). Since most of the women who get abortions are unmarried, have had no children, and are under twenty-five, one would assume that for them, sterilization is not an acceptable alternative to abortion.

Some family planners apparently do not agree. Hypothesizing a model of "rational" fertility control in which most women will use the pill or the IUD (the "medically preferred" methods) for several years, followed by one or two children spaced closely together, followed by sterilization, they regard sterilization as a reasonable alternative to abortion for women of *all* ages—those who have "had all the children they want" plus those who do not want any.[24] This view of "family planning rationality" is abstracted from reality. People change their minds, and have a right to change their minds, about childbearing; life circumstances change in ways one cannot always foresee. Studies of women who regret their sterilization, for example, have found that many chose this avenue to resolve a troubled marriage, later got divorced, and wished to have more children in a subsequent relationship.[25]

Moreover, while sterilization and abortion rates rose along a similar curve during the 1970s, and reflect a similarly complex weave of economic, medical, and social conditions, they are nonetheless clearly distinct phenomena. For one thing, the medical histories of sterilization and abortion are extremely different. Sterilization was always an alternative initiated through institutionalized medical means. Today it is an increasingly technical and complicated procedure, administered necessarily in a medical setting and requiring specialized surgical skill. Abortion was traditionally a procedure that remained in women's and lay practitioners' hands and only belatedly was incorporated—and then halfheartedly—into regular medical practice. Although technically defined as surgery, abortion in the early stages of pregnancy is a relatively simple procedure that could be performed adequately by trained nurse-midwives working under sanitary conditions with good hospital backup in case of complications. As explained in earlier chapters, the legalization of abortion grew out of a rising popular demand resisted by many in the medical profession; abortion providers are predominately freestanding clinics, not hospitals. The shift in sterilization trends and policies, however—from a cautious, restrictive policy twenty years ago to one of strong advocacy beginning in 1970—was largely *initiated* by physicians and family planners. This shift directly reflects adverse reports and women's own fears about the health hazards of the pill, particularly for older women, and the search by clinicians for a medically controlled substitute.[26] Thus, while they represent parallel trends, the recent increases in sterilization and abortion really grow out of different dynamics in the political dialectic of reproductive control.

An important part of the history of sterilization that sets it apart from abortion is the incidence of coercive sterilization and sterilization abuse among mainly poor, immigrant, and minority women in the United States. While instances of coercion or pressure on women to get an abortion surely occur, they have nothing of the systematic, state-sanctioned character of involuntary sterilization, as a look at public policy immediately makes clear. Legislative proposals to allow the involuntary sterilization of certain groups on eugenic grounds have a long history, linked to private upper-class organizations promoting "racial betterment and WASP purity."[27] Today sterilization programs are more subtle but nonetheless motivated by population control objectives aimed at particular groups—the "surplus" poor. A deliberate policy of manipulation if not coercion is involved when medical associations and family planning agencies advocate sterilization as a preferred form of birth control, particularly to low-income women and women of color, while withholding or minimizing information about other methods of fertility control. Such a policy is evident in the continued reimbursement by Medicaid, along with most commercial and employment-related health insurance, of 90 percent of the costs of contraceptive sterilization, while funds for abortions are cut off in most states.[28] Practices such as the failure to inform patients adequately, in their own language, that sterilization is irreversible; the failure to provide full information about nonpermanent alternatives (including abortion); the threat of withholding welfare or Medicaid benefits to a woman or her children if she refuses "consent" to sterilization; making permanent sterilization the condition of a voluntarily sought abortion (the notorious "package deal"); using hysterectomy—with its enormously increased risks and drastic consequences—as a form of sterilization; or sterilizing minors or the mentally incompetent are all forms of sterilization abuse prohibited by the 1978 Federal Sterilization Regulations.[29] Yet auditors' reports on federally funded sterilizations in a number of states suggest that such abuses continue in many hospitals that service the poor, largely because of the lack of effective government enforcement machinery.[30]

Nearly all of the documented or court-adjudicated instances of sterilization abuse during the 1970s involved women who were poor and either black, Mexican-American, Puerto Rican, or Native American, or women who were incarcerated or mentally incompetent. Neo-eugenic policies and abusive practices may have played a part in effecting class and race differences in sterilization rates. National survey data from 1975–76 indicate that low-income women and women with little education (high school or lower) have significantly higher rates of sterilization than their middle-class counterparts. Moreover, among low-income, black, and Hispanic groups, it is much more likely to be women rather than men who become sterilized, for reasons that have to do with ethnic culture and history as well as clinical practices; vasectomies occur primarily among white middle-class married men.[31] A recent report by researchers with the federal Health Care Financing Administration shows that female Medicaid recipients are between *two and four times more likely* (depending on geographical region) to be sterilized than are women not dependent on Medicaid; and nearly all Medicaid sterilizations are performed on women.[32]

Abortion rates too tend to be higher among Medicaid-dependent and minority women than among white middle-class women. How, then, can we argue that these differentials indicate women's self-determination in the one case and abuse or nonchoice in the other? Surely the higher *rates* of sterilization among poor women reflect some of the same social and economic constraints and class divisions within the medical care system that structure the abortion decision among poor women (who are disproportionately women of color). In both cases, the decision is more often than not the product of a conscious, rational determination by poor women to deal with the situation at hand, rather than of manipulations or lies by doctors. In some cases sterilization may be viewed by a woman as a definite relief, a solution to her birth control problems that eliminates fear of pregnancy and hassles with men.

Generally speaking, it is not the technology of a birth control method that makes it abusive or malevolent, but the social arrangements in which that technique is embedded—the degree to which those arrangements allow for the user's conscious participation and control and respond to her personal and biological needs. Sterilization or even hysterectomy may satisfy these criteria in particular cases, depending on the situation.[33] The same may be said for abortion. Yet, recognizing this, we also have to recognize that sterilization has been and remains distinct from abortion both in its historical uses and its practical consequences for women. In the case of sterilization, it is possible to imagine, as some demographers do, that logically, because the method is permanent, its use *always* connotes voluntary choice to terminate childbearing.[34] In reality, we have to deal with a well-documented history in which surgical sterilization has been imposed on women without their knowledge or consent, or without their understanding that the procedure was permanent. This has not occurred with abortion, at least not in the United States or Western Europe. Involuntary sterilization, not involuntary abortion, has been the nucleus of state-sponsored eugenic and neo-eugenic population control policies precisely because it is medically controlled and is permanent. It eliminates a potential "breeder," not just a potential child; and it does not have a long-standing tradition of popular practice behind it. From the point of view of a neo-eugenicist public policy the coincidence of antiabortion and prosterilization programs is not contradictory but rather class and race specific.

Given recurrent patterns of abuse and worsening economic conditions for poor women in the United States, it seems reasonable to expect that denial of abortion funding and further restriction of legal abortions will result in higher rates of sterilization among poor women; abortion cutbacks and sterilization abuse are in this sense "opposite sides of a coin."[35] Yet, at this writing—it may be too soon to predict what will happen—Medicaid-dependent women denied abortion funds do not seem to have turned to sterilization as an alternative.[36] Rather, they continue to seek abortions using any means they can. This indicates that sterilization is not an adequate substitute for abortion for most women, in most circumstances; its irreversibility entirely transforms the meaning of "costs" and "risks," putting not a pregnancy but a woman's whole reproductive capacity on the line. It also indicates that political struggles over sterilization abuse by feminists and Third World groups apparently have had an impact on women's consciousness.

Irreversibility is the major fact distinguishing sterilization from abortion, but the risks are different in other ways as well. The mortality, morbidity, and complication rates for tubal ligation are much higher than the rates for a first-trimester induced abortion. For a tubal ligation, the estimated annual mortality rate is 25–30 per 100,000 users, whereas that for a first-trimester abortion is 2.5–3.0 per 100,000.[37] Standard female sterilization operations involve hospitalization of up to a week and general anesthesia, which always increases surgical risk, whereas first-trimester abortions are done on an outpatient basis. Even the new outpatient methods of sterilization involving laparoscopy and hailed by population planners as easy and safe ("Band-Aid surgery") involve risks of ectopic pregnancies (which may be fatal to a woman), menstrual irregularities, and, in the case of electrocoagulation, "extraordinary" destruction of tissue and burns to the abdominal wall and bowel that have resulted in several deaths.[38] Even an older woman who wishes to have no more children might think twice about preferring sterilization to the combination of (nonchemical) contraception and abortion.

The Pill and the IUD

Because of their more than 98 percent reliability and their requirement of a physician's services to be obtained and used, oral contraceptives and IUDs (intrauterine devices) are known as "medically effective" methods.[39] Next to abortion and surgical sterilization, the method of fertility control used most frequently among American women since the mid-1960s has been the oral contraceptive pill. It is not my intention here to offer a detailed analysis of the health risks of the pill, since that is available elsewhere, but to examine how publicized evidence of those risks, as well as daily disturbances and side effects, have influenced women's pill use and increased their reliance on abortion.[40]

Before reviewing the risks, however, it is important to note that the health picture for women as a result of the pill is a mixed rather than an unredeemably negative one. Between 1955 and 1975, the proportion of reproductive deaths related to pregnancy and childbearing declined from 99 percent to 48 percent (not counting abortion-related deaths, which fell even more sharply), whereas by 1975 "complications of contraception" (mostly from the pill) had become the cause of 47 percent of reproductive deaths. Thus federal researchers have stated that "pregnancy prevention [in the U.S.] now causes about as many deaths as pregnancy itself."[41] But this 47 percent represented many fewer deaths than had occurred among previous generations of women from all pregnancy-related causes. That is, the pill accounts for relatively more deaths in a context of declining maternal mortality. Moreover, insofar as that decline is due to decreased childbearing, the pill is partly responsible for *saving* women's lives by curtailing pregnancies.

Evidence about the pill's sometimes fatal hazards to health, particularly in regard to cardiovascular and circulatory disease, was reported in 1969 in British medical journals and was rapidly transmitted to the American public through the press, Senate hearings (1970), and Barbara Seaman's widely read exposé, *The Doctors' Case Against the Pill*.[42] Since then, evidence of serious or fatal risks associated with oral contraceptives and estrogens generally, especially for women over thirty-five and those who smoke, has grown substantially and has come to include a long list of conditions extending beyond the original concern with thromboembolisms. Extended pill use has now been associated with myocardial infarction, metabolic disorders, liver tumors, gall bladder complications, and possibly breast and cervical cancers, particularly in women whose family histories make them more susceptible to these conditions.[43] These studies and the tireless efforts of feminist health advocates led the Food and Drug Administration (FDA) in 1977 to require the insertion by manufacturers of warning information in pill packages.

Attempting to salvage the pill's reputation in the wake of adverse publicity and a decline in pill use, researchers and family planners go to lengths to emphasize the importance of "synergistic effects" and "predisposing factors," especially age and smoking behavior, in determining levels of risk. Among such spokesmen, it is now the commonly accepted view that the pill may be contraindicated for women who smoke, women over thirty-five, and women who have personal or family histories of diabetes or hypertension. It has become standard clinical practice in many places not to prescribe the pill for such women.[44] Epidemiologists at the Centers for Disease Control in Atlanta, studying age-specific reproductive mortality for American women since 1955, found that the reproductive mortality rate had declined by 73 percent for women generally but only by 41 percent for women aged 35–44. This difference was "because of the relatively high mortality rate associated with oral contraceptive (OC) use in this age group" since 1960.[45] While recommending that reproductive deaths related to contraception be included in national surveillances of maternal mortality, these researchers nonetheless conclude that "for the vast majority of younger women who do not smoke the pill is very safe." Similarly, based on her survey of world literature on health risks to adolescents from contraceptive use, Dr. Adele Hoffman, testifying before the Senate Subcommittee on Aging, Family and Health Services, concluded that risks are "minimal." "Fifteen- to nineteen-year-olds, whether or not they smoke, are at the lowest risk" of any group of women using oral contraceptives, particularly with regard to strokes or clotting disorders (not a single case has been reported). While the incidence of cervical cancer has risen among sexually active adolescents and young adults, Dr. Hoffman does not believe there is sufficient evidence to associate this rise with pill use, as opposed to sexual frequency and multiple partners.[46]

There seems little doubt that the health hazards of pill use rise enormously for women in relation to age and smoking and that the risks for younger, nonsmoking women may for many be worth taking. It is also true that longitudinal studies of the pill's relation to cancer, especially among younger women using lower-dosage pills, remain unsatisfactory and inconclusive. But the ways in which researchers interpret existing mortality and morbidity data, if not the studies themselves, are open to serious question.[47] For one thing, the emphasis on compounded risks for smokers diverts attention from the disturbing fact that the risk of cardiovascular mortality for women who use the pill but *do not smoke* are three to five times greater than for women who do not use the pill.[48] Second, the wider range of diseases now associated with the pill suggests that "the cumulative absolute risk" of all of them may pose a greater overall danger to a woman's general health over time than any one factor taken singly.[49] Third, the argument that family planning analysts continually make on behalf of the pill—that, except for women smokers over forty, there are fewer risks associated with the pill than with pregnancy—is specious. It assumes that the alternative to pill or IUD use for most women is multiple pregnancies and births, ignoring the reality that most women in developed countries who go off (or never start) the pill end up using some combination of more traditional—and safer—methods and early abortion.[50] In fact, the most definitive conclusion that Christopher Tietze drew from his available data on birth-control-related mortality (shown in Figure 5-1) was not the "relative" safety of the pill, but *"the very low mortality combined with 100 percent effectiveness that can be obtained by use of the condom and diaphragm when these methods are backed up by early induced abortion."*[51]

Finally, the lack of conclusive evidence about a relationship between oral contraceptives and cancer, or other long-range risks to health for younger women, cuts two ways. At this point, we do not know as much as we need to know to make an informed judgment about such risks, particularly the "synergistic effects" that might be caused not only by smoking but by many other environmental agents, when combined with synthetic hormones. Yet, if the risks for pill users who are today in their teens and early twenties turn out to be small, that very fact owes a lot to the active struggle waged by feminists, who publicized the cancer link to estrogen during the 1970s and forced the companies to produce a lower-dosage and safer pill. Not until the mid-1970s did drug companies begin to manufacture pills with substantially lower doses and did reproductive researchers come up with the "knowledge" that lower-dosage

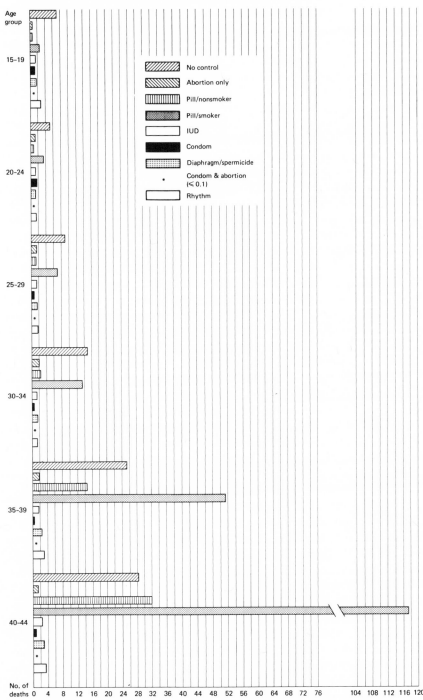

FIGURE 5-1. ANNUAL NUMBER OF DEATHS PER 100,00 WOMEN
ASSOCIATED WITH FERTILITY CONTROL METHODS.

SOURCE: Howard W. Ory, "Mortality Associated with Fertility and Fertility Control: 1983," *Family Planning Perspectives* 15 (March/April
1983).

pills were as "efficacious" as those high in estrogen. Like the important pill package inserts describing risks and side effects, this was obviously a response to the public outcry about pill hazards and shifted the ground of reproductive rights conflicts.[52] As with any technology, the science and the health impact of fertility control methods develop within and in reaction to politics.

How the data on mortality and health risks are used and transformed is thus an important part of the political arena in which doctors and family planners, feminist health advocates and women patients contend in their struggle to negotiate fertility control practices. In a political context dominated by right-wing attacks on abortion, the medical and family planning establishment would seem to be engaged in a campaign to allay women's doubts about the pill, partly to make an end run around the abortion issue. It is significant that in all the discussions of contraceptive hazards and benefits, abortion is rarely mentioned except to say how it may be avoided. A blatant example is an article by Charles Westoff and others that estimates the number of "preventable" abortions based on the hypothetical assumption that all contraceptive users rely on the pill, the IUD, or surgical sterilization.[53] The article is a piece of wishful thinking that totally ignores the practical reasons why many women do *not* see these methods as reasonable alternatives to abortion; the problems of the methods themselves make continued reliance on abortion a necessity.

My argument here is not that abortion is "safer" than the pill or IUD, although since suction methods have replaced sharp curretage for first- (and early second-) trimester abortions, the health dangers of abortion are mainly social and political (the causes of delay or poor sanitary conditions) rather than method related.[54] If we look at mortality alone, as presented in Figure 5-1, early abortion and the pill for women under thirty who do not smoke appear to involve similar levels of risk. But women stop taking the pill not only because of fears about severe or fatal health risks but also because of less dangerous but bothersome side effects that doctors and family planners tend to dismiss or trivialize. That pill use has declined among certain groups of American women since the early 1970s seems clear. Almost as soon as the pill became "number one" among contraceptives, a significant rise in the pill "drop-out" phenomenon occurred. As the House Select Committee on Population reported in 1978, "potential health hazards associated with the most highly effective contraceptives—the pills and IUDs—have discouraged increasing numbers of adult women and adolescents from using them."[55] A substantial part of the decline among older married women is accounted for by the rise in surgical sterilization; for women over thirty who do not wish to have more children, the serious hazards and side effects of the pill may make sterilization seem a "medically necessary" or "medically advisable" alternative.[56] But younger women too have participated in the pill "drop-out" in substantial numbers. Among American adolescents "use of the pill and IUD declined by 41 percent [between 1976 and 1979], while use of withdrawal and rhythm rose by 86 percent. In 1976, the three most popular methods [among teenagers] were condom, pill and withdrawal, in that order; in 1979 they were withdrawal, condom and the pill."[57] This "flight from the pill" occurred among both white and black teenagers, but was much sharper among whites (a 46 percent decline as compared with 21 percent among blacks). This difference may reflect the greater susceptibility of white teenagers to popular media, the trend toward "naturalness" ("it's no good to put drugs into your body"[58]), and generalized fears of cancer. It is also likely that some of the decline, among all teenagers, is due to misinformation and rumors about the pill, which may feed into an already present ambivalence about using contraception regularly. At the same time, attributing the pill "drop-out" to a media-concocted scare is a way of discrediting the judgment of women and of distorting facts.

In fact, the pill "drop-out" represents not so much an absolute decline in users as a pattern in which a persistently large number of users goes on the pill for a few years and then discontinues its use. What is rarely noticed is that this pattern has existed almost from the beginning of the "pill era" and belies the notion that pill discontinuation is mainly the result of feminist or Black Power propaganda, or scare tactics by the media. Feminists who see women pill users as simply the victims of the male-dominated medical profession and drug companies have their counterpart in family planners and population-oriented physicians who see pill "drop-outs" as simply the dupes of the press. Since clinicians emphasize "efficacy" above all other measures in their evaluation of fertility control methods, they are likely to see deliberate cessation of an "efficacious" method by a woman who is not seeking to become pregnant as irrational or manipulated—a psychological rather than a social problem. A recent article in *Family Planning Perspectives,* for example, attempts to assess "the influence of the media" on pill and IUD discontinuation between 1970 and 1975, through a series of graphs that rather mechanically correlate "peaks" in discontinuation with prime media events (e.g., Nelson committee hearings, FDA warnings).[59] In the same article, however, these authors present findings from the 1975 National Fertility Survey indicating that the overwhelming reason women give for their termination of the pill is not "worry about reports of danger to health," but "experienced physical problems."[60] The tacit implication is that these physical problems must be imagined, the product of women's suggestibility to media influence.

But there is ample evidence that they are not imagined, that while many women (and men) are justifiably worried about the long-range health risks of oral contraceptives (by 1977 only 29 percent of men and

25 percent of women still believed the pill to be safe), the reason why they stop taking the pill has to do with the day-to-day, immediate discomforts the pill causes them. These include weight gain, depression, diminished sexual response, headaches, nausea, and recurrent vaginal infections. One basis for this conclusion is the fact that the pill "drop-out" as a major trend (an over 40 percent discontinuation rate) began in 1967, three years *before* the "media barrage" publicizing the pill's hazards, and continued to rise steadily thereafter.[61] No matter what year women began using the pill throughout the 1960s, the probability of dropping the pill rose sharply after one year and still more sharply after the second and third year of use. The reason given for discontinuation by between two-thirds and three-fourths of every age and racial group in 1970 was, again, "personally experienced physical problems."[62] More recent studies confirm these findings.[63] The flurry of recent articles in family planning journals that try to reassure women about the pill, however, focuses exclusively on mortality issues; the side effects and less-than-fatal health risks that constitute the basis for most women's discontinuation are regarded as psychosomatic or negligible.

In the case of the IUD, it has been much harder to ignore the experience of unpleasant side effects because they are so pervasive and pronounced. Women who have IUDs inserted continue to be plagued by problems such as vaginal bleeding, cramps, heavy periods, and expulsion of the device, which account for high rates of discontinuation.[64] Although "these local symptoms have been generally considered innocuous and a common accompaniment of IUD usage"[65] by clinicians and researchers, for most women there is nothing "innocuous" about such symptoms, and one avoids them if possible. It is thus not surprising that only 6 percent of all American women and 2 percent of teenagers use the IUD as their method of contraception.[66] Much more serious is the association of IUD use with ectopic pregnancies or pregnancies resulting in septic trimester abortions that have led to women's deaths. Above all, there is now conclusive evidence that women who use IUDs, particularly if they are young and have multiple sexual partners, run a three to four times greater risk of developing pelvic inflammatory disease (PID)—an infectious, sexually transmittable disease that often leads to tubal inflammations, damage to organs in the pelvic area, and infertility.[67] This is the most dangerous health complication for teenagers from any form of contraception.[68]

Abortion and Contraception—The Necessary Link

The standards that pit "efficacy" against women's health and well-being are at odds with feminist standards of reproductive freedom as they evolved in the 1970s. Both the contraceptive practices of women, as embodied in their increasing caution about the pill, and feminist ideology, as articulated by the women's health movement, reject the notion that women must sacrifice their physical health, a necessary condition of their liberation, to access to reliable fertility control. In part, this view takes the form of a demand that society, particularly its highly politicized medical research structures, place an immediate priority on developing a genuinely safe and effective method of contraception. Family planners now tend to dismiss this demand as utopian (a "panacea"), but women are understandably dismayed by the failure of modern science to conquer reproductive biology, while space travel and weapons of global destruction have long been routine. Short of a "technological fix," however, the insistence on *both* reliability and safety grows out of the material conditions of fertility control that already exist, even though their potential is limited by current political forces. For we *have* a 100 percent effective and reasonably safe form of birth control: the diaphragm or condom (and now a new vaginal sponge) backed up by early legal abortion.

I do not believe women are "substituting" abortion for contraception, but I do believe they are less and less willing to trade off their health and physical well-being for technical reliability. As Marx pointed out, the standard of human needs is determined not only by technology but by a "historical and moral element" reflected in social consciousness. The need for abortion grows, not only as further medical complications of the pill and the IUD are "discovered," but also as women's consciousness changes about the level of risk or discomfort that *ought* to be tolerated. If this is "hedonism," this concern with personal health and safety, it is surely the kind that Herbert Marcuse talked about as a necessary precondition to the development of social and sensual human beings. We can understand the pill "drop-out" and the rise in abortions as a historically particular form of resistance to the idea that it is "woman's nature" to suffer.

Can still better contraceptive technologies be expected to relieve the necessity of abortion? In a sensible and sobering article, Malcolm Potts and Robert Wheeler demonstrate convincingly that within the context of existing biomedical research the quest for perfect fertility control in one package (a "magic bullet") is fraught with dangers for women's bodies. There tends to be an "inverse association" between technical effectiveness (measured in pregnancy rates) and dangerous or troubling side effects: "In the case of oral contraceptives, the higher the dose and the more extensive the systemic effects, the greater the effectiveness and also the greater the probability of problems among users."[69] This dilemma extends to most experimental techniques. Nearly every "revolutionary" contraceptive method now on the drawing board—chemical methods of female sterilization, injectables, female and male analogs of hormone-releasing hormones (LHRH); prostaglandins to induce menses—involves the use of chemicals that may carry as much risk to health as currently used contraceptives.[70] Experiments with newer methods of tubal sterilization, such as plastic clips and silicone plugs, seem to promise a safer approach to fertility control and reversibility, since little damage is done to the Fallopian tubes; but these methods are still regarded as virtually permanent by researchers and have failed to work in 10 to 15 percent of the women tested.[71]

More important, women using the supposedly most effective methods of nonpermanent contraception now available may have *greater* likelihood of needing an abortion at some time than women who use less effective methods because of the pill's and the IUD's side effects and the consequent discontinuation rate. Using computer simulation techniques, Potts and Wheeler calculate that fewer conceptions will occur with "use of a traditional or simple method with a good continuation rate" than among pill and IUD users, who have a lower continuation rate.[72] As I argued initially, the "contraceptive revolution," especially the pill, has increased rather than decreased women's need for access to abortion. This is true because of two interacting developments: the widespread availability of the pill and legal abortion, reinforcing women's awareness of fertility control as their right; and a newer political consciousness that refuses to accept risks to reproductive health as fate's decree. The current status of contraceptive techniques underlines more than ever that as long as it remains possible for a woman to become pregnant without wanting to be, abortion will be a necessity and its denial a punishment of women—for having sex.

That rising abortions and increased contraceptive use are related trends contradicts the widely held impression that many women are substituting abortion for contraception. Among teenagers, a high proportion use some method of contraception prior to a pregnancy, and 7 out of 10 become regular contraceptive users after a first pregnancy.[73] For some teenagers, an abortion becomes a *rite de passage* toward regular contraceptive use; the great majority of abortions in any given year are first-timers rather than "repeats." This is not to deny that some young, mainly poor teenagers continue to get pregnant after one or two abortions. But most of them have no intention of getting pregnant; they do so because contraception fails or because they are ignorant of reproductive processes. Even if they are "between" methods because of having "dropped out" of pill or IUD use, they do not usually "consider abortion either a primary or a backup method of birth control—indeed not a method of birth control at all."[74]

Something more general needs to be said here about the politics of "taking risks." The need to balance the dangers of individualism (exposure to exploitation or unfair risk) against the dangers of protection (invasion of privacy, paternalism, exclusion) is a favorite subject of philosophical and public health discourse.[75] For feminists, however, it is not an academic conflict but one that lives and breathes in the history of the movement and of the treatment of women by those who exercise power. Historically, it comes up most bitterly in the split between feminists who supported the Equal Rights Amendment and women trade unionists who feared it would abolish hard-won protective legislation in employment. But it has resurfaced from time to time around issues related to sexuality—prostitution, rape, pornography—where one group of feminists fought to expose and regulate the dangers to women in the trafficking and exploitation of their bodies, their need for "protection," while others foresaw the dangers of protection, its tendency to be used as a pretext for denying women their capacity to be sexual, to work, or even to walk on the street.[76] And, of course, both groups have been right, as we have learned recurrently in the case of "protective legislation" when its presence has been used as an exclusionary device to keep women out of male occupational strongholds, whereas its absence has left women vulnerable to economic and sexual abuse. Neither individualism—formulated as the "right to privacy" in liberal constitutional tradition—nor paternalism has ever provided adequate solutions to women's collective oppression.

In reproductive politics, the tension between individual choice, which involves individual risk taking and responsibility, and protection from abuse, which may involve the socialization of responsibility and perhaps surveillance or suppression of choice, takes specific and sometimes dramatic forms. Feminists have confronted the contradictions implicit in the liberal rhetoric used to defend "reproductive choice" as it gets thrown back at them by the very power structures that oppose feminist goals. As in the history of women's employment, we find the ideas of individual freedom and consumer choice brandished by drug companies and the medical establishment in their rigid opposition to government regulation of oral and injectable contraceptives and of sterilization abuse.[77] Meanwhile, employers such as chemical corporations invoke the benevolent "protection" principle as a reason to screen pregnant women, or all women, out of jobs that carry reproductive hazards—or to require them to be sterilized. The Reagan administration and the New Right likewise claim to be "protecting" teenage women from "health hazards" by imposing a federal requirement that their parents be notified every time they seek birth control services.[78]

It is obvious that these uses of "individual freedom" and "protection from abuse" are rhetorical and specious. Drug companies and doctors, in the tradition of all capitalist defenders of "free market" principles, seek to expand their freedom to do business and make a profit, rather than the freedom of individual women to avoid "red tape." American Cyanamid and other corporations seek to protect themselves, not women workers, from lawsuits in behalf of damaged fetuses or liability for cleaner workplaces.[79] And if the Reagan administration and Jeremiah Denton seek to "protect" teenage girls, it is not their health they are worried about but their virginity. Still, while feminists recognize and continually need to expose the distorted and self-serving uses of "reproductive freedom" ideology by those who oppose it, this does not resolve the dilemmas inherent in the ideas.

On one level, reproductive freedom must involve an element of socially determined need, which implies common standards and general principles that are socially enforced. There is a degree of risk that is intolerable for anyone, certain products that ought not to be sold, a standard of health and well-being that the society ought to expect for all its members whether they consciously seek it or not. On the other hand, needs are particular to ages, occupations, genders, conditions of health, and a whole range of circumstances. The medical risks a woman runs from taking birth control pills are affected to an important degree by her age, the state of her health, and whether she smokes.[80] For some younger women, the pill may be the best birth control option now available, the one that gives them the most possibility for sexual self-determination *and* good health.[81]

While I do not think the tension between individual control and social protection will ever be totally resolved, there is a helpful conceptual process for bringing them more closely together. This involves establishing the *necessary preconditions* for individual control or consent within the immediate social context. The Federal Sterilization Regulations exemplify public policy, drafted by feminists and health activists, that embodies this notion of preconditions, including the more familiar "right to know" (full disclosure, orally and in writing, of all risks, consequences, and alternatives) and prohibiting a range of contextual situations that would effectively eliminate choice. The threat, real or imagined, that one's livelihood— welfare or medical benefits, or one's job—may be lost as a penalty for refusing sterilization diminishes choice, no matter how thorough one's knowledge of the risks. In an analogous way, as long as the contraceptive alternatives available to women (or men) involve irreversible sterility, an irreducible element of risk to health, or an indeterminate risk of error, the availability of cheap, legal, and safe abortion is a necessary precondition for any of those methods to be a real choice. *Without* safe, legal abortion as a backup, being "free" to decide against the pill or sterilization is like being "free" to lose your job to avert sterility or miscarriage. One is not choosing to take risks if there is no viable alternative.

The Failure of Institutional "Delivery Systems"

Not only the quality or safety of the prevailing contraceptive methods is problematic but also the institutional contexts through which these methods are administered. What we might call the social relations of the clinic, as they apply to reproductive health care, directly affect women's contraceptive use in ways that in some instances impede rather than facilitate contraceptive effectiveness. This is particularly true for teenagers, with whose special needs gynecological practice and clinical bureaucratism are sometimes out of touch.

Physicians and clinics function as "gatekeepers" to accurate knowledge and assurance about contraceptive alternatives for teenage girls,[82] and their authority (to prescribe or withhold) can sometimes have a negative influence on contraceptive use. What this has meant for teenage patterns of contraception is a pervasive tendency toward pill use and then discontinuation that may result from the procedures of doctors and family planning clinics as the sole sources of birth control information and services. Zelnik and Kantner document the "massive shift to oral contraception" that occurred among U.S. teenagers in the 1971–76 period, which coincided with the doubling of federal funds for family planning services. While private physicians are still the providers of birth control for the majority of white teenagers, 58 percent of black teenagers and 44 percent of white teenagers are serviced by organized clinics.[83] It is interesting to compare patterns of contraceptive use among teenage clinic patients with those among the teenage population as a whole, including those who rely on "drugstore methods." While the pill is the most frequently used method among teenagers who use contraception, there would appear to be a large difference in its frequency depending on where birth control is obtained. According to a National Center for Health Statistics survey of visits to family planning clinics, 77 percent of teenage clinic patients in 1978 became or were pill users.[84] In contrast, Zelnik and Kantner's survey of teenage contraceptive use in metropolitan areas, which includes teenagers who have never visited clinics or gynecologists as well as those who have, indicates a 46 percent decline between 1976 and 1979 in pill and IUD use among white teenagers, who have a total rate of pill use that is only 38 percent, compared with 51 percent among black teenagers.[85] Black teenagers, who rely on family planning clinics in significantly higher proportions than whites do, have a 40 percent greater likelihood than whites (in the 15–17 age group) of using the pill and are twice as likely to use the pill at first intercourse.[86]

The ironic thing about this institutionalized reliance on the pill is that, rather than result in more effective contraception among teenage women, it may result in less. This is so because when women stop taking the pill, as they frequently do because of unpleasant side effects or because of doctors' recommendations, no viable alternative is presented or seems acceptable. With regard to private physicians as birth control dispensers, studies have documented a pattern of systemic "M.D. mismanagement" of young women's contraception: recommending the pill and the IUD virtually to the exclusion of other methods; prescribing the pill as a means of "regulating" women's menstrual periods without sufficient discussion of birth control; and periodically taking patients off the pill, or removing their IUD, because of clinical contraindications or just "for a rest," without providing information or advice about contraceptive alternatives. The failure of physicians to counsel patients thoroughly about safer alternatives to the pill may be even greater than usual among teenage women, poor women, and non-English-speaking women, whom doctors tend to regard as incompetent to handle such methods as the diaphragm.[87] Another researcher quotes a number of subjects whose pregnancies resulted from having been told by their doctors they should "go off" the pill periodically, or having experienced nausea or depression or other symptoms that discouraged continuation and not having succeeded in finding an acceptable alternative. One woman reported: "I went and got a regular gynecologist— you know, here in town—and he told me that you are supposed to go off your pills every two years and some doctors say every four years, because, I guess, you become sterile. That's what he made it sound like— you would become sterile if you didn't go off of them. So, I went off of them for three months and that's when I got pregnant."[88]

Having surveyed this pattern of misinformation and neglect among one hundred repeat abortion patients at his clinic in Nassau County in 1974–75, Dr. Joel Robins concluded that their contraceptive failures were mainly due not to "reliance on abortion as a substitute for contraception" but to "inadequate or inaccurate advice" from their doctors. He recommended, among other things, that physicians be educated about how to provide contraceptive and reproductive information to young patients, that "nonprescription methods of contraception" be made "widely and easily available," and that "paraprofessional counselors" substitute for physicians or other medical personnel whose "lack of interest or time" so impedes their ability to deliver birth control services adequately.[89]

It is not only misinformation that results in contraceptive failure but also the intricate social processes through which bits of information about reproductive biology and birth control techniques are perceived and either absorbed or shelved away. It comes closer to the truth to say that "although sex is a social act, contraception is rarely thought of as a set of social skills. Thus, teenagers learn about the pill or the condom, but they do not learn how to apply this knowledge in social situations"[90] or how to connect the technique with the experience (real or fantasied) that the social situation conjures up. The question for feminists is not simply whether physicians or clinic personnel "manage" women's reproductive lives poorly or adequately; rather, it is whether or under what conditions "management" by professionals allows young women, and men, to know what they need to know to make their way through the thicket of sex and reproduction.

The very notion of family planning is obviously inappropriate to the sexual and contraceptive needs of young unmarried people, who are not "planning families" but negotiating relationships and/or sexual adventures (including the *separation* from family). Moreover, the atmosphere and professional/bureaucratic procedures of the clinic or the "sex education" classroom may have the effect of containing birth control within a sterile discourse on "sex hygiene" and medical problems that severs it from its real connections, especially for teenagers, with sexuality as it is constructed for *them*—a sexuality formed out of relationships, love, and danger. From a feminist perspective, the separation of birth control from sex may inhibit knowledge that is useful, that connects the experience of the body to feelings and to sensual social life. Birth control as a knowing and effective "social act" thus requires a basic transformation of the modes through which knowledge is transmitted; the understanding and choosing of techniques have to be integrated with discussions of gender relations and heterosexual experience in the concrete world. In fact, the feminist health movement began during the 1970s to make such a transformation, to transcend the isolation of birth control *techniques* from sexual and social experience.

At first glance, it would seem that nearly every available technique is ill suited to the sexual and contraceptive conditions of young teenagers. The pill, the most widely promoted method, seems to imply that sex has become part of one's daily life, like brushing your teeth, and it requires frequent contact with physicians, who may not be sympathetic or sensitive. In addition, we still do not have adequate long-term clinical studies to show conclusively that the pill is *not* hazardous for younger women if taken over a number of years. The problems of the IUD (bleeding, pain, expulsion, PID) make it intolerable for most teenagers. The condom and withdrawal rely centrally on male cooperation, which is even less likely from men who are young and uncommitted; and the diaphragm implies an ease of communication with male partners and a comfort with one's own body that may be in direct opposition to the tentativeness and sense of mystery and change that characterize the adolescent girl's body image. Also, many women (of all ages) dislike the diaphragm because they find it "messy" and unromantic. Only about 4 percent of U.S. teenagers who use contraception use a diaphragm.[91]

Earlier, however, I argued against this focus on techniques as misplaced, as a technological determinism that disregards the underlying social relations that give birth control methods a particular function and context. The association of the pill not only with heterosexual activity but with sexual availability is a cultural artifact, not a pharmaceutical given. Moreover, it is the endemic social relations of the clinic in an age- and gender-stratified society, and particularly the relationship between male gynecologists and adolescent girls, that makes the procedures surrounding "medical methods" (apart from their health risks) an onerous experience. Those relations are not intrinsic to the methods or to any technical form. Similarly, how young women understand and relate to their bodies is a social question, subject to radical change, as the impact of feminist ideas and practices about birth control and sexuality during the 1970s began to show.

Our Bodies, Ourselves represents a radical transformation of traditional modes of "knowing" about the intimate realms of women's reproductive and sexual life. Reduced to its essentials, the feminist way of knowing places technical information (medical, method related, resource oriented) in the context of personal and bodily experiences of women as they are lived and reexamined in the social frameworks of gender, class, and hetero- or homosexuality. The body is "reorganized" within its social situation; women are given access to what they need to know, to gain control over their fertility and sexuality, through what they already know (e.g., about what relations with boys and men have been like).[92] This is a way of knowing, a discourse, that has become accessible to millions of young women, not only through a popular book, but also through a network of feminist self-help clinics in cities where feminist organization is strong; and, probably most important, through the penetration of the clinics by feminist ideas and personnel. Symptomatic of this influence are modes of counseling and group discussion that reveal a feminist commitment to simultaneously assuring women's health, maximizing their control, and expanding their consciousness about their conditions as women.

One example of this process occurred in an established, mainstream clinical setting. It illustrates that a safe and highly effective method such as the diaphragm can be accommodated to the sexual patterns and needs of most women in a learning context where openness about sexuality, collectivity rather than isolation, and careful instruction and counseling are emphasized. In the early 1970s, with feminist consciousness and concern about the pill in full swing, researchers at the Margaret Sanger Research Bureau in New York studied a group of more than two thousand mostly unmarried women, around 10 percent of them teenagers and 10 percent nonwhite, who became diaphragm users through the bureau's program. Most of the women were high school graduates or attending high school, and "some 28 percent were either low- or marginal-income women. . . ." These women were counseled fully, in a group discussion led by a nurse, about all available methods of contraception and their "advantages and disadvantages." They were instructed precisely in the use of the diaphragm, their own anatomy, self-examination, and every precaution necessary to maximize the diaphragm's effectiveness and ease. Most of this occurred in a group setting. The results were an overall continuation rate, over a period of twelve months, of around 84 percent.[93]

In the youngest group, aged 13–17, only two pregnancies occurred—the lowest number for any age group—and only 25 percent of the women (44 out of 175) discontinued the method, for "personal reasons," during the two-year period of observation. The authors of the study attribute this success to the thorough counseling, "which bolstered the patient's self-confidence," and "the participation of personnel who believed in the method and who possessed the skill and patience to teach it. . . ."[94]

If the methods of contraception inherently discourage effective teenage use, then one would be hard pressed to explain why a steadily growing *majority* of teenagers who engage in sexual intercourse use contraception successfully and avoid unwanted pregnancy. The development of a "new and imaginative approach" to contraception designed for teenagers (e.g., a "morning-after" device that can be easily hidden from parents, doesn't rely on men, and doesn't require a prescription) would not transform the social relations and cultural mixed messages that impede some women from using contraception.[95] We need to account for the fact that, especially among very young women, the rise in abortions sometimes results from using no contraception of any sort, safe or unsafe. At the same time, we need to understand that problem as basically rooted in social, sexual, and political arrangements, not moral or technological failure; to see technological failure as growing out of the politics of sexuality and reproduction. But even after those arrangements are transformed in ways we have not yet begun to imagine, abortion will remain necessary for women. For "perfect" contraception—that defies human error, unforeseen circumstances, or medical risk—is an illusion.

NOTES

1. See Christopher Tietze, "New Estimates of Mortality Associated with Fertility Control," *Family Planning Perspectives* 9 (March/April 1977): 74–76; and Howard W. Ory, Allan Rosenfield and Lynn C. Landman, "The Pill at 20: An Assessment," *Family Planning Perspectives* 12 (November/December 1980): 278–83.

2. Carl Djerassi, *The Politics of Contraception* (New York: Norton, 1979), pp. 77–78. In the days when abortion was illegal, most U.S.-based research on chemical contraception was conducted in Third World countries. This was not only because Third World women were preferred as "guinea pigs" but also because abortions in their countries could be obtained more easily.

3. Susan Scrimshaw, "Women and the Pill: From Panacea to Catalyst," *Family Planning Perspectives* 13 (November/December 1981): 260.

4. Gregory Pincus, *The Control of Fertility* (New York: Academic Press, 1965), pp. xii–xiii, 5–6.

5. Barbara Seaman and Gideon Seaman, *Women and the Crisis in Sex Hormones* (New York: Bantam, 1977), pp. 80–86.

6. Compare my account of the complex conditions responsible for the rise of surgical sterilization in the 1970s, " 'Reproductive Choice' in the Contemporary United States," in Michaelson, as well as the arguments by L. Gordon, *Woman's Body, Woman's Right*, pp. 317–19; Himes, *Medical History of Contraception*, pp. 326–30; and McLaren, *Birth Control in Nineteenth Century England*, pp. 221–22, 232ff., showing that the commercialization of a birth control industry in the 1930s was likewise a response to popular demand.

7. Lee Rainwater, *And the Poor Get Children* (Chicago: Quadrangle, 1974), p. 127.

8. Toni Cade (Bambara), "The Pill: Genocide or Liberation," in *The Black Woman*, ed. Toni Cade (New York: New American Library, 1970), p. 168.

9. Kristin Luker, *Taking Chances: Abortion and the Decision Not to Contracept* (Berkeley: University of California Press, 1975), pp. 124–27.

10. Cf. the discussion in Chap. 1 of Flandrin's view that so-called male methods, particularly coitus interruptus, in eighteenth-century France actually involved a high degree of female influence.

11. Luker, p. 127.

12. See Pincus, pp. 187–89, 194; Seaman and Seaman, pp. 81, 325–27; Djerassi, pp. 136–39; M. and M. Briggs, "Oral Contraceptive for Men," *Nature* 252 (13 December 1974): 585–86; and "Male Contraceptive Is Tested but Side-Effects Prohibit Use," *New York Times*, 17 September 1981, p. A18.

13. See Seaman and Seaman; Boston Women's Health Book Collective *Our Bodies, Ourselves;* and National Women's Health Network, *Newsletter*, published bimonthly and available from National Women's Health Network, 224 Seventh Street SE, Washington, D.C. 20003.

14. Pincus, p. 281.

15. Ibid., pp. 171, 275–76.

16. Ibid., pp. 285, 301–2.

17. Wertz and Wertz, *Lying-In*, Epilogue; and Barbara Katz Rothman, "Women, Health, and Medicine," in *Women: A Feminist Perspective*, 2d ed., ed. Jo Freeman (Palo Alto, Calif.: Mayfield, 1979), pp. 27–40.

18. This point was made by several participants at a conference on "Cultural Issues in Family Planning," sponsored by Development Associates, New York City, 23 March 1979, and attended by several hundred family planning counselors.

19. Information for this section was taken from Rachel Benson Gold and Peters D. Willson, "Depo-Provera: New Developments in a Decade Old Controversy," *Family Planning Perspectives* 13 (January/February 1981): 35–39; and Stephen Minkin, "This Is Science?" *Mother Jones* 6 (November 1981): 34–39, 50–54.

20. Minkin charges that Dr. Malcom Potts of the IFRP and his colleague, Dr. Edwin McDaniel of Chiang Mai, Thailand, where over half the female population had been given Depo-Provera, failed to follow through an investigation of 60 Thai women hospitalized with endometrial cancer in the mid-1970s. ". . . the study *never* determined how many of the women were injected; and the alarming information about the young age [most were of reproductive age, which is unusual in cases of endometrial cancer] of many of the cancer victims was not revealed." The study eliminated all but nine cases and concluded on the basis of those cases that Depo-Provera was not related to the women's cancer.

Meanwhile, according to Minkin, a World Health Organization report was released subsequent to the Potts-McDaniel study indicating "a marked increase in admissions for cancer of the cervix and breast [in Chiang Mai]" (Minkin, pp. 38–39, 54).

21. See Petchesky, in Michaelson; and idem, "Reproduction, Ethics, and Public Policy: The Federal Sterilization Regulations," *Hastings Center Report* (1979).

22. "Reversing Female Sterilization," *Population Reports* 8, Series C, No. 8 (September 1980): C-97 and C-108, concludes that "reversal is still a long, difficult, and costly operation" whose prospects for the future are "not good."

23. See Henshaw et al., "Abortion in the United States," *Family Planning Perspectives* 13, p. 17, Table 10; Forrest, Tietze and Sullivan, "Abortion in the United States," *Family Planning Perspectives* 11, p. 337, Table 4; U.S. Department of Health, Education, and Welfare, Center for Disease Control, *Surgical Sterilization Surveillance: Tubal Sterilization,* Publication No. (CDC) 79–8378 (Atlanta, July 1979), pp. 5–6; and U.S. Department of Health and Human Services, National Center for Health Statistics, "Induced Terminations of Pregnancy: Reporting States, 1977 and 1978," *Monthly Vital Statistics Report* 30 (28 September 1981): 1 (data based on eight reporting states).

24. For example, Charles Westoff et al., "Abortions Preventable by Contraceptive Practice," *Family Planning Perspectives* 13 (September/October 1981): 218–23, estimates the number of "preventable" abortions by assuming that all "contraceptive users"—women not interested in getting pregnant—were either on the pill or IUD or had been sterilized.

25. R. M. L. Winston, "Why 103 Women Asked for Reversal of Sterilization," *British Medical Journal* 2 (July 1977): 305–7.

26. Petchesky, in Michaelson, pp. 67–69.

27. See Chapter 2.

28. CARASA, *Women Under Attack,* pp. 51–52; and Charlotte Muller, "Insurance Coverage of Abortion, Contraception, and Sterilization," *Family Planning Perspectives* 10 (March/April 1978): 71–77.

29. *Federal Register* 43 (8 November 1978): 52146–75; and Petchesky, 1979.

30. U.S. Department of Health and Human Services, Office of the Inspector General, "Audit of Sterilizations and Hysterectomies Funded by the DHHS, Reports on Colorado, Illinois, Kansas, Maine, Massachusetts, Michigan, North Carolina, Oregon, Pennsylvania, and California" (mimeo, 2 March 1981); and Howie Kurtz, "Sterilization Abuses Discovered in Nine States, Including Kansas," *Wichita Eagle-Beacon,* 8 February 1981.

31. Petchesky, in Michaelson, Tables 2–4.

32. Jeanette H. Johnson, "Special Report: Tubal Sterilization and Hysterectomy," *Family Planning Perspectives* 14 (January/February 1982): 28–30; and Michele Gerzowski, Scott Berlucchi, and Allen Dobson, "Medicaid Sterilizations (1976–1980)" (paper presented at the meeting of the American Public Health Association, Los Angeles, 1981).

33. At a workshop on "Childbearing Rights of the Mentally Handicapped" during a conference on Childbearing Rights held at Worcester, Mass., 18–19 November 1978, several retarded persons spoke of their conviction that individuals classified as "mildly retarded" were capable of exercising voluntary informed consent to sterilization. One young woman reported having chosen, in consultation

with her parents but of her own will, to undergo hysterectomy in order to avoid the difficulties she experienced with menstrual periods.

34. For example, Charles F. Westoff and James McCarthy, "Sterilization in the United States," *Family Planning Perspectives* 11 (May/June 1979): 147–52, 150.

35. CARASA, p. 49.

36. See Chapter 4. Preliminary data gathered by the Health Care Financing Administration (HCFA) show an erratic pattern of Medicaid-funded sterilizations since 1978 in states that previously were heavy providers of Medicaid abortions and have since restricted their funding of abortion. In some states, reported Medicaid sterilizations have gone up since 1978, but in others they have gone down. The meaning of the figures is complicated by differences in reporting procedures, especially in local interpretations of the 1978 Federal Sterilization Regulations. I am grateful to Dr. Allen Dobson of HCFA for kindly providing me with these data.

37. C. B. Arnold, "Public Health Aspects of Contraceptive Sterilization," in *Behavioral-Social Aspects of Contraceptive Sterilization,* eds. S. M. Newman and Z. E. Klein (Lexington, Mass.: Lexington Books, 1978), Table 2-1.

38. See Petchesky, in Michaelson, pp. 72–74; Arnold, in Newman and Klein, pp. 10–12; C. W. Porter and J. F. Hulka, "Female Sterilization in Current Clinical Practice," *Family Planning Perspectives* 6 (Winter 1974): 31; Herbert B. Peterson et al., "Deaths Associated with Laparoscopic Sterilization by Unipolar Electrocoagulating Devices, 1978 and 1979," *American Journal of Obstetrics and Gynecology* 139 (1981): 141–43; and "Female Sterilization—No More Tubal Coagulation," *British Medical Journal* 1 (12 April 1980): 1037.

39. For a medically reliable summary of currently available methods of contraception, their advantages and risks, see *Our Bodies, Ourselves,* 3rd ed., forthcoming.

40. Among the more useful reviews and studies of the health hazards of the pill are Christopher Tietze, "The Pill and Mortality From Cardiovascular Disease: Another Look," *Family Planning Perspectives* 11 (January/April 1979): 80–83; Ory, Rosenfield and Landman; Robert Hoover et al., "Oral Contraceptive Use: Association with Frequency of Hospitalization and Chronic Disease Risk Indicators," *American Journal of Public Health* 68 (April 1978): 335–41; Shanna H. Swan, "Critique of the Walnut Creek Contraceptive Drug Study: Monograph III" (ms., n.d.); Becky O'Malley, "Who Says Oral Contraceptives Are Safe?" *Nation,* 14 February 1981, pp. 170–72; Seaman and Seaman; John J. Sciarra, Gerald I. Zatuchni, and J. Joseph Speidel, eds., *Risks, Benefits, and Controversies in Fertility Control* (Hagerstown, Md.: Harper & Row, 1978); and Marian Cleeves Diamond and Carol Cleaves Korenbrot, eds., *Hormonal Contraceptives, Estrogens, and Human Welfare* (New York: Academic, 1978).

41. Benjamin P. Sachs, Peter M. Layde, George L. Rubin, and Roger W. Rochat, "Reproductive Mortality in the United States," *Journal of the American Medical Association* 247 (28 May 1982): 2792.

42. New York: Dolphin, 1969. See also Seaman's vivid history of these early developments in Seaman and Seaman, pp. 84–96.

43. See Diamond and Korenbrot, pt. 3; articles by Bruce A. Barron, Alphonse T. Masi, and Michael H. Briggs, in Sciarra et al.; and M. P. Vesey et al., "An Epidemiological Study of Oral Contraceptives and Breast Cancer," *British Medical*

Journal 1 (1979): 1757. The association with breast cancer is disputed, and there is evidence that the pill helps to ward off benign breast disease.

44. See Ory, Rosenfield, and Landman. They state the caveats with noticeable reluctance: "Beginning at age 30, women *might wish to review* their fertility control needs and consider moving to other effective methods" (p. 279).

45. Sachs et al., pp. 2789–90.

46. Adele Hoffman, testimony before Senate Subcommittee on Aging, Family and Human Services on "risks to adolescents from contraceptive use," 19 April 1982, pp. 3–4.

47. For example, the widely promoted Walnut Creek Contraceptive Study, financed by G. D. Searle and proclaimed in the press in late 1980 as showing that health risk from birth control pills had been "exaggerated," was apparently flawed. The study lost nearly one-third of its under-30 population in follow-up and was biased in its selection process toward older women and toward healthier women than the normal user population. See Swan; and O'Malley.

48. Ory, Rosenfield and Landman, p. 278, gloss quickly over these figures.

49. Judith Blake, "The Pill and the Rising Costs of Fertility Control," *Social Biology* 24 (Winter 1977): 270.

50. Ibid., p. 269.

51. Tietze, 1977, p. 76; emphasis added.

52. There is a clear analogy here with the introduction of a safer (vacuum aspiration) method of abortion than the dilation and curettage method, in 1973—the year of *Roe* v. *Wade*. See Susan Harlap et al., "A Prospective Study of Spontaneous Fetal Losses after Induced Abortions," *New England Journal of Medicine* 301 (27 September 1979): 680.

53. Westoff et al.

54. Harlap et al.; and Cates et al., "Mortality from Abortion and Childbirth," *Journal of the American Medical Association* 248.

55. U.S. House of Representatives, Select Committee on Population, *Final Report,* 95th Congress, 2d sess. (Washington, D.C.: Government Printing Office, 1978), p. 12.

56. One out of five white women and one out of four black women in the 1973 National Survey of Family Growth replied that they had gotten tubal ligations for "medical reasons." Either their doctors had advised them that it would be unsafe to undergo future pregnancies or they feared the medical consequences of taking the pill. William F. Pratt, "Sterilization in the United States: Preliminary Findings from the National Survey of Family Growth, 1973" (paper presented at the meeting of the Population Association of America, Seattle, Washington, 1975); and personal communication, W. Pratt, Family Growth Division, National Center for Health Statistics.

57. Melvin Zelnik and John F. Kantner, "Sexual Activity, Contraceptive Use and Pregnancy Among Metropolitan-Area Teenagers: 1971–1979," *Family Planning Perspectives* 12 (September/October 1980): 236.

58. See Kathryn Watterson Burkhart, *Growing into Love: Teenagers Talk Candidly about Sex in the 1980s* (New York: Putnam, 1980), p. 257.

59. Elise F. Jones, James R. Beniger, and Charles F. Westoff, "Pill and IUD Discontinuation in the United States, 1970–1975: The Influence of the Media," *Family Planning Perspectives* 12 (November/December 1980): 293–300. See also Blake,

who argues that the Nelson Committee hearings in 1970, as well as other instances of publicity about the pill's hazards, sharply affected people's attitudes toward the pill, resulting in "a precipitous drop in confidence," without inferring a direct link between press reports and pill use.

60. Twenty-three percent of the women gave "physical problems" as a reason, compared with 6 percent who gave "worry about reports." Jones, Beniger, and Westoff, p. 294, Table 1.

61. Charles F. Westoff and Norman B. Ryder, *The Contraceptive Revolution* (Princeton: Princeton University Press, 1977), p. 47, Fig. 2-2; and p. 45, Table 3-9.

62. Ibid., p. 43, Table 3-7; and p. 44, Table 3-8.

63. See Hoover et al.; Seaman and Seaman, pp. 95–96; and reports in Sciarra et al. concerning "blood pressure effects" and amenorrhea. Seaman claims to have received many letters from women who got vaginal infections while on the pill.

64. "IUDs—Update on Safety, Effectiveness, and Research," *Population Reports,* Series 8, No. 3 (May 1979); and Prabodh K. Gupta, "Intrauterine Device (IUD) and Actinomyces," testimony before Senate Subcommittee on Aging, Family and Human Services (19 April 1982), p. 3.

65. Gupta, p. 3.

66. U.S. Department of Health and Human Services, National Center for Health Statistics, *Contraceptive Utilization—United States, 1976, Vital and Health Statistics,* Series 23, No. 7 (March 1981): 20, Table 4. The percentage is much higher in other countries, especially Asia, where family planning programs have stressed this method.

67. Gupta, pp. 4–5; and "PID Risk Increased Sharply Among IUD Users, British Cohort, U.S. Case-Control Studies Affirm," *Family Planning Perspectives* 13 (July/August 1981): 182–84.

68. Hoffman, p. 6.

69. Malcolm Potts and Robert Wheeler, "The Quest for a Magic Bullet," *Family Planning Perspectives* 13 (November/December 1981): 269.

70. See John M. Benditt, "Current Contraceptive Research," *Family Planning Perspectives* 12 (May/June 1980): 149–55; Linda Atkinson et al., "Prospects for Improved Contraception," *Family Planning Perspectives* 12 (July/August 1980): 173–92; and idem, "The Use of PGs in Human Reproduction," *Population Reports* 8, Series G, No. 8 (March 1980).

71. C. W. Maranker, "Thread-Like Plug May Be Reliable as Birth Control," *Bergen Sunday Record,* 29 November 1981, p. H24, quotes researcher Dr. Robert Erb as stating that "we can only expect to place a normal plug 85 percent to 90 percent of the time."

72. Potts and Wheeler, p. 270. This is precisely the opposite conclusion to that of Westoff et al. The latter study is falsified by its failure to take into account both actual pill "drop-out" rates and the side effects that motivate them. It *pretends* that the pill and sterilization are safe and acceptable and then hypothesizes what would happen to abortion rates if *all* women used the pill regularly until they reached a certain age and then became surgically sterilized—a population-controller's dream, but not reality.

73. Melvin Zelnik and John F. Kantner, "Contraceptive Patterns and Premarital Pregnancy Among Women Aged 15–19 in 1976," *Family Planning Perspectives* 10

(May/June 1978): 139–41; and Laurie Schwab Zabin and Samuel D. Clark, Jr., "Why They Delay: A Study of Teenage Family Planning Clinic Patients," *Family Planning Perspectives* 13 (September/October 1981): 211. Ellen W. Freeman, "Abortion: Subjective Attitudes and Feelings," *Family Planning Perspectives* 10 (May/June 1978): 155, found that 93 percent of her sample were using contraceptives four months after their abortion.

74. Barbara Howe, H. Roy Kaplan, and Constance English, "Repeat Abortions: Blaming the Victims," *American Journal of Public Health* 69 (December 1979): 1244. Forrest, Sullivan, and Tietze, Table 4; and Henshaw et al., Table 10, show that while the ratio of repeat to first-time abortions has gone up every year, first-time abortions in 1978 were around 75 percent of the total. Jaffe, Lindheim, and Lee, pp. 12–13, explain that the fact that the proportion of "repeaters" goes up each year reflects the annual rise in the pool of women who have ever had an abortion.

75. Tom L. Beauchamp, "The Regulation of Hazards and Hazardous Behaviors," *Health Education Mongraphs* 6 (Summer 1978): 242–57; and *Hastings Center Report*, published bimonthly by the Hastings Center, Hastings-on-Hudson, N.Y.

76. See William H. Chafe, *The American Woman: Her Changing Social, Economic, and Political Roles, 1920–1970* (London: Oxford University Press, 1972), Chap. 5; and Gordon and DuBois.

77. See quotation from the Upjohn Company representative at the 1978 hearings of the House Select Committee on population. Introduction, p. 8, above.

78. E.g., Senator Jeremiah Denton, press release, 19 April 1982.

79. "Workers, Reproductive Hazards, and the Politics of Protection," *Feminist Studies* 5 (Summer 1979). See articles by C. Bell, W. Chavkin, R. Petchesky, and M. Wright.

80. See Ory, Rosenfield, and Landman, p. 278.

81. See Dr. Hoffman's testimony.

82. The notion of professionals as "gatekeepers" comes from a preliminary paper presented by Constance A. Nathanson at the annual meeting of the Population Association of America, April 1982.

83. Melvin Zelnik and John F. Kantner, "Sexual and Contraceptive Experience of Young Unmarried Women in the United States, 1976 and 1971," in Furstenberg, Lincoln, and Menken (1981), pp. 81–83, 88; and Bettie L. Hudson, "Visits to Family Planning Service Sites: United States, 1978," National Center for Health Statistics, *Advancedata*, No. 72 (29 June 1981): 3–5.

84. Ibid., Table 3.

85. Zelnik and Kantner, 1980, p. 236 and Table 10.

86. Zelnik and Kantner, 1981, p. 87 and Tables 13–14.

87. See "Blame MD 'Mismanagement' for Contraceptive Failure," *Family Planning Perspectives* 8 (March/April 1976): 72–76; and Mary Kay Zimmerman, *Passage Through Abortion* (New York: Praeger, 1977), p. 83.

88. Zimmerman, p. 83.

89. Joel Robins, "Failures of Contraceptive Practice," *New York Journal of Medicine* 76 (March 1976): 361–65.

90. Furstenberg, Lincoln, and Menken, p. 302.

91. National Center for Health Statistics, "Contraceptive Use Patterns, Prior Source, and Pregnancy History of Female Family Planning Patients: United States,

1980," *Advancedata,* No. 82 (16 June 1982): Table 1; and Zelnik and Kantner, 1981, Table 11.

92. *Our Bodies, Ourselves* contains sections not only on the predictable topics of reproductive health (e.g., abortion, venereal disease, birth control, pregnancy, menopause) but also on the social and sexual contexts of these issues.

93. Mary E. Land, Rosalinda Arceo, and Aquiles J. Sobrero, "Successful Use of the Diaphragm and Jelly by a Young Population: Report of a Clinical Study," *Family Planning Perspectives* 8 (March/April 1976): 81–86, esp. 81–83.

94. Ibid., p. 86.

95. As this book was going to press, the FDA approved a new nonprescription sponge contraceptive that claims the same rate of effectiveness as the diaphragm, but without the diaphragm's messiness or inconvenience; the spermicide is already contained in it and it remains effective for around 24 hours. (Robert Pear, "FDA Approves New Sponge Contraceptive," *New York Times,* April 6, 1983, pp. A1 and A20.) Because it will be available over the counter, and is apparently safe and untroublesome, this method is likely to become a more useful method for teenagers than the diaphragm or the pill. Nevertheless, this does not affect my argument that it is mainly the social relations surrounding sexuality and pregnancy, and not technology, that determine patterns of contraceptive use. Moreover, feminist health organizations have questioned the adequacy of clinical trials and the haste with which the FDA approved the sponge before its safety has been assured.

Abortion and Heterosexual Culture: The Teenage Question

6

He's not really worrying about what's going to happen to you. He's only worrying about himself. This time I think what I really thought was if you don't think about it, maybe you'll get something out of it. So I guessed it wouldn't be a hassle, I wouldn't worry about it. And I did get a lot more out of it, not worrying about it. I had thought about getting birth control pills with the boyfriend before, but that worked to where it was a one-way street for his benefit, not for mine. It would be mine because I wouldn't get pregnant, but safe for him, too, because I wouldn't put him on the spot. So I get sick of being used. I'm tired of this same old crap, forget it. I'm not getting pills for his benefit. So I never got them and I never thought I would have to 'cause I wasn't looking for anyone since I was tired of being used. Sex was a one-way street. He gets all the feelings, girls have all the hassles. She gets more emotional and falls head over heels while he could give a damn. I'm sick of it, so I thought hang it all.

LUKER, *Taking Chances*

"No *Pill* when you were in high school? What did you *do?*" a high school senior in Queens exclaimed. "Oh, that's terrible!" . . . I found myself feeling like a historical relic when I told them in college, we had curfews, weren't allowed apartments of our own and could be expelled for setting foot inside a boy's apartment! High school and college girls alike shrieked and hooted when I told them that girls in my high school were automatically suspended from school if they were pregnant, even if they got married. And they sobered when told that abortions were illegal and available only at great risk to a girl's life.

BURKHART, *Growing into Love*

205

A number of women, especially young women, engage in heterosexual intercourse neither using birth control nor intending to get pregnant. That fact is undeniable. Not all of them are victims of "contraceptive failure," even broadly defined. Why they get pregnant when pregnancy is avoidable, when relatively safe and reasonably effective contraception is available, has usually been approached from a psychological perspective: The woman's "noncontraceptive behavior" is the consequence of "unresolved conflicts" or "unconscious motives" that make her act in contradictory ways. Even the conceptual framework of "risk-taking," I would argue, is essentially behavioristic in orientation, focused on the individual woman and her strategy for resolving the dilemma of an unwanted pregnancy (though here the strategy is seen as conscious and rational rather than irrational).[1]

My approach to the problem of noncontraception is one that understands its psychological and irrational dimensions in cultural terms. The more subtle and unacknowledged roots of unwanted pregnancy have to do with the contemporary heterosexual culture and the dilemmas it poses for women. They develop through patterns of meaning, dominant moral values, and social relationships—between parents and children, between women and men—that are by and large learned and that bear down with a heavy weight on the "choices" of individuals. Like the social, economic, and medical circumstances we considered in assessing the underlying conditions of abortion, these cultural norms and patterns—the social relations and ideology of sexuality—play an important part in constructing women's reproductive behavior. They too exist objectively in the society and act on individuals sometimes in spite of their conscious "will."

This chapter explores the relationship between abortion, noncontraception, and some of the cultural dilemmas, or double binds, of heterosexuality, particularly for unmarried teenage women. There are two reasons for focusing on teenagers: (1) because the issues of sexual identity, and therefore of socialization into the dominant sexual culture, are most concentrated for them; and (2) because politically it is their sexuality that has been the object of so much of the recent abortion debate.

Defining Sexuality—The Role of Abortion

Both feminists and antifeminists understand birth control and abortion as necessary conditions for women's sexual freedom, but they are far from sufficient; and the practical connections between birth control/abortion and sexuality are by no means clear. Relief from the fear of unwanted pregnancy remains for most women an end in itself, but one that does not in itself assure satisfying or "liberated" sexual relations. At the same time, in a culture in which heterosexual relations are usually dominated by men, family relations by fathers, and personal life by heterosexual patriarchy, the circumstances surrounding an unwanted pregnancy are as often ridden with conflict and strife as with desire. Such conflict may undermine consistent birth control use. The young woman quoted at the beginning of this chapter says that she "gets a lot more out of [sex]" when she doesn't bother about birth control or making herself "safe" for the man's "benefit." This strategy may be rational within the terms of the dominant sexual ideology, which lags behind social conditions, and in terms of a woman's life circumstances. "Subjective reasons" for not using contraception (e.g., wanting to "test the man's commitment" or "prove you are a woman") may be a tactical, if self-defeating, response to real disparities in power.[2]

Two principal themes run through the analysis that follows. The first is that unwanted pregnancy and abortion often occur among those with traditional values about sexuality rather than what one could call a "liberated" consciousness; or they may represent accommodations to older values in changed circumstances. The second is that the relationship between birth control/abortion and sexuality takes historically specific forms, reflecting the shifting dynamics through which gender, class, and generational conflicts get played out. From this standpoint, the outcome of a sexual encounter or a pregnancy is less important than the social process and the consciousness that define its meaning in terms of a given power relationship. "Having sex" may be an act of resistance or an act of deference and accommodation. (It may also, of course, be an act of mutuality and pleasure.) Similarly, getting pregnant, having a child, or getting an abortion has no intrinsic social or political meaning; it receives its meaning from the historical and political context in which it occurs and the circumstances (class, age, marital status, employment conditions) of the woman involved. For adolescents, sexuality, pregnancy, and abortion are densely mediated by agendas other than what they appear; they become the terrain for negotiating gender, child and adulthood, and gender-specific class and race. At the same time, in late-twentieth-century heterosexual culture, birth control and abortion are crucial signifiers of female adolescent sexuality, particularly, I argue, for white middle-class teenagers.

In developing what follows, I am applying certain theoretical assumptions about sexuality drawn from the work of Michel Foucault, Jeffrey Weeks, and other historians of sexuality.[3] This work contains several shared premises summed up most clearly by Weeks. First, it questions whether for human beings there is any such thing as "pure" sexuality, "sex as such," or raw libido unsocialized or unmediated by social relations and history. Critiquing the "drive-reduction" model of sex as biological instinct formulated by Freud and adopted uncritically by many leftist-Freudians and sex radicals (e.g., Reich, Marcuse, Havelock Ellis), this perspective understands sexuality primarily in historical and cultural terms. Human sexuality exists always in a context of social relations from which it derives its meanings, both conscious and unconscious; it is mainly a social, not biological, activity.[4]

Second, the historical theory of sexuality calls into question the assumption of most feminists and sex radicals that control over sexuality—through the family, the church, or the state—takes the simple form of "repression," the other side of the "instinctual drive" model. Rather, Foucault in particular suggests a more complicated model in which various centers of power attempt to define, categorize, organize, regulate, and even "incite" sexuality in specific directions so that the very definition of what is "sexual" becomes an area of contestation. It is not that sex is "repressed"; rather, its terms and varieties, its agents and boundaries, are intricately patrolled. Moreover, the particular ways that sexuality is channeled or "deployed" not only change historically but differ according to one's age, class, race, and gender. (Foucault mentions class alone.) Sexuality may be defined in relation to procreative ends in some cultures or periods but not in others, may be associated with pleasure in some and with danger and taboos in others, may be organized mainly across genders in some or within genders (homosocially) in others; there are no universal or transhistorical sexual forms.[5] What is specifically modern (and presumably Western) in the cultural meaning of sex is its existence from the eighteenth century as a privatized act, an assertion of self and individuality.[6] But we have to note that sexual ideology thus becomes prototypically male, in a misogynist culture epitomized by Rousseau, which abhorred the idea of female self-assertion and defined "individualism" as a male prerogative. Hence the notorious double standard, linking sex for women with reproduction and sex for men with *self*-expression.

In the nineteenth century, neither feminists nor Malthusians saw in birth control a means toward the sexual self-expression of women, particularly unmarried women. During the radical decades of the 1910s and 1920s, people like Emma Goldman, Margaret Sanger, and various sex reformers proclaimed women's rights to full sexual autonomy as the basis of birth control demands; but by the 1940s, "sex without fear" and "marital fulfillment" through sex therapy and counseling became the province of a now respectable family planning profession. The new professionals carefully restricted their attack on "sexual dysfunction" and "unwanted pregnancy" to the traditional framework of marriage, motherhood, and "family stability," removed from any notion of male power within marriage or women's right to a sexual existence outside it.[7] Today, the idea of women as sexual agents, sexual initiators, either in a lesbian or a heterosexual context, is still a dangerous one in the dominant culture. While feminists articulate an ideological link between birth control and abortion and women's "sexual freedom," the content of this link remains unspecified. We sense that larger issues about women's sexuality—its boundaries, subjects, forms, and age limits—are being distilled into the conflict over abortion, but without fully understanding why, or why *now*.

The *specificity of abortion* from the 1960s through the 1980s, as contrasted with earlier times, lies in two important features we have already observed. First, on the level of ideology the right to abortion has been connected, by some feminists, to the right of women to sexual self-determination. (This is not the understanding of all feminists, certainly not of many liberal feminists and religious feminists who think of abortion as a matter of "private conscience" rather than social and sexual need.) Those who oppose abortion, particularly policy makers, make the same connection in a negative sense: The rise in abortions represents promiscuity, immorality, and hedonism (see Chapter 7). Second, on the level of popular practice, abortion has become, perhaps for the first time in history, a phenomenon predominantly of young unmarried white women, a large proportion of them teenagers, many living with their parents. One-third of all women receiving abortions in 1978 were teenagers, another one-third were aged 20–24 (mostly unmarried), and 70 percent of all pregnant teenagers getting abortions were white.[8] These facts create a reality that helps to construct the social meanings of sexuality in contemporary American culture and politics. Abortion—organized legal abortion—is associated with sex because it is seen to reveal sex; it is a signifier that helps make sex *visible* and therefore subject to scrutiny and an inevitable defining of limits between the licit and the illicit. Above all, it helps identify and categorize a new sexual subject: the "promiscuous" white teenage girl.

In the context of an (lawful, clinical) abortion, the sexuality of a teenage girl takes on a very different meaning from what it has in the context of an out-of-wedlock birth, especially for white middle-class teenagers. The common characteristic of "shotgun weddings," unwed motherhood, illegal abortions, and "petting" is the invisibility, the secrecy with which they mantle sex. The unwed pregnant (white) girl who drops out of school is pathetic, victimized by her folly or by an unscrupulous male; she remains an outsider, a mystery.* The girl who has a legal abortion, on the other hand, returns as a reminder of the *possibilities* of sex, sex that is penalty-free. One-half million unmarried teenagers a year

---

* When I was growing up in Tulsa, Oklahoma, the local home for unwed mothers was as shrouded in horror and mystery as an asylum or leper colony. Located outside of town in a field off a rural highway, unmistakably "institutional," it drew my fascination by the lifelessness outside its walls and the miserable types I imagined must dwell within. The windows always seemed closed. There were stories of unknown origin that circulated in our high school about a hatchet-wielding killer named "Sparky," a crazy man who haunted the outskirts of town in search of innocent girls or couples who parked on deserted roads to hack to pieces. Somehow the two symbols of lost innocence and the terrors of sex—Sparky and the "home"—became closely connected in the dark shadows in my mind.

getting legal abortions represent a "sexual event" that cannot be concealed and therefore must be measured, sealed off, studied, categorized, organized, regulated, and contained. This is exactly what family planning professionals, journalists, and conservative politicians have been up to in the frenzied debate over teenage sexuality and pregnancy.

The Rise in Teenage Sex and Pregnancy— A Revised View

Two explanations are offered in the demographic literature for the increase in adolescent pregnancies and abortions since 1970: that of mainstream demographers, who proclaim a "rise in teenage sexual activity"; and that of feminist sociologists, who emphasize a continuity of traditional sexual norms in the midst of changing conditions. Both are focused primarily on issues of sexuality rather than the socioeconomic conditions we considered as the essential "background" to this increase in Chapter 4. Both give us pieces of useful information, but are ultimately unable to explain historical transformations in sexuality and their connection to abortion trends.

Family planners and demographers tend to explain the rise in teenage pregnancies and abortions in terms that are strangely akin to those of their political adversaries on the right. For both, the source is an *increase in teenage sex,* defined as heterosexual intercourse; and for both this is seen as a "problem"—a moral problem for conservatives, a public health problem for liberals.[9] The main programmatic difference between them is that the New Right and the conservatives in the Reagan administration would like to stop this activity, whereas liberals and family planners take the view that stopping it is impossible and that its negative effects should be curtailed through birth control and abortion services, sex education, and V.D. prevention. According to the right-wing position, the availability of birth control and abortion is a major *cause* of increased sexual activity (along with "permissiveness," feminism, etc.), whereas for liberals availability is a necessary consequence of this activity. As far as a *concept* of sexuality is concerned, however, there is nothing in the liberal family planners' position that diverges much from certain traditional assumptions that I presume most conservatives share: a view of sex as organized around genital intercourse, not pleasure; a view of heterosexuality as normative (family planners just don't know what to do with homosexuality, since they believe it falls so thoroughly outside their domain, whereas the New Right declares war against it); and an implicit view that what is recognized as sex is inappropriate behavior for certain age groups.[10]

The hysteria about teenage sexuality and pregnancy characteristic of the Reagan administration and the New Right originated among liberal demographers and family planners, who "discovered" an "epidemic" of teenage sexual activity in the mid-1970s. After the 1976 publication of the pamphlet "Eleven Million Teenagers: What Can Be Done About the Epidemic of Adolescent Pregnancies in the U.S.,"[11] the image of rampant teenage promiscuity linked to rising pregnancy and illegitimacy rates was quickly absorbed by the media and policy makers. The result was the creation, in 1978, of a federal Office of Adolescent Pregnancy and the rechanneling of government family planning resources into research and outreach programs involving teenagers. It is ironic that today that office is headed by a staunch antiabortionist who opposes giving teenagers access not only to abortion but to sex education and birth control services without their parents' permission. But while the program has changed, the focus on teenagers is just as aggressive and the underlying theme, the sexual visibility of teenage girls, just as pronounced. As we saw earlier, the alarm signals about an "epidemic" were exaggerated given the actual trends in teenage childbearing. But the "eleven million" in the pamphlet's title referred neither to teenage pregnancies nor to illegitimate births but to the estimated number of "sexually active" young women. In other words, the family planning and media campaign itself helped define and demarcate the "sexual" teenage girl in the 1970s. The language of an epidemic provides not merely a label but a whole system of organization and containment. An epidemic calls for data gathering, subcategorization, and public strategies of control; it defines an area of "sexual life" as a domain of social intervention. The object of this sexual-social construction is clearly *girls,* as evidenced by the fact that the interventions are aimed exclusively at abortion, prescription birth control, and pregnancies.

In their own terms, which are normative as well as quantitative, the estimates of demographers are not incorrect. More teenage white women in the 1970s apparently did engage in premarital heterosexual intercourse, and at earlier ages, than their parents' and grandparents', and even their older sisters' generation, as indicated in Table 6-1. It is clear from these data that the increasing incidence and frequency of premarital intercourse among white teenage girls was as great or greater during the 1970s as it was in the whole period from the "stable" 1940s to the 1970s. What this means, according to adolescent sex researchers, is that girls' "sexual behavior" has "caught up" to that of boys, which has not increased in nearly the magnitude of girls'. Moreover, the increase in more recent years has been especially great among young *white* women. This, indeed, is what much of the political disturbance about adolescent pregnancy and sexuality is about.

Zelnik and Kantner base their highly influential conclusion about a rise in sexual activity among white American teenage girls on the following changes: (1) a 30 percent increase in the number who had ever engaged in premarital intercourse; (2) a lowering age at which sex (heterosexual intercourse) is initiated; and (3) "less exclusivity in the choice of partners."

TABLE 6–1. PERCENTAGES OF TEENAGE WOMEN WHO HAVE EVER HAD PREMARITAL INTERCOURSE, BY AGE AND RACE, SELECTED YEARS

Age	1938–49[a]	1971		1976		1979	
		White	Black	White	Black	White	Black
15	1.0	11.3	31.2	13.8	38.9	18.3	41.4
16	2.0	17.0	44.4	23.7	55.1	35.4	50.4
17	8.0	20.2	58.9	36.1	71.0	44.1	73.3
18	14.0	35.6	60.2	46.0	76.2	52.6	76.3
19	18.0	40.7	78.3	53.6	83.9	64.9	88.5
Total	—	23.2	52.4	33.6	64.3	42.3	64.8

[a] Data available for white women only.
SOURCES: Theodore Caplow et al., *Middletown Families: Fifty Years of Change and Continuity* (Minneapolis: University of Minnesota Press, 1982), Appendix A, Table 8-1; and Melvin Zelnik and John F. Kantner, "Sexual Activity, Contraceptive Use and Pregnancy Among Metropolitan-Area Teenagers: 1971–1979," *Family Planning Perspectives* 12 (September/October 1980), Table 1.

By 1979, an apparently record-breaking 50 percent of all teenage women—substantially higher among those eighteen and nineteen—were "sexually active," with well over a third using no form of contraception and two-thirds of these becoming pregnant.[12]

Now, even if all these young women used contraception, it would still be true that more heterosexual intercourse would result in more unwanted pregnancies and hence in a higher incidence of abortion. But beyond that, there is little we can conclude from this crude and narrow data about "incidence" and "frequencies" of intercourse. The data tell us nothing about the actual ways in which sexuality among teenagers is lived and understood, the circumstances in which noncontraception is "chosen" as a sexual strategy, or whether anything resembling a "sexual revolution" has occurred. Because they are primarily concerned with predicting unplanned pregnancies and births, population specialists define "sexual activity" in the narrowest terms—sex that can result in pregnancy. They assume that "the 'sexual revolution' is in the end just about more sexuality," rather than "different ways being developed of organizing sexual behavior."[13]

The focus of demographic studies on numbers of women who have ever, even once, experienced heterosexual intercourse masks more than it reveals about sexual practices and consciousness—for example, the possibility that having such an experience once, at a certain age, under certain circumstances, may make a girl *less* rather than more "sexually active."

It is based on the "drive" model of sex and assumes that sex is a kind of energy that gets stored up and then "activated." Zelnik and Kantner qualify their finding of a rise in sexual activity with the almost contradictory statement that *"many sexually experienced teenagers are relatively inactive sexually."* Over half of the 1976 interviewees had no sexual intercourse in the month preceding the interview; and all showed a decline in the frequency of intercourse between 1971 and 1976, despite the rise in the proportion who had "done it" at least once.[14] This is particularly true in the first year after "sexual initiation" and for the youngest teenagers, who are the least likely to use contraception.

Zabin, Kantner, and Zelnik found that "half of all initial premarital teenage pregnancies occur in the first six months of sexual activity, and more than one-fifth in the first month." They attribute this pattern to the tendency among "younger adolescents especially" to delay contraceptive use until they have become more sexually experienced, explaining nonuse by the "intermittent and sporadic" and "largely unplanned" character of sex in the lives of many young women, especially those in the early teen years. A major reason such women give for nonuse is not lack of access to or information about contraception, but that "they had not expected to have intercourse."[15] Interviews with teenagers in the early 1980s confirm this pattern, with many of the young women reporting having had sexual intercourse once at age 13–15, then avoiding it for many months.[16]

These studies of teenage sexuality lead to the ironic conclusion that teenage unwanted pregnancies may occur because these young women are "relatively inactive sexually"! More precisely, they indicate that "sexual experience" has different meanings for women at different stages of development, since the pattern of sporadic and unanticipated intercourse is especially prevalent among teenagers age seventeen and under. This is significant, for it is among this age group that most of the decade's increase in teenage out-of-wedlock births is concentrated. That this pattern of sporadic sexual encounters has resulted in rising rates of unwanted pregnancy among young white teenagers is not surprising, given (1) the shift away from early marriage and toward higher college attendance and labor force participation; (2) the earlier age at menstruation and increased fecundity of today's teenage girls relative to their mothers and grandmothers, due largely to improved health and nutrition;[17] and (3) the continued prevalence of "traditional" norms and expectations about appropriate female behavior. In fact, if we look again at Table 6-1, we find that the highest percentages of teenagers to experience "premarital intercourse" are eighteen- and nineteen-year-olds, most of whom would have been married thirty years ago. Thus, although teenage women, especially whites, are more likely to get pregnant unintentionally than they were in the past, neither their higher illegitimacy and abortion rates *nor* their "higher frequencies" and "earlier onset" of sexual intercourse may be indicators of greater sexuality or sexual awareness.

Continuities in Heterosexual Culture

Attempts to get at the meanings of adolescent sexuality and not just the frequency of intercourse seem to elude family planners and sex researchers. One review of reported studies on adolescent behavior from the mid-1940s through the mid-1970s warns "that we know little about normal adolescent sexual behavior," that existing data is incomplete and subject to numerous reporting and other errors (e.g., teenagers' tendencies to exaggerate or fantasize, or their misunderstanding of critical terms such as "sexual intercourse").[18] Nevertheless, even with sparse data, we may assume that, for teenagers as for adults, sexual experience includes not only genital intercourse but a wide range or continuum of erotically stimulating experiences and social situations—oral, anal, autoerotic, homosexual, "touching," as well as genital and heterosexual.[19] Seen from this broader understanding of sexuality, the historical significance of current rates of teenage pregnancy, abortion, or even heterosexual intercourse is much less clear. At the least, the notion of "promiscuity," its ebbs and flows, is grossly simplistic. How does one draw a moral line, or a quantitative line, between a single incident of intercourse on the living room sofa in the 1970s and the intensely eroticized "petting" in parked cars that typified white middle-class teenage life in the 1950s—even if you didn't "go all the way"? What basis is there for asserting, from this perspective, that teenage sexual activity has increased or for maintaining that the difference between the present and the past is "promiscuity" rather than pregnancy?

To assume that the teenagers of the 1940s and 1950s were "sexually inactive" because they "abstained" (but not always) from heterosexual intercourse or got married to legitimate it is absurd. Rather than point to a "sexual revolution," this analysis suggests an "evolution" over the past thirty to forty years.[20] In fact, the variety of sexual forms that young people put into practice in the past may have been as erotic, imaginative, and absorbing as any practiced today; the difference is that they were less visible, and therefore more acceptable, to adults. The popular custom of petting, for example, which according to studies of Kinsey and others increased significantly during the 1920s (with the spread of the automobile), then "stabilized in the mid-1930s and persisted through the 1950s,"[21] involved an intricate hierarchy of codified pleasures, usually enforced by the girl, and doled out in portions that advanced with the status of the relationship.[22] Like "bundling," its long-ago precursor, petting was (and is) an exciting form of erotic play. Undoubtedly, the teenage girl of the 1950s learned the sexual code from wiser peers or older sisters;

it was passed down as custom in a closed and secretive teenage sex subculture, structuring the popular reality ("folkways") of teenage sex even as the image of the "unwed mother" structured its moral and political discourse.[23] Burkhart found the petting custom alive and well among today's teenagers:

> . . . although it's not talked about very much, many [teenagers] make decisions about a great deal of sex that stops short of genital union but is very exciting, passionate and satisfying. In our culture, people for many generations have remained "virgins" and still found sexual satisfaction in hours of erotic play that involves everything from kissing to exploring each other's mouths with their tongues, to petting and massaging one another, to "dry humping"—simulating intercourse but with clothes on—to oral sex and mutual masturbation. All of this sexually exciting play can lead to orgasm that involves no threat of pregnancy.[24]

Yet the petting culture probably represents a specific historical reality and a specific class reality. One might speculate about the extent to which it grew out of not only an attempt to accommodate traditional morality to sexual desire and the parsimonious mentality of the middle class (waiting and saving) but also the material availability of the automobile as a private and secretive space in a sexual culture whose requirement was secrecy above all else. While working-class and lower-class youth of the 1920s through 1950s attempted and were expected to accommodate the same dominant morality, they usually did not have cars, and they lived in more crowded and less private conditions, which made sex unavoidably more visible. A classic study of adolescents in a midwestern town in the early 1940s makes it clear that the "principle of secrecy" and professions of chastity were as important to lower-class boys and girls and their parents as to middle-class ones, although in reality the modes of accommodation may have been different. Heterosexual intercourse played a larger role than petting among the lower-class youth, resulting in a much higher proportion of unwanted pregnancies, high school dropouts, and "shotgun weddings."[25] Mainly because of economic circumstances, secrecy and discretion were simply *less possible* among working-class and lower-class teenagers. (The haste toward marriage in case of an "accident" was itself an effort to maintain a veil of silence over sex.)

Access to birth control and abortion have brought important changes in the conditions of sexuality for young unmarried women, especially among the middle and working classes. We saw in Chapter 4 how those changes were part of a larger set of transformations that involves delaying marriage and childbearing in favor of education and work. But growing numbers of teenagers who use birth control and get abortions, and even higher rates of heterosexual intercourse, do not necessarily indicate "revolutionary" changes in the experience and meanings of sexuality. The *continuities* in teenage sexual culture may be as important as the changes in behavior, which quantitative studies often exaggerate.

In a comparison of "Middletown" families in the 1970s with those studied by the Lynds in the 1930s, sociologists emphasize that the values and relational contexts surrounding sexual behavior have remained surprisingly constant: "Monogamic heterosexual marriage is still the nearly universal norm, and most nonmarital sexual behavior involves the possibility of eventual marriage."[26] The principal changes in sexual attitudes and practices among "Middletown" residents since the mid-1930s are (1) the appearance of XXX-rated film houses, massage parlors, porn shops, and easily available "soft porn" magazines; (2) the enrollment of one-third of the county's teenage girl population in the local Planned Parenthood clinic, where the "pill pick-up" scene has the casualness of a gym roll call; and (3) numerous sex education and other activities of Planned Parenthood in local schools and other "community settings."[27] It is fascinating that these are the "sexual changes" the recent "Middletown" study highlights. Of course none of them is about sex as sensual experience or as relationships; rather, it is about historically particular and public ways of displaying, organizing, and regulating sex. Fifty years earlier the Lynds had observed that "Middletown" residents feared sex as "a force" that "might break loose and run wild," and so had tried to keep it "out of sight and out of mind as much as possible."[28] In the 1970s and 1980s, sex has become *visible* through certain political-economic and cultural mediations: birth control and abortion services for young, mostly poor and working-class, women; commercial pornography; and a gay culture that is "out." It is hardly an accident, then, that abortion and teenage birth control, pornography, and homosexuality have become the focal issues of sexual politics in the public arena. But what about sexual *relations?* Is this public battleground all there is of sex, or has there been a revolution in sexual values and practices, especially among unmarried teenagers, since the 1950s?

To feminists of the 1960s and 1970s, claims about a sexual revolution are a male fantasy. Historically, we can know little about sexual values or behavior from quantitative data such as illegitimacy rates. Looking particularly at France and England in the eighteenth and nineteenth centuries (when a tremendous rise in illegitimacy did occur), feminist historians show that upturns in illegitimacy or even sexual activity often reflect, not the quest for adolescent "self-discovery," but the greater vulnerability of young working women to seduction because of increasing social mobility and the proletarianization of male workers; deteriorating economic conditions that hinder marriage; and the breakdown of community customs sanctioning nonprocreative forms of erotic play (e.g., "bundling").

Under such conditions, out-of-wedlock pregnancy may represent an "expression of the traditional wish to marry," but in circumstances that weaken the normative and the economic enforcements of marriage.[29] The lesson of history is that the sexual behavior and values of young people may change little, whereas the social and economic context in which sex occurs—the security of a marriage promise or the social consequences of an out-of-wedlock pregnancy—may change a great deal.

Feminist social scientists interested in explaining contemporary patterns of noncontraception and rising abortion also criticize the myth of the sexual revolution and stress the persistence of traditional sexual values in the midst of changing conditions. Luker and Zimmerman document the pervasive view among teenage and other unmarried young women who got abortions in the 1970s that "sexual activity should occur in the confines of a permanent or potentially permanent relationship" (read, "love") and that sexual planning or premeditation—signaled by pill or diaphragm use—by a noncoupled woman advertises her as "loose" or "available."[30] These are two sides of a single ideological coin, ways of accommodating different realities to the dominant value of heterosexual monogamy. Nearly all the qualitative studies of unwanted pregnancy and abortion in the 1970s stress the association between contraceptive use patterns and the nature or intensity of the sexual relationships in which the women are engaged. Studies of both black and white unmarried young people have indicated that a relational context that is stable and steady is more likely to generate regular contraceptive use than is a context of unstable or "casual" relationships or infrequent sexual encounters.[31]

The intimate association for many women between a sense of their own sexuality and the emotional quality of sexual relationships ("she gets more emotional and falls head over heels while he could give a damn") is undoubtedly a product of a particular sexual and gendered culture. It is nonetheless deeply rooted. Studies of abortion patients find two patterns, the two heterosexual realities mentioned above. In the first, the women were involved, or claimed to be involved, in monogamous relationships with men; their nonuse of contraception, resulting in unwanted pregnancy, grew out of a desire to test the love or commitment of the male partner, or even of themselves, and sometimes an expectation of marriage. Its basis was the traditional culture of the romantic heterosexual couple and the woman trying to please or hold on to "her man." Here, the sexual act and its consequence are primarily signifiers in the playing out of "the relationship," rather than events with purpose in themselves. Using sex, and the risk of pregnancy, to test the limits of commitment helps define the future (which may indeed be precarious) and creates an aura of romanticism in which "a willingness to accept the possible consequences" becomes a test of one's "faith in the relationship."[32]

The second pattern involved women who were not in such relationships, whose sexual encounters were either casual or infrequent. These women, usually younger teenagers, maintained a "conviction of the inappropriateness of contraceptive preparedness."[33] Contraceptive nonuse and unwanted pregnancy grew out of a clear sense that while sexual pleasure for women is all right within the confines of a "steady" relationship, a woman who pursues her own pleasure outside of "a relationship," as evidenced by regular birth control use, is "bad" and makes herself vulnerable to sexual exploitation:

> . . . contraception forces a woman to define herself as a person who is sexually active. Planning specifically suggests not only that a woman has been sexually active once, but that she intends to be so again. A woman who plans is actively anticipating intercourse; in the terminology of the women interviewed, she is "looking to have sex." . . .
>
> If she is frankly expecting sex, as evidenced by her continued use of contraception, she need not be courted on the same terms as a woman whose sexual availability is more ambiguous. For many women, the loss of this bargaining position outweighs all the benefits of contraception.[34]

Both situations represent anything but a posture of sexual revolt; rather, they reflect the persistence of a sexual ideology and social reality that persuades women that the only true measure of their worth/existence is a romantic attachment to a man. The ironic conclusion to which we are led is that it may be the young women who are most faithful to conventional morality, rather than the liberal-minded or consciously feminist ones, who predominate among women getting abortions. These young women are apparently caught in a double bind; they are trying to accommodate a traditional morality about "love" and feminine virtue, yet are pulled in another direction by their sexual curiosity, the entreaties of boys, and social conditions—including the availability of birth control and abortion—that devalue early marriage and childbearing and place few sanctions on males for "lack of commitment." The contradictions in young women's consciousness about sexuality flow out of continuities with traditional morality as much as from changing opportunities for contraceptive use and abortion.

Recent interviews with 150 teenage girls about their sexual experiences found that they never mentioned anything concerning *pleasure* (although they might say "it didn't hurt"). Rather, the meanings of sex that they talked about were entirely bound up in the "story," the *relationship*—what happened with the boy, their girl friends, and so on. This was true even though most of them seem to have accepted heterosexual intercourse as a normal or predictable event in their lives, a matter of course.[35] Another set of interviews with 250 teenagers across the country in the 1980s reflects similar contradictions in consciousness about sexuality. These girls, from different class, racial, and geographic backgrounds, generally evince an expectation that they will engage in premarital sex, and not only with the person they intend to marry or an exclusive partner.[36] Their attitudes about sex are remarkably wide-ranging and frequently characterized by openness, self-confidence, and sophistication about their bodies and a variety of erotic pleasures; some even demonstrate the kind of bravado and rivalry about sexual conquests traditionally typical of teenage (and older) boys. At the same time, these "liberated" attitudes coexist with many traditional-sounding expressions of guilt and shame, and the persistence of the belief among some that one ought to be a virgin when one marries. Many of the girls retain a gnawing fear of pregnancy, which interferes with their sexual enjoyment, despite the availability and their use of contraception. Some even put off having intercourse because of that fear, citing stories about contraceptive failure or the side effects of the pill and the IUD as reasons for "not taking any chances."[37] Is the threat of pregnancy or medical side effects being used as a defense by some girls to stave off pressures (from peers, boys, popular culture) to have sex before they feel ready? Or is it a kind of internalized punishment, an echo of centuries of the double standard?

The social patterns as well as the norms of adolescent sexuality exhibit continuities with a presumably more "disciplined" past. For example, Zelnik and Kantner's 1976 study showed that by far the most frequent place where teenagers have sexual intercourse is at home (their own home or their partner's).[38] This reflects a material reality—dependent teenagers have few resources of their own—but also an understandable ambivalence about "leaving home." Moreover, whatever variations it takes, teenage sexuality seems to generate its own quasi-familial structures and moral codes. In her interviews, Thompson found that peer groups dictated rules for permissible and impermissible behavior that, while differing regionally and by class and race, nevertheless provided a set of limits on sexual activity (e.g., in many cases oral sex was considered taboo, even though intercourse was not). While the content of the rules may have shifted, it seems clear that such peer-group rules may be working as effectively among teenagers today as did the charivari in nineteenth-century Europe or the petting codes of the 1940s and 1950s to *restrict* sexual behavior. Thompson also mentions the elaboration, through sexual activity, of quasi kin networks involving boy friends and girl friends, former boy friends and best girl friends, in a triangle or nexus that reconstructs a family form rather than reflecting an abrupt separation from it.

The ambiguity in the teenage girl's sexual situation is enormously encouraged through the media and popular culture. First, even as a preteen she finds herself—or her idealized counterpart—commercially sexualized in films, advertising, and television. The image of the "promiscuous" teenage girl, as young as twelve or thirteen, is an outgrowth, and an ancient one, of a male-dominant culture. Its recent propagation through the media, child pornography, advertising, and the multi-billion-dollar packaging of Brooke Shields proceeds in tandem with the paternalistic fervor of the New Right and the courts, who seek both to "protect" young women from the ravages of abortion profiteers, pornographers, and seduction, and to punish them for succumbing. Patriarchal societies have traditionally served up a double mystification of women—mother and temptress, virgin and whore. Like its more traditional counterparts, the current commercial image of preteen sexuality is not one of female self-assertion or sexual autonomy but one of availability to fantasized male desire. To the extent that young women attempt to conform to that image, it does not reflect a radical change in sexual values or practices but a variation on the old patriarchal theme of "pleasing Daddy."

At the same time, teenagers have become the market for a multi-million-dollar bonanza of the publishing industry: paperback romances with titles like *Dreams Can Come True, P.S. I Love You,* and *Flowers for Lisa.* The formula for these books, based on similar ones published in the 1950s, is devoid of not only sex but race, class, and, for the most part, working mothers. Girls never make the first move; they wait to see what boys will do. And boys—a "relationship"—take priority over all else in life.[39] Feminist writer Brett Harvey aptly identifies these teen romances as a *reactionary* literature to the more sexually explicit teen fiction of the early 1970s; the new romances are "morality plays," whose message is that sex goes with marriage (or, at least, the "real thing") and "a woman is incomplete without a man."[40] The persistence of these traditional sexual values alongside the ambiguous social position of teenage girls—independent in some ways and dependent in others—compounds the conditions leading to unwanted pregnancy and abortion: "The 'problem' is not an absence of 'morality' among teenagers, but rather the persistence of a morality based on the sexual restraint of women presumed to be independent and responsible."[41]

On the other hand, if teenagers today exhibit complicated attachments to the sexual morality of the past, those of an earlier generation may have engaged in a degree of sexual inventiveness and subterfuge that rivals the sexually active teenagers of today. In his 1940s study, Hollingshead captures the sense of this dynamic complexity in his distinction between the "mores" and "folkways" of sexuality; between what people adhere to as beliefs and what they do and know in practice; between formal lines of moral authority and informal grids of complicity:

> . . . [many] play an intricate game of outward conformance to the publicly professed sex mores while they violate them in secret.

. . . In this game some adults aid and abet the adolescents,
while others work against them and attempt to maintain
the mores; one sex plots against the other, not infrequently males
outwit males and females hoodwink females; adolescents defy
adults, and children their parents. The churches try to uphold
the mores; the taverns and public dance halls aid in their
circumvention. Although the police are charged with the
maintenance of the mores, they regularly compromise between
their strict enforcement and their open violation.[42]

In this analysis of an earlier generation, Hollingshead suggests that
the conspiracy of silence and verbal adherence to the prescribed code is
more important than the actual prevention of a taboo behavior. Thus,
while marriage was the normative goal of sexual relations, in practice it
was understood that "going together" did not have to lead to marriage;
while "nice girls" were not supposed to like going to "petting parties,"
in practice many did; while parents and authorities were expected to
censure teenage sexual activity, in practice they loaned the car or looked
the other way. These perceptions are useful when we attempt to understand the sexual and reproductive politics of the 1980s, for it would seem
that those politics are aimed once again at silencing, reprivatizing, the
outward *signs* of sexuality (most conspicuously, abortion) more than its
actual practice.

Grids of Conflict and Sources of Change

Sexuality is not merely symbolic, an acting out of fantasies and norms
received from the dominant culture (family, church, media, films, and
novels). It is primarily social and is experienced through social relationships, not only with immediate sexual partners but also with the agents
of sexual authority and classification: parents, peers, religious figures,
and medical professionals. The social relations of sex, which involve class
and race as well as generational and gender divisions, are riddled with
conflict, differences in power, and sometimes resistances to power; these
are at least as important as the weight of traditional morality in determining the meanings of sexual encounters and the likelihood of contraception
or unwanted pregnancy.

This social content makes sexual experience historical—subject to
change over time—as well as specific to age, gender, and other social
categories. Sexuality for contemporary teenage women may function as
a theater in which gender-specific behavior is learned and practiced (waiting for a phone call, seeing what will "happen" to you, fearing rejection
if you don't accommodate—all the rituals of female passivity and compliance). At the same time, it is an area for staking out individual identity,

for risk taking and "gamesmanship" in exploring the self, the body, and the boundaries between one's self, one's parents, and "boys."[43] The accessibility of birth control and legal abortion has not generated a sexual revolution in the sense of a transformation of traditional norms of female sexual passivity. But it has widened the latitude for such explorations to take place, providing a "safety net." The widespread availability of birth control and abortion to teenagers has made it possible for sexuality and pregnancy to become an *extension* of adolescence, or a dimension of it, rather than a passage or threshold to "growing up." From the survey literature, one derives a striking picture of not only sex (including sex talk as well as sex performance) but also its concomitants—birth control, pregnancy, and abortion—as critical arenas in which dependent young women map out their identities and sense of separateness. As a large-scale social phenomenon, this may be historically new. I shall first describe some of the dynamics that construct these grids of conflict and self-exploration, then ask what might be their basis in the common and different social circumstances of contemporary teenage women.

A powerful teenage subculture—known to social scientists as "peer pressure" and to conservatives as "dope and sex"—was certainly not the product of birth control and legal abortion. But access to birth control and abortion, without parental knowledge or approval, might well have strengthened the sense that teenagers, particularly women, have of their collective identity. The influence of peer norms about sexual behavior is complex; it may help define a sphere of "otherness" from parents, which is both separate and safe, or it may pull some teenagers in directions that make parental sanctions a not unwelcome protection. Some of the teenage girls interviewed by Burkhart found themselves confronted with new codes, new standards of performance, which put pressure on them to "lose their virginity" and garner sexual conquests as a way to "score points" with girl friends.[44] If they feel unready for such "performance," the terrain of sexuality may still serve the purpose of defining the adolescent's separate (peer-related) identity through sex talk, even through boasting or lying about sexual experiences.

In the struggle to assert independence from parents or explore the boundaries between childhood and adulthood through sexual events, pregnancy itself may become a kind of resource. Some of the frequently cited psychological reasons why teenagers have sexual intercourse without using birth control (thinking "it can't happen to me" or wondering whether it can, confusion about when pregnancy may occur or wondering whether it might)[45] may be a kind of test of the borders of "maturity," of one's separateness from or connection to the family. All of the contraceptive nonusers in Zimmerman's study were high school students living at home. In terms that echo Luker's description of the "benefits of pregnancy," particularly in reaction to parents, she quotes young women who enjoyed their pregnancy (prior to abortion), using it as a time to fantasize about moving out of their mother's house and in with their boy friend; perceiving it as a way of "rebelling against" parents and asserting their own separateness, or alternatively (and sometimes simultaneously) of winning parents' attention and sympathy. ". . . I was doing everything I could possibly think of and I thought if I would have got pregnant or if I told them that I was pregnant or something like that, then maybe they would sit down and finally just listen to me for awhile. . . ."[46] Again, the fact of pregnancy and not its outcome is the focus[47]—pregnancy as a visible sign of sexual initiation, sexuality as a sign of individual identity. And at the same time a warning that will bring daughter and parents "closer," warding off for a while the separateness that neither yet fully wants. Using contraception renders the sexuality, the "act," invisible and thus undercuts its efficacy as a medium of self-assertion. "She didn't think I was like that," comments one of the young women about her mother's reaction to her pregnancy and its mutually understood meaning.[48]

The resolution of pregnancy, either through abortion or childbirth, also serves as a means to negotiate relations with parents, or between parents and boy friends, a means that is frequently hostile and perceived (correctly) as dangerous. Many different combinations of negotiated outcome appear in the survey literature—all of them involving explicit conflicts with parents and sometimes with peers. In some cases, peer pressure, instead of supporting young women's decision to get an abortion, seems to be heavily against it. In some cases parents insist on immediate abortion as a means of reasserting their control; in others, they reject abortion as "murder," in a volley of hostility that plainly reflects feelings about their daughter's sexuality.[49] In some cases young girls living at home who get pregnant are clearly not interested in bearing a child so much as in commanding their parents' attention; in others, they express a strong desire to have a baby in defiance of parental wishes and see themselves as weaker, less determined, for having relented to get an abortion.[50]

In a study of black rural teenagers, the cultural fact that pregnancy and childbirth would ultimately win these young women enhanced prestige and "adult status" within the household and community was often tempered by the initial experience of resistance, anger, and abuse from adult female kin. If this hostile reaction grew too overbearing, the women would redefine their situation by seeking an abortion or looking to the male partner for protection.[51] Whatever the outcome, it is clear that, at least during a particular stage, a pregnancy and its resolution represent a critical struggle for power and control between young women and their parents and between them and their male partners. Working through this struggle is an emotionally charged, powerfully affecting experience that usually leaves teenage girls feeling older, transformed, on the other side of childhood. Notice, however, that they are active participants in constructing the sexual terms of the struggle and not just passive victims.

But why should sexuality and pregnancy or abortion be the crucible through which teenage women individuate from their parents, discover who they are? The ambiguity in sexual power relations and the fact that teenage women may experience sex as the arena in their lives in which they feel the *most* powerful, even though that arena remains circumscribed by age, gender, and class hierarchies, helps to explain this phenomenon. I wish to argue that the reasons why sexuality and pregnancy function in this way, in the present historical context, are not only psychoanalytic in origin—and certainly are not just the by-product of "immorality"—but can be mapped in the ambiguous social situation of most teenage women today. This situation differs for different groups, yet there are conditions that the majority of teenage women share. For one, as suggested above, they are in the anomalous position of being at once infantilized by the cult of virginity (codified, for example, in statutory rape and "age of consent" laws) and objectified by the media's cult of "Lolita"; at the same time, they have few real resources for independence. "Not independent in society (and therefore not responsible for the consequences of their actions), [some] teenaged girls accept the risk of pregnancy rather than consciously separate sexual intercourse from procreation. . . ."[52] If they are poor or working class, their sense of limited alternatives may extend into an indefinite future. As Nick Freudenberg points out, based on clinical work with pregnant adolescents, "at some level . . . teenagers consider their other options for adult roles—through education, employment, social networks, etc.—and see their prospects as pretty bleak. Sex [and pregnancy] becomes one of the few ways to be like adults that isn't stamped down by the broader social structures."[53]

Objective limits on teenage women's social power may help construct the "outcomes" of sex and birth control. The modes and resources for seizing sexual and contraceptive initiative—including locations and opportunities for sex, birth control methods and delivery systems, and money—are intrinsically the tools of the powerful (i.e., adults, parents, doctors), but not young teenage women. Most teenagers, male or female, are essentially poor; having the money for condoms, pills, or a visit to a doctor or a clinic—even if you have the motivation—is no small matter if you are fifteen (i.e., Brooke Shields is a media fantasy in the tradition of Horatio Alger). Moreover, nurses, physicians, and clinics function as gatekeepers to accurate knowledge and assurance about contraceptive alternatives for teenage girls, and their authority (to prescribe or withhold) can have a negative influence on contraceptive use. For some teenagers, their lack of funds and minority status, as well as the bureaucratic requirements of clinic services, create sufficient barriers to prevent the acquisition of "contraceptive skills":

> . . . if they went to a government-funded "family planning" clinic (the very name is enough to turn most teenagers off), they would have been required to document parental income to obtain subsidized services. Given the guilt and ambivalence surrounding the introductory phase of sexual activity, it is not surprising that many younger teenagers chose, under these circumstances, to engage in sexual intercourse without contraception and take their chances with pregnancy.[54]

Teenage women living at home are inevitably influenced by their parents' power over them and control of their time, resources, and future. While this power does not and will not deter most teenagers from engaging in sex, it does affect the levels and timing of their birth control use and their need for abortion. Some girls, for example, shy away from getting contraceptives for fear their mother will "find them lying around the house."[55] Lack of privacy acts as a deterrent against contraception. A study of twelve hundred teenage family planning clinic patients (all female) in large cities around the country found that 42 percent delayed their first visit to a clinic for a period of between three months and several years after their "first intercourse." Thirty-six percent came only when they suspected they were pregnant. The *main reason* given for this delay, other than suspecting pregnancy, was the fear that their parents would find out.[56] Similar fears motivate many teenagers who get abortions not to tell their parents about it. A recent survey of teenage patients in five thousand abortion clinics found that 55 percent of those surveyed had informed their parents that they were going to obtain an abortion, but only 38 percent had told them voluntarily, since some were required to do so by the clinic's regulations or state law. The study concluded that nearly one-quarter would not have come to the clinic if required to tell their parents, "that a sizeable proportion of teenagers believe that the notification of parents would put them in a desperate situation and that they would be forced to resort to desperate measures to deal with it" (presumably, illegal or self-induced abortion or worse).[57]

The depth of teenage women's fears of "telling parents" reflects the continued mystification of sex by the dominant culture, particularly for young women. Along with the series of double messages discussed earlier, this mystification includes parental resistance to the idea of their daughters' sexual being and their strategies to control or, more often, ignore it. These strategies present cues that set up sexuality, contraception, and abortion as areas of potential conflict and provoke the anticipation—not at all irrational—of some terrible consequence, perhaps not physical violence but mental and emotional stress and disapproval. Such dynamics are particularly relevant in the case of fathers and their authority in the intrafamilial sexual power struggle. Evidence suggests that the relationship of the two parents to a daughter's abortion experience is not the same and that mothers are more likely to be told and more likely to extend sympathetic support. In Minnesota, where parental notification is required by state law, seeking an abortion becomes a common struggle of mother and daughter:

> Easily 25 percent of Meadowbrook's clients are minors, and for many the abortion itself is preceded by a harrowing day in court trying to secure a waiver from a judge against having to tell parents. Not uncommonly, mother and daughter are thrown into a conspiracy against a wrathful father who they fear will never be able to understand how his daughter came to such a sorry pass.[58]

The sexual shame and fear associated with abortion for a young teenage girl, it would seem, is deeply locked into parental authority. Shame and fear contribute to her need for abortion (her delay in getting contraception) and are reinforced through the paternal anger and disappointment that the abortion evokes. More serious still is the likelihood that many out-of-wedlock births among teenage girls—it is impossible to estimate how many—result from the fact that they "deny the reality as long as possible, often until it's too late even to consider an abortion."[59] This denial/delay syndrome is the direct by-product of a fear bred of a still punitive, female-blaming sexual culture whose agents are often fathers.

Relations with male sexual partners may also generate conflicts that discourage rather than encourage contraceptive use. In most of the abortion surveys, male partners neither knew nor cared about contraception, considering it the "woman's responsibility." This attitude is reinforced by most birth control and abortion clinics, which cater to a female clientele, as well as by the culture at large. But the conflict is usually experienced as an interpersonal one, with the woman perceiving that, given the availability of abortion, the man thinks of sex as something that has no painful consequences for her. Many of the men surveyed refused to use condoms or had a basic misunderstanding of the biological aspects of women's reproductive cycle and distanced themselves from it (even though they might later, if the woman became pregnant, feel they ought to have some say in whether she got an abortion). In this context, the woman's nonuse of contraception may be a kind of resistance, though a primitive and self-defeating one. "The structural situation . . . 'sets up' a man to be detached and noncommitted to this vital part of the sexual relationship, and women often feel not that they have 'control over their own bodies' but that they are being used."[60] One of Luker's respondents expressed annoyance at the idea of being a "sexual service station" that regular pill use seemed to imply. And one in Zimmerman's group complained:

. . . I just felt like if I took [the pill] he'd know, "Well, she's taking the pill. I can do it all the time." I didn't want that. I wanted him to be with me because he wanted to be with me, not to fool around. [Did you ever discuss condoms?] Yeah. He went and bought some one time, but he just—he didn't like it. He'd just take it right off.[61]

This kind of statement should not be read as a rejection of sex or sexuality, but as a rejection of a particular mode of sexuality with which the pill has become identified. That mode is fixated on genital intercourse (and thus male-oriented) and emotionally noncommittal (thus disconnected from "the relationship," or caring). It is not only that teenage girls may be coerced or pressured into having sex with boys or fear rejection if they refuse, although that is surely part of the reality.[62] It is also that many young men—who are using the terrain of sexuality to test out their identity as "masculine" in a sexist and male-dominant culture—may not be the most adroit or sensitive sexual partners. When pitted against young women's continued concern with affection and a "relationship," male sexual posturing may account for the "sporadic" pattern of young teenage women's early sexual activity and their failure to associate sex with pleasure. Resistance to the idea of herself as sexual object, wanting confirmation, within the sexual experience, of her worth and needs as a person, may be the other face of sexual and contraceptive "noncommitment" for some teenage women. It is a contemporary echo of the sentiments of Victorian feminists who distrusted birth control and abortion as tools that would further sexual abuse by men. The difference is that today access to safe, legal abortion has become a condition making it possible both *to be sexual* as a young woman and to avoid a sexual "availability" that traditional morality and female prudence find troublesome.

In the context of sexual and familial power relations, then, both noncontraception and abortion may represent a woman's resistance to, rather than her compliance with, dominant norms of behavior. For some women surveyed, the main point of deciding on an abortion seemed to be an assertion of their autonomy and needs vis-à-vis the men with whom they were involved. They would decide, not he. This was certainly the case among women who found themselves under pressure from male partners to have the baby and get married regardless of the impact that early marriage and childbearing would have on their lives.[63]

Yet, having said all this about the cultural and social-structural bases of teenage *non*contraception, it is time to emphasize that this is not the dominant reality but a diminishing one. The majority of sexually active (meaning heterosexually active) teenagers do *not* get pregnant—indicating that many use birth control effectively. Over 60 percent of teenage women negotiate sexuality and birth control without unwanted pregnancies or abortions, despite conflicting cultural and ideological pressures; despite parental disapproval or avoidance; despite the guilt-laden messages of religious organizations and the New Right; despite male irresponsibility and presumption; despite lack of resources, money and privacy; and despite bureaucratic and medical barriers to decent information and care.[64] Moreover, despite the persistent conditions of sex and gender conflict, many men and women—including teenagers—manage to cooperate in birth control and abortion use, enjoy sex together, and get along.

There were men who played a supportive and comforting role in the abortion experience and its emotional stresses.[65] Some young men definitely "felt birth control was the girl's responsibility not theirs," but others had a strong sense of mutual responsibility and concern (which, however, seemed to be more intense when the girl involved was a "girl friend" and not just any "girl"). Against what Burkhart calls "the myth of the macho male," many of the boys she interviewed manifested concern "with the quality of a relationship as a prerequisite for sexual intercourse." (Many, however, didn't, and their attempts to show "the gang" their prowess, as well as their resentment of sexually assertive women, suggest that the "macho male" is alive and well.) Boys resented social pressures on them "to prove themselves sexually" or to "prove their masculinity" through sex; they also preferred sex when they were "really in love," setting limits based on their feelings about the relationship, and not wanting to be used or objectified sexually by girls.[66]

All this is not to suggest that heterosexual relations among teenagers are without conflicts but that sexuality and gender relations may develop along somewhat different trajectories. A teenage girl in a relationship or sexual encounter with a teenage boy confronts a male whose situation is not very different from her own. With little more money or likelihood of having a job, just as little autonomy from parents and teachers, and equivalent adolescent uncertainty about who he is or what he will become, he is perhaps more her equal than most men are likely to be ever again in her life. Macho culture, high school sports, teen romances, and rock music may mystify these realities, but as ideological props of male superiority, they are constructed on a rather tenuous economic and social base.

Just as the image of the macho teenage male needs to be qualified, the image of female passivity and "noncommitment" to heterosexual sex may be inappropriate today. The rural black teenagers in Dougherty's study, for example, are impressive in the freedom, versatility, and self-assertion with which they organize their sexual lives. Using complex strategies and the support of female kin and peer networks, stressing "diversity in partners" and the desire not to be "tied down," their view of sexual relations is one that straightforwardly aims at optimizing pleasure and maximizing their own control.[67] One is struck by aspects in the sexual lives of these Florida teenagers and their marked contrast to the values and modes depicted in the (mainly white) groups surveyed in abortion studies. For one thing, the sexual experiences of these young black women seem much less isolated, much more integrated into relations with girl friends (the "peer group"), who lend advice and support throughout the "initiation phase" of sex; the male is not the total focus of the experience. For another, romanticism, as opposed to eroticism, would seem to be at a minimum here; courtship is strongly infused with an "element of play," and the idea of linking one's future to one man is disdained. "Most girls do not talk about 'love.' They speak about 'being crazy' about a man, meaning that they cannot keep their mind off of him, feel that they want him permanently, and would 'do anything' to 'get him.' "[68]

Studies of black women's kinship and sexual arrangements make it clear that young black women's attitudes toward sex and men often grow out of both the realities of racism and black male unemployment and the positive image of black women in charge of matrifocal households. They document the prevalence in black female cultural networks—urban and rural, intrapeer and intergenerational—of skepticism about how much you can rely on men and advice to daughters or younger kin to be self-reliant and resourceful in their relations with men.[69] These values, emphasizing women's sexual self-reliance as well as the communal value of babies and motherhood, also reinforce the general support among black kin networks for out-of-wedlock childbearing and their opposition to forced or precipitous marriage.[70] The strength of female support networks to help raise a child and the positive value attached to motherhood as that which perpetuates the community and signifies a woman's ascent to adulthood may be incentives not to use contraception nor seek abortion. But clearly, in this case, noncontraception has nothing to do with "noncommitment to sex."

What is relevant to the current "crisis" around teenage sexuality is that this kind of playful, self-assertive sexual code exists among some white middle-class teenage girls as well. There is reason to suppose that a changing sexual consciousness has accompanied the changing conditions analyzed in Chapter 4. For many young women surveyed, the assumption that nonmarital sex is a fact of life is taken for granted, just like the expectation that they will work most of their lives and share any household or child-care duties with their "equal" male partner. Often girls are "more afraid of commitment than boys," leery of being "tied down," eager to explore their sexual possibilities. Many of them have no compunction about making the first move in a sexual encounter or taking risks. "I was really curious, and I really wanted to do it to see what it was like. I wasn't in love with him at all."[71] The main reason they become involved in sex is because it *feels good*. Some teenagers (girls and boys) interviewed were highly experimental and imaginative, as well as considerate of the other person, in their sexual play. Indeed, contrary to the idea that petting may be becoming a lost art, many of them seemed to have experienced important and extensive phases of petting, touching, and oral sex, intense and exploratory heterosexual experiences that involve mutual pleasure giving but not intercourse.[72]

The picture drawn here suggests a model of sexuality that is developmental, a process learned through social interactions rather than a force or a "drive" that is either released or contained. Such a developmental, process-oriented concept helps distinguish between the images of a dominant patriarchal-heterosexual culture (e.g., the "Lolita syndrome") and the everyday sexual practices of various teenage subcultures; between fantasy and reality. It is difficult to sort out the reality of the sexualized teenage girl from her ideological construction, since the two affect one another. But the empirical evidence suggests that the sexual experience of teenage women, even the very young, is more complex and more organic—rooted in a process of growth—than the label of promiscuity implies. The construction of "promiscuous teenage girls" as a social crisis is a projection of adults' fears. It ignores not only the specific developmental character of teenage sex but the adeptness with which teenage subcultures often establish sexual rules and limits. Disrupting that process, either by forbidding sex or by forcing young teenagers into an "adult" organization of sexuality for which they are developmentally unprepared (e.g., "going steady" or marriage), may be futile or destructive. Sporadic risk taking or exploratory formats of sexual behavior may be endemic to early adolescence, which makes a *post*conceptive method of fertility control most appropriate. Not telling parents may be precisely the point of adolescent sexuality, insofar as that mode or phase of sexuality is precisely not a "family affair" but about breaking out of the family, defining one's own territory of intimacy.[73] While adolescents need to be helped to protect themselves from sexual *abuse* (sex that is coercive or imposed), venereal disease, and unwanted pregnancy, no adult has the right to "protect" them from the pleasurable sensations and explorations of their own bodies. Feminists and family planners share the view that to provide birth control, abortion services, and sex education—not to withhold them—is the sensible way to offer protection; although family planners are mainly interested in preventing pregnancy, while feminists are concerned with empowering young women, giving them more control over their lives.

Greater visibility and openness in the public discourse of sex, then, have undoubtedly entailed real changes in sexual practices among teenagers. "The actual act of sexual intercourse does not seem to be thought of as an act of rebellion anymore but rather as a normal part of life that comes either before marriage or with marriage. . . ."[74] The most striking fact about these changes, and politically the most charged, is that they break down some of the entrenched cultural divisions between white women and women of color, between middle-class and working-class and poor women, that have long been rooted in sexual stereotypes. While all women have been affected by the availability of legal and funded abortion, it is the white middle-class teenage woman who has been visibly "sexualized," both in her image and in her experience (see Table 6-1).

As long as it was black or poor white women who were having sex or showing up on hospital wards with complications from illegal abortions, the events were perceived not as sexual but as the "natural" consequences of poverty and race. These events, in a white-dominated and bourgeois culture, become visible to that culture, hence definers of "changing (or deviating) sexual mores," only when they involve masses of white middle-class young women. This is a shift of some importance in the history of class-race-gender relations in capitalist patriarchal society. In the nineteenth century, sexual "excess," like procreative "excess," became a badge of "otherness" that middle- and upper-class white women used to dissociate themselves from immigrant working-class and black women. "Slut" or "whore" implied black or lower-class ethnic, whereas the white middle-class woman accused of "whoring around" might be identified with "niggers."[75] The innocence and "purity" of his daughters was also a badge of the white male patriarch's authority and control over his household, his place in the racist and class-divided social structure. The illusion of the "petting culture" was to maintain these race and class divisions in the realm of sexuality. In the pre-pill, pre-*Roe* era, the working-class girl was more vulnerable than both the working-class boy and the middle-class girl. (Middle-class white boys were always expected to have sex with prostitutes—most of whom were blacks or poor whites.) Not protected by the safety and facade of "respectability" that the petting culture offered the middle-class girl, if she chose to be (hetero)-sexual, she walked a thin line between "having a good time" or "having a few romances" before "settling down" and being stigmatized as "loose" or "common property." Alternatively, she might be hastened into, or take refuge in, a life-determining early marriage and series of pregnancies. Contraceptives (i.e., condoms) among unmarried high school students in the 1940s were apparently well known, easily accessible, and cheap—for boys; Hollingshead makes no mention of contraception in relation to girls.[76] Meanwhile, the working-class girl tended to seek support through more open sex talk with girl friends of her class, thus risking the violation of secrecy codes and the ostracism of middle-class girls, who considered her "filthy-minded" and "dirty."[77]

Today, the availability of legal abortion and birth control services has created material conditions that have to some extent begun to equalize the sexual situations of young unmarried women across lines of class and race. On the one hand, for the working-class or poor young woman, access to safe, funded abortion avoids the stigma and burden of early pregnancy and so makes "respectability" and privacy in sexual relations a more universal good. On the other hand, for the middle-class young woman, access to abortion diminishes the penalties of sexual intercourse and, bolstered by the prospect of education and economic self-sufficiency, makes the rewards of chastity less compelling. For both groups, the context of a changing sexual consciousness and practice is the expansion of educational and earning opportunities, which has affected many working-class and black as well as white middle-class women. Traditional culture's tie between "sex" and "marriage" cannot withstand this cluster of changes.

In addition to birth control and abortion services, another change that may have contributed toward "democratizing" the teenage heterosexual culture has been a shift in the "geography of sex." Surveys of teenage women of all classes in the late 1970s found that nearly 80 percent of the heterosexual activity of these women occurred either in the girl's home or her partner's. Thus the family home, now empty and private during the day because of the rise in "working mothers," has become the central location of teenage heterosexual activity.[78] Moreover, if the culture of matrifocal households has reinforced sexual autonomy and self-determination among many black women, then the rising proportion of such households among white families may have a similar impact: encouraging young white women—out of their experience—to develop sexual self-reliance. These are trends not lost on the New Right, who see them as further reason to blame women, and feminists, for teenage abortion and sexuality. Mothers, particularly white middle-class mothers, are no longer at home policing their daughters' chastity, and fathers are out of the picture. What is significant is that, between 1967 and 1978, married women's labor force participation rates increased across the whole spectrum of economic groups, but *most sharply among middle- and upper-class wives.*[79] The home as a private space, more commodious than the automobile, has become another "leveler" of teenage sexual culture, no longer the guardian of young middle-class women's virtue.

But once the older culture of sexual subdivision and secrecy, of "nice women" and "bad women," begins to break down, and the sexual practices of black and white, lower- and middle-class teenage girls are no longer obviously different, what happens to the terms of race and class division as they have traditionally been expressed? What happens to the authority position of the white male father? The availability of birth control and abortion to all teenage girls, the real changes in their sexual behavior as both cause and consequence of that, and the *visibility* of those sexual changes through *white* teenage pregnancy and abortion rates challenge not only patriarchy but the sexual bases of racism and class domination. They are thus triply dangerous, which is why they have become the object of such vociferous attack. In the following chapters, we look at how these dangers to traditional gender, sexual, race, and class relations have been refracted into the abortion question through right-wing ideology and politics; and how feminist ideology and politics respond.

NOTES

1. Kristin Luker, *Taking Chances: Abortion and the Decision Not to Contracept* (Berkeley: University of California Press, 1975), pp. 25–33. Luker presents an incisive critique of what she calls the "intrapsychic conflict theory" of noncontraception, as well as the "contraceptive ignorance theory." Her argument is "that unwanted pregnancy is the end result of an informed decision-making process" that is "rational" and is aimed at "more diffuse goals than simply preventing pregnancy" (p. 32). While she thus intends to put "social-structural explanations" at the center of her analysis of "the decision not to contracept," and in part does so, the conceptual framework she chooses—"risk-taking models"—in combination with her survey methodology, actually detracts from this aim by focusing almost exclusively on the individual woman and her circumstances. Where she attempts to integrate the discrete experiences of her subjects through an analysis of broader cultural norms, it is almost entirely in ideological terms. She does not consider ways in which noncontraception may reflect, not only the internalization of traditional values about "nice girls," but also objective circumstances and conflicts existing in the social situation of young unmarried women.

Mary Kay Zimmerman, in *Passage Through Abortion* (New York: Praeger, 1977), is somewhat more successful in developing a social, as opposed to a psychological or psychoanalytic, explanation of unwanted pregnancy. Zimmerman's framework is interactionist, focused on the woman's relationships and symbolic communications with a series of "significant others" through which her abortion experience is structured. Again, a larger social and historical perspective is mostly lacking from this work.

2. See Luker, Chap. 4 and pp. 67–73.

3. See references cited in Introduction, note 24.

4. See Weeks, *Sex, Politics, and Society,* pp. 2–4; and Foucault, *History of Sexuality,* Vol. 1, Chap. 1.

5. Weeks, pp. 4–5, 9, 11; and Foucault, pp. 10–12 and 81–91.

6. Weeks, p. 12.

7. See L. Gordon, *Woman's Body, Woman's Right,* Chap. 10.

8. See Chap. 4.

9. For a theoretical critique of the complicated relationship between moralistic-punitive and therapeutic modes of "managing" deviant behavior by social welfare agents, see R. Petchesky, "Treatment as a Model of Social Control" (Ph.D. dissertation, Columbia University, 1974).

10. Camille Bristow, oral presentation, Workshop on Teenage Sexuality, The Scholar and the Feminist Conference 9, Barnard College, New York City, 24 April 1982. See also letters and editorials in the *New York Times* on this subject in March and April 1982, in which liberals tell conservatives that curtailing abortion and birth control services for teenagers will not stop them from having sex, and conservatives ask liberals how *they* propose to stop them.

11. Alan Guttmacher Institute, New York.

12. Zelnik and Kantner, "Sexual and Contraceptive Experience of Young Unmarried Women," in Furstenberg, Lincoln, and Menken, *Teenage Sexuality, Pregnancy, and Childbearing,* pp. 69 and 79; and idem, "Sexual Activity, Contraceptive Use and Pregnancy . . . ," (1980), pp. 230–33.

13. Weeks, p. 23; see also Kathryn W. Burkhart, *Growing into Love: Teenagers Talk Candidly About Sex in the 1980s* (New York: Putnam, 1981), p. 201. She critiques the statistical approach to defining "sexual activity."

14. Zelnick and Kantner, "Sexual and Contraceptive Experience of Young Unmarried Women," pp. 77–78 and Table 6.

15. Laurie Schwab Zabin, John F. Kantner, and Melvin Zelnik, "The Risk of Adolescent Pregnancy in the First Months of Intercourse," *Family Planning Perspectives* 11 (July/August 1979): 215–22; and Melvin Zelnik and John F. Kantner, "Reasons for Nonuse of Contraception by Sexually Active Women Aged 15–19," *Family Planning Perspectives* 11 (September/October 1979): 289–96, 289–92 and Tables 1-3. Over half the white teenagers gave as their reason that they "thought they could not get pregnant," because of either the time of the month, their youth, or the infrequency with which they had intercourse.

16. Burkhart, pp. 205–6, 276. Another recent study found that 44 percent of the "sexually active" teenagers in the clinic ($N = 1200$) abstained from sex for periods "lasting four months or more." Laurie Schwab Zabin and Samuel D. Clark, Jr., "Why They Delay: A Study of Teenage Family Planning Clinic Patients," *Family Planning Perspectives* 13 (September/October 1981): 205–7, 211.

17. Phillips Cutright, "Illegitimacy in the United States: 1920–1968," in *Demographic and Social Aspects of Population Growth,* ed. Charles F. Westoff and Robert Parke, Jr. (Washington, D.C.: Commission on Population Growth and the American Future, 1972), pp. 392–93.

18. John Diepold, Jr., and Richard David Young, "Empirical Studies of Adolescent Sexual Behavior: A Critical Review," *Adolescence* 14 (Spring 1979): 45–64, esp. 45–49.

19. Compare this analysis of different sexual patterns among black and white teenagers: ". . . facts show that Black youngsters are becoming pregnant more frequently than white. What does this mean when placed in the Black perspective? It tells *me* that the researchers have counted pregnancies rather than assessed sexual activity. White teenagers engage in more types of what we in the field of Sex Education call non-procreative sex. Such behavior by definition cannot lead to pregnancy. Non-procreative sex means stimulation accomplished by any means other than direct genital contact. Its source can be manual, oral, anal, autoerotic, or by artificial means, such as a vibrator. White youngsters engage in all these types of sexual activity at earlier ages and for a longer portion of their lives than do their Black counterparts." June Dobbs Butts, "Adolescent Sexuality and the Impact of Teenage Pregnancy from a Black Perspective" (paper presented at the Family Impact Seminar, October 1978), p. 15.

20. Diepold and Young, pp. 57 and 62; and Theodore Caplow et al., *Middletown Families: Fifty Years of Change and Continuity* (Minneapolis: University of Minnesota Press, 1982), p. 168.

21. Caplow et al., p. 165; and Diepold and Young, pp. 57–58.

22. "The more deeply a boy and girl cared about each other, the "further" they considered it all right to go. The standard enforced by the girls and grudgingly accepted by the boys held, in a general way, that kissing was all right if the two merely liked each other; "deep" or "French" kissing if they felt romantic about each other; breast touching through the clothing if they were halfway "serious" about each other, and with the bra off if they were somewhat more serious than that; and explorations "below the waist" . . . only if the couple considered themselves really in love." Quoted in Caplow et al., pp. 165–66, from Morton Hunt, *Sexual Behavior in the 1970s* (Chicago: Playboy Press, 1974).

23. Male sexual culture is a standard subject of fiction of the period, epitomized by Holden Caulfield and evoked nostalgically by William Styron's autobiographical character "Stingo" in *Sophie's Choice*. But the sexual experience of young women in the period, and the shared female subculture that defined it, remains without an acknowledged *female* voice in American fiction.

24. Burkhart, p. 200.

25. A. B. Hollingshead, *Elmtown's Youth* (New York: Wiley, 1961), pp. 414–17, 430. Hollingshead could confirm that the woman was not premaritally pregnant in only 20 percent of the high school marriages in his population; in at least 67 percent, she was.

26. Caplow et al., p. 168.

27. Ibid., pp. 161–63, 174. Burkhart, pp. 19–21, also stresses these outward "signs" of sex in the 1980s.

28. Quoted from R. Lynd and H. Lynd, *Middletown in Transition: A Study in Cultural Conflicts* (New York: Harcourt, Brace, 1937), in Caplow et al., p. 161.

29. Louise A. Tilly, Joan W. Scott, and Miriam Cohen, "Women's Work and European Fertility Patterns," in Rotberg and Rabb, *Marriage and Fertility,* pp. 219–48. They critique the "sexual revolution" theories of historian Edward Shorter. In the same vein, see Cissie Fairchilds, "Female Sexual Attitudes and the Rise of Illegitimacy: A Case Study," ibid., pp. 163–204.

30. See Zimmerman, p. 81; and Luker, p. 49.

31. See Frank F. Furstenberg, Jr., "The Social Consequences of Teenage Parenthood," in Furstenberg, Lincoln, and Menken, p. 190; Lucille Newman, "Unwanted Pregnancy in California: Some Cultural Considerations," in *Culture, Natality and Family Planning,* ed. John F. Marshall and Steven Polgar (Chapel Hill, N.C.: University of North Carolina, 1976), pp. 156–66; and K. G. Foreit and J. R. Foreit, "Correlates of Contraceptive Behavior Among Unmarried U.S. College Students," *Studies in Family Planning* 9 (June 1978): 169–74.

32. Steinhoff, "Premarital Pregnancy and the First Birth," in Miller and Newman, *The First Child and Family Formation,* p. 183; and Zimmerman, p. 76.

33. Newman, in Marshall and Polgar, p. 159.

34. Luker, pp. 46, 49. Compare Burkhart, p. 263, and Zimmerman: "Because it is not proper to do so, unmarried women do not generally think of themselves as sexually active persons. They may engage in sexual activity, but that is viewed differently from being a sexually active person . . . reliable methods of birth control suggest a commitment to sex" (p. 85).

35. Sharon Thompson, oral presentation, Workshop on Teenage Sexuality, The Scholar and the Feminist Conference 9, Barnard College, New York City, 24 April 1982.

36. Burkhart, p. 28.

37. Ibid., pp. 47–50.

38. Zelnik and Kantner, "Sexual and Contraceptive Experience of Young Unmarried Women," p. 75, Table 5.

39. N. R. Kleinfield, "New Heroines: Teenagers," *New York Times,* 17 September 1981, p. D1; and Brett Harvey, "Boy Crazy," *Village Voice,* 10–16 February 1982, pp. 48–49.

40. Harvey, p. 49.

41. Smith and Hindus, "Premarital Pregnancy in America . . . ," in Rotberg and Rabb, *Marriage and Fertility,* p. 360.

42. Hollingshead, p. 417.

43. See Molly C. Dougherty, *Becoming a Woman in Rural Black Culture* (New York: Holt, Rinehart and Winston, 1978), p. 81, regarding "strategy" and "gamesmanship" in adolescent sex.

44. Burkhart, pp. 44–45.

45. See Zelnik and Kantner, "Sexual and Contraceptive Experience of Young Unmarried Women," pp. 72–73, 85–88; Harriet B. Presser, "Guessing and Misinformation About Pregnancy Risk Among Urban Mothers," ibid., pp. 317–26; and Burkhart, pp. 259, 266–68, 278.

46. Zimmerman, pp. 91, 112. Luker too quotes one of her respondents who used pregnancy as a way of getting her mother to listen to her and bringing them "closer together" (p. 73).

47. Luker, p. 72.

48. Zimmerman, p. 129.

49. Ibid., pp. 129–32.

50. See Steinhoff, in Miller and Newman, pp. 195–97; and Zimmerman, p. 132.

51. Dougherty, pp. 90–91.

52. Smith and Hindus, in Rotberg and Rabb, p. 360.

53. Personal communication.

54. Evans, Selstad, and Welcher, "Teenagers: Fertility Control Behavior and Attitudes . . . ," in Furstenberg, Lincoln, and Menken, *Teenage Sexuality, Pregnancy, and Childbearing.* p. 370.

55. Zimmerman, p. 88.

56. Zabin and Clark, pp. 205, 213–15.

57. Aida Torres, Jacqueline Darroch Forrest, and Susan Eisman, "Telling Parents: Clinic Policies and Adolescents' Use of Family Planning and Abortion Services," *Family Planning Perspectives* 12 (November/December 1980): 284–92, 288. Zimmerman's survey, though much smaller, also found that 52 percent of the women had confided in a parent or parents about the abortion (p. 116, Table 6.2).

58. "Abortion: Women Speak Out," *Life* 4 (November 1981): 48; emphasis added.

59. Katie Leishman, "Teenage Mothers Are Keeping Their Babies—With the Help of Their Own Mothers," *Ms.,* June 1980. She quotes Pauline Seitz, a nurse-midwife in Cleveland: "The girl loses her childhood and many of her secret ambitions. Her father is often furious and then disappointed in his daughter, who

may have been the first woman the family had expected to go to college. Her mother loses her fantasy about what her daughter might have become—a fantasy that perhaps arose because she herself had a baby as a teenager and never got back on track. She also must surrender her dream that, in a few years, her mothering job will be over. No wonder they all deny the reality as long as possible, often until it's too late even to consider an abortion" (p. 64).

60. Luker, p. 127. Her argument (Chap. 6) that abortion and "female-oriented contraception" have diminished men's responsibility for the consequences of pregnancy, since they take the pressure off men to marry the woman or acknowledge paternity, is misleading and ahistorical. It blames abortion and birth control, rather than the gender hierarchy which long predates them, for women's unfair reproductive burdens. It also ignores that women were always blamed for unwanted pregnancy, whether abortion and "modern" contraception were available or not.

61. Luker, p. 49; and Zimmerman, p. 88.

62. See Burkhart, pp. 205, 273, and 276.

63. See especially Zimmerman, p. 145. But cf. Ellen W. Freeman, "Abortion: Subjective Attitudes and Feelings," *Family Planning Perspectives* 10 (May/June 1978): 154–55. Many of her respondents expressed heavy reliance on the male partner for emotional support, or sharp disappointment at the lack of it.

64. See Figure 4-2, above.

65. See Freeman, p. 154; Burkhart, p. 272; and Pamela Black, "Abortion Affects Men, Too," *New York Times Magazine,* 28 March 1982, pp. 76–78, 82–83.

66. Burkhart, pp. 29, 57–58, 61, 64–65.

67. Dougherty, pp. 77, 81–82.

68. Ibid., p. 82.

69. See Joyce A. Ladner, *Tomorrow's Tomorrow: The Black Woman* (Garden City, N.Y.: Doubleday, 1971), pp. 131–32, 166; Carol Stack, *All Our Kin: Strategies for Survival in a Black Community* (New York: Harper & Row, 1974), pp. 113; Dougherty, p. 84; and Gloria I. Joseph, "Black Mothers and Daughters: Their Roles and Functions in American Society," in Gloria I. Joseph and Jill Lewis, *Common Differences: Conflicts in Black and White Feminist Perspectives* (Garden City, N.Y.: Anchor, 1981), pp. 112–14.

70. "Most women agree that girls should not be pushed into marriage or any permanent relationship if they are not ready or do not feel that they have found 'the right man.' It is better for a girl to have a child who is wholly dependent on her family than to force her into a relationship with a man with whom she is not happy" (Dougherty, p. 92).

71. Burkhart, pp. 37–40.

72. Ibid., pp. 200–205, 214–19.

73. Ibid., p. 14.

74. Ibid., p. 41.

75. See Elaine Tyler May, *Great Expectations: Marriage and Divorce in Post-Victorian America* (Chicago: University of Chicago Press, 1980), pp. 109–10.

76. Hollingshead, p. 421.

77. Ibid., pp. 415, 419.

78. Zelnik and Kantner, "Sexual and Contraceptive Experience of Young Unmarried Women," pp. 59–60 and Table 5.

79. U.S. Department of Labor, Women's Bureau, *1969 Handbook on Women Workers,* Bulletin 294 (Washington, D.C.: Government Printing Office, 1969), p. 33; U.S. Department of Labor, Women's Bureau, *1975 Handbook on Women Workers,* Bulletin 297 (Washington, D.C.: Government Printing Office, 1975), p. 23; and Beverly L. Johnson, "Marital and Family Characteristics of Workers, 1970–78," *Monthly Labor Review* 102 (April 1979): A28. Determinations of family "economic levels" in these sources are based on husband's income only.

PART

III

SEXUAL POLITICS IN THE 1980s

7

The Antiabortion Movement and the Rise of the New Right

Abortion derives its meanings, not from any theological text or abstract moral code, but from the particular historical conditions surrounding it. In the 1970s, those conditions—delayed marriage and increased college attendance and labor force participation, an active and vocal women's liberation movement, and open dissemination of birth control—dramatically affected young unmarried women. Moreover, their impact on the socioeconomic position of such women and on their sexual ideas and practices form a related whole, as both feminists and antifeminists are aware. Thus abortion came to represent in the 1970s much more than either a "terminated pregnancy" or a "murdered fetus." To feminists and antifeminists alike, it came to represent the image of the "emancipated woman" in her contemporary identity, focused on her education and work more than on marriage or childbearing; sexually active outside marriage and outside the disciplinary boundaries of the parental family; independently supporting herself and her children; and consciously espousing feminist ideas. Insofar as the "typical" abortion patient was white, middle-class, young, and unmarried, the circumstances surrounding and defining her abortion presented an unquestionable threat, not only to traditional gender and sexual relations, but to traditional racial and class relations as well.

Given the powerful scope of this threat to a white capitalist patriarchy, it was to be expected that a movement to reverse legalized abortion and delegitimate its ideology would arm itself. The failure of feminists to anticipate and prepare for a counterattack was a reflection of a naive faith in liberal institutions more than the unexpected potency or origins of the attack. As early as 1970, the Catholic church began to organize "right-to-life" committees to stop the tide of legalization, and after *Roe* v. *Wade* in 1973 it launched a full-scale campaign to secure a "human

241

life amendment" to the U.S. Constitution that would declare the fetus to be a "human person" and abortion (for the first time in American legal history) to be murder. In 1977, the first Hyde Amendment curtailing federal Medicaid funding for abortion was passed, and by 1979 no federal funds could be paid for abortion or abortion-related services except when the woman's life was in danger. Meanwhile, local and state laws began to require parental and spousal consent or notification before allowing abortions to be performed on unmarried minors or on wives; and the drive in Congress to pass a constitutional amendment or statute that would recriminalize abortion, while making little headway in the early 1980s, nevertheless remained on the agenda.[1]

More than the attack on legal abortion, what needs to be explained is, first, why it succeeded in altering the public policy that had apparently prevailed only a few years earlier; and, second, why the campaign against abortion was taken up as the battering ram in a much broader offensive against nontraditional families, feminism, teenage sexuality, the welfare state, socialism, and every other target of the right. Finally, we need to understand the essentially cultural and ideological nature of this anti-abortion counteroffensive, for its legislative form is only one measure, not necessarily the most powerful, of its political effectiveness.

Launching the Neoconservative State

The politics of the family, sexuality, and reproduction—and, most symbolically, of abortion—became a primary vehicle through which right-wing politicians sought to achieve state power in the late 1970s and the 1980 elections. In particular, the crusade against legal abortion was taken up by an ascendant New Right as the pivotal issue in a drive to impose conservative thinking on many areas of policy making and social life.[2] But this ideological thrust predated the Reagan administration; it made important dents in state policy—in the executive branch, Congress, and the courts—during the Carter administration. Although by 1982, amid a deepening recession and the preoccupation of politicians with a stagnant economy, it seemed to have lost much of its steam in the legislative arena, its impact on administrators, courts, media, and public consciousness was (and is) profound. At this writing, abortion is still legal in the United States, but its legitimacy has been shaken, access to it has been curtailed, and the larger climate of feminist and liberal values that spurred its legalization has been called into question.

Why were abortion and sexual and family issues so centrally the focus of a resurgent conservatism? Is the connection between opposition to abortion and other, more traditional conservative political goals merely an opportunistic diversion (e.g., to take people's minds off the economic crisis),[3] or is there a more fundamental connection between abortion politics, sexual politics, and the economic and military policies of the New Right? It is my contention that antiabortion and more broadly antifeminist politics played a critical role in legitimating the transition from the liberal to the neoconservative state.

Attacks on sexual deviance and feminism historically have been a part of right-wing, or backlash, movements. Nativist and anti-immigrant sentiments helped fire crusades against abortion, obscenity, and birth control in late-nineteenth-century America. The early Ku Klux Klan and other right-wing groups in the 1920s attacked not only "cohabitation between whites and blacks" but "bootleggers, pimps, . . . wife-beaters, family-deserters, home-wreckers," as well as jazz music and short skirts.[4] The Nazis marked homosexuals for extermination along with Jews, Bolsheviks, Slavs and gypsies. The witch-hunters of the McCarthy period persecuted homosexuals as well as communists, liberals, and other "un-Americans," lumping them into one "subversive" list.[5] Modern authoritarian, fascist, and anticommunist movements have not failed to link a rigid patriarchal family structure, including the repression of sex outside heterosexual marriage and procreation, with the values of militarism, national and racial chauvinism, and sacred private property; and, as feminists know, they are perversely correct. It is not merely that there are "cultural" aspects to right-wing politics but that those aspects are connected to the "economic" and "political" aspects in deep-lying and complicated ways. What Reich called "organized mysticism" creates a mentality that is susceptible to authority, that displaces bodily needs into "fantasized substitute gratification" and racist hatreds, and that is easily diverted from the miseries of everyday life.[6] But the connections between right-wing economic policies and right-wing sexual-racial policies, at least in the current context, have an important social as well as psychological base. To analyze these connections means looking at the relations between antiabortion politics, antifeminism, and a declining capitalist economy.

Economic recession and massive unemployment provide a fertile context in which the ideas and politics of the right can thrive. A climate of soaring inflation, constant layoffs, retrenchment of social programs, and general insecurity helps explain popular susceptibility to conservative values and the defensiveness or weakness of left and feminist movements in response. The expansion in higher education and employment, especially in the public sector and professional jobs that opened to many women in the 1960s and 1970s, has eroded. As women, particularly younger and poorer women and single and divorced mothers, become more vulnerable to unemployment and cuts in social programs that have allowed them a margin of independence from traditional marriage, their sense of reproduction as a domain of conscious control may diminish. As corporate interests and the capitalist state accelerate their drive to rechannel resources from the public to the private sector, to increase profits in a period of decline, they perceive the "social experimentation" programs of the past two decades—including affirmative action, food stamps, battered women's shelters, legal services, environmental protection, occupational safety and health, and government-sponsored family planning and funded abortion—as expendable. The economy "cannot afford" social justice or the equality of women.

But while they gain momentum in times of economic distress, backlash movements are not primarily economic but political and ideological forces. In economic crises, antifeminist, racist, anticommunist, antiwelfare, and other stock conservative values—which are always there, always "in the wings" of American politics[7]—become not just a "diversion" but an essential means of legitimating the policies that deepen that crisis. They not only spring from it but propel it onward. In this manner, the campaign against abortion has played a specific and important role in propelling the right-wing economic and political resurgence of the late 1970s and the 1980s.

Backlash movements derive their ideological core from their existence as reactions to social movements and ideas of the left, including liberal and radical feminism. In American history, complicated as it has been by feminist participation in moral purity, eugenicist, and other semi-rightist or racist tendencies, those movements have typically assumed a moralistic fervor, often garbed in evangelical religiosity. Witness Father Coughlin, the fundamentalist Anti-Communist Christian Crusade, the Reverend Billy James Hargis, and others. Extreme right-wing movements are typically an expression of the "preservatist" impulses of social groups that feel their way of life threatened:

> Desperately preservatist or restorative movements—that is backlash movements—require an aggressively moralistic stance and will find it somewhere. There needs to be invoked some system of good and evil which transcends the political or social process and freezes it.[8]

What this "system of good and evil" is, however, is not arbitrary but a product of the historical moment and of a conjunction of forces that bring specific social conflicts to the fore. If the embodiment of absolute evil for an earlier generation of the right was international communism, the left, and labor movements, in the recent period it is feminism and homosexuality. Both represent movements for transcendence of a patriarchal form of family and for sexual liberation. This shift is not surprising given the weakness of the left and labor movements at the present time; whereas the feminist movement in the 1970s was the most dynamic force for social change in the country. And of all feminist demands, the right to abortion and to sexual freedom appears most threatening to traditional sexual and social values.

The antiabortion movement, which began in the Catholic church and, despite disclaimers, has remained an essentially religious movement, has been a central vehicle through which the New Right has crystallized and developed its mass base and mass ideology. This particular crusade, which predates the New Right, has provided the perfect issue to "freeze" the political process into an absolute struggle between good and evil; it is something "positive to fight for." But while the religious, moralistic, and often mystical terms in which this crusade is couched resonate for many of its followers, religion should not be mistaken for the content of right-wing politics. Religion provides an "apocalyptic framework which validates [moral] absolutism,"[9] but this framework is political in the most conventional sense: It has to do with how and by whom power is exercised in the economy, the state, the family, and the churches. In addition, religion supplies a language and symbolism through which the right lays claim to the righteousness and purity of its vision. Abortion represents all the satanic evils the right seeks, and Scripture beckons it, to destroy (communists, feminists, homosexuals, liberal welfare advocates); the fetus symbolizes the pristine and the innocent, which must be protected and saved (family, children, God, the American way). Paul Weyrich, New Right theoretician and political kingmaker, conveys the apocalyptic character of this vision and the full sweep of the cast of enemies it implicates:

> . . . from our point of view, this is really the most significant battle of the *age-old conflict between good and evil,* between the forces of God and forces against God, that we have seen in our country.
>
> We see the antifamily movement as *an attempt to prevent souls from reaching eternal salvation,* and as such we feel not just a political commitment to change this situation, but a moral and, if you will, a religious commitment to battle these forces. . . .
>
> Among the antifamily forces are hardcore socialists who see it as a means by which they can attain greater state control. One of the Communists' chief objectives has always been to break down the traditional family.
>
> There is also a group of economic opportunists who profit by the decline in traditional values, through pornography, abortion clinics, the contraceptive mentality, drug sales.
>
> Then there are people who want a different political order, who are not necessarily Marxists. Symbolized by the women's liberation movement, they believe that the future for their political power lies in the restructuring of the traditional family, and particularly in the *downgrading of the male or father role in the traditional family.*[10]

This appeal to evangelical religion and populism reflects traditional ingredients of American right-wing ideology; what is distinctly new is that abortion is the occasion of the crusade, and "the family"—more centrally and passionately than "free enterprise" or national defense—its sacred object. This shift in emphasis is unmistakably the product of feminist ideas and their powerful impact in the 1970s on popular consciousness. Feminists are the "communists" of the 1970s.[11]

The simplest and most obvious explanation for the New Right's existence and success in influencing public policy is that the political values and social changes its members are fighting against are real and pervasive. The women's and gay liberation movements and structural changes in the family that have been both cause and effect of those movements represent a genuine threat to the family system and sexual morality the New Right is seeking to preserve. While New Right language and symbolism often take a mystical and irrational form, their ends are coherent and clear; the conflict between the values of the New Right and those they oppose, as they perceive better than many liberals, offers no compromise. In this sense, the antiabortion/antigay/anti-ERA/profamily current is indeed a backlash movement to turn back the tide of the major social movements of the 1960s and 1970s. It is aimed primarily at organizations and ideas that have directly confronted patriarchal traditions regarding the place of women in society and the dominant norms of heterosexual love and marriage. But it is also a reaction to the New Left and the counterculture generally, which many white middle-class parents experienced as having robbed them of their children, either literally or spiritually. The strength and determination of this backlash, particularly in regard to abortion, homosexuality, and the ERA, is in part a measure of the effectiveness of the women's and gay movements, the extent to which their ideas (and various distortions of their ideas) have penetrated popular culture and consciousness, if not public policy.

The "profamily" movement is reacting to dramatic changes in family life that have occurred most sharply during the past fifteen years. When we add together the changes in marriage, fertility, women's labor force participation, and household composition discussed in Chapter 3, the result is that only around 10 percent of all American households consist of the "normative" model: husband-wife families with two or more children at home and the husband as the sole breadwinner.[12] Although marriage and remarriage rates are higher than ever before, the combination of postponed marriage and high divorce rates means that marriage becomes a phase of the life cycle rather than a lifetime proposition, with continually increasing numbers of women spending years of their adult lives heading households or alone. Delayed and declining fertility and the growing tendency to work during pregnancy and childrearing years have made active motherhood a shrinking part of most women's daily life and overall life cycle. While most women will raise one or two children in their lives, they will do so in a context of nearly continuous work outside the home and, for many, of decreasing economic dependence on men. Meanwhile, one out of five Americans lives as a single individual—not in a "family"; and a growing proportion of households (still a small minority) consists of young unmarried couples.[13]

These demographic trends undoubtedly conjure up for many people untold fears of sexual deviance and the absence of "safe" boundaries. Whatever the gap between conservatives' fantasies and the reality of people's lives, it seems unquestionable that the demographic changes have been accompanied by significant cultural shifts. In particular, they have brought greater openness about homosexuality, nonmarital heterosexuality, living arrangements, and childrearing that fall outside the traditional (normatively sanctioned) heterosexual-married-household pattern. Moreover, we should remember that they are changes whose major upswing has occurred only during the last twenty years, less than one generation, and whose impact on people's lives and expectations for themselves and their children has undoubtedly been unsettling.

Absorbing that impact has been difficult for all people, including committed feminists. For one whose belief has remained unshaken in his prerogative, as a man, to "have the authority and make the decision," or her privilege, as a woman, "to be happy with it," it must seem a very alien and treacherous world. For many more, the economic strains and social changes of the contemporary period are experienced as personal crises, as "family" crises: loss of job, loss of children, loss of a sense of security, or loss of mother (or wife) at home. Thus the construction of a "profamily" politics, with the embattled fetus as its motto, appeals, or is intended to appeal, to a level of longing and loss (homelessness) buried deep in the popular subconscious. To argue that the New Right's focus on sexual and family issues is a diversionary tactic to lure people's attention away from unemployment and other economic distress is to deny the social reality of changes in the family and their effect on people's sense of who they are, particularly in a climate of economic insecurity. At the same time, women's employment outside the home, as well as the women's liberation movement, is once again blamed for the economic crisis, for taking jobs away from men, and this adds fuel to the New Right's antifeminist attack and people's susceptibility to it.

Embedded in the New Right's "moral" offensive are two interlocking themes. The first is the antifeminist backlash, aimed initially at abortion but extending from abortion to all aspects of sexual freedom and alternatives to traditional (patriarchal) family life. The second is the anti-social-welfare backlash, aimed at the principle (given a certain legitimacy during the New Deal and the 1960s) that the state has an obligation to provide for economic and social needs through positive government-sponsored programs. What we need to understand is the relationship between these two aspects of the right's current politics, how they reinforce one another.

For it is becoming clear that the moralistic fervor applied in the antiabortion campaign is being extended to political goals that seem unrelated to sex, religion, or the family—to traditional right-wing goals such as racial segregation, welfare cutbacks, and militarism. The analysis that follows attempts to show not only the centrality of antifeminism and antiabortion politics to the New Right's ideology and political organization but also some connections between antifeminism and the attacks on liberalism and social welfare. In particular, I stress the ideology of "privatism" and "private morality" as that element of the antiabortion/antifeminist thrust that has provided the critical link between family and sexual politics and traditional economic and social conservatism.

Historically, the concept of privacy for American conservatives has included not only "free enterprise" and "property rights" but also the right of the white male property owner to control his wife and his wife's body, his children and their bodies, his slaves and their bodies. It is an ideology that is patriarchal and racist as well as capitalist.[14] Part of the content of the formal appeal to "states' rights" is the idea of the family as a private, male-dominated domain. Control over families (one's wife and children) and over local and state power structures are closely related conservative values, insofar as the latter is the means whereby the former is sought as an end. Thus what seem to be attacks on federalism or federally sponsored social services are simultaneously attacks on movements by women, the poor, and young people to assert their right to resources, services, and a viable existence outside the male-dominated family and the ghetto.[15]

Privatism and the welfare state in American capitalist society have not opposed but in many ways have reinforced one another.[16] Public programs to bestow social benefits have frequently functioned to subsidize private (market) interests (e.g., Medicaid, manpower training, or tax benefits to proprietary day-care centers and nursing homes). The very concept of welfare in the United States contains within it the idea that the well-being of people and providing for their basic needs is an essentially private matter, that the state should act as provider only in situations of extremity or helplessness. Thus, unlike welfare clients, individual workers "earn" their social security benefits by working hard and paying into the program. In the last two decades, however, the sizable expansion of social welfare programs has reached into new substantive areas of "entitlement"—health care, food, housing, legal services, higher education, protection from abusive husbands and toxic environments, and abortion—as a result of demands by organized popular movements. These gains, though limited, have helped individual women, poor men, teenagers, workers, and communities exposed to environmental hazards gain independence and security in their lives. They have also created a political climate in which the *idea* that basic human needs *ought to be met* through public, social instruments has begun to achieve popular acceptance. For this reason—political rather than mainly economic, for many of the programs being cut back are among the least costly—the social welfare apparatus has come under attack, not only by the New Right, but by businessmen and centrist policy makers.[17] Thus the push to reprivatize or "deregulate" certain public programs has been highly selective, aimed specifically at domains of social service created through the struggles of working people, blacks, the poor, and women in the 1960s and 1970s to expand their sphere of autonomy within a capitalist patriarchal society.

Legitimating this push is the neoconservative notion of "excessive government." It argues that what's wrong with busing programs or Medicaid abortions or the Occupational Safety and Health Administration (OSHA) is that the federal government is meddling in our "private business." It assumes, indeed, that there exist some private, safe places— "our" neighborhoods, "our" private schools, "our" churches, and, above all, "the family"—that would give us everything we needed if only the government would stay out. But, although the language of New Right ideology evokes the sentiment of personal freedom from state interference, what distinguishes that ideology from classical conservatism is that it is spoken on behalf of corporate bodies rather than individuals. It is corporate privatism—in the service of business, church, private school, and patriarchal family—that is intended, not individual privacy. Moreover, it is put forward in the name of a particular class—white middle-class Christians—whose relationship to "private" institutions is one of ownership. In both these aspects, the New Right's appeal to privatism is much closer to fascism than to classical libertarian doctrine and is thus perfectly compatible, in theory as well as practice, with a program of state control over individuals' private lives. For example, requiring that both parents be informed when teenage girls seek abortion or birth control services has created serious contradictions in the policies of the Reagan administration. It attempts to support traditional conservative principles of individualism and states' rights and at the same time dictates how states should regulate relations between parents and their children as well as the sexual behavior of young people. But such contradictions are apparently of little consequence to the New Right and the Reagan administration, whose concern is polemical appeal rather than coherent policies. By focusing on realms that have the greatest *appearance* as "private" or "personal" in our culture—sexuality, abortion, the relations between parents and children—the New Right has been able to achieve a certain ideological legitimacy for its policies of racist and sexist exclusion and denial.

Nowhere is this clearer than in measures to cut off Medicaid funding for abortions, which in 1977–78 helped prepare the way for the conservatization of the state. The Hyde Amendment and the Supreme Court's decision upholding that amendment contain the antifeminist and the antisocial welfare components of New Right politics in a nutshell. For these measures undermine the idea that women's "right to choose" abortion is fundamental and the idea that the state is obligated to pay for the health needs of those who cannot do so themselves.

Restriction of Medicaid abortions was one of the first in a series of escalating cutbacks in social services, adopted in the context of economic and fiscal crisis, military buildup, and environmental and business deregulation. Involving an activity that seems most deeply associated with a private, personal realm and affects the most vulnerable, least powerful group in society—poor women, many of them women of color or teenagers—this policy has provided a politically acceptable wedge for the agenda of "reprivatization" to be applied on a larger scale. The assault on Medicaid abortions helped provide more than a pragmatic fiscal argument for social service cutbacks; it provided a "moral" argument. Women who seek abortions are accused of "selfishness" and "hedonism," a theme extended to welfare clients, food stamp recipients, legal services clients, and all who are dependent on social welfare programs to survive (though not those on social security or unemployment insurance). And these are predominantly women—poor divorced, widowed, separated, and single women, those who live outside the patriarchal nuclear family, recently called the "nouveau poor."[18] Abortion is "evil" not only because it represents women seeking their "selfish" ends rather than their procreative "duty" but also—and this is the dimension of popular "morality" that the New Right has tapped most successfully—because it represents women who "get away" with something, who get a "free ride." Medicaid funding for abortions gives poor women a "license" for illicit sex. They don't have to "pay" for their sins, they get something (sex) for nothing, courtesy of the taxpayers. That, far more than the killing of fetuses, makes not only conservative politicians but many working-class and middle-class people angry.

The campaign against abortion funding—and abortion generally—I would argue, exploited both the "taxpayer revolt" and the rightward-drifting sexual morality. It was instrumental in propagating the ethic of self-sacrifice and belt tightening that the corporate ruling class and the capitalist state attempted to impose on workers, consumers, and, most of all, the poor, as a means of "controlling" the economic recession. In this way, antiabortion politics played midwife to the neoconservative state and its business-oriented economic policies.

At first sight, a policy that restricts abortion access for poor women seems in direct contradiction to a decade-long policy of state-sponsored population control among the poor, as a means of diminishing welfare dependency. But neoconservative and New Right thinking about welfare cutbacks and abortion does not represent a pronatalist doctrine so much as a formula for restoring the traditional patriarchal family and the authority of men within it, among the poor as among the middle class. In the forefront of this thinking is President Reagan's favorite neoconservative, George Gilder, whose *Wealth and Poverty* is a singularly unoriginal recapitulation of the ideas of Malthus, Mandeville, and Daniel Patrick Moynihan.

To Gilder, the central cause of poverty, apart from the failure of the poor to work hard, is the weakness of "the male role in poor families," the "breakdown of family responsibilities among fathers." The solution to poverty, then, is to "strengthen" male authority, to return women to their "maternal horizons," thereby tying poor men to the family and to a long-term future of "work and thrift."[19] The implicit objective here, however, is not unlimited childbearing but the imposition on the poor of a bourgeois ethic and culture of saving and, no doubt, abstemiousness. Shades of Malthus. Similarly, Hyde Amendment restrictions seem irrational and contradictory to fiscal conservatism (reducing the numbers of people on the welfare rolls) only if we ignore the fact that saving money is not the primary function of either abortion or welfare cutbacks. Reaganomics involves cutting back those social programs that affect the poorest and most vulnerable people and yet are smallest in terms of total outlays.[20]

Social welfare cutbacks, including funding for abortion, are less a matter of increasing revenues or achieving a balanced budget than they are of imposing discipline, social control. But who is the object of discipline, and for what ends? Piven and Cloward argue that the major purpose of social welfare cutbacks in the 1980s is to discipline workers by tightening the income-maintenance programs that make loss of employment less onerous, less threatening to *all* workers, not only the unemployed. Thus the cutbacks are ultimately directed at restoring the power of the capitalist class over the working class as a whole.[21] This argument, while not wrong, ignores the fact that the great majority of the beneficiaries of those programs undergoing the severest cuts are women—female family heads who are in poverty, poor women seeking legal help for divorce, paraprofessional and professional workers in the public sector, and sexually active teenagers. It seems undeniable that a major goal of the conservative state's effort to contract if not dismantle social welfare is to discipline and punish women who try to survive, and be sexual, outside the bounds of the traditional family.

Here the denial of funding for and access to legal abortion is obviously key. The crisis of capitalism and the capitalist state provides only half the explanation for the antiabortion campaign; the other half comes from the crisis of patriarchy. Abortion is not simply an aspect of social welfare; it is a condition of women's liberation, and by the 1970s it had become recognized by advocates and foes as deeply symbolic of feminist aspirations, a paradigmatic feminist demand. The reasons for this, as we have explored, are rooted deep within the actual conditions of women in industrial society and the culturally assigned responsibilities of women for children. While unarticulated, often even by feminists, the meanings resonating from abortion politics have more to do with compulsory heterosexuality, family structure, the relationship between men and women and parents and children, and women's employment than they do with the fetus. Thus the campaign against abortion in the courts, the legislatures, and through electoral politics is—in some ways that are more devastating than the defeat of the ERA—a challenge to the changes in women's conditions that are identified with the feminist movement. The campaign against legal abortion reflects and reinforces the swelling counterattack against feminism.

The Organizational Base: Churches and Reproductive Politics

In contrast to the peace, environmental, and antinuclear movements, which also contain many religious activists and groups, the antiabortion movement, which encompasses not only Catholics and fundamentalist Protestants but also Orthodox Jews, Mormons, and Black Muslims, is narrowly religious and antisecular. As Judge Dooling commented in *McRae* v. *Harris,* "the right-to-life movement . . . does use religious language, invokes religious motivations, and enlists prayer as an aid."[22] Nevertheless, its leadership is hostile to those it associates with "social" or "liberal" Christianity, such as the National Council of Churches or the left-wing Catholic clergy in Latin America. This is hardly a position of ecumenism. While various denominations participate, the unquestioned direction of the "right-to-life" movement—doctrinal, organizational, financial—has from the outset come from the Catholic church hierarchy.[23]

> Roman Catholic clergy and laity are not alone in the prolife movement, but the evidence requires the conclusion that it is they who have vitalized the movement, given it organization and direction, and used ecclesiastical channels of communication in its support. The union of effort with representatives of other denominations is based on shared religious conviction.[24]

The "right-to-life" movement was originally a creation of the Family Life division of the National Conference of Catholic Bishops (NCCB), the directing body of the Catholic church in America. Immediately following the Supreme Court decision in *Roe* v. *Wade,* the NCCB Pro-Life Affairs Committee declared that it would not "accept the Court's judgment" and called for a major legal and educational battle against abortion. Since then, in numerous documents the bishops have summoned Catholics, both lay and clergy, to enter the antiabortion struggle: to defeat liberal abortion laws and proabortion candidates and work for a constitutional amendment that would, in accordance with Roman Catholic doctrine, declare the fetus a full human person from the moment of fertilization and abortion thus a homicide.[25] In 1975 the NCCB presented a detailed strategy for the church's antiabortion crusade, its "Pastoral Plan for Pro-Life Activity." It called for the establishment of a network of "prolife committees," based in the parishes, that would (1) effect the passage of a "prolife" amendment, (2) elect "prolife" sympathizers to local party organizations, (3) monitor officials on their abortion stands, and (4) "work for qualified candidates who will vote for a constitutional amendment and other prolife issues."[26] From the outset, the "right-to-life" movement was set up to be a political action machine to influence national and local elections, but working primarily through the churches and the financial and organizational leadership of the hierarchy.

Churches constitute the most important strategic base for carrying out the antiabortion crusade. Pastoral letters have been read from pulpits, urging parishioners to get involved in "prolife" political work of all kinds. Church services have become a regular source of financial support for the movement, with hundreds of thousands of dollars collected annually through Sunday mass collections and then channeled to local and national "right-to-life" committees.[27] More important than financial assistance, local churches and parishes provide the "right-to-life" movement with the organizational and communicational system that allows it immediate access to material resources and recruits. Churches supply rooms for meetings, telephones, duplicating equipment, buses and bodies for rallies and demonstrations, and highly effective organizers in the person of priests. Clergy distribute "prolife affirmation cards" at mass and hold prayer meetings, masses, and diocesan rallies to coincide with electoral and lobbying efforts.

It is important to note the key role that many (though not all) priests and pastors have played in the building of the "right-to-life" movement. Recruited through the hierarchy, they have served as organizers, theoreticians, and militants. Above all, they have used their pastoral authority to engage in moral exhortation, in terms clearly evoking religious guilt and linking "prolife" activity with Christian duty and eternal salvation. The pulpits and parochial schools have become the central platforms from which antiabortion statements are delivered regularly; parishioners and students are directed to attend marches, rallies, clinic sit-ins, and other activist events.[28] For Roman Catholics and fundamentalist Christians who believe in the metaphysical reality of the soul and the "innocence" of "fetal life," this appeal receives a powerful stimulus from the concern for one's own salvation.[29]

The most politically crucial function of the churches has been their contribution to the "right-to-life" electoral strategy. "Prolife" Catholic and Protestant clergy have not hesitated to use the power of the pulpit to condemn political candidates targeted by antiabortion "hit lists," attempting to influence votes on the very eve of elections.[30] More generally, the churches serve as recruiting grounds from which voters of both major parties are enlisted into "right-to-life" electoral politics. "Prolife" political action manuals give local organizers detailed instruction about how the electoral process works at every level and how to penetrate it.[31] Because of the steadily declining voter turnout in the United States, most political candidates are elected or defeated by a very small margin. The antiabortion movements in the mid-1970s thus adopted a complicated electoral strategy whose nucleus was the "voter identification survey":

> The 1980 right-to-life strategy [was] to pack the state legislatures with antiabortion representatives as a means of getting as many of the requisite 38 states as possible to call for a Constitutional Convention . . . [or, failing that,] to use this leverage to force Congress to report the Human Life Amendment out of Committee. In either case, their electoral goals [were] on the state level, where they [felt] they [had] a better chance of having immediate impact. Toward this end, they . . . conducted voter identification surveys in 36 states. In New York State alone, they . . . canvassed over a quarter of a million primary voters to locate those people who [would] vote against proabortion candidates in 1980.[32]

The organized antiabortion movement, however, in its political and ideological roots is distinct from the New Right and should not be confused with it. Unlike the National Right to Life Committee (NRLC) or the Catholic bishops, the individuals, organizations, publications, and political action committees that define themselves as the New Right are not ultimately concerned with fetal souls or moral purity but with achieving state power. Formed in 1974–75 in reaction to what they perceived as the liberal dominance of the Republican party, this cluster revolves around a small core of political strategists—"technicians," not themselves politicians—allied with a group of right-wing fundamentalist preachers who serve primarily as propagandists and fund raisers and a cohort of conservative politicians in Washington largely of their own promotion.[33] Though strongly tied to the organizations of the old right—most New Right leaders have long affiliations with groups like the Young Americans for Freedom, the John Birch Society, or the World Anti-Communist League—the New Right is "new" in a number of ways. First, their aim is unlike that of the old right, for example the Birchers, who maintained an essentially reactive, defensive politics.[34] The New Right is on the offensive to create a national political machine that cuts across the major political parties, wins elections, initiates legislation and policy, and eventually dominates the state. Second, the means through which they have pursued this aim have been innovative as well as effective (at least in 1976 and 1980). Targeting every conservative single-issue cause in the country—antiabortion, "right-to-work" committees (antiunion), gun owners, antibusing groups, school prayer advocates, "creationists," textbook censorship groups, anti-ERA and antipornography groups—they have attempted to fuse these causes into broad-based coalitions that can be mobilized politically in support of right-wing candidates and issues.[35] In this process the fundamentalist churches and preachers recruited into the New Right's organizational structure have provided an important institutional base. In addition, the use of computerized mailing lists, compiled from all these conservative groups, to do direct-mail fund raising among some 25 million Americans has transformed the nature of American political techniques.[36]

Finally, the New Right may be distinguished—and distinguishes itself—by its ideology. While faithful to traditional conservative themes such as the right to bear arms, high taxes, a balanced budget, and America's failing military strength, it initially focused its energies on issues related to the family and sexuality, rather than "economic" issues. In other words, it defined itself primarily in reaction to feminism and identified abortion as its number-one target. At the 1980 Republican convention, it was through sexual/reproductive politics that New Right forces made their strength felt on the platform committee and among the delegates. Throughout the campaign, it was not an aggressive defense-spending and tax-cutting program (which Democrats supported as well) but opposition to abortion and the ERA that identified the New Right's politics.

Of course, Reagan's election in 1980 was not the doing of the New Right nor can it be read as a popular "mandate" for conservatism; the popular vote was a rejection of Carter and a complaint about economic conditions more than anything else.[37] What the 1980 elections suggest is not so much the susceptibility of voters to antifeminism, but the determination of the right to construct a political phalanx around it. Building on the emotional response that abortion and invocations of "the family" and Scripture generate, the organized Moral Majority intends to move on to other, less obviously "moral" agenda items: "The alliance on family issues" will "look at the morality of other issues such as SALT and the unjust power that has been legislated for union bosses."[38] Sexual and family politics, then, beginning with abortion, become for the New Right intrinsic elements in a larger program that encompasses more traditional right-wing aims: anticommunism; support for increased armaments and opposition to arms control; and resistance to affirmative action, unions, and government-sponsored social services. The strategic assumption is that a newly defined constituency called the "Christian right" can share a common political outlook; the same people who oppose abortion and homosexuality are also the parents of "private Christian" schoolchildren, the foes of unions, and the friends of the Panama Canal.

The New Right could not help but be drawn to the winning ingredients of the "right-to-life" electoral strategy: a tightly controlled organization geared to recruiting and influencing voters across party lines, an alleged 11 million members and 3,000 chapters throughout the United States, and a sense of moral righteousness on behalf of conservative values and a cause. Through a vigorous use of these conservative religious organizations, the New Right—and indirectly the Reagan forces—sought to gain votes and funds, active recruits and foot soldiers, and ideological legitimacy—the elements of political power. By 1978, its spokesmen were claiming that the religious tie would give them potential access to 100 million voters, and they were confident of commanding sufficient votes in the elections to give them control over the Senate, the Republican party, and the presidency.[39] Regardless of how one analyzes the deeper causes of right-wing electoral victories in 1980, it is undeniable that a key element in the right's strategy was to use the "right-to-life" movement as an organizational model and base. Conservatives in the 1980 elections were direct beneficiaries of mass antiabortion organizing, which has helped create a constituency and a consciousness that is both responsive to the New Right's "profamily" ideology and committed to participating in the electoral process. In a political climate in which many liberals and radicals are disaffected nonvoters, such political socialization undoubtedly contributed to the right's margin of victory. The 1980 elections brought not only Ronald Reagan, a conservative Republican and opponent of legal abortion and the ERA, to the presidency but also a shift in the balance of power in the Senate to a conservative Republican majority for the first time in twenty-six years, as well as the chairmanship of many key Senate committees by conservatives.[40]

By 1978 the New Right had begun to absorb the antiabortion movement within its network of "prolife" Political Action Committees (PACs), leadership conferences, and conservative Christian organizations, all under the rubric of the "profamily" movement. The strategy, adopted in 1977, was to consolidate "groups devoted to preservation of the traditional social roles of the family, the churches, and the schools" (i.e., groups that were antiabortion, antibusing, anti-ERA, and antigay rights) into a single coalition organized around four main planks: "prolife," "profamily," "promoral," and "pro-American," with "family" as the keystone.[41] New Right organizers launched direct-mail campaigns aimed at politicizing the country's fundamentalist preachers, and organized a series of leadership conferences and religious coalitions. In addition to the highly publicized Moral Majority, conferences and groups with names like Religious Roundtable, Christian Voice, and American Family Forum proliferated, with the same speakers and leaders appearing continually on their rosters: Paul Weyrich, Phyllis Schlafly, Richard Viguerie, and Howard Phillips; Senators Jesse Helms (R.-N.C.), Gordon Humphrey (R.-N.H.), Paul Laxalt

(R.-Nev.), Orrin Hatch (R.-Utah). Representatives Jake Garn (R.-Cal.), Henry Hyde (R.-Ill.), and Larry McDonald (R.-Ga.); and the Reverend Jerry Falwell and Pat Robertson. Moreover, New Right strategists set up a number of "prolife" organizations outside the framework of the National Right to Life Committee (NRLC), such as the American Life Lobby (ALL) and the National Pro-Family Coalition. Organizations such as these, used to appeal to sympathizers on behalf of a "moral" cause, may "function as fronts for direct-mail campaigns and primarily to make money for themselves." New Right–sponsored single-issue organizations became conduits both for campaign funds for right-wing candidates (including Reagan) and for building a well-financed political organization.[42]

The main constituency "profamily" leaders have sought to organize is the estimated 50 million "born-again" Christians in this country, reached through evangelical church pulpits and a vast broadcasting network (13,000 radio stations, 36 television shows) to which the evangelical churches have access. As in the "right-to-life" movement, the key to this strategy is the preachers, particularly the nationally known Bible-preaching broadcasters. For millions of evangelical Protestants, who are the most frequent listeners to religious broadcasts, radio and television have taken the place of the local church, reaching people in their cars and homes, not only on Sunday but every day all across America. Religious broadcasting for right-wing political purposes has long been a tool of right-wing preachers, but today the use of high-wave frequencies and satellite technology magnifies the potential impact of such broadcasting tremendously.[43] What is of interest is not the high-powered technology of fundamentalist broadcasters but the financial backing that allows the application of that technology on a massive scale and the political and ideological purposes for which the "electronic church" has been created. An important example is Rev. Jerry Falwell, founder of the "profamily" Moral Majority, which has a mailing list of 70,000 pastors. Falwell broadcasts daily over 300 television stations and 280 radio stations in 31 states. The message he communicates is not only the doctrinal one of the Bible's "inerrant truth" as literally interpreted, "salvation by faith alone and the premillennial return of Christ." It is also the essence of "profamily" ideology: against homosexuality ("the bisexual and homosexual movements in America are antifamily, . . . the number one offender . . . in traditional man-woman relationships"), against feminism ("we believe in superior rights for women"), and against abortion and divorce.[44]

An alliance between Protestant fundamentalist preachers and the political right is not new. I grew up in Tulsa, Oklahoma, in the 1950s, where Anita Bryant was the football queen of the rival high school; where fundamentalists (Oral Roberts, Billy James Hargis) maintained their headquarters; where Athletes for Christ made regular rounds to the schools;

and where the connection of these groups with anticommunism and the John Birch Society was commonly known. That connection is documented in an article by David Danzig, who describes "extreme Protestant fundamentalism," linked to ultra-right organizations, as "a growing socio-religious force in America."[45] In the early 1960s this force, regional (based mainly in the South/Southwest) and fiercely anti-Catholic, cut across various Protestant sects. Fundamentalist thinking contains "an anti-historicism which readily supports the conspiracy theory of social change," and an "apocalyptic conception of the world" that sees everything in terms of "the unending struggle between God and the devil." It may thus lend itself to a political ideology that is similarly absolutist and apocalyptic, projecting a vision of society as ridden by demons (communists, homosexuals, "liberated" women) from whom the innocent and God-fearing must be saved.

It is important not to exaggerate the association between Protestant fundamentalism, and certainly the much broader and more disparate array of evangelical Christian churches, and right-wing politics in America. In a sharp critique of Danzig's study, Carol Virginia Pohli argues that he ignores the opportunistic uses of religious fringe groups by the right and the continued resistance of many fundamentalists to *any* sort of political change or involvement.[46] In the contemporary mobilization of fundamentalist religiosity in the service of right-wing causes, it is crucial to understand that this is a political calculation, not a prophecy. Political and social conservatism are not necessarily spontaneous or organic outgrowths of Christian evangelicism, which has existed throughout this country's history and has on occasion played an important role in progressive reform movements. The New Right looks to fundamentalist and evangelical churches as its principal organizing base mainly for three purposes: ideological coherence and legitimacy, constituents and organized networks, and money. For those churches are not only potentially sympathetic to conservatism but, on the whole, affluent.

By the late 1950s and early 1960s, the class base of Protestant fundamentalism in the South and Southwest had changed. It was no longer mainly the rural poor, but included wealthy beneficiaries of what later would be known as the "Sunbelt revival":

> Many fundamentalist churches are modern and imposing, financed by wealthy oilmen from Texas and Oklahoma and prosperous farmers in the wheat and corn belts. Rich and influential lay leaders . . . now make their influence felt in the power structure of the community and state. The fundamentalists also operate a vast network of colleges, training schools, Bible institutions, Bible prophecy conferences, prayer meetings, and study groups. They have many large publishing houses which blanket small towns with conservative tracts and pamphlets.[47]

Since the 1960s, right-wing fundamentalists have developed a formidable base of financial support, stemming not only from publication and broadcasting revenues and the contributions of small donors but also from an array of business "fronts" and corporate backers.[48] This support has in some cases been channeled into politics, defying the traditional fundamentalist inclination to shun worldly matters. The main purpose of "profamily" organizing prior to the 1980 elections was to mobilize the growing social force of Christian fundamentalism into conservative political activity and weld it to the politicized and Catholic-dominated "right-to-life" movement. An alliance between conservative Catholics and Protestants would be historically unprecedented in the United States. New Right leaders believe that the politics of morality—that is, conservative family and sexual politics—is the key to forging such an alliance and uniting "100 million Americans" into right-wing political identity and votes.[49]

Yet the assumption of a direct line between popular religious conservatism and popular social and political conservatism on all issues is unfounded. Take the abortion question. The relationship between the conservative politicians and political promoters who call themselves the New Right and the "right-to-life" movement is a complicated one, involving close ties and deep divisions. From its origins in the early 1970s, the "right-to-life" movement has found itself lured into a symbiosis in which New Right organizers lend to "prolife" groups their expertise in direct mailings, targeting candidates, and managing PACs in return for securing a mass base of voters and local organizers. Rhonda Copelon, attorney for the plaintiffs in *Harris* v. *McRae,* speculates that New Right politicos see the "right-to-life" movement as genuinely broad-based and thus a vehicle through which conservative forces can make inroads into the (majority) liberal-democratic electorate.[50] At the same time, the New Right's political aims go well beyond the abortion issue. The goal of their electoral strategy is to get rid of legislators considered liberal on any of the right's favorite issues, including environmental regulation, welfare, defense spending, and civil rights. This connection of abortion to a larger and more traditional set of rightist political ends has sown seeds of difference between hard-core "right-to-lifers" and their New Right and fundamentalist patrons. Even prior to the 1980 elections, some antiabortion leaders expressed suspicion of the New Right's motives and were reluctant to let their single-issue focus become absorbed in the larger "profamily"/ "pro-America" agenda.[51] Indeed, much of the rhetoric and organizing of the NRLC has attempted to appeal to liberal and "humanist" religious people who identify with the poor and the oppressed, to connect the "rights of the unborn" to other human rights issues. (There is even a "Prolife Feminists" caucus, as well as a small but growing left wing of the movement that opposes population control and nuclear power and favors welfare benefits.[52])

On a practical level, a too-close association with the New Right could be damaging to the "right-to-life" movement's support among liberal Catholics and others who identify with humanist and pacifist traditions, who strongly favor many of the services and institutions (day care, labor unions, environmental protection laws) that the New Right condemns. An editorial in the liberal Catholic journal *Commonweal* gave prophetic warning to the Church hierarchy about the fellows it was bedding down with in the antiabortion campaign:

> The anti-abortion amendment is a right-wing issue, and the bishops will quickly become the tools of conservative so-called "pro-life" (and perhaps anti-busing, anti-"welfare chislers," pro–arms race, pro-CIA) candidates in the 1976 elections. The effort will fizzle and the church will have been had.[53]

As if responding to this warning and the concerns of its liberal laity, the hierarchy has more recently taken a series of outspoken stands in direct opposition to the policies of the Reagan administration and the New Right: opposing U.S. intervention in El Salvador, nuclear weapons, and cutbacks in social welfare budgets.[54] Moreover, the hierarchy is challenged from within on the abortion question. The 1,800-member National Coalition of American Nuns announced its opposition to a Human Life Amendment and its view that the abortion decision ought to be the choice of "those who are directly and personally involved."[55] Also, recent statements from among the broad and disparate assortment of Christian evangelists—some of whose churches have opposed the Klu Klux Klan, joined with the black freedom movement, or staunchly maintained an indifference to politics—distinguish themselves from right-wing fundamentalists and Falwell's reactionary Moral Majority.[56] The group of self-defined leftist, pacifist, and "feminist" Christians who also define themselves as "prolife" (a disturbing phenomenon for feminists in the reproductive freedom movement) have emphatically dissociated themselves from the New Right and its politics. Thus the leftist Christian *Sojourners Magazine,* in proclaiming its conversion to "prolife" doctrine, writes:

> The political strategy of these Christian groups is being formulated by long-time Washington veterans of the extreme right wing who have not been known for their religious devotion. Their motivations have always had more to do with military and economic goals than with abortion. Their pro-military and pro-business agenda is decidedly anti-poor, anti-black, and anti-feminist. . . . The unholy alliance between the anti-abortion movement and the right wing must be directly challenged by those who seriously and consistently espouse a pro-life commitment.[57]

Divisions within evangelical Christianity and the New Right belie its pretensions of being a "moral majority" or a unified political monolith.

Pohli points to two factors: "biblical arrogance"—a belief in the assured-ness of their own salvation and righteousness that renders them aloof from the concerns of society—and a long tradition of "Protestant individu-alism" and separatism of denominations and congregations that tend to undermine the New Right's unity and its potential political effectiveness. The Moral Majority "is comprised of people whose loyalties to their local church are far stronger than their political ambitions." As a result, "political solidarity among Evangelicals" is a harder thing to achieve than rhetorical fervor.[58]

This inherent tendency toward divisiveness surfaced in failed at-tempts by New Right leaders and antiabortionists to unify around an antiabortion legislative strategy in 1981–82. After the 1980 elections, it seemed that as the Reagan forces had used the New Right to develop a popular electoral base, so the New Right had used the antiabortion move-ment. By 1981, the initiative for legislative actions to stop abortions had clearly passed from the National Right to Life Committee and the Catholic church hierarchy to New Right politicians in Congress, who showed them-selves more interested in winning votes and trading favors than in purity of doctrine. In 1982 serious conflicts, not only between New Right politicos and "right-to-life" forces, but within both groupings, emerged around various proposals in the Senate for an antiabortion amendment or statute. The paramount goal of the "right-to-life" movement had been a constitu-tional amendment that would not merely recriminalize abortion but ex-pressly declare the fetus a "human person" from the moment of concep-tion, enjoying all human rights including the right to life. Congressional committee hearings in 1981 on a statute sponsored by right-wing Senator Jesse Helms, containing such language, had proven so problematic and politically disastrous for the right that by the next year some New Right leaders in the Senate had decided to defer the "human life amendment" or statute in favor of various compromise proposals which would make it possible for individual states to pass "human life" statutes. Nevertheless, hard-liners in the "right-to-life" movement denounced the "compro-mises" and warned that they would consider their endorsement "a pro-abortion vote." The open warfare that developed involved a split between the National Conference of Catholic Bishops and the president of the NRLC, on one side, and a large segment of the NRLC board, on the other.[59] This division reflected a deepening conflict in the antiabortion movement between the practical political need to win a victory and the ideological need to hold on to the "human life amendment" as a vision, a goal, that gives their movement coherence and popular momentum.[60]

One compromise proposal finally made it to the Senate floor: an amendment to a bill on the national debt ceiling that would have made a declatory (nonbinding) statement about fetal "personhood," imposed a permanent ban on federal funding of abortion services, and encouraged the Supreme Court to reverse its decision in Roe v. Wade (S. 2148). After a vigorous filibuster, the proposal was defeated by one vote.[61] Antiabortion forces blamed the Reagan administration for lack of full support, and Reagan blamed the antiabortion forces for lack of unity; on all sides, however, there was an understanding that for the present, the constitutional amendment strategy had met its demise.

The immediate reason for the failure of the New Right/"right-to-life" legislative campaign in the early 1980s was not only the divisions within the "prolife" camp. In addition, a determined coalition of liberal "prochoice" groups, their congressional friends, and feminists organized effectively to defeat the campaign. Through lobbying, letter writing, and militant demonstrations—national television cameras showed feminists bearing placards and shouting inside the committee hearing rooms, "A woman's life is a human life!"—the pressure politicians felt to pass some antiabortion legislation was defused and deflected.[62] This victory for liberal and feminist groups must be read as only one round of a much more complicated struggle; the victory itself grows out of an ambiguous political context that is perhaps more foreboding than a "human life amendment." I would argue that such an amendment never had much chance of passing, for we live in a dominant political and moral culture that is overwhelmingly secular and for which, in most people's understanding, "abortion morality" has always signified sexual and gender issues more deeply than it has "fetal rights." By 1981, and certainly after the hearings on the human life statute, the dominant public discourse in the abortion debate had shifted ground, away from the abstract question of "fetal personhood" toward more social questions about the family and teenage sexuality. This shift was largely the product of the political and cultural struggle between the New Right's "profamily" ideology and feminism.

The Ideological Message: Reprivatizing Sexuality and "Preserving the Family"

Organized opposition to abortion has never been a single-issue movement. The underlying message of the crusade against abortion—the message the New Right has embraced as its ideological centerpiece—is conveyed in the defensive response by Dr. J. C. Willke, president of the NRLC, to accusations about firebombings and the harassment of abortion clinics:

> It is they who are doing violence to our beloved nation by their systematic undermining of the basic unit of our society, the family. They do violence by their so-called sex education which is encouraging sexual promiscuity in our children and leading to more and more abortions. They do violence to us by

driving wedges, barriers, and suspicion between teenagers and parents. They do violence to marriage by helping to remove *the right of a husband to protect the life of the child he has fathered in his wife's womb.*[63]

Abortion, Willke suggests, is the opening wedge in an avalanche of "moral" assaults on the traditional nuclear family, including sex education, teenage sexuality and autonomy, and the sexual and reproductive freedom of women. Preservation of the fetus is not the central issue here; rather, it is the patriarchal dominion of the husband over "his wife's womb," the restoration of a patriarchal family form. As Ellen Willis noticed some years ago, "the nitty-gritty issue in the abortion debate is not life but sex."[64] A set of unmistakably conservative sexual values lies at the core of antiabortion politics, dictating that "God did not ordain sex for fun and games."[65]

Over and over again in antiabortion and "profamily" literature, one is struck with a defiantly traditional middle-class morality regarding sexual behavior and an undisguised antipathy toward *all* forms of sexuality outside the marital, procreative sphere. Sociologist Donald Granberg's study of a national sample of "prolife" activists found no correlation between opposition to abortion and "a more generalized prolife stance," as reflected in opposition to capital punishment, war, and military spending. "Prolifers" tend to favor these forms of death. On the other hand, Granberg found the greatest correlation to exist between opposition to abortion and "a conservative approach to matters of traditional morality," that is, disapproval of premarital sex, birth control for teenagers, sex education, and divorce.[66] Sharon Thompson also found particular sexual biases when she attended a workshop on sex education at a local "right-to-life" convention:

> In a sense, theirs is a movement championing the asexual in a post-Freudian era. The fetus is their purest symbol for that reason. Even babies are sexual, they now admit, but surely not the fetus. (If we could get a photo of a fetus masturbating, we might be able to short-circuit their whole movement.) They hate Planned Parenthood in large part because they perceive it as pro-sex. "Planned Parenthood even thinks old people should have sex!" one speaker called out at lunch, and the whole room exploded with laughter.[67]

More than anything else, the subject that excites "prolifers" is premarital sex among teenagers. Increasingly, antagonism to abortion stems less from concern for protecting the fetus than from a desire to prevent teenage sexuality. "Right-to-life" advocates assume a causal relationship between legalized abortion and a rise in sexual promiscuity and illegitimacy, particularly among teenagers. Not only abortion but also birth control and sex education programs are seen as giving official government sanction to "illicit" sex and therefore as interfering with parents' control over the moral behavior and values of their children. Conversely, the way to eliminate premarital sexuality is to eliminate abortion, teenage contraceptive programs, and sex education. This has been the unenlightened opinion of Ronald Reagan for years, judging from remarks he made in 1973 while vetoing (for the third time) proposed legislation in California to allow teenagers to obtain contraceptives without parental consent:

> Simply because sexual permissiveness may exist among certain young people does not mean the state should make it easier for them. . . . The state has no right to even tacitly seem to condone such behavior, particularly among children who, in too many instances, are not yet mature enough to understand the full implications of their actions.[68]

In a time demanding economic restraint and self-sacrifice, women who get abortions are the ultimate hedonists, the paradigm of "selfishness," and thus represent a defiance of both the patriarchal family and the patriotic state. Moreover, their action bears witness to the fact that sexuality may be exercised apart from procreation. And if apart from procreation, then—as the church has long understood—why not apart from marriage or from heterosexual relations? Thus, "lesbianism and abortion . . . are inextricably linked, not only as issues of self-determination for women, but . . . [as] powerful acts of female autonomy . . . that . . . defy the principal lessons of culture: heterosexual romance, marriage and motherhood."[69] The idea of "control over one's body" is not dangerous simply, or even mainly, in relation to fetal life; the ultimate objective of that idea is sexual freedom. Historically, the inability to control her pregnancies has been a major restriction on a woman's sexual activity, in a way that is obviously not the same for men. It is important to note that "right-to-life" ideology is not simply antisex; the point is not wholesale repression but the *rechanneling* of sexuality into patriarchally legitimate forms, those that reinforce heterosexual marriage and motherhood. If a woman can control her pregnancies, there is no built-in sanction against her having sex when, how, and with whom she pleases—and this, for the "profamily"/"prolife" movement, is the heart of the matter: "free" sex.

The bastion of traditional values around sex, values that encumber sex with innumerable conditions of age, gender, and status, is and ever has been the patriarchal family. To ward off the threat to the family and consolidate its social and economic goals, the New Right developed its own program for a conservative family and social policy, contained in comprehensive form in its showcase legislation, the so-called Family

Protection Act.[70] Introduced in both houses of Congress in 1979 and in a revised version in 1981, the FPA was initially drafted by the New Right's Library Court legislative group. As a whole, it remains a guiding model, though many of its specifics have already become policy under the Reagan administration through legislative action, budgetary cutbacks, or executive fiat. Designed "to preserve the integrity of the American family, to foster and protect the viability of American family life . . . and to promote the virtues of the family," the FPA aims basically at removing federal jurisdiction over "parental rights" and the "rights" of churches and private schools. Specific provisions use the state's taxing and spending powers to promote a public policy favoring not only marriage and childbirth but also heterosexuality and the role of the husband as household head. They are meant as disincentives to divorce and female-headed households. Thus, various tax benefits would be provided to married couples only if they file joint returns, a special tax deduction would be available to a married "individual" who sets up an individual retirement plan for (his) "non-earning spouse," and a $1,000 tax exemption would be given to *married couples only* for the birth or adoption of a child during the fiscal year ($3,000 if the child is born handicapped—an obvious disincentive to abortion). A similar exemption for the support at home of aged or handicapped relatives would also seem to be restricted to married couples (Secs. 203, 205, and 207). Moreover, the family to be "preserved" is clearly intended to be not only patriarchal but authoritarian. The act would abolish federal jurisdiction over child abuse and spouse abuse, exempting from the definition of child abuse the application of corporal punishment (i.e., spanking).

The major provisions of the bill, however, have to do with education. They would authorize parents to "review" (i.e., censor) any textbooks intended for use in public school classrooms and reauthorize sex segregation of "sports or other school-related activities" by rescinding federal authority to withhold funds to locales that prohibit such segregation on affirmative action grounds. Awareness of the power of ideas in shaping sexual politics is much in evidence here, as is the fear the New Right has of feminists, radicals, homosexuals, or anyone who questions traditional ideas about sexual divisions. This is sharply underlined in a blanket provision that would prohibit federal funding to any program that supports "educational materials . . . [that] tend to denigrate, diminish, or deny the role differences between the sexes as it [*sic*] has been historically understood in the United States," a clear reference to women's studies programs and courses (Sec. 301). More straightforward still is the provision that bars federal funds for "homosexual advocacy," that is, for the support of "any public or private individual or entity," not only schools, which presents "that male or female homosexuality is an acceptable lifestyle" (Sec. 108). This homophobic provision, though revised in the later version to exclude discrimination against homosexuals in regard to welfare, social security, veterans, or student benefits, nonetheless lays bare that the core of the FPA is not so much the maintenance of families but the repression of sexual deviance and the hegemony of a patriarchal form of family.

These measures supplement the vigorous national campaign initiated by Falwell's Moral Majority to censor television programming and school books; for example, the feminist bestseller *Our Bodies, Ourselves*—a comprehensive manual on birth control, abortion, sexuality, pregnancy, and gynecological health—has been the target of a witch-hunt.[71] Similarly, the New Right has reinforced its legislative campaign against feminism in the schools with "direct action" tactics at the local level to harass, defund, and discredit campus women's centers and women's studies programs around the country.[72] The emphasis on "materials" is tactical and deliberate. Although radicals and feminists justifiably fear a recurrence of McCarthyism, at this stage the aim is primarily to purge, not teachers, but children's minds of any ideas that are critical of racism, sexism, homophobia, or class divisions. Hence the stress on supporting, through government subsidies, parochial and private schools and even "parental" or "Christian" schools. While federal support for parents who teach their children at home was dropped from the revised version of the FPA, it remains a live part of the "profamily" agenda. At a recent meeting of the American Family Forum, the largest national gathering of New Right "profamily" forces, the idea that parents (i.e., *mothers*) should keep their children at home until the age of eight or ten, teaching them out of sanitized 1950s textbooks—and, of course, staying home with them, where they belong—was warmly received.[73]

In addition to control over the schools for right-wing ideological purposes, the FPA reasserts parental control over education in the service of middle-class economic interests. It provides special tax deductions (a form of tuition tax credits) for parents who contribute up to $2,500 per year per child to an "education savings account" (Sec. 201), a measure, along with one regarding "tax exempt schools," aimed at granting federal support to private and parochial education. These provisions are not merely class biased; they are also fundamentally racist. Their aim is to support schools whose reason for being is racial segregation and religious sectarianism. The bill would bar the federal government from regulating not only religious schools but "church-operated child care centers, orphanages, foster homes, social action training schools, juvenile delinquency or drug abuse treatment centers," mainly for the purpose of immunizing them from federal affirmative action regulations (Sec. 501). It would also prohibit the use of Legal Services funds for litigation involving busing or other programs for "the desegregation of any elementary or secondary school or school system" (Sec. 305).

All these ends—tuition tax credits, racial segregation, reinforcing religion in schools, banning textbooks that question traditional patriarchal and sexual values, and preventing "homosexual advocacy"—are interrelated. Parents among fundamentalist and Catholic conservative constituencies to whom the New Right appeals want control over local schools for reasons that are in part religious, in part class-based, in part racist, in part sexist and homophobic, and in part expressive of their fears, as parents, of loss of control over their children. Overall it may be that, in a time of economic and political insecurity, the desire to control one's children (since other aspects of life seem out of control) becomes a conduit for other fears. In this context, invocations of "the family" communicate complex meanings and moral sanctions. "The family" provides a new moral thrust, a new legitimation for older right-wing aims such as racial segregation and prayer in the public schools, which, since the 1960s and the civil rights movement, are no longer so easily justified. The sexual component of this ideological thrust cannot be overstressed. For the "freedom" that white parents want is clearly the "freedom" to keep their children away from black children; their fears of "racial mix" are in no small part bound up with sexual-racial stereotypes and the fear of their children's sexuality.[74]

The idea of protection runs heavily throughout the "profamily" literature—protection not only of fetuses and minors but of adult women, who are meant to remain dependent on husbands. This idea was used continually to discredit the ERA, which Phyllis Schlafly claimed would "strike at the heart of women's family support rights."[75] Just as the Reagan administration promises to protect corporations from the "shackles" of regulation, and to protect fascist regimes in El Salvador and Guatemala from popular rebellion, so the New Right seeks to protect the traditional patriarchal family. The fetus "in his wife's womb" becomes a symbol of the besieged sanctuary of patriarchy. "Protection" encounters contradictions, however, in regard to domestic violence: how to protect women from the physical dangers that exist *within* the family? One of the major legislative campaigns of the New Right has been directed against the Domestic Violence Prevention and Services Bill, which would expand federally funded programs to assist domestic violence victims.[76] Behind the New Right's opposition to the bill is a desire to shut down a national network of battered women's centers, often run by feminists, which encourage battered women to leave home. While acknowledging that wife battering exists, the "profamily" alternative is to return women to the authority of their spouses, offer them counseling, and remove domestic violence services from the public back to the private (preferably church-sponsored) domain. In a related attempt to bolster the patriarchal family structure, the FPA restricts federal legal assistance or Legal Services funds for litigation in which clients, who are nearly always poor women, are seeking to obtain an abortion or a divorce; or in which homosexuals, male or female, are seeking the adjudication of their rights (Sec. 106). It also requires that no family planning agency "may receive federal funds unless prior to providing a contraceptive device or abortion service (including abortion counseling) to an unmarried minor, the parents or guardian of such minor are notified" (Sec. 102).

The Family Protection Act must be read, not as a legislative instrument likely to be adopted as it stands, but as a conservative political program to reverse the radical family and sexual politics of the 1960s and 1970s. Its elements constitute a nearly point-by-point response to the piecemeal but potentially radical program for school desegregation, women's studies, equality within families, public support for alternative family forms, gay and lesbian rights, and services for battered women, which grew out of the civil rights, women's, and gay liberation movements over the past twenty years. The practical social and political impact of this New Right agenda is to wipe out many existing feminist and gay rights programs that depend heavily on federal funds: to reconstitute the family and private agencies, such as the church, as the main institutions to which women and teenagers, especially if they are poor, must look for support.

Although the FPA remains on a back burner in Congress, many of its key provisions have, bit by bit, become public policy under the Reagan administration. It became apparent during 1982 that some of President Reagan's advisers regarded the "social program" of the New Right—including an antiabortion amendment—as a politically losing proposition in Congress in the midst of an embattled economy.[77] But that political judgment, characteristically opportunistic, did not mean any fundamental lack of sympathy for right-wing positions on abortion, sexuality, the family, or education. In fact, the stalemate in Congress around some of the right's major issues (abortion, teenage pregnancy and sexuality, busing, tuition tax credits) has simply fortified them, with ample support from the executive branch, in utilizing other routes—administrative orders, judicial rulings, heavily funded media and propaganda campaigns—to achieve the same ends more circumspectly.

The requirement of parental notification prior to delivering contraceptive services or devices to unmarried teenagers emerged in an executive regulation issued, amid tremendous public protest, by the Department of Health and Human Services. Through a combination of legislative riders and Reagan's cutbacks in the social welfare budget, federal legal services to homosexuals were curtailed and the Legal Services Corporation budget was decimated.[78] Conservative-minded courts succumbed to right-wing pressure, rescinding court-imposed orders to enforce busing to desegregate the schools[79] and endorsing, with qualifications, state and local requirements of parental consent or notification for teenage abortions (see Chapter 8). In regard to abortion, on one level the New Right's legislative assault floundered badly, leaving it hopelessly divided and with less support for *any* antiabortion amendment in 1982 than it had in 1980. At the same time, the Reagan administration engaged in a strategy of bureaucratic guerrilla warfare that systematically harassed and intimidated abortion providers and restricted access, particularly for young unmarried women, to abortion and birth control services.

Rather than annihilate abortion rights through a constitutional amendment, this strategy whittles them away. In the latest foray, the Department of Health and Human Services issued "guidelines"—unlike regulations, these require no public hearings or public response prior to formalization—imposing the complete segregation of abortion facilities and services from other family planning activities in federally funded clinics and hospitals. This meant that "family planning clinics could not provide any assistance to women seeking abortions," causing the fragmentation rather than integration of care and the duplication of offices, equipment, and personnel in a period of stringent budgetary restraints.[80] It was an act of administrative fiat whose intent is to circumvent the legislative process and wield the threat of denial of funding so that clinics and hospitals will suspend abortion services. In this way, the New Right and the state may intend less to recriminalize abortion than to delegitimize it by rendering it inaccessible and marginal once again.

Reagan administration officials were from the outset open about their intention to curtail such services and that their reasons had to do with sexual politics. Reagan appointed staunch conservatives and "prolife" political figures to all the senior positions in the Department of Health and Human Services related to family planning, reproductive health, and adolescent sexuality. When Marjorie Mecklenberg, the administration's head of the Office of Family Planning and deputy of Population Affairs, was asked how she, an ardent "right-to-lifer," would handle the problem of adolescent pregnancy, she responded that teenagers should "postpone sexual involvement." Similarly, Richard Schweiker, secretary of Health and Human Services, remarked publicly that the "federal government should not be in the sex education business."[81] This federal policy to discourage teenage sex culminated in the enactment of federal regulations under Title X of the Public Health Services Act requiring federally funded family planning projects to notify both parents or the legal guardian of all minors within ten days after issuing prescription birth control devices or pills.[82]

It is noteworthy that the "squeal rule" focuses on the "health risks" of contraceptives as ground for "protection" of young women and for parental intervention. Feminists are again seeing their protests about the health hazards of oral contraceptives lifted out of context and used against women's autonomy. The goal of "protecting" young women is not aimed at health hazards, however, but at sexual activity. Targeting prescription methods not only provides a pretext thought acceptable to liberals but, and this is more important, restricts the impact of the regulations to females. As with parental consent and notification requirements for abortion, reporting to *both* parents is a system of surveillance meant to mitigate the authority of health and family planning professionals, to enhance that of fathers, and to intimidate heterosexually active young women. Right-wing Senators Orrin Hatch and Jeremiah Denton expressed the sexual ideology of the rules' sponsors when they replied to the liberal *New York Times:*

> And what of chastity? Personally, we still think it should be considered, even in 1981. The most effective oral contraceptive yet devised is the word "no." It costs nothing, has no harmful side effects and is 100% effective.[83]

The theme of protecting children has also been applied in the movement's virulent, heavily financed campaign against homosexuals and lesbians.[84] On the pretext that male homosexuals and lesbians are child molesters, New Right offensives have sought, with some success, to defeat gay rights ordinances in cities around the country, to deny federally funded legal services to homosexuals, and to bar homosexuals from teaching in the public schools (e.g., in the defeated Briggs Amendment campaign in California).[85] They have revived the ideology, abandoned even by the American Psychiatric Association, that homosexuality is "pathological" and "perverse." A longer-range goal is to prohibit the employment of homosexuals not only in education but in *any* "public sector" or "high visibility public jobs,"[86] as well as to prohibit federal funding of any organization that "suggests" that homosexuality "can be an acceptable lifestyle" (FPA). A section of the original FPA, deleted from the amended version and so blatantly unconstitutional that probably even the right's congressional agents were loathe to defend it, would have added to the 1964 Civil Rights Act the following:

> . . . the term "unlawful employment practice" shall not be deemed to include any action or measure taken by an employer, labor organization, joint labor-management committee, or employment agency with respect to an individual who is a homosexual or proclaims homosexual tendencies. No agency, bureau, commission, or other instrumentality of the Government of the United States shall seek to enforce nondiscrimination with respect to individuals who are homosexuals or who proclaim homosexual tendencies.

The ideas behind the New Right's campaign against homosexuals reveal the political values that motivate the "profamily" movement, including the movement against abortion. They suggest that while "prolifers" appear hostile to sexuality as such, it is really the social aspects of traditional gender identities, particularly the position of male paternal and heterosexual authority, that they are determined to protect. Male homosexuality is even more dangerous than female in the "profamily" view because it signals a breakdown of "masculinity," or what one neo-conservative calls the "male spirit" or "the male principle."[87] What is at stake in the New Right campaign against homosexuality is the idea of what it means to be a "man" or a "woman," as well as the structure and meaning of the traditional family. These two concepts are clearly related, for "masculinity" has been defined historically through the structure of the family and the dominant position of the father within it. Paul Weyrich expresses an awareness of this reality when he decries feminists for seeking "the restructuring of the traditional family and particularly . . . the downgrading of the male or father role in the traditional family."

Taking feminist ideas more seriously than many liberals do, the doctrinal leaders of the New Right relate women's sexuality to their place in society—only they reverse the feminist vision. Connie Marshner, another prime mover of the "profamily" movement, assures women that all they need is "to know 'that somebody will have the authority and make the decision, and that your job is to be happy with it.' "[88] This is exactly what Schlafly and her anti-ERA forces have been promoting since 1973: that it is women's "right" to be dependent, cared for, subordinate to men, and defined by marriage and motherhood. Anti-ERA and "profamily" ideology assumes that it is destructive of the family for married women to work outside the home. Pat Robertson, a New Right fundamentalist preacher and head of the Christian Broadcasting Network, decries the calamity of working mothers and offers the "Christian solution":

> Deficit spending, from the 1940s through the 1970s, put an intolerable burden on the American people. . . . So it became necessary for women to enter the work force not because they wanted to but because they had to. Twenty-five million children under school age are dumped into day care centers by their mothers. Teenagers come home and there's no one there, so they think, "How about a little marijuana and a little sex." When mother gets home she's tired, and squabbles with her husband. They get divorced, the children lose their role models, there is more rebellion in the schools and homosexuality, and the children of divorce get divorced themselves.
>
> The solution? . . . A Christian marriage. . . . Being a housewife is a noble profession. My father was a Senator, but my mother stayed home to tell me about Jesus Christ.[89]

Here, in a mythical rewriting of the recent past, are coupled the twin evils of Keynesianism (the liberal state) and working mothers, and their "good" counterparts, supply-side economics and the pious mother at home. Her absence, not the economy, is blamed for every demon that plagues the family: teenage pregnancy, drugs, homosexuality, divorce, and "rebellion in the schools." At bottom, "prolife"/"profamily" ideology represents the urge to restore the bourgeois values of motherhood as they have been propagated since the late eighteenth century. One could speculate at length on the deeper cultural and psychological roots of the "motherhood" backlash, yet it obviously touches something very profound: in men, an ingrained expectation of being taken care of, which feminism seems to threaten; and in women, an ingrained vulnerability to guilt, which antifeminism evokes.

The men of the "profamily" movement, mainly upper-middle-class professionals,[90] are not immune to the sense of personal loss and threat provoked by feminism and recent changes in the family and women's work. Restoring the virginal purity of unmarried daughters is an assertion of bourgeois paternalism and an effort to avert the baneful influence of feminism on a younger generation of women. Weyrich again captures the essence of the middle-class patriarchal *ressentiment:* "The father's word has to prevail."[91] With this unambiguous call to arms, he speaks not only as a New Right general but also as a husband and father. And he speaks, too, as a leading patriarch in his church, aware of the Sonia Johnsons and the Sister Theresa Kanes and the other powerful religious women who would turn traditional church governance upside down.

We should not underestimate the directive impact of conservative churches on the sexual values and practices of young people. A study of "premarital pregnancy in America" confirms that, historically, "restrictive sexual attitudes" and "lower levels of premarital sexual activity" have been associated with active "religious involvement" (i.e., church attendance). But this association is not automatic or one-way: "Religion can be said to have an impact on the overall incidence of premarital sex only when it is an *encompassing and controlling force* in the lives of the young and not merely an option."[92] Certainly it is a goal of the Moral Majority and other New Right organizations to establish "Bible-believing" churches as an "encompassing and controlling force" over young unmarried people, particularly over their sexual values and habits. Smith and Hindus note that the "age-stratified institutions" that help construct a separate teenage culture (e.g., nonsectarian high schools, rock music, television, and family planning and VD clinics that cater to the needs of teenagers) weaken the power of "modern parents . . . to be oppressive in an effective way." Teenagers today are "psychologically enmeshed in but not controlled by their families of orientation."[93] Aided by "Christian academies," censorship campaigns against feminist writings and programs, and government restriction of teenage girls' access to abortion and birth control, the leaders of right-wing sects like the Moral Majority are attempting to break down the "age-stratified" culture, especially the teen-sex culture, to reestablish direct lines of control through reabsorption of young people into the family and the church.

In the Catholic church, one could argue that feminism, within the church and outside it, explains the singlemindedness and fury with which the church hierarchy has engaged in the current crusade against birth control and abortion. The hierarchy and the pope have expressed strong concern about feminist and Marxist stirrings within the church's ranks and the need to impose "discipline" and patriarchal authority in its own house. This was made clear in the pope's visit to the United States in 1979 and his outspoken endorsement then, and during the recent Synod of Bishops, of the most conservative views on women, birth control, sexuality, and marriage—even in the face of widespread lay nonconformism and public appeals by nuns for a more modern approach.[94] Feminism represents a threat of insubordination and depopulation. Not only have Catholic birthrates (and parochial school enrollments) gone down as much as those of other groups, but American Catholics apparently approve of and practice abortion in nearly as large numbers as do other groups.[95]

The "prolife"/"profamily" campaign cannot be written off as religious fanaticism or mere opportunism. It has achieved a popular following and a measure of national political power because it is a response to real social conditions and deep-lying personal fears. New Right organizers understand all too well that the main threats to maintaining a traditional family structure in which men dominate women and children and women seek their identity in motherhood are women's economic independence from husbands, teenagers' cultural independence from parents, and the existence of a strong feminist movement. The massive rise in women's labor force participation and, on a smaller but still important scale, the existence of feminist alternatives outside the home (e.g., battered women's shelters, lesbian communities, "returning women's" programs in colleges, and feminist health networks) create the possibility for women to function outside traditional married life. For married women too, these possibilities have changed how they think about marital relations and motherhood and whether to remain married (most of them do). Far more than an opportunistic appeal to the "irrational," the New Right represents a conservative response to these broad and changing social conditions. Moreover, the popular phobias it attempts to harness and channel toward reactionary ends are real, if misplaced. Above all, the fear that homosexuality and feminism will erase the "differences" between women and men, make everyone "the same," while inflamed by the New Right, is not of their making but is embedded deeper in the culture than feminists sometimes want to believe.

It is not only those conditions and fears that have given the New Right its leverage. It is also the failure of the left and feminist movements to develop an alternative vision that provides a sense of orientation in dealing with the personal insecurity and disruption brought about by recent changes in the family and sexual norms. The disjunction in relations between parents and teenagers painfully illustrates this lack of vision. For the concerns of parents about their children getting pregnant, having abortions, abusing drugs, and being encouraged toward "sexual freedom" without any social context of sexual and reproductive responsibility are rational. Neither the left nor the women's movement has offered a model for a better, more socially responsible way for teenagers to live. The "prolife" movement's critique of a certain "hedonism," the cult of subjective experience and "doing whatever feels good," with no sense of values outside the self, is in part a response to the moral failure of contemporary capitalist culture.

In addressing these cultural dislocations, the New Right answers with the reassurance of moral absolutism: To deal with the problems of abortion, teenage sexuality, and conflicts in female-male relations, simply abolish them. There are no decisions to make, no hard choices, no ambiguities. But this is not morality because it absolves human beings, especially those lacking patriarchal authority, of moral agency and plays on people's weakness and insecurity. Moreover, it puts its own followers (e.g., the activist women of the "right-to-life" and "profamily" movement) in a terrible dilemma because the meaning of political activism, to which they are being called, is to think, to act, and to be responsible. Indeed, the most stinging contradiction embodied in the "prolife" movement may be that confronting its large numbers of female rank and file, most of them white, middle-class, and middle-aged. On the one hand, these are the very women for whom the loss of a protective conjugal family structure and motherhood as the core of woman's fulfillment is a menacing specter. On the other hand, what can it mean to be active as a woman in a political movement, or a church, that stands for women's passivity and subordination? How will the women of the New Right confront this dilemma?

Anita Bryant, for three years national symbol and leader of the campaign against gay rights and a devout fundamentalist, may be the harbinger of a gathering storm. Finding herself divorced, jobless, and denounced by the male-dominated church that has made millions of dollars off her name, by 1981 Bryant claimed to "better understand the gays' and feminists' anger and frustration." She sees "a male chauvinist attitude" in "the kind of sermon [she] always heard" growing up in the Bible belt—*'wife submit to your husband even if he's wrong'*—and thinks that "her church has not addressed itself to women's problems":

Fundamentalists have their head in the sands. The church is sick right now and I have to say I'm even part of that sickness. I often have had to stay in pastors' homes and their wives talk to me. Some pastors are so hard-nosed about submission and insensitive to their wives' needs that they don't recognize the frustration—even hatred—within their own households.[96]

We need more insight into the potential "cracks in the high walls" around the evangelical churches and their women, Carol Virginia Pohli reminds feminists. She observes that in the process of engaging its congregants in politically controversial discourse, debate, and activism, New Right churches introduce a contradiction into their internal belief system and power structure; they thereby unwittingly expose their members to conflicting ideas and values and thus open up "potentially subversive" windows of change within their ranks.[97] Only by ignoring the forces of radical change and creating a hermetically sealed world of separate institutions, teachings, schools, culture, and services can the New Right "protect" their women from feminism. Engaging them with the "enemy" has a dangerous side. This becomes even truer to the extent that evangelical women too are the victims of sexual abuse, job discrimination, and chauvinist treatment.

Material and ideological contradictions may undo the "prolife" movement in the long run. The New Right's rejection of the now dominant ideology of the "working mother," their determination to bring women back into the home, represents a basic misunderstanding of current economic realities, including the long-range interests of the capitalist class as a whole, which continues to rely heavily on a (sex-segregated) female labor force. Corporations are unlikely to fill low-paying, part-time, unprotected, high-turnover jobs in the clerical and service sectors—"women's work"—with white male workers; yet these are still the growing areas of the economy. More important, the vast majority of families will continue to depend on at least two wage earners. While the "profamily" movement is reacting to social changes that have caused disruptions in people's lives, its "solutions" are relevant to only a tiny privileged minority. The family model the New Right would like to restore—in fact, to make mandatory—has become practically extinct in America. The three-fourths of all married women who currently work outside the home, nearly half of them with preschool children, do so primarily for the same reasons that men work: to enable themselves and their families to live decently, and in the realization that being an adult member of a capitalist society involves having a job and earning money. Meanwhile, the numbers of female-headed households, unmarried cohabiting couples, homosexual partners, and single individuals not living in "families" continue to increase. Are all these people "immoral" or "un-American"? What will the Moral Majority do about the real majority?

Some of these contradictions may have begun to surface by the 1982 congressional elections. Those elections saw *not a single* New Right candidate win in any state, while the conservative Republican base in the House was eroded by the loss of twenty-six seats to candidates considered liberal on every major economic and social issue, including abortion.[98] Political observers have speculated a good deal about the degree to which these results can be attributed to a growing "gender gap"—the greater tendency for women to vote for Democrats and liberals and to support government spending for social welfare, nuclear disarmament, and a non-interventionist foreign policy. Even White House advisers have expressed concern that the disproportionate impact of budget cuts on women, particularly those who are single and divorced, has led to their growing antagonism toward the Republican administration.[99] Will this shifting political consciousness reject conservative "social" (family-sexual) policies as it has rejected conservative economic and fiscal policies? Is the disarray besetting New Right antiabortion tactics a sign of their eroding popular base? If women are disassociating themselves from the militaristic, antisocial values of Reaganomics, they may also be disassociating themselves from the idea that the male, or the male-dominated state, has a right of paternity to intervene in a woman's womb.

Finally, neither the practice of abortion and birth control nor the expression of sexual desire has ever been successfully stamped out by repressive religious or legal codes. As Jill Stephenson comments with regard to the failure of Nazi "motherhood" ideology to raise the German birthrate:

> The long history of birth control in Germany, with widespread resort to abortion if contraception had been unavailable, or had failed, could not be eliminated from popular consciousness by a few laws and even a mass of propaganda. . . . Repression could only drive these practices underground, where popular demand ensured that, somehow, they survived.[100]

In the United States in the 1980s, social needs and popular consciousness will also assure the survival of these practices. But whether survival will transform into political struggle will depend on the existence and strength of an organized popular movement.

NOTES

1. For more detailed analyses of these policies, see Jaffe, Lindheim, and Lee, *Abortion Politics;* Richard Lincoln et al., "The Court, the Congress and the

President: Turning Back the Clock on the Pregnant Poor," *Family Planning Perspectives* 9 (September/October 1977): 207–14; CARASA, *Women Under Attack;* and Planned Parenthood–World Population, *Washington Memo,* 1977–81.

2. Early attempts to assess the New Right as a political force include Linda Gordon and Allen Hunter, "Sex, Family, and the New Right: Anti-Feminism as a Political Force," *Radical America* 11–12 (November 1977–February 1978): 9–25; Sasha Gregory-Lewis, "Danger on the Right," *Advocate,* published as a series, 1977, and available from Liberation Publications, San Francisco; Peggy A. L. Shriver, "A Briefing on the Right Wing" (report prepared for the Office of Research, Evaluation and Planning, National Council of Churches, Spring 1978); and Dana Naparsteck, "The Politics of the Right-to-Life Movement," *Interchange* (Interchange Resource Center: Washington, D.C., 1979). More recent studies are Allen Hunter, "In the Wings: New Right Organization and Ideology," *Radical America* 15 (Spring 1981): 113–38; Alan Crawford, *Thunder on the Right: The "New Right" and the Politics of Resentment* (New York: Pantheon, 1980); Michael Miles, *The Odyssey of the American Right* (New York: Oxford University Press, 1980); and Frances FitzGerald, "The Triumphs of the New Right," *New York Review of Books* 28 (19 November 1981): 19–26.

3. Crawford, whose critique of the New Right reflects what he calls "responsible conservatism," implies that a politics focused on abortion, gay rights, and opposition to the ERA and busing is opportunistic because these issues are "symbolic" and "nonpolitical, fringe issues at best" (pp. 8–10 and 149).

4. See David M. Chalmers, *Hooded Americanism: The History of the Ku Klux Klan* (Chicago: Quadrangle, 1965), pp. 56–57; and Seymour Martin Lipset and Earl Raab, *The Politics of Unreason: Right-Wing Extremism in America, 1790–1970* (New York: Harper & Row, 1970), pp. 116–18.

5. See Jonathan Katz, *Gay American History: Lesbians and Gay Men in the U.S.A.—A Documentary* (New York: Crowell, 1976); David Caute, *The Great Fear: The Anti-Communist Purge under Truman and Eisenhower* (New York: Simon and Schuster, 1978), pp. 36–37, 303, 335, 422; and Heinz Heger, *The Men with the Pink Triangle* (Boston: Alyson, 1980).

6. Wilhelm Reich, *The Mass Psychology of Fascism,* trans. Vincent R. Carfagno (New York: Farrar, Straus & Giroux, 1970), pp. 126–31.

7. Hunter, "In the Wings."

8. Lipset and Raab, p. 117.

9. Ibid., p. 111.

10. Interview, *Conservative Digest* 6, No. 6 (June 1980): 12.

11. The easy transition that long-time anticommunists such as Phyllis Schlafly have made to antifeminism (without abandoning their anticommunism) reflects a conservative view of feminism as communistic, that is, an association between the traditional patriarchal family structure and capitalism. On Schlafly, see Fitzgerald; Carol Felsenthal, *The Sweetheart of the Silent Majority: The Biography of Phyllis Schlafly* (New York: Doubleday, 1981); and Zillah Eisenstein, *Feminism and the State: Reagan, Neoconservatism, and Revisionist Feminism* (New York: Monthly Review, 1984, forthcoming).

12. U.S. Department of Commerce, Bureau of the Census, Current Population Reports, *Household and Family Characteristics: March 1980,* Series P-20, No. 366 (Washington, D.C.: Government Printing Office, 1981), Table 1; and U.S. Depart-

ment of Labor, Bureau of Labor Statistics, Bulletin 2080, *Perspectives on Working Women: A Databook* (Washington, D.C.: Government Printing Office, 1980), Table 26. The 10 percent calculates the percentage of all U.S. households in 1980 (79.1 million) that were married-couple families with two or more children and then halves that to account for the more than 50 percent of wives in such families who work outside the home.

13. U.S. Department of Commerce, Bureau of the Census, Current Population Reports, *Marital Status and Living Arrangements: March 1980*, Series P-20, No. 365 (Washington, D.C.: Government Printing Office, 1981), pp. 1–4 and Tables B–G.

14. For an analysis of capitalism and patriarchy as distinct but interrelated ideological traditions, see Zillah Eisenstein, *Capitalist Patriarchy and the Case for Socialist Feminism* (New York: Monthly Review, 1978), Intro.

15. In the "profamily" movement's most successful campaign, the battle against the ERA, a connection between "family rights," "property rights," and "states' rights" was made continually. The *Conservative Digest* characterized the ERA as a "federal power grab," charging that "it would shift vast amounts of power from states to the federal government" (*Conservative Digest* 4, No. 7 [July 1978]: 16). Similarly, in a Florida fund-raising letter for "Stop-ERA" Orrin Hatch wrote that the ERA would "allow federal bureaucrats to answer and dictate areas of yours and my personal lives where they have never been able to intrude before. . . . Under ERA, our states will have to surrender to the federal bureaucrats their law-making rights covering marriage, divorce, property settlements and even the raising of our children."

16. See Eli Zaretsky, "The Place of the Family in the Origins of the Welfare State," in *Rethinking the Family: Some Feminist Questions*, ed. Barrie Thorne and Marilyn Yalom (New York: Longman, 1982). He argues that the welfare state in the U.S. has historically functioned to shore up and legitimize the "private" family more than it has intruded on it: "The issue is not whether the welfare state eroded the family, but rather in what form it preserved it. My argument is that the family has been preserved as an economically private unit and that most of the normative aspects of state policy are based on that" (p. 195).

17. See Frances Fox Piven and Richard A. Cloward, *The New Class War* (New York: Pantheon, 1982), Chap. 1.

18. Barbara Ehrenreich and Karin Stallard, "The Nouveau Poor," *Ms.* 11 (July/August 1982): 217–24.

19. George Gilder, *Wealth and Poverty* (New York: Basic Books, 1981), pp. 69–71.

20. Piven and Cloward, pp. 3–4, 15, 19.

21. Ibid., pp. 15, 26, 39.

22. *McRae v. Califano*, 491 F.Supp. 630 (1980), p. 711.

23. Ibid., pp. 703–7; *McRae v. Califano*, 76 Civ. 1804, U.S. Dist. Court, Eastern Dist. of N.Y., Plaintiffs' First Amendment Brief, pp. 70–106, hereafter cited as McRae Brief; Thomas B. Littlewood, *The Politics of Population Control* (Notre Dame: University of Notre Dame Press, 1977), pp. 148–49; and Naparsteck, pp. 2–4.

24. *McRae v. Califano*, p. 712.

25. The 1974 declaration allows certain "permissible exceptions," even though it says that "no reason, even the death of the mother, is sufficient to

'confer the right to dispose of another's life.'" This general prohibition does not cover "unintended abortion" consequent to treatment or surgery because of grave or life-threatening conditions such as a cancerous uterus or an ectopic pregnancy. But if the fetus is alive in such cases and dies *in utero*, it must be baptized. More significantly, in rape or pregnancy following "involuntary intercourse," medical treatment soon afterward—when there is doubt that the egg has implanted—is allowed within Catholic doctrine. Note that these are precisely the exceptions written into law in the earliest Hyde Amendment.

26. *McRae* v. *Califano*, pp. 703–5; and McRae Brief, pp. 78–79.

27. Evidence in *McRae* revealed an agreement between the New York Right-to-Life Committee and Cardinal Cooke that funds collected in churches on "Respect Life Sunday" would be split three ways between "the local group," the state committee, and the National Right-to-Life Committee (McRae Brief, pp. 101–3). According to the *National Catholic Reporter* (cited in the brief), the National Committee for a Human Life Amendment (a NCCB lobby) received its largest contribution in 1979 from the New York archdiocese.

28. Examples abound of exhortation from the pulpits in antiabortion organizing. In St. Louis, the *Cathedral Bulletin* urged parishioners to picket a local abortion clinic with the message: NO CHRISTIAN WILL EXCUSE HIMSELF LIGHTLY ON THIS DUTY (cited in McRae Brief, p. 93). See also "Cardinal Condemns Abortion," *Catholic Register* (12 August 1977); and R. Petchesky, "Face-to-Face with the Far Right: Tradition, Family, Property," *Heresies*, No. 6 (Summer 1978): 59.

29. In an address before a Maryland right-to-life convention, Rep. Henry Hyde, a sponsor of the Hyde Amendment, conveyed the awesome otherworldliness of this belief: "When the time comes, as it surely will, when we face that very terrible moment, the final judgment, I've often thought . . . that it is a terrible moment of loneliness, you have no advocates there, you are there alone standing before God and a terror will rip your soul like nothing you can imagine. I really think that those in the prolife movement will not be alone. I think there'll be a chorus of voices that have never been heard in this world but are heard very beautifully and very loudly in the next world and I think they will plead for everyone who has been in this movement and they will say to God, 'Spare him, because he loved us.' And God will look at us and say not 'Did you succeed?' but 'Did you try?'" (McRae Brief, p. 117).

30. Michael Knight, "Cardinal Cautions Voters on Abortion," *New York Times* (16 September 1980), p. A20; and John Herbert, "Anti-Abortionists' Impact Is Felt in Elections Across the Nation," *New York Times* (19 June 1978), pp. A1, B10.

31. See, for example, Robert G. Marshall, *Bayonets and Roses: Comprehensive Pro-Life Political Action Guide* (Robert G. Marshall, 1978).

32. Sharon Thompson, "The Anti-Abortion Movement in New York State: Fall 1979" (ms.). Thompson's report is based on personal observations and interviews. I am grateful for having had access to this unpublished work.

33. What follows is based largely on information provided by Crawford, Fitzgerald, Hunter, and the *Conservative Digest.*

34. The John Birch Society, one of the most vocal right-wing organizations of the 1950s and 1960s, has been mainly secular in its approach and focused on economic issues and anticommunism. Moreover, the Birch Society "never seri-

ously attempted to build a mass appeal of any kind" but saw itself as a "striking force" trying to influence other conservatives and especially the Republican party. (See Lipset and Raab, p. 269.) Right-wing anticommunist movements rooted in churches (e.g., the Anti-Communist Christian Crusade, Rev. Billy James Hargis, and even Father Coughlin in the 1930s) developed a mass following; they crusaded around "moral" and "family" issues such as sex education and prayer in the schools, as well as espousing anticommunism. But these movements were never highly organized to move into national arenas of power. See ibid., pp. 262, 273; and David Danzig, "The Radical Right and the Rise of the Fundamentalist Minority," *Commentary* 33 (April 1962): 291–98.

35. See Crawford, Chap. 1.

36. Fitzgerald, pp. 19, 26.

37. See Adam Clymer, "Displeasure with Carter Turned Many to Reagan," *New York Times*, November 1980, p. A28; and Zillah Eisenstein, "Antifeminism in the Politics and Election of 1980," *Feminist Studies* 7 (Summer 1981): 187–205.

38. Paul Weyrich, "Building the Moral Majority," *Conservative Digest* 5 (August 1979): 18–19. See also William Billings, *The Christian's Political Action Manual* (Washington, D.C.: National Christian Action Coalition, 1980), pp. 33–34.

39. Steve Manning, " 'New Right' Forces Expect to Win," *Guardian*, 3 October 1979, p. 3; and "Mobilizing the Moral Majority," *Conservative Digest* 5 (August 1979): 15. I am indebted to a talk given by Meredith Tax on "The New Right and the Right-to-Life Movement" before a meeting of New York CARASA, 8 November 1979; and to a chart developed by Tax and Bettie Wallace, "The Interlocking Directorate," which documents connections between "prolife" leaders and other conservative political organizations. Chart available from Bettie Wallace, Center for Constitutional Rights, 853 Broadway, New York, NY 10003.

40. For further breakdown of these developments, see Steven V. Roberts, "New Conservative Coalition," *New York Times*, 7 January 1981, p. A15; Martin Tolchin, "Republicans Prepare for Senate Leadership," *New York Times*, 6 November 1980, p. A28; and Marjorie Hunter, "Democrats Keep Control of the House," *New York Times*, 6 November 1980, p. A29. See also William Schneider, "Realignment: The Eternal Question," *PS* 15, Summer 1982, pp. 449–57.

41. Crawford, p. 36; and *Conservative Digest* 6 (May–June 1980). See detailed profiles of the "profamily" movement's leaders, organizational networks, and goals.

42. Crawford, pp. 57–70.

43. Billy James Hargis was broadcasting his anticommunist messages over one hundred radio stations by the mid-1960s, having learned the technique for organizing a "radio-based movement" from Gerald Winrod, a virulent anti-Semite and pro-Nazi of the 1930s and 1940s. See Lipset and Raab, pp. 167–69, 273–75. For information on the large financial assets and technical capacity of the Christian Broadcasting Network, see Ernest Holsendolph, "Religious Broadcasts Bring Rising Revenues and Create Rivalries," *New York Times*, 2 December 1979, pp. 1, 36.

44. *Moral Majority Report* 1 (14 March 1980): 3; and 5 (26 May 1980): 5.

45. Danzig, pp. 292–93.

46. Carol Virginia Pohli, "Church Closets and Back Doors: A Feminist View of Moral Majority Women," forthcoming in *Feminist Studies* 9 (Fall 1983), n. 14.

47. Danzig, p. 293.

48. Deborah Huntington and Ruth Kaplan, "Whose Gold Is Behind the Altar?" *Press-On! Evangelical Study* 1, No. 4; and 2, No. 1 (1980): pp. 1–12. Available from California Student Christian Movement, 2311 Bowditch Avenue, Berkeley, CA 94704. Interchange Resource Center, "The Right Wing and 'Where It's At' in the Business Community" (xerox). Available from Interchange Resource Center, 2027 Massachusetts Avenue, N.W., Washington, DC 20036.

49. Weyrich, p. 15, reaches this figure by adding together "50 million born-again Protestants, 30 million morally conservative Catholics, 3 million Mormons, and 2 million Orthodox Jews."

50. Personal communication.

51. For example, the director of the NRLC in Washington left the organization to form the American Life Lobby, reportedly because of NRLC President Carolyn Gerster's opposition to close ties between the organization and Viguerie. The former director is Judie Brown, wife of Paul Brown, who directs LAPAC; her American Life Lobby has become Viguerie's first direct "prolife" client. See "The Right-to-Life Movement: Major Force or Guerrilla Movement?" (report prepared for Planned Parenthood Federation of America, 16 October 1979). Ellen McCormack, leader of the Right-to-Life party in New York, apparently favors federally funded child care, gun control, and détente with the Soviet Union. When she insisted on running for president in 1980 on a strict antiabortion platform, she met hostile resistance from Reagan supporters both within and outside the "right-to-life" movement. See Frank Lynn, "Anti-Abortion Groups Split on Reagan's Candidacy," *New York Times*, 22 June 1980, p. 28; "Will McCormack Cost Reagan the Election?" *Human Events* 40, No. 29 (19 July 1980): 1 and 8; and Crawford, p. 36.

52. The most coherent statement is John Lippis, *The Challenge to Be "Pro Life"* (Santa Barbara: Pro Life Education, 1978), pp. 1–3. Workshops at the 1979 National Right to Life Convention in Cincinnati included "Pro-Life—Truly a Liberal Cause" and "Poverty, Abortion and Genocide." A resolution passed at the convention links the "right to life" of the unborn to that of "the retarded, mentally ill, physically handicapped, abused children, educationally deprived, the poor, the aged, unmarried parents, the incurably ill, drug dependent persons including alcoholics, victims of discrimination or [crime], the hungry all over the world." There has been an attempt to appeal to minorities by identifying abortion with "genocide" and publicizing antiabortion views of well-known leaders such as Jesse Jackson and Cesar Chavez.

53. Editorial, *Commonweal*, 2 January 1976, quoted in *McRae* v. *Califano*. p. 709.

54. Richard Halloran, "U.S. Tells Bishops Morality Is Guide on Nuclear Policy," and Kenneth A. Briggs, "Majority of Bishops Said to Back Arms Letter," *New York Times*, 17 November 1982, pp. 1, B4; and Bernard Weinraub, "U.S. Catholic Conference Asks Shift on El Salvador," *New York Times*, 8 March 1983, p. A6.

55. "Nuns' Group Opposes Abortion Strategy of Bishops," *New York Times*, 28 May 1982, p. A28; and Iver Peterson, "Nun Defies Archbishop on Medicaid Abortions," *New York Times*, 8 March 1983, p. A10. Sister Agnes Mary Mansour defied the order of her archbishop that, in her capacity as state director of social services in Michigan, she denounce state-funded abortions for poor women. Her

view that it is "immoral" to deny funding to the poor for a service that is the "legal right" of others was in such sharp conflict with the church that she finally gave up her vows rather than resign her position or face expulsion from her order. (Iver Peterson, "Michigan Nun Quits Order to Keep Welfare Post," *New York Times,* May 12, 1983, p. A14.)

56. See Timothy L. Smith, "Protestants Falwell Does Not Represent," *New York Times,* 22 October 1980; and Robert Booth Fowler, "Evangelical Christians and Women's Liberation" (paper presented at the meeting of the American Political Science Association, Washington, D.C., August 1980).

57. Jim Wallis, "Coming Together on the Sanctity of Life," *Sojourners Magazine* 9, No. 11 (November 1980): 4.

58. Pohli, "Church Closets and Back Doors."

59. See Planned Parenthood–World Population, *Washington Memo* W-14 (12 February 1982): 5; and W-2 (25 August 1982): 1–2. The NRLC issued a statement calling for Dr. Willke's resignation over this issue.

60. Rhonda Copelon, personal communication.

61. Steven V. Roberts, "Senate Kills Plan to Curb Abortion by a Vote of 47–46," *New York Times,* 16 September 1982, pp. 1, B13; and idem, "Reagan Backs Anti-Abortion Bill as Opponents Resume Filibuster," *New York Times,* 9 September 1982, p. A24.

62. See *CARASA News,* June 1981 and September 1981, regarding demonstrations by feminists at Senate hearings on S. 158 and the subsequent arrest and trial of five women. This event marked a real turning point in feminist efforts to hold back the right's antiabortion crusade.

63. Memorandum, National Right to Life Committee, 21 February 1978, signed by J. C. Willke. Willke was at the time national vice-president of the committee. By "they" he is referring specifically to Planned Parenthood but more generally to abortion advocates, liberal family planners, and feminists.

64. Ellen Willis, *Village Voice,* 5 March 1979, p. 6.

65. Anonymous woman participant interviewed by Bonnie Bellow and Nick Egleston at the 1979 National Right-to-Life Convention. Audiovisual slide presentation on abortion politics. My thanks to Bellow and Egleston for permitting me to screen this material before its release.

66. Donald Granberg, "Pro-Life or Reflection of Conservative Ideology? An Analysis of Opposition to Legalized Abortion," *Sociology and Social Research* 62 (April 1978): 421–23. Granberg's findings were confirmed by a study of Catholic "right-to-life" advocates done at the Quixote Center for Justice in Washington, D.C. Maureen Fiedler and Dolly Pomerleau, *Are Catholics Ready?* reviewed in *National Catholic Reporter,* 14 November 1978.

67. Thompson (1979), p. 11.

68. Quoted in Littlewood, p. 138.

69. "A Lesbian Perspective on Abortion," *CARASA News* 5 (December 1981): 12.

70. The earlier version of the bill (96th Cong.) was known as S. 1808, the later version as the Family Protection Act of 1981, co-sponsored by Sens. Roger Jepsen (R-Iowa) and Paul Laxalt (R-Nev.). *Moral Majority Report* 1 (11 April 1980): 16, describes the bill's purpose as "to strengthen the family, the home, the church, and the private school" against "big government's . . . constant intrusion into family matters."

71. A widely circulated letter addressed to Moral Majority supporters, signed by Rev. Falwell, and dated January 1, 1981, targets *Our Bodies, Ourselves* for a major censorship drive. The letter excerpts passages from the book, blacking out key passages; solicits funds for the campaign against it; denounces "secular humanism"; and asks people to try to expunge this and other "obscene" books from their local school libraries.

72. "Witch Hunt Knocks Out Women's Studies Program," *Ms.* 11 (February 1983): 19; and personal communication from Princeton University Women's Studies faculty.

73. Nadine Brozan, "Swapping Strategies at Forum on Family," *New York Times*, 2 August 1982, p. A13.

74. Conservative members of Congress in 1980 were applying the moralistic scare tactics and "profamily" rhetoric developed in the antiabortion campaign to busing. Steven V. Roberts, "Senate Votes to Bar Justice Department Suits Asking for Busing," *New York Times*, 18 November 1980, pp. 1, B10. "Busing" evokes a whole array of fears related to the autonomy of families and parental control over children. Right-wing politicians and judges use "family rights" and the defense of "the family" against "government meddling" to justify racial segregation. Senator Strom Thurmond, the antibusing bill's cosponsor, maintained: "We're not favoring discrimination. We're simply saying, 'Let the children go to the nearest school, whether it's all white or all black or whatever.' " (Martin Tolchin, "Antibusing Measure Approved by Senate," *New York Times* [Nov. 14, 1980], p. A18.) In his judgment defying a federal district court order to enforce desegregation in a Louisiana school, Judge Richard E. Lee (who subsequently became a right-wing and segregationist hero) held "that the case *no longer involves desegregation but is solely a matter of 'family law'* over which he, not the Federal Government, has jurisdiction." (John M. Crewdson, "Judge's Stand on Busing Divides Louisiana Town on Racial Lines," *New York Times* [Jan. 9, 1981], p. A10.)

75. Phyllis Schlafly, "ERA Means Unisex Society," *Conservative Digest* 4, No. 7 (July 1978): 14–16; and *Eagle Forum—The Alternative to Women's Lib* (Alton, Ill., n.p., n.d.).

76. Onalee McGraw, "Federally Funded Domestic Violence Centers," *Moral Majority Report* 1, No. 4 (11 April 1980): 14–16; and "Senate Jeopardizes Family Values," idem, 5, No. 3 (14 March 1980): 8.

77. Senator Max Baucus, a liberal, called Reagan's endorsement of the currently favored antiabortion legislation "a token appeasement for the right wing" and claimed "that his heart is not in it." Roberts, "Reagan Backs Anti-Abortion Bill," p. A24.

78. William Robbins, "Legal Aid Centers for Poor Hampered by Budget Cuts," *New York Times*, 14 December 1981, p. A22.

79. Nathaniel Sheppard, Jr., "Chicago Upheld on School Plan Without Busing," *New York Times*, 7 January 1983, pp. A1 and A16.

80. Robert Pear, "New Rules Seek to Separate Abortion and Family Clinics," *New York Times*, 7 December 1982, p. A18.

81. David E. Rosenbaum, "Abortion Foe Is Chief Candidate to Lead Birth Control Programs," *New York Times*, 18 February 1981, p. 16.

82. *Federal Register* 47 (1982): 7699; Asta M. Kenney, Jacqueline D. Forrest, and Aida Torres, "Storm over Washington: The Parental Notification Proposal," *Family Planning Perspectives* 14 (July/August 1982): 185–97; Robert Pear, "U.S. Issues

Rule on Warning Parents on Birth-Curb Aids," *New York Times*, 20 February 1982; and "U.S. to Require Notice to Parents If Children Receive Contraceptives," *New York Times*, 25 January 1983, p. A23. The latter reports the Reagan administration's intention to pursue the "squeal rule" despite enormous public opposition.

83. Letter to the *New York Times*, 15 June 1981, p. A22.

84. See Gregory-Lewis for information on funding campaigns against gay rights and the ERA.

85. See "Sexuality and the State: The Defeat of the Briggs Initiative and Beyond," interview with Amber Hollibaugh, *Socialist Review* 9 (May–June 1979): 55–72.

86. *Conservative Digest* 5 (March 1979): 10.

87. Michael Novak, "Homosexuality: A Social Rot," *Conservative Digest* 5 (January 1979): 44–45.

88. Quoted in Leslie Bennetts, "Conservatives Join on Social Concerns," *New York Times*, 30 July 1980, pp. 1, B6.

89. Quoted in Nadine Brozan, "Parley Asserts U.S. Undercuts Family," *New York Times*, 28 July 1982, p. A18. This was part of a speech before the 1982 American Family Forum Conference.

90. This is an inference based on P. Leahy, *The Anti-Abortion Movement: Testing a Theory of the Rise and Fall of Social Movements* (Ann Arbor: University Microfilms, 1975), pp. 50–52; and on descriptions of the "profamily" and "right-to-life" leadership contained in their own literature and provided through personal observations by individuals of their national meetings.

91. Quoted in Bennetts (July 30, 1980), p. B6.

92. Smith and Hindus, "Premarital Pregnancy in America," in Rotberg and Rabb, *Marriage and Fertility*, p. 349.

93. Smith and Hindus, p. 360.

94. See Francis X. Clines, "Pope Ends U.S. Visit with Capital Mass Affirming Doctrine," *New York Times*, 2 October 1980, p. A14.

95. Jaffe, Lindheim, and Lee, p. 106, summarizing national survey data through 1977; and Chap. 4 in this volume.

96. Quoted in Cliff Jahn, "Anita Bryant's Startling Reversal," *Ladies' Home Journal* 97 (December 1980): 62–68.

97. Pohli.

98. See Hedrick Smith, "New House Seems Less in Tune with Reagan," *New York Times*, 4 November 1982, pp. A1, A18; and Adam Clymer, "Democrats Victors in Key Races in a Wave of Reagan Discontent," *New York Times*, 3 November 1982, pp. A1, A20. A New York Times/CBS News study showed that three-quarters of the newly elected representatives opposed a constitutional amendment allowing states to prohibit abortions, opposed a constitutional amendment permitting prayer in public schools, and favored the ERA. These are also majority positions in the House of Representatives as a whole. "The New House: Shifts in Attitudes on Major Issues," *New York Times*, 4 November 1982, p. A18.

99. See Kathleen A. Frankovic, "Sex and Politics—New Alignments, Old Issues," *PS* 15 (Summer 1982): 439–48; and Adam Clymer, "Warning on 'Gender Gap' from the White House," *New York Times*, 3 December 1982. But a New York Times/CBS News poll after the elections showed that margins of opposition to conservative candidates were as great among single men and young married

men as they were among women. In fact, except for young married men, there seems to be a political gap between single people of both genders and married people that is greater than that between women and men. This "marital gap" may also be read as an "age gap." While it certainly reflects the greater susceptibility of younger people to unemployment, it may also be true that young single people, particularly unmarried and divorced women, find it more difficult to identify with the New Right's "profamily" sexual politics. Adam Clymer, "Poll Shows a Married-Single Gap in Last Election," *New York Times*, 6 January 1983, p. A12.

100. Jill Stephenson, *Women in Nazi Society* (New York: Barnes and Noble, 1975), p. 71.

8

Protecting Family Integrity: The Rightward Drift in the Courts

This right of privacy . . . is broad enough to encompass a woman's decision whether or not to terminate her pregnancy.

JUSTICE BLACKMUN, *Roe* v. *Wade,* Jan. 1973

People misunderstand. I am not for abortion. I hope my family never has to face such a decision.

JUSTICE BLACKMUN, press interview, Jan. 1983

Antiabortion forces consider January 22, 1973, the date on which *Roe* v. *Wade* was decided, to be a day of infamy. They see the Supreme Court and other federal courts as bastions of liberalism in regard not only to abortion but to policies such as affirmative action, racial integration, and the prohibition of school prayer. In reality, the role of the federal courts, including the Supreme Court, in mediating and interpreting public policy is much more complex than any conspiracy theory would suggest. On the broadest level, the courts more often *follow* than initiate political trends. Within that framework, the courts play a specific part in constructing the ideology that legitimates the policy. In particular, they provide legal and conceptual tools that *accommodate conservative cultural and political tendencies to a prevailing tradition of liberal institutions and liberal procedures.*

Liberal tradition is not static but changes as historical conditions change. At the moment, there are several principles in the ideology of the liberal state that have been incorporated into popular understanding and that New Right and neoconservative politicians find it difficult to dislodge even from their own rhetoric. They include (1) deference to medical authority and medical rationales for policy; (2) the legitimacy of state intervention in matters affecting population, reproduction, and sexuality; and (3) voluntary consent and freedom of choice. In reproductive rights litigation, the courts have functioned to accommodate an increasingly conservative social content to these formal liberal principles.

This is not to deny that the courts are essentially arenas where political struggles are fought and, sometimes even on progressive terms, are won. Radical groups and feminists sometimes win victories in the courts because the courts reflect political currents, and at certain moments progressive movements are strong. In the long run, however, the courts play a predominantly ideological role, using legal language and techniques to resolve the tension between liberal and conservative elements in the capitalist state. This tension has existed throughout the history of capitalism, regardless of political parties, and persists today in a climate of right-wing resurgence. An image of New Right policies suddenly superimposed on the capitalist state is false. It obscures both the process of accommodation through which conservative revisions of the dominant liberal ideology get hammered out and the conservative values and practices contained within the liberal state all along. No president, we should recall, has ever publicly supported legal abortion; and the state-sponsored attack on abortion rights was initiated under a Democratic-controlled Congress and a Democratic administration. (President Carter's refusal to support Medicaid-funded abortions was premised on the sanctimonious observation that "some things in life are just unfair."[1])

Similarly, the Supreme Court began its backtracking from *Roe* v. *Wade* well before a conservative administration was in office. In fact, liberal principles, those applied by the courts in rationalizing their decisions, contain conservative as well as radical potentialities. "Medical necessity" or "health reasons" may be used to expand women's access to necessary reproductive health services or to restrict women's sphere of action in favor of parents' or physicians' authority. "Privacy" may be invoked to defend a woman's right to decide about abortion and the state's obligation to provide access to abortion, or it may be invoked in the name of abandoning public services to the private sector. Even "consent" may be turned around so that the "freedom to choose" is subordinated to the *'capacity* to choose." The *social content* of well-being or freedom is never determined by liberal principles. Politics determine that content, and the courts use legal doctrine and procedures to legitimate it.

The recent history of abortion decisions underscores this political role of the Supreme Court and demonstrates a "pendulum" theory: The Court's views swing whichever way it perceives the dominant trends in national politics to be going, and it functions largely as a barometer of those trends.[2] From *Roe* v. *Wade* onward, Supreme Court pronouncements on abortion may be read as a series of knots and fences, drawn increasingly tighter, hedging in the "right" to abortion with qualifications and exceptions that limit its practical availability among the women most in need of it: poor women and teenagers. Even in periods of heightened liberalism and attention to social welfare, the feminist concept of abortion as rooted in women's right/need to control their bodies was never accorded legitimacy by the state.

This skeptical interpretation of recent state policy making regarding abortion and the Supreme Court's role in it is very different from the view that "with the advent of a new national administration and a new Congress, the abortion debate shifted from the courts to Congress."[3] The implication here is that the courts were the "liberal" force in national abortion politics and that the conservative trend was inaugurated with the Reagan administration in its ties with the New Right, whose stronghold since the 1980 elections has been the Senate. In fact, Congress began engaging in "the abortion debate" in 1977 with its passage of the first of an increasingly restrictive series of amendments to limit Medicaid funds for abortion. During the congressional debates on the Hyde Amendment and when the right-wing, antifeminist current was in full swing, *no one* in Congress stood up and defended a woman's right to decide about abortion *because* it is her body and she is the one who will bear the consequences of pregnancy and childbearing. On the contrary, the most liberal congressmen scrambled to assure their constituents that they were opposed to "abortion for convenience."[4] The Supreme Court responded with characteristic deference, anxious to smooth over rather than accentuate the more liberal dimensions of *Roe* v. *Wade.*

Thus the reactive shifts in abortion politics must be seen in terms not of a constitutional balance of powers but of the totality of political forces that by the late 1970s had come to determine reproductive issues. The reasons for a backsliding so rapid, so "bipartisan," and so massive have been a constant theme in this book. These reasons were not constitutional but social and sexual. They expressed a reaction in all the "centers of power" to abortion, not as an antidote to unwanted pregnancies, but as a condition and a signifier of women's social and sexual autonomy. Any analysis of the legal definitions of abortion policy has to be situated in this larger setting.

Roe v. *Wade* was certainly the most expansive and libertarian of the Court's decisions concerning abortion. But, as we saw in Chapter 4, that "landmark" decision was the product, not of judicial invention or fiat, but of a groundswell of popular feeling and practice that was given powerful political expression by the feminist movement, liberal professionals and politicians, and the population control establishment. It was the product of a social and political moment, which was transformed all too quickly by the backlash described in Chapter 7. Soon after the *Roe* decision, policy makers and courts began to chip away at the formal legalization of abortion under the Constitution, reducing it through one restriction after another. This process, even before the rise of a nationally powerful antiabortion movement, reflects the fact that public policy to liberalize abortion was *nowhere framed in feminist terms*—declaring access to abortion a *social right and need of all women*. Rather, it was framed in terms either of a concept of "medical necessity" or medical prerogative or of an abstract "right of privacy" that, in practice, has often excluded those too poor or too young to exercise their rights without public support. These terms left legalization open to a welter of exceptions: "conscience clause" statutes that exempted medical professionals with religious objections from the obligation to provide abortions, parental and spousal consent or notification requirements, compulsory waiting periods, and retraction of public funds and abortion-related services. Through the courts and through bureaucratic maneuvers, a "counterrevolution" is occurring that is attempting to re-create the austere conditions of pre-*Roe* days when a woman's judgment was considered suspect, and she had to pass medical and bureaucratic hurdles for her abortion to be deemed "necessary."

The following guidelines, fundamentally at odds with abortion as a "woman's right," have surfaced in post-*Roe* revisionist case law: (1) women should not get abortions unless they are "medically necessary"; (2) even when abortions are "medically necessary," the state has no obligation to pay for them (i.e., they do not qualify as a "welfare right"); (3) abortion is not generally a medical or health issue but a "religious" and "moral" issue; (4) women, particularly if they are unmarried teenagers, may be incompetent to choose between abortion and childbirth. With this increasingly prevalent line of reasoning, the Supreme Court has moved ever closer to the right-wing position on abortion.

"Medical Necessity" Versus Women's Autonomy:
Roe v. Wade

The concept of "medical necessity," or "therapeutic abortion," defines nonmedical abortions as "elective," meaning they are somehow frivolous, unnecessary.[5] This bifurcated view distorts reality; it denies that familial, economic, and sexual conditions, as well as those of physical health, create genuine needs that justify abortion. It also reduces the meaning of health, ignoring the extent to which medical problems are related to social, economic, and family-sexual conditions, a point made by Judge Dooling in *McRae* when he argued that "poverty is itself, persistently, a medically relevant factor."[6]

Above all, "medical necessity" makes the physician the final arbiter of the abortion decision. Within this framework, it contains the old eugenic idea of childbearing as a "scientific" undertaking for which only certain women are "fit." Thus it can allow abortions in some cases because women are seen as too poor, too young, or too mentally or physically incompetent to bear children. Abortion and contraception become not a *right* of women to self-determination but a *duty* (to the nation, the "race," the family, or even the self). In this way, therapeutic-eugenic discourse about fertility control, including abortion, allows the liberal state to accommodate without legitimating feminist demands. *Roe* v. *Wade* granted women the "right" to choose abortion in a spirit that was imbued with the "medical necessity" concept. Indeed, how the court defined the "private choice" of abortion hinged very much on the role of medical authority.

The most important legal doctrine invoked to support women's "right to choose" abortion is that of a "right of privacy." Though not granted explicitly in the Constitution, the right of privacy has been found by the courts to reside inherently in various amendments and the "penumbras of the Bill of Rights," particularly with regard to activities related to sexuality and reproduction (marriage, contraception, procreation, homosexuality, childrearing).[7] It was given its most far-reaching expression in Justice Brennan's opinion in *Eisenstadt* v. *Baird* (1972), which involved a ban on the sale of nonhazardous contraceptives to unmarried persons:

> If the right of privacy means anything, it is the right of the *individual,* married or single, to be free from unwarranted governmental intrusion into matters so fundamentally affecting a person as the decision whether to bear or beget a child.[8]

This was not a majority opinion, and so it carried no precedential weight. Moreover, the qualifying term "unwarranted" implied that there might be situations in which "governmental intrusion" into the privacy of reproductive decisions would be justified. In 1973, what the Supreme Court was doing was not so much securing the privacy of a woman's right to choose abortion as defining the scope and limits of the state's authority to intervene.

Roe v. *Wade* and *Doe* v. *Bolton* were very clear in stating that the "privacy right" involved in abortion decisions was not "absolute." In its most positive formulation, the Court held that "this right of privacy . . . is broad enough to encompass a woman's decision whether or not to terminate her pregnancy" and went on to enumerate—in terms it would lay aside in 1980—the serious health consequences that may result for women if this right is denied, including "a distressful life and future," "psychological harm," and harm to "mental and physical health."[9] Nevertheless, it also concluded that the constitutional right of privacy does not entail "an unlimited right to do with one's body as one pleases," or "abortion on demand"; the abortion decision may be limited by certain "important state interests in regulation."[10] These interests include that of "preserving and protecting the health of the pregnant woman," on the one hand, and "protecting the potentiality of human life," on the other. According to the Court's complicated formula—in actuality, the heart of *Roe* v. *Wade*—these two state interests are "separate and distinct," each becoming "compelling" at a different *stage* of pregnancy. Thus the Court implied that during the first trimester, state regulation of abortion was unconstitutional; during the second trimester, the state might intervene for reasons of "protecting the woman's health"; and in the final trimester, which the Court associated with fetal "viability," the state's "interest in potential life" could justify a *prohibition* of abortion "except when it is necessary to preserve the life *or health* of the mother."[11]

May we nonetheless presume that women were being granted an unqualified "right to choose" abortion in the first stage of pregnancy? Here is how the Supreme Court clarified it in *Roe:*

> The decision vindicates *the right of the physician* to administer medical treatment *according to his professional judgment* up to the points where important state interests provide compelling justifications for intervention. Up to those points, *the abortion decision in all its aspects is inherently, and primarily, a medical decision, and basic responsibility for it must rest with the physician.*[12]

Thus the Court "was not upholding a *woman's* right to determine whether to bear a child, as abortion proponents and feminists had argued. Instead, it was upholding a *doctor's* right to make a medical decision!"[13] This was even clearer in *Doe* v. *Bolton.* There the Court's opinion seemed to reject the "medical model" by invalidating statutory requirements that abortions be performed only in accredited hospitals with the approval of the hospital abortion committee and two outside physicians. Although the Court was paring away some of the more cumbersome medical restrictions on abortion maintained by AMA policy and past medical practice, it did so explicitly on behalf of *"licensed physicians."* Nurses, counselors, paramedicals, and other potential providers were denied standing to sue in the case, since they "are in no position to render medical advice."[14] The bureaucratic restrictions were struck down by the Court because they were held to infringe on *"the woman's right to receive medical care in accordance with her licensed physician's best judgment and the physician's right to administer it"—"the physician's right to practice."*[15]

Roe v. *Wade* and *Doe* v. *Bolton* therefore simply confirmed the model of abortion decisions being made within a private, confidential doctor-patient relationship—a model that already prevailed in clinical practice for white middle-class women. But the Court was not saying anything about a woman's right to *have* this kind of medical care. If anything, it was upholding the traditional professional autonomy of private practicing physicians over determinations of when (and for whom) medical care is warranted. It was explicitly fitting abortion within the market-oriented

medical paradigm. Moreover, it was reserving the legitimacy of state interference with this professional autonomy in the interests of "protecting
women's health" or "preserving potential life." With regard to this last
point, while the Court in *Roe* v. *Wade* is widely read as dismissing the
notion of "fetal personhood" or "fetal rights" as constitutionally relevant
(which essentially it does), still another carefully veiled hedge foreshadows
Harris v. *McRae*. Acknowledging that abortion is covered by the constitutionally protected right of privacy, the Court nevertheless suggests in
an ominous aside that abortion may not be a right to the same degree
as other rights:

> The pregnant woman cannot be isolated in her privacy. She carries
> an embryo, and, later, a fetus. . . . The situation is thus
> *inherently different* from marital intimacy, or bedroom possession of
> obscene material, or marriage, or procreation, or education. . . .[16]

Why, then, was the 1973 abortion decision so widely interpreted
as a victory for women's right of privacy and the language about "medical
judgment" and "inherent difference" from other privacy rights overlooked? Again, we have to look at the political and social context in
which the decision was rendered. The strength of the women's liberation
movement and the broad approval in the society for liberal feminist ideas
about equality and self-determination meant that *Roe* would be interpreted
by the lower courts and policy makers, as well as by the general public,
as giving women a "fundamental right" to abortion. I would also argue
that, despite its limitations, *Roe* v. *Wade* genuinely reflected this liberal
climate. It established the legality and legitimacy of abortion, and it did
so within a normative framework that emphasized women's health, very
broadly defined, rather than abstract moralism or "fetal rights." In this
sense, it was progressive, and its immediate impact was to expand women's
access to abortion significantly.[17]

In fact, the concept of "medical necessity" or "protecting women's
health" cuts in different ways. It may be interpreted as, simply, whatever
doctors decide is necessary; this outcome is reinforced by the absence,
in a private, profit-oriented medical system, of any socialized, uniform
processes for determining standards of need. But it may also refer to
the standards themselves, their material content, as Judge Dooling did
when he enumerated with great sympathy and detail the array of physical
and psychological difficulties that unwanted pregnancy may provoke.
These two criteria, *medical authority* and *health needs,* may come into conflict
(e.g., in the passage of "conscience clause" statutes that allow doctors
to refuse to perform abortions on grounds unrelated to women's health).
Understood expansively, however, "health reasons" for abortion may provide the broadest *practical* basis for abortion services *within the health-care*

system as it is currently structured. This is why the medical emphasis in *Roe v. Wade* may have been, at a particular moment, relatively progressive for women. In the broad language of the Court, the injuries to *health* that women suffer from being denied access to abortion may even include "a distressful life and future," and at *no* time during a pregnancy is the state justified in withholding legal abortion if such injuries to health would result.[18]

While feminist thinking sees the medical necessity criterion as restrictive of women's rights in principle, increasingly since *Roe v. Wade* the opposite is true in practice. It has been a hard fight to get abortion recognized as a legitimate health concern at all. Within the health-care system, only conditions defined as "disease" usually receive insurance coverage, even though many nonpathological conditions (i.e., much of reproductive health and all preventive services) require the same costly medical facilities and personnel. If abortion was clearly understood as health related, it would be much more difficult politically to exclude it from Medicaid coverage. (The Supreme Court was able to rationalize denial of Medicaid funding for abortion in 1980 only by choosing to ignore its own strong language about health consequences in 1973.)

The pressure that the health-care system exerts to define abortion in medical terms was spelled out in a memorandum by the late Frederick S. Jaffe, director of Planned Parenthood's Center for Family Planning Program Development, shortly after *Roe v. Wade.*[19] He argued for the "need to develop rapidly a viable concept of 'medical necessity' or 'medical indications' for fertility control (and particularly abortion)—and that we have to find a way to have such a concept adopted by the medical profession and the insurance industry." The alternative was that abortion would "be shut out of U.S. health financing mechanisms." Jaffe was aware of the problems in urging "medical indications" as the basis for abortion services for institutional and funding purposes. He acknowledged that it was "repugnant" to the idea of women's "constitutional *right* to avoid involuntary pregnancy . . . for her own reasons, without the need for any external justifications." But to define most abortions as "elective" (i.e., a question of individual choice) is *ipso facto* to disqualify them "from public or private financing," thus to "win the battle and lose the war."[20] The contradiction between abstract, formal "right" and practical access to services is structured into the existing health-care system.

In 1976, with the debut of the interminable Hyde Amendment debates that marked the escalation of the "right-to-life" movement's antiabortion crusade to the national level, low-income women watched grimly as what they thought was their court-approved constitutional right to choose abortion was systematically whittled down by a legislative body composed almost entirely of men: first to "medically necessary" abortions; then to those indicated by a risk of "severe and long-lasting *physical* health damage," as certified by two physicians, or to those precipitated by (duly reported) rape or incest; and finally, to those necessitated by actual danger to the woman's life. These restrictions were subsequently adopted by all but 14 states and the District of Columbia, which provided 92 percent of the public funds used to finance abortions for poor women in 1981.[22] At the federal level, funds are restricted not only to Medicaid-dependent women but to military dependents, Peace Corps volunteers, and working women dependent on employment-related pregnancy disability benefits.[23]

From the beginning of this massive legislative assault on abortion funding, the posture of liberals in Congress and the courts was to retreat into a defense of "medical necessity." A review of early legislative debates on the Hyde Amendment suggests that feminists' apprehensions about the limits of this framework as a way of thinking about abortion, even in a period of repression, are well founded. Throughout the debates, liberal senators who were most outspoken against the "right-to-life" proposals and in favor of retaining Medicaid funding based their arguments on a strict notion of medical autonomy. Senator Brooke, who introduced an amendment that would have attached the phrase "where medically necessary" to the provisions, clarified the concept thus: "The only alternative was to allow the doctors to make the decisions that only they were qualified to make, and that [the principle of medical necessity] would leave the medical decisions where they so clearly belonged . . . [he] made clear that the doctor would have to make a medical determination, however, and not take the word of the pregnant woman."[24] Brooke's position, considered the most liberal in Congress at the time, is immediately recognizable as the official AMA policy since 1967 on abortion. Similarly, other liberal senators, such as Javits, Bayh, and Kennedy, declared their support for federal funding for abortions where *doctors* determine there are "sound medical reasons" (Javits) or "in cases of genuine medical necessity" (Kennedy), but decidedly *not* for "abortion on demand" or "as a method of family planning or for emotional or social convenience."[25] Even opponents of the Hyde Amendment in the Senate were infected by the rapidly mounting antifeminist backlash, the view that abortion rates were a reflection of women's "selfishness."

On the other hand, "right-to-lifers" in Congress were resolutely opposed to any reference to "medical necessity" or even medical approval as part of the Hyde Amendment exceptions, arguing that this would open the door to "abortion on demand." By 1979, they had succeeded in eliminating all medical criteria from the amendment, reducing Medicaid-funded abortions to those where a woman's life is threatened and thereby virtually wiping out publicly financed abortions for most poor women. In this new political context the defense of "health reasons" for abortion seemed not only vital but relatively progressive.

Privacy Rights Versus Social Justice: Medicaid Funding

By defining abortion as an individual privacy right under the liberty clause of the Fourteenth Amendment, the Supreme Court in *Roe* v. *Wade* managed to evade the more complicated social realities that may prevent women from securing safe abortions, regardless of their formal "rights." ("Pro-choice" advocates effect the same evasion when they define "abortion rights" as an individual matter, one of "conscience" rather than socially determined need.) The right of privacy is a "shaky" constitutional basis for women's abortion rights insofar as it lends itself to interpretations favoring the professional and proprietary claims of doctors.[26] Another reason why the right of privacy is a dubious principle for asserting women's need for reproductive freedom is that the principle asserts the *personal* and *individual* character of pregnancy and childbearing; it provides no basis for demanding that women, as a "class," are entitled to abortion services and that denial of access to those services is prejudicial to the legitimate interests and needs of women collectively.[27] In turn, the denial of a collective or social basis of women's need and right of access to abortion, its portrayal as a "private choice" rather than a condition of a decent life, serves to perpetuate class divisions *among* women. In a class-divided society, leaving individuals to their own private resources to secure a right means inevitably to exclude those who lack the resources.

The constitutional doctrine used to show that some group, or "class," has been treated unfairly is the equal protection clause of the Fifth and Fourteenth Amendments. But, incredibly, the Supreme Court, in its spate of decisions affecting women's rights, has not seen fit to consider women a "suspect class" for purposes of "equal protection"—for purposes of showing that a law or policy discriminates against women without any "compelling state interest" that would justify such discrimination. (Racial groups and illegitimate children have been accorded such status, but not women nor, for that matter, the poor.[28]) Yet, logically, it would seem that an "equal protection" argument would be necessary, within the framework of American constitutional law, to make the case that abortion rights must be made available to *all* women equally and not simply to "individuals" abstractly.

By early 1977, the political pendulum had swung to the right. The women's movement was fragmented and on the defensive; the "right-to-life" movement was engaged in a well-funded and well-organized political offensive; and Congress was embroiled in debate over provisions of the Hyde Amendment, which would curtail federal financing of abortions. The Supreme Court responded accordingly. In June it issued three decisions related to state Medicaid programs to reimburse abortions: *Beal* v. *Doe, Maher* v. *Roe,* and *Poelker* v. *Doe.*[29] Essentially, it set the stage for *Harris* v. *McRae* and the denial of an "equal protection" basis for guaranteeing that poor women would have the same access to abortion services as middle-class women. The linchpin of its rulings was the distinction—"revived with a vengeance," as Willis put it—between "medically necessary" and "nontherapeutic" abortions. Pennsylvania was justified, said the Court, in excluding "nontherapeutic abortions from Medicaid coverage"; this did not constitute a denial of equal protection to Medicaid-dependent women because of the state's "valid and important interest in encouraging childbirth" and in "protecting the potentiality of human life."

What, then, had happened to the woman's "fundamental right," in consultation with her doctor, to choose abortion for any reason without state interference, at least in the first trimester of pregnancy? By 1977 the Court was apparently denying the existence of such a right, instead incanting the state's "valid and important interest," its "significant" interest, its "unquestionably strong and legitimate interest" in childbirth[30] in a litany that all but drowned out the woman's and the physician's right of decision as laid down in *Roe*.

The Court distinguished its 1977 rulings from *Roe* v. *Wade* by an extraordinary piece of verbal agility. The right to choose became, instead, the "freedom to decide whether to terminate her pregnancy" free from "unduly burdensome interference" by the state. There is no such "interference," the Court held in *Maher*, when the state refuses to allocate public funds to support abortions for poor women or implements policy "favoring childbirth over abortion." Such policy is different from statutes that impose "obstacles," such as criminal penalties; the state is under no obligation to provide women with the means necessary to realize their constitutionally protected rights, only to refrain from putting any "obstacles" in their "path":

> An indigent woman who desires an abortion suffers no disadvantage as a consequence of Connecticut's decision to fund childbirth; she *continues as before to be dependent on private sources* for the service she desires. The State may have made childbirth a more attractive alternative, thereby influencing the woman's decision, but it has imposed no restriction on access to abortions that was not already there. *The indigency that may make it difficult—and in some cases, perhaps, impossible—for some women to have abortions is neither created nor in any way affected* by the Connecticut regulations.[31]

Of course, the Court's reasoning here is built on a pile of misconceptions: that state policy "favors childbirth" for indigent women, when in fact it favors sterilization (for which Medicaid funds 90 percent of the costs); that there is "no discrimination" because neither poor women nor poverty in general constitute a "suspect class . . . so recognized by our cases";[32] and that "an indigent woman who desires an abortion" could always obtain "private sources for the services she desires." The legalistic burden/benefit distinction distorts reality, conditioning a woman's right in a way that virtually dissolves it for poor women. Although "medical necessity" still seemed to be the cutting edge of abortion politics, the profound class bias exhibited in the 1977 decisions demonstrates that the Supreme Court was merely keeping pace with the regressive currents that were sweeping the country.

Some federal judges resisted the reactionary political trends. Most remarkable among these was the late John F. Dooling of the federal district court in New York, who in *McRae* v. *Califano* heard and rejected the government's arguments for the constitutionality of the Hyde Amendment. While Judge Dooling's expansive understanding of medically necessary abortions seems courageous, the content of the decision reflects the tireless work of feminist lawyers in the case, trying to stretch existing legal constraints to meet the needs of women for abortion.[33]

On one level, Dooling's opinion was framed in terms of the amendment's exclusion of medically necessary abortions. The Hyde Amendment, he concluded, was a denial of a poor woman's statutory rights under the Social Security Act (Title XIX) and her constitutional rights under the First and Fifth Amendments—but viewed in both cases as medical entitlements exercised under medical auspices:

> Since the recommended abortion is medically necessary to safeguard the pregnant woman's health, and her basic statutory entitlement is to appropriate medical assistance, the disentitlement to medicaid assistance impinges directly on the woman's right to decide, *in consultation with her physician and in reliance on his judgement,* to terminate her pregnancy *in order to preserve her health.*

Even Judge Dooling's most ringing statement of women's rights was linked to a therapeutic situation:

> A woman's conscientious decision, *in consultation with her physician,* to terminate her pregnancy *because that is medically necessary to her health,* is an exercise of the most fundamental of rights, nearly allied to her right to be. . . .[34]

On the other hand, Judge Dooling's decision was solidly rooted in reality, especially the serious health consequences of pregnancy. Extensive testimony on the health impact of the denial of Medicaid funds for abortion had determined that poor women—a disproportionate number of whom are minority women—were left with the unviable "choices" of going through with their unwanted or dangerous pregnancies, resorting to illegal or self-induced abortions, or seeking practically nonexistent alternative services, all of which result in serious complications or risky delays. Dooling's summary strongly emphasized the health risks involved in delay, particularly for poor women who are mainly dependent on large public or teaching hospitals and "as a class are not well served medically."[35] Also important is the broad meaning Dooling gives to the concept of health. "Medical" indications, he suggests, cannot be separated from a wide spectrum of conditions including psychological and emotional factors, age, family situation, the woman's attitude toward the pregnancy, her general health and nutritional level, and poverty itself, which "takes its toll on pregnant women's general health and in the heightening of the health risks of pregnancy."[36] "The unwanted pregnancy [*never occurs*] *as an abstraction or in isolation from the woman's total life circumstance. . . .*"[37] At the same time, the copious evidence concerning the health risks and complications of pregnancy, especially those associated with poverty, youth, or chronic disease, on which Dooling's decision largely turned, reminds us that pregnancy is for many, perhaps for most women, a profoundly health-disrupting condition.

One final point should be stressed about Judge Dooling's decision in *McRae:* It placed the woman's health needs above any "state interests" in "preserving the fetus." No such interests could "justify withdrawing medical assistance," *even* "in the extremely rare third trimester case."[38] Dooling's decision against the Hyde Amendment grew out of this basic set of priorities and his perception, stated early in the opinion, that a "fetal rights" position and a "woman's rights" position on abortion are fundamentally, unalterably "irreconcilable." The Hyde Amendment could have no other purpose than "to prefer the life of the fetus over the health interests of the pregnant woman," since the only other "rationally related" purpose, "encouraging normal childbirth," was never discussed in the congressional debates, nor does it exist in federal policy regarding the poor. The Hyde Amendment, then, discriminated against poor women, subordinating their health needs to the survival of the fetus:

> The relevance of the woman's poverty is that medicaid is her health care reliance, and when she is excluded from receiving under medicaid the therapeutic abortion that is to her a medical necessity, there can be no assurance that she will receive the medically necessary abortion elsewhere. She is effectively denied assurance of *a basic necessity of life.*[39]

In reviewing and reversing Dooling's decision in *McRae,* the Supreme Court saw it differently, rejecting Dooling's fundamental principles: that a woman's health must take priority over fetal survival and that health care itself must be considered "a basic necessity of life." We need to look at the Court's reasoning with regard to each of these principles and to review the political reasons why their rejection is coupled.

Harris v. *McRae* strikes two blows at once. It attacks the idea that women's right to abortion is so fundamental that *no* woman should be denied it and attacks the idea that decent health care is a basic human need that the society should meet regardless of ability to pay. No matter how one reads it, and in spite of the loopholes in *Roe* v. *Wade,* it is impossible to reconcile the position the Court took in 1980 with its opinion in 1973. There, a distinction was drawn between the early stages of pregnancy and "viability." Before that point, the Court held, the *only* "compelling interest" the state might justifiably claim for interfering in the abortion decision was to "protect the woman's health"; after that point, it might claim a "legitimate interest" in preserving the "potentiality of human life," *except* when abortion "is necessary to preserve the life *or health* of the mother." In *Harris* v. *McRae*, the "viability" distinction gets dropped, the exception to protect women's health gets dropped, and the Court upholds the Hyde Amendment's curtailment of federally funded abortions at *any* stage of pregnancy, for *any* reason other than to save a woman's life.[40]

There is also a subtle but politically significant shift in the Court's language regarding the relative weight of the woman's health versus the survival of the fetus. In 1973, the "compelling interest" that the Court suggested the state might claim *in the third trimester of pregnancy only* was "the potentiality of human life." In 1980, a new verbal formulation is introduced: "Abortion is inherently different from other medical procedures, because no other procedure involves *the purposeful termination of a potential life.*"[41] This formulation marks a significant departure from the Court's previous language concerning this politically sensitive issue. It is the closest the Court has come to recognizing the doctrine of fetal "personhood." At the least, the Court's majority is now declaring that the fetus has priority over a woman's health—a total retreat from *Roe* v. *Wade.*

There was, of course, a technical difference between *Roe* and *McRae.* The former involved removing a criminal prohibition, whereas the latter involved the denial of federal funding under Medicaid. But the only way the Court could consider this difference decisive was by flatly denying the truth that Judge Dooling underscored: Without Medicaid funding, many poor women are left with no abortions, for "Medicaid *is* [their] health care reliance."[42] The Court's majority opinion is based almost entirely on its reasoning in *Maher;* it rests on the distinction between a "governmental obstacle" or "unduly burdensome interference," on the one hand (e.g., criminal penalties), and governmental "benefit," or subsidization, on the other. Acknowledging that the Hyde Amendment (unlike the regulations in *Maher*) curtails payment for *medically necessary* abortions and that access to such abortions at *all* stages of pregnancy is protected by "the constitutional liberty identified in *Wade,*" the Court nevertheless holds that even in the case of medically necessary procedures, a "constitutional right" does not entitle anyone to the *material means* needed to exercise that right in practice:

> . . . it simply does not follow that a woman's freedom of choice carries with it a constitutional entitlement to the financial resources to avail herself of the full range of protected choices. The reason why was explained in *Maher:* although government may not place obstacles in the path of a woman's exercise of her freedom of choice, it need not remove those not of its own creation. Indigency falls in the latter category.[43]

Strange as it may seem, the Court is not denying that the Hyde Amendment and its own decision result in discrimination against poor women. Rather, it is saying that such discrimination is not in violation of the Constitution's equal protection clause because (1) it is "related to a rational, constitutionally permissible purpose" (i.e., the protection of the fetus), which the Court *now* regards as sufficiently "rational" and "compelling" to justify subordinating poor women's health and well-being; and (2) the Constitution does not protect against such discrimination anyway, since neither poor people nor women are a "suspect class." Repeating its position in *Maher,* as well as previous "social welfare" cases, the Court delivers the judicial mechanism for disregarding class, or economic differences, as a relevant category in the American administration of "justice":

> An indigent woman desiring an abortion does not come within the limited category of disadvantaged classes so recognized by our cases. Nor does the fact that the impact of the regulation falls upon those who cannot pay lead to a different conclusion. In a sense, every denial of welfare to an indigent creates a wealth classification as compared to nonindigents who are able to pay for the desired goods or services. But this Court has never held that financial need alone identifies a suspect class for purposes of equal protection analysis.[44]

The illogical and unfair notion that the state is obligated to uphold certain rights but not to provide the material means to make them real (we didn't create poverty, we're not responsible) is in perfect accord with the neoconservatives' and the Reagan administration's policies against social welfare. Indeed, the idea that the state is socially responsible, through its public agencies, to provide not only abstract formal rights but real, concrete services, universally accessible and at uniformly high standards, implies a total transformation of the social system. Yet the concept of "basic human needs," or "basic necessities of life," and the state's obligation to meet them is not alien to Supreme Court decisions.

It has been applied in cases analogous to Medicaid abortion cases, most effectively in a case decided the same year as *Roe* v. *Wade,* one that underlines the political nature of the Court's twists and turns, especially its most recent turn toward conservatism.

In *Memorial Hospital* v. *Maricopa County,* [45] the Supreme Court confronted the issue of determining the "basic necessities of life" whose denial to particular groups constitutes an infringement of "equal protection of the laws." Expanding its previous judgment that access to "welfare aid upon which may depend the ability . . . to obtain the very means to subsist—food, shelter, and other necessities of life"—could not be denied in the absence of a "compelling state interest," the Court held that *"medical care is as much a basic necessity of life to an indigent as welfare assistance."* It therefore struck down a county residency requirement for nonemergency hospitalization.[46] It is not a coincidence that this judicial doctrine of society's responsibility to provide the "basic necessities of life" to the poor was developed in the late 1960s and early 1970s when there was an active left as well as a vocal welfare rights movement in this country, and the notion of social responsiveness to human needs had wide political legitimacy. While the Court refused to apply its ruling to poor people as a "suspect class," it presented a broad notion of health-care rights: Medical procedures need not be of an "emergency" (i.e., life and death) nature to qualify for constitutional protection; they need only be necessary "for the preservation of [a person's] health and well being."[47] Moreover, in a way that clearly influenced the health issues raised in *McRae,* the Court emphasized the serious risks to health and general well-being if treatment is delayed. It suggested that health, for purposes of constitutional protection, must be viewed as a continuum, a process, not a static category, which is intimately related to other material conditions in a person's life: "The denial of medical care is all the more cruel in this context," it held, "falling as it does on indigents who are often without the means to obtain alternative treatment."[48]

Apparently, "cruelty" and lack of material alternatives were constitutionally relevant factors in 1973 but not in 1980. By *Harris* v. *McRae,* the lone conservative dissent of Justice Rehnquist in *Maricopa* had become the view of the majority: The state is not responsible for economic inequality; it has only to avoid creating "unduly burdensome obstacles" to the enjoyment of rights. Social welfare needs (e.g., reproductive health care) are a matter of "balancing competing interests" through "social policy," not of determining legal and social justice through the courts.[49] Clearly, this reasoning might be extended to "de-fund" the entire Medicaid program or dissolve any social service legislatures have chosen by statute to confer and may by statute choose to take away. One of the Court's messages in *McRae* is that the state is under no constitutional obligation to provide benefits necessary to make good the social welfare rights it has bestowed (or to redress the social evils it has not created).[50] Those benefits must come from the private sector if they are to come at all. Reestablishing the primacy of the private sector (the medical profession, the churches, the nuclear family), not "promoting childbirth," is the real meaning of the "compelling state interests" vaguely defined by the Court. In 1980, then, the Supreme Court bent its earlier precedent to accommodate the new conservatism and in fact gave the New Right's antifeminist, antiwelfare politics the weight of law.

Sexual Freedom Versus "Authority in Their Own Household": Parental Notification

> . . . every human being of adult years and sound mind has a right to determine what shall be done with his own body.
> JUDGE CARDOZO, *Schloendorff* v. *The Society of New York Hospital* (1914)

> Many minors, like appellant, oppose parental notice and seek instead to preserve the fundamental, personal right to privacy. . . . Involving the minor's parents against her wishes effectively cancels her right to avoid disclosure of her personal choice.
> JUSTICE MARSHALL, *H.L.* v. *Matheson* (1981, dissenting)

The desire to engage freely and comfortably in heterosexual sex is a major reason why women seek reliable birth control and abortion. But the language of medical necessity, individual privacy, and "procreative rights" favored by the courts deliberately avoids acknowledging this fact. They avoid it because they do not wish to seem approving of behavior that the state has never publicly endorsed: sex outside marriage. As a result, legal abortion and birth control were from the start burdened with an ambiguity reflected in various public statements, including judicial opinions, that extended rights in the name of reproductive "privacy" and then restricted them in the name of moral "protection." This pattern was most intense with regard to unmarried minors. As Chapter 6 showed, the legalization of contraception and abortion contributed to the image of a wave of sexual permissiveness, particularly among young unmarried people; this visibility called forth overt political responses from policy makers and judges. As teenage sexuality and pregnancy became the major focus of the abortion debate, so the regulation of teenage sexuality, through the requirement of parental consent or notification for abortion and contraception, became a major focus in the courts.

In *Roe* v. *Wade* and *Doe* v. *Bolton*, the Supreme Court left undecided whether "unemancipated" (legally dependent) minors could be prohibited from obtaining an abortion without their parents' knowledge or consent.[51] In subsequent cases, however, the Court came up against the conflict between its liberal principles in *Roe* and the "understood" policy of discouraging nonmarital sex. This conflict was always embedded in government-funded family planning programs, particularly for adolescents and unwed welfare recipients, since the prevention of unwanted pregnancies and the prevention of "promiscuous sex" seemed at odds. But through much of the 1970s, state policy leaned toward pregnancy prevention. Title X legislation, enacted in 1970 to make "comprehensive voluntary family planning services readily available to all persons desiring such services," was amended in 1978 by the Adolescent Health, Services, and Pregnancy Prevention and Care Act, through which Congress mandated the executive to provide special services for adolescents—encouraging consultation with parents, but by no means requiring it.[52] Almost simultaneously, the predictable sexual control backlash emerged, through an array of state and federal court cases and local ordinances challenging the right of women under eighteen to obtain an abortion or contraceptive services. Couched in terms of parental rights (to know about and administer their children's "health") and "family integrity," these challenges were brought by the same forces whose stated goals are to recriminalize abortion and legislate "teenage chastity." Their clear purpose is to make abortions harder to get and heterosexual activity penalty-ridden for unmarried teenage girls. Yet the means they use often involve an accommodation of liberal rhetoric about "health reasons" and "consent."

The response of the Supreme Court to this onslaught was cautious at first but gradually has become more receptive. The balance between its position "that minors have rights . . . to access to sex-related health care"[53] and its position that the state should protect "parental consent to or involvement in important decisions by minors"[54] increasingly tends toward the latter. In fact, what the Court has done is attempt to accommodate both principles, in a doctrine freighted with ambiguity.

On the one hand, its decisions cast the issue of whether minors ought to decide for themselves about abortion and contraception within the standard legal framework of "informed consent" to medical treatment. Thus, the Court has evolved the notion that, as with any other treatment, informed consent requires that a person be "sufficiently intelligent and mature to understand the situation and the explanation" and that "mature minors" be distinguished, in this regard, from "immature" ones.[55] Its recent case law has exempted "mature minors" from statutory requirements of parental consent or notification regarding abortion and has required a speedy judicial or administrative process to determine maturity if it is in question.[56] But the emphasis on "informed consent" to abortion contains all the inadequacies of the medical, or therapeutic, model from which it derives. It ignores that the decision whether to get an abortion or have a baby is not only a health issue and that the competence of a teenage girl to make that decision is altogether different from her competence to decide whether to undergo major surgery.

On the other hand, the Court's increasing deference to "family integrity" and the authority of parents over their children[57] cuts in a different direction from the therapeutic model, which implies that children's interests (health and well-being) supersede parental discretion and may be protected by the state. The "parental authority" principle derives from a *moral* model of abortion and assumes that abortion is a matter that "raises profound moral and religious concerns" more than medical ones,[58] concerns that parents rather than doctors or judges should oversee. In this part of its reasoning, the Court ignores the reality that access to abortion affects women's health and well-being dramatically, particularly so for younger women. But neither the therapeutic nor the moral model contains much space for the notion that the abortion decision ought to belong to the young woman herself, as a fundamental right "nearly allied to her right to be." What the two approaches have in common is their assumption that dependent minors must, like the mentally incompetent, be protected at any cost.

The tension between a state-oriented and a parent-oriented approach to protecting children has a long history. The doctrine of the state as *parens patriae,* or its protective role over those unable to care for themselves, predates that of the family as protector, going back to the Middle Ages and the Elizabethan Poor Laws.[59] In the United States in the late nineteenth and early twentieth centuries, particularly during the Progressive era, the common-law idea that parents have ownership of their children's bodies became increasingly subordinate to the power of the state to intervene to protect children when parents were deemed incompetent or the state's interest paramount. In this period the juvenile justice system was established—to prevent as well as to punish juvenile crime—and child neglect and child abuse statutes were introduced in many states. Numerous laws were passed requiring parents to send their children to school, to provide them with necessary medical care, and not to exploit their labor—laws that the courts upheld in a line of constitutional cases emphasizing the power of the state to protect children even when this interfered with parents' religious or personal beliefs.[60] But these laws and judicial rulings were directed at certain families, those thought to be innately "dependent" and "delinquent" and in need of state supervision—that is, immigrants and the poor in ghetto communities. In practice, the state's *parens patriae* control has always been exercised selectively.[61]

A second line of cases and policies has emphasized the state's obligation to preserve parental authority and "family integrity," the rights of parents against undue interference by the state in "family privacy," and the relations between parents and children. But these cases, more recent and more limited than the *parens patriae* cases, also have been applied selectively; a particular kind of family situation or family interest has usually been protected. A classic case cited as precedent for the Court's concern for "parental authority" is *Pierce* v. *Society of Sisters* (1925). This case involved the complaint of two private schools—a Roman Catholic parochial school and a profit-making military academy—against Oregon's compulsory education statute, which the appellants argued violated their private property rights, including "the right to conduct schools," under the Fourteenth Amendment. In a way that is strikingly reminiscent of right-wing "profamily" legislation in the 1980s, "parental rights" were used here to support a conservative attack by private interests on public education.[62] Similarly, the often cited and more recent parental authority case, *Wisconsin* v. *Yoder* (1972), which upheld the right of Amish parents to withdraw their children from school after the eighth grade in accordance with their religious beliefs, hinged on an argument, not about "parental rights," but about the rights of a distinct religious subculture to survive.[63] Although different from one another, these two cases are not about "a constitutional parental right" but about the rights of private, established religious groups—seen here as agents of order and authority.

Yet in the late 1960s and the 1970s, the Supreme Court came increasingly to pay deference to "the parents' claim to authority in their own household to direct the rearing of their children."[64] The context of this shift was a growing emphasis, not only in appellate briefs but in the country at large, on "children's rights," the "youth culture," and a widespread student civil rights and antiwar movement that reached even into the high schools. The Court's initial reaction to this political and social pressure was mixed; it began to acknowledge that minors may have constitutional rights,[65] but seemed determined to "balance" this acknowledgment with a repeated invocation of parental authority. The "mature minor" doctrine is an attempt to resolve this conflict; to say that *some* minors may independently exercise constitutional rights upholds the general principle of parental authority over dependent minors. It is a pragmatic and flexible doctrine because it recognizes that young people have different rates of development and different capacities for handling difficult problems, such as an unwanted pregnancy. At the same time, it is an administrative device that redistributes the jurisdiction over young women's reproductive decisions between parents and the courts.[66]

After having held, in *Planned Parenthood of Central Missouri* v. *Danforth* (1976), that no "blanket provision" requiring parental consent to abortion or "parental veto" was constitutionally permissible, the Supreme Court developed its position on parental notice and consent in *Bellotti* v. *Baird* (known as *Bellotti II*) in 1979.[67] This decision is a masterpiece in the art of the double message. Its holding is far more liberal than the Massachusetts statute, which required all unmarried minors, regardless of maturity or dependency status, to have either the consent of both parents or a court authorization to obtain an abortion. As pointed out in one of the opinions (there was no majority—a further sign of the Court's ambivalence on this issue), "young pregnant minors, especially those living at home, are particularly vulnerable to their parents' efforts to obstruct both an abortion and their access to court." Thus, states must allow a teenage girl "to go directly to a court without first consulting or notifying her parents," in order to determine either (1) that she is sufficiently mature "and well enough informed to make the abortion decision intelligently on her own" or (2) that an abortion "would be in her best interests."[68] But what this resolution does is to shift the weight of authority from parents to judges. The decision of an unmarried minor woman to seek an abortion is "her own" only after a court determines that she is legally "mature."

Subsequent experience with parental consent provisions has shown that they put a substantial obstacle in the way of young unmarried girls getting abortions safely and promptly. Pregnant teenagers who manage to bring their petition before a court under these restrictions, while they usually succeed, sometimes are faced with offensive or inappropriate questions from judges about their morality, their sexual lives, or the description of the fetus. In a Long Island case, a judge denied the petition of a fourteen-year-old because of her "immaturity," while acknowledging her "lack of significant life experiences, her lack of any understanding of the responsibilities of motherhood and the likelihood that she could be further along in the pregnancy than she suspects." In other words, a girl may be "mature" enough to bear a child, although too "immature" to understand the implications of having an abortion. For many teenagers, the burdens involved in dealing with court appearances and attorneys—costs, transportation, having to maintain secrecy and the appearance of normality at home—are beyond their scarce resources. Thus, the practical impact of *Bellotti II* is to create not only "a hassle . . . that increases the trauma to the minor"[69] but an effective obstacle to her obtaining an abortion.

Apart from putting the abortion decision of unmarried minors in the hands of judges, *Bellotti II* contains a conservative ideological tone. While rejecting parental consent and notification laws *under certain conditions,* the Court does so in language that, throughout, strongly affirms the principle of parental authority and "a family resolution" of the teenage girl's abortion decision. *Bellotti II* affirms the idea of parental consent; it simply spells out procedural qualifications under which such laws will be valid:

> . . . parental notice and consent are qualifications that typically
> may be imposed by the State on a minor's right to make
> important decisions. As immature minors often lack the ability
> to make fully informed choices that take account of both
> immediate and long-range consequences, a State reasonably
> may determine that parental consultation often is desirable and in
> the best interests of the minor. It may further determine, as

a general proposition, that *such consultation is particularly desirable with respect to the abortion decision—one that for some people raises profound moral and religious concerns.*[70]

In its recent decisions regarding teenagers and abortion, the Court has emphasized that the "abortion decision is unique," that it differs from other decisions, including medical decisions, a minor might make. But what exactly is unique about abortion is not made clear. At one point the Court seems to suggest that it is simply the timing factor, the necessity of avoiding delay, the fact that it is too late for preventive methods or high-minded moralizing.[71] More often, this sensible approach gives way to a moralistic and implicitly punitive language that rests the denial of decision-making autonomy to young women on "moral" or "religious" issues. Parents should be consulted about abortion, it seems, because of a teenage girl's *moral* interests, not her medical interests; it is *moral* judgments that she is deemed incompetent to make for herself. These two views create a tension in the parental consent and notification cases that one suspects is both deliberate and politically motivated.

Finally, it may be more accurate to describe the tenor of the Court's ruling in *Bellotti II* as "profather" rather than "profamily," for it held valid "as a general rule" the Massachusetts requirement that both parents' consent be obtained. Earlier we saw that teenage girls who confide in a parent about pregnancy are much more likely to tell their mother and are fearful of telling their father. A requirement that both parents be informed affirms paternal authority and power over young women's sexual lives. In the concrete reality of many family situations, this may amount to undermining the mothers of teenage daughters, including their custody rights.[72]

Relative to the parental (patriarchal) approach to teenage sexuality and birth control, the state-oriented, or public welfare, approach seems potentially more attentive to young women's needs, if still in a "protective" mode. This approach directly contradicts the notion in *Bellotti* and *Matheson* that "moral and religious concerns" are a special preserve of parental jurisdiction and unlike matters of "health." In *Prince* v. *Massachusetts,* the Supreme Court said that "the family itself is not beyond regulation in the public interest, as against a claim of religious liberty . . . that the state has a wide range of power for limiting parental freedom and authority in things affecting the child's welfare; and that this includes, to some extent, matters of conscience and religious conviction."[73] In this spirit (though unrelated to religion), the Supreme Court of New Jersey denied the view of a lower court and a retarded girl's parents that "no one has a better right or responsibility and no one is in a better position nor is better equipped than the child's parents to decide what course to pursue."[74] In an important case involving the reproductive rights of retarded minors, that court rejected the ultimate right of parents to decide on the sterilization of their retarded daughter, asserting instead the duty of the state to protect the constitutional right to "personal autonomy over procreation and contraception" that belongs to "all individuals."[75] Basing its decision on both the "sordid" history of sterilization abuse in American history and the Supreme Court's doctrine on privacy as expressed in *Eisenstadt, Danforth, Roe,* and *Doe,* the New Jersey court took the position that a decision about reproduction "belongs to the child"; where the child is incapable of exercising choice, her "best interests" must be protected through rigorous "procedural safeguards" under the supervision of the court. But the main emphasis was on personal autonomy: "What is at stake is not simply a right to obtain contraception or to attempt procreation. Implicit in both these complementary liberties is the right to make a meaningful choice between them."[76]

Though perfectly consistent with its earlier decisions, this liberal direction is not the one the Supreme Court has chosen. Its most recent decision concerning teenagers and abortion illustrates sharply its tendency to abandon or grossly distort issues of health and social needs and to stress the state's interest in preserving "family integrity" and (in theory) favoring childbirth. In *H.L.* v. *Matheson* (1981), the Court followed *Bellotti II* by issuing a narrowly construed ruling couched in sweeping "profamily authority" antilibertarian ideology. It upheld the constitutionality of a Utah statute requiring a physician to notify "if possible" a minor's parents prior to performing an abortion on her, only insofar as the minor is "living with and dependent on her parents," "unemancipated," and "immature." But alongside these narrow guidelines, which still involve the formal burdens of securing a court judgment of "maturity" or "best interests," it enunciated principles that in effect reversed the *Roe* idea, applied so faithfully by the New Jersey Supreme Court, that "all individuals" should have "personal autonomy" over reproduction. The rationale on which the decision turns is that of *Bellotti II,* upholding the state's interest in preserving parents' "authority in their own house"; and the special "moral and religious" connotations of abortion. But the decision goes further and announces that *"there is no logical relationship between the capacity to become pregnant and the capacity for mature judgment concerning the wisdom of an abortion."*[77]

This is the true meaning behind the legalism and apparent liberalism of the "mature minor" doctrine. It brings to the abortion conflict an aspect not present in *Roe* v. *Wade,* the question of "adequate capacity to give a valid and informed consent." The "right to choose" may exist in principle, but a woman must have not only the material means but also the proven intellectual and moral capacity to exercise it. If the *"capacity* to choose" may be disqualified by age, however, may it not also be conditioned upon "emotional stability," previous history, or other indicators of "competence"? There is a sharp political edge to the issue of "choice" once particular categories of women are told that they are not sufficiently competent or mature to decide whether to have a child.

Of course the actual formulation in *Roe* v. *Wade* and *Doe* v. *Bolton* did not stress the woman's right or capacity to choose so much as the physician's; they were decisions that relied on and bolstered medical authority. That this was the Court's intention is affirmed in a footnote in *Bellotti II*, which reemphasizes "the importance of the role of the attending physician" and even justifies parental notice and consent provisions on the ground that, to the Court's dismay, physicians actually have little contact with patients and are relatively uninvolved in the "counseling process," in the everyday reality of most abortion clinics.[78] Such counseling and auxiliary services are provided ordinarily by nurses and trained paraprofessionals, who may be more skilled and sensitive in this area than doctors, and who often encourage the consultation of a parent or family member in the abortion.[79] What the Court is doing here, as it did in 1973 when it denied nurses and counselors standing as litigants, is to discredit not only the capacity of minors to decide on abortion but the capacity of clinic personnel (mainly women and nonphysicians) to provide services.

Unlike the courts, the "right-to-life" movement is suspicious even of doctors, whom they see as accomplices with their patients in murderous acts.[80] The image they evoke is one of medical authorities—public school officials, social workers, federal courts, or other state agencies—subverting the traditional family, particularly the authority of husbands over wives and children. Thus the effort to secure parental and spousal consent requirements in state and local abortion laws is aimed not only at women's decision-making autonomy but at that of doctors. At the same time, antiabortionists have not been able to abandon medical legitimations, for the power of medical discourse and medical authority in the dominant culture, including legal and judicial rhetoric, is much too great. Even "right-to-life"-sponsored legal briefs, which are reflected in court decisions favoring parental consent or notification, contain "medical" arguments. Accordingly, the second justification (after "family integrity") offered by the majority opinion in *Matheson* is that parental notification is necessary to "protect adolescents" by allowing parents "an opportunity . . . to supply essential medical and other information to a physician." However, as Justice Marshall wrote in his dissent:

> It seems doubtful that a minor mature enough to become pregnant and to seek medical advice on her own initiative would be unable or unwilling to provide her physician with information crucial to the abortion decision. In addition, by law the physician already is obligated to obtain all information necessary to form his best medical judgment, and nothing bars consultation with the parents should the physician find it necessary.[81]

The "medical" rationale in *Matheson* is a liberal, benevolent gloss over a conservative ideology. Like many in the organized antiabortion movement, the Court's majority here uses the argument about "potentially traumatic and permanent [medical, emotional, and psychological] consequences" of abortion for teenage women to prop up an underlying argument about the *moral,* particularly *sexual,* dangers of abortion. This "medical" argument, which implies that abortion is more dangerous to young women's health than childbearing, is in diametric opposition to medical fact, as well as to the Court's own recognition of the medical and social consequences of early childbearing in *Roe* v. *Wade.* In a recent examination of data comparing mortality from legal abortion and from childbearing in the United States, researchers at the Centers for Disease Control found an almost seven times greater risk of dying as a result of childbirth, for women of all ages.[82] While the mortality risks in childbirth and abortion are lower for younger than for older women, teenagers' childbirth-related mortality is much higher than their mortality from legal abortions, and, as we have seen, they confront more serious life disruptions and social-psychological deficits as a result of early childbearing. Yet in a statement that left some of the justices as well as the medical profession stunned, the Court's majority declared in *Matheson:* "If the pregnant girl elects to carry her child to term, the *medical* decisions to be made entail few—perhaps none—of the potentially grave emotional and psychological consequences of the decision to abort."[83]

It is important to understand what is going on here, what familiar ideas about women and childbearing are concealed behind the Court's pretense that parental notification is primarily a medical matter and that immature minors must be protected from their choice not to give birth. For the Court's concern with the "emotional and psychological consequences" of abortion, and its unfounded assumption that childbearing for a young teenager involves no such problems, rest on deep-lying misogynist and pseudo-biological views about pregnancy and "woman's nature." Behind the belief that a teenage girl can be too young or immature to understand the implications of abortion but mature enough to bear a child is the ancient patriarchal idea of childbearing as woman's "natural" biological function, whatever her age or situation; abortion is a violation of her "nature." Obviously, this idea is in tension with the dominant liberal notion of a few years ago, embodied in the federal government's Adolescent Pregnancy Prevention program, that teenage pregnancies were an "epidemic" and must be halted through public intervention. The Court's position in *Matheson* both echoes and reinforces the increasing cult of maternity found in mass media and neoconservative state policies, encouraging childbearing and adoption programs rather than abortion for pregnant teenagers. In this sense the Court has turned dramatically from *Roe* v. *Wade,* acting once again as a barometer of rightward political trends. I am not denying that abortion is a health-related issue or that having an abortion or repeated abortions may involve health risks, mental as well as physical, for certain young women.[84] Yet, in a society that has vacuum aspiration, antibiotics, and widely dispersed sanitary public health facilities, it is surely even truer than it was in Stella Browne's day that blocking young women's access to abortion because of "health hazards" is a red herring.

Another legal doctrine used in defense of parental notification or consent to abortion emphasizes, not the state's "compelling interests,"[85] but the minor's "best interests." Thus the Supreme Court in *Bellotti* insinuates that "an abortion may not be the best choice for the minor."[86] In what circumstances, we must ask, can it be in an unmarried teenager's (or any woman's) "best interests" to go through pregnancy and childbirth if she does not wish to do so? What pretext can justify the attempt to persuade her to become a mother against her will, other than the parents' sense of moral virtue or religious duty? In an early stage of pregnancy, what "medical" rationale can exist? We may agree that children, including young adolescents, should have "the right not to be forced into self-reliance, the right to be supported [and taken care of] by adults,"[87] without this implying a duty to seek such "help" or limiting "helpers" to parents. If consulting parents were meant simply to help a young girl make a difficult decision, then it would seem as important to "consult" them when a minor seeks to have a baby but parents counsel her to get an abortion. This is obviously not the intention of conservatives. The parental notification and consent cases are by definition situations in which a teenager has decided on her own to seek an abortion (hence her visit to a doctor or clinic in the first place), but parents and the state wish to prevent her, or to put serious obstacles in her way.

The insistence on parental notification is connected to sexual, not medical, supervision; parents are to be consulted because of the "moral" nature of the issue. The truth about abortion and teenagers is that being able to get an abortion without one's parents' knowledge or consent means being able, even at age twelve, to have sex without their knowledge or consent. Thus, notification and consent provisions are fundamentally *sexual deterrents.* If deterrence fails, the impact of parental consultation and, possibly, intervention against abortion is to reinfantilize the teenage girl, to increase her dependency on her parents (and her mother's domestic obligations, if she is the one expected to raise the child); to absorb her sexual "initiation" into the virtues of motherhood or the trappings of shame.

In an earlier case, the Supreme Court conceded that the deterrence strategy in regard to contraceptives for teenagers does not work and may render harm.[88] But it never denied—nor has it since denied—that the state may legitimately regulate or "discourage" the "promiscuous" sexual activity of minors. While it affirms in principle (with significant exceptions) that minors share in "the right to privacy in connection with decisions affecting *procreation,*" this does not imply any right to *sexual* self-determination. The analogy drawn by at least one justice between "young persons" engaging in sex and "young persons" driving motorcycles is revealing of a deep-rooted view of teenage sex as an unredeemably *dangerous* activity.[89] From this standpoint, the state's posture should be one of either prohibition or cautious protection—surely not permission.

This prohibitive-protective stance emerges most obviously in a companion case to *Matheson* in which the Supreme Court denied that a California "statutory rape" law was unconstitutional because it discriminated on the basis of gender.[90] A statute that "makes men alone criminally liable for the act of sexual intercourse" when both "perpetrators" or the woman alone are under age eighteen, the Court held, is not discriminatory (against men) "because virtually all of the significant harmful and inescapably identifiable consequences of teenage pregnancy fall on the young female." In other words, since men cannot get pregnant, criminal penalties are necessary to deter them from engaging in premarital intercourse; but for minor females, "the risk of pregnancy itself constitutes a substantial deterrence. . . ."[91] (Strange reasoning, since the "risk of pregnancy" is supposedly the "danger" from which the Court wishes to "protect" young women!) Of course, the "risk of pregnancy" becomes a "substantial deterrence" in a world where access to legal birth control and abortion services is curtailed. This is the underlying premise of the Court's decision: Young women become "victims" who must be "protected" from sexual intercourse and its consequences under conditions where such services, particularly abortions, are viewed as an undesirable option; conversely, punishing sexual intercourse among teenagers is a way of preventing abortions.[92] Reproductive and sexual policies are thus pushed back twenty years.

In his concurring opinion in *Michael M.,* Justice Blackmun is the most straightforward in pinpointing the common aim of statutory rape laws, parental consent and notification provisions, and the courts that enforce them. "Both Utah's statute in *Matheson* and California's statute in this case are legislatively-created tools intended to achieve similar ends and addressed to the same societal concerns: *the control and direction of young people's sexual activities.*"[93] As in *Carey* v. *Population Services,* the majority of the justices have no objection on constitutional grounds to the state's authority to exercise such control and the desirability of its doing so. Echoing the position of the California Supreme Court, Rehnquist emphasizes that the main purpose of such control is "to prevent illegitimate teenage pregnancies" rather than to preserve "female chastity."[94] Yet this concern to present a "therapeutic" rather than a moralistic purpose cannot conceal the ultimate objective of sexual policing. Indeed, this opinion creates a new category of deviance: "illegitimate pregnancy" (as opposed to the traditional "illegitimate birth"). Abortion is thus implicitly contained in the proscribed behavior, and underneath the "protective" gloss is the assumption, which we meet over and over again, that restricting abortions and restricting heterosexual activity go hand in hand.[95]

A shift in the dominant sexual discourse reflects, and is a response to, changes in behavior; at the same time, its intention is to contain that behavior within certain limits. The currently prevailing policy among male judges and policy makers, both liberal and conservative, concerning young female sexuality is to attempt its prevention or containment rather than its punishment, but in no way to condone it as a "right." One of the more conservative members of the Supreme Court dissents from its plurality opinion in *Michael M.* because it does not punish women equally with men, evoking the theme of "equality with a vengeance" that has always been the other face of protective legislation:

> . . . as a matter of constitutional power, . . . I would have no doubt about the validity of a state law prohibiting *all* unmarried teenagers from engaging in sexual intercourse. . . . In this case, the fact that a female confronts a greater risk of harm than a male is a reason for applying the prohibition to her—not a reason for granting her a *license to use her own judgment* on whether or not to assume the risk.[96]

In fact, however, there is no quarrel between Justice Stevens and his brethren about the end to be achieved, but only about the efficacy of the means.

Neither statutory rape laws nor rules inhibiting teenage girls' access to abortion and birth control services are likely to stop teenage sex. They are likely to resurrect the climate of guilt, furtiveness, and fear of pregnancy that traditionally infused the experience of sex for unmarried women—and that is their point. Stevens accurately defines what is at issue here: whether women of any age, but especially young unmarried women, are to be granted a "license to use their own judgment" about abortion, sexuality, and how to live their lives. At bottom, the struggle between feminism and the array of rightist political and ideological forces *is* about the "right to choose," insofar as antifeminism, whether as paternalist "protection" or misogynist punishment, involves the denial of women's capacity for moral judgment and hence for "choice."

One of the most insidious legal forms, disguised in a liberal-therapeutic idiom, this denial has taken is in provisions enacted in several locales—most notably, in Akron, Ohio, in 1978—requiring "informed consent" to abortion. Later invalidated by the Supreme Court, the Akron ordinance required a twenty-four-hour waiting period after a woman signed a consent form, thus creating further delay and stress and compounding the difficulties of women who had to travel from out of town for an abortion.[97] In addition, it imposed a hospitalization requirement on all second-trimester abortions, thus doubling their cost and increasing the likelihood that women would have to travel to procure services. Most controversial of all, however, the ordinance required a physician to "inform" an abortion patient, among other things,

> that the unborn child [sic] is a human life from the moment of conception and that there has been described in detail the anatomical and physiological characteristics of the particular unborn child at the gestational point of development at which time the abortion is to be performed, including, but not limited to, appearance, mobility, tactile sensitivity, including pain, perception or response, brain and heart function, the presence of internal organs and the presence of external members.
>
> That her unborn child [sic] may be viable, and thus capable of surviving outside of her womb, if more than 22 weeks have elapsed from the time of conception. . . .[98]

Informed consent is a clinical-legal concept meant to protect patients from unknowing risks to *themselves.* Its use in this way to "warn" women of the "dangers" (which are self-evident) of abortion to the fetus is a gross distortion and a confusion of medical with unprovable moral or religious claims; it is another intimidation tactic meant to scare women from having abortions or to make them feel guilty if they do.[99] Above all, its implication is that women as a group lack the capacity for moral judgment, lack the capacity for consent, since what they are being "informed" of here is transparently a particular moral view of abortion under a pseudo-medical mantle. Indeed, an *amicus curiae* brief submitted to the Supreme Court by the AMA, the ACOG, the American Academy of Pediatrics, and the Nurses Association of the Obstetrical College asserts that the "information" presented in the Akron ordinance is "inaccurate, baseless or irrelevant," and "a serious obstacle to sound medical practice."[100]

On June 16, 1983, the Supreme Court rendered a decision in the *Akron* case that surprised people on both sides of the abortion question. Apparently returning to its earlier liberal position, it strongly rejected all parts of the Akron ordinance as unconstitutional and reaffirmed *Roe v. Wade.* Emphasizing both the "right of privacy" as formulated in *Roe* and current medical standards of women's health, the Court declared, in a majority opinion written by Justice Lewis Powell, that "Akron has imposed a heavy, and unnecessary, burden on women's access to a relatively inexpensive, otherwise accessible, and safe abortion procedure." This applied particularly to the hospitalization requirement, which the Court held was invalidated by "present medical knowledge" and the reality that second-trimester abortions with D. and E. (dilation-and-evacuation) may be performed perfectly safely in an outpatient clinic at half the cost. With regard to the so-called informed consent provision, the Court found that the "information" it conveyed was "designed not to inform the woman's consent but to persuade her to withhold it altogether." Here, too, medical criteria and medical authority were the cutting edge of the decision. This provision, said the Court, was objectionable because it "[intruded] upon the discretion of the pregnant woman's physician." It inserted the state's authority regarding "what information a woman must be given" in place of the authority of the medical profession.[101]

The *Akron* decision is a distinctly progressive one for women, relative to the Court's position of the past several years. Evoking the liberal spirit of *Roe* v. *Wade*, it declares that abortion *is* a woman's constitutional choice and that no state shall put burdensome obstacles in her way. But it is important to be aware of the limitations of this liberal stance and the mixture of political forces responsible for this "pro-choice" victory. True to *Roe*, the *Akron* decision affirms not only a woman's right to choose abortion but the physician's right to define its terms and conditions. It places emphasis not only on women's health but on medical authority.

Why did the Court decide now to reaffirm *Roe* v. *Wade* so strongly, after apparently retreating from it for several years? There are two levels on which to answer this question. First, the *Akron* decision resulted from certain intersecting political influences that were not as evident in prior cases. These included (1) the active organization of the medical profession against state-imposed restrictions on abortion services, which it perceived as a threat to its autonomy; (2) a growing threat to the independence of the federal judiciary (especially in abortion and desegregation cases) from the New Right and the Reagan administration, against which the Court asserted its authority and (3) the recent weakening and divisions among antiabortion forces in Congress and elsewhere. (The strength of "pro-choice" and feminist advocates, on the other hand, was not significantly greater in 1983 than in 1977 or 1980.) Both the galvanizing of the medical profession and the weakening of the "prolife" influence are rooted in the social realities of women's need and demand for abortion, a need and demand that stubbornly refuse to go away.

On another level, if *Akron* was consistent with *Roe*, *Roe* itself was limited, as we saw, by its emphasis on both "privacy" and medical authority. It never declared abortion either a "social right"—a right that society must support through funds and services as well as legality—or a "sexual right" that is open to women of all ages, as a condition of sexual self-determination. As a result, the decision left the way open for serious exceptions and qualifications that would limit abortion access in practice for some groups of women. While *Akron* significantly expands the meaning of "access," particularly for second-trimester abortions, it does not alter the limitations on teenagers' abortion rights (through parental consent and notification rules, with exceptions for "mature minors"[102]) or on those of low-income women (through the denial of Medicaid funds). Although progressive in its emphasis on women's choice and their health, the Supreme Court's decision in *Akron* can and will accommodate a conservative sexual ideology and welfare policy.

It is noteworthy that the "informed consent" and parental consent restrictions, and excessive hospitalization requirements, frame antiabortion measures similarly in terms of the state's role in "protecting health." A conservative sexual politics cannot impose itself wholesale on a framework of liberal political and legal institutions and a popular political culture firmly laced with liberal concepts (e.g., "voluntary consent" and deviance as "sickness"). It must accommodate its social ends to those concepts, create an ideological fusion perceived as natural and "true to life." This ideological fusion occurs not only in the courts but also in conservative organs of mass culture that, unlike the *Conservative Digest* or *Moral Majority Report*, written for a committed hard core, must concern themselves with the receptivity of a broader, and essentially liberal, mass public.

An example is a story published in *Families* magazine—a *Reader's Digest* publication distributed in supermarkets—entitled "Daddy, I'm Sorry—The Story of a Teen-Age Pregnancy."[103] Pretending to be a "stark account" of one teenager's abortion experience, the story begins with a photograph of a white middle-class father, concerned but stern-looking, gripping the shoulders of a weeping and abject daughter. It is a morality play in which the father, who with the assistance of two other male authority figures (a priest and a church youth counselor), tells how he "rescued" his teenage daughter from a situation—unwanted pregnancy—described as an unimaginable white middle-class horror. "It couldn't happen in our family," he laments, clearly referring to their class, race, and staunch Baptist identity. "She had been taught right from wrong by word and example." Her pregnancy was an inexplicable deviation, a mystery like a bad dream. Throughout the story we are kept in the dark about the circumstances of the pregnancy, the sexual experience of the daughter, whether she had a boy friend, or even who the "perpetrator" was. A pervasive sense of innocence and asexuality prevails. It is her innocence that ultimately becomes the object of "rescue."

In managing the "crisis," the narrator-father takes firm command. His wife is presented as uncaring, hysterical, and utterly incompetent to handle the situation; like her daughter, she needs patriarchal-pastoral "guidance." Shepherded by the male triumvirate, the girl is taken out of town to get her abortion; significantly, abortion *is* chosen as the best solution under the circumstances, even though the story urges us to see it as a vale of misery, clinically and geographically remote. The *Families* story thus accommodates a liberal view of legal abortion as a "choice" while integrating it within a patriarchal, moralistic, and punitive image

of abortion as a lived experience. Grimness, shame, penitence, and forgive-
ness are communicated by the story's title ("Daddy, I'm Sorry") and
the constant theme of redemption, which signifies a return to infancy
and the familial nest ("We've got to . . . save our daughter"; "you're
my little baby"). The lesson is that patriarchal control, in a benevolent-
protective mode made palatable to the modern ear by psychotherapeutic
language, can divert teenage daughters from sex: "Overcoming the emotional trauma and re-establishing a positive self-image, regaining trust
and reaffirming old values can *prevent young women from turning to sex as a
means of bolstering their self-esteem.*"[104]

What is happening in this *Families* story is that, while legal abortion
is retained and its availability assumed, the social and emotional context
of the event is displaced; it is removed from the clinic and put back
into "the family." The message of the story is less about the incidence
of abortion than about the restoration of a traditional patriarchal family
form, but in a recognizably late-twentieth-century idiom. "Daddy knows
best," but what he knows is primed in the discourse of developmental
psychology rather than holy writ. As in the 1950s, with its curious blend
of motherhood revival and mother hatred, neo-Freudianism is enlisted
in the service of antifeminist ideology.[105] The difference is that then the
sexual deviant was the married woman, whereas today she is the unmarried teenager whose sexuality has become too visible, too out of control.

It is important to understand the complicated ideological presenta-
tions in which conservative ideas about sexuality and abortion are couched
because of the political power they have, but also because of the power
they lack. There is something ingenious in the fusion. Conservative morality and liberal therapeutics come together in a dominant ideology that
permits legal abortion, but under the most infantilizing, shame-ridden
terms. Since this is a likely scenario, we have to pay attention to it. At
its core is an image of the chastened, submissive daughter, surrounded
by male authority figures and abandoned by an ineffectual mother. It is
a recognizable patriarchal fantasy, but a fantasy whose power to get inside
of women as well as men remains daunting. Whether the combination
of restrictive public policies and cultural backlash will help reconstruct
this fantasy in young women's consciousness and successfully undermine
the elements, now widespread in the culture, of a (liberal) feminist consciousness depends on the future direction of feminism. Nevertheless,
it is significant for the feminist future that conservative ideology, in its
popular mode, has had to try to accommodate liberal consciousness. Despite its power to reach into the psyches of women and men, daughters
and parents, poor and middle class, the ideology of sexual conservatism
remains *in tension* with social reality even as it affects that reality by
affecting the consciousness of the people who live it. All the abortion
opinion polls suggest that the majority in this society, faced with an

unwanted pregnancy (their own or a young daughter's), will choose abortion.[106] The liberal gloss over conservative policies and propaganda related to abortion and birth control is an effort to accommodate that reality. At the same time, it reinforces the message that abortion and nonmarital sex are evils for which a girl must pay.

Another reason why conservative reproductive and sexual policies must try to accommodate liberal ideology is that liberal ideology has become vested in the state apparatus and the professions. Conservative and New Right policies attacking government-sponsored family planning services for teenagers are a direct challenge to a complex network of public and private agencies; demographers, family planners, and social welfare bureaucrats; and institutionalized norms regarding the legitimacy of state intervention in "family life." They are also threatening to the long-standing prerogatives of the medical profession and its well-guarded autonomy. Thus, in spite of their medical-protective guise, the parental and informed consent provisions have aroused the strong opposition of all major medical associations and many local governments, as well as that of feminists and family planners. In addition to the brief filed by the four medical associations against the Akron ordinance, state governments have exhibited tremendous reaction against the Title X parental notification requirement for teenage birth control services (the "squeal rule"). Three-quarters of all the states and several governors filed written comments objecting to the regulation as an intrusion of the federal government into "the state's responsibility and authority to make its own decisions and policies regarding" the provision of confidential services to minors.[107]

The irony of this massive defection of the state governments from the policy of an administration supposed to stand for a new federalism and states' rights should not be lost. Neither should the fact that what is occurring here is a battle between the liberal welfare state and the neoconservative state for control over sexual, reproductive, and population politics. Like restrictions on abortion, the "squeal rule" became both a test of the Reagan administration's commitment to New Right social programs and an arena in which the terms and limits of the dominant discourse of sexual politics would be defined. The enormous opposition to the rule was broadly based and contained many expressions of the idea that reporting to parents about birth control amounted to an invasion of privacy and a denial of the legitimate self-determination of young women. An anonymous student, writing in the *New York Times*, undoubtedly echoed the sentiments of thousands of letters and feminist protests:

> It wasn't that my parents had unshakeable religious or moral convictions opposed to premarital sex, or to birth control. It wasn't that they were unable even to discuss the issue: My mother

had explained all the technical details long before. It wasn't that my father was going to beat me, or lock me in my room or forbid me to see my boyfriend. But I knew my parents would disapprove. I knew that their disapproval wasn't going to make me stop, no matter how much "family communication" we had. And I didn't see any reason to throw my actions in their faces, to create the discord that would have followed such a revelation. There was also the matter of my privacy: I didn't want my sex life to become a matter of dinner table debate.[108]

Recently, a federal district court judge in New York enjoined the "squeal rule," a temporary victory for "reproductive choice" advocates. Yet, instead of the values of privacy and sexual autonomy expressed above, he chose reasons that reflect the very different purposes of the New York State Attorney General and Department of Health. The rule would "subvert the intent of Congress" because it would "increase unwanted adolescent pregnancies" and thus "the financial burdens of additional persons in need of public assistance," as well as violating the "confidentiality" between doctor and patient.[109] In blocking a conservative regulation, the court is once again invoking the interests of the liberal state in population control and the medical profession in its autonomy. In the process, these criteria become the legitimating principles for women's access to birth control, and the feminist idea of women's reproductive choice is muted and contained.

Feminists and radicals do not control the courts. Except in rare instances, their language does not become the courts' language, nor their reasons the courts' reasons. This is not an argument for abandoning the courts as an arena for political struggle in a progressive cause. But it does say that feminist ideas and the feminist movement must find a louder, stronger voice in popular culture and consciousness before they can have a lasting impact on state power.

NOTES

1. Press conference, 12 July 1977, quoted in Jaffe, Lindheim, and Lee, *Abortion Politics*, p. 132.

2. This is also the sense of Kristin Booth Glen, "Abortion in the Courts: A Laywoman's Historical Guide to the New Disaster Area," *Feminist Studies* 4 (February 1978): 1–26. Much of my analysis of Supreme Court decisions regarding abortion from 1973 to 1977 is based on Glen's incisive work.

3. Mary C. Segers, "Can Congress Settle the Abortion Issue?" *Hastings Center Report*, June 1982, p. 20.

4. See *Congressional Record* 123 (1977): S11051–53. The debates are also summarized in an appendix in *McRae* v. *Harris*, 491 F.Supp. 630 (1980), pp. 787–95.

5. See my summary of the feminist critique of this concept in Chapter 3 of this volume.

6. *McRae* v. *Califano,* 491 F.Supp. 630 (1980), pp. 689–90.

7. See *Roe* v. *Wade,* 410 U.S. 142 (1973), pp. 152–56 and cases cited. The most famous case was *Griswold* v. *Connecticut,* 381 U.S. 479 (1965), where the Court denied the constitutionality of state laws prohibiting the sale of contraceptives to married couples.

8. *Eisenstadt* v. *Baird,* 405 U.S. 438 (1972), p. 453; Glen, p. 8.

9. *Roe* v. *Wade,* p. 153.

10. Ibid.; and *Doe* v. *Bolton,* 410 U.S. 179 (1973), p. 189, where the Court says outright: "a pregnant woman does not have an absolute constitutional right to an abortion on her demand."

11. *Roe* v. *Wade,* pp. 162–63. This formulation is ambiguous on the question of "viability." While the Court associates viability with the third trimester, its language leaves open the possibility that, should viability be pushed forward as technology for sustaining a fetus outside the uterus "advances," then the "state's important and legitimate interest in potential life" may become operative at a point earlier than the third trimester.

12. Ibid., p. 166; emphasis added.

13. Glen, p. 9.

14. *Doe* v. *Bolton,* p. 189.

15. Ibid., pp. 197–99; emphasis added.

16. *Roe* v. *Wade,* p. 159; emphasis added.

17. See Forrest, Tietze, and Sullivan (1978); Lindheim (1979); and Jaffe, Lindheim, and Lee. They give precise accounts of the expansion of abortion services after *Roe* v. *Wade* and the important geographic and demographic variations in availability of services.

18. 410 U.S. 142, pp. 162–163.

19. Frederick S. Jaffe, memorandum, 4 January 1974, Center for Family Planning Program Development, Planned Parenthood–World Population, New York. My thanks to Rhonda Copelon for this valuable document.

20. Ibid., p. 6.

21. Ibid., p. 8.

22. Beginning in FY 1977, the Hyde Amendment (named for Rep. Henry Hyde, R.-Ill., its original sponsor) has been attached to the annual appropriations bill for the Departments of Health and Human Services (formerly, Health, Education and Welfare) and Labor. Except for its first year, when a court order enjoined its enforcement, and a 7-month period in FY 1980, when the *McRae* court ordered the federal government to fund all medically necessary abortions, the amendment has become increasingly restrictive; by 1981, the only criterion left was life endangerment. At this writing, medically necessary abortions are being funded by 10 states and the District of Columbia voluntarily (Alaska, Col., D.C., Hawaii, Md., Mich., N.Y., N. Car., Ore., Wash.); and 5 states under court order (Cal., Ga., N.J., Pa., W. Va.). See Rachel Benson Gold, "Publicly Funded Abortions in FY 1980 and FY 1981," *Family Planning Perspectives* 14 (July/August 1982): 204–207 and Tables 1–2.

23. These restrictions are embodied in amendments to the Defense Appropriations Acts of 1978 and 1979; the Foreign Assistance Program regarding Peace

Corps volunteers; and the Civil Rights Act of 1964, as amended in 1978, which excludes abortion coverage from pregnancy disability benefits (the "Beard Amendment").

24. *Congressional Record* 123 (1977): S11050.

25. Ibid., pp. S11052–53.

26. Glen, pp. 9–10.

27. Ann Corinne Hill makes this point forcefully in "Protection of Women Workers and the Courts: A Legal History," *Feminist Studies* 5 (Summer 1979): 266–67. Commenting on the Supreme Court's 1974 decision, which struck down forced maternity leave policies as an unjustifiable interference in a woman's "freedom of personal choice in matters of marriage and family life," Hill notes that this emphasis on pregnancy as a "personal matter" totally ignored the fact "that the forced leave policy was sex discriminatory."

28. See ibid., p. 267, and Glen, pp. 10–11. Glen provides a clear explanation of the equal protection clause and the various rules applied by the courts to determine when laws discriminatory in their effect may nevertheless be valid. The ultimate absurdity of the Court's position that refuses to treat women as a "suspect class" became clear in two decisions, *Geduldig* v. *Aiello,* 417 U.S. 484 (1974), and *Gilbert* v. *General Electric,* 429 U.S. 125 (1976). The Court declined to find any violation of the equal protection clause in employment health and disability insurance plans that do not cover pregnancy and childbirth, on the ground that "pregnant persons," not women per se, were the object of discrimination in the statute!

29. *Beal* v. *Doe,* 432 U.S. 438; *Maher* v. *Roe,* 432 U.S. 464; and *Poelker* v. *Doe,* 432 U.S. 519. All are 1977 cases.

30. See *Beal* v. *Doe,* p. 446; and Glen, pp. 12–13. The Court's determination that this "significant state interest" exists "throughout the course of the woman's pregnancy" clearly contradicts its sharp distinction in *Roe* between the first and second trimesters.

31. *Maher* v. *Roe,* 432 U.S. 464, p. 474; emphasis added.

32. Ibid., pp. 470–71.

33. *McRae* v. *Califano,* 491 F.Supp. 630 (1980). The lawyers who prepared this important case were Rhonda Copelon of the Center for Constitutional Rights and Janet Benshoof and Judy Levin of the American Civil Liberties Union's Reproductive Freedom Project.

34. Ibid., pp. 737, 742.

35. Ibid., pp. 660, 673.

36. Ibid., pp. 668–69, 689–90.

37. Ibid., p. 675; emphasis added.

38. Ibid., p. 737.

39. Ibid., pp. 737, 739.

40. *Harris* v. *McRae,* 448 U.S. 297 (1981).

41. Ibid., p. 325.

42. This judgment was based on evidence from preliminary estimates by family planning officials and the Department of Health and Human Services about the potential impact of Hyde. Subsequently, more systematic surveys indicated that in states where Hyde had gone into effect, the majority of Medicaid-dependent women needing abortions were finding ways to get them financed. But

this does not in the least negate the spirit of Dooling's judgment nor the overwhelmingly discriminatory effect of the amendment.

43. *Harris* v. *McRae*, p. 316.

44. Ibid., p. 323; and *Maher* v. *Roe*, p. 471. That *gender* is the relevant category for "suspect class" analysis in abortion cases was never argued during the *McRae* proceedings, obviously because plaintiffs knew the Court would not accept it. Even Judge Dooling treated the "equal protection" argument around "suspect class" cautiously, holding that the "class" most prejudicially affected by the Hyde Amendment was *teenagers* dependent on Medicaid.

45. *Memorial Hospital* v. *Maricopa County*, 415 U.S. 250 (1973).

46. Ibid., pp. 254, 259.

47. Ibid., p. 260*n*.

48. Ibid., p. 261.

49. Thus, in *Harris* v. *McRae*, the Court retreated into classic judicial conservatism: "It is not the mission of this Court or any other to decide whether the balance of competing interests reflected in the Hyde Amendment is wise social policy" (p. 50). If we take a long-term view, discounting an exceptional case like *Maricopa* and the progressive decisions of the New Deal period, conservatism has been the fairly consistent position of the Supreme Court. It came out most sharply in *Dandridge* v. *Williams*, 397 U.S. 471 (1970), p. 484, where the Court distinguished between "freedom of speech cases" and "those involving social welfare" for purposes of constitutional protection. The state, said the Court, is under no constitutional obligation to meet some given "standard of need" or to meet people's "social and economic" needs at all.

51. The first case to deal with this issue directly was *Planned Parenthood of Missouri* v. *Danforth*, 428 U.S. 52 (1976), in which the Court approached the question of parental consent and notification requirements still very much in the spirit of *Roe*. The state may not impose a "blanket requirement of parental consent" on unmarried, unemancipated women under eighteen who wish to get an abortion or use contraception, since *"the right to privacy in connection with decisions affecting procreation extends to minors as well as adults"* (p. 74; emphasis added). It was notably "procreative" rights, however, not sexual rights, that the Court was endorsing.

52. Asta M. Kenney, Jacqueline D. Forrest, and Aida Torres, "Storm Over Washington: The Parental Notification Proposal," *Family Planning Perspectives* 14 (July/August 1982): 187. Recommendations of the House Select Committee on Population, whose hearings in 1978 paved the way for the act, were liberal to the point of including a proposal for mass distribution of condoms and foam through vending machines. See U.S. House of Representatives, Select Committee on Population, 95th Cong., 2d sess., *Final Report* (Washington, D.C.: Government Printing Office, 1978), p. 19.

53. Eve W. Paul and Harriet F. Pilpel, "Teenagers and Pregnancy: The Law in 1979," *Family Planning Perspectives* 11 (September/October 1979): 297.

54. *Bellotti* v. *Baird*, 443 U.S. 622 (1979), p. 637.

55. Paul and Pilpel, p. 300.

56. These were the two major holdings in *Bellotti* v. *Baird*.

57. Ibid., pp. 637–38.

58. *H. L.* v. *Matheson*, 450 U.S. 398 (1981), 101 S.Ct. 1164, p. 1171.

59. Mary Jo Bane, *Here to Stay: American Families in the Twentieth Century* (New York: Basic Books, 1976), pp. 98–101.

60. *Jacobson* v. *Massachusetts,* 197 U.S. 11 (1905), on compulsory vaccination; *People* v. *Pierson,* 196 N.Y. 201 (1903), on medical care; *Prince* v. *Massachusetts,* 321 U.S. 158 (1944), on child labor; and *Ginsberg* v. *New York,* 390 U.S. 629 (1968), on sale of "obscene material" to minors.

61. See Bane, p. 104; Rosalyn Baxandall, Linda Gordon, and Susan Reverby, *America's Working Women: A Documentary History, 1600 to the Present* (New York: Vintage, 1976), pp. 139–41; and Barbara Ehrenreich and Deirdre English, *For Her Own Good: 150 Years of the Experts' Advice to Women* (Garden City, N.Y.: Anchor, 1979), pp. 170–77, 205–10.

62. *Pierce* v. *Society of Sisters,* 268 U.S. 510 (1925). "The fundamental theory of liberty upon which all governments in this Union repose excludes any general power of the state to standardize its children by forcing them to accept instruction from public teachers only" (p. 535).

63. *Wisconsin* v. *Yoder,* 406 U.S. 205 (1972).

64. *Ginsberg* v. *New York,* 390 U.S. 629 (1968), p. 639.

65. *In re Gault,* 387 U.S. 1 (1967), extended to minors the right to legal counsel in criminal proceedings, while *Tinker* v. *Des Moines Independent Community School District,* 393 U.S. 503 (1968), upheld the right of high school students to wear armbands to school protesting the Vietnam war. Nevertheless, Justice Douglas was the sole dissenting voice in behalf of the constitutional rights of minors in *Ginsberg* and *Yoder.* In the former, he argued against the constitutionality of a statute prohibiting the sale of materials defined as "obscene" to minors as a violation of their sexual freedom. In the latter, he argued that the issue was the obligation to respect the "desires" of children as "persons" who, if "mature enough," should have a say in a matter so life determining as the forfeiture of schooling.

66. Patricia Donovan, "Your Parents or the Judge: Massachusetts' New Abortion Consent Law," *Family Planning Perspectives* 13 (September/October 1981): 224–28, presents a similar view.

67. *Bellotti* v. *Baird.*

68. Ibid., pp. 647–48; and Paul and Pilpel, p. 300.

69. Donovan cites as ignorant or ill-considered questions by judges: "If she knows that she may never be able to have another child if she has an abortion . . . ; if she knows who the father is and if she has considered marrying him; what her parents will do if they find out about the abortion at a later time; or whether her parents are young enough to raise her baby" (pp. 225–26).

70. *Bellotti* v. *Baird,* p. 640.

71. Ibid., p. 642.

72. ". . . when parents are separated or divorced and have fought over child custody, knowledge of the child's sexual activity communicated to the non-custodial parent [who is usually the father] could be used to deprive the other parent of custody on the grounds of improper supervision." Kenney, Forrest, and Torres, p. 193.

73. *Prince* v. *Massachusetts,* 321 U.S. 158 (1943), pp. 166–67.

74. *In the Matter of Lee Ann Grady,* 170 N.J. Super. 98 (1979), p. 125.

75. *In re Grady*, 85 N.J. 235 (1981), p. 247, pp. 11, 14.

76. Ibid., p. 250. The New Jersey Supreme Court mistakenly attributes to the U.S. Supreme Court's decisions about abortion and contraception an intention to grant "the right to control one's own body" (p. 15), but this is reading the Court's meaning too broadly.

77. *H. L.* v. *Matheson*, pp. 1170–71.

78. *Bellotti* v. *Baird*, p. 642n.

79. Kenney, Forrest, and Torres, p. 192.

80. Some "right-to-life" literature pictures pregnant women and their doctors plotting in secret to "get rid of" an unwanted fetus. See, for example, the pocket comic book *Who Killed Junior?* published in 1976. On the other hand, the antiabortion movement has also recruited prominent physicians to its service, for example, Dr. C. Everett Koop (U.S. surgeon-general under Reagan) and Dr. Bernard Nathanson (former long-time abortionist who "converted").

81. *H. L.* v. *Matheson*, p. 1189.

82. Cates et al., "Morality from Abortion and Childbirth" (1982).

83. *H. L.* v. *Matheson*, p. 1173.

84. See Cates et al., Tables 3 and 4; "Gestation, Birth-Weight, and Spontaneous Abortion in Pregnancy after Induced Abortion" (report of collaborative study by WHO Task Force on Sequelae of Abortion), *Lancet,* 20 January 1979, pp. 142–45; and "Repeated Abortions Increase Risk of Miscarriage, Premature Births and Low-Birth-Weight Babies," *Family Planning Perspectives* 11 (January/February 1979): 39–40.

85. On the surface, a third rationale for parental notification given in *H. L.* v. *Matheson* is an apparent defense of pronatalism, under the rubric "compelling state interests." In answer to why the state might require parental notification for abortion when it does not do so for other medical procedures, including childbirth, the Court replies that it is justified in doing so in order to further a policy of "promoting childbirth" (p. 1173). As we have seen, however, pronatalist arguments have historically concealed a complicated mix of antifeminist and racist elements. There is no official public policy in the United States of "promoting childbirth," since "curbing population growth" is still the avowed policy. But there may well be an unofficial one, in reaction to numerous 1980 census reports about higher rates of population growth among racial and ethnic minorities.

86. *Bellotti* v. *Baird*, p. 643.

87. Bane, p. 112.

88. *Carey* v. *Population Services International,* 431 U.S. 678 (1977), pp. 715–16.

89. Ibid., p. 716; and Paul and Pilpel, p. 299. The majority opinion upheld only the constitutional right of minors sixteen years of age and over to acquire nonprescription contraceptives. It also upheld the state's right to *prohibit* the sale of nonprescription contraceptives to minors under 16, in *"furtherance of the state's policy against promiscuous sexual intercourse among the young"* (p. 690).

90. *Michael M.* v. *Superior Court of Sonoma County,* 450 U.S. 455, 101 S.Ct. 1200 (1981).

91. Ibid., p. 1206.

92. Ibid., p. 1205.

93. Ibid., p. 1211.

94. Ibid., p. 1205n.

95. In their dissent, Justices Brennan, White, and Marshall point out that the "protective" purpose of California's statutory rape law was always aimed explicitly at young women's sexual "virtue" and not at the "risk of pregnancy" and that this is a new justification reflecting the recent shift in public discourse about female sexuality. See ibid., p. 1217n, where they quote from a California Supreme Court decision as recent as 1964: "An unwise disposition of her sexual favor is deemed to do harm both to herself and the social mores by which the community's conduct patterns are established."

96. Ibid., pp. 1218–19.

97. *Akron Center for Reproductive Health* v. *City of Akron,* 479 F.Supp. 1172 (N.D. Ohio 1979); affirmed in part, reversed in part, 651 F 2d 1198 (6th Cir., 1981); Supreme Court—cert. granted, 73 L.D. 2d 1282 (1982).

98. Linda Greenhouse, "Medical Groups Opposing Curbs in Abortion Law"; and idem, "Excerpts from Akron, Ohio, Abortion Law," *New York Times,* 31 August 1982, pp. A1, A12.

99. CARASA, *Women under Attack,* pp. 24–25. Information about the *Akron* case reported here is from Linda Greenhouse, "Court Reaffirms Right to Abortion and Bars Variety of Local Curbs," *New York Times* (June 16, 1983), pp. A1 and B11; and "Excerpts from Court's Opinion and Dissent on Abortion Case," *New York Times* (June 16, 1983), p. B10.

100. Greenhouse, p. A12; and Editorial, *American Medical News* (AMA), 10 September 1982, pp. 1, 4.

101. "Excerpts from the Court's Opinion," p. B10. In a dissent that the majority opinion found "rejects the basic premise of Roe," Justice Sandra Day O'Connor, joined by Justices White and Rehnquist, argued "that the state's interest in protecting potential human life exists throughout the pregnancy." This view is tantamount to the right-to-life position, rejected by the Court in *Roe,* and marks Justice O'Connor as a spokesperson for antiabortion forces on the Court. Likewise, President Reagan expressed his "profound disappointment" in the decision, calling on Congress to enact an antiabortion amendment or statute. (Francis X. Clines, "Reagan Urges Congress to Nullify Supreme Court's Abortion Rulings," *New York Times,* June 17, 1983, p. A16.) The unstated threat here is that, if reelected in 1984, Reagan needs only two appointments to pack the Supreme Court with an antiabortion majority.

102. The majority in *Akron* rejected the provision of the ordinance requiring the "informed written consent" of a parent or guardian of a minor woman under the age of 15 seeking an abortion, because it did not make an exception for "mature" minors. This is consistent with the Court's position in *Bellotti* v. *Baird.*

103. Robert Deaton, "Daddy, I'm Sorry—The Story of a Teen-Age Pregnancy," *Families,* June 1982, pp. 87–94. It is worth remarking that a "teenage pregnancy" has in the 1980s become a "story."

104. Ibid., p. 94.

105. See Chafe, Chap. 9; and Ehrenreich and English, Chap. 7, on the cult of motherhood and "momism" (mother-hatred) in the 1950s.

106. See Chap. 10, below, and sources cited in note 6.

107. Kenney, Forrest, and Torres, p. 193.

108. "The 'Squeal Rule,' " *New York Times,* 11 February 1982, p. A27.

109. Arnold H. Lubasch, "Judge Bars Federal Birth-Control Rule for Minors," *New York Times,* 15 February 1983, pp. 1, B2.

9

Morality and Personhood: A Feminist Perspective

I choose to side with women, because they will have the responsibility
for the results of that decision, and I trust their ability to weigh
the alternatives carefully. The "pro-life" side picks fetuses, because
they have little confidence in the moral judgment of women. These
women have, after all, "gotten themselves pregnant," as one state
legislator put it. They have obviously sinned and are deserving of
punishment. A fetus, on the other hand, is virginal and pure.

MARY KAY BLAKELY, New York Times

Feminism as a perspective stands squarely in a humanist philosophical
and historical tradition. Because feminists are "defenders and advocates"
of women who live in the real world, their vantage point is necessarily
historical as well as humanist.[1] Generations of earlier feminists subscribed
to a set of moral principles that were abstract and universalist, drawn
from the natural rights doctrine of the Enlightenment or from religious
faith. They were arguing for the application of those principles (including
the right of "selfhood") to the other half of the human race. Yet in
practice, they found themselves having to discard all traditions, all moral
"authorities." They had to rewrite the Bible, as Elizabeth Cady Stanton
did, and to redraft every legal code because *all* sources of traditional
morality, even enlightened republicanism, originated in patriarchal power
and "maligned" women.

Thus, even as they drew from a male-dominated culture for the
language and perhaps some of the conceptual framework of a feminist
moral sensibility, "women's rights" advocates in the past also looked to
the actual conditions of women—their work, their marital and sexual
relations, their education or lack of it—to determine the elements of a
new, antipatriarchal moral vision. Their perspective, in other words, was

326

implicitly *contextual* and *social,* its references being the relations between women and men, women and children. Similarly, many feminists today, locked in the abstract moral language of "prochoice" and "privacy" derived from a male-dominated tradition of liberal individualism and property rights, nevertheless ground their practical morality about abortion in the real relations in which the necessity for abortion arises. This is the often inchoate, unarticulated perspective I refer to as "moral praxis," and it is that perspective that informs the discussion of abortion morality in this chapter and the one to follow.

My approach to understanding the moral problems of abortion is premised on the conviction that prevailing ideas about morality are inevitably shaped by their historical and cultural contexts. This is as true of the concept of "personhood" as it is of the concepts of "murder" or "maternal duty"; such concepts change historically and across cultures, which is evidence that they are neither biologically rooted nor divinely ordained. Our only reliable source of verification for their rightness or wrongness is their impact on human life and on the welfare and consciousness of human beings. Willis points out that the distinction between "to kill" and "to murder" is itself understood by most legal and ethical systems, including that of the Catholic church, as relative to particular situations. "It makes no sense to discuss whether abortion is murder without considering why women have abortions and what it means to force women to bear children they don't want."[2] The changing conditions of women are part of the total context of the morality of abortion. No amount of scientific measurement or reading of ancient theological texts can determine the "social, political and moral" meanings either of the act of abortion in a given case or of what it is to be a "person" in today's society: "Nothing outside the practice of a human group can decide or determine its membership, since it is comprised of just those individuals who have reciprocal practical relations with each other."[3]

Any serious discussion of the moral and ethical issues of abortion must be prefaced by a clear understanding that the status of the fetus and whether it shall be regarded as a "person" or a "human life" do not exhaust the bases for moral inquiry about abortion. Whether anyone can be compelled to carry and nourish a fetus she does not want is also a moral issue. Philosophers and moralists who assume that the "humanity of the fetus" is the bottom-line issue in the "abortion dilemma" close their eyes to the fact that in many cultures and historical periods this way of framing the abortion question (fetus *versus* woman) was unknown. While abortion practices seem to have existed in all recorded times and cultures, the values and sanctions attached to them have been remarkably variable. Devereux's survey of primitive and ancient societies, for example, uncovers a tremendous variety of attitudes toward abortion and the fetus, "[ranging] from mild resignation to deep horror," with a corresponding range of social signs and sanctions expressing approval or disapproval. Burial customs give evidence of such differences; some cultures bury fetuses "like adults," others distinguish between miscarried and aborted fetuses for burial purposes, still others discard them indiscriminately "in the refuse heap," and at least one cannibalizes them "in times of famine."[4]

Significantly, in primitive and ancient societies that have regarded abortion as wrong, it is not usually the fetus that is considered the wronged party. On the contrary, sanctions against abortion are invoked more often on behalf of the family, the tribe, the state, or the husband or maternal uncle, depending on the prevailing basis of patriarchal authority. Under Roman law, an imperial decree declared that if a woman obtained an abortion, she should be exiled, "for it may be considered dishonorable for a woman to deprive her husband of children with impunity."[5] Thus, ancient patriarchal law valued the fetus as it valued children, slaves, and wives: as the father's property rather than in its own right.

Most current literature on the morality of abortion and on how pregnant women understand that morality is striking for its historical amnesia. It assumes that moral discourse is static and given rather than socially constructed. As we saw earlier, the major historians of abortion in nineteenth-century England and America find a widespread popular acceptance of the practice prior to "quickening," an assumption that there was no "murder" until then because there was no "child" until then. Abortion "was simply a fact of American life," and if it was thought to raise any moral issues, those had to do with women's "health and safety" rather than the status of the fetus.[6] Knowing the particular conditions in which abortion came to be seen as immoral, its association with lapsed "maternal duty," and the instrumental role of physicians in promoting those ideas gives us a useful historical perspective. It helps us to see that the "moral agonies" and guilt cited by "right-to-lifers" as the *intuitive* effects of abortion are the product of historically distinct cultural norms. Specifically, the idea that abortion is "murder" and you are "killing a baby" is a culturally generated one, not shared by many eras and peoples.

Contemporary moral discourse about abortion is constructed out of "a distinct moral language," one that may be identified with a particularly female regimen of socialization and moral development: "the language of selfishness and responsibility, which defines the moral problem as one of obligation to exercise care and avoid hurt."[7] This language is recognizable as the discourse of *maternalism,* which women in modern industrial societies, whether they become mothers or not, are trained to internalize and to embody in their behavior toward others.[8] Social historians document that the modern definition of motherhood as total and selfless devotion to one's biological children was not shared by our preindustrial forebears in Western Europe and that the "preciousness" of each child is a modern—and thoroughly ideological—invention.[9] As feminist analysis shows, however, this "modernization" of motherhood, its "civilization" within the property relations of the bourgeois family, may be seen as unqualifiedly "progressive" only if we exclude the vantage point of the mother herself.

Similarly, the idea of "fetal personhood" and of the fetus as the primary protagonist in the abortion conflict is relatively new to secular thought. Where that idea has emerged historically, it has been linked with an attack on the social position and morality of women. Indeed, I argue that the moral construction of the "abortion dilemma" as one that pits the fetus against the woman in an adversarial relationship of two separate "persons" is not only a relatively recent concept but also a distortion of reality. Even within Catholic doctrine, the precise moment when the fetus became "animated" with a soul was for centuries the source of some dispute; Catholic moral theologians throughout the early modern period argued for various exceptions and qualifications to the abortion prohibition. Not until the mid-eighteenth century did the papacy, facing a decline in its authority and a rise in the use of birth control and abortion, impose a much stricter doctrine; and not until 1869 was abortion at any stage of pregnancy, for any reason, declared a mortal sin punishable by excommunication.[10]

Of course, the recent provenance of an idea does not attest to its truth or falsehood. Nor can we infer what is right from popular belief and practice alone, as borne out by innumerable examples of popular compliance in moral atrocities. Jacques Maritain is unanswerable when he says: "All this proves nothing against natural law, any more than a mistake in addition proves anything against arithmetic, or the mistakes of certain primitive peoples, for whom the stars were holes in the tent which covered the world, prove anything against astronomy."[11] Without subscribing to a theory of natural law, it is possible to posit a humanist moral philosophy that is *principled* yet defines good and evil in terms of the real needs of human beings as they exist in their relations with one another. It is false to link *relativism* irrevocably with *amorality*. An awareness of the historical particularity of moral concepts also allows us a healthy caution about absolutist positions and to question the very terms of ongoing moral debate; that is, it makes critical inquiry possible. Who or what constitute "persons"—beings who share rights and duties within a human legal and moral community—is preeminently a moral, legal, and philosophical question and therefore subject to the historical and cultural variations I have been talking about.

The concept of personhood prevalent in modern Anglo-European legal and political thought from the seventeenth century on has reflected the bourgeois values of rationalism, intellectualism, individualism, and property ownership—as opposed, say, to the value of kinship or lineage that prevailed in the Middle Ages. As a result, in its practical applications, the concept has often excluded certain groups of mature human beings, insofar as they were defined as irrational, primarily emotional or "sensual," dependent, and propertyless. Based on such criteria, women, blacks, prisoners, the pauperized and institutionalized, and, until relatively recently, most wage-earning men as well, were alienated from the community of moral and legal persons in many Western societies and prevented from exercising their full social capacities.[12] Nevertheless, the liberal humanist tradition associating personhood with rationality and consciousness has had a liberating aspect as well, since it invokes a universalistic standard to which all, presumably regardless of social rank, can lay claim. It provided the philosophical basis for the antislavery and feminist movements in the nineteenth century, which argued that neither rationality nor moral autonomy was the exclusive province of white male property owners. Those movements did *not* argue that *because* women and slaves breathe, have human bodies, or are able to copulate and produce human offspring, they should be accorded full rights as citizens. Such an argument would have been perceived as intrinsically degrading, in a rationalistic-humanistic culture, and yielding to the very stereotypes used to oppress women and blacks. Rather, it was the dignity and *humanity* of possessing reason, consciousness, and free will that feminist and black leaders invoked in asserting their claim to full personhood.[13]

This concept of personhood has been incorporated into the common law and the U.S. Constitution, which, it is worth observing, have never recognized the unborn as "persons." While in the 1860s and 1870s many states adopted statutes making abortion a felony, thereby reversing the long-standing leniency of the law, abortion was nowhere declared a homicide.[14] In *Roe* v. *Wade,* the Supreme Court explicitly refused to find constitutional sanction for the view that the fetus is a full human person from conception or otherwise, declaring that this view has no basis in the constitution or "in the law," nor any consensus within "medicine, philosophy and theology." Moreover, the Court found that the use of the word "person" in the Fourteenth Amendment carries no meaning that "has any possible prenatal application."[15]

It should be remembered that the Fourteenth Amendment was passed by Congress after the Civil War expressly to protect the rights to life and liberty of adult males of African descent.[16] *Personhood* was equated in the amendment with *citizenship,* from which all adult women were excluded because they were deemed to lack the capacity to reason and to exercise independent political judgment. Nevertheless, it was not the definition of "persons" embodied in the amendment to which feminists objected, but the exclusion of women from that definition. Today, the promise of the natural rights concept of personhood remains unfulfilled, even in a formal sense; witness the defeat of the Equal Rights Amendment in 1982. Groups such as blacks and women, who were presumably "emancipated" by the Thirteenth, Fourteenth, and Nineteenth Amendments, remain economically, socially, and politically less than full persons in American society. The "right-to-life" movement seeks to alter radically the rationalistic concept of personhood inherited by the U.S. Constitution from the Enlightenment. Without embracing that concept, we can nonetheless see that, in this effort, "right-to-lifers" degrade the political struggles of large groups of living, mature, conscious human beings who still have not won the rights of full persons, even in the bourgeois liberal sense. "Right-to-lifers" correctly perceive that such a change in the legal meaning of personhood could be effected only through a constitutional amendment.[17] As the Supreme Court recognized in *Roe* v. *Wade,* however, the concept of "fetal personhood" raises moral and philosophical problems that go beyond the capacity of legislative or judicial mechanisms to resolve.

Fetuses and Persons

> The paramount right to life is vested in each human being from the moment of fertilization without regard to age, health, or conditions of dependency.
>
> PROPOSED TEXT, HUMAN LIFE AMENDMENT

The position that a fetus at any point in a pregnancy, beginning at conception, is a full human person bearing the panoply of rights available to all persons under the Constitution broaches no compromise. It is not a position based on "scientific evidence," but rests crucially on religious, philosophical, and moral premises. Stated in the absolutist terms in which "right-to-lifers" almost invariably couch it, that doctrine has the consequence that every abortion, under any circumstances, is murder, the fetus being regarded in all instances as not merely human but also uniquely "innocent," or, in the more theologically correct formulation, "helpless." Thus, abortion can be nothing other than a wanton form of human killing: "When the mask is lifted from the liberty of abortion, it is seen that the liberty consists in a freedom to knife, poison, starve, or choke a human being differing only in his or her degree of helplessness from the one who kills and the judge whose decree makes the killing possible."[18] Emotionally charged rhetoric such as this is aimed at reclaiming the terms of moral judgment and righteousness from what are seen as the individualistic, libertarian values of the last two decades. More than a battle to save fetal lives, more even than a battle over the limits of legitimate sexuality, the antiabortion movement must be understood as the battle for *moral hegemony* and control over popular consciousness accompanying a right-wing economic and political resurgence. One surmises that it is not so much the *act* of abortion that "right-to-lifers" and the Catholic church hierarchy are worried about as it is the legitimation and visibility of abortion and the "permissive" sexual morality they seem to uphold. As Blanche Cook observes with regard to homosexuality, it is not the committing of sin but its politicization and public display that are the threat.[19] Abortions, like gay bars, can stay in back alleys. Three constitutive elements in this struggle over morality need to be sorted out if we are to understand the emotional power and ethical fallacies in "right-to-life" ideology: religious symbolism, biological reductionism, and maternal revivalism.

Religious Symbolism

"Right-to-life" spokespeople strenuously oppose the characterization of their movement as primarily religious, despite all the evidence (see Chapter 7) about the centrality of religious personnel and institutions in antiabortion organizing. Many liberal Catholics are sensitive to the charge that the antiabortion cause is led by the church hierarchy, or to the association of the "right-to-life" movement with the church, seeing behind it a veiled expression of anti-Catholic bigotry.[20] In fact, the argument made again and again about the cross-denominational character of both antiabortion attitudes and antiabortion activism is valid. Yet the emphasis on interdenominationalism obscures the importance of religious symbolism in abortion politics, especially in regard to "fetal personhood." A pluralism of sects does not necessarily mean an absence of doctrinaire religious values and motifs inspiring that idea. It is not religion that is objectionable in "right-to-life" ideology but conservative, antihumanist religion, which contradicts its claim to rest on "science" and reveals its fundamentally narrow, sectarian character. An important part of the struggle for moral hegemony is that being waged *within* the major religious groups (Catholic, Protestant, and Jewish), between their liberal and sometimes feminist tendencies and their orthodox or fundamentalist tendencies.

The religious doctrines underlying antiabortion ideology, taken as a related cluster, are more characteristic of fundamentalist and orthodox sects. These religious doctrines include (1) belief in the existence of an immortal soul; (2) belief that the soul is "implanted" in the fetus from the moment of conception; (3) belief in the doctrine of original sin or the innate sinfulness of human beings, who are "conceived in sin"; (4) belief therefore that souls "killed unbaptized" are lost to eternal salvation and that death before birth is an especially horrible "curse"; (5) belief in divine creation and in the fetus as the "bearer of God's image"; and (6) belief in the doctrine of "stewardship," that human bodies belong neither to themselves nor to their parents nor to society, but to God, their creator, who alone has the right to kill the "innocent."[21]

While there is little theological content or consistency to the idea of fetal innocence,[22] it is used continually by the antiabortion movement as a symbol to mobilize, not just moral outrage, but religious sentiment, in an attempt to justify an absolute prohibition against abortion. A polemical device that draws on religious signifiers, the notion of innocence constructs the view of abortion as murder and the fetus as helpless victim. It also implies that the fetus is an object of preference—holier, closer to God, than women and their families. Thus, the "absolutist" or "one-dimensional" position of the Catholic church and the "right-to-life" movement on abortion "gives the fetus the overwhelming advantage," making conflicting concerns, such as the health or well-being of pregnant women, negligible.[23] The church's 1974 Declaration on Abortion, denying that even danger to a woman's life is sufficient justification for abortion, makes this perfectly clear:

> We do not deny these very great difficulties. It may be a serious question of health, sometimes of life or death, for the mother; it may be the burden represented by an additional child, especially if there are good reasons to fear that the child will be abnormal or retarded; it may be the importance attributed in different classes of society to considerations of honor or dishonor, of loss of social standing, and so forth. We proclaim only that none of these reasons can ever objectively confer the right to dispose of another's life, even when that life is only beginning.[24]

To a moral tradition that celebrates renunciation and turning away from the human world, the woman who dies in childbirth becomes the supreme "exemplar" of blessed motherhood and Christian "self-sacrifice."[25]

As represented in testimony in *McRae*, religious groups that tend to be more progressive, liberal, or humanist in their interpretation of Scripture take a different view of the fetus and the moral issues involved in abortion. Certain Baptist, Methodist, and Reformed Jewish groups, for example, stress some version of the idea of "responsible parenthood" as the ethical basis of abortion decision making, implying that in special circumstances abortion may be seen as a religious *duty*. These groups, and the Lutheran Church–Missouri Synod, hold unequivocally that the woman's life, health, and well-being and her family's welfare must take precedence over the survival of the fetus. According to one Baptist clergyman testifying in *McRae*: "It is for the people themselves to decide on the number of their children, because that is a value judgment. Conscience means moral awareness, and liberty of conscience means the exercise of one's moral awareness. Abortion presents a matter for individual moral decision, in a matter of ultimate concern respecting bringing a life into the world." In the Reformed Jewish view, "Abortion is mandated to preserve a woman's health and is permitted in the interest of the wellbeing of the woman and her existing family. The position on abortion is seen as a part of the larger principle of choosing life, that is, life in this world, not in the next."[26] Liberal Catholic thinking, too, particularly the natural-law tradition represented in the ideas of Jacques Maritain, while indeed not condoning abortion, contains a humanistic concept of personhood that conflicts sharply with that of conventional "prolife" dogma. Religion, then, or religious sectarianism masquerading as "universal morality," cannot be summoned to settle the "abortion question."

Biological Reductionism

Increasingly, in response to accusations of religious bias and violations of church-state separation, the evidence marshaled by antiabortionists to affirm the personhood of the fetus is not its alleged possession of a soul but its possession of a human body and genotype. In addition, by relying on biological, or genetic, determinism, the "right-to-life" movement asserts a claim to scientific objectivity. Biological determinism grows out of the social Darwinism and eugenics of the nineteenth and early twentieth centuries, which were applied in the service of racism, class domination, and population control. Its essential core is an attempt to explain the meaning and direction of human society, behavior, and values in terms of biochemistry and what we can observe about heredity: "For sociobiologists and believers in natural aristocracies of class and sex, the properties of society are determined by the intrinsic properties of individual human beings, individuals are the expression of their genes, and genes are nothing but self-replicating molecules."[27] All human life is reduced to its chemical bits. It is no accident, of course, that the "right-to-life" movement draws on mechanistic biological explanation as well as religion to legitimate its moral and social philosophy. For it does so in a general ideological climate that has seen the revival of genetic "theories" of race and reductionist theories of genetics; the rise of sociobiology in the social sciences; and, as part of the backlash against feminism, the renewed respectability of biological arguments supporting gender distinctions.[28]

"Fetal personhood" doctrine draws upon biological determinism in several ways. Its crudest expression is the profusion of antiabortion imagery presenting the fetus as "baby." It is a propagandistic tour de force to have taken the notion of "personhood" (a metaphysical, moral idea) and translated it into a series of arresting visual images that are utterly physiological and often just plain morbid. Various techniques are used to convey the idea that the fetus is literally a baby from the moment of conception: (1) photographs of fetuses at different stages of development, revealing recognizable physiological features; (2) photographs of aborted (bloody, gory) fetuses, particularly those aborted late; (3) clinical descriptions of fetal development, with special emphasis on the formation of heartbeat, fingerprints, fingers, and toes; (4) juxtaposition or alternation of pictures of fetuses with pictures of live babies, reinforcing the idea of their identity; and (5) the constant use of language referring to fetuses as "babies," "children" or "unborn children."[29]

The fetus as an image of the small, the helpless, and the mortal is made to *embody* one's desire for protection, for the safety of the womb; hence its power as a symbol to manipulate emotions. Through an erroneous attempt to portray the fetus as a miniature replica of you or me, this imagery not only denies the subtle processes of biological development but also seeks to arouse one's sense of identity with the fetus. Indeed, continually stressing the "small fingers and toes" or the capacity of the fetus to "feel pain" excites this kind of identification, through a psychological mechanism that reduces the sense of "humanity" to its most primitive biological and sentimental manifestations. The purpose of shocking, scaring, and eliciting morbid fears is connected to the biologistic reduction of the meaning of "human life." "Right-to-life" rhetoric communicates the worst horrors of our age; abortion is "killing babies," clinics are "death camps" and "abortion chambers," clinicians who perform abortions are "death peddlers" and "Nazi murderers." Their emphasis on fetuses "hacked to pieces" or "burned" in saline solution is polemical, since it refers to only 5 percent of all abortions. For people who claim to uphold "life," as critics have frequently noted, "right-to-lifers" are enormously preoccupied, even obsessed, with death and the remnants of aborted fetuses, apotheosizing and even displaying them in public rituals.

This symbolic representation of fetal "personhood" in the guise of human embodiment (in contrast, note, to "ensoulment") is reinforced on a more sophisticated level through an appeal by antiabortionists to biological science. Thus Jesse Helms, in introducing the "human life statute" (S. 158) in the Senate, cited, not moral and religious authorities, but sources on human embryology; and Noonan takes for granted that the argument for fetal personhood is established in "biological knowledge common to all Americans."[31] Using biological and theological language almost interchangeably, "prolife" spokesmen, in supporting the Helms statute in the Senate, argued that science is now able to determine "when human life begins" and that this settles the matter of the moral and legal status of the fetus.[32] Because it can be shown that every fertilized human egg is genetically unique, possessing a distinct human genotype, they claim, it can be inferred that the zygote is a human person in a moral sense. The Protestant theologian and opponent of abortion Paul Ramsey expounded this argument, which Peter Steinfels calls the "genetic package" argument, back in the 1960s:

. . . microgenetics seems to have demonstrated what religion never could, and biological science to have resolved an ancient theological dispute. The human individual comes into existence first as a minute informational speck, drawn at random from many other minute informational specks his parents possessed out of the common gene pool. This took place at the moment of impregnation. There were, of course, an unimaginable number of combinations of specks on his paternal and maternal chromosomes that did not come to be *when they were refused and he began to be.* Still (with the exception of identical twins), no one else in the entire history of the human race has ever had or will ever have exactly the same genotype. Thus, it can be said that the individual *is whoever he is going to become from the moment of impregnation.* Thereafter, his subsequent development may be described as a process of becoming the one he already is.[33]

Ramsey's statement is a wondrous example of theological opinion masquerading as biological fact. Into the randomness of human fertilization and genetic pairing he conveniently reads the Calvinist doctrine of predestination: We are all that we can ever be from the moment of conception. Indeed, there is even the suggestion, in the image of millions of possible combinations "refused" and only one selected, of a divine and inscrutable will. Such an interpretation is peculiarly alien to the stance of modern science, including molecular biology, which is one of rigorous *indeterminacy:*

> . . . the traditional opinion, which most of us are still unconsciously guided by, is that the child conceived on any one occasion is the unique and necessary product of that occasion: *that* child would have been conceived, we tend to think, or no child at all. This interpretation is quite false. . . . Only over the past one hundred years has it come to be realized that the child conceived on any one occasion belongs to a vast cohort of Possible Children, any one of whom might have been conceived and born if a different spermatozoon had chanced to fertilize the mother's egg cell—and the egg cell itself is only one of very many. *It is a matter of luck then, a sort of genetic lottery.* And sometimes it is cruelly bad luck—some terrible genetic conjunction, perhaps which once in ten or twenty thousand times will bring together a matching pair of damaging recessive genes. Such a misfortune, *being the outcome of a random process,* is, *considered in isolation, completely and essentially pointless.* It is not even strictly true to say that a particular inborn abnormality must have lain within the genetic potentiality of the parents, for the malignant gene may have arisen *de novo* by mutation. The whole process is *unhallowed*—is, in the older sense of that word, *profane.*[34]

Abortions occur continually in nature, and we do not experience them as sacred events—quite the contrary. Even in a narrowly biological sense, it is impossible to say with certainty that a particular embryo will develop into a particular human being, since it may be spontaneously aborted or may turn out to be a decidedly unhumanlike mutation.[35]

If molecular biology cannot be relied on to ascertain the sanctity of genetic uniqueness, how much less can it tell us about the relationship between the *genotype* and the *person*. The most striking fallacy in the genetic arguments of antiabortionists is their leap from the *fact* of genetic individuality—a characteristic not only of humans but of all living things, including cows and chameleons—to the *value* of human personhood. This is a problem, in part, of confusing the self, the person, with her or his genetic basis, ignoring the enormously complex interaction between genes, environment, and development that ultimately determines who or what an actual person becomes. To say that who I am is codified from the moment of my conception is to deny most people's common-sense assumptions about who they are, their selfhood, and its roots in conscious experience. But it also contradicts the caveats of well-known geneticists (those of a humanist persuasion) against confusing genetic *potentiality* with *actual* human personality and character, which are highly influenced by culture.[36] Manier sums up this genetic fallacy with great elegance:

> Since our general concept of humanity is more than a biological concept, no amount of biological evidence can provide adequate warrant for any claim concerning the starting point of individual life. . . . Further, it is misleading to assert that "a being with a human genetic code is a man," as if there were specific evidence from molecular biology warranting that assertion. In fact, it has no more empirical significance than "a rose is a rose," since the only means of identifying genetic material as human is by direct comparison with DNA already identified as human.[37]

Thus the broader problem with the idea that the fetus is a "person" from conception is its concept of personhood, or even humanity, for it either rests on a theological premise—"ensoulment"—or it reduces to a crude, mechanistic biologism. In legal and moral terms, this means that the concept of "person" (moral) is totally collapsed into the concept of "human life" (biological, or generic).[38] In fact, as Dr. Leon Rosenberg testified in the Senate hearings on S. 158, there is *not* agreement among scientists about the question of "when human life begins," nor any way to determine the answer definitively.[39] But I submit that *the beginning of human life is not the issue,* for it can be argued that fetuses, even if they are "human life," are still not human *persons.* It might be conceded that the fetus is a *form* of life insofar as it is alive (as established by EEG readings, heartbeat, and other biological responses) and it is human (in the narrow and morally insignificant sense that it is composed of authentically human genes or DNA, derived from genetically human parents). Yet, agreeing on this reduction of the fetus' identity to its genetic material does not move us one step toward knowing what *value* to give the fetus, what *rights* it has (either as a class or in a particular case), or whether to regard it as a person in the moral and legal sense (which is the only sense there is).[40]

That the fetus is human and may even have a "right to life" does not prove that abortion is "morally (im)permissible," because being "human in a genetic sense" is distinct from being "human in a moral sense"— that is, from being a person. The fetus is not a human person in this latter sense; therefore, whatever rights it may have "could not possibly outweigh the right of a woman to obtain an abortion, since the rights of actual persons invariably outweigh those of any potential person whenever the two conflict."[41] This position suggests that we may acknowledge the fetus' "potentiality" and its "sanctity of life" while rejecting its "personhood." To deny that the fetus is a "full human person" does not necessarily mean denying that the fetus, as a *potentially* human and presently sentient being, is morally deserving of consideration, or even that it can make moral or emotional claims on those in charge of its care— mainly pregnant women. The problem is that whatever those claims may be, they frequently come into conflict with the rights and needs of women and others with whom they are connected who *are* (in the opinion of feminists and humanists) full human persons. But the "right-to-life" position either denies such conflict or dissolves it into a definition of "motherhood" that makes the fetus' life determinant of the woman's.

Maternal Revivalism

Like its view of the fetus, the "right-to-life" view of motherhood is a remarkably Victorian mixture of religious and biological-determinist elements. On the one hand, there is the Augustinian image of woman as ordained by God to procreate; the passive receptacle of the male seed, "selfish" and "sinful" if she evades that destiny and directs her sexuality to nonprocreative ends. Abortion, from this view, is a sin against God in defiance of woman's nature, for which she is morally culpable. Hence the message communicated in "right-to-life" literature, demonstrations, and harassment of women at abortion clinics. Women who get abortions are "murdering their own children," putting their "selfish desires" before their "own children's lives," and will suffer terrible guilt. But what if the woman does not feel agony or guilt but, like many women after an abortion, feels mainly relief that a difficult problem has been put behind her? One antihumanist, "prolife" writer insists that the woman's feelings have nothing to do with whether or not she *is* guilty, which is determined by her objective relation to the "moral law" and not by "subjective experience." She *"ought* to feel guilty" because she has in fact committed "an evil of incomprehensible dimensions."[42] The fundamentalist doctrine that "man's nature is wholly corrupt" is opposed here to "the humanist tenet that man is basically good." The very idea of human progress and social or moral development or "enrichment" in history is anathema to this doctrine, which asserts "the wickedness of man" (and, assuredly, of woman) as the source of every human (i.e., social) problem. Hence, "why have mothers, in the name of the liberation of womanhood, demanded the death of their own children?" For the antihumanist "prolifer," the answer is quite simple: "human wickedness."[43]

The "right-to-life" doctrine of the fetus' "personhood" and the aborting woman's "selfishness" is akin to the antihumanist philosophy of the New Right. Antihumanism, as professed by the "right-to-life" and "pro-family" movements, pits itself squarely against every intellectual and philosophical tradition that grew out of the Enlightenment and secularism. Marxism and feminism are of course denounced by the right, but so are all philosophies, including radical Christian movements such as liberation theology, whose central focus is social change on this earth or even human, as opposed to divine or scriptural, ends. When Weyrich describes the Moral Majority as "a Christian democratic movement rooted in the authentic Gospel, not the social gospel," he is attacking and distinguishing his politics from those Christian movements in the United States and Latin America that ally with the poor to change oppressive social conditions.[44] All social movements, including labor movements, peasant uprisings, anticolonial struggles, civil rights, and antinuclear protests, would thus be categorized by the New Right under "materialistic, atheistic humanism," charged with the sin of making human life and human pleasure on earth the measure of all value. But a particular condemnation is reserved for feminism and the movement for sexual liberation. The New Right associates this branch of humanism most closely with hedonism, equated with "doing whatever feels good," with "moral perversity and total corruption."

By the end of the 1970s, some "right-to-lifers" began to promote the view that women who get abortions are themselves victims—of profiteering doctors or coercion by Planned Parenthood—and should be offered protection and Christian compassion.[45] In this view, abortion is depicted as contrary to women's true desires and interests as mothers, invariably a source of anguish and "ambivalence." Yet this profession of "compassion" and support for pregnant women is simply a more paternalistic version of the idea of an innate maternalism, which abortion violates. In a major "right-to-life" propaganda piece, Francis A. Schaeffer, a fundamentalist minister, and C. Everett Koop, U.S. surgeon general and head of the National Institutes of Health under Reagan, refer to women who have had abortions as "aborted mothers" and "bereft mothers" filled with bitterness and "sorrow":

> With many of the women who have had abortions, their "motherliness" is very much present even though the child is gone. . . . One of the facts of being a human being is that in spite of the abnormality of human beings and the cruelty of their actions, there still exist the hopes and fears, the longings and aspirations, that can be bundled together in the word *motherliness*. To stamp out these feelings is to insure that many women will turn into the kind of hard people they may not want to be.[46]

Like the fundamentalist fire-and-brimstone view, the implication of the "Christian compassionate" view of abortion is the basic precept of all patriarchal ideology: Motherhood—and indeed "motherliness," a *state of being* and not just a social role or relationship—is the primary purpose of a woman's life. Abortion is thus "abnormal," "unnatural"; a woman who undergoes an abortion is subverting her own nature and will surely suffer or become "hardened" (read, unmotherly, *unwomanly*). Whether the "prolife Christian" confronts her "suffering" with pity or hatred, the point is that suffer she must, for procreation and childrearing are woman's "privileged position and purpose in human history" and to renounce them—whether once or for good—is to place herself outside female nature and "human history."

More ancient than the idea of the fetus as person, the primacy and necessity of woman as Mother has been a continuous ideological thread in antiabortion pronouncements since the nineteenth century. Callahan quotes the Catholic theologian Bernard Häring, writing in 1966 in terms that lay bare the deeper passions underlying "right-to-life" sentiments:

> If it were to become an accepted principle of moral teaching on motherhood to permit a mother whose life was endangered simply to "sacrifice" the life of her child in order to save her own, motherhood would no longer mean absolute dedication to each and every child.[47]

Because the pregnant woman is Mother, she must be ready to die for the fetus. More than the survival of the individual fetus, what is ultimately at stake in the abortion struggle, in this view, is the "moral teaching" of motherhood as "absolute dedication." It is the *idea* of woman as Mother, and of the fetus as the tie that binds her to marital chastity and selflessness, that takes precedence over anything else. The woman who has an abortion makes a clear statement about her life and her understanding of her moral and social commitments relative to a potential maternal relationship; she renounces, defies the concept of motherhood as total self-sacrifice for the sake of others. On some level, perhaps, she even asserts her capacity to exercise control over life and death—and this makes her particularly, ineffably dangerous.[48] Thus does antiabortion ideology reveal its association, not only with antifeminism, but with the most primitive traditions of misogyny.

Contemporary opponents of abortion reflect these elements of misogynist thinking in their perpetuation of the myth that women who get abortions do so mostly for reasons of "convenience" and to repudiate motherhood.[49] We have seen that the social reality behind this perception is complex; motherhood has assumed a *different* place in many women's lives during the past decade, interwoven with work and study, deferred but hardly abandoned. What is important here is the tremendous emotionalism and hostility toward women that the perception of change has apparently generated. The cry that women are "killing their children" (you too, it seems to say, might have been an abortion) signals a new wave of "momism" and "motherhood revivalism," a fundamental current of the New Right's moral offensive. This cry touches deep nerves—fears of maternal abandonment, fears that women will no longer mother. The assumption behind it, that woman's purpose is to exemplify "unselfishness" through motherhood, is not often challenged even by those who claim to favor "choice."[50] Recently, a rash of disclaimers and apologies by liberals, leftists, and even some feminists in the popular media, confessing "ambivalence" about abortion,[51] reveal the extent to which "right-to-life" ideology has penetrated the dominant culture and fostered guilt, even without a change in the law. More than ever, we need a feminist morality of abortion, one that addresses the issues that "right-to-lifers" raise in human, social terms and moves well beyond them.

Toward a Feminist-Humanist Concept of Personhood

The doctrine of fetal personhood is morally offensive from a feminist, socialist, and humanist standpoint because what makes human life distinct is its capacity for consciousness and sociability. To reduce it to genetics, to equate Holocaust victims with aborted fetuses, is to demean human life and the moral value of consciousness. It is, moreover, to demean pregnant women, who are treated in this perspective as the physical vessels for genetic messages rather than responsible moral agents. Motherhood in this sense becomes, not a socially determined relationship, but a physiological function, a "fact of life." At the same time, "right-to-life" ideology equates pregnancy with motherhood as it has been defined in modern Western patriarchal culture—as a moral and social duty. Although pregnant nulliparous women do not usually regard themselves as "mothers," since in their experience there is no "child" with whom they have a relationship, this doctrine tells them they should become instantaneously "motherly" from the moment of conception.

Reducing motherhood to a passive biological state is a way of dehumanizing it, stripping it of dependence on women's consciousness. Oddly enough, however, imposing an absolute maternal duty on pregnant women induces the same deadening passivity. Biological determinism and moral absolutism arrive at the same end. The antiabortionists' charge that women who get abortions are invariably "selfish" and "irresponsible" insults not only women as moral agents but motherhood as a human practice and a conscious, demanding activity. By insisting that the abortion question has only one answer, the "right-to-life" position denies the role of human will and judgment in moral decision making, particularly in decision making about childbirth and sex. It thus denies the full human personhood of women.

What is necessary to personhood, it would seem, is *personality*—the existence of a self, which implies a psychological and a social component beyond mere biological integrity or vitalism, involving some degree of self-awareness in relation to others. What it means to be human involves an irreducible social or relational basis without which the very concept of humanity, or persons as actual or developing moral beings, makes no sense. Now, a difficulty we run into here is the tendency of liberal moral philosophers, following in the classical and particularly Kantian tradition, to associate personhood with attributes of developed human beings—not only "consciousness" but "reasoning," "self-motivated activity," even the ability to "judge between right and wrong."[52] One problem with this rationalist-individualist concept of personhood, as I suggested earlier, was always its use in the interests of a ruling elite to exclude those considered insufficiently "rational" or "motivated" or "civilized" from the civic or even the moral community: slaves, women, children, the colonized. In this respect, the concerns of some of those who oppose abortion contain a decent, though I believe mistaken, moral impulse. They are concerns shared by many liberals, especially Catholics, who disapprove of abortion, although they do not identify with the conservative politics of the organized "prolife" movement. That impulse is (1) to affirm the Kantian principle of a "person" as one who is a being in and for herself, an end rather than a means; and (2) to deny that this involves a set of intellectual or cognitive prerequisites that would exclude or disqualify a whole range of human beings considered "inferior" or "unfit." These are concerns meant to appeal, not unreasonably, to leftists and especially feminists, sensitive to the political consequences (for women, for blacks) of a "moral" tradition that elevates mind and reason and denigrates the body.[53] Antiabortionists frequently raise the prospect of a "slippery slope" (always a polemical device) that leads from fetuses to "euthanasia" among the mentally disabled, the physically disabled, the elderly, and so on. More persuasive perhaps is their argument that the classical definition of personhood leaves no way to distinguish between infants and fetuses and therefore would allow infanticide:

If to be human *means* to be a person, to be a self-conscious subject of experience, or if it means to be rational, this state of affairs does not come to pass until a long while after the birth of a baby. A human infant acquires its personhood and self-conscious subjective identity through "Thou-I" encounters with other selves; and a child acquires essential rationality even more laboriously. If life must be human in these senses before it has any sanctity and respect or rights due it, infanticide would seem to be justified under any number of conditions.[54]

What concept of personhood would avoid biological reductionism yet include newborn babies, as well as allowing for the developmental variations in the fetus at different stages; that is, would accord with the common-sense notions about who has a "right to life" and who does not that most people in fact apply in everyday life? While there are practical historical reasons why infanticide has mostly fallen into disuse (not the least of which is access to legal birth control and abortion!), there is a coherent philosophical explanation for why most people treat babies differently from fetuses, and late fetuses differently from early ones. This explanation lies in a theory of personhood whose elements are humanist, socialist, and feminist.

The Kantian principle of treating persons as ends in themselves, with intrinsic value, is an elegant version of the bourgeois myth of atomized individuals; it disregards that the necessary premise for such persons to exist is the prior human world of interrelationships, interdependence— in short, of social life. Philosophers of diverse persuasions have understood that the preformed, self-sufficient monad—of which the fetus as person is a vulgarization—is not only philosophically but socially (*and biologically*) implausible. The Catholic humanist Jacques Maritain presents a concept of the person that is insistent in its emphasis on not only spirituality but sociability: "The person is a whole, but it is not a closed whole, it is an *open* whole. . . . It tends by its very nature to social life and to communion . . . demands an entrance into relationship with other persons. To state it rigorously, the person cannot be alone."[55] The Marxist humanist Agnes Heller clarifies the necessary interrelationship or "synthesis" between "self-consciousness," or "I-consciousness," and consciousness of being part of a larger whole, a "species-being" in Marx's sense: "The Individual is a person who 'synthesises' in himself the chance uniqueness of his individuality with the universal generality of the species," who has a *consciousness* not only of himself/herself as an end but of "his (her) world. Every person forms his world and thus himself too."[56] "Personhood" or "humanism" in this view is not static, not a set of physical or even intellectual "properties"; rather, it is a *process,* a continual *coming to consciousness.* We *become humanized,* in a never-ending development that involves, as consciousness, rational and "moral" faculties but, more primally, feelings, sensations, the body—and always in a context of *relationship* with others. It is this relationship, this interdependence, that humanizes us; the particular physical, verbal, or intellectual mode of relating is secondary. Seen from this perspective of humanization as a continual process of "movement toward liberation"[57] or greater consciousness, personhood must inevitably involve some differences of degree. Moral philosophy cannot avoid distinguishing "between the human and the 'truly human,' "[58] as for example when we speak of the "inhumanity of man." More important, this theoretical perspective on personhood may help us to formulate a more precise philosophical approach to the meaning of fetuses and infants at different stages of development than either the "right-to-life" or the rationalist-individualist position allows.

We begin to see, then, why antiabortionists jump so easily between two apparently contradictory positions—the "ensoulment" argument (that the fetus has a perfectly independent soul from the moment of conception) and the "genetic package" argument (that all we are and can be is perfectly contained in our DNA). Both arguments rest on the false premise of totally isolated, self-sufficient individuals connected only to God or their own biochemical structure. Both explicitly reject any *social* conception of human beings or humanness; any other person, including the biological mother, becomes inconsequential. But the idea of "persons" as self-contained atoms is a fallacy at any stage of human development and certainly at its inception. Without consciousness, awareness of others, or ability to communicate its needs, the fetus cannot be a being "in and for itself" (a person); it is less so even than a mature animal. Its identity as a "human life" is thus all the more inevitably endowed or bound up with contextual meanings; it *is* the social context and the value placed on the fetus by those immediately concerned in its care that determine to a large extent its value in the world and even its rights.

Nothing could illustrate more clearly the fallacy in "right-to-life" thinking about personhood than the frequently voiced claim that the fetus exhibits "sensitivity to pain" and therefore should be recognized as human. This is equivalent to saying that the fetus "feels bad" when we abort it, which is absurd, since we do not know, nor can we know, what the fetus "feels." Pain as a concept refers only to subjective feelings, not to biological responses that can be measured; sensitivity to touch and reflex actions, on the other hand, can be found in plants and have little to do with pain. It is precisely because the fetus is not a subjectivity and therefore cannot take cognizance of or communicate its "bad" feelings that we cannot recognize it as a person. We can only recognize its value in a context of relationships with others, defined by *their* subjectivity. For loving "expectant parents," an unwanted abortion is an event occasioning mourning and a deep sense of loss because of the social context of longings, care, and expectations that envelop the pregnancy. The scarcity of children available for adoption to infertile couples, or the desires of a potential father or grandparent for a child, may be other circumstances that endow the fetus with value. But those are as extrinsic and utilitarian (i.e., bound to particular interests) as are the pregnant woman's wants and needs, and cannot be used to argue that the fetus has value in and of itself.

If, however, a relational concept of personhood requires an existent self-awareness, then it becomes difficult indeed to include the newborn infant. Where can we derive any moral principle against killing small babies other than from the subjective reality that babies are nice and responsive and we like them better than fetuses? The problem here results from assumptions about consciousness and the humanization process, shared by Marxists as well as liberals (and all who have not broken fully from the Enlightenment tradition), that focus exclusively on verbal and "rational" modes of communication. To correct these outmoded assumptions, we can look at theories of developmental and object relations that psychologists have proposed about the formation of the "self" in the infant; we can even look at the lived experience of pregnant women, which supports those theories.[59] They tell us that the emergence of a "self"—the psychological process of individuation in which the child begins to acquire a consciousness of itself in relation to, and separate from, others, and thus a consciousness *of* others—occurs, and *can only occur*, in an interactive and social context.

The relationship with others constructs the self in a complex and sometimes protracted process of reciprocal perceptual and later emotional cues, so that the "self" could not possibly be a genetic or inborn property. Thus, the antiabortion argument that "I cannot will that my mother should have had an abortion when she was pregnant with me," so I cannot "consistently deny to others the right to life that I claim for myself," is illogical. There was no self, no "me," during my mother's pregnancy with me, with whom my present self is continuous.[60] The fetus has no interest in preserving its body because it has no "self," no consciousness: ". . . while you have interests regarding your body, your body and its parts have no interest of their own, and in its earliest stages a fetus is only a body and not a self at all. . . ."[61] While the self, the *person,* cannot exist separately from its body and its sensory apparatus, which is the biological precondition for its consciousness, the body predates the self and may survive its extinction (as consciousness).

What, then, of the "preindividuated" infant prior to its development of self-awareness, and of the fetus in its later stages? A social, relational concept of personhood, because it is focused on process rather than some illusory substance or property, allows us the possibility, the only humanist possibility, of encompassing such beings within our moral framework. It gives human content to the otherwise mystical, abstract notion of "potentiality." Human pregnancy, like any other human experience, is never raw biology; its biological dimensions are mediated by the social process of coming into relationship, in this case the earliest, most elemental relationship, which is what humanizes it. "Relationship" means, first, that there is *interdependence;* and, second, that there is *consciousness* of this, even if that consciousness is one-sided for a time. Willis captures the human reality of pregnancy when she says: "There is no way a pregnant woman can passively let the fetus live; she must create and nurture it with her own body, a symbiosis that is often difficult, sometimes dangerous, uniquely intimate."[62] The idea of a "symbiosis," however, can only refer to a social or cultural construct, a learned response. On the level of "biology alone," the dependence is one-way—the fetus is a parasite.[63] Not only is it not a part of the woman's body, but it contributes nothing to her sustenance. It only draws from her: nutrients, immunological defenses, hormonal secretions, blood, digestive functions, energy. Even the concept of "viability," *whenever* it may occur, is meaningless—a device to protect doctors against lawsuits and to denigrate the role of the pregnant women in prenatal nurturing. What does it mean to speak of viability in a society that has no intention of providing care for the children of working mothers, much less aborted fetuses? More important, the fetus is never viable insofar as it remains utterly dependent for its survival on the mother or another human caretaker until long after birth.

Yet pregnancy, like all relationships, is characterized by mutual dependency in a social and moral sense. For the pregnant woman, whether she wants the fetus or not, is caught up irrevocably in a condition of intimacy with and perhaps longing for it as well. The experience of going through a full-term pregnancy, bearing a child, and giving it up for adoption is punitive and traumatic for a woman because the relationship by then is real; it exists. No woman who has ever borne a child needs to be told that its "personality" and certainly its relationship to her begin to emerge well before its birth. It is not surprising that until relatively recently (and perhaps still) the moment of "quickening" was considered by most women the dividing line between the nonexistence and existence of a "child." The movements of the fetus are signs, communications, that denote to the pregnant woman its life and its dependence on and relationship to herself. Certainly up until that time a pregnant woman is in no sense a "mother," for the simple reason that motherhood is a *socially* constructed relationship, not a biological condition alone (the situation of adoption is an obvious example). She is not yet a mother any more than the man who has inseminated a fertile ovum with his sperm becomes from that moment a "father." With the onset of movement in the uterus, the woman begins to develop her consciousness of interrelatedness. That consciousness, emerging out of reciprocal sensory activity, marks the beginning of the social relationships that are the necessary and sole basis through which the fetus' development of a "self," its *humanization,* is possible.

The point is not that the fetus now has a "subjective" relationship with this particular "mother" but that it has objectively entered the community of human beings through its social interaction with (and not only its physical dependency on) *an* other. Its earliest "socialization" occurs through its body and the interdependence of its body with a conscious human being. The fact that the (post-"quickening") fetus or the early infant is not yet a "self" does not negate this reciprocal quality. Piaget, for example, discovered that the three-month-old infant, in the process of "assimilating" visual images (a hand) to motor activity and sucking, engages in imitation of the caretaker's movements, even before there is any recognition "of another's body and his own body. . . ."[64] But of course, the existence of the other and its (her/his) *attentive consciousness* is the necessary precondition for the imitative activity to occur. What is irreducible and indispensable in this humanization process (the formation of the "person") is *the subjectivity of the pregnant woman,* her consciousness of existing in a relationship with the fetus. Short of artificial wombs and Brave New World laboratories (which may be the "final solution" "right-to-lifers" have in mind), there is no getting around this, no eliminating the pregnant woman as active agent of the fetus' "personhood." For it is *her* consciousness that is the condition of its humanization, of its consciousness evolving from the potential to the actual.

In the everyday practices of abortion and childbearing, more clearly than in opinion polls or surveys of attitudes, we can read the social record of a moral sense about abortion that comes close to the one I have just presented. If 1.5 million abortions a year indicate a compelling need and desire for abortion among women, we may also notice that between 92 to 96 percent of those abortions occur within the first trimester, and over half within the first eight weeks.[65] These data are significant in understanding popular values about "fetal life." They confirm the sense that most women have, in term pregnancies, of developmental differences that correspond to differences, changes, in their relationship/obligation/bond to the fetus. This sense determines, too, that a miscarriage often has a different meaning when it occurs in the first or second month of a pregnancy, when it may not even be noticed, than when it occurs in the fifth or sixth month, when it becomes the occasion of mourning— the *loss* of "someone." Even our ordinary language expresses this. We say, "She had a miscarriage," in the earlier case, and after some hard-to-define but real point later on, "She lost her baby."

Peter Steinfels, editor of *Commonweal* and a forceful spokesperson for liberal Catholic opposition to abortion, urges liberal Catholics to admit "quite frankly that the moral status of the fetus in its early development is a genuinely difficult problem. . . ." Steinfels acknowledges that to equate "a disc the size of a period or an embryo one-sixth of an inch long and with barely rudimentary features" with "Albert Einstein and Anne Frank as human beings" is "based on bad biology." He thereby opens up the possibility of different degrees of "life" or "personhood," for such acknowledgment implies that humanization is a developmental process rather than a distinct moment or quality.[66]

Looking again at the data for 1978–79 regarding the gestational period in which abortions occur, the impression of a kind of implicit moral code among women is strengthened if we break down who are the small number of women who get "late" abortions (after twelve weeks) and why. As we might expect, the 5 to 8 percent of abortions in those years that occurred after the first trimester tended to be among teenagers.[67] Delayed abortions among teenagers are mainly the result not of personal attitudes so much as of public policies that (1) create legal and administrative obstacles for teenagers who seek abortions, (2) restrict Medicaid funding for abortion, and (3) support a dominant culture and "morality" that punish the sexuality of unmarried young women. In a different sexual culture with unrestricted availability of legal, publicly funded abortion services, nearly all abortions (except in a small number of health-related cases) would occur early in a pregnancy. This would be desirable from the standpoint of women's health and well-being as well as sensibility to the fetus and its development.

Given this developmental view of pregnancy and its moral implications, what would be a feminist-humanist position on amniocentesis and other forms of prenatal diagnosis? For amniocentesis usually implies an intention to abort if the fetus does not meet certain specifications, and to abort at a relatively late stage of fetal development. (The procedure cannot be performed earlier than at sixteen weeks of gestation.) "Right-to-lifers" have opposed these techniques almost as strongly as abortion, citing them as support of the "slippery slope" argument and inevitable contributing factors to the escalation of abortion. But this has little basis in fact. In the gestational data cited earlier, pregnant women aged 30–39 had lower percentages of abortions after nine weeks than other age groups, indicating that abortion following amniocentesis is not a frequent occurrence among them.[68] In short, amniocentesis would seem to have had a negligible impact on abortion rates. This is not to say that abortion following amniocentesis in the second trimester raises no moral questions or poses no hard dilemmas for women (or prospective parents). It does not follow from the feminist position that holds that only a pregnant woman can decide about abortion that abortion raises no moral issues, or that the fetus makes no moral claims on the pregnant woman.

Here we need to distinguish between the *political question*—who should decide—and the *moral question*—whether abortion is right or wrong in a given instance—and begin to enunciate feminist principles for the latter as well as the former. The situation of prenatal diagnosis followed by a decision to abort is a specific one because it nearly always involves a context in which pregnancy is desired but a *particular* fetus is rejected for its characteristics. That such choices may be morally ambiguous or even immoral in certain cases seems unquestionable. Choosing to abort solely on the basis of gender preference, whether for male or female, would be grossly sexist and therefore antifeminist and immoral. A different case is that of Down's syndrome, one of the most common concerns of women undergoing amniocentesis. Down's syndrome represents a wide-ranging disorder in terms of its symptoms, although the chromosomal abnormality detected through amniocentesis is always the same, and one can never know with certainty that one is rejecting a "nonfunctional" individual. Similarly, with neural tube defects such as spina bifida, it *may* turn out that one chooses abortion when surgical correction is possible. And, of course, the question of what is "humanly" functional is a morally laden one.[69] A decision to undergo abortion in such cases is probably always made in terms of competing moral claims to those of the fetus: limited family or community resources; obligations to other children; or the pregnant couple's sense of the limits on their capacity for, and vision of, parenting. It could hardly be otherwise, since pregnancies always exist in a context of social relations and moral commitments, not in isolation.[70]

The other side of the matter is the immeasurable human benefit of a social and medical context in which such a choice exists. For the 5 percent of tested women who receive a positive amniocentesis result, the prospect of ending the pregnancy and undergoing a second-trimester abortion is undoubtedly painful and anguished; some prefer to go through with the pregnancy. But for most, it seems nothing short of miraculous that what used to be a question of ill fate—the responsibility for a child born with severe, incapacitating handicaps—is now subject to human intervention and choice. Like safe, legal abortion, amniocentesis may be an occasion of sorrow *at the same time* as it is a condition of expanded human freedom and consciousness.[71]

The point here, then, is not the particular outcome of the decision one way or the other so much as it is that such moral decisions are *inevitably hard;* they must be approached with the fullest attention and care given toward all their consequences on the part of those immediately involved. This might be called the "ethic of people being allowed to work out their own ethic," to take their own moral judgments seriously.[72] In this regard, a feminist morality of abortion cannot totally separate the political question of who decides from the moral question of what decision to make, any more than it can prejudge what is "right" in a particular case by reference to some holy writ. For it is women whom the culture trains in "maternal thinking," to exercise care in regard to questions about life; it is pregnant women themselves whose consciousness is closest to the reality of the fetus and the total circumstances in which it exists. In the last analysis, their decisions are most likely to be morally informed. What the antiabortion movement is about is the discrediting of women's moral judgment.

Fetal Politics and False Dilemmas

Under the impact of "fetal personhood" ideology, women's autonomy in pregnancy and decisions related to it has been subjected to new kinds of challenges in workplaces, clinics, and courts. These have included (1) employer actions to exclude women from jobs where there may be substances hazardous to reproductivity, (2) medical "advances" that treat the fetus as "patient" and the pregnant woman as the "maternal environment," and (3) "custody" suits in which the husband or male partner seeks recognition as an equal party in the abortion decision. Employers, doctors, and potential fathers have claimed "relationships" with the fetus that conflict with the pregnant woman's and preempt her claim to autonomy. In this effort, they have drawn support from the idea that the fetus is a "separate person" with an existence independent of the pregnant woman. Behind this ideology, what is going on here is a struggle, not over the contents of the womb, but over the meaning of maternity and the competence of adult women to exercise judgment.

Employers in the auto, steel, chemical, and rubber industries, which have traditionally employed primarily men and have been severely affected by plant shutdowns and layoffs, began in the late 1970s to adopt a policy of excluding women workers from jobs that involve substances, such as benzene and lead, known to be hazardous to the developing fetus.[73] A highly publicized case involved five women chemical workers at an American Cyanamid plant in West Virginia who were sterilized in 1979 when the company's managers told them their only other alternatives were to be transferred to low-paying janitorial jobs or to be fired.[74] This and similar cases raised fundamental questions, not only about "choice" or "consent," but also about the relationship between women and pregnancy and the uses of "fetal personhood" ideology to restrict the social mobility of women.

The pretext for excluding *all* women of childbearing age who are fertile, not just those who are actually pregnant or might expect to be, is an ostensibly "protective" one: that potential harm to the fetus may occur in the early weeks of pregnancy, before a woman knows she is pregnant. General Motors, DuPont, Goodyear, Firestone, and Allied Chemical, among others, have stated two motives for imposing such wholesale (and sex-discriminatory) "protection," both related to the idea that the fetus exists as a "person" independently of the pregnant woman.

One motive is legal, the alleged concern about employer liability for damaged offspring and future lawsuits by them or on their behalf. The other is "moral," the alleged concern with "protecting the unborn child" from harm.[75] Of course, as labor and feminist activists opposed to such exclusionary policies have emphasized, the actual motive is to shift the costly burden of reducing workplace hazards from the companies onto the employment status of working women. But it is important to see how this evasion of corporate responsibility to provide a safe and healthy work environment for *all* workers draws legitimacy from the idea of the fetus as a separate "person" with rights and standing in the courts. Thus, according to reports in 1971 and 1977 by the National Council on Radiation Protection, a private, nongovernmental organization that helps to set radiation exposure levels:

> The need to minimize exposure of the embryo and fetus is paramount. It becomes the controlling factor in the occupational exposure of fertile women. . . . For conceptual purposes the chosen dose limit [of radiation] essentially functions to *treat the unborn child as a member of the public involuntarily brought into controlled areas.*[76]

Opponents of female-exclusionary "protection" as an approach to the problem of reproductive hazards in workplaces have revealed many arbitrary and discriminatory aspects of the policy. First, it is highly selective, focused on female employment in heavy industry but so far totally unconcerned with the reproductive hazards to women in traditional, often risky occupations (e.g., hospital work, laundries, and clerical work involving radioactive computer terminals).[77] This underscores that at least one aim of the policy is to eliminate gains in employment made by women under Title VII in "nontraditional" job sectors and to reinforce sex segregation in production.

Second, the policy ignores the fact that harmful mutagenic and teratogenic agents may be transmitted to the fetus through the male's sperm, or may render him sterile; thus, as "protection" for the fetus or for reproduction, sex-exclusive policies are bound to be partly ineffective.[78] This too suggests that the main purpose of the policy is to exclude women rather than to protect "the unborn," but there is an additional reason why the effects of reproductive hazards on men as well as women are overlooked in corporate policy. Because of the gender bias built into reproductive biology and medicine, "scientific studies have focused largely upon the placental transmission of harmful substances." The male role in reproduction is treated as though it did not exist; thus there is little "scientific evidence" to show the harmful effects through exposure of male workers.[79]

Above all, the treatment of *all* "fertile women" as potentially pregnant and potentially vulnerable both resurrects the patriarchal ideology of women's destiny as childbearers and constructs the issue of reproductive hazards as one in which women's employment rights and the "rights of the fetus" are diametrically opposed. That construction is false because it ignores that male workers too may transmit and be damaged by hazardous substances; because it disregards various arrangements whereby workers (both male and female) and their offspring might be protected without losing their jobs or seniority;[80] and because it ignores the fact that most working women at any one time are not pregnant, have no intention of becoming pregnant, and in fact use reliable birth control regularly to make sure that they do not become pregnant. The real issue is that, once again, the woman's capacity to evaluate risks, make judgments, and exercise care is being maligned; she cannot even be "trusted" to know whether she is likely to be at risk of pregnancy.[81] It is worth pointing out that such an assumption is bolstered by a context in which abortion is *not* considered a ready option; in which full, thorough disclosure of hazards to workers is *not* a usual practice; and in which some reasonable job transfer or leave in case of pregnancy is *not* available. The focus on excluding all women from jobs involving harmful exposure evades the reality that no women, and no men, wish to have their offspring or potential offspring exposed to hazardous substances; but neither do they wish to lose decent jobs. It is an untenable dilemma.

The medical profession, along with corporations, has begun to assert a "protective" relationship to the fetus, both clinically and legally. This too is an ambiguous area. For couples who desire a child, the possibility of medical interventions to cure fetal defects *in utero* may be extremely heartening. What is far more problematic is the use, by doctors or social workers, of child abuse statutes to stop abortions or impose on pregnant women certain forms of prenatal care, and the use of court orders to force women into cesarean sections without their consent "because physicians testified that a vaginal delivery would endanger the fetus."[82] An article in a 1981 issue of *Obstetrics and Gynecology* describes the case of a Colorado welfare mother, pregnant with her third child, who refused to undergo a cesarean section. The hospital called in a judge, a psychiatrist, and two lawyers—one to represent the fetus. Under this pressure, the woman finally acquiesced. Defending the hospital's position, the authors claim

> . . . that the state had . . . a duty to protect the children within its jurisdiction—including an unborn child—notwithstanding the wishes of the parents . . . that the state has an obligation . . . to intervene . . . to ensure that a child, even while unborn, is given the necessary medical treatment to protect its life over the unreasonable objection of the parents.[83]

The growing tendency of ob-gyn practitioners to view the fetus as their "patient" independently of the woman who carries it may, like corporate exclusionary policies, reflect fears of potential lawsuits, in this case for malpractice, by or on behalf of deformed children. But one senses that such fears are only part, perhaps an insignificant part, of the story. "Fetal surgery" is clearly becoming a new and heroic frontier of medical conquest, despite its enormous risks and costs. Although to date surgeons have rarely succeeded in saving a defective fetus, intricate techniques for removing the fetus from the uterus, treating it, and replacing it, or for catheterizing or operating on it *in utero,* are now considered "feasible," and some are widely available. "Any trained obstetrician with an ultra-sound machine and a long hollow needle is entitled to try to treat a fetus."[84]

These technologies by their very existence seem to "deprivatize" the womb; it is no longer a woman's "private space," and she is no longer the only or even the main patient in an obstetrical situation.[85] The application of the techniques seems to give concrete reality to the idea of the fetus as "person," even as that idea is used to promote the prestige and heroism of the techniques. But this relationship is a purely symbolic or apparent one. The existence of medical technology that can treat the fetus *in utero* is no more evidence of the fetus' "personhood" or "viability" than is the existence of maternity leaves; nor does it tell us when and whether the technology ought to be used and who should decide. Whether it is beneficial or unduly risky in any given case, it is currently being used *ideologically* to discredit or circumvent the decision-making autonomy of pregnant women, in consultation with doctors, about whether to carry through a pregnancy and through what medical means. It is a pretext for denying women's capacity to consent and defining them as merely the biological vessels of the "unborn." Here again, women are put into an impossible dilemma: If the damaged fetus can be treated, does that mean it *must* be? Is the woman guilty of "neglect" if she refuses and complicit in denying her own autonomy if she doesn't?

Finally, attempts to secure spousal consent and notification require-ments for abortion, and court judgments supporting a "father's" right to veto his wife's abortion decision (thus far all unsuccessful), have ex-tended the "fetal protection" banner to individual husbands. In one recent case in Maryland, apparently a test case brought by "prolife" forces, a circuit court judge upheld a husband's argument that the Maryland Equal Rights Amendment (1972) gave husbands an equal say in decisions to terminate a pregnancy and granted an injunction against the wife's abortion.[86] (The wife in this case got the abortion anyway during a brief period while the injunction was stayed by an appeals court; the case is being heard on appeal.) The idea of the "father's right to decide," though not definitively granted in the courts, is similar to the recent tendency of judges to apply "sex-neutral" child custody statutes in favor of fathers when custody is disputed.[87] In both situations the concept of women's "equality" is used as a device to reduce women's control, in a way that is analogous to judicial repudiation of "protective" minimum wage laws for women in the backlash period of the 1920s.[88] This is in interesting contrast to the "protective" strategy used in regard to reproductive hazards and women's employment at the moment, indicating that both "equality" and "protection" can be turned into political weapons to deny women the conditions of autonomy. In both the custody and the abortion situation, the actual inequality in women's and men's long-term and socially defined responsibilities for children and in their access to the means of support is disregarded in assigning legal rights.

This is not to say that potential fathers may never have any moral claim to be consulted about an abortion. But under what circumstances does such a claim arise; what makes it valid? It should be evident that a feminist-humanist morality, which opposes biological determinism, cannot support a view that gives the male a legal or a moral right of consent or notification on the basis of his genetic connection to the fetus alone or the biological contribution of his sperm. Nor can the "marriage bond" be the basis for such a claim without implying a kind of ownership of the woman's body and its procreative capacity inherent in patriarchal authority. The only basis for such a claim to have moral weight is *through the social relationship established between the man and the pregnancy*—the actual demonstration of care and involvement and responsibility in the situation, or in prior coparenting experiences. For the experiences of everyday life tell us that the potential for further socializing, further humanizing, the pregnancy process and the fetus' development within it is very large. Some men mourn deeply the loss of a wanted pregnancy in a spontaneous or therapeutic abortion; they may participate in the reciprocal sensory and emotional consciousness I described earlier, feeling the fetus' movements and integrating a sense of its being and potential "personhood" into their own identity. Similarly, they may share, out of their understanding of the immediate conditions enveloping a pregnancy, in the moral judgment prompting an abortion decision. That this is so simply confirms that the process of bringing-into-consciousness or selfhood that we call "nurturance" or "maternity" is not mainly a biological but a social one. But the presumed right of the man to be informed or consulted should not override the woman's right to make the final decision; it should not be exercised as a veto because there remains a biological dimension of this process that is irreducible. Apart from the question of social responsibility for children after they are born, pregnancy is a condition specific to women; the consequences, at least during the period between conception and delivery, and the contingent rights are not and cannot be equalized.

If we concede that male partners have certain contingent (but not equal) rights in the pregnancy experience, although those rights cannot preempt the woman's, can they be legally enforced? Like parental consent and notification rules, those regarding spouses have to be seen in the context of existing social and power relations. A court-enforced system requiring consent or notification of the husband when a woman seeks an abortion would be redundant and unnecessarily invasive in the case of couples who have a cooperative and loving relationship; it would become a means of punitive surveillance over women's sexual behavior in the case of those who do not. In fact, such proposals are intended by their right-wing sponsors as a deterrent to both abortion and "illicit" sex. Paternal claims "to protect the life of the child he has fathered in his wife's womb" rest not only on the ideological premise of "fetal personhood"—that the fetus exists and has rights independently of the pregnant woman—but also on a traditional proprietary interest in the wife's body and its progeny.

Yet there is a troubling problem here. How are men to exercise greater responsibility and care in the processes of reproduction if women insist on exclusionary control? Increasingly, male partners voice complaints about feeling excluded, by both female partners and clinic personnel, from the abortion decision and the procedures surrounding it.[89] Meanwhile, feminists criticize the gender bias in reproductive health care and its persistent definition as a "woman's" problem. Responding to these pressures, some abortion and family planning clinics have opened their counseling sessions to male partners and even allowed the male to accompany the woman throughout the procedure. But the reality is that this supportive role is not forthcoming from many men.[90] Even the nurturant, sharing behavior of some men receives little enforcement from the dominant culture and reproductive politics. If women sometimes act to reinforce gender divisions around reproduction, concealing their pregnancies and their abortions and taking on all the responsibility, they do so in a larger social framework in which women are still blamed for both unwanted pregnancy and abortion. It is a culture in which male supportiveness and shared responsibility in any aspect of maternal work are still considered exceptional and noble rather than a matter of course. Current legislative and judicial measures challenging women's "right to choose" in the name of paternal rights are not in the least motivated by a spirit of support for women or shared responsibility but by an adversary posture in which the woman is pitted against the fetus and its "protective father." There is no intention by the right or the state of questioning the existing arrangements whereby primary responsibility for most aspects of reproduction and the care of children remains with women. Nor is there concern about the implications that involuntary pregnancy and childbearing may have for a woman's life and that of a prospective child. Perhaps we are left to conclude, then, as Margaret Sanger did in 1920:

In an ideal society, no doubt, birth control would become the concern of the man as well as the woman. The hard, inescapable fact which we encounter today is that man has not only refused such responsibility, but has individually and collectively sought to prevent woman from obtaining knowledge [and resources] by which she could assume this responsibility for herself.[91]

Again, we return to the principle that morality cannot be separated from the social conditions and concrete situations in which moral judgments take place. As long as pregnancies occur in women's bodies, change their bodies, and restructure their lives, there can be no conditions in which women will not need access to safe abortions and the ultimate right of decision. In a different world, in a different set of social arrangements where men's care and responsibility for children are a matter of customary practice and public policy and women have a full measure of power in the political economy, then a social dialogue about men's relation to the abortion (and birthing and childrearing) process will have a different and fuller meaning. In the meantime, on the levels of both personal relationships between women and men and public policy, we seem locked into the dilemma with which this book began: How do women negotiate between the social (yet personal) need to extend responsibility for reproduction to men and the state and the personal (yet social) need to defend their control over the terms and conditions of reproduction? How do we create radically new arrangements of shared responsibility for children, including the power over whether they are born, in a world where women still have power over little else?

This arouses in us an awareness of the "injustice in the very occurrence of the dilemma."[92] We must, finally, take a moral stance that is also a political stance: to refuse the terms of the dilemma, to reject being caught between unviable "choices." This is very different from demanding the "right to choose." We are saying that we reject the choices: We reject a system of production in which childbearing and jobs with decent pay are incompatible, and in which workers have no control over the health hazards to which they are subjected. We reject a medical-care system in which it is possible or thinkable for physicians to treat fetuses as separate, and adversary, medical subjects from pregnant women and to evade the woman's right to informed consent on that ground.[93] We reject a dominant sex-gender system in which men assert power over women and children without being obliged to learn the painstaking, ambiguous discipline of "maternal thinking," while women's practice of that discipline, however flawed, is never rewarded with social power (as participation, not domination). In short, making authentic moral judgments about abortion and having choices that are real involve changing the world.

NOTES

1. The framework for thinking about feminism that I am drawing from here comes from the groundbreaking work of the late Joan Kelly, especially her essay "Early Feminist Theory and the Querelle des Femmes, 1400–1789," to be published in her posthumous book, *Women, History and Theory* (Chicago: University of Chicago Press, forthcoming); and her unpublished notes on feminist theory.

2. Ellen Willis, "Abortion: Is a Woman a Person?" in *Beginning to See the Light: Pieces of a Decade* (New York: Knopf, 1981), p. 207.

3. Edward Manier, "Abortion and Public Policy in the U.S.: A Dialectical Examination of Expert Opinion," in *Abortion: New Directions for Policy Studies*, ed. Edward Manier, William Liu, and David Solomon (Notre Dame: University of Notre Dame Press, 1977), p. 5.

4. Devereux, *A Study of Abortion in Primitive Societies*, pp. 43–45.

5. Cited in Noonan, *Contraception*, p. 27.

6. Mohr, pp. 73–74; McLaren, *Birth Control in Nineteenth Century England*, pp. 34–35, 124.

7. Carol Gilligan, *In a Different Voice: Psychological Theory and Women's Development* (Cambridge, Mass.: Harvard University Press, 1982), p. 73.

8. See Nancy Chodorow, *The Reproduction of Mothering* (Palo Alto, Calif.: Stanford University Press, 1978).

9. See, e.g., Shorter, *The Making of the Modern Family;* Stone, *The Family, Sex and Marriage in England;* Badinter, *Mother Love;* and Flandrin, *Families in Former Times.*

10. Noonan, pp. 86–90, 362–65, 404–5; and Callahan, *Abortion: Law, Choice and Morality*, pp. 307–308 and 413.

11. Jacques Maritain, *The Rights of Man and Natural Law* (London: Geoffrey Bles, 1958), p. 36.

12. See Macpherson, *The Political Theory of Possessive Individualism;* Elizabeth Spelman, "Woman as Body," *Feminist Studies* 8 (Spring 1982): 109–31; and references cited in note 4, Chapter 2, in this volume.

13. See, e.g., Sarah M. Grimké, "Letters on the Equality of the Sexes and the Condition of Woman" and "Declaration of Sentiments and Resolutions, Seneca Falls," and Frederick Douglass, "Editorial from *The North Star,*" all in *Feminism: The Essential Historical Writings*, ed. Miriam Schneir (New York: Vintage, 1972); and Frederick Douglass, "Self-Elevation—Rev. S. R. Ward," in *Black Nationalism in America*, ed. John H. Bracey, Jr., August Meier, and Elliott Rudwick (Indianapolis: Bobbs-Merrill, 1970), pp. 60–62.

14. *Roe v. Wade*, 410 U.S. 142 (1973), pp. 138–41; and Mohr, pp. 200–202.

15. *Roe v. Wade*, pp. 156–59.

16. The amendment reads: "All *persons born* or naturalized in the United States, and subject to the jurisdiction thereof, are citizens of the United States and of the State wherein they reside. No State shall make or enforce any law which shall abridge the privileges or immunities of citizens of the United States; nor shall any State deprive any *person* of life, liberty, or property, without due process of law; nor deny to any *person* within its jurisdiction the equal protection of the laws" (emphasis added). See *Slaughter-House Cases*, 16 Wall. 36, 21 L. Ed. 394 (1873), regarding the historical origins of the amendment.

17. Rhonda Copelon, "Constitutional Analysis of S. 158 . . . and H.R. 900" (memorandum prepared for the Center for Constitutional Rights, March 1981). My thanks to Rhonda Copelon for providing me with this and other unpublished documents related to S. 158.

18. John T. Noonan, Jr., *A Private Choice: Abortion in America in the Seventies* (New York: Free Press, 1979), p. 171.

19. Keynote address, Scholar and the Feminist Conference 8, Barnard College, New York, 11 April 1981.

20. For example, Peter Steinfels, "The Search for an Alternative," *Commonweal* 108 (30 November 1981): 660–61.

21. John M. Frame, "Abortion from a Biblical Perspective," in *Thou Shalt Not Kill: The Christian Case Against Abortion* (New Rochelle, N.Y.: Arlington House, 1978); John T. Noonan, Jr., "Abortion and the Catholic Church," *Natural Law Forum* 12 (1967): 85–131; Callahan, pp. 310, 414–21; and *McRae* v. *Califano*, 491 F.Supp. 630 (1980), p. 695. I do not mean to suggest that any one of these points, taken by itself, is particular to right-wing fundamentalist sects but that as a chain of interconnected reasoning it reflects their doctrinal position. According to Noonan, there is "no relation" between "the Christian position" on fetal personhood beginning at conception and "theories of infant baptism" (p. 125). But there is no doubt that this vulgarization of that position is embedded in "right-to-life" ideology.

22. At least in Roman Catholic theology, fetal "innocence" is a heresy or highly contradictory, since it conflicts with the doctrine that all human beings are "conceived in sin." As Dr. Beverly Harrison, author of *Our Right to Choose* (Boston: Beacon Press, 1983), explained to me, it cannot both be true that "personhood" has nothing to do with consciousness or moral awareness and that the fetus is innocent, which implies the capacity for guilt. "Innocence" in this usage must be a metaphorical, polemical, and ultimately "nostalgic" (Harrison's term) use of the notion of "helplessness," the concept preferred by Noonan. My thanks to Beverly Harrison for discussing this question with me, and to Janet Gallagher, who brought the issue to my attention.

23. Callahan, pp. 419, 430–31.

24. Cited in *McRae* v. *Califano*, p. 693.

25. Noonan, 1967, pp. 130–31.

26. *McRae* v. *Califano*, pp. 695–98.

27. R. C. Lewontin, "The Corpse in the Elevator," *New York Review of Books* 29 (20 January 1983): 34.

28. One nasty example is Michael Levin, "The Feminist Mystique," *Commentary* 70 (December 1980): 25–30.

29. This synopsis is based on examination of dozens of pieces of antiabortion propaganda material produced between 1975 and 1980 by "prolife" groups and widely available through churches and National Right-to-Life Committee chapters.

30. Drusilla Burnham, "Induced Terminations of Pregnancy: Reporting States, 1979," U.S. Department of Health and Human Services, National Center for Health Statistics, *Monthly Vital Statistics Report* 31 (Oct. 25, 1982), Table 9.

31. See *Congressional Record*, 19 January 1981, p. S287; and Noonan, 1979, p. 59.

32. The text of the "human life statute" reads: "1. The Congress finds that present day scientific evidence indicates a significant likelihood that actual human life exists from conception.

"The Congress further finds that the 14th Amendment to the Constitution of the United States was intended to protect all human beings.

"Upon the basis of these findings, . . . the Congress hereby declares that for the purpose of enforcing the obligation of the States under the 14th Amendment not to deprive persons of life without due process of law, human life shall be deemed to exist from conception, without regard to race, sex, age, health, defect, or condition of dependency; and for this purpose 'person' shall include all human life as defined herein." In addition, the bill would deny to federal courts jurisdiction over abortion. It was this aspect, so blatantly in violation of the Constitution, that lost the bill the support of even many conservatives.

33. Paul Ramsey, "The Morality of Abortion," in *Life or Death: Ethics and Options*, ed. Edward Shils et al. (Portland, Ore.: Reed College, 1968), pp. 61–62. The same mystification of molecular biology is contained in C. Everett Koop, "A Physician Looks at Abortion," in Ganz: "That one cell with its 46 chromosomes contains the whole genetic code, written in molecules of DNA, that will, if not interrupted, make a human being just like your or me, with the potential for God-consciousness" (p. 9).

34. P. B. Medawar, "Genetic Options: An Examination of Current Fallacies," in Shils et al., pp. 99–100.

35. Callahan, pp. 377–82, makes this point with great cogency.

36. For example, Theodosius Dobzhansky writes: ". . . human behavior is in the main genetically unfixed; it shows a remarkably high degree of phenotypic plasticity. It is acquired in the process of socialization, of training received from other individuals. Its base is set by the genes, but the direction and extent of its development are, for the most part, culturally, rather than biologically, determined." *The Biological Basis of Human Freedom* (New York: Columbia University Press, 1956), p. 130. Similarly, C. H. Waddington: "The first step in the understanding of heredity is to realize that what a pair of parents donate to their offspring is a set of potentialities, not a set of already formed characteristics. . . . Any one genotype may give rise to many somewhat different phenotypes, corresponding to the different environments in which development occurs." *The Nature of Life* (Chicago: University of Chicago Press, 1961), p. 29.

37. Manier, p. 170.

38. Thus the legal memorandum that provided the theoretical ammunition for "prolife" sponsors of S. 158 justifies Congress' authority to override the Supreme Court in *Roe* v. *Wade* on the unexamined assumption that "if Congress decides that unborn children are human life for the purpose of the fourteenth amendment's protection of life, it follows logically that for this purpose they are persons as well. By common usage of language, any human being must be recognized as a person." Stephen H. Galebach, "A Human Life Statute," *Congressional Record*, 19 January 1981, p. S289. It by no means "follows logically" nor is it a matter of "common usage" to equate fetuses with persons in this way.

39. Bernard Weinraub, "Senator Agrees to Extend Hearings on Abortion Bill," *New York Times*, 25 April 1981, p. A7. See also Walter Sullivan, "Onset of Human Life: Answer on Crucial Moment Elusive," *New York Times*, 4 May 1981, p. B12;

and Harriet S. Meyer, "Science and the 'Human Life Bill'," Commentary, *Journal of the American Medical Association* 246 (21 August 1981): 837–39.

40. Callahan, pp. 377–78, 388–89.

41. Mary Anne Warren, "On the Moral and Legal Status of Abortion," in *Today's Moral Problems*, ed. Richard A. Wasserstrom (New York: Macmillan, 1979), pp. 37–39, 48.

42. Richard L. Ganz, "Psychology and Abortion: The Deception Exposed," in Ganz, pp. 30, 33.

43. Ibid., pp. 35–36.

44. *Conservative Digest* 5 (August 1979): 18. Typical of fundamentalist right-wing attacks on "secular humanism" in relation to abortion are Ganz, in Ganz, pp. 26–42; and Francis A. Schaeffer and C. Everett Koop, *Whatever Happened to the Human Race?* (Old Tappan, N.J.: Fleming H. Revell, 1978). In a like-spirited address before the Institute on Religious Life's Conference in St. Louis, 22 April 1978, Rep. Henry Hyde expressed concern over the rise of left-wing and feminist dissidents within the church who are critical of the church's social policies—a trend he sees as posing "serious problems for the church." The text of this speech is available from Rep. Hyde's office.

45. One practical manifestation of this view has been the attempt to expose abortion clinics as "exploiters" of women. Another is the effort to provide "positive alternatives" to abortion through such vehicles as the counseling group Birthright and the "pregnancy hotline."

46. Schaeffer and Koop, p. 52.

47. Callahan, p. 421.

48. On the ancient origins and continuities of myths embodying men's fear of women's power over mortality, see Simone de Beauvoir, *The Second Sex* (New York: Bantam, 1961), Chap. 9; Rich, *Of Woman Born*, Chaps. 3 and 4; and Philip E. Slater, *The Glory of Hera* (Boston: Beacon, 1968), Chaps. 8 and 9.

49. Thus, for example, one social scientist refers to abortion as "an easy alternative for women who perceived that having children was no longer one of the attractive feminine roles." William T. Liu, "Abortion and the Social System," in Manier, Liu, and Solomon, p. 147.

50. Callahan, a liberal supporter of women's "right to decide," expresses diffidence toward women who get abortions for what he considers to be "selfish" or not "serious reasons," which turn out to be any reasons not grounded in maternal duty, either to other children or to "the good of mankind" (pp. 429–31). This contradicts the strong arguments he makes later on about women's right to define the abortion situation as they see fit.

51. See, for example, Betty Friedan, "Feminism's Next Step," *New York Times Magazine*, 15 July 1981, pp. 14–15; Mary Meehan, "Abortion: The Left Has Betrayed the Sanctity of Life," *Progressive* 44 (September 1980): 32–34; Leslie Savan, "Abortion Chic: The Attraction of 'Wanted-Unwanted Pregnancies,'" *Village Voice*, 4–10 February 1981, p. 32; and Elizabeth Moore and Karen Mulhauser, "Pro and Con: Does Free Abortion Hurt the Poor and Minorities?" *In These Times*, 28 February 1979, p. 18. (This "debate" stirred an angry exchange of feminist criticisms and editorial rejoinders in subsequent issues of *In These Times*, considered a leading left-wing newspaper.) For a trenchant critique of this trend on the left, see Stacey Oliker, "Abortion and the Left: The Limits of 'Pro-Family' Politics," *Socialist Review* 56 (March–April 1981): 71–95.

52. See Warren, pp. 45–47; Callahan, pp. 497–98; and Steinfels, quoting Charles Hartshorne, p. 661, for this sort of thinking.

53. See Spelman for an excellent feminist critique of this dualist tradition.

54. Ramsey, p. 60.

55. Maritain, pp. 6–7, 10, 27, 37.

56. Agnes Heller, "Marx's Theory of Revolution and the Revolution in Everyday Life," in Hegedus, Heller, Markus, and Vajda, *The Humanisation of Socialism*, pp. 46–47.

57. Maritain, p. 27.

58. Steinfels, p. 661.

59. See, for example, Jacques Lacan, "Le Stade du Miroir comme Formateur de la Fonction du Je," in *Ecrits I* (Paris: Editions de Seuil, 1966); Chodorow, pp. 46–51; W. R. D. Fairbairn, *An Object-Relations Theory of the Personality* (New York: Basic Books, 1952); Alice Balint, "Love for the Mother and Mother-Love," in *Primary Love and Psycho-Analytic Technique*, ed. Michael Balint (New York: Liveright, 1965), pp. 91–108; idem, *The Early Years of Life: A Psychoanalytic Study* (New York: Basic Books, 1954); and Jean Piaget, *The Origins of Intelligence in Children*, trans. Margaret Cook (New York: Norton, 1952).

60. Quoted from Alasdair MacIntyre, in Manier, p. 20.

61. Roger Wertheimer, "Philosophy on Humanity," in Manier, Liu, and Solomon, p. 130.

62. Willis, p. 208.

63. My thanks to Randy Reiter for helping me to clarify this point.

64. Piaget, pp. 108–9.

65. Burnham, "Induced Terminations of Pregnancy," Table 4; and U.S. Department of Health and Human Services, Centers for Disease Control, *Abortion Surveillance*, Annual Summary 1978 (Atlanta, Ga., 1980), Table 15. It is for this reason that the "viability" issue would seem blown out of proportion by both feminists and antiabortionists. New technology that "pushes forward" the so-called point of "viability" will not affect the vast majority of abortions.

66. Steinfels, p. 663. See also Callahan's interesting discussion of the "developmental school's" approach to understanding the fetus, pp. 384–390.

67. *Abortion Surveillance*, p. 4 and Table 15.

68. Around 95 percent of women undergoing amniocentesis have negative results, and among those who test positively for any of the one hundred defects currently diagnosable with this procedure, not all elect to undergo abortion. Robert F. Murray, Jr., "Technical Issues and Problems Related to Amniocentesis" (lecture given at Symposium on the Dilemmas and Decisions of Prenatal Diagnosis, New York City Community College, Division of Continuing Education, 26 April 1980). Much of my thinking about amniocentesis and prenatal diagnosis is based on having attended this excellent conference. My thanks to Dean Fannie Eisenstein for inviting me to attend.

69. Ruth Hubbard, "Prenatal Diagnosis and the Problematic Quest for Certainty" (keynote address, New York City Community College Symposium on Prenatal Diagnosis); and Wendy Carlton, "'Wrongful Life,' 'Wrongful Birth,' Antenatal Testing: The Silent Revolution in Children's Rights" (paper presented at the American Sociological Association meeting, Toronto, 24–28 August 1981), pp. 8–9.

70. A different perspective from the one presented here is that of parents of a fetus diagnosed to be severely hydrocephalic (brain damaged and enlarged by buildup of fluid, causing retardation or death), who gladly consented to every heroic pyrotechnic the medical profession can offer. After a marathon of brain shunts, catheters, needles, etc., the infant was born with compounded anomalies and malformations and died at the age of five weeks. The father observed: "We're sad that Mark's gone. . . . But I can't feel guilty about anything we did or didn't do. Mark suffered a lot, both before his birth and afterward. But I felt that if I had asked him, 'Do you want to go through with this?' if he had been able to answer he always would have said yes." Robin Marantz Henig, "Saving Babies Before Birth," *New York Times Magazine,* 28 February 1982, p. 46. This is an expression of "fetal personhood" ideology: the apotheosis of life under any conditions, the more suffering the holier; the projection of the parent's moral illusions on to the unconscious, unknowing fetus. Whether parents *should* have this "choice," whether society's already inequitably distributed medical resources should be deflected into "saving" such fetuses, is another question.

71. I do not subscribe to the view that the existence of a technique limits choice because it compels its use. This is an antitechnological form of technological determinism, attributing to the technique magical power over people's relation to it. My sense is that in this case the technique potentially widens the framework for moral praxis and a more conscious life; there is nothing wrong with individuals wanting "certainty." The very real potential for *abuse,* on the other hand (e.g., pressure on women to undergo the procedure when it may be unnecessary or risky), is a function not of the technique but of the organization and politics of existing medical care.

72. My thanks to Marty Fleisher for this observation.

73. Wendy W. Williams, "Firing the Woman to Protect the Fetus: The Reconciliation of Fetal Protection with Employment Opportunity Goals under Title VII," *Georgetown Law Journal* 69 (1981): 641–704; Ronald Bayer, "Women, Work, and Reproductive Hazards," *Hastings Center Report,* October 1982, pp. 14–19; and "Workers, Reproductive Hazards, and the Politics of Protection," *Feminist Studies* 5 (Summer 1979). In this special issue, see articles by R. Petchesky, Wendy Chavkin, Vilma R. Hunt, Carolyn Bell, and Michael J. Wright.

74. R. Petchesky, in *Feminist Studies* 5 (1979), p. 237; Williams, pp. 641–642; and Bayer, p. 14.

75. Williams, pp. 644, 647, 697n.

76. "Occupational Exposure of Fertile Women," Measurement Report No. 53, quoted by Vilma Hunt, *Work and the Health of Women* (Boca Raton, Fla.: CRC Press, 1979), p. 63.

77. See Carolyn Bell, "Implementing Safety and Health Regulations for Women in the Workplace," *Feminist Studies* 5 (1979), 296–97.

78. Michael J. Wright, "Reproductive Hazards and 'Protective' Discrimination," *Feminist Studies* 5 (1979): 304–5; and Wendy Chavkin, "Occupational Hazards to Reproduction: A Review Essay and Annotated Bibliography," *Feminist Studies* 5 (1979): 313.

79. Williams, p. 687.

80. See Equal Employment Opportunity Commission, "Interpretive Guidelines on Employment Discrimination and Reproductive Hazards," *Federal Register*

45 (1 February 1980): 7514–17; and the farsighted approach taken by the United Steelworkers of America and the labor-oriented Committee for the Reproductive Rights of Workers (CRROW), summarized by Wright, pp. 306–8.

81. Williams, pp. 696–97.

82. See Nancy E. Bellon, "Court Decision Erodes Abortion Rights," *Guardian,* 6 October, 1982, p. 5; and Ruth Hubbard, "Legal and Policy Implications of Recent Advances in Prenatal Diagnosis and Fetal Therapy," *Women's Rights Law Reporter* 7 (Spring 1982): 201–18, esp. footnotes written by Janet Gallagher, pp. 56–60, and cases cited therein. A Louisiana law requires that every pregnant woman examined in an abortion clinic undergo an ultrasound test; and a Florida omnibus antiabortion bill, if passed, would require that the fetus be given anesthesia before an abortion. See also Ruth Hubbard, "The Fetus as Patient," *Ms.* 9 (October 1982): 32.

83. Quoted in Hubbard, "Legal and Policy Implications," pp. 212–13. The original article is Bowes and Selegstad, "Fetal versus Maternal Rights: Medical and Legal Perspectives," *Obstetrics and Gynecology* 58 (1981): 209–13. The authors of this article, a physician and a lawyer, cite *Roe* v. *Wade*—the state's interest in protecting "potential life" in the third trimester!—as the legal basis of the Colorado cesarean case.

84. Henig, p. 48.

85. Hubbard, "The Fetus as Patient," p. 32.

86. Bellon.

87. See Nancy Polikoff, "Why Are Mothers Losing?: A Brief Analysis of Criteria Used in Child Custody Determinations," *Women's Rights Law Reporter* 7 (Spring 1982): 235–43. Polikoff argues that, since the late 1970s, when fathers sue for custody they are winning about fifty percent of the time. This is because judges devalue the mother's caretaking functions in favor of the father's higher earnings or greater likelihood of remarrying and have a wife at home—a reaction against working mothers.

88. See Hill, "Protection of Women Workers and the Courts," *Feminist Studies* 5; and William Chafe, *The American Woman* (London: Oxford University, 1972), Chap. 5.

89. Arthur B. Shostak, "Men and Abortion: Survey Data and Human Needs" (paper presented at the meeting of the Eastern Sociological Society, New York City, March 1981); and Pamela Black, "Abortion Affects Men, Too," *New York Times Magazine,* 28 March, 1982, pp. 76–78, 82–83, 94.

90. Ibid.; and Freeman, "Abortion: Subjective Attitudes and Feelings," *Family Planning Perspectives* 10:153–55.

91. Sanger, *Woman and the New Race,* p. 96.

92. Gilligan, p. 103.

93. Cf. Hubbard, "Legal and Policy Implications": "It makes no sense, biologically or socially, to pit fetal and maternal 'rights' against one another" (p. 215). She argues this on the basis of the "organic unity" of the fetus and the pregnant woman, which is similar to what I am arguing here, except that it ignores what I have also acknowledged as the "parasitic" dimension of the fetus' dependence on the woman and an element of tension in that relationship as well.

10

Women's Consciousness and the Abortion Decision

[Women] make their own history, but they do not make it just as they please; they do not make it under circumstances chosen by themselves, but under circumstances directly encountered, given and transmitted from the past.

KARL MARX, *The Eighteenth Brumaire of Louis Bonaparte*

. . . it is not simply that there is a disjunction between what people say they do and what they in fact do. The more cogent point is that the meaning people attach to action . . . is an integral component of that action and cannot be divorced from it in our analysis.

JANE COLLIER, MICHELLE Z. ROSALDO, AND SYLVIA YANAGISAKO,
"Is There a Family? New Anthropological Views,"
in *Rethinking the Family*

Doing and Believing—The Morality of Praxis

Constructing a feminist politics of reproductive freedom, including abortion, requires that we analyze women's consciousness in relation to the abortion decision. But that is not an easy thing to do. How women act to resolve an unwanted pregnancy is not in itself expressive of their consciousness; we cannot comprehend their reasons and their understandings from their actions alone. In sorting through the available evidence of what women who undergo abortions usually think and feel, we have to untangle the frequent contradictions between what women *say* and what they *do,* and between different things they say at once. This complexity immediately suggests the difficulty in assuming a "reproductive consciousness" that is "universal" among women.[1] First, no "universal consciousness" grows out of the conditions of reproduction, for abortion, pregnancy, and childbearing are different in different social circumstances and consciousness will reflect those differences. Depending on whether or not they already have children, their age, the quality of their sexual relationships, their class and ethnic position, their involvement in work or school, women's understanding of their abortion or childbearing experience may vary. Class and ethnically divided policies of the state in regard to reproduction may contribute to this varied consciousness—as, for example, when coercive sterilization and abortion practices arouse resistance among the targeted women; or when racist policies generate an oppositional nationalist or ethnic birth campaign among an oppressed ethnic minority and the group's women comply.[2]

Even within the same circumstances and the same woman, consciousness about abortion is likely to be multilayered or contradictory. The same woman who avers that abortion is "terrible" or "wrong" may also insist on her need or right to have one; at the very least, she will act on that belief, whatever her professed convictions. Escalation of the "right-to-life" propaganda campaign depicting abortion as murder and fetuses as innocent babies has apparently influenced how people feel and talk about abortion, but not what they choose to do about it.[3] This disjunction between belief and behavior is evident from recent attitude surveys that indicate "that a much greater proportion of both Catholics and Protestants would have an abortion themselves (or advise their wives to have one) than advocate legal abortion on principle."[4] The opinions expressed in these surveys clearly reveal the gap between moral prescriptions and real-life perceptions in popular consciousness. There is a striking contrast between the fact that percentages approving abortion in opinion polls have stayed roughly the same or even slightly declined since the initial surge of approval prior to 1975, while abortion rates for American women rose every year during the 1970s. Further, the reasons why most women, especially young unmarried women, get abortions are not usually the dire indications (e.g., life endangerment, health, fetal defect) that most Americans "approve" of verbally, but the more controversial "socioeconomic" ones: being too young, too poor, without a job; needing to finish school; wanting "to have a life for herself."

Even in opinion surveys, an apparent confusion about the morality of abortion contrasts sharply with a strong consensus about its legality. Surveying a cross section of more than a thousand American women of varying ages, geographical regions, races, income groups, religions, and political persuasions, a recent *Life* magazine poll found that "not one major grouping—including the most politically conservative—believes that a woman should be legally denied the right to choose to have an abortion if she determines that the procedure is necessary." While 56 percent of the respondents felt that having an abortion was "morally wrong," 67 percent thought that "any woman who wants an abortion should be permitted to obtain it legally"; this percentage was considerably larger among urban women, women of color, and women living in the western states. A majority (62 percent) of women identifying themselves as conservatives agreed that abortion should be legal. When asked to relate the moral issue to concrete situations, two-thirds of all women interviewed agreed that women they knew who had had abortions had done "the right thing."[5] Apparently, what is "right" in real-life circumstances differs from abstract morality.

The fact that large numbers of Catholics are getting abortions reinforces the impression of a moral ethos divorced from social reality. Catholic birth control practice is now nearly equivalent to that of the rest of the population, in clear opposition to church teaching.[6] This cultural shift has apparently affected Catholic abortion practice as well. Catholics in many countries get abortions nearly as frequently as do non-Catholics, despite the adamant position of the church; "one of the main effects of religion [is] not to stop abortion but to create problems of conscience."[7] Abortion-clinic operators and counselors in the United States confirm this view. Clinics located in areas with heavily Catholic populations report that their clientele is approximately two-thirds Catholic. Clinic operators speculate on the possibility that the church's prohibitive policy on artificial contraception actually works to *increase* abortion rates among young Catholic women.[8] Two abortion counselors working in a Boston clinic report that their predominantly Catholic patients, "when faced by a problem pregnancy," choose abortion as the lesser evil in a situation where the alternative to guilt is leaving school, lifelong poverty, or shame.[9]

What this suggests is that different levels of consciousness are operating at once and that people's understanding of the dictates of morality and their understanding of their own situation and needs are in conflict. Women internalize the dominant ideologies about abortion, blame themselves and get blamed, even though their economic conditions and other social pressures dictate a different course of action and a conflicting set of values. As one young woman put it, "I am saying that abortion is morally wrong, but the situation is right, and I am going to do it."[10] Rather than indicate "selfishness" or moral confusion on the part of individual women, however, this double-think may be interpreted as strong evidence that the current antiabortion view of morality is disconnected from the needs that people experience in everyday life. Indeed, when we penetrate beneath the conventionally articulated ideas about what is "morally correct," we find another, more popularly understood set of moral values that reflects a sense of immediacy and personal responsibility in ethical decisions and an attentiveness to the practical demands arising out of concrete circumstances.

Building on the work of the late Sarah Eisenstein, I understand consciousness as a dynamic process of accommodating the pressures of conflicting ideologies and values imposed by the dominant culture and various oppositional cultures on one's own sense of felt need. That sense, in turn, grows out of material and social constraints that may disrupt ideological preconceptions, constraints rooted in class and life situations and in the unconscious and the body. Consciousness is thus a series of "negotiations" back and forth between ideology, social reality, and desire.[11] These negotiations result not only in a "decision," a discrete act, but often in an unarticulated *morality of situation, of praxis*, which incorporates social and individual need into the shifting ground of moral values. There is nothing predetermined about the outcomes of this process; we have to analyze it through the specific situations that construct it, as well as the choices and understandings to which they lead. This chapter suggests that the consciousness of most women who get abortions, far from being amoral or irresponsible, is rooted in the "morality of praxis."

Recent research on "abortion attitudes" among women who undergo abortion provides a basis for analyzing the consciousness of some women about their abortion experience.[12] This material refutes certain stereotypes: that abortion patients are "careless" or morally insensitive; or, on the contrary, that they are steeped in guilt and despair. The surveys describe a remarkably wide-ranging mixture of attitudes about the abortion experience: Many women report feeling "fine," others experience various degrees of being "troubled"; some become strong prochoice advocates afterward, others shrink from thinking about it or weep and are solitary and mournful; some find it "very hard," others insist they do not "feel guilty" in the slightest. While many women experience feelings of loss, ambivalence, anxiety, and regret around the time of an abortion, particularly when they are making a decision about it, the majority feel mainly "relief" several months afterward.[13] "Clearly," as one researcher concludes, "their abortions resolved a distressing event in their lives which they could not and did not accept casually."[14]

The first thing that must be said about guilt is that it does not exist in a vacuum but in a context shaped by history, politics, and religious and moral codes. A century of legal and religious condemnation, along with the lived reality of abortion as sinister, secret, dirty, and dangerous, inevitably stamps women's "moral sense" of abortion as wrong or deviant. For many women who got abortions during the period of early legalization, that image was very vivid and infused their self-judgment. The "shady, back-alley context in which abortion was typically cast," the "cloak of secrecy," and the "butcher with a big knife" created "a subtle yet powerful lens through which most of the women had formed their prior abortion attitudes as well as one through which they were to perceive the events of their own abortion passage."[15] The strong moral antagonism toward abortion of many women in black communities may be inseparable from the long experience of dangerous, unhygienic, "quack" methods to which black women were disproportionately exposed; their sense of "wrongness" is imprinted with the reality and the fearful tales of danger and death.

Over a decade after legalization, in a climate of vociferous antiabortion propaganda, the legacy of deviance still hangs over women's heads. It is manifested not so much in what people do about abortion as in what they say, in the apologetic tone that even feminists and liberal "prochoice" advocates adopt in statements supporting legal, funded abortion. Thus, an editorial in the *New York Times*, which has consistently supported abortion as a need and right of all women, characterizes "America's high abortion rate" as "a national tragedy" and women's decision to terminate a pregnancy as "a decision they are *invariably reluctant to make*."[16] This assumption of "reluctance" is a bow by liberal journalism to the ideological power of the right wing and not a reflection of fact. The passage of time and the assimilation of abortion into the routinized and sanitary procedures of the clinic have created a new context that must be helping to structure a new moral consciousness, especially among women too young to remember the "old days." This context makes possible a more subtle analysis of women's feelings about having an abortion, since those feelings are no longer drowned in terror.

Yet there is no escaping the fact that abortion is frequently a painful experience for the woman; it signifies a loss. What is interesting is that so many women choose it anyway, and are able to separate their *feelings* from their moral judgment about what is best to do. As with divorce or separation, feelings about an abortion may be in conflict without this spelling a sense of "guilt." The much-discussed "ambivalence" of many women toward the *experience* of abortion (not the *right*) is a smokescreen that obscures a dense web of losses and sorrows related to aging and childbearing and the precariousness of sexual relationships, as well as the longings for family ties and emotional commitment that a "baby" may symbolize. These feelings are not necessarily "irrational" but may reflect conscious desires thwarted by harsh realities. Older women following an abortion may mourn the loss of children growing up as much as the aborted fetus.[17] Women whose relationship did not survive the abortion may also be mournful, regretting not only the fetus but the whole emotional fabric from which they have separated. Teenage women may "wish" a child—to establish adulthood or have someone of their own to love—but may feel a responsibility to finish school or become self-supporting. Many subjects in abortion studies "want a child" but say that abortion is the necessary and harder choice because of external circumstances.

But conflicted feelings should not be confused with guilt. None of the women surveyed would be likely to confuse her complicated feelings about abortion with her right to get an abortion or the moral justification for her decision. Many if not most women seeking abortions are not reluctant or ambivalent about the abortion and the need for it. If they are "reluctant" about anything, it is the prospect of having a baby, which is why a resurgent pronatalist/promotherhood culture imposes guilt on them. A focus on subjective "attitudes" tends to cloud the central issue in determining moral consciousness: the reasons and objective circumstances that motivate the decision, often in spite of ambivalent feelings.

Where ambivalence occurs, it may in fact be a perfectly appropriate response to a situation in which parents are unsupportive or condemning, boy friends angry or withdrawn, school peers taunting and stigmatizing.[18] It may be a response to conditions in which the genuine desire for a child is thwarted by poverty, inadequate housing, lack of a supportive partner, or the unavailability of child care.[19] Yet the decision remains firmly to get the abortion; from the moral standpoint, the oppressiveness of the conditions does not negate the authenticity of the decision. The insinuation that women who get abortions do so out of "self-indulgence" must strike many women as ironic. For they are aware of the truism that one's own needs, one's responsibility to self as well as others, may conflict with one's desires:

> What I want to do is have the baby, but what I feel I should do which is what I need to do, is have an abortion right now, because sometimes what you want isn't right. Sometimes what is necessary comes before what you want. . . .[20]

Interviews with women contemplating an abortion provide powerful evidence that the "morality of praxis" guides ordinary women's abortion decisions. Its center is the "taking of responsibility upon oneself," claiming "the power to choose . . . and [accept] responsibility for choice":

> I think you have to think about the people who are involved, including yourself. You have responsibilities to yourself. . . .
> To me it is still taking a life. But I have to think of mine, my son's and my husband's. . . . To me it is taking a life, and I am going to take that upon myself, that decision upon myself and I have feelings about it. . . .[21]

One's needs exist and have validity along with the needs of significant others to whom one is responsible, in a context of interpersonal relations for which the decision to have an abortion or have a child has irrevocable consequences. Other children, sexual partners, coworkers, and kin have claims on one's time and resources; parents have legitimate expectations that their daughters develop the tools of independence; indeed, a potential child may be thought to have certain rights not to be delivered into an environment that is sure to be unloving, unhealthy, or insecure.

For teenage women, the consequences of early childbearing include sharply heightened risks of maternal morbidity and mortality, as well as an irreparable loss of education and work experience. For their infants, there is a greater risk of low birth weight and developmental as well as economic difficulties in later years.[22] I am not arguing the inevitability of these consequences but simply that they are consequences for *others*. Women perceive them to exist, and that perception affects their consciousness of their moral responsibility.

On the other hand, the background to an abortion decision may be a situation, not of accommodating the demands of others, but of *conflict* between a pregnant woman and those with whom she feels the greatest connection, particularly her sexual partner and her parents (if she is a young teenager). Her immediate social reality may reinforce a strong sense of being alone in her responsibility. As things stand, *she* is the one whose life will be most drastically affected by an early marriage; *she* is the one who will be required to care for or separate from the infant; *she* is the one who will have to undergo a ritual and physical loss and pain, in the abortion process. Small wonder, then, that most women who get abortions would prefer to ensure their control over the decision than to rely on "male responsibility." In one group of abortion patients surveyed, among the unmarried couples it was not the women but predominantly the men who wanted to get married to "legitimate" the pregnancy. Moreover, among both married and unmarried couples, it tended to be the women rather than the men who urged the necessity of abortion because of financial problems, the man's inability to support a family, or because the "time was not right."[23] Using traditional criteria, the men were being "responsible," but the women evidently had a different notion of responsibility, and they pursued it in spite of the men.

Whatever the circumstances, the evidence suggests that most women's abortion decisions ultimately get made on the basis, not of received moral or religious doctrine and still less out of sheer "selfishness," but of the social conditions and relations that define their lives. Whether we look at the outcome of an abortion decision or the consciousness of the women making it, the stereotype of that decision as careless, immoral, and selfish is not only false but malicious. In the painful self-searching and deliberation of abortion clients interviewed by Carol Gilligan and others emerges a picture of a moral consciousness that is sensitive to a many-faceted reality and to "the actual consequences" of an action "in the lives of the people involved." Ultimately, the "reconstructed moral understanding" that grows out of attentiveness to concrete reality results in an awareness of the "injustice . . . manifest in the very occurrence of the dilemma."[24] In other words, the very situation of a pregnancy that one "wants" but cannot have, or that one does not want and is made to feel guilty for not having, is an unjust one, whose terms and conditions must be refused.

For some women, awareness of the injustice built into the context of abortion may develop slowly, prompted by what Gilligan identifies as the "conventional voice" of "doing good" and "helping others." Indeed, women's own ways of thinking about the abortion decision may be couched, not in feminist or libertarian terms, but in traditional religious or "feminine" values. There are complex layers through which women negotiate the tensions between a sense of morality (perceived as externally imposed), the pull of external circumstances (necessity), and an acknowledgement of responsibility. Reconciling the abortion, the clear decision to do it, with a surrounding (political, familial, or church) climate of moral condemnation is handled by some women, not by agreeing to their own moral worthlessness nor affirming the moral rightness of abortion, but by a strategy of "denying [their] own responsibility." Echoing the woman who thought that "abortion is morally wrong but the situation is right," some abortion patients cast their position in terms of compulsion or nonchoice: "I was being forced to do something . . . that I didn't want to do"; "It was the only way out, and you have to accept that"; and "I had no choice."[25] This denial of responsibility is a tactic intended to accommodate a received view of abortion as immoral and wrong to "the reality of [the woman's] own participation in the abortion decision." Thus it embodies a contradiction, an evasion.[26]

But the problem of consciousness is further complicated by the fact that competing moral and cultural values that pervade the dominant culture coexist within an individual woman's consciousness and may contradict one another. Abortion morality is not monolithic. Alongside the right-wing views of abortion as murder and women defined by maternal self-sacrifice and procreation is a liberal view that justifies abortion in the name of "quality over quantity." This is a legacy not only of eugenics but of eighteenth- and nineteenth-century bourgeois morality that prescribed a model of childbearing geared to the economics of an expanding consumer market and the idea that "maternal duty" involved rational planning and budgeting, of children as well as household economies. Though seldom recognized as such, the idea that childbearing ought to wait until one is "financially sound" because children have a right to a certain standard of living is a powerful *moral* doctrine in contemporary American society. Today, not only most family planners but many ordinary people agree with John Stuart Mill's dictum "that to bring a child into existence without a fair prospect of being able, not only to provide food for its body, but instruction and training for its mind, is a moral crime, both against the unfortunate offspring and against society. . . ."[27]

Women clients of contemporary abortion clinics are motivated by a sense of "maternal duty"—or sometimes filial duty. Economic constraints were the "most frequently cited circumstance" necessitating abortion for both married and unmarried women in one study.[28] In the concept of "planning" or "timing" that many women internalize, the main component seemed being able to "afford" a baby. Time and again in interviews this idea was put forward; needing to finish school or improve one's financial situation was taken to be an unassailable, universally recognized justification for avoiding parenthood even among those who adhere to the view that abortion is "murder."[29]

Like the idea that "unwanted" children are likely to be abused, the concept of "planned births" is justified in the name of children's rights, not women's. What is confusing here is that the notion of "financial necessity" is counterposed to "morality," as a kind of external, almost natural force, rather than understood to be a shorthand for a complicated set of alternative moral values that have been both internalized and occasionally transformed by working-class and middle-class women as they contemplate what to do about an unwanted pregnancy. But both streams of the dominant ideology about abortion—the conservative-procreational and the liberal-utilitarian—contain an underlying theme of female self-denial and maternal duty. For the liberal, it is not the woman who gets an abortion who is "selfish" but the one who doesn't—when she is too young or too poor or too "incompetent." For both, the ethic of maternal responsibility, rather than women's liberation, constructs abortion morality.

Are we, then, to conclude that the prevailing consciousness that informs women's abortion decisions is one of accommodation to traditional "female" (patriarchal) norms? Are most women who seek abortions really saying: "Rest assured, we are as moral and maternal as ever you wish us to be. Abortion isn't something we really want; if the 'circumstances' were different, we'd choose babies"? If this is the case, it is difficult to reconcile with the social reality we examined earlier, which showed that the background for rising abortions among most women in the past decade was a set of circumstances that *improved* their lives, making abortion more of a choice than a "desperate measure." It would also seem alien to a feminist consciousness about abortion, insofar as that means an assertion of women's collective rights and needs, not just a resignation to grim necessity. Can we locate a resistant and transformative moment in women's consciousness about abortion, one that is not only "female" but feminist,[30] that asserts not only an accommodation to what exists but an aspiration toward change?

An analysis of consciousness that attends only to words, ignoring the social situations those words conceal or that give them a specific meaning, will never understand consciousness as more than an accomodation to what exists.[31] People's words in most instances seek to accommodate the dominant ideology; the language itself reverberates with it. Yet their words may also be strategies for fitting the dominant ideas into a contradictory reality and perception. In assessing women's consciousness about abortion, it is important to determine how their social circumstances may alter the meanings of words. An idea such as "child spacing" or "responsible motherhood" may originate among bourgeois family planners and social reformers yet have different implications when applied by working-class women to themselves. Similarly, concerns such as financial constraints or "respectability" clearly have a different content for different classes. For a woman deciding on an abortion to say, "I don't want to bring up a child with nothing,"[32] may mean a staunch refusal of her conditions, if she is poor. It may reflect a long-standing tradition of working-class parents to strive to make their children's lives better, thereby *both* accommodating bourgeois assumptions about upward mobility *and* determining to push beyond the limits of their situation. Under cover of a bourgeois ethic that has become so universalized that it is no longer recognizable as "morality," working-class and poor women may be saying: I want a better life; whereas young middle-class women may be simply conforming to the timetables their parents and their class have laid out for them.

For middle-class women, too, the abortion decision may represent a consciousness and a reality that are complex. The language of self-assertion embodied in the themes of "taking control of my life," assuming "a responsibility to myself," and "claiming the power to choose"[33] may reflect a distinct class privilege, for the *"power* to choose" is clearly more accessible to women whose future contains a Radcliffe degree and a career. At the same time, insofar as the dominant patriarchal ideologies about abortion are based on maternal duty and self-denial, then for *all* women the language of self-assertion contains an oppositional dimension. For a woman of any class to say, in regard to abortion, *"I* will decide, based on *my* needs as well as those of the (living) persons to whom I am immediately responsible," is by definition an act of resistance in the context of a dominant ideology and culture that define her in terms of the needs of others.

Critics on the left as well as the right have identified elements of the ideology of "self-discovery" and "self-duty" as a form of bourgeois individualism packaged through the media and popular psychology, including their feminist versions.[34] Yet, within a bourgeois individualist culture, women generally have been denied their claims to individualism on behalf of a biological or spiritual determinism that relegates them to the realm of nature rather than autonomous will. It is thus not surprising that feminist aspirations tend to take an individualist form.[35] We have to recognize such aspirations as expressions of resistance (in a patriarchal context) and their articulation by individual women as expressions of a feminist or prefeminist consciousness. When a woman says, "It is *my* responsibility and nobody else's," responsibility begins to edge into a conviction of right. Seen from this perspective, it may be that a feminist, or resistant, consciousness emerges as the consequence more than the cause of a decision to get an abortion. This may become increasingly true in a political context where legal abortion has existed for well over a decade yet is increasingly under attack.

It is complicated indeed to sort out the relationship between freedom and necessity in women's attempts to negotiate the abortion decision. For women of all social classes and age groups, the necessity of abortion is often perceived to be, and is, the result of external conditions—whether economic, social, medical, or interpersonal—they did not choose. From the standpoint of a concept of consciousness as metabolically related to social reality and needs, the act of choosing to deal with those conditions through an abortion is one of self-determination and therefore self-empowerment. In a culture that still underwrites women's powerlessness in the face of maternity and moral decision making, it is also in most cases an objective assertion of moral praxis. Let me add, however, that the decision to go ahead with a birth, to decline abortion, in spite of difficulties or the resistance of others, may also express the morality of praxis. It depends on the circumstances and on how the woman assesses her situation and commitments. Only "right-to-lifers" caricature the feminist position as dogmatic "proabortionism" or some crazed baby-hatred. For feminists, it is not the outcome that is at issue, but women's autonomy over the *process* of choosing. And I believe that most women, whether or not they call themselves feminists, aspire to that autonomy.

Yet one may have other, less optimistic thoughts on this question. Whether, afterward, a woman understands her decision to get an abortion in accommodationist or oppositional terms; whether she perceives it as a duty ("I had no choice") or a right ("It was *my* choice") is the issue of consciousness that is hardest to predict, and is most crucial for feminist politics. For, if "the meaning people attach to action . . . is an integral component of that action and cannot be divorced from it,"[36] then women's own understandings about the *justice* of abortion will have an important impact less on their willingness to get abortions than on their willingness to fight for them. As feminists are keenly aware, legal changes are fragile indeed without a "revolution in consciousness." On this level, we know little about women's consciousness regarding abortion because we have not asked the right questions. Opinion polls and survey research frame their questions in terms borrowed from the dominant discourse ("Do you think abortion is moral?" "Is the fetus a 'person'?" "How did you feel during/after the abortion experience?"), not in feminist terms ("What would it mean to you to be pregnant when you didn't want to be and not have abortion available?" "Do you think whether you have an abortion or bear a child should be up to your husband/boy friend/priest/parents?"). The *absence* of feminist questions is part of the cultural force that helps shape women's consciousness and maintain the continued gap between their actions and their political understanding. Ten years of legal abortion in many states have surely contributed enormously to abortion practice and its cultural legitimacy. But a feminist politics rooted in an explicit feminist morality of abortion has not penetrated popular consciousness, which still views abortion as a "necessary evil" rather than a right. In this regard, abortion has not achieved the status of a liberal, much less a radical, demand. Thus Betty Friedan believes she speaks for masses of women when she compares abortion to mastectomy, rather than to, say, education or a living wage.[37]

If abortion is to be understood as a "social right"—a necessary service that society ought to make available to all women—and not just an individual right, much less a fatality or a duty, it must be connected to women's social power. There is a basis for making this connection in popular consciousness by relating the "morality" of abortion to the "morality"—and power—of motherhood as a social practice.

Maternal Practice and Reproductive Consciousness

It is frequently overlooked or dismissed in the debate about the "morality" of abortion that the corollary of "fetal personhood" is forced motherhood. For all the antiabortionists' insistence that the fetus is biologically distinct from the woman and not part of her body, the fact remains that human embryos and infants are completely dependent on a primary caretaker, who in most cultures is the biological mother. The fetus has no resources to take care of itself; indeed, its condition of dependence, as mediated by the pregnant woman's consciousness, illustrates that human biology is always determined in part by social experience. Thus, if the fetus has an automatic and absolute right not to be killed, this implies that "it also has a right to be nurtured by the pregnant woman and raised by her"—a fact that irrevocably changes the course of a woman's life.[38]

Maternity, if chosen, is not servitude; it is in many ways pleasant and satisfying, socially as well as personally. But it is at the same time a *service* that every childbearing woman performs for others, whatever her personal stakes in the matter. Moreover, it is a service that requires an irreducible physical burden: the renunciation of bodily health and well-being for many months, perhaps with permanent physical consequences—a demand that under any circumstances other than criminal punishment is seen as absolutely necessitating the person's voluntary consent.[39] On this ground alone—the consequences of pregnancy and childbirth for a woman's own body and health—her autonomy in regard to the abortion decision is justified. This is the core of what I have identified as the "feminist" basis for abortion. But in popular consciousness the "social consequences" rationale may hold greater sway than this feminist principle at the present time. That is the notion that, as long as women are assigned the major burdens and tasks of children's care, then women must retain control over the terms and conditions of their birth. There is a long-standing tradition of female, if not feminist, outrage at male claims to know better than they the "duties of motherhood." Echoing the nineteenth-century proponents of "voluntary motherhood," many women today would probably agree that the morality of abortion is women's business, a kind of knowledge they can lay claim to by virtue of their knowledge of motherhood:

> There is nothing moral about giving birth to children we cannot feed and care for. *Forced* sterilization and genocide aren't the same thing as *choosing* to have an abortion. . . . It is precisely because women take lives sacredly—our own as well as our children's—that some of us choose not to bring into the world those we cannot take care of.[40]

Speaking out of a similar urge to defend women's moral integrity, eighteen hundred nuns publicly dissociated themselves from the church's position on abortion, declaring: "While we continue to oppose abortion, in principle and in practice, we are likewise convinced that the responsibility for decisions in this regard resides primarily with those who are directly and personally involved."[41] Noting the irony "that the same leaders who are currently demanding that women bring their babies to term are simultaneously voting to cut off food stamps, child nutrition programs and related benefits essential for the health and well-being of our children," these nuns put themselves on the side of all women who ground "woman's choice" in the social realities of children's care.

From a more theoretical perspective, feminist philosophers have begun to explore a concept of motherhood that links women's consciousness about mothering to the actual knowledge they acquire through practice. It is a concept that restores the centrality of women's consciousness to decisions about all dimensions of reproductive activity, including abortion and birth control. Sara Ruddick explains "maternal thinking" as a "discipline" and a "conception of achievement," involving a coherent logic and particular skills.[42] "Maternal practices," from this perspective, correspond to certain conscious "demands" and "interests," like any science or art, and have specific standards, particularly an attentiveness to "the real situation," or "the real children" and their needs, rather than some abstract set of rules or extrinsic goals.[43] This concept of motherhood is explicitly not a biological one; it focuses on the social and the practical dimensions of maternal activity that arise out of women's gender-specific socialization. Motherhood, or nurturance, is here seen in its *human* form, not as an "instinct" but as a craft, a set of traditions and skills that are both learned and transferable. (The implication is, of course, that, given a different socialization, men too could acquire these skills.)[44]

Ruddick's concept of maternal thinking provides one philosophical basis, aligned with the felt understandings of many women who do mother or think about mothering, for defending women's control over the abortion decision. The point is not that women's attentiveness to "real situations" is automatic or that their maternal practices never fail to measure up to the standards of their discipline.[45] Authentic maternal thought is not applied scrupulously in all cases. Nevertheless, it exists as a standard and is frequently present in women's reproductive practices. With respect to abortion, there is reason to believe that, not an "innate" sense of morality, but their social positioning as mothers or potential mothers creates in most women deciding on abortion a sense of moral care. Gilligan found a strong sensitivity to conflict and moral ambiguity among the abortion patients she interviewed. She uses the example of abortion decision making to argue that the cultural gender division that roots women's perceptions and judgments more deeply than men's in "contextual" and "relational" concerns may result in "a different social and moral understanding."[46] Women's traditional "concern about hurting others," about the immediate interpersonal and social context, is not necessarily a "lower" stage of moral development than a morality that equates goodness with abstract laws or with "universal ethical principles." Indeed, women's tendency to fix on real problems and particular needs in deliberating moral questions may be a model for a kind of moral decision making that is more humane, more attentive to people's well-being and less to their "goodness."[47]

But there is a real danger for feminism in a position that rests women's claim to autonomy over abortion decisions on their maternal thinking. To defend women *as* mothers or reproducers inevitably risks perpetuating the patriarchal ideology and institution of motherhood as exclusively woman's "sphere," romanticizing or idealizing maternity. That is not what I am advocating. Rather, it is a social principle that says control over decisions ought to be exercised by those whose work and concern have been most consistently involved in the activity in question. We may find an analogy in the application by a few courts of a "primary caretaker presumption" in resolving child custody disputes. This principle assigns custody on the basis of which parent has provided daily nurturance and care—prepared meals, attended to medical and clothing needs, helped with homework, consoled, and so on. As we would expect, that parent is still generally the mother, but there is no reason why the principle should reinforce a traditional gender division of labor. Its thrust could be to encourage fathers to enter more actively into the routine caretaking of their children, since not doing so would assure their loss of custody in the event of a dispute.[48]

In the case of abortion, the "social reality" principle ought to leave wide latitude for greater involvement of men than currently exists in responsibility for birth control and reproduction. At the same time, as I have argued, the work and service of a woman's body in pregnancy put her in a special situation regarding abortion that can never be "equally shared." Feminist theory must develop a concept of equality in which special needs are recognized yet not allowed to become the pretext for social liabilities. In this respect, women's right to autonomy over abortion is similar to the right of disabled persons to barrier-free public spaces; it is a necessary condition of their equality.

A feminist morality of abortion adapts to historical and personal circumstances. In a predominantly patriarchal culture, its point of departure is the lived experience of women as those charged with the bearing and raising of children. This reality constructs a "female consciousness" that connects women's "right to choose" to their "duty," and practical capacity, to engage in maternal work. But a feminist approach to abortion must contain within it the possibility of transcending and transforming the existing sexual division of labor, *at the same time as* it recognizes women's specific situation in reproduction. Ultimately, this means rejecting "maternal thinking" as a gender-specific practice while persistently defending abortion as a gender-specific need.

Liberals give many utilitarian reasons for making abortion a matter of women's individual choice, including the unenforceability of criminal sanctions; the need to limit poverty, population, child abuse, and birth defects; and the idea that the law should not intrude on individual behavior that causes no "social harm."[49] The reason for feminists, however, has to do with none of these things but with the essentially moral question whether women are to be allowed "authenticity," the power to act with moral freedom, to listen to one's own voice. I suggested in the Introduction that reproductive freedom is not so much a "right" in the abstract juridical sense as it is a basic human need, a need that is indispensable to being a person. The compression of abortion into "privacy rights" obscures this larger issue, implying a negative or exclusionary principle and the analogy of one's body to bourgeois property. To be sure, the right to be free from unwanted or forced invasions of one's body for the purposes of others is an essential component of the need for "control over one's body" and for personhood. The repugnance of rape, torture, forced sterilization, or other involuntary medical intervention makes that very clear.[50] But the need goes far beyond one of "self-defense" or proprietary claims, and it even goes beyond "the body."

Control over one's body—including, for women, control over whether, when, and in what circumstances they shall bear children—is not just a libertarian "right" (i.e., a private space in which I am free to maneuver so long as I do no other person any harm). It is, rather, a positive and necessary enabling condition for full human participation in social and communal life. The principle of "control over one's body" raises the fundamental issue of the relationship between the body and the self: whether the self (the "person") shall be defined as a disembodied, asexual soul belonging only to God or a bundle of self-replicating genetic information—or rather as a *consciousness* that is *embodied,* with its own sensate needs, desires, and history. As such, it establishes a compelling moral claim, insofar as one's self and one's body are not separable. If things can be done to my body and its processes over which I have no control, this undermines my sense of integrity as a responsible human being and my ability to act responsibly in regard to others. Sometimes such loss of control is unavoidable, as in the case of chronic debilitating disease. But when it is inflicted on another by human will, it can only be understood as a *punishment.* As long as there is any possibility that I might get pregnant against my will, for whatever reasons, then the denial of access to safe abortion must indeed be regarded as a form of punishment analogous to involuntary servitude; there is no other way to read it.[51]

The attempt to discredit women's capacity to make moral judgments about abortion is part of a much broader attack on the terms of moral discourse that feminism (along with other radical and left-wing social movements) represents. That discourse surfaces in ordinary people's attention to the realities of their situation and to the full range of conflicting human needs that claim their responsibility and their love. Right-wing polemics against "secular humanism" reflect an awareness (a hostile one) of this alternative, subterranean morality. Abortion is wrong, in their view, not only because it "destroys innocent life," but even more because it rests on and validates a principle of morality that assumes that individuals must make choices for themselves and ought to do so in terms of the concrete situations in which they live. According to "prolife" ideology, whatever a woman's family and sexual relationships, whatever her age or marital or economic condition, whatever the state of her health or that of the fetus, and whatever the society has (or has not) provided in the way of child care and related benefits, abortion is taboo. Yet these are precisely the conditions that most directly impinge on the meaning of childbearing in the lives of women, who are still the ones mainly responsible for children after they are born. And it is these conditions that, in the last analysis, construct the practical morality, as well as the practice, of abortion.

I am saying, then, that on a fundamental philosophical level, women's "choice" or control over reproduction *is* the central issue in the political controversy over abortion. It is an issue, however, not of women as private individuals, but of women as a collectivity, whose common needs, social-sexual position, and consciousness are organized around the relations and tasks of reproduction.[52] For it is women collectively whose competence to make moral judgments is maligned and whose sexual and maternal practices are circumscribed by and through the state. Women collectively, through an organized feminist movement, have to meet this challenge.

NOTES

1. See Mary O'Brien, *The Politics of Reproduction* (London: Routledge and Kegan Paul, 1981), pp. 50, 189–90.

2. Floya Anthias and Nira Yuval-Davis, "Contextualizing Feminism—Gender, Ethnic and Class Divisions," forthcoming in *Feminist Review* (Fall 1983).

3. Manier, "Abortion and Public Policy in the U.S.," in *Abortion: New Directions for Policy Studies*, ed. Manier, Liu, and Solomon, pp. 19, 22.

4. Jaffe, Lindheim, and Lee, *Abortion Politics*, p. 101; see also Granberg and Granberg, "Abortion Attitudes, 1965–1980." The Granbergs offer an overview of opinion poll data, concluding: "Polls suggest that most Americans cannot be characterized as antiabortion or proabortion. The majority, apparently, believe that abortion should be available under a variety of circumstances, and very few would prohibit it in all cases. People's attitudes, however, tend to be complex and ambivalent" (pp. 251–52).

5. "Abortion: Women Speak Out," *Life* 4 (Nov. 1981), pp. 45–48.

6. Jaffe, Lindheim, and Lee summarize the recent data on Catholic attitudes toward abortion, from which they conclude that "the majority of Catholics increasingly both support the availability of legal abortion and voice a willingness—under certain conditions—to avail themselves of that option" (p. 106).

7. Malcolm Potts, Peter Diggory and John Peel, *Abortion* (Cambridge, England: Cambridge University Press, 1977), pp. 119, 121.

8. Kathleen Kerr, "Study: Teens Mum on Abortion," *Newsday*, 8 January 1981, reporting on a study of 1,100 patients in clinics run by Bill Baird in Boston and Long Island.

9. Ilene S. Hauck and Nancy Talbot, "Alone and Afraid: The Dilemma of Catholic Abortion," *Equal Times*, 14 August 1978, p. 10.

10. Gilligan, *In a Different Voice*, p. 86.

11. The ground-breaking thought of Sarah Eisenstein on working women's consciousness was in process of development at her untimely death in 1978. I first thought about the problems of consciousness through talking with Sarah and reading her early essays "Bread and Roses: Working Women's Consciousness, 1905–1920" and "Working Women's Consciousness in the U.S., 1890–W. W. I" (dissertation proposal, 1976). These essays and other parts of Sarah's work, along with an introduction and explanatory appendix by Harold Benenson, are contained in her posthumous book, *Bread and Roses: Working Women's Consciousness in the United States, 1890 to World War I* (London: Routledge and Kegan Paul, 1983).

12. The observations that follow are based on my composite study of published surveys and interviews, particularly those by Gilligan, Luker, Zimmerman, and Freeman. See also Howe, Kaplan, and English, "Repeat Abortions . . . "; Henry P. David, "Psychosocial Studies of Abortion in the United States," in *Abortion in Psychosocial Perspective*, ed. Henry P. David et al. (New York: Springer, 1978), pp. 77–115; and Linda Bird Francke, *The Ambivalence of Abortion* (New York: Random House, 1978).

13. See esp. Zimmerman, *Passage through Abortion*, pp. 181–84, 110.

14. Freeman, "Abortion: Subjective Attitudes and Feelings," *Family Planning Perspectives* 10, p. 153.

15. Zimmerman, pp. 10, 63–64. Cf. Ladner, *Tomorrow's Tomorrow*, p. 258.

16. "In Memoriam," editorial, *New York Times*, 30 May 1982, p. 14E; emphasis added. The subject of the editorial was a planned "memorial service" in Los Angeles for 17,000 aborted fetuses.

17. These observations are based on discussions with several persons who have done abortion counseling.

18. Zimmerman, p. 185.

19. One psychiatric case study of black and Hispanic "repeat" abortion patients at Kings County Hospital in Brooklyn reveals that some of the women had come to New York as economic migrants from the Caribbean and had had to leave their children behind. One reported feeling depressed because she could not afford care for her present child, although she wanted another child. Nearly all had experienced heavy pressure from male partners, desiring proof of their "manhood," to "bear them" a child, and at the same time faced the severe economic constraints oppressing black and migrant women. See Michael Blumenfeld, "Psychological Factors Involved in Request for Elective Abortion," *Journal of Clinical Psychiatry* 39 (January 1978): 17–19, 23–25.

20. Quoted in Gilligan, p. 77.

21. Ibid., p. 78.

22. See Moore and Waite, "Early Childbearing and Educational Attainment," *Family Planning Perspectives* 9, pp. 220–225; Wendy Baldwin and Virginia S. Cain, "The Children of Teenage Parents," *Family Planning Perspectives* 12 (January/February 1980): 34–43; and Chapter 4 in this volume. Baldwin and Cain argue that, while the association between early childbearing and low birth-weight babies is mainly the result of poor prenatal care, other "deficits" (cognitive, emotional, economic) accrue to the children of teenage women due to the "context of childrearing." For another view, see D. Rothenberg et al., "Relationship between Age of Mother and Child Health and Development," *American Journal of Public Health* 71 (August 1981): 810–17. They conclude that "when relevant background characteristics are controlled, children of teenage mothers are as healthy and develop as well as children of older mothers."

23. Zimmerman, pp. 123–24, 140.

24. Gilligan, p. 103.

25. Zimmerman, pp. 192–193.

26. Gilligan, p. 85.

27. *On Liberty* (New York: Dutton, 1951), p. 216.

28. Zimmerman, p. 139.

29. "I can't afford to have a baby right now, so I had to terminate it. . . . But I think it's murder. It's part of you; it's like a child." Quoted in Leslie Bennetts, "In an Abortion Clinic: Ambivalence, Guilt and Relief," *New York Times*, 27 March 1981, p. B4. This young woman had just had an abortion. In a recent set of televised interviews, however, a couple who had been persuaded by "right-to-life" views and decided to have the baby and put it up for adoption expressed much the same feeling; being "financially sound" was the prerequisite for raising a child. "Abortion Clinic," *Frontline*, Public Broadcasting System and Public Television Stations, 18 April 1983.

30. See Temma Kaplan, "Female Consciousness and Collective Action: The Case of Barcelona, 1910–1918," *Signs* 7 (Spring 1982): 545–66. This article is an

elaboration of the distinction between "female" and "feminist" consciousness and an interesting historical case study.

31. I was helped very much in thinking about this question by a discussion with Liz Ewen and Roz Baxandall.

32. Steinhoff, "Premarital Pregnancy and the First Birth," in *The First Child and Family Formation,* ed. Miller and Newman, p. 187.

33. Gilligan, pp. 94–95.

34. See, for example, Daniel Yankelovich, "New Rules in American Life: Searching for Self-Fulfillment in a World Turned Upside Down," *Psychology Today* 15 (April 1981): 36, 46, 50. Yankelovich traces "the strange moral principle that 'I have a duty to myself' " to the baneful influence of the 1960s and its preoccupation with "inner psychological needs." See also, on the right, Schaeffer and Koop, *Whatever Happened to the Human Race?*, and, on the left, Christopher Lasch, *Haven in a Heartless World* (New York: Basic Books, 1977).

35. Cf. the discussion in Zillah Eisenstein, *The Radical Future of Liberal Feminism.* She calls for "a feminist individualism that recognizes the necessity of independence and autonomy within women's (and men's) lives" (p. 191).

36. Jane Collier, Michelle Z. Rosaldo, and Sylvia Yanagisako, "Is There a Family? New Anthropological Views," in *Rethinking the Family,* ed. Thorne, p. 37.

37. Betty Friedan, "Feminism's Next Step," *New York Times Magazine,* 5 July 1981, p. 15. Friedan admonishes feminists to take the sex out of sexual politics, to cool it on issues such as abortion and homosexuality, which she sees as "inflammable" and connoting "permissiveness." In so doing, she certainly takes a giant step toward "neoconservative feminism." See Zillah Eisenstein's critique in her forthcoming book, *Feminism and Sexual Equality: The Crisis of Liberal America.*

38. Martha Brandt Bolton, "Responsible Women and Abortion Decisions," in *Having Children: Philosophical and Legal Reflections on Parenthood,* ed. Nora O'Neill and William Ruddick (New York: Oxford University Press, 1979), p. 42. See also Jaggar, "Abortion and a Woman's Right to Decide," in *Women and Philosophy,* ed. Gould and Wartofsky, for a similar argument.

39. See Donald H. Regan, "Rewriting *Roe* v. *Wade,"* *Michigan Law Review* 77 (August 1979), pp. 1579–1581, for a chilling summary of the clinical picture.

40. Campbell, "Abortion: The New Facts of Life," *Essence* 12, p. 129.

41. "Nuns' Group Opposes Abortion Strategy of Bishops," *New York Times,* 28 May 1982, p. A28.

42. Ruddick, "Maternal Thinking," in *Rethinking the Family,* ed. Thorne, p. 77.

43. Ibid., pp. 82, 87.

44. Ibid., p. 89. A comprehensive and useful feminist critique of biological and psychological theories of "maternal instinct" is in Chodorow, *The Reproduction of Mothering,* pp. 17–28. Chodorow's own analysis of the reproduction of gender in childrearing is less attentive to cross-cultural, and certainly to historical, variations than it might be. One could compare, for example, the rural black women in southern Florida whom Dougherty talked to, among whom biological mystification of motherhood seemed nonexistent. There, motherhood is clearly seen as an achieved status and a learned authority, not an instinct. If younger women do not prove their mettle or concern for their children, the older women of the

community take over. See Dougherty, *Becoming a Woman in Rural Black Culture*, p. 103.

45. Ruddick, p. 84.

46. Gilligan, pp. 17–18, 73.

47. An argument of this sort is made by Jean Bethke Elshtain, "Antigone's Daughters," *Democracy* 2 (April 1982): 46–59.

48. See Polikoff, "Why Are Mothers Losing?" *Women's Rights Law Reporter* 7, pp. 241–42.

49. See, e.g., Callahan, *Abortion: Law, Choice, and Morality*, pp. 473–75; and Bolton, pp. 43–44.

50. Cf. Willis, p. 208; Hubbard, "Legal and Policy Implications . . . ," pp. 216–217 and n. 59; Judith Jarvis Thomson, "A Defense of Abortion," in *The Rights and Wrongs of Abortion*, ed. M. Cohen, T. Nagel, and T. Scanlon (Princeton: Princeton University Press, 1974), pp. 8–22; and Jeffrey H. Reiman, "Privacy, Intimacy and Personhood," in *Today's Moral Problems*, ed. Richard A. Wasserstrom (New York: Macmillan, 1979), p. 380. Each presents a variation of the argument that a woman's body is her "property" and cannot be invaded without her consent.

51. Steinfels ("The Search for an Alternative," *Commonweal* 108) is very straightforward about admitting that the consequence of his proposal to make all abortions illegal after the first eight weeks would result in involuntary maternity: " 'Would you then use the law to *force* a woman to carry through a pregnancy to term?' That is the challenge liberal Catholics must be willing to face if they are to make any difference at all in the moral controversy. Their answer will have to [be] 'Yes.' Not for every pregnancy . . . but for many pregnancies, yes" (p. 662).

52. The idea of women as a reproductive collectivity is developed in O'Brien, esp. Chap. 6.

Conclusion: The Feminist Movement and the Conditions of Reproductive Freedom

> The right to have or not have children; the right to have both children and a selfhood not dependent on them; these are still being fought for, and this fight threatens every part of the patriarchal system. We cannot afford to settle for individual solutions. The myth that motherhood is "private and personal" is the deadliest myth we have to destroy, and we have to begin by destroying it in ourselves.
>
> ADRIENNE RICH, *On Lies, Secrets, and Silence*

There are no individual solutions to the dilemmas posed by reproductive politics because "choices" are not merely the product of self-motivated desires but depend on conditions existing in the society. The ultimate dilemma for those who seek to enhance reproductive and sexual freedom is how to create a sense of collective purpose—of feminist and social solutions—concerning matters that seem so intrinsically personal and private. Since 1970, feminist activism and the right-wing reaction against it have succeeded in deprivatizing the abortion issue and have brought it squarely within the arena of political discourse. Moreover, the practical content of feminist abortion politics has implied social solutions. To demand that the state provide uniform, funded, and high-quality abortion services to all women has been to acknowledge that abortion should be a matter of public responsibility and not of "private choice" alone.

Yet feminist thinking about abortion continues to reflect two assumptions that obscure the ways in which abortion is a basic need of women, which is different from either a "necessity" (unchosen) or a "choice" (unnecessary). These dubious assumptions are, first, that abortion is a "necessary evil" that, with changing conditions, will disappear; and, second, that the freedom to have children and the freedom not to have them are equivalent "rights." In what follows, I offer a critical view of both assumptions. I then consider areas of future practice for feminists concerned with translating reproductive "choices" into social and cultural realities.

1. *The need for abortion will not disappear.* In writing a book about abortion, it was not my intention to inflate its significance. Abortion in itself does not create reproductive freedom. It only makes the burdensome and fatalistic aspects of women's responsibility for pregnancy less total. It does not socialize that responsibility, empower a woman in her relations with men or society, or assure her of a liberated sexuality. It only allows her the space to move from one point in her life to the next, if she is a heterosexual woman; to navigate some of the more oppressive patriarchal and institutional forces that are beyond her control. Abortion is but one of many social conditions that encompass women's education, employment, health, reproductive choice, and economic and sexual self-determination. As such, it is both minimal and indispensable.

Yet, since the late 1970s, a negative view of abortion seems to have penetrated the feminist movement as well as the dominant culture. Typically, it takes this form: "Of course, nobody likes abortion; we just think there should be a choice." Sometimes this defensiveness grows out of a pragmatic concern to win a broad base of support. Even committed feminists in the movement for reproductive rights lament that abortion is "a hard issue to organize people about," one that fails to uplift people's spirits or generate joyful, proud symbols (the coathanger is seen as a "last resort"). Sometimes feminist ideas themselves absorb and reflect cultural forces that project abortion as a "necessary evil." Thus Adrienne Rich wrote in the mid-1970s: "No free woman, with 100 percent effective, nonharmful birth control readily available, would 'choose' abortion"; and "abortion is violence: a deep, desperate violence inflicted by a woman upon, first of all, herself."[1]

The basis of this victimizing, victim-blaming position is a perspective that reduces women's condition universally to "male violence." It is also a strain of feminist tradition that idealizes motherhood, implying that the termination of every unwanted pregnancy is somehow a tragedy. Whatever its intention, this view does not accord with the facts. Many, perhaps most, abortions performed today (and, as far as we can tell, through much of history) are not the product of "grim, driven desperation," as Rich calls it, but of women's sober determination to take hold of their lives and, sometimes, of a sense of enlarged power for being able to do so. That abortion may be painful or unpleasant does not make it "violence against oneself" any more than a painful divorce or a mastectomy is "violence against oneself." My point is not to deny that abortion often involves pain in the experience of individual women, but to understand that experience in social terms.

Nor can we expect that "in a society where women entered sexual intercourse willingly, where adequate contraception was a genuine social priority, there would be no 'abortion issue.' "[2] This echoes the view of nineteenth-century feminists that abortion will be "unnecessary in a future world of egalitarian respect and sexual discretion."[3] For the reasons discussed in Chapter 5, we cannot assume that there will ever be a "100 percent effective, nonharmful" contraceptive in a human (not merely a technical) sense. While the terms of the need for abortion will change as technology and social conditions change, the "abortion issue" will not go away.

The view of abortion as a necessary evil born out of desperate circumstances is a liberal accommodation to recent waves of antiabortion (and antifeminist) ideology. It is a clearly mistaken view, since the conditions underlying rising abortion rates in the 1970s and 1980s have on the whole involved a greater expansion of women's relative power in American society than at any other time. Indeed, the historical material presented in this book seems to suggest a rough hypothesis: The easing of women's access to birth control and abortion (which are positively related) coincides with periods of their increased social power and status; while restrictions on that access usually indicate a broad-scale attack on women's sexual and social autonomy and on feminist movements.

The "necessary evil" concept oddly forgets the spirit of buoyancy infusing not only feminists but masses of women after *Roe* v. *Wade*. Suddenly the years of terror, of silently fearing pregnancy, of sneaking off to possible sterility or death, and of sex ridden with shame were with a few judicial words going to end. It was a naive faith, for the last several years have shown that deep-rooted ideology and noncompliant administrative and clinical practices were too powerful for a Supreme Court ruling to reverse. The buoyancy was there nonetheless because abortion—easily available, cheap, administered under safe, hygienic conditions early in a pregnancy and in an ambience free of stigma and guilt—*is* a component (not just a condition) of women's liberation. What makes abortion "awful" is the shame and guilt caused by two heavily ideological notions that all women in the society still learn to some degree: (1) the association of fetus with "baby" and the aborting woman with "bad mother," and (2) the assumption that sex for pleasure is "wrong" (for women) and that women who indulge in it have to pay a price. Leaving aside these timeworn misogynist ideas, the circumstances in which abortion occasions misery and suffering are (1) when it is delayed or illegal and results in serious medical complications; or (2) when a pregnancy and child are desired, but social or economic conditions weigh against it. Under the second set of circumstances and most of the first, the surrounding *condi-*

tions—those that prevent people from having wished-for children securely or from having abortions safely—are tragic and impede freedom, not the abortion itself. Along with a heterosexist culture in which a woman feels she must "prove her adequacy as a woman by getting pregnant" or "look for economic security to a man, getting pregnant as a by-product,"[4] these are the conditions that a movement for reproductive freedom must seek to transform.

Rather than apologize for abortion, feminists must proclaim loudly— as they did in the late 1960s and early 1970s—that access to safe, funded abortion is a *positive social need* of all women of childbearing age. Abortion is a necessary, though far from sufficient, condition of women's essential right and need, not only for bodily health and self-determination, but also for control over their work, their sexuality, and their relations with others—including existing children. From this perspective, abortion conducted under safe, affordable, and stigma-free conditions is neither a necessary evil nor a matter of private choice. Rather, it is a positive benefit that society has an obligation to provide to all who seek it, just as it provides education and health benefits. Put another way, abortion is not simply an "individual right" (civil liberty) or even a "welfare right" (for those "in need") but a "social right."[5]

What does it mean to talk about abortion as a social right or, more accurately, a social need? First, it means that *access* to abortion (as distinct from the actual experience) is necessary to women's well-being and self-determination; therefore, it is closer to a "necessary good" than a "necessary evil," whatever discomfort it may entail. The farther a society moves toward transforming the oppressive socioeconomic and cultural conditions that encumber the meaning/experience of abortion, the more will abortion become a genuine tool of freedom rather than an occasion of misery. In this regard, it is similar to work or divorce. Second, it means that the need for abortion is universal in the sense that its availability is essential to *all* women, for it defines the terms and conditions of "womanhood" in the society; and it is specific in the sense that the need grows out of a particular set of problems. Not being able to get an abortion when she needs it presents a woman with irrevocable consequences for her sexuality, her body, and her relation to maternity. These are very different consequences from those confronted by a woman whose *desire* for children is thwarted by economic, political, or biological circumstances.

2. *The "right to have children" and the "right not to have them" are not equivalent rights.* An expansive view of the conditions of reproductive choice has typified the feminist movement for reproductive rights that emerged in the 1970s. Many feminists have understood reproductive freedom as involving much more than access to safe, legal abortion. The Committee for Abortion Rights and Against Sterilization Abuse (CARASA), for example, was formed in 1977 in New York with the idea that the "right to

have children," as well as the right to avoid pregnancy, was essential to women's control over reproduction. It recognized that access to abortion services was the chief problem for some women, but for others, particularly for women of color or handicapped women, state policies to restrict their childbearing could be more pressing. Thus CARASA's organizational principles spelled out the conditions of reproductive freedom in the broadest terms: "No category of women—poor, young, handicapped—should be excluded from reproductive freedom. To really have that freedom, we require: abortion services for all women, regardless of income; safe, well designed birth control; sex education in the schools; good and accessible pre- and post-natal and maternal health care; and the right to conduct our sex lives as we wish and with dignity." CARASA also called for basic economic and social changes: equal wages for women, decent housing, adequate welfare benefits, reliable child care and good schools, an end to toxic environments that threaten fertility, and an end to government-sponsored sterilization abuse.[6]

This perspective usefully shifted the focus of abortion debate from individual (moral) choice to social need. But in order to assimilate what were thought to be the different reproductive needs of different groups of women within a common conceptual framework, it assumed a mistaken symmetry between "the right to have children" and "the right" (as it was ineptly called) "not to have them." It never questioned whether these two dimensions of reproductive politics and life-activity do not involve qualitatively distinct problems. Nevertheless, not only are the conditions of reproductive freedom different in each case, but whatever we mean by "freedom," its exercise and the limits on it, is different when we consider "having children" and when we consider women's specific need to control the conditions and timing of childbearing. To construct a false equation between them suggests a market model of "reproductive rights" in which "choices" are a grab bag of discrete personal desires (get pregnant, do not get pregnant, have children, do not have children, choose a method of birth control, choose a partner, etc.). All that a *politics* of reproduction is concerned with, in this view, is allowing individuals to "maximize" their desires. What is missing from this essentially libertarian (or utilitarian) picture is an awareness that different reproductive strategies have different social meanings and consequences.

As I have demonstrated, the compulsory pregnancy and childbearing that the denial of abortion implies is incompatible with the existence of women as moral agents and social beings. Access to safe abortion is a fundamental need of women as persons, and circumstances justifying an exception are difficult to imagine. The desire to have a child represents a different kind of claim. Having and raising children is a fundamental dimension of *human*—as opposed to gender-specific—fulfillment and social life, one that a just society must support for all those who wish to have children. But this desire is frequently complicated by conflicting social needs, which any society must also accommodate. One is the need of a woman to have control over pregnancy, which may conflict with her partner's (sincere, legitimate) desire to procreate. On a deep cultural level, it is this conflict (between Woman as Person and Man as Father) that the current abortion crisis is about.

Another source of social conflict in the freedom of individuals to have children, quite apart from the need of women to have control over their fertility, is the existence of real children, who have separate needs from parents. The principle that society has an obligation to provide its children with not only the best possible health care, education, housing, and nutrition but also with protection from abuse may justify public intervention in parents' "rights" over their children. Perhaps this may even be true of policies, applied universally without race, class, or gender bias, that limit the number of children per family or individual. Sociologist Alva Myrdal urged in 1941 "that Sweden's social policy be predicated on 'the desire to safeguard for all children, born and unborn, what are now average environmental conditions for children with regard to housing, food, medical attention, schooling, and so forth. Such a policy has strong moorings in our predilection for greater social justice. If the nation's resources or the social ingenuity for redistribution cannot ensure such average conditions for all children, no additional children should be sought.' "[7]

There are, however, difficulties in reconciling society's obligation to support people's desire to have children—their procreative freedom—with its responsibility to provide resources for those children. Where the state and family are still predominantly patriarchal and women have little power in formulating national policy, the practical application of childbearing restrictions may be coercive and discriminatory.[8] Yet, even if we lived in a society where gender as well as class and racial equality had been achieved, a *politics* of reproduction would still exist, in the tension between "social right" as defined by those in power and the desires of individuals. Should we encourage (as indeed the "right-to-life" movement does) a young teenager without resources or education to have and raise a baby because she "wants someone to love"? Should an alcoholic or drug-addicted woman be allowed to carry her pregnancy to term "in privacy," as her "lifestyle" dictates? Social policies that would impose a nondiscriminatory, nonpunitive, temporary pregnancy leave or transfer in reproductively hazardous workplaces; or policies that would provide pregnant women with good nutrition, regular prenatal checkups, and use of fetosafe drugs—these are policies that might reasonably supersede "individual choice." Such "protective" measures would not pit the fetus against the pregnant woman, who *has* chosen to have a child. Rather, they would impose a standard of good nurturance in behalf of a new generation's chances for the best possible life.

I shall be accused of grave contradictions. After all, didn't I argue strongly against the denial of women's moral judgment in such matters, the importance of the "right to choose"? The political context makes all the difference. In a society where women collectively, and especially women of color and the poor, are still essentially powerless, even the most benign protections seem susceptible to abuse; we are understandably cautious about them. What I am saying is that the tension between individuals' desires to have children and raise them "freely" (I assume that wanting them means wanting to raise them) and the establishment of social standards and resources for children's welfare is not merely a product of a sexist and racist power structure. Even in a society built on socialist-feminist principles and practices, some of that tension would remain. Moreover, the principles on which we negotiate the tension are not the same when it is a question of a woman's desire *not* to have a child.

But we are far from such a society today. Before we can consider giving up the principle of women's autonomy over reproduction, a number of fundamental changes will have to take place. The immediate problem for feminists seeking to create reproductive freedom is to fight for the conditions of equality; to remove the political, institutional, and cultural obstacles to realizing a social concept of women's reproductive needs. As long as a right-wing government is in power and the legitimacy of the state's obligation to provide social welfare is in question, feminist activities to secure reproductive freedom will invariably be defensive (e.g., struggling to maintain legal abortion rather than expanding the availability and quality of abortion services), and individual women will necessarily defend their "private choice." Beyond the New Right and Reaganism, however, a feminist program of transformation toward reproductive freedom will carry a weighty agenda.

Creating equality of conditions for reproductive choice means, first, a wide range of social supports that will make having and raising children, or not doing so, a real alternative for *all* people: high-quality, publicly funded health, maternal, and child care; the elimination of reproductively hazardous environments; and the provision of adequate jobs, incomes, housing, and education. Above all, changes in the social arrangements of child care and reproductive decision making will have to be accompanied by basic changes in the sexual division of labor in the economy and the state. As long as women work in segregated jobs, for low pay and with subordinate status, and must negotiate a political system controlled by men, there can be no "equality" in reproduction.

Second, the conditions of reproductive freedom will have to include cultural as well as socioeconomic changes, specifically changes in the social and sexual relations of reproduction. The feminist idea of sharing responsibility with men for sexuality, birth control, and child care must be fused with the socialist idea that society bears collective responsibility for the well-being and futures of children; and this ideological synthesis must be put into practice on a national scale. Unlike capitalism, under socialist transformation there is a normative basis for maintaining the principle of collective (transgender) responsibility in the activity of reproduction and childrearing, as in everything else. The historical fact that in socialist societies birth control and child care remain women's domain should not be taken as evidence of an inherent incompatibility between socialism and women's liberation but should be seen as one dimension (among others) in which a full socialist revolution has failed to occur.

To implement shared parenting in a gender-neutral way involves changes in consciousness and values as well as changes in public policy. "Maternal practices" will have to become contributions that men as well as women not only value but achieve. Such changes go way beyond legal reforms such as parental leave benefits, flex-time, child-care centers staffed by men and women, and the like. They require a revolutionary commitment to a cultural revolution that will take hold of families, schools, the media, and ordinary ways of life, even among those in power. The meanings of sex as well as gender will be called into play in such a revolution. Not only the standards of nurturance and who shall provide it are at stake but the socially sanctioned expressions of desire. In particular, we shall need to develop a set of standards and practices for a revolutionary "sex education." What should be its goals? What new kinds of knowledge, social more than technical, should it generate? How is the sexuality of teenagers to be allowed space while its specific needs are respected? These questions, which are distinct from questions about gender equality, have barely begun to be asked from a feminist perspective. Nor does the introduction of social reforms (including child care, birth control, and abortion services) guarantee that they will be.

Even during the most liberal years of teenage access to abortion and contraception, the potentially liberating impact of that access was muffled by the persistence of a male-dominant culture and social relations of sex. The openness and legitimacy of nonmarital heterosexual activity continued to be encumbered with traditional risks and pain for young teenage women, insofar as they played for different stakes (commitment, love, romance) than males, and often lost. A clear feminist vision, an alternative culture of sexuality embracing passion and play as well as love, has not penetrated the consciousness of younger generations; indeed, for heterosexual women, it has not even been articulated. While a lesbian subculture has flourished, the cultural forms—the stories, plays, songs, novels— feminists have created during the past ten years that might have spoken to younger heterosexual women about a different vision of sex and relations with men have mainly revealed women's anger over what now exists as "love and romance." Yet, as Alexandra Kollontai understood, a revolution in women's social place and in the relations of reproduction is impossible without a "new morality" of sex and love.[9] I do not know what the content of that morality is, except that it must integrate a broad, ecumenical acceptance of multiple forms of pleasure with the principle of respect for another's body and well-being (which is not necessarily the same as accommodating *any* of another's desires). We have responsibilities to others in sexual relationships, as well as our own desires and needs. We must know much more than this, however, before we can teach a "new morality," a feminist morality, to the young.

Within such a culturally and socially transformed setting, reproductive choices will still occur within institutional frameworks. These institutions—above all, the health-care system—must also undergo sweeping and specific changes before reproductive freedom for all women can exist. Institutionalized reproductive services and their political settings, even at their most expansive, have been monopolized by medical and family planning professionals whose concept of "social need" has often been different from that of feminists or women as reproductive health consumers. To defeat the policies of the New Right simply to reinstall a family planning bureaucracy whose priorities are population control and "medically effective" but hazardous contraceptive techniques would be a small victory for feminists. But to contest the medical and family planning monopoly over reproductive politics is not to deny that reproduction and abortion are health related.

It is appropriate to encompass "abortion rights" within a broad and expansive definition of women's health for two reasons. First, pregnancy *is* a health issue for women—sometimes in dramatically life-changing or life-threatening ways. To affirm this is to say that access to decent health care and the conditions of physical well-being for all people is a moral question; health and morality cannot be dichotomized. Second, the fact that the reproductive and fertility control services to which most women have access are at present contained within medical institutions means that it is within those institutions that we must challenge the quality and availability of the services. This means challenging the modes of organization and authority within the institutions—transforming the medical system and its dominant ideologies from within.

Abortion is *not* analogous to tuberculosis inoculations or indeed mastectomy; it has to do with women's sexual and moral autonomy as much as their physical integrity. At the same time, the appeal to an "individual rights" (moral) framework, in the context of the capitalist state and a privatized medical market, is as inadequate as the appeal to a narrow concept of "medical necessity" to satisfy women's reproductive and abortion needs. Even during the halcyon days of legal, funded, and presumably unrestricted abortions, medical control over reproductive health services determined in practice the extent of the "personal choice" of abortion, especially for poor women. Individual rights in American constitutional law, as the Supreme Court insists on reminding us, guarantee only that the state will erect no "obstacles," no roadblocks, in our path—for example, will not arrest us on the way to the doctor's office or shut down the (free market) abortion clinics. Nor may the state, as the Court held in *Akron*, saddle abortion with unnecessarily burdensome requirements such as waiting periods and hospitalization rules. These rights will not assure us of money to pay for abortions or that state hospitals will provide them, or will provide them in a decent and humane setting; or even that private clinics will be protected from vandals, arsonists, and exploitative hucksters. And they will not be applied in the name of sexual (as opposed to "procreative") autonomy, since the state reserves the authority to "protect" young women from the sexual consequences of legal abortion. While arguing for an individual rights position, Willis recognizes its limits when she says:

> . . . doctors have always been free to withhold treatment they consider unnecessary or harmful. If there were no abortion laws, doctors and hospitals could still deny women "unnecessary" abortions, or even argue (as many antiabortionists do) that abortion causes guilt and depression and is therefore bad for women's emotional health.[10]

The abortion experience of the past hundred years confirms that realizing the right to abortion requires putting an end to privatized, class-divided medicine and socializing medical care. This will mean, first, that health needs become one essential ground for abortion and that medical personnel who fail to provide essential services will be publicly called to account. Second, it will mean that, rather than twist abortion into the restrictive framework of pathology and cure, we will broaden the dominant meanings of "medical" (and consequently standards of reimbursement) to include *all* aspects of health—preventive, reproductive, and socioeconomic as well as remedial. This expansive approach to a concept of reproductive health will affect public and private financing not only of abortion but of contraception, pregnancy, and prenatal and child care.

The concept of a social approach to reproductive health care not only requires a socialist transformation of the health care system, its standards of care, and its methods of distribution but also a new definition of the meaning of "health," a feminist definition. Returning to the social-contextual concept of Judge Dooling in *McRae*, we may posit that sexual self-expression is itself a basic human need so allied to a person's physical and emotional well-being as to constitute an aspect of "health" in the widest sense.[11] Further, the principle of control over one's body must also be incorporated into an expanded concept of health needs, since if things can be done to my body over which I have no control (e.g., forced pregnancy or involuntary sterilization), this impairs my ability to function as a fully responsible (i.e., healthy) human being.

A feminist and socialist approach to reproductive health will transform not only the ideology and methods of medical care in Western capitalist societies but their hierarchical structure as well. If "health needs" include those that will save an individual from death or disease and those that refer to basic well-being, then they are the province not only of professionals but of individual "consumers" and social organizations designed to "enforce more uniform—and more liberalized—standards of practice throughout the country."[12] These organizations will become part of a larger movement to democratize political control over social welfare programs. The historical conditions in which women may anticipate sharing reproductive responsibility with men, or with the "community as a whole," must be those in which democratic principles and processes are built into reproductive (and all) decision making. That is, we will need a radical social democracy in which domination by bureaucrats and medical professionals is not allowed to repress those whose lives are immediately affected by decisions. What this will mean in practice is an active feminist movement that retains its autonomy from a socialist state and even a socialized health-care system. Feminists will need to be organized politically as advocates of women's needs even in a society whose institutions formally embrace the equality of women.

Given such a context, we can imagine concrete situations in which collectively organized social intervention into reproduction, or even "population" matters in a narrower sense, will be not only legitimate but necessary. Society will have to deal with economic and social questions concerning the allocation of resources to communal child-care facilities, the mobilization of men on a systematic basis into child-care activity, and, most difficult of all, the relationship between the responsibilities of collective organizations and those of parents or other related adults for children. Indeed, unless we adopt a crude anti-Malthusian position that refuses to acknowledge any such thing as population problems, we will have to deal with certain "quantitative" concerns—for example, the ways that the age structure of the population affects its capacity to provide collective child-care and educational resources.[13] The view of reproduction and parenting as essentially social relationships implies not only a commitment to the legitimacy of social regulation of those areas of human activity but also a rejection of the idea that there is a "natural right" to procreate indefinitely or to procreate at all. That idea must be distinguished sharply from the idea of a socially determined need (of both men and women) to participate in the care and rearing of children, as a distinct and special part of human existence. The latter is essential to a feminist and socialist vision of the future. The former is a remnant of biological determinist thinking (akin to "mother-right") that should have no place in feminist thought.

Yet, even in a society where the collective responsibility for reproduction and childrearing is taken seriously at all levels of public and interpersonal life, will there not still be aspects of reproductive and sexual relations that remain a "personal affair"? In particular, will women not still retain a preemptive claim to reproductive autonomy, especially around questions of abortion and childbearing, based on the principle of "control over one's body"? Even in the context of revolutionary social relations of reproduction, it will never be legitimate to compel a person to have sex or to bear a child, to have an abortion or be sterilized, to express or repress sexuality in some prescribed way, or to undergo surgical or chemical or other bodily intervention for reproductive or contraceptive purposes. A sense of being a person, with personal and bodily integrity, will remain essential to the definition of social participation and responsibility, under any historical conditions I can imagine.

To deny that there will always be a residual conflict between this principle—which is the idea of concrete individuality, or subjective reality—and that of a social and socially imposed morality of reproduction seems not only naive but dismissive of an important value. In any society, there will remain a *level of individual desire that can never be totally reconciled with social need*[14] without destroying the individual personalities whose "self-realization" is the ultimate object of social life. How will an individual woman's desire to have a child, or not to have a child, be harmonized in every case with a social policy that determines, on the basis of social need, the circumstances in which people should or should not have and raise children? Even if reproduction and pregnancy are technologically relegated to the laboratory, there will no doubt remain women who resist the "technological revolution" as usurping a process that belongs to them individually, personally, to their bodies. The provision of adequate, universal child-care services or male sharing in childrearing will eliminate neither the tension between the principles of individual control and collective responsibility over reproduction nor the need to make reproductive choices that are hard. But this very tension can be, for feminism—and through feminism, socialism—a source of political vitality.

NOTES

1. Adrienne Rich, *Of Woman Born*, pp. 268–69.
2. Ibid.
3. Mohr, *Abortion in America*, p. 112.
4. Adrienne Rich, *On Lies, Secrets, and Silence* (New York: Norton, 1979), p. 272.

5. This distinction is developed by Chiara Saraceno in "Changing Collective Identities Through Protest and Reform: The Case of Women as Mothers and Women as Teachers in the Seventies" (1983), p. 8, forthcoming in *Feminist Studies*.

6. CARASA, *Women Under Attack*, p. 60.

7. Quoted in Carolyn Teich Adams and Kathryn Teich Winston, eds. *Mothers at Work: Public Policies in the United States, Sweden, and China* (New York: Longman, 1980), p. 211.

8. See ibid., pp. 141–48 and 167–69.

9. Alexandra Kollontai, *Selected Writings*, ed. Alix Holt (New York: Norton, 1980), pp. 201–15, 225–31, 237–49.

10. Ellen Willis, *Village Voice*, March 3, 1980, p. 8.

11. Cf. Frank Brodhead, "Reproductive Rights and the Peace Movement," *Resist*, No. 147 (April 1982): "By now we should see sexual expression as a basic human need, akin to food, air, or shelter. What would be our attitude towards an alliance with an organization which sought to abolish political rights or civil liberties for women, or made their right to shelter contingent on the approval of two doctors?" (p. 7).

12. Jaffe memorandum (January 1974), p. 8.

13. See Steven Polgar, "Birth Planning: Between Neglect and Coercion," in *Population and Social Organization*, ed. Moni Nag (The Hague: Mouton, 1975), p. 197.

14. Heller, *The Theory of Need in Marx*, p. 45.

Index